The Practical Endgame Bible

Guidelines for the Fundamentals of the Endgame

Boroljub Zlatanovic

First edition 2023 by Thinkers Publishing

All sales or enquiries should be directed to Thinkers Publishing, 9850 Landegem, Belgium.

Email: info@thinkerspublishing.com
Website: www.thinkerspublishing.com

Editorial Director: Adrien Demuth

Assistant Editor: Daniël Vanheirzeele

Proofreading: Kai Tan

Software: Hub van de Laar

Cover Design: Iwan Kerkhof

Graphic Artist: Philippe Tonnard

Production: BESTinGraphics

ISBN: 9789464201741
D/2023/13732/8

The Practical Endgame Bible

Guidelines for the Fundamentals of the Endgame

Boroljub Zlatanovic

Thinkers Publishing 2023

Thanks to my lovely wife Marijana
for her wholehearted support

Key to Symbols

!	a good move
?	a weak move
!!	an excellent move
??	a blunder
!?	an interesting move
?!	a dubious move
□	only move
N	novelty
⟳	lead in development
⊙	zugzwang
=	equality
∞	unclear position
=∞	with compensation for the sacrificed material
⩲	White stands slightly better
⩱	Black stands slightly better
±	White has a serious advantage
∓	Black has a serious advantage
+−	White has a decisive advantage
−+	Black has a decisive advantage
→	with an attack
↑	with initiative
⇆	with counterplay
Δ	with the idea of
⌓	better is
≤	worse is
+	check
#	mate

Table of Contents

Foreword

In his new book Boroljub Zlatanovic is reviewing a variety of endgame strategies. The various moves (good and bad), critical moments, future strategy for both sides are well explained and emphasized by the author. It includes topics such as “The Center", "Exchanging Pieces", "The Active King", and "Activity and Harmony". I really like that the book is focused on human thinking and explanations and not just on plain computer analysis. The book is great for starting and professional players alike.

Kiril Georgiev, 2022

Preface

It is a well-known fact that endgames are the basis of chess. Simply, you must know endgames, for instance to be able to build a good plan in the middlegame (and even in the opening if you are a true master). Good opening theory knowledge and the decision-making process and planning in the middlegame would just not be enough if you do not know how to convert in the endgame. This is why all serious chess education from its beginning must start with the endgame. Of course, one starts with trivial and simple endgames, to be later upgraded with typical ones. However, after reaching a certain level it is necessary to investigate endgames much more deeply – to pay attention to more universal and complex elements, ideas and principles. Not surprisingly some universal principles (such as activity, harmony, controlling the open file etc.) are valid not only in the middlegame but they still keep an important role in the endgame!

There are many books devoted to basic endgames, even from the Middle Ages. Principles of typical endgames (such as keeping the rook behind a passed pawn, not setting pawns on the same colored squares as your bishop's, distant pawns being more dangerous than central ones etc.) are well known too. But what about "complex endgames"? I have in mind endgames with at least two pieces on each side; well I don't find them often nor sufficiently well-explained in the past! It is exactly this fact (together with my passion and great endgame experience) that has motivated me to write this book (many friends simply call me *"Endgame Wizard"*).

Over two decades of working as a coach has confirmed my opinion that endgames are the biggest problem for young players. Today, in the computer era with a lot of information easily provided, youngsters all over the world rather play blitz, or solve some tactical puzzles in a manner that is "the faster the better" (or even spend time on some other chess disciplines). All of this neglects the basis of chess – the importance of endgames! It is not uncommon that everyday you can be witness to some strange endgame misunderstanding, even at the top level.

This is why I consider some of my favorite endgame books based on logic as the best I've ever read – I learned the endgame from some of the best endgame players and authors. And this is why I want to fill that gap in chess literature and to share my devotion, ideas, principles, opinions with you! I hope you will enjoy this material and I am pretty sure you will broaden your endgame horizons.

The material is separated into 15 chapters that I found essential to cover all the ideas that I had in mind. Logically, I started with more important principles (like the center and activity of the king) which will be widely used later in the book as well. The most specific principles are analyzed at the end. So, for this reason I suggest that you should not skip examples.

Finally, I would be grateful if you would deliver all your opinions, criticisms, suggestions to my mail borzlat@gmail.com. Enjoy and welcome!

Boroljub Zlatanovic, November 2022

The Center

The center is considered to be the ultimate principle of chess in the middlegame. This is also the case in the opening, because we must fight for the center as quickly as possible. Furthermore a series of exchanges in the middlegame will not affect at all the center's importance!

Moreover, the center remains a leading chess principle in the endgame. Indeed, the presence of empty space in the center of the board (this is a usual situation in endgames) would simply reinforce the importance of centralization.

Game 1

♙ Znosko Borovsky, Eugene
♟ Alekhine, Alexander
Paris 1933

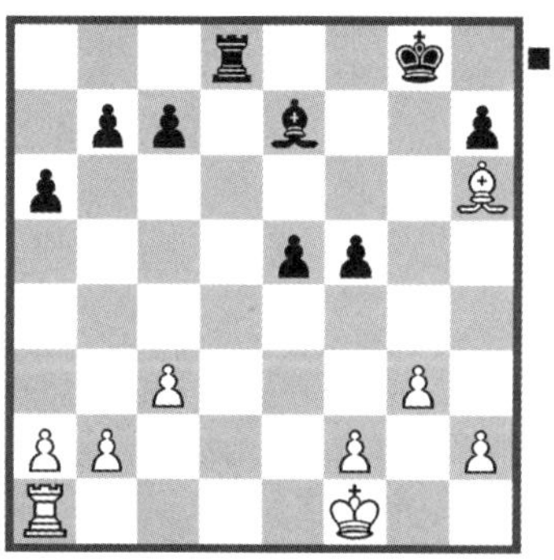

Our first (and in general, the most important) topic starts with a classic and relatively simple example. Alekhine's play in this endgame produces a strong impression. First, Black activates the king.

19... ♔f7 20. ♗e3

White instinctively moves the bishop back to base. However, of course, it was safe on h6. It was better instead to play 21. ♔e2.

20. ♔e2 f4 21. gxf4 ♔g6

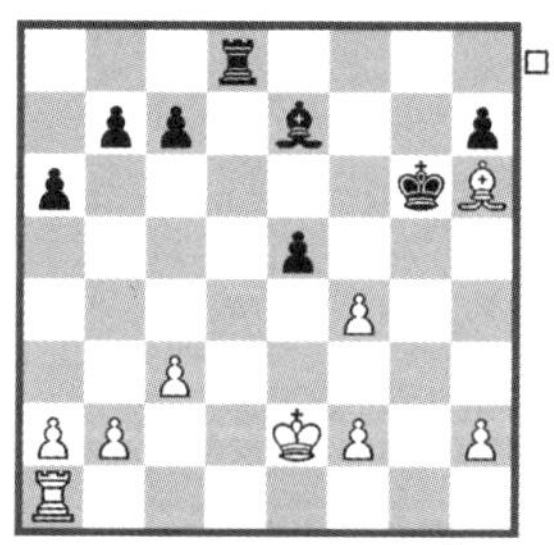

Position after: 21... ♔g6

This would give nothing to Black after the following. 22. ♗g5 ♗xg5 23. fxg5 ♔xg5 24. ♖g1+ White even has a small advantage.

20... h5!

He who stands better in the center can play on the flanks! Although this is more a psychological rather than a truly dangerous approach, it is in any case logical. Black wants to put annoying pressure after ...h4. Usually the logical response with gxh4 creating an outside passed pawn would be simply bad because the black central pawn armada would dangerously constrict White's army.

21. ♔e2

21. h4 f4 22. gxf4 exf4 23. ♗xf4 ♗xh4 24. ♔e2 ♖e8+

Position after: 24... ♖e8+

25. ♔f3 ♗d8 26. ♖h1 h4

21... ♔e6 22. ♖d1

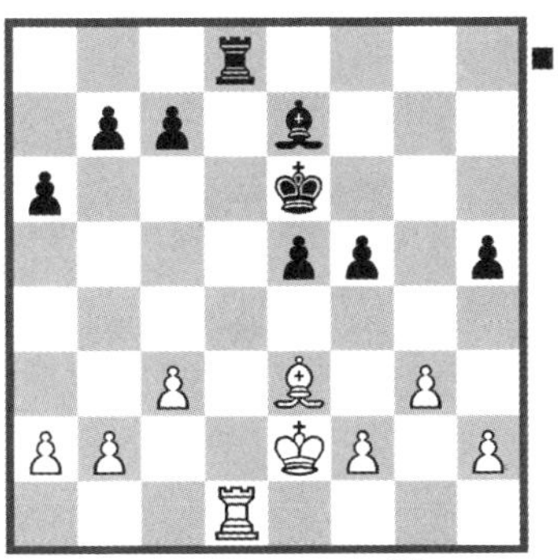

Position after: 22. ♖d1

22... ♖g8

22... ♖xd1 This engine move with the idea to advance ...c5-c4 and fix the white pawns on the bishop's color is not good enough because after 23. ♔xd1 ♔d5 24. f3 White should hold without problems. In any case, Black can trade rooks at any moment, so why trade the more active rook for its counterpart?

23. f3 h4

An unpleasant contact.

24. ♗f2

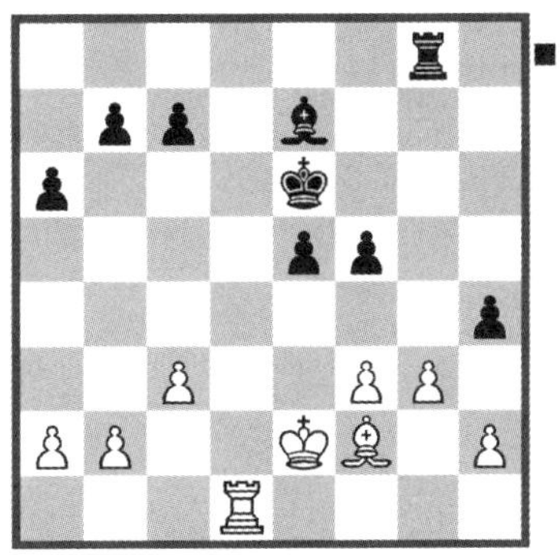

Position after: 24. ♗f2

An interesting moment. Since White should not capture on h4 Black should not hurry. It would have been more appropriate to start with activities on the other side.

24... hxg3?!

24... b5 Further expanding on the queenside would have been more logical. Control of the center would give Black solid chances for play on both flanks.

25. hxg3 ♖h8

Black has the h-file but there is nothing to achieve if White plays precisely.

26. ♗g1 ♗d6

Position after: 26... ♗d6

A small improvement. The bishop closes the d-file and keeps an eye on the potential target g3.

27. ♔f1?!

White switches to defense.

27. a4 This would have been a better choice. Now Black's expansion on the queenside would result in trading some pawns – a good strategy for the side playing for a draw. Also, White would then have the a-file for his rook.

27... ♖g8 28. ♗f2 b5!

White has missed the moment for a4 and Black gains space.

29. b3 a5 30. ♔g2

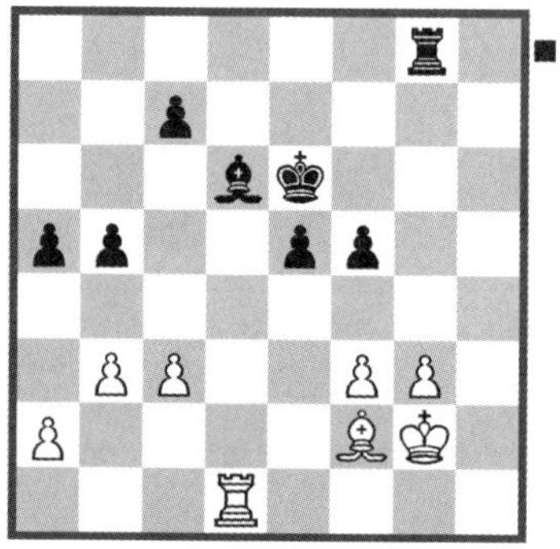

Position after: 30. ♔g2

30. a4?? This leads to disaster after the following. 30... bxa4 31. bxa4 ♖b8

30... a4

Strong and direct play by Alekhine.

31. ♖d2?!

Too passive.

A) 31. bxa4 bxa4 32. ♖b1 This is bad in view of 32... ♔d5.

B) 31. ♖h1 This was simply necessary. White must create some activity by seeking counterplay. 31... axb3 32. axb3 ♖a8 33. ♗e1

Position after: 33. ♗e1

33... ♖a2+ 34. ♔f1 This should hold. White would have counterplay against the f5-pawn.

31... axb3

With White's passive king driven far from the queenside, and with the black king active and well centralized together with the bishop, Black opens up a front on the queenside.

32. axb3 ♖a8

Position after: 32... ♖a8

33. c4?

This is already a direct mistake. White cannot achieve simplification without losing material.

33. ♗e1! ♖a3 34. ♖b2!? This would have been a good defensive construction. Black dominates but there is nothing apparent.

33... ♖a3! 34. c5?

If White must play this, then it is clear that his "strategy" has failed.

A) 34. cxb5? ♖xb3–+

B) 34. ♖b2 bxc4 35. bxc4 ♖c3

Position after: 35... ♖c3

This wins material but White would be able to fight for a draw in a rook endgame after the following. 36. c5 ♗xc5 37. ♗xc5 ♖xc5 38. ♖b8!

34... ♗e7 35. ♖b2 b4!

The pawn on c5 is separated and may fall soon.

36. g4

Position after: 36. g4

It is too late for this.

36... f4!

Not typical but the strongest response. This move cuts off the white king and bishop from play. Black in return has the possibility of ...e4 while the white passer at g4 is not dangerous at all.

37. ♔f1 ♖a1+ 38. ♔e2 ♖c1 39. ♖a2 ♖c3!

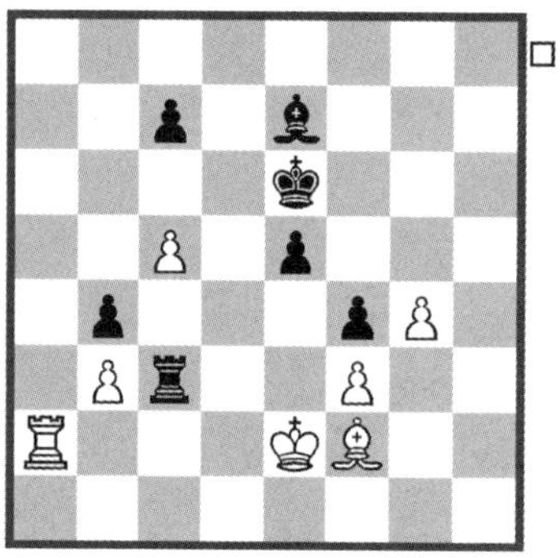

Position after: 39... ♖c3!

The pawn on b3 is the more important one. The pawn on c5 will fall anyway. It provides a shield for the black king for now.

40. ♖a7 ♔d7 41. ♖b7 ♖xb3 42. ♖b8 ♖b2+ 43. ♔f1 b3

Black converts with no particular problems.

44. ♔g1 ♔c6 45. ♔f1

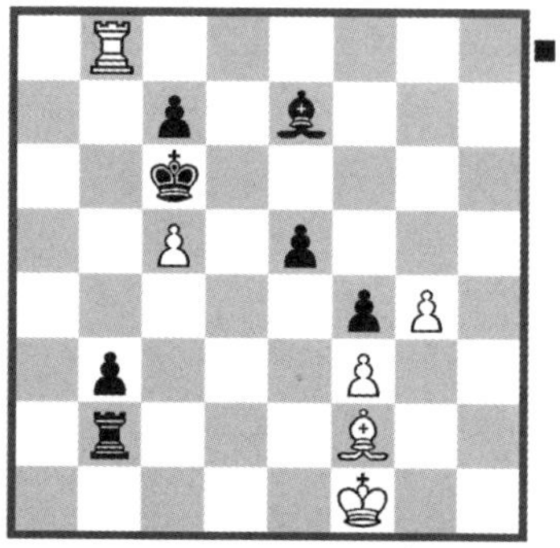

Position after: 45. ♔f1

45... ♔d5

Again Alekhine prefers direct play – this time against the white king!

45... ♗xc5? This is less precise due to the following. 46. ♗xc5 ♔xc5 47. g5 There is no need to calculate the arising rook endgame.

46. ♖b7 e4 47. fxe4+

47. ♖xc7 ♔e6 48. fxe4 ♖c2–+

47... ♔xe4 48. ♖xc7 ♔f3

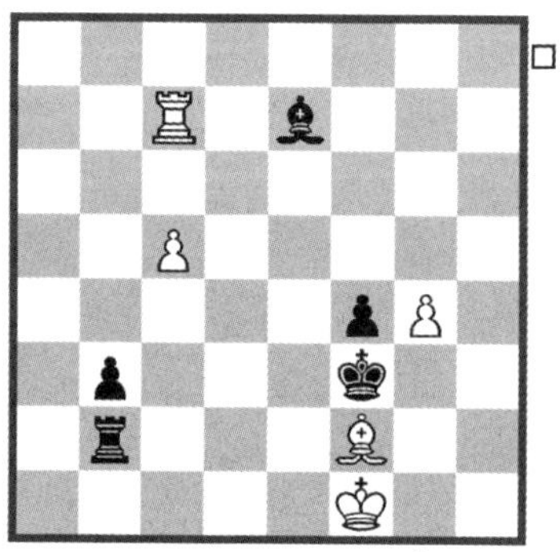

Position after: 48... ♔f3

The quickest win.

49. ♖xe7 ♖xf2+ 50. ♔e1 b2 51. ♖b7 ♖c2 52. c6 ♔g3 53. c7 f3 54. ♔d1 ♖xc7 55. ♖xb2 f2

0-1

Game 2

♙ Kasparov, Garry (2595)
♟ Natsis, Trifon (2240)
🌍 Valetta 1980

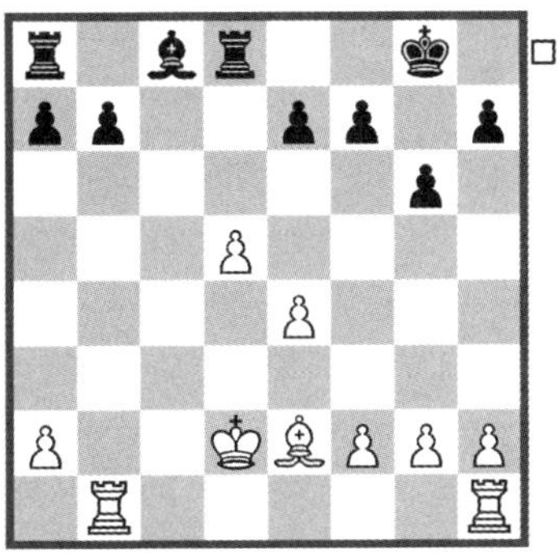

White is evidently better. The evaluation is clear from his better development, space advantage, active king and domination in the center.

17. ♔e3

Kasparov naturally removes his king from the pin and makes it more active.

17... b6?!

Natural-looking, but very static and passive.

17... e6 This was practically a necessity. 18. ♗c4 exd5 19. ♗xd5 ♖d7 20. ♖hc1

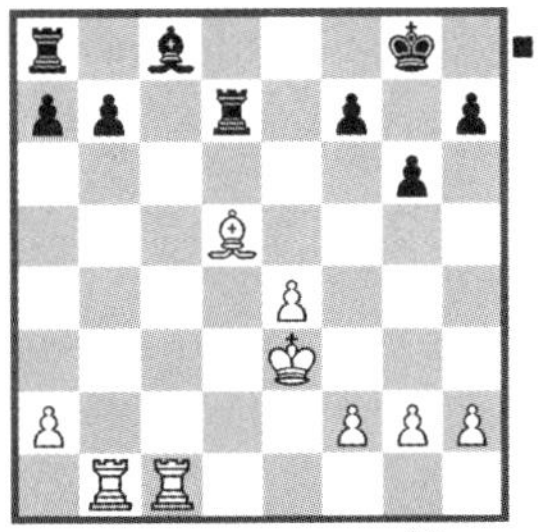

Position after: 20. ♖hc1

20... ♖e7 Now this would give Black chances to defend persistently.

18. ♖bc1!?

Kasparov decides that the other rook belongs on d1. It is a matter of style.

18... e6

Now this is not so efficient. Black has lost a very important tempo.

19. ♗c4

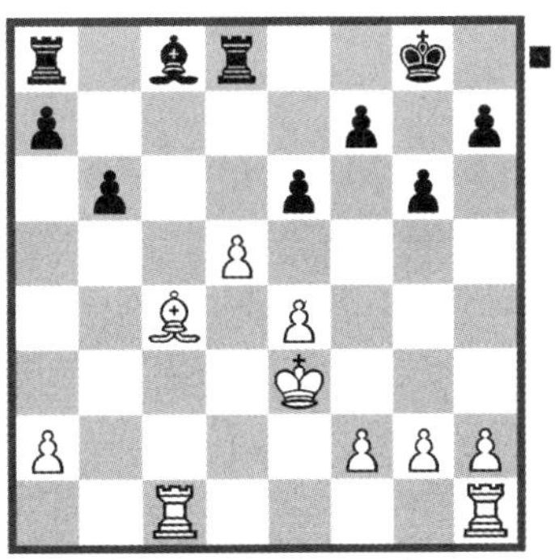

Position after: 19. ♗c4

19... e5?

If Black must play this after he has already played ...e6, then everything is clear. Black's defensive strategy is bad – if one actually exists. No wonder Kasparov exploits it with great energy.

A) To be fair, it is difficult to give Black good advice. 19... exd5? 20. ♗xd5 ♖b8 21. ♖c7+–

B) 19... ♖b8!? 20. dxe6 ♗xe6 21. ♗xe6 fxe6 22. ♖c7 This is awful for Black.

20. ♗b3 ♗d7 21. ♖c7 a5

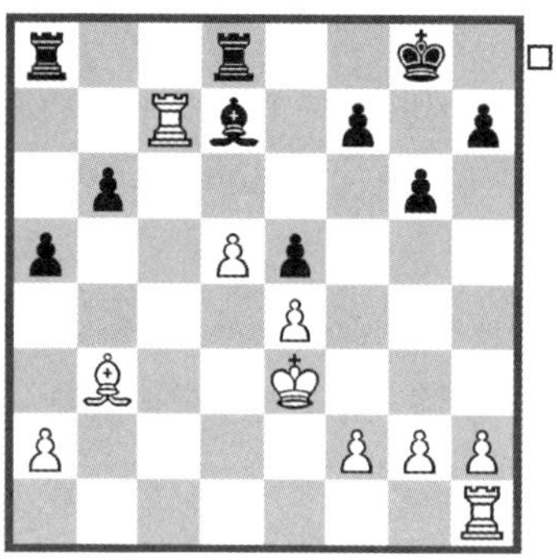

Position after: 21... a5

22. d6!

It is necessary to open the diagonal to attack f7 and to place the bishop on d5.

22. ♖hc1 This is less effective because of 22... a4! 23. ♗d1 b5.

22... b5 23. f4!

White chooses a good moment to attack on the opened f-file. Black's pieces are stuck and cannot regroup to defend the f7-spot.

23... exf4+ 24. ♔xf4 ♖a6 25. e5

Of course. Picturesque. Take a look at White's centralized army and Black's disorganized troops.

25... a4 26. ♗d5

Position after: 26. ♗d5

26... a3

Black's advance on the queenside misses the mark. It is game over.

26... b4 27. ♖f1 b3 28. axb3 a3

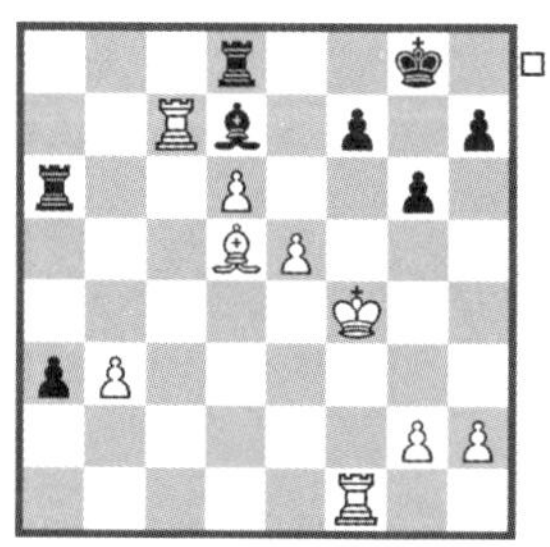

Position after: 28... a3

This gives nothing. White would simply continue as follows. 29. ♔e3 a2 30. ♗xf7+ ♔g7 31. ♗e6 White has an easy win.

27. ♖f1 ♖a4+ 28. ♔e3 ♗e6 29. ♗xe6 fxe6

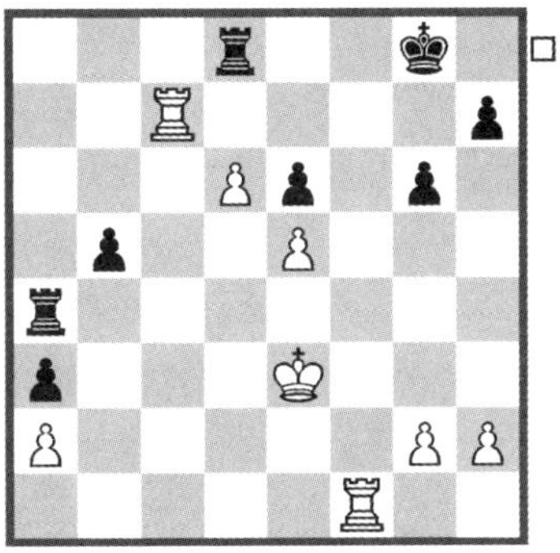

Position after: 29... fxe6

30. ♖ff7 ♖h4 31. ♖g7+ ♔h8 32. ♖ge7

1-0

Game 3

♙ Amos, Bruce M
♟ Martz, William E
🌍 Mayaguez 1971

White is absolutely dominant, with full control over the center, his centralized king and the natural possibility to advance his pawns to constrict Black. Black's theoretically "better" majority is useless – furthermore, advancing the b-pawn has only weakened the c5- and c6-squares.

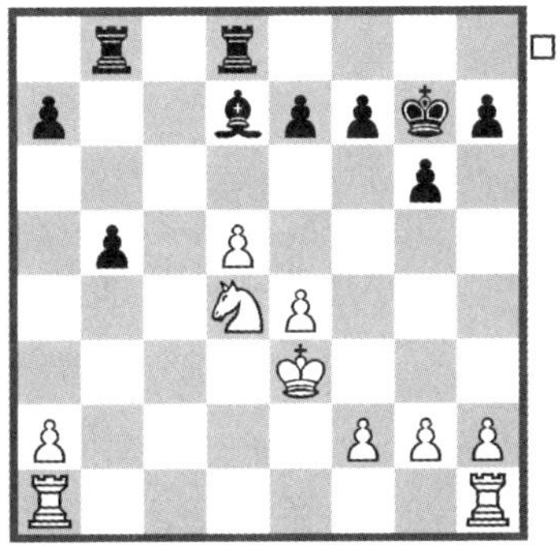

20. ♖hc1 ♖b6

20... ♖dc8 21. ♘b3 White has full control after ♘c5 and ♔d4, with further doubling on the c-file and advancing the pawn phalanx in the center.

21. ♖c7 ♖a6 22. ♖b7?

An inaccuracy.

22. a3 This was needed to prevent the check on a3. Now 22... b4 fails to 23. ♘b3+–.

22... ♖a3+ 23. ♔f4

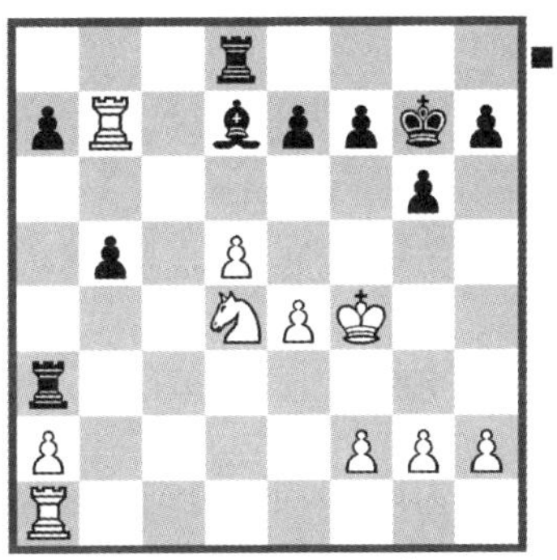

Position after: 23. ♔f4

23... a6?

23... ♖a4! This would have kept the tension, delivering threats on the 4th rank with sufficient counterplay.

24. ♖c1!

White immediately takes his chance.

24... ♖a4

It is not the same to do it now.

24... ♖xa2? 25. ♖cc7+–

25. ♘c6?

This allows a nice tactical line. 25... g5 26. ♔g3 ♗c6, 27. dxc6 ♖c8 Nothing is clear.

Position after: 25. ♘c6

25. ♘b3 This is also good. 25... ♖xa2 26. ♖cc7 ♖xf2+ 27. ♔e3 ♖b2 28. ♘d4! White should win.

25... ♗xc6?

A fatal mistake.

25... g5+! 26. ♔g3 [26. ♔xg5? ♖xe4∓; 26. ♔e3 ♖a3+ 27. ♔d4 ♗xc6 28. ♖xc6 ♖e8 This leads Black to safety.] 26... ♗xc6 27. dxc6 ♖c8 Black should not lose.

26. dxc6 ♖c8 27. c7 ♖c4

The only move to delay resignation.

28. ♖xc4 bxc4 29. ♔e3

Position after: 29. ♔e3

Of course the c4-pawn is exposed. White wins without problem.

29... e5

Black prevents an immediate infiltration by the white king.

29... ♔f6 This would not help because of the following. 30. ♖b6+ [But not 30. ♔d4? ♔e6 31. ♔xc4 ♔d6 and Black can show long resistance.] 30... e6 31. ♖c6 ♔e7

Position after: 31... ♔e7

32. ♔d4 ♔d7 33. ♖xc4 White wins.

30. ♔d2 ♔f6 31. ♔c3 ♔e7 32. ♔xc4 ♔d6 33. ♖a7

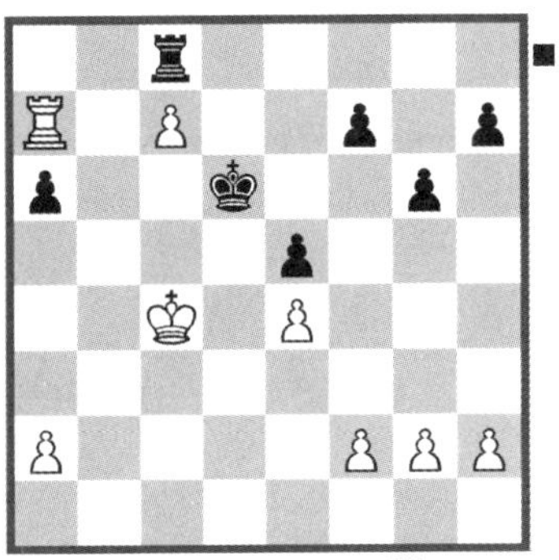

Position after: 33. ♖a7

The game is over. No further comment is necessary.

33... ♔c6 34. ♖xa6+ ♔xc7 35. ♔d5 ♔d7 36. ♔xe5

36. ♖a7+ This would have been a finer win.

36... ♖c2 37. ♖f6 ♔e7 38. a3 ♖c5+ 39. ♔d4 ♖g5 40. ♖f3 ♖xg2 41. a4 ♖g5 42. ♖a3 ♔d6 43. a5 ♔c7 44. a6

1-0

Game 4

♙ BioWaffen (2510)
♟ Zlatanovic, Boroljub (2407)
Playchess 2013

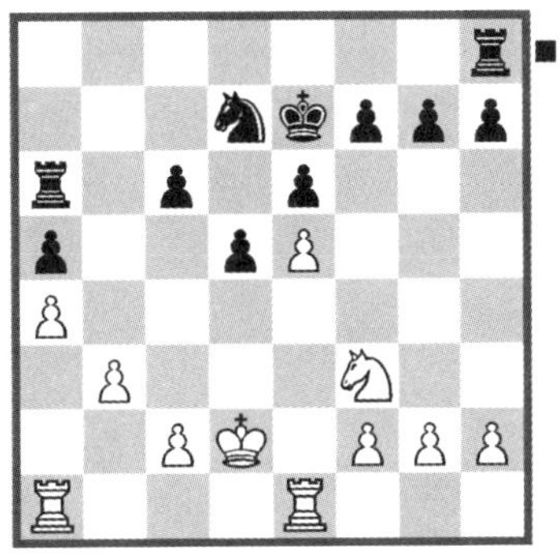

Black's advantage is undisputed. The evaluation is clear, with his better pawn structure, better prospects for the rooks and the possibility for pawn play on the queenside. Despite the fact that this was a friendly blitz internet game, Black was dedicated and focused on strategy. Alas, he went in too early to build the center.

17... f6?!

Premature.

17... c5 Evidently this was a better choice. Black would deliver the powerful threat of ...c4 (after ...♖c8). A crushing center with ...f6 can be on the agenda later.

18. exf6+ gxf6 19. ♘d4

This is the point. Now whatever Black advances, the white knight would get a solid spot.

19... e5?!

19... c5 This would have been a better option. 20. ♘b5 ♖g8 Black keeps the advantage.

20. g4?

20. f4! ♖g8 [Alternatively 20... ♔f7 21. fxe5 fxe5 22. ♖f1+ with rich play would be okay for White.] 21. g3 h5 This should be preferable for Black, but with nothing apparent.

20... ♘c5?

Position after: 20... ♘c5?

Returning the favor.

20... h5! This would have given Black a huge initiative.

21. f3?!

21. ♘f5+! ♔e6 22. ♖ad1 ♖a7 This would have been a better option for White.

21... ♔f7 22. ♘f5

With excellent control of the center, it is possible and timely to act on the flanks.

22... h5

Again this crushing move secures Black a lasting initiative.

23. h3 ♘e6

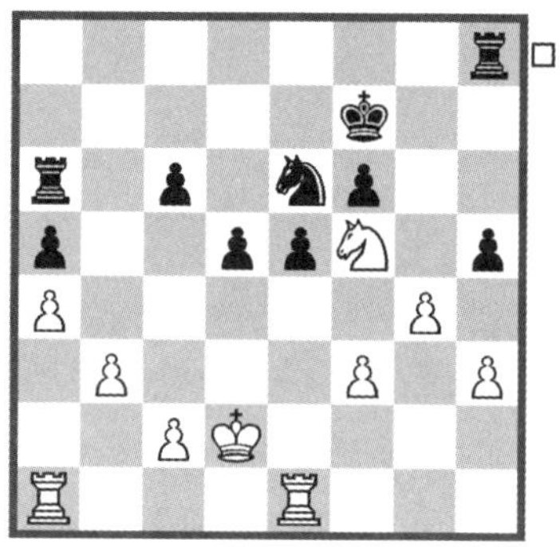

Position after: 23... ♘e6

24. ♘g3?

24. ♖h1 This was necessary. White wanted somehow to force play. Of course it is unpleasant to wait for the opponent to open the file – however, having such an uncentralized army against one that is so centralized means it is important to play very carefully.

24... hxg4 25. hxg4 ♖h3

Black's rooks will invade via the h-file and the game is practically over.

26. ♖g1 ♖a8

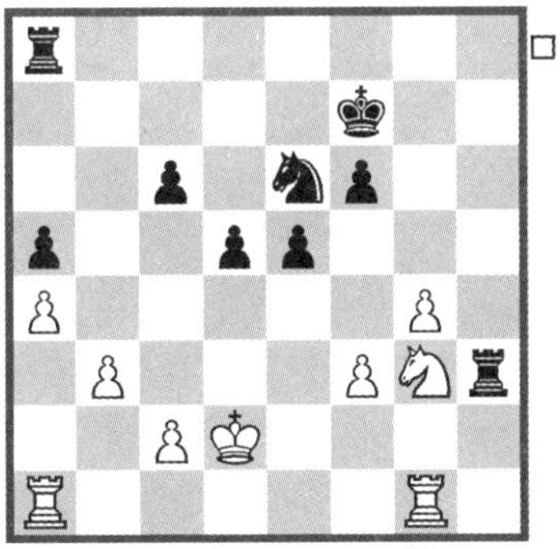

Position after: 26... ♖a8

Another rook joins the attack on the h-file.

27. ♖af1 ♖ah8 28. ♘e2 ♖h2! 29. ♔e3 ♖8h3

Picturesque. White's pieces are stuck in the center without any action or tasks. At the same time Black's artillery triumphs on the flank – all this is a consequence of the strong control of the center.

30. c3 ♘c5

Alternatively 30... c5 with the idea of ...d4 would have been even stronger.

31. b4

An act of desperation.

31... axb4 32. cxb4 d4+

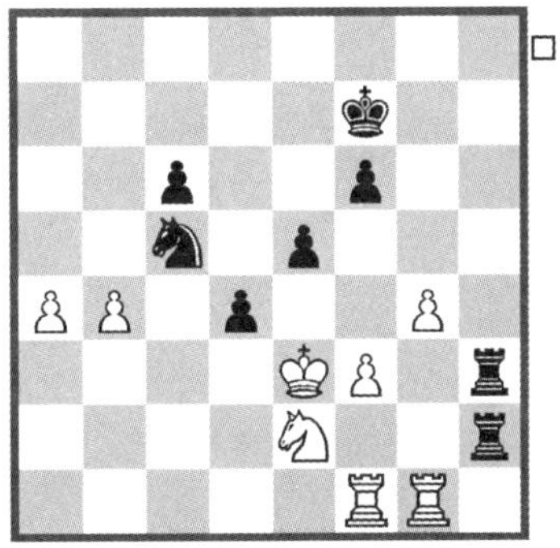

Position after: 32... d4+

33. ♔d2 ♘xa4 34. ♔d3 ♘b2+ 35. ♔d2 d3

White resigned.

0-1

Game 5

♙ Kotov, Alexander
♟ Eliskases, Erich Gottlieb
Saltsjobaden 1952

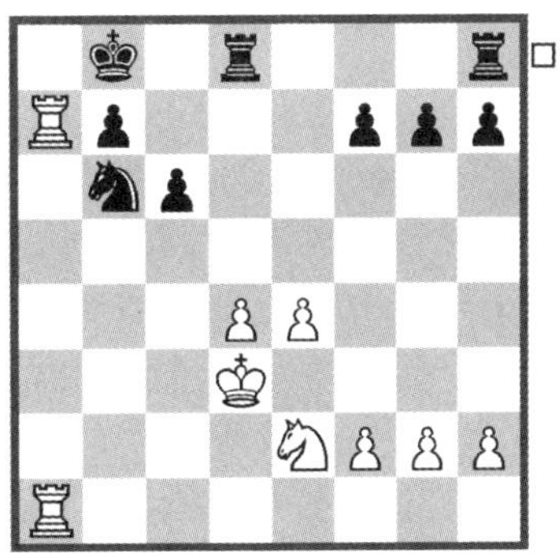

White has accumulated some advantages: gained space and active pieces after finishing development.

However most importantly there is control of the center. With his next move White follows the motto "he who controls the center may attack on the flank", at the same time preventing any possible attempt by Black to crush the center.

23. g4

Preventing ...f5.

23... ♔c7

A) 23... h5 This would face the obvious 24. g5.

B) 23... g5 This cannot be an option because the knight may jump to the weakened squares f5 and h5.

24. f4 ♖d7 25. ♖7a5!

Position after: 25. ♖7a5!

An excellent decision. The rook has more to do on the 5th rank.

25... ♖hd8

Black does not have many options, but he has a stable position. In order to accumulate more pluses White decides to provoke some weaknesses on the kingside.

26. ♖g5

26. h4 This is a good move in the same direction but with an alternative implementation.

26... f6?!

26... g6 This looks somehow more flexible and logical.

27. ♖ga5 ♘c8

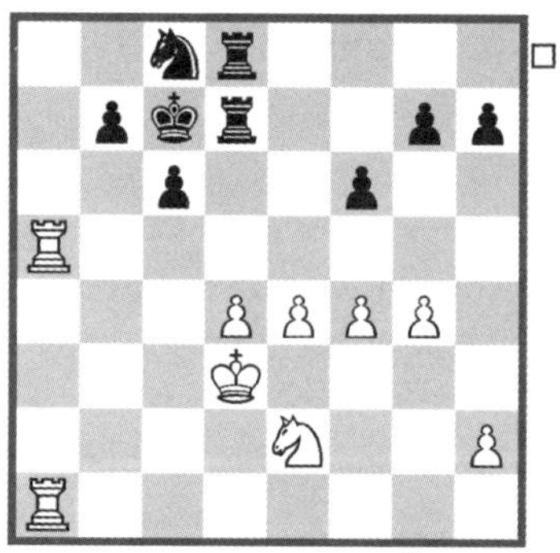

Position after: 27... ♘c8

28. f5

This was White's intention and the point of the rook's maneuver.

28... g5!

The knight must not come to f4.

29. h4

An instinctive reaction.

29... h6

29... gxh4 30. ♖h1 This does not deserve any consideration by Black.

30. hxg5 hxg5 31. ♖h1 ♘d6 32. ♖h6 ♖e7

It may look as if Black has solid counterplay against the e4-pawn. However White has predicted the upcoming play.

33. ♘c3!

33. ♘g3 This is not as good because of 33... ♖ed7!.

33... ♖de8

Position after: 33... ♖de8

34. e5!

An excellent move. Only this move gives chances to play for a win.

34. ♖xf6 ♘xe4 35. ♘xe4 ♖xe4 This will soon lead to a clear draw.

34... fxe5 35. ♘d5+?!

However this is already a dubious decision.

35. d5! This would have been a logical continuation. 35... e4+ 36. ♔e2 White would keep some chances.

35... cxd5 36. ♖c5+ ♔b8

36... ♔d7 37. ♖xd5 White would gain time taking the knight with check.

37. ♖xd6 exd4 38. ♖cxd5 ♖e3+ 39. ♔c4

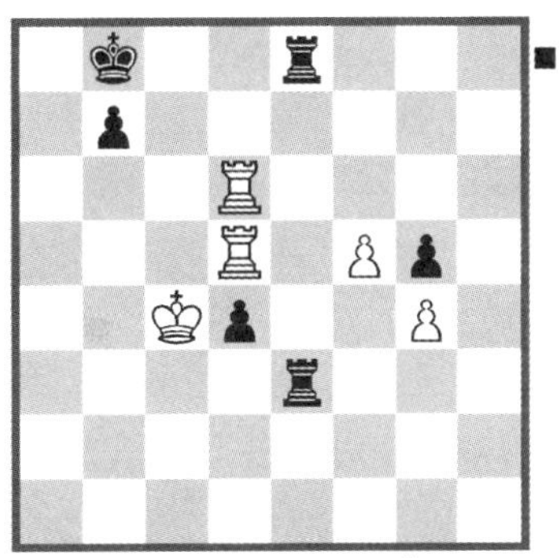

Position after: 39. ♔c4

39. ♔xd4 This would give a clear draw after the following. 39... ♖8e4+ 40. ♔c5 ♖c3+

39... ♖c8+?

A mistake. 39... ♖3e4! Why not this?

40. ♔xd4 ♖g3?!

This simplifies White's task.

40... ♖e1 This would be met as follows. 41. f6 ♖f1 42. ♖e6!

41. f6 ♖xg4+ 42. ♔e5 ♖f4 43. ♖d8?

43. ♔e6! This is precise. 43... ♖e8+ 44. ♔f7 ♖e1 45. ♖xg5 White wins easily.

43... ♖xd8 44. ♖xd8+ ♔c7 45. ♖g8

Position after: 45. ♖g8

45... ♔d7?

Black errs at last and the game is over now.

45... ♖f1! 46. ♔e6 ♖e1+ 47. ♔f7 ♔d6 This would lead to a study draw.

46. ♖g7+ ♔e8 47. ♖xb7 ♖f2 48. ♔e6 ♖e2+ 49. ♔f5 g4 50. ♔g6!

(see diagram next column)

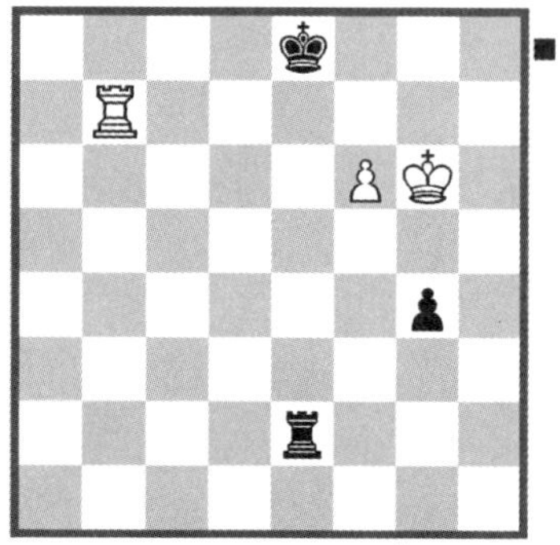

Position after: 50. ♔g6!

50... ♖f2 51. f7+ ♔f8 52. ♖b8+ ♔e7 53. ♖e8+

Black resigned.

1-0

Game 6

♙	Jussupow, Artur	(2665)
♟	Khalifman, Alexander	(2650)
🌍	Ubeda 1997	

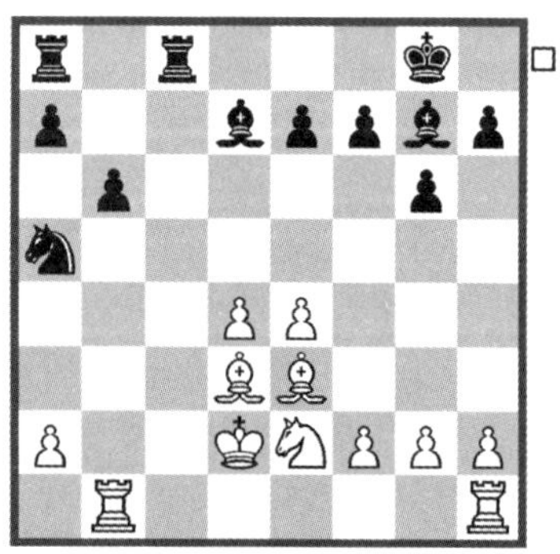

White is obviously better. His pawn center is very powerful and creates a perfect shield for his pieces and king.

Black does not have a well organized army at the moment.

16. ♗a6

White gets control over the c8-square, fighting for the c-file.

16. ♖hc1 Another logical approach with the idea to directly switch to a minor piece endgame.

16... ♖d8

16... ♖c7 This would be worse. 17. ♖hc1 ♖xc1 18. ♖xc1 White keeps a clear plus after gaining a serious advantage.

17. ♖hc1 ♗c8

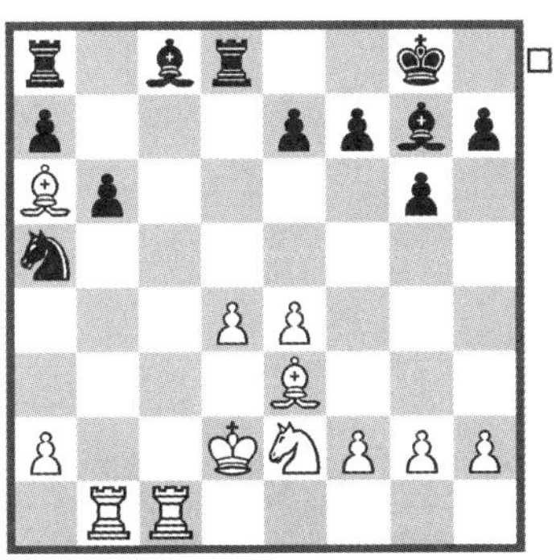

Position after: 17... ♗c8

18. ♗d3

With an advantage in space and mobility, it is useful to keep the pieces on the board.

18... ♗b7 19. ♖c7 ♖ac8 20. ♖bc1

20. ♖xe7? ♗f8

20... ♖xc7 21. ♖xc7 ♖c8

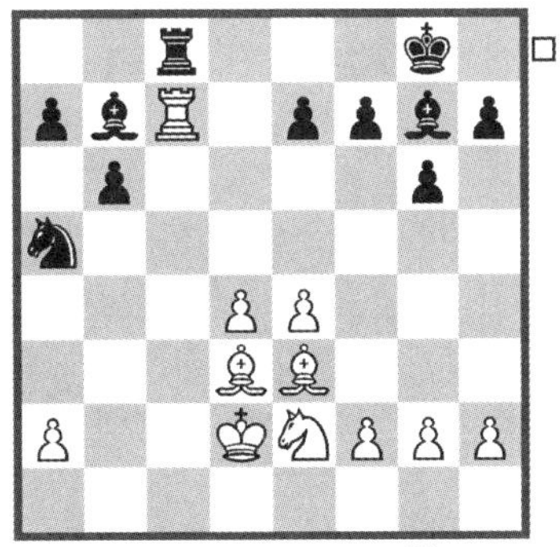

Position after: 21... ♖c8

22. ♖xc8+

22. ♖xe7? ♗f8 23. ♖e5 [23. ♖d7? ♗b4+ 24. ♔d1 ♗c6–+] 23... ♗b4+ 24. ♔d1 ♗c6∞

22... ♗xc8

The situation is defined. White has kept his bishops on the board but the rooks are gone. White has a stable advantage due to his better mobility and more space. All of this is due to the powerful pawn center. However White must take care with any further exchange of pieces – Black traditionally has the better majority. In this firmed situation centralization and space would prevail over the majority.

23. ♘c3

Eyeing the b5- and d5-squares.

23... ♘c6 24. ♘b5

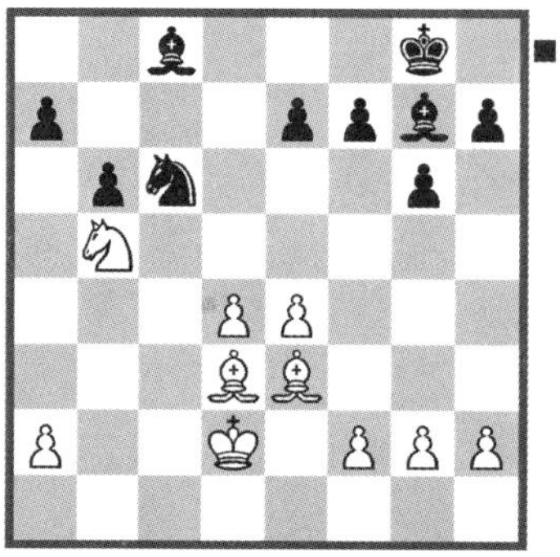

Position after: 24. ♘b5

White has the idea to provoke an advance of the black pawns which will make infiltration easier.

24... ♗a6 25. ♔c3 ♔f8?!

The king goes toward the center, although Black should have started with something more careful.

25... e6!? Another logical move. Black would try to prevent White's further expansion and reactivate his bishop via f8.

26. a4!

This pawn is safe here and liberates the bishop.

26... ♗b7

(see diagram next column)

Position after: 26... ♗b7

27. g4!?

A well-known approach from the previous game. White expands on the kingside according to the principle of playing on the side where he is stronger, at the same time preventing Black's crush with ...f5.

27... ♔e8 28. ♗c4

Better is 28... ♗c8 with the idea of targeting the white phalanx and reactivating the bishop.

28...♘b8 29. ♔d3

Of course not 29. ♘xa7 ♗xe4.

29... a6

The knight is under attack. White has provoked ...a6 and now targets the b6-pawn.

30. ♘c7+! ♔d8 31. ♘d5

Position after: 31. ♘d5

31... ♘d7

Black's pieces are more and more passive. The knight on d7 is just a sore defender, restricted by the d4-pawn.

31... ♗xd5 32. ♗xd5 e6 33. ♗c4 This would lead to a hopeless position for Black. White will add the bishop pair to the list of advantages.

32. ♘b4!

Simultaneously attacking both the a6- and f7-pawns.

32... a5

A necessity.

33. ♗d5

This was Artur's point.

33. ♘d5 However, this would keep the domination due to the more mobile majority and brutal centralization.

33... ♗xd5

Both of the following lines look awful for Black.

A) 33... ♔c8 34. ♗xb7+ ♔xb7 35. ♘c2

B) 33... ♗c8 34. ♘c6+ ♔e8 35. ♗c4

34. ♘xd5 e6 35. ♘c3 ♔c7 36. ♘b5+ ♔c6 37. ♔c4 ♗f8

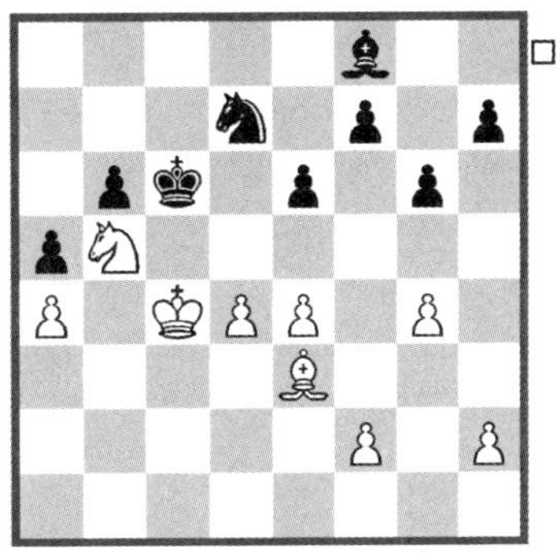

Position after: 37... ♗f8

After a series of clear moves White has simply enlarged his advantage. Black's majority is neutralized and useless. White has stable control of the b5- and c4-squares and is ready to use his majority. However before doing so, it is useful to fully activate his pieces.

38. ♗f4 ♗b4 39. f3

Another small improvement. There is no need to rush.

39... ♗f8 40. d5+ exd5+ 41. exd5+ ♔b7 42. ♘d6+!

The most direct way to win.

42... ♗xd6 43. ♗xd6

Position after: 43. ♗xd6

White's bishop is dominant. White is practically a pawn up with a paralyzed black knight. He has precisely evaluated the upcoming consequences of exchanging the minor pieces.

43... g5

A) Waiting is no good because of the following. 43... ♔a6 44. g5! ♔b7 45. ♔b5

Position after: 45. ♔b5

Black faces a zugzwang. The game is over after the following. 45... f6 46. h4 f5 47. f4

B) 43... ♘f6 44. g5 The knight is trapped in all lines. 44... ♘e8 [44... ♘h5 45. ♗e5+–; 44... ♘g8 45. ♔b5+–] 45. ♗e5+–

44. ♗g3

Position after: 44. ♗g3

44... ♘f6

44... ♔a6 This is not good enough in view of the following. 45. d6 h6 [45... ♔b7 46. ♔b5 ♘f6 47. ♗e5 ♘d7 48. ♗d4+– Zugzwang!] 46. ♗f2 ♘e5+ 47. ♔d5+–

45. ♗e5 ♘d7 46. ♗d4 ♔c7 47. ♔b5

Position after: 47. ♔b5

47... f6

A) 47... ♔d6 48. ♗xb6 ♘xb6 49. ♔xb6 ♔xd5 50. ♔xa5 ♔c5!

Position after: 50... ♔c5!

51. ♔a6 ♔c6 52. a5+–

B) 47... ♔b7 48. d6+–

48. ♗f2 ♔d6 49. ♗xb6 ♘e5 50. ♗xa5 ♘xf3 51. ♗c3

1-0

Game 7

♙ Bogoljubow, Efim
♟ Reti, Richard
Moravska Ostrava 1923

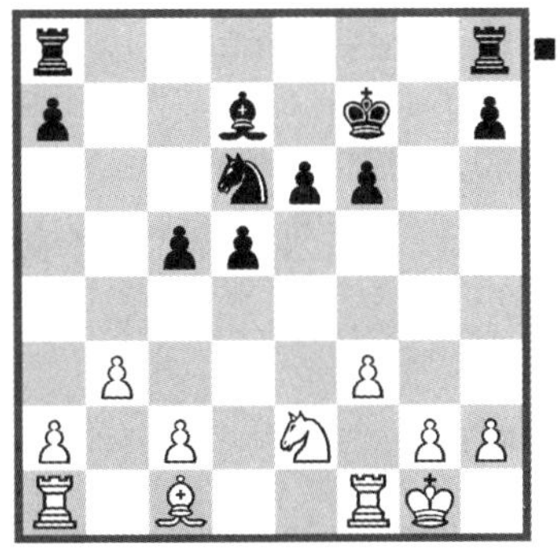

On our next diagram the position is much better for Black. The position arose as a result of White's diversion early in the opening. His "strategy" has failed. Black's central pawns will soon put enormous pressure onto White's position forcing his troops to retreat in panic. Black will easily finish development, setting his pieces behind the pawns and supporting them.

19... e5 20. ♗a3 ♖ac8

This rook is the correct one to move – the other rook will be needed on the d-file in order to advance pawns.

21. ♖ad1 d4

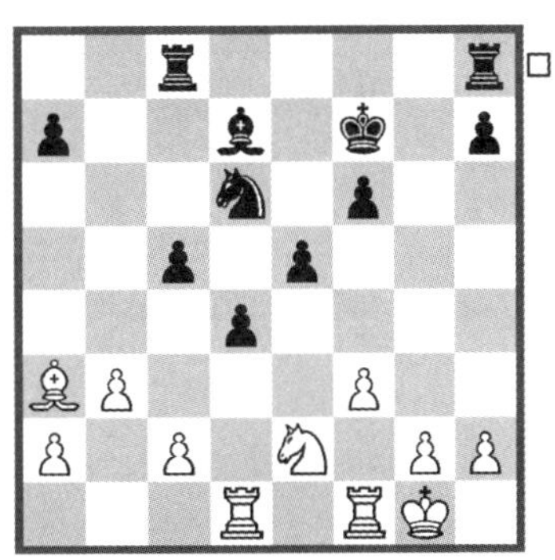

Position after: 21... d4

An instructive moment. In order to achieve full harmony, the pawns and knight should be placed on squares of the same color and the bishop placed on the opposite one! At the same time Black restricts White's minor pieces, especially the bishop, and secures the e3-spot for the knight.

22. ♘c1 ♘f5

Black has found the target: the pawn on c2.

23. ♖f2 ♘e3 24. ♖e1 c4

Direct play. White is just lost – the triumph of centralization.

24... ♗f5 This was also a good move, but the played move should be preferred.

25. b4

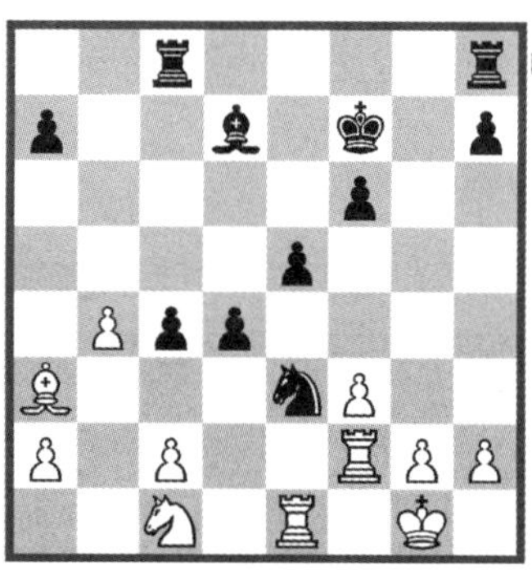

Position after: 25. b4

In this hopeless situation for White there are many winning plans. Black found a very beautiful maneuver.

25... ♗a4! 26. ♖ee2 ♘d1 27. ♖f1 ♘c3 28. ♖ef2

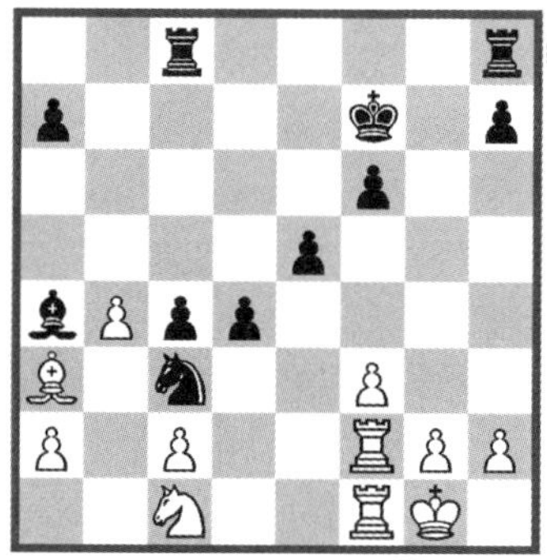

Position after: 28. ♖ef2

28... ♘b1?

But then... realizes it is the wrong way. He missed White's 30th move.

28... ♘b5 29. ♗b2 c3 30. ♗a1 Instead this line would have led to an easy win. White plays without a bishop – a perfect example of how a centralized army easily crushes the opponent's troops. This time it is not about destroying but about imprisoning instead.

29. ♗b2 c3 30. ♘b3!

This move delays resignation. Black is forced to find more good moves to convert.

30... ♗xb3! 31. axb3 ♘d2 32. ♖e1 ♖hd8!

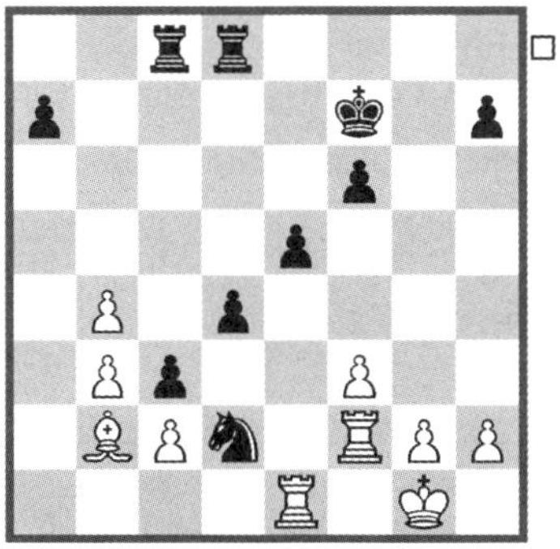

Position after: 32... ♖hd8!

33. ♗c1 d3! 34. cxd3 ♖xd3

The series of forced moves is over and the dust has settled. White is in any case close to defeat.

35. ♗xd2 ♖xd2

Black transposes into an easy endgame.

36. ♖a1 ♔e6 37. ♔f1 ♖xf2+ 38. ♔xf2 c2 39. ♖c1 ♔d5 40. ♔e3 ♖c3+ 41. ♔d2 ♔d4

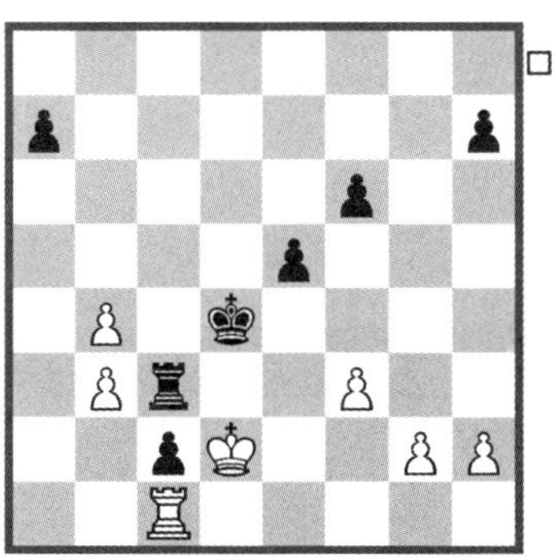

Position after: 41... ♔d4

White is in zugzwang.

42. h4 ♖d3+

0-1

Game 8

♙ Rubinstein, Akiba
♟ Schlechter, Carl
San Sebastian 1912

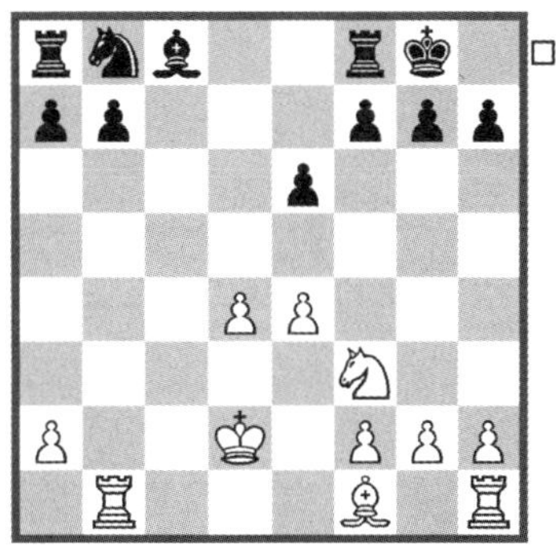

Black has just made his only mistake in this game, but it was a serious one – he castled. Of course, it would have been correct to keep his king in the center on e7, to develop and to gradually reach equality. For Rubinstein such a mistake is enough for him to win convincingly. Black's king is now far from the center and harmony in Black's camp will be broken due to the scattered army. There must be some good response here that leads to a serious advantage! Rubinstein found a great move which decades later became one of his trade-marks.

13. ♗b5!

An amazing move! One of the finest I have ever seen! It looks like a waste of time but in actual fact, White will win one tempo! The move has two points. First, it prevents Black's natural developing moves ...♘c6, ...♘d7 and ...♗d7. Secondly, it forces the move 13... a6, weakening the b6-square.

13. ♗d3 b6 14. ♖hc1 ♗a6 15. ♖c7 ♗xd3 16. ♔xd3 ♘a6 This looks okay for Black.

13... a6

What else?

14. ♗d3

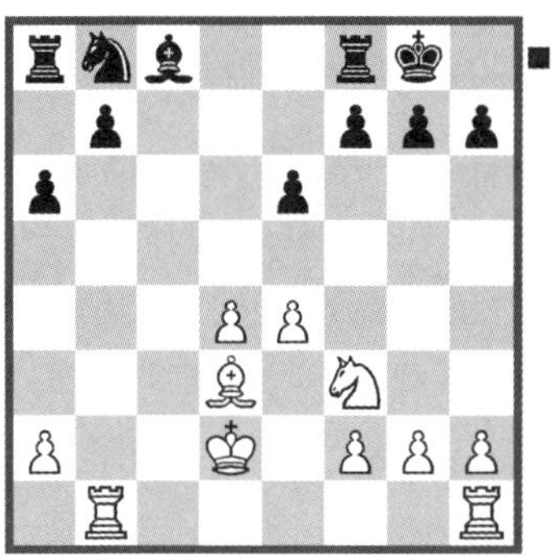

Position after: 14. ♗d3

The move ...b6 is not possible now. The pawn will be going to b5, creating new weaknesses.

14... ♖d8

14... ♘c6 15. ♖b6 This is very bad for Black. His queenside would be paralyzed.

15. ♖hc1 b5

This is necessary sooner or later. Now the stopped pawns on a6 and b5 will be good targets. There is also the weak dark complex on the queenside.

16. ♖c7 ♘d7 17. ♔e3! ♘f6 18. ♘e5!

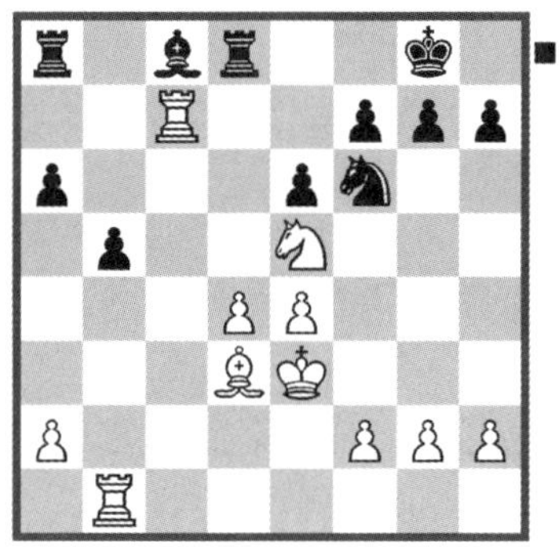

Position after: 18. ♘e5!

What a centralization! Take a look at White's last moves. First with 17. ♔e3 he protected the d4-pawn, getting the knight ready for action. This pawn protects the knight on e5. With his next move he prevents the check on g4 – thus the king, pawn and knight perfectly collaborate and help each other. The principles of centralization and harmony were always the foundation of Rubinstein's strategy.

18... ♗d7 19. g4!

He who dominates in the center can go for flank activity.

19... h6 20. f4!

The correct decision! White renews the threat of g5. The alternative 20. h4 is not so good – the f-file is more important than the h-file! You should establish your decisions as to how to recapture based on the importance of the file you open.

20... ♗e8 21. g5 hxg5 22. fxg5 ♘h7 23. h4

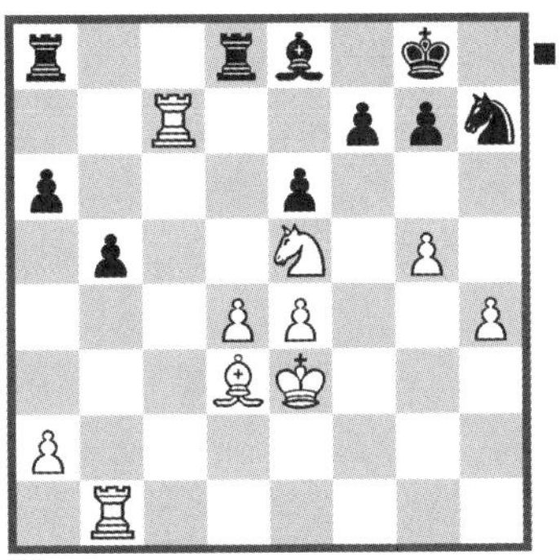

Position after: 23. h4

Please take a look at the black army, scattered and stuck in corners. At the same time White's army is perfectly centralized, mobilized and active. Strategically, Black is completely lost.

23... ♖dc8 24. ♖bc1 ♖xc7 25. ♖xc7 ♖d8 26. ♖a7

Finally converting the enormous positional advantage to a material one. Conversely the black army may simply be subjected to humiliation.

26... f6

Reducing the pawn material and with the idea to liberate the pieces somehow.

26... ♖d6 This allows for a beautiful finale as follows. 27. ♖a8 ♔f8 28. g6 fxg6 29. ♘xg6+

Position after: 29. ♘xg6+

29... ♔f7 30. ♘h8+ ♔f8 31. e5 Now the white pieces are placed in corners, but this set-up decides the game!

27. gxf6 gxf6 28. ♘g4 ♗h5 29. ♘h6+ ♔h8

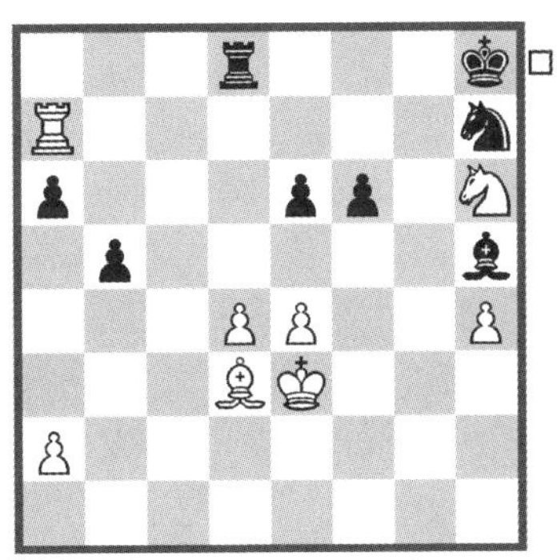

Position after: 29... ♔h8

30. ♗e2!

Black's bishop achieves liberation, but only for a moment. It must go back to prison.

30... ♗e8 31. ♖xa6 ♔g7 32. ♘g4 f5 33. ♖a7+! ♔h8

33... ♔g6 This is bad; there is a risk that Black's king will be mated. 34. h5+ ♔g5 35. ♖g7+ ♔h4 36. exf5 exf5 37. ♘h6

Position after: 37. ♘h6

Winning – now the following leads to mate. 37... ♘f8 38. ♘xf5+ ♔h3 39. ♗f1+ ♔h2 40. ♖g2+ ♔h3 41. ♖g3+ ♔h2 42. ♔f2

34. ♘e5 fxe4

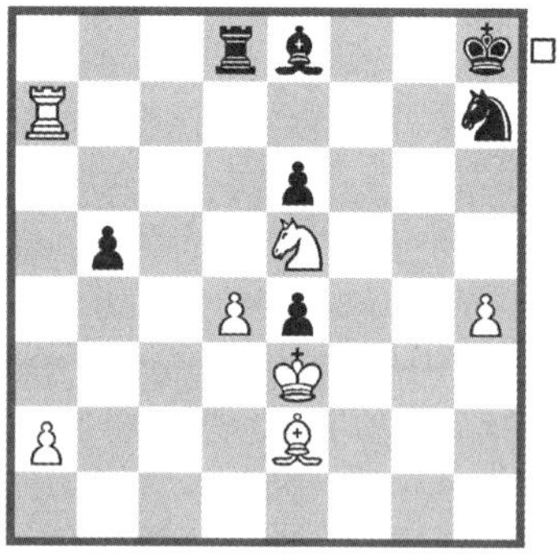

Position after: 34... fxe4

It looks like Black has consolidated his position by reducing some material. However Rubinstein's next move proves that Black is desperately lost. After conducting the game perfectly in a strategic way, there must be some hidden tactics!

35. ♗xb5! ♘f6 36. ♗xe8 ♖xe8

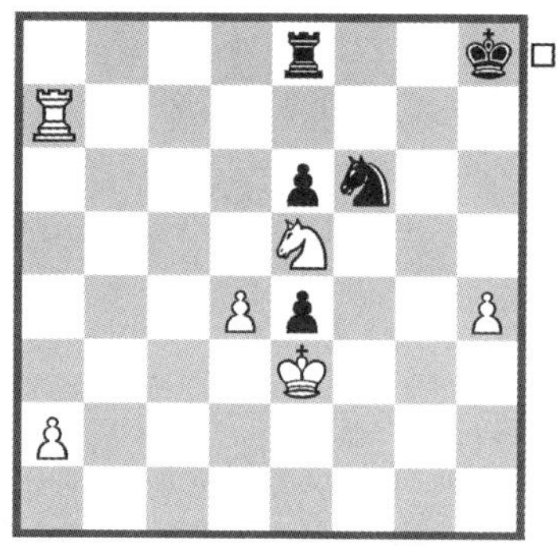

Position after: 36... ♖xe8

37. ♔f4!

White chooses the quickest plan. Black's king is in danger and White goes directly for mate.

37... ♔g8 38. ♔g5 ♖f8 39. ♔g6

1-0

Game 9

♙ Zlatanovic, Boroljub (2331)
♟ Zivanovic, Zoran M (2062)
Serbia 2006

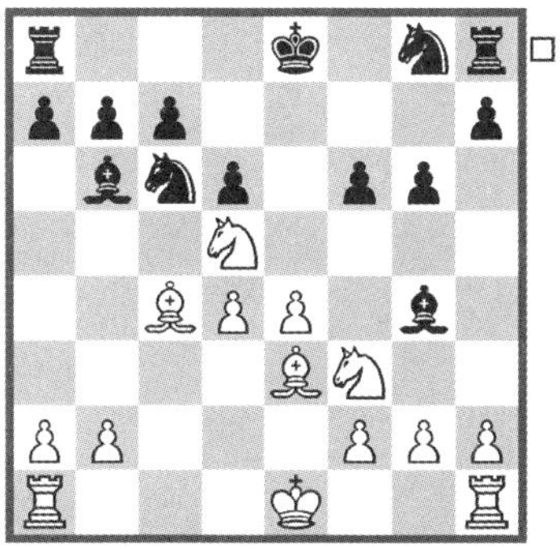

The position on this diagram can hardly be classified as an endgame. However it is still very instructive to follow. The evaluation may be drastic – Black is (almost) hopeless. He is backward in development, without any chance to complete it quickly. At the same time White enjoys strong centralization and dominant activity. The knight on g8 cannot come into play. On the queenside White threatens to prepare a4-a5 which will provoke an advance of Black's a-pawn, and destroy the pawn structure after ♘xb6 cxb6.

First White removes the knight to avoid damaging the pawn structure and at the same time directs it to b3, to prepare for the a4-a5 advance.

12. ♘d2!

This simple retreat proves Black's inability to do anything. The knight goes to b3 and the pawn to f3 to strengthen the center again.

12... 0-0-0 13. ♘b3 ♗a5+

Black, already strategically lost, goes desperate.

14. ♔f1!

Why trade pieces? Black's bishop would be a target.

14. ♘xa5 ♘xa5 15. ♗d3 This does not spoil anything, but White plays a more methodical move.

14... ♔b8 15. ♖c1 ♗b6 16. a4

Alternatively 16. f3 with ♔f2 was another trivial method to improve the initiative. However White is standing perfectly in the center and decides to attack immediately on the flank. This can go ahead when there is such a comfortable situation.

16... ♗d7

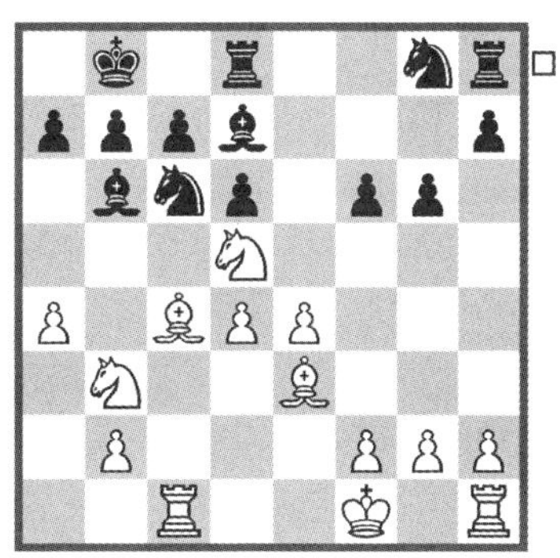

Position after: 16... ♗d7

17. ♗b5?!

17. ♖a1! A clearer and simpler solution.

17... ♗a5 [17... ♘a5 18. ♘xa5 ♗xa5 19. b4+–] 18. h4! Transferring play to another front further underlines Black's helplessness.

17... ♘a5?!

An inaccuracy.

A) 17... f5!? This was better although White keeps the advantage after the following. 18. exf5 gxf5 19. g3

B) 17... ♗e6!? This was another better solution. White would keep all the advantages after 18. ♗c4!.

18. ♘d2!?

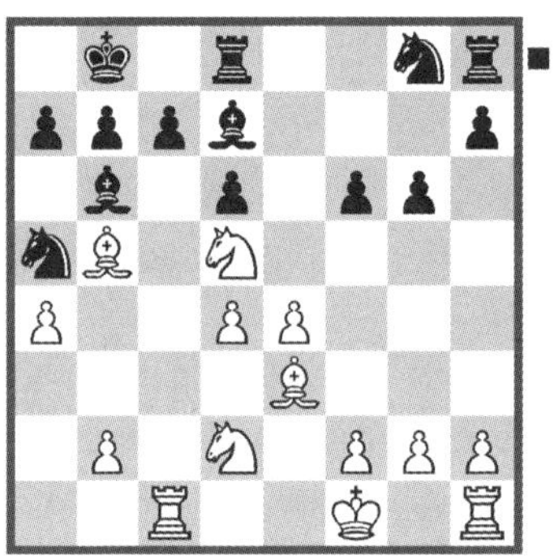

Position after: 18. ♘d2!?

White is consistent in keeping his pieces on the board.

18. ♘xa5 This would have been more direct. 18... ♗xa5 [18... ♗xb5+ 19. axb5 ♗xa5 20. h4! Black is hopeless.] 19. b4

(see analysis diagram next column)

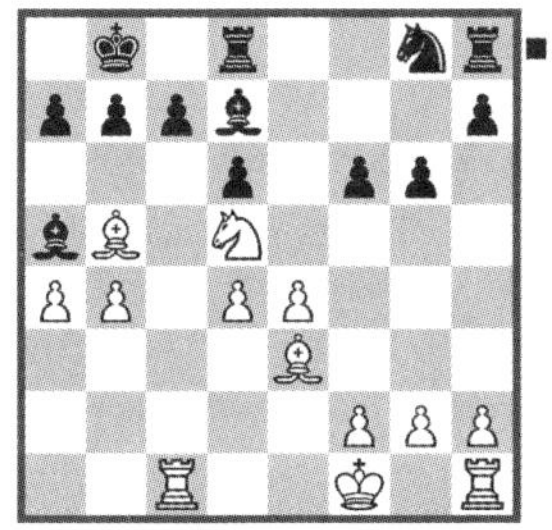

Position after: 19. b4

19... c6 20. ♗f4 White keeps a huge advantage.

18... c6?

Black wanted to radically get rid of White's active pieces, contravening Nimzowitsch's advice to do so patiently, resulting in disaster.

18... ♘c6 This was necessary, but after 19. ♘b3 Black has problems.

19. ♘xb6 axb6

19... cxb5 20. ♘xd7+ ♖xd7 21. axb5+–

20. ♗d3 c5

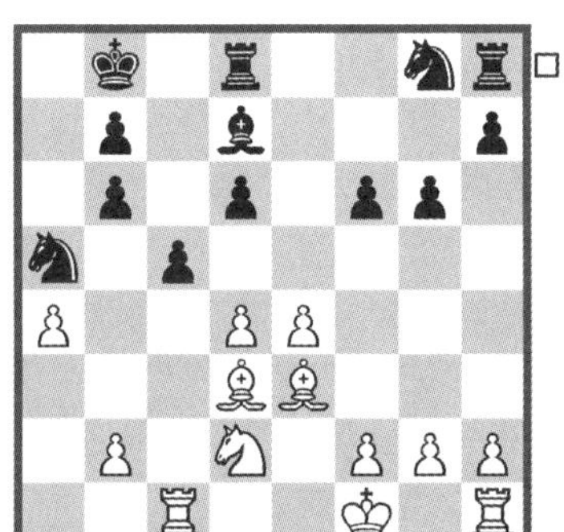

Position after: 20... c5

In order to rescue the knight.

21. ♗f4

21. b4! cxb4 22. d5 This would have led to a beautiful win and crown the centralizing strategy. After 22... ♔a7 23. ♖b1 Black will collapse on the b6-square.

21... ♗xa4 22. ♖a1 ♗c6?

22... c4 This would have delayed resignation. However the result is clear after the following: 23. ♖xa4 cxd3 24. h4 with ideas of h5 and ♖h3-d3.

23. dxc5 g5 24. ♗xd6+ ♖xd6 25. cxd6

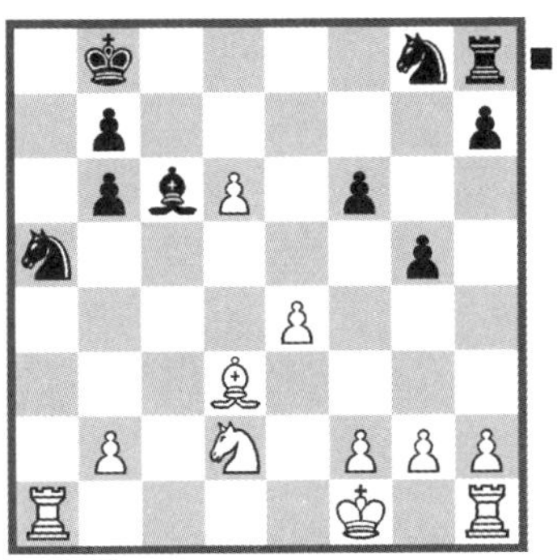

Position after: 25. cxd6

The rest does not require comment.

25... ♗d7 26. b4 ♘c6 27. ♘c4 ♗e6 28. ♘xb6 ♘a7 29. ♔e2 ♘h6 30. ♖a5 ♖d8 31. ♖ha1 ♖xd6 32. ♘d5 ♗xd5 33. exd5

1-0

Game 10

♙ Karpov, Anatoly (2755)
♟ Seirawan, Yasser (2585)
Skelleftea 1989

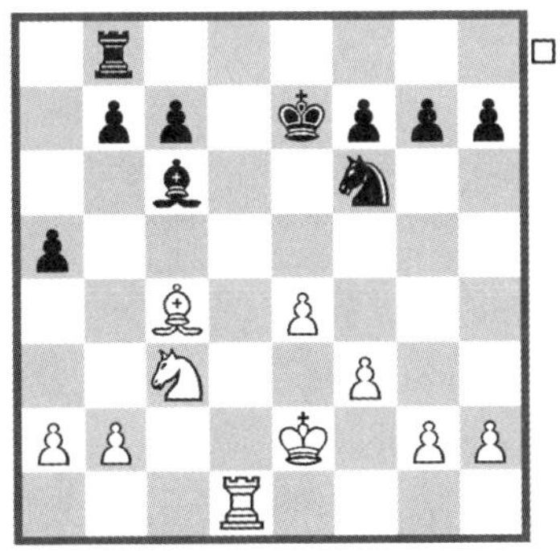

Black did not centralize well in the development phase of the opening, and so the arising endgame is clearly in White's favor. There is clear domination in the center. Black is simply unable to go for simplification by offering the exchange of rooks due to the loss of the f7-pawn. Thus White can comfortably organize play in the center and on the kingside.

17. ♔e3

Supporting the centralization.

17... g6

17... b5 18. ♗f1 b4 19. ♘e2 This is bad for Black. White moves the knight to d4 and the rook to c1 with various threats.

18. ♗b3

A patient move that renders Black's 18... b5 ineffective.

18... ♖a8

Black continues wandering, although it is difficult to suggest anything else. Should the bishop on c6 move, White's next move would be the crushing e5. On the kingside Black also cannot find a single reasonable move. He is forced to wait.

19. ♖d4!

A typical move by Karpov. Whenever any opponent moves somewhere far away from the center, he answers with a strong centralizing move, applying stronger and stronger pressure, both positionally and psychologically. The rook on d4 prevents the move ... a4 and is also ready to be transferred to the kingside after advancing the e-pawn.

19... ♘d7

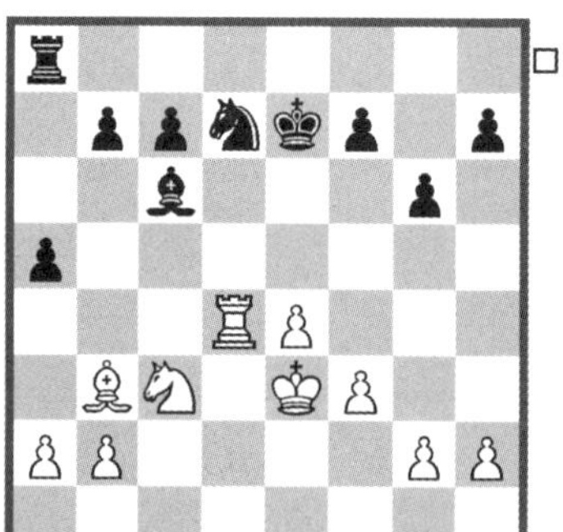

Position after: 19... ♘d7

What else?

20. ♗d5

Black has voluntarily relinquished control over the d5-square and White immediately takes his chance.

20. ♘d5+ This is wrong. 20... ♗xd5 21. ♗xd5

Position after: 21. ♗xd5

21... ♘e5! [21... c6 Another good solution. Now it would be bad for White to play the following. 22. ♗xf7 ♘b6! 23. ♗b3 a4 24. ♗c2 c5 25. ♖d3 ♘c4+ 26. ♔e2 ♘xb2 In this double-edged position Black cannot be worse with such advanced pawns on the queenside.] 22. ♗xb7 ♖b8 Black is not worse. His pieces have finally become active.

20... ♖a6 21. f4!

Improving the kingside position and preparing. Of course, this lets the opponent capture first.

21... f6

Position after: 21... f6

22. h4!

22. g4? An instructive mistake. Always be careful with three connected pawns placed on the same rank. The opponent may strike at the middle one and create holes and outpost for his pieces! 22... g5! The black knight finally gets a perfect outpost on e5.

22... h6

Once again Black is ready to play ...g5.

23. g3

Don't rush!

23. g4? g5!

23... ♗xd5 24. ♘xd5+ ♔d8 25. ♘c3

Every simplification would be in Black's favor. Black wants to play ...♖d6 followed by ...c6. White must keep his centralized pieces. With any exchange a large part of the advantage would dissipate.

25... ♖b6

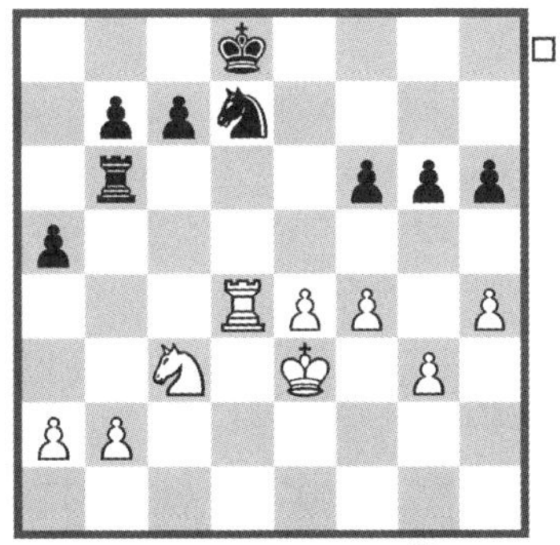

Position after: 25... ♖b6

26. ♖d2!

The rook's job on the 4th rank is done. Now it goes to the 2nd rank to support the move h5. The point is that White wants to eliminate Black's g6-pawn and create an outpost on f5! With three connected pawns on the same rank it is natural to attack the middle one – if it is either exchanged or advanced, an outpost would be created (see comments on White's move 22).

A) 26. b3? The wrong move order. 26... ♖c6 After this, whatever White chooses the rook cannot be easily placed on the 2nd rank. If Black moves the rook to some other square, the move b3 would not be needed.

B) 26. h5 Of course this was strong too but Karpov did not want to change the rhythm of play. Really, why complicate matters if everything is going smoothly?

26... c6 27. h5! g5 28. ♔f3

Both the knight and the king are ready to occupy the f5-square.

28... ♔e7 29. ♘e2?!

29. ♘d1! This is much better – the knight inevitably gets f5.

29... c5 30. ♘c3 ♖d6

Position after: 30... ♖d6

31. ♖d5

31. ♖xd6 ♔xd6 32. ♘d5 This is perhaps a simpler win. However the played move is more methodical – let Black take first. [Alternatively 32. e5+ ♔e6 would complicate White's task. The game move leaves Black in a hopeless situation.]

31... ♖xd5

What else? Black is paralyzed.

32. ♘xd5+ ♔e6 33. ♘e3

The rest is simple and requires no comment.

Position after: 33. ♘e3

33... b5 34. ♘f5 ♘b6 35. ♘xh6 ♘c4 36. ♘f5 ♔f7 37. b3 ♘d2+ 38. ♔e3 ♘f1+

1-0

Game 11

♙ Botvinnik, Mikhail
♟ Vidmar, Milan Sr
Groningen 1946

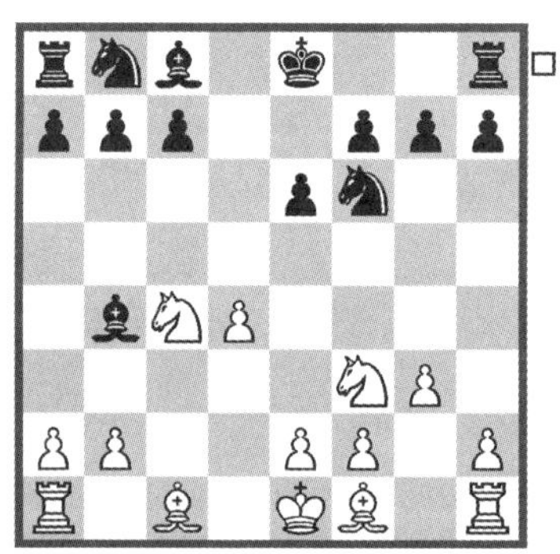

We can hardly call this an endgame. However very soon some pieces will be traded and this is an important moment to start with. White has better development and some chances to establish control over the center. Naturally, he played the following.

9. ♗d2 ♗xd2+ 10. ♘fxd2!

A critical moment and a very instructive move. White does not take with the king although it may look natural with the idea to connect the rooks. Instead White opens the diagonal for the bishop after being placed on g2 and uses the moment to transfer his knight towards the queenside. Black's queenside will be targeted by all of the white pieces. At the same time White makes it possible to establish pawn control over the center with e4 and a possible f3 or f4.

10. ♔xd2 ♘e4+

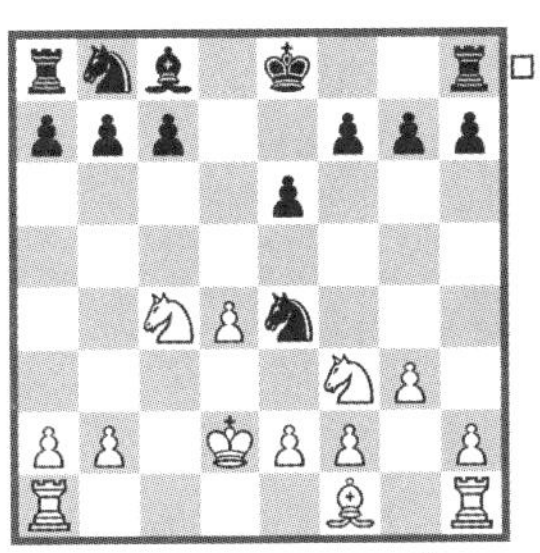

Position after: 10... ♘e4+

[Alternatively simply 10... b6.] 11. ♔e3 ♘d6 This does not look as promising for White as the game continuation.

10... ♘c6

Black suddenly has problems with finishing development of his queenside.

10... ♗d7 11. ♗g2 ♗c6 12. 0-0 This gives White better chances.

11. e3

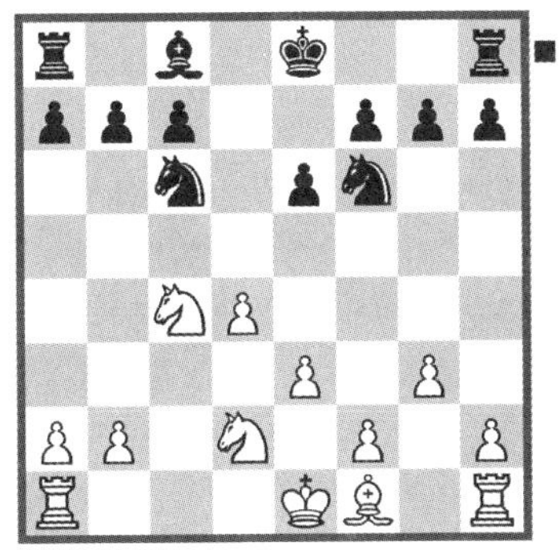

Position after: 11. e3

11... ♘b4?!

This is a diversion. With the lack of space and undeveloped pieces, this cannot be a good solution. The played move results in a waste of time.

11... ♗d7 This was needed. 12. ♗g2 0-0-0 13. ♔e2 White is evidently (much) better, but it is the lesser evil for Black.

12. ♔e2!

Eliminating the primitive threat while supporting development and centralization.

12... ♗d7 13. ♗g2 ♗c6

(see diagram next page)

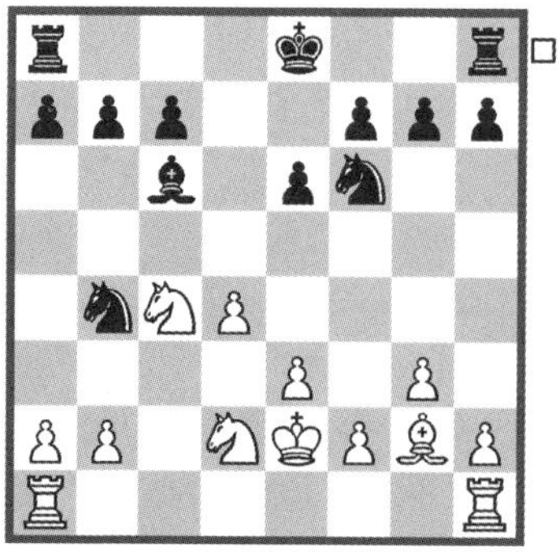

Position after: 13... ♗c6

14. f3!

I like this move very much. It may look as if White has made his own bishop passive and at the same time allowed the black bishop to be an "attacker" – yes, but after the inevitable e4, White will launch his central phalanx. In this case it would be good to keep the pieces on the board – a powerful phalanx will drive back Black's minor pieces, at the same time converting the white pieces to becoming very active! And of course, the b4-knight would be in trouble – the c6-square is taken.

14... ♘d7 15. a3

White starts with the above-mentioned procedure!

15... ♘d5 16. e4 ♘5b6

(see diagram next column)

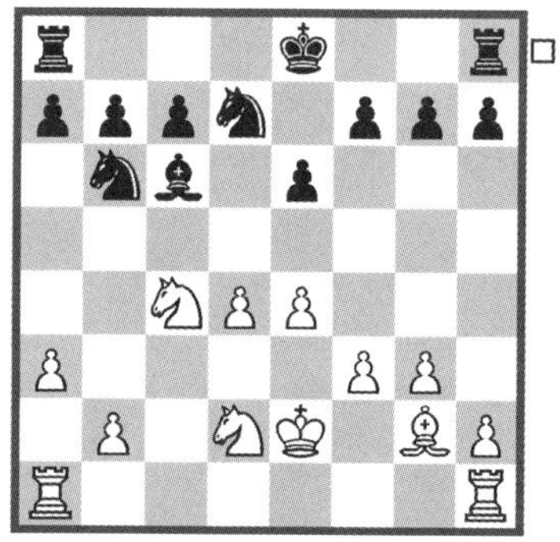

Position after: 16... ♘5b6

17. ♘a5!

After causing disorder in Black's camp, White keeps the knight on the board – a very simple and excellent move. White attacks both the bishop and the b7-pawn, threatening to crush Black's queenside. The a5-square is a very comfortable spot for the white knight which will, together with the bishop placed on g2, put tremendous pressure on the b7-spot and Black's queenside overall.

17... ♗b5+ 18. ♔e3 0-0-0

Black has eliminated the direct threats but his position remains awful.

19. ♖hc1 ♘b8

19...f5 This would have been worth a try, to complicate the game by targeting the white king, intending to destroy the shield or to paralyze the white phalanx.

20. b3 ♗d7

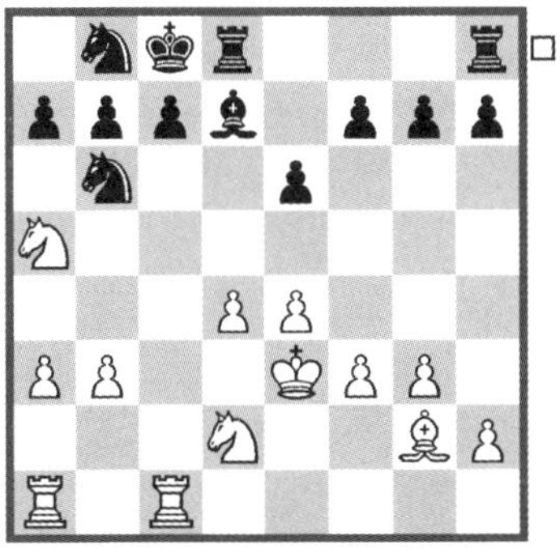

Position after: 20... ♗d7

If Black must go for this, then it is clear that his opening strategy has been a disaster. Pause for a moment to compare the white and black armies – a centralized versus a scattered army.

20... ♘c6 21. a4!+–

21. ♗f1 ♘c6!

Black naturally reduces White's pressure by trading his passive piece for an active one.

22. ♘xc6 ♗xc6 23. a4!

White drives the black pieces back, gaining more and more space.

23... ♗e8 24. a5

(see diagram next column)

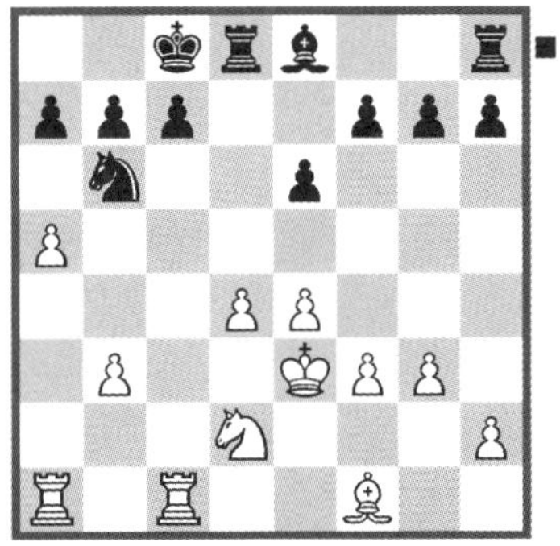

Position after: 24. a5

24... ♘a8

24... ♘d7 25. a6 b6 26. ♖c3 ♔b8 27. ♖ac1

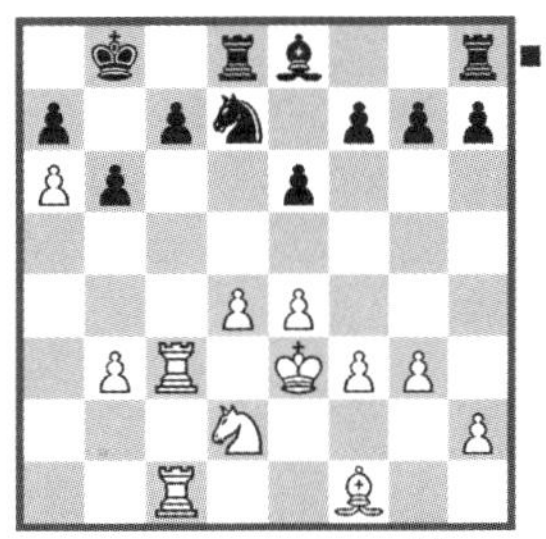

Position after: 27. ♖ac1

27... ♖c8 28. ♘c4 White's idea is ♘d6 and he is simply winning. Black's position is tragicomic.

25. a6 b6 26. b4

While the white army is centralized and harmonized, the black army creates a tragicomic impression.

26... ♔b8

26... c6 27. ♗b5 ♔c7 28. ♗xc6+–

27. ♖c3

27. b5! White will finally lock up the entire black army.

27... c6 28. ♖ac1 f6

Preventing ♘d2-c4-e5.

29. ♘b1

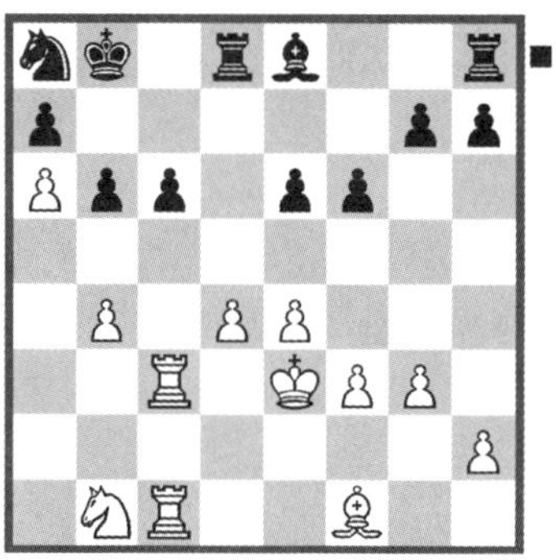

Position after: 29. ♘b1

White’s knight finds another route.

29... ♗d7 30. ♘a3 ♘c7 31. b5! ♘xb5 32. ♗xb5?

32. ♘xb5! cxb5 33. ♖c7 This leads to a clear win after the following. 33... ♖c8 34. ♖b7+ ♔a8 35. ♖xc8+ ♗xc8 36. ♖xg7 ♗xa6 37. ♖f7

32... cxb5 33. ♖c7 ♖c8

This loses.

33... ♗c8! The best defense. 34. ♘xb5 ♖d7! 35. ♖xd7 ♗xd7 36. ♘xa7 ♔xa7 37. ♖c7+ ♔xa6 38. ♖xd7 ♖c8 This is better for White with some small chances for Black to survive.

34. ♖b7+ ♔a8

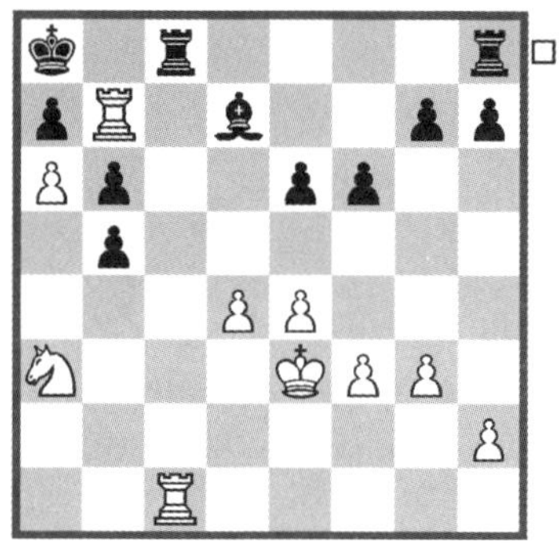

Position after: 34... ♔a8

35. ♖xd7!!

This was White's point. The knight and rook will create a deadly battery and Black is simply hopeless.

35... ♖xc1 36. ♘xb5 ♖hc8 37. ♖xg7

37. ♖xa7+ ♔b8 38. ♖xg7 This was, of course, also winning.

37... h6 38. ♖xa7+ ♔b8 39. ♖b7+ ♔a8 40. ♖a7+ ♔b8 41. ♖b7+ ♔a8

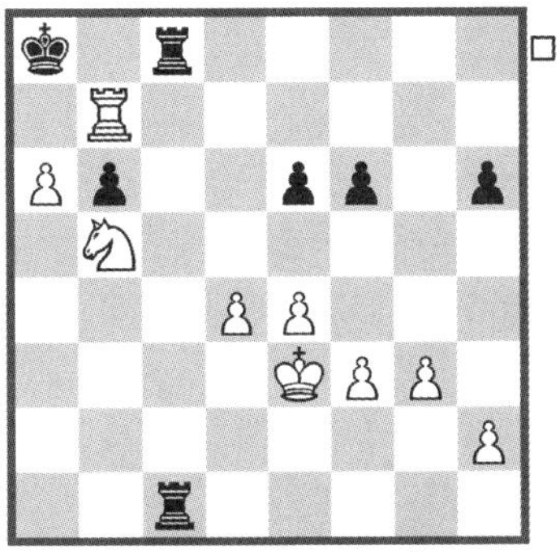

Position after: 41... ♔a8

42. g4

42. ♖e7 This was more methodical.

42... e5

Black tries to organize something with complications.

42... ♖b1 43. ♘c7++–

43. d5 ♖1c5 44. ♖a7+ ♔b8 45. ♖b7+ ♔a8 46. ♖xb6

Position after: 46. ♖xb6

46... ♖b8 47. ♖xb8+ ♔xb8 48. a7+ ♔b7 49. ♘d6+

Simpler and a more prosaic win.

49. d6 This would also win as follows. 49... ♖c8 50. ♔d3 ♖c1 51. h4 Black is hopeless.

49... ♔xa7 50. ♘e8 ♔b6 51. ♘xf6+–

Position after: 51. ♘xf6+–

51... ♖c3+ 52. ♔f2 ♖c7 53. h4 ♖f7 54. ♘h5 ♔c7 55. g5! hxg5 56. hxg5 ♖h7 57. ♘f6 ♖h2+ 58. ♔g3 ♖h1 59. ♔g2 ♖h8 60. g6

Black resigned.

1-0

The Active King

It is clear that the king should be well protected in the opening and middlegame – but what about the endgame? Of course, that is completely different; the king must become active in the endgame – it is one extra piece for the ending. Even in some queen endgames, the king can be an important weapon. Having a passive king in the endgame simply means that you would be a piece down! The fewer pieces there are on the board the more important it is to activate the king – and of course, this is critical in a pawn endgame!

Game 12

♙ D'Amore, Carlo (2425)
♟ Polgar, Sofia (2295)
Rome 1989

In our first example Black is clearly winning. Her pieces are very active and support the dangerous passer which will decide the game. White is desperately passive and must control the infiltration squares c1 and c2. The passer on the a-file is not a significant factor. Black's active pieces need help which must be the job for the king.

44... ♔g7

The king itself goes forward to help the passer.

45. a4

This is just an act of desperation.

45. ♖b4 This would lead to a nice finale after the following. 45... e2+ 46. ♔f2 e1=♕+

Position after: 46... e1=♕+

47. ♔xe1 ♘c2+

45... ♔f6 46. a5

46. g4 g5 Opening a path to the king! 47. ♖b6+ [47. f5 ♔e5] 47... ♔f7 48. f5 e2+

Position after: 48... e2+

49. ♔e1 ♖c2 Mate will soon follow.

46... ♔f5 47. a6

Position after: 47. a6

47. h3 e2+ 48. ♔e1 [48. ♔f2 e3+] 48... e3 Black will follow with ...♔e4 and an easy win.

47... ♔g4

The king gets full activity.

48. ♔g2 e2 49. h3+ ♔f5 50. ♔f2 e3+

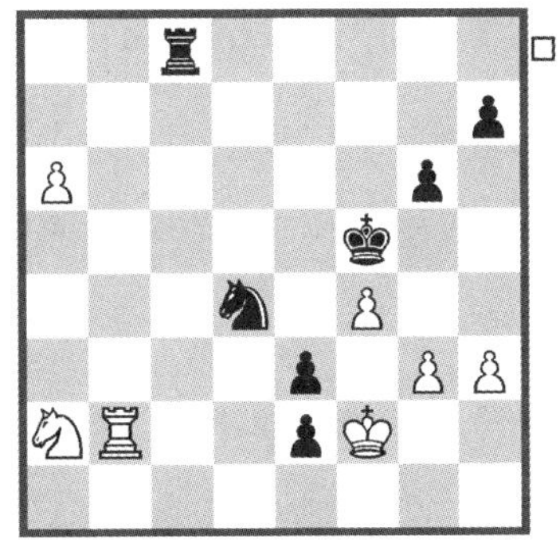

Position after: 50... e3+

Now the king definitely invades.

51. ♔e1 ♔e4 52. ♖b4 ♔d3 53. ♖xd4+ ♔xd4 54. ♘b4 ♔c4 55. ♘c2 ♔c3 56. ♔xe2 ♔xc2 57. f5 gxf5 58. ♔xe3 ♖a8 59. ♔f4 ♖xa6 60. ♔xf5 ♖g6 61. ♔f4 ♔d3

0-1

Game 13

♙	Smyslov, Vassily V	(2550)
♟	Fuller, Maxwell L	(2355)
🌍	Copenhagen 1980	

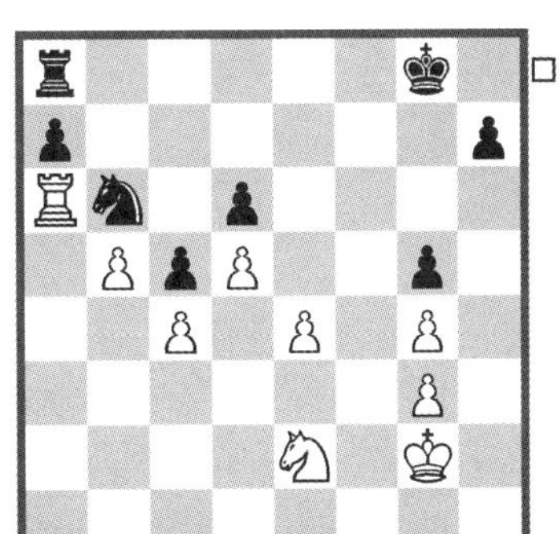

White is a pawn up, but how can he save the c4-pawn? After it falls Black will have even chances to opt for more than equality. Was Smyslov wrong to decide to go for this endgame?

31. e5!

This blow was predicted by the great champion. Black's position will collapse soon.

31... dxe5

31... ♘xc4 32. exd6 This changes nothing.

32. ♔f3 ♘xc4 33. ♔e4

On the surface Black is a pawn up but White's active king decides the game.

33... ♖d8

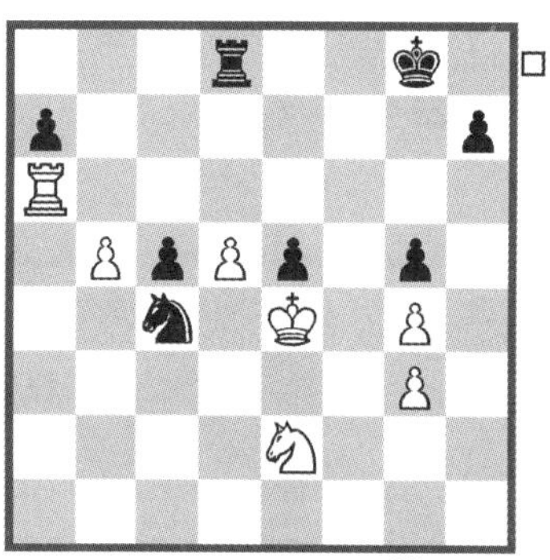

Position after: 33... ♖d8

33... ♔f7 34. ♖c6 White gains material with a winning positional advantage.

34. ♘c3

Preparing even ♔f5 and possibly ♘e4 afterwards.

34... ♖d7 35. ♖c6 ♔g7 36. ♖xc5

Position after: 36. ♖xc5

The game is over. The rest needs no comment.

36... ♘d6+ 37. ♔xe5 ♔f7 38. ♘e4 ♘xe4 39. ♔xe4 ♖e7+ 40. ♔f5

1-0

Game 14

♙ Mazzoni, Guy
♟ Larsen, Bent
Le Havre 1966

The compact pawn structure (White's b-pawn is useless, while at the same time Black has a plan of advancing in the center and to attack on the kingside with ...h4) and Black's inability to install the knight makes the evaluation clear – Black is better. His first task is to improve the king – this is especially important because its white counterpart may not take part in the struggle.

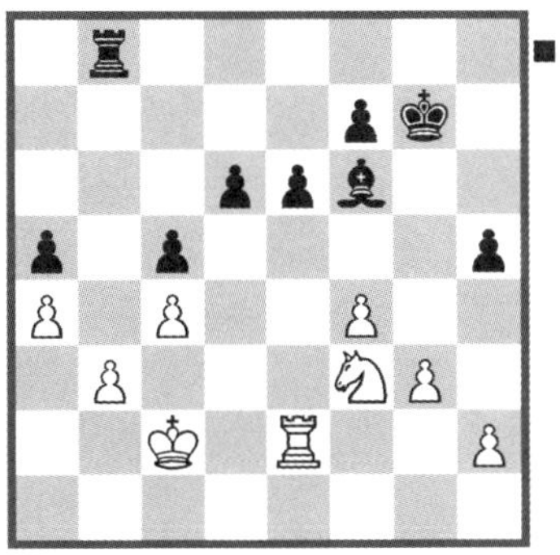

37... ♔g6 38. ♖d2 ♗e7 39. ♖e2

White is practically forced to hold a waiting policy.

39. ♖d3!? ♔f5 40. ♘g5!?

Position after: 40. ♘g5!?

This would be interesting and a somewhat wild attempt at active resistance. However after 40... ♖f8 Black would keep the advantage due to the threat of ...h4.

39... ♔f5

And this is a good exercise to you, dear reader. Although the engine evaluates the position as only "slightly better" for Black, in a real game it is almost impossible for White to hold. Well, can you find Black's plan for a win and try to convert the advantage against White's various defensive plans?

40. ♘d2?!

White switches to passive defense.

40. ♖d2 This would be better instead because now: 40... h4?! [40... ♖d8 would have been, of course, normal resuming the threat of ...h4] is met by 41. ♘xh4+!.

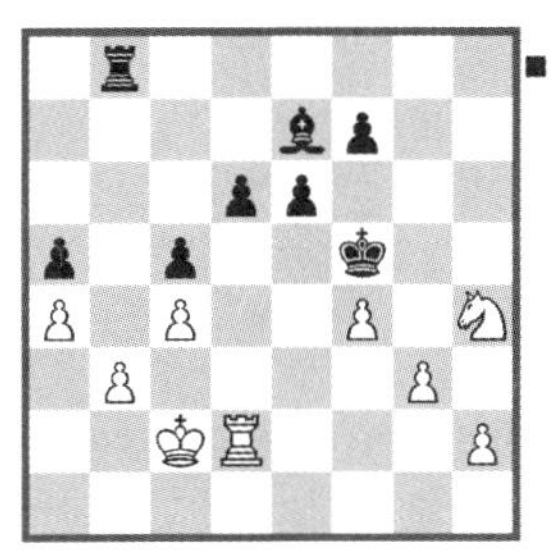

Position after: 41. ♘xh4+!

41... ♗xh4 42. gxh4 ♖d8 43. h3 Surprisingly, this would keep the balance.

40... h4 41. ♘f1

(see diagram next page)

41. ♘e4 This would have been better. If the knight needs to control g3, let it do so from the center.

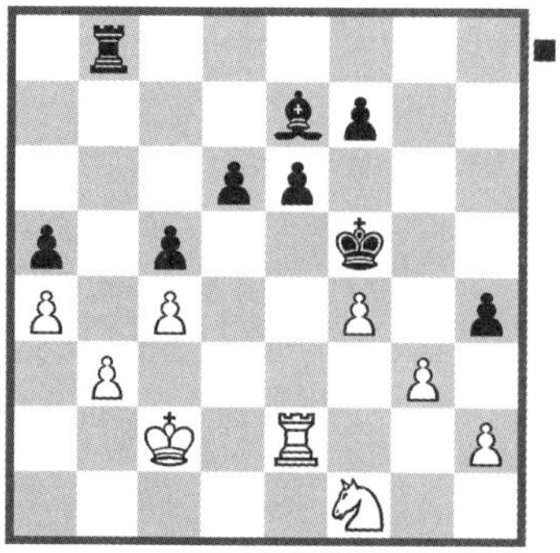

Position after: 41. ♘f1

41... ♔g4?

Activating the king, but still wrong.

41... hxg3 42. hxg3 ♗f6 Setting the bishop on d4 and activating the rook via the h-file would be more direct and better.

42. ♖e3?

Returning the favor.

42. ♖f2 hxg3 43. hxg3 ♖h8 44. ♔d3 White can put up more resistance.

42... ♗f6 43. ♔d2 ♗d4 44. ♖d3 hxg3 45. hxg3 ♖h8

Black is winning. White's pieces are cramped and without chances to put up any resistance.

46. ♔e2 ♖h1 47. ♘e3+ ♔xg3!

(see diagram next column)

Position after: 47... ♔xg3!

48. ♘f5+ ♔xf4 49. ♘xd6 ♖h2+ 50. ♔d1 f5

The tricks are gone. It is time to resign.

51. ♘b7 e5 52. ♘xa5 e4 53. ♖d2 ♖h1+ 54. ♔e2 ♗c3

0-1

Game 15

♙ Kasparov, Garry (2630)
♟ Beliavsky, Alexander G (2620)
🌍 Frunze 1981

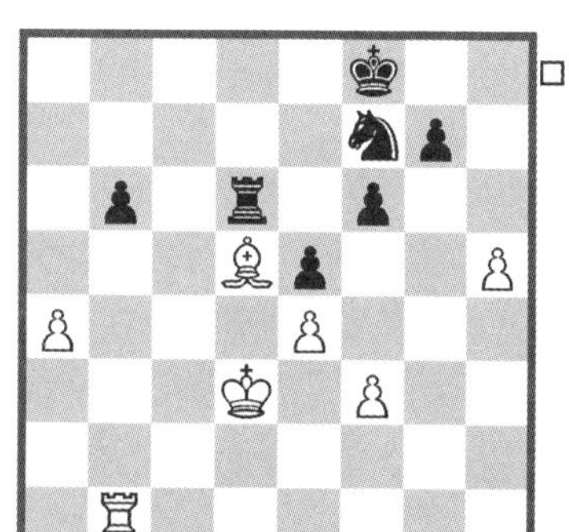

White is dominant due to his strong bishop and more active rook and king. Still, the king should become more active. Kasparov plays directly invading with the king.

48. ♔c4 ♘g5 49. ♖b3

There is no reason to complicate. White will easily win after the maneuver ♔b5-a6.

49... ♔e7

49... ♘h3 This is slow. White wins after the following. 50. ♔b5 ♘f4 51. ♗c4! Δ 52.♔a6 + –

50. ♔b5 f5

Seeking any counterplay.

51. ♔a6 f4

Position after: 51... f4

52. ♔b7!

A move in advance. The king liberates the path for the a-pawn.

52. ♖xb6? This is a mistake because of 52... ♘xf3 and surprisingly Black is okay after the following. 53. ♔b7

Position after: 53. ♔b7

[53. ♖xd6 ♔xd6 54. ♔b6 This is horrible in view of 54... ♘d2 where White must save the draw with 55. ♗b7!.] 53... ♖d7+

52... ♖h6

52... ♔d7 53. ♖xb6 ♘xf3 This loses after 54. a5.

53. ♖xb6 ♖xb6+ 54. ♔xb6

Position after: 54. ♔xb6

The game is over. There are some technical issues which is not a problem for Kasparov.

54... ♘xf3 55. a5 ♘d2 56. a6 f3 57. a7 f2 58. a8=♕ f1=♕

Position after: 58... f1=♕

It may look like mutual promotion is an achievement for Black but he is simply lost – the white king helps to knit a mating net around its counterpart.

59. ♔c7

59. ♕a3+ ♔f6 60. ♕g3 This is another, even simpler, win.

59... ♕c1+

59... ♕f8 This fails to 60. ♕a3+ with a forced mate which you may find yourself.

60. ♗c6 ♘xe4 61. ♕e8+ ♔f6 62. ♕g6+ ♔e7 63. ♕xg7+ ♔e6 64. ♕g4+

(see diagram next column)

Position after: 64. ♕g4+

64... ♔f7 65. ♕g6+ ♔f8

65... ♔e7 66. ♕xe4

66. h6

1-0

Game 16

♙	Damljanovic, Branko	(2534)
♟	Velimirovic, Dragoljub	(2558)
🌍	Subotica 2000	

Although it may look as if Black is fine here due to his majority on the kingside and the beautiful knight with most of the white pawns fixed on the bishop's color, in actual fact the white king's activity is the dominant positional factor here.

34. ♔c3 a5

Black, pursuing his active-playing style, tries to change the character of the battle with some active moves. Alas, there is nothing to achieve – White has a centralized army and more importantly, the far more active king.

34... ♔f7 35. ♘c6 a5 36. ♔d4

Position after: 36. ♔d4

36... ♘b7 37. ♔e5 This is winning.

35. ♘c6 ♗a6 36. ♘e5 ♔g7 37. ♔d4

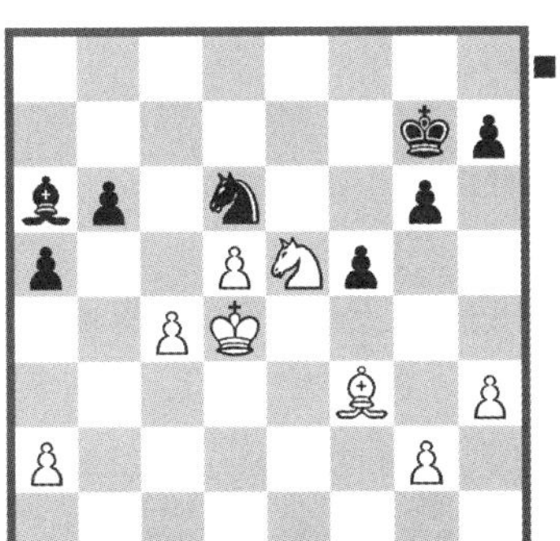

Position after: 37. ♔d4

37... g5

Alternatively 37... f4 with the idea to deliver check from f5 would have been the last chance to prolong resistance. However 38. ♗g4 with the further a4 to prepare c5 would be winning.

38. a4

Eliminating the check on b5 and preparing c5.

38... f4 39. ♗g4! ♗c8

An act of desperation.

40. ♗xc8

The simplest win.

40... ♘xc8 41. c5+–

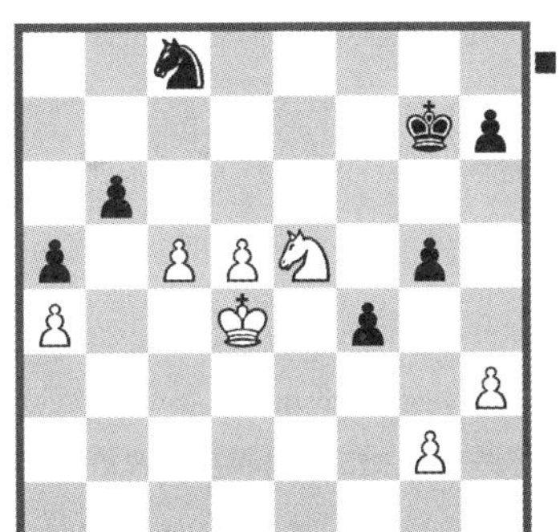

Position after: 41. c5+–

41... bxc5+ 42. ♔xc5 ♔f6 43. ♘c4 h5 44. ♘xa5 g4

Black's counterplay on the kingside comes too late.

45. hxg4 hxg4 46. ♘c4

Position after: 46. ♘c4

46... ♘e7

46... f3 This changes nothing. White wins after the following. 47. gxf3 gxf3 [47... g3 48. ♘e3 ♔e5 49. ♘g2+–] 48. ♘d2+–

47. a5 f3 48. gxf3 gxf3 49. ♘d2 f2 50. d6

Black resigned.

1-0

Game 17

♙ Andersson, Ulf (2623)
♟ Hansen, Sune Berg (2558)
Helsingor 1999

White is evidently better here due to the excellent activity of all his pieces. It may look as if there is nothing apparent, but White gets the moment for an excellent maneuver.

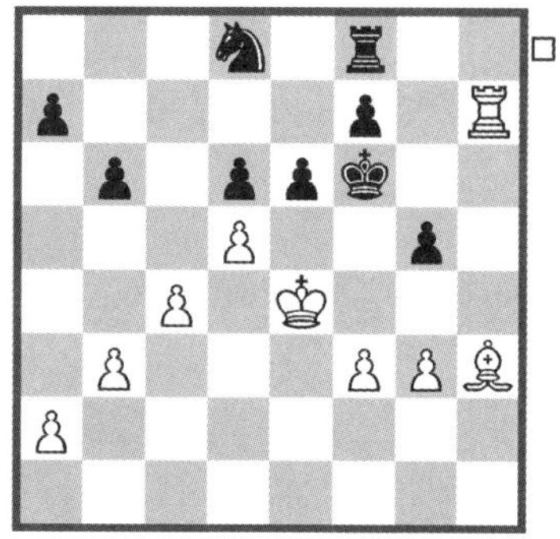

29. dxe6! ♖e8

A) 29... ♘xe6 30. ♗xe6! ♔xe6 31. ♖h6+

Position after: 31. ♖h6+

31... f6 32. ♖h7! Black is clearly about to collapse.

B) 29... fxe6 This is bad because of 30. ♖xa7.

30. ♗g4!

Liberating the rook. At some point, ♗h5 will be a threat.

30. ♔d5?? ♔g6 White must save the draw after the following. 31. ♔xd6 ♔xh7 32. e7

Position after: 32. e7

32... ♘c6 33. ♗d7! The position is balanced.

30... ♘xe6

30... a5 31. ♔d5+–

31. ♔d5

The result of the fine maneuver is a fully active king and Black is lost. There is nothing to oppose the white king's demolition of Black's queenside.

31... ♔g6

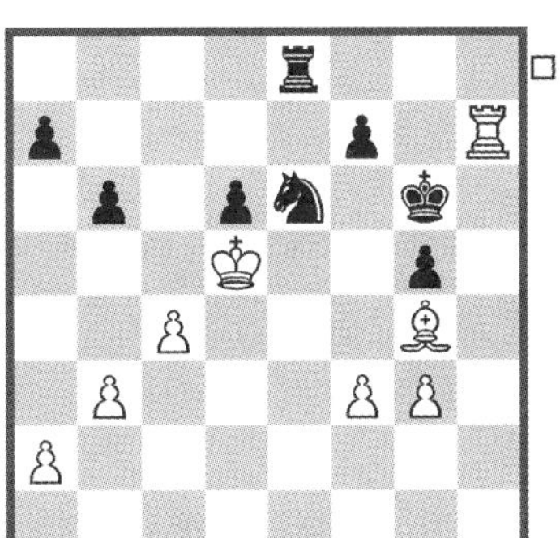

Position after: 31... ♔g6

32. ♖h2!

A precise retreat.

32... ♘g7 33. ♗d7

But not 33. ♔xd6? f5 34. ♗h3 ♖h8 and Black has counterplay.

33... ♖e3 34. ♖f2

There is no need to rush.

34... ♘h5 35. g4 ♘f6+ 36. ♔c6

Position after: 36. ♔c6

White's king finally invades.

36... ♔g7

36... ♘xd7 This would achieve nothing. 37. ♔xd7 ♖d3 [37... f5 38. ♔xd6 fxg4 39. fxg4

Position after: 39. fxg4

39... ♖g3 40. b4 ♖xg4 41. ♖c2+–] 38. ♔c6 f5 39. ♔b7 d5 40. cxd5!+–

37. ♗f5 ♘e8 38. ♗e4 ♘f6 39. ♗d5 ♘e8

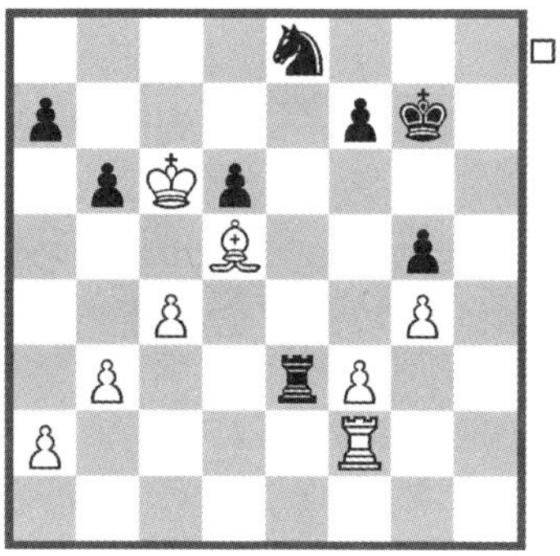

Position after: 39... ♘e8

Black fights with great energy, but it will not change anything.

40. b4?!

40. ♔b7 ♖e7+ 41. ♔b8 or 40. ♔d7 ♔f8 41. ♖h2 are both clearly better ways to continue.

40... ♖e7 41. ♖d2 ♔f8 42. ♗e4 ♖c7+ 43. ♔b5

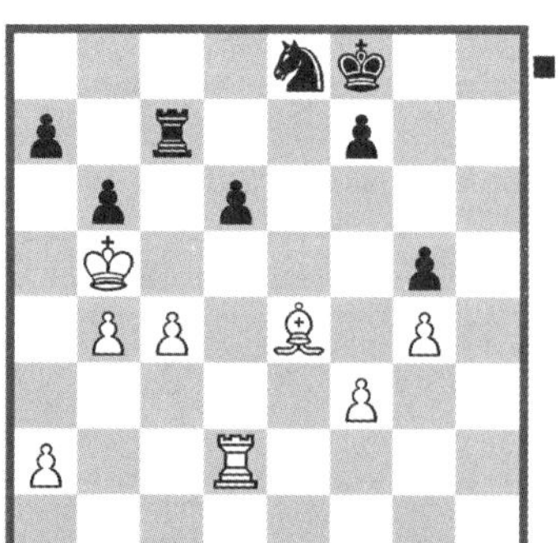

Position after: 43. ♔b5

43... ♖c8

This does not look the best but already there is no rescue.

43... ♔e7 44. ♗d5 ♘f6 45. ♖e2+ ♔d8 46. ♔a6+–

44. ♗b7! ♖c7

44... ♖b8 45. ♔a6+–

45. ♗c6 ♘g7 46. ♖xd6 ♔e7 47. ♖d2 ♘e6 48. ♗d5 ♘f4 49. ♗e4 ♔f6 50. c5

Position after: 50. c5

The rest is simple.

50... bxc5 51. bxc5 ♘e6 52. c6 ♖c8 53. ♖d7 ♘c7+

Here Black resigned.

1-0

Game 18

♙ Lebel Arias, Julia (1724)
♟ Osmak, Iulija (2405)
Batumi 2018

Although the position may look quite balanced with many pawns on the board and a restricted bishop, in actual fact Black is completely winning. Advanced players will undoubtedly assess the difference in the kings' activities as the decisive factor.

31... ♖c1+

So simple. Black first kicks the white king out of play.

32. ♔h2 ♔f8

... And now activates his own. Black's king goes towards the queenside. Black will easily win the game, having an extra unit.

33. ♖d2 ♔e7 34. ♖a2

34. ♔h3 If White plays this at any moment, he would be faced with a nice reaction. 34... ♖h1+ 35. ♘h2 f5 Black is about to provide for ...g5-g4 with a win.

34... ♔d7 35. ♘d2 b6

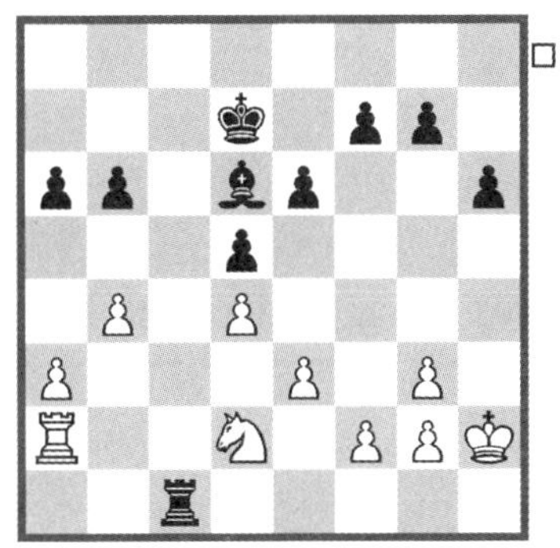

Position after: 35... b6

36. ♘b3 ♖c3 37. ♘d2 ♔c6 38. ♘b1 ♖c1 39. ♖b2 ♔b5

Picturesque. The game is over.

40. ♘d2 ♔a4 41. ♘b1 e5

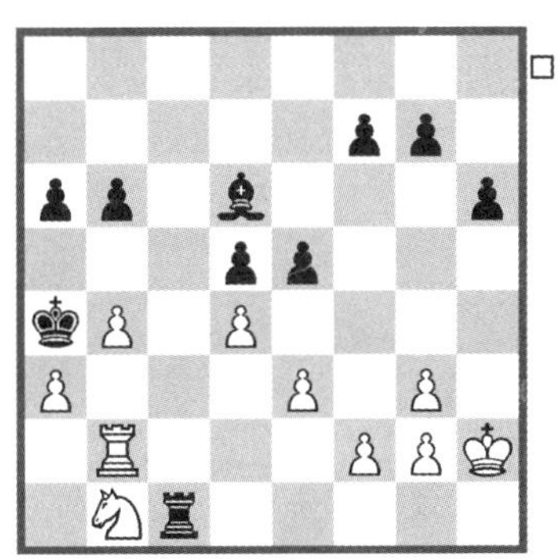

Position after: 41... e5

Black uses the fact that the white troops are paralyzed to strike on the opposite flank. Everything wins.

42. f4 exd4 43. exd4 f5 44. ♘d2 ♔xa3 45. ♖b3+ ♔a4 46. ♖e3 ♗xb4 47. ♘f3 a5

Position after: 47... a5

48. ♖e5 ♔b3 49. ♖xd5 a4 50. ♖d7 a3 51. d5 a2 52. ♘d4+ ♔b2

0-1

Game 19

♙ Butnorius, Algimantas (2392)
♟ Delchev, Aleksander (2640)
Turin 2006

Black is absolutely dominant due to his better rook, better bishop, and better pawn structure fitting with the bishop. It is time to activate the king.

35... ♔e7

35... ♗xe4? Of course, not this move when White has two good replies: 36. ♖f2+ and 36. ♖e2. Both of them will lead to a balanced position.

36. ♗d5

White protects the pawn. He is unable to activate his king to the desired e3-square due to Black's discovered check with ...♗c2 and winning.

36... ♔d6 37. ♔g2 ♔c5 38. ♔f2 ♔d4

Exactly on time. An instructive example on the topic of centralization and active king. The game is decided.

39. ♗g8 h6

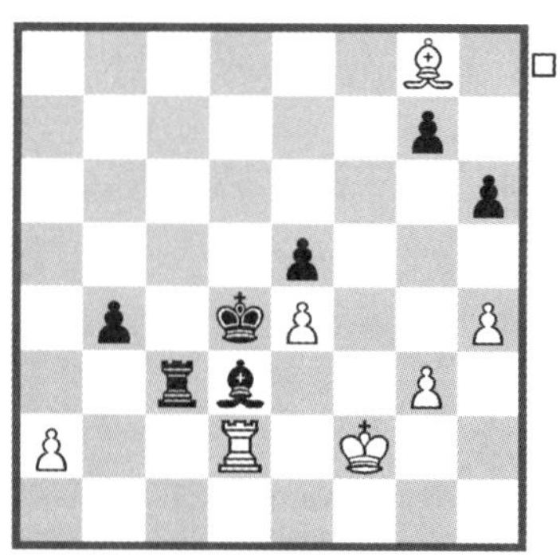

Position after: 39... h6

40. ♗b3

40. ♗d5 ♖c2 The simplest win. 41.

♖xc2 ♗xc2 42. ♔f3 ♗d3 A zugzwang is coming up.

40... ♔xe4 41. ♗d1 ♔d4 42. ♖b2 ♔c5 43. ♔e1 e4

With an extra pawn and maintaining his positional domination Black wins easily.

44. ♔f2 ♖c1 45. ♗e2 ♖c2!

Position after: 45... ♖c2!

46. ♖xc2+ ♗xc2 47. ♔e3 ♗b1 48. ♗d1 ♗xa2 49. ♔xe4 b3

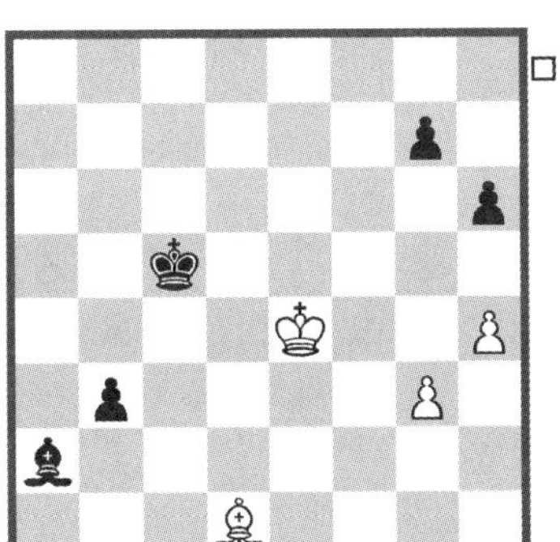

Position after: 49... b3

50. ♔f5 b2 51. ♗c2 ♔d4 52. ♔g6 ♗c4

0-1

Game 20

♙ Kosashvili, Yona (2560)
♟ Psakhis, Lev (2625)
Haifa 1995

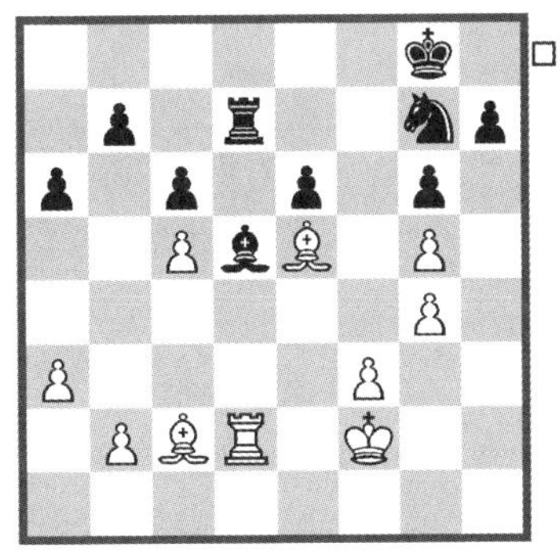

White's domination is evident. The bishop pair dominates. Black's bishop must not move, and his knight and rook are without prospects. White can even exchange his bishop for the knight and easily play with his better bishop. However of course, before any such action the king should be activated – the knight can be taken at any moment.

39. ♔e3 ♖f7 40. f4 ♔f8+– 41. ♗d1

There is no need to rush. White prevents a possible ...♗f3.

41... ♘e8 42. ♔d4 ♖d7

(see diagram next page)

Position after: 42... ♖d7

43. ♔c3

Now White's plan becomes crystal-clear – his king will invade Black's queenside.

43... ♔e7 44. ♔b4 ♔d8 45. ♔a5 ♘c7 46. ♔b6 ♔c8 47. a4

With all the pieces on their most active squares it is time for pawn action. White starts with organizing it on the queenside.

47... ♖f7 48. ♗c2

... But now switches to the kingside.

48... ♗f3 49. ♗xc7!

(see diagram next colum,)

Black wants to activate the knight, so this is the right moment to eliminate it. White has no problem giving away his powerful bishop.

Position after: 49. ♗xc7!

49... ♖xc7 50. f5 ♗xg4

50... gxf5 51. gxf5 This changes nothing.

51. f6

Picturesque. Look at how the black pawns are all placed on the light squares. The extra pawn means nothing with such a bad structure. White wins easily.

51... ♖f7 52. ♖d6 e5 53. ♗b3 ♖f8 54. ♗e6+

Position after: 54. ♗e6+

54... ♗xe6 55. ♖xe6 ♔d8 56. ♔xb7

Black resigned.

56. ♔xb7 ♖e8 Leading to a nice mate after 57. ♖d6#.

1-0

Game 21

♙ Polugaevsky, Lev
♟ Tal, Mihail
Leningrad 1971

Here it is evident that White dominates. Strangely, Tal allowed his opponent to fix with a5, missing playing ...a5! himself. As a result, the chronic weaknesses on the dark squares will decide the game. A perceptive reader will guess White's plan.

23. ♔b2!

Of course, White intends to directly invade the holes on the queenside.

23... ♗e6 24. ♔c3 ♖ac8 25. ♔b4! h5

Already an act of desperation. There is nothing to oppose White's infiltration. In any case, this action will change nothing.

25... c5+ This would stop the king but now the b7-pawn is in danger. 26. ♔c3 ♖c7 27. ♖d6 Black is hopeless.

26. ♗f3! hxg4 27. hxg4 ♖cd8

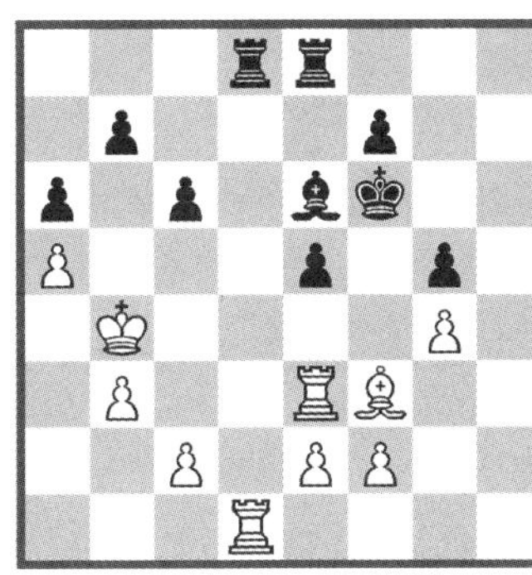

Position after: 27... ♖cd8

A usual approach won't be enough to win here.

28. ♖xd8 ♖xd8 29. ♔c5 ♖d4

29... ♖d2 30. ♔b6 ♖xc2 31. ♔xb7+–

30. c4!

So beautiful. White closes the fourth rank and goes to destroy Black's queenside.

30... ♗xg4

30... ♖d7 31. ♖d3!+–

31. ♗xg4 ♖xg4 32. ♔b6 ♖f4 33. f3 e4 34. ♔xb7!

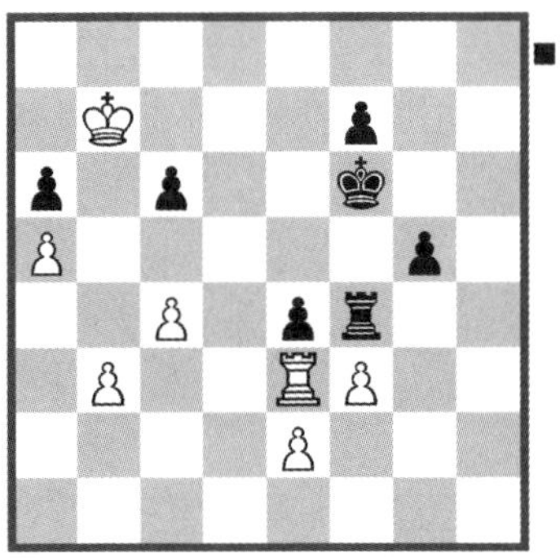

Position after: 34. ♔xb7!

Of course!

34... ♔e5 35. ♔xa6 ♔d4 36. ♖xe4+ ♖xe4 37. fxe4 g4

No, there is no chance for Black. White has calculated precisely.

38. ♔b7 g3 39. a6 g2 40. a7 g1=♕ 41. a8=♕

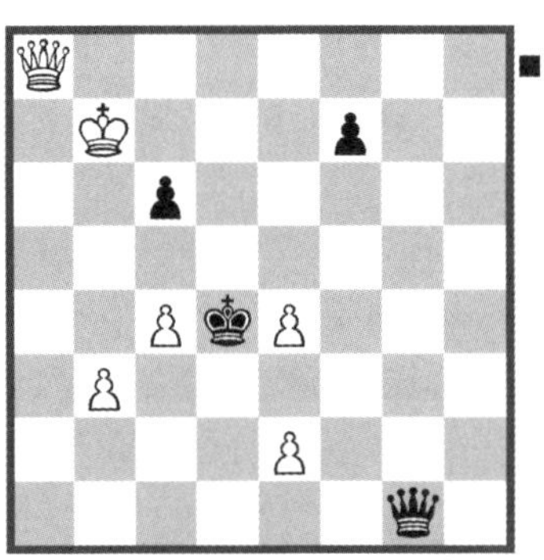

Position after: 41. a8=♕

41... c5

What else?

42. ♔b6!

Having a newborn queen does not force you to move it!

42... ♔c3 43. ♕d5 ♕g8

43... ♔xb3 44. ♕xc5 Black is lost. His king is in the wrong place. White's king will easily find shelter.

44. ♔xc5 ♔xb3

44... ♕c8+ 45. ♔b6 ♕b8+ 46. ♔a6 This gives Black nothing.

45. ♕d3+ ♔b2

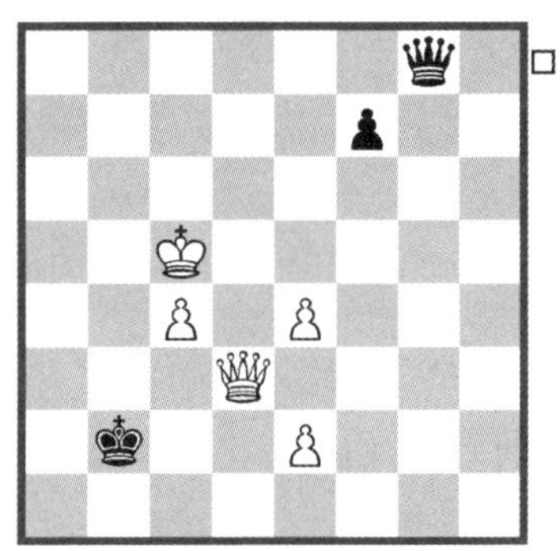

Position after: 45... ♔b2

46. ♕d6!

Instructive. Before launching the passer in a queen endgame it is important to re-establish harmony, set the queen on the best spot and prevent checks.

46... ♔b3

46... ♕c8+ 47. ♕c6 ♕f8+ 48. ♔b6+–

47. ♕b6+ ♔c2 48. ♔b5 ♕g4 49. ♕d4

Centralization is still the leading chess principle here.

49... ♕xe2 50. ♔b6 ♕h2 51. e5!

Position after: 51. e5!

51... ♔b3 52. c5 f6 53. c6! fxe5 54. ♕d5+ ♔a4 55. ♕b5+ ♔a3 56. c7

Black resigned.

1-0

Game 22

♙ Tal, Mihail
♟ Uhlmann, Wolfgang
🌍 Moscow 1967

With such amazing activity White must be dominant. But how should he improve? Tal was always a master of concrete play, so his next move suggested itself and was not difficult for him to find.

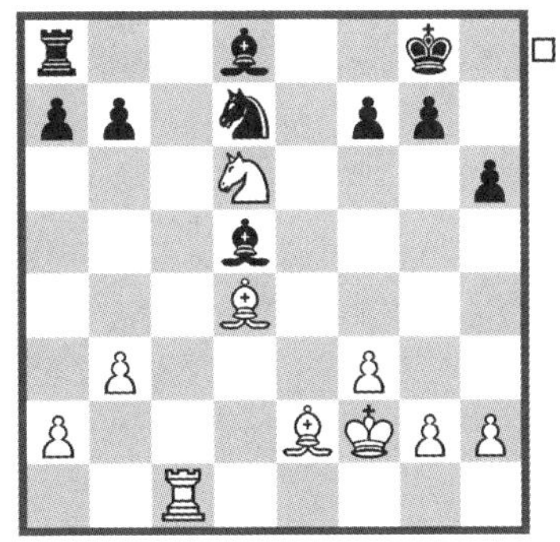

24. ♗c4!

A simple idea to eliminate the best defender! If you observe more deeply you will see that White is now able to activate his king!

24... ♗xc4 25. ♖xc4 b6

25... ♗b6 This is practically the last chance to organize any defense.

26. ♔e3

What a triumph of activity! The king itself joins the attack to deliver a devastating strike after exchanging rooks.

26... g6

There is in fact nothing to oppose.

27. ♔e4 ♗e7 28. ♖c8+

(see diagram next page)

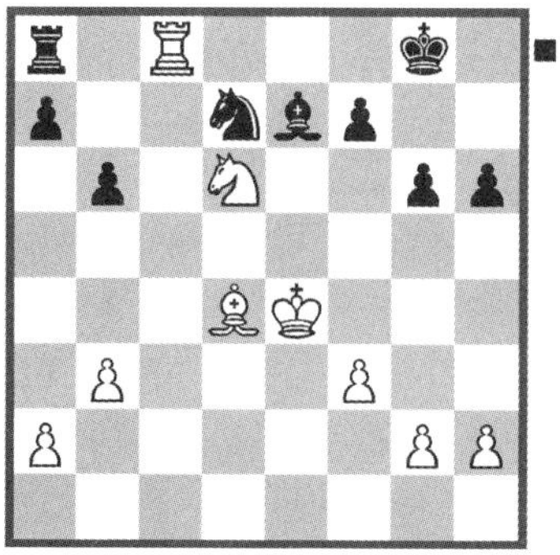

Position after: 28. ♖c8+

White cannot further delay trading the rooks. In any case, this is the simplest way to convert.

28... ♖xc8 29. ♘xc8 f5+ 30. ♔d5 ♔f7

1-0

Game 23

♙ Tal, Mihail
♟ Lisitsin, Georgy M
🌍 Leningrad 1956

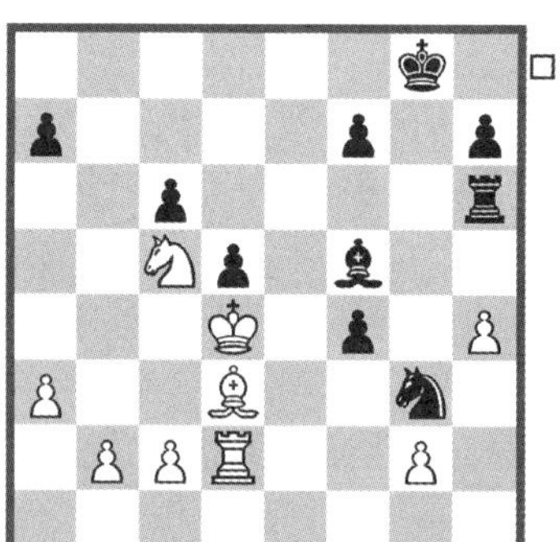

This is a very unclear position. Black is formally a pawn up, and threatening another pawn. Furthermore, after the h4-pawn falls Black will threaten ...♖h2 and ...f3! White must find something quickly.

30. ♔e5!

This time the active king keeps the balance!

30... ♗xd3 31. cxd3

31. ♘xd3 This is not good. After 31... ♔f8 Black is much better with an extra pawn.

31... ♖xh4 32. ♔d6?!

Tal goes towards the queenside pawns prematurely.

It would have been better to use the fact that the king is attacking the f4-pawn, and start pushing on the queenside.
Now, for instance the following line will lead to a dynamic balance. 32. b4 ♖h6 33. ♔xf4 ♖g6 34. ♘d7

Position after: 33... ♖g6

32... ♖h6+ 33. ♔c7

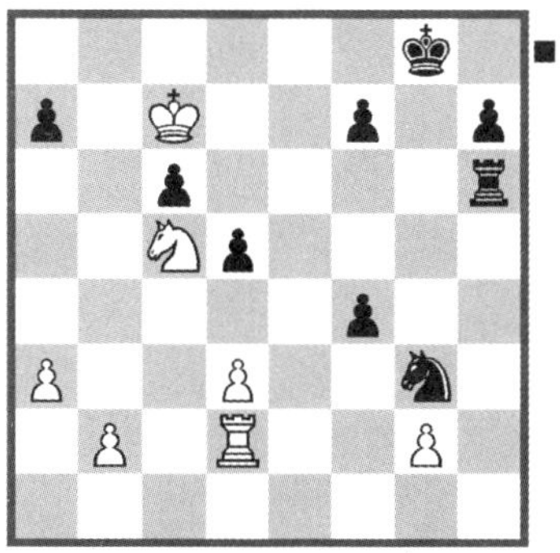

Position after: 33. ♔c7

33... ♘f5?

Returning the favor. Now the initiative goes to Tal.

33... ♖h2! 34. ♖f2 h5! Black would have the advantage.

34. ♔b7?!

34. ♖f2 Why not this move?

34... ♘d4?

All this looks natural for Black. The centralized knight protects c6. However White has a direct way to improve.

34... ♘d6+! 35. ♔xa7 ♖h2 36. ♖f2 f3

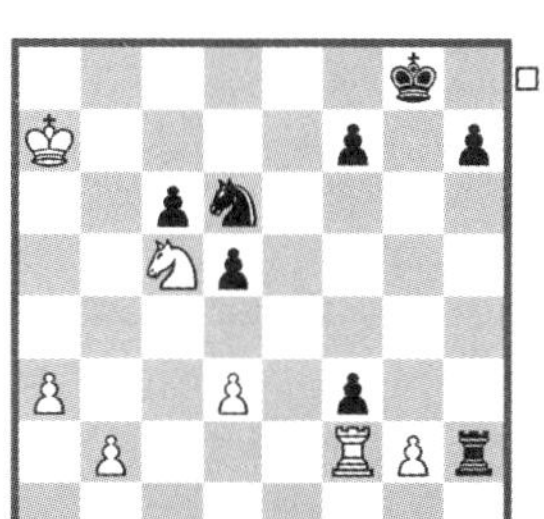

Position after: 36... f3

37. ♖xf3 ♖xg2 This is unclear.

35. ♖f2!

Black's play on the kingside would now come too late.

35... a5 36. ♖xf4 ♘e6 37. ♖g4+!

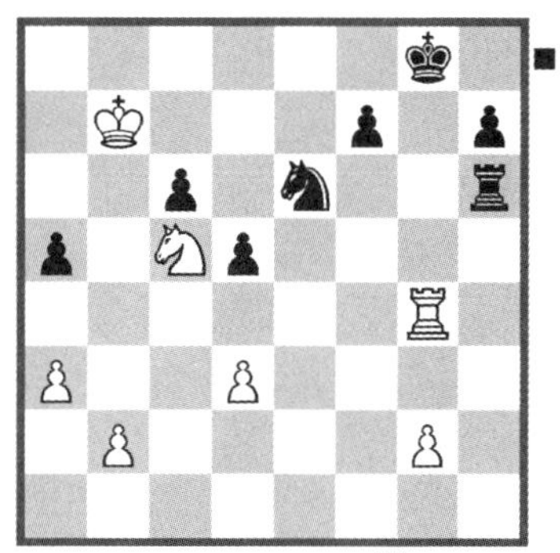

Position after: 37. ♖g4+!

37... ♔f8 38. ♔xc6!

Tal's class is demonstrated through some tactics.

38... ♘xc5+ 39. ♔xc5

The result is a winning position for White due to his very active king.

39... ♖e6 40. ♔xd5 ♖b6 41. b4 axb4 42. axb4 ♔e7 43. ♔c5 ♖f6

(see diagram next page)

Position after: 43... ♖f6

44. ♖d4!

Instructive – cutting off the black king.

44... ♖f5+ 45. ♔b6 ♖f6+ 46. ♔c7 ♖f5 47. ♖e4+ ♔f6 48. ♔c6 ♖f2 49. g4

Position after: 49. g4

Full control over the position!

49... h5 50. gxh5 ♔g5 51. b5 f5 52. ♖b4 f4 53. b6 f3 54. b7

Black resigned.

1-0

Game 24

♙	Sveshnikov, Evgeny	(2535)
♟	Browne, Walter Shawn	(2555)
🌍	Wijk aan Zee 1981	

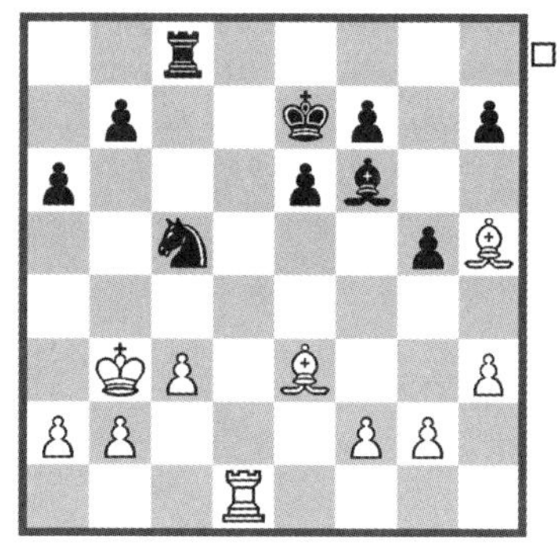

The bishop pair and better majority give White a lasting advantage. However, being under check, he must make a decision here.

29. ♔b4!?

With his king already active White decides to use it properly. If the king can be safe on its journey, then why not?

29. ♔c2 This would also have been good, but not aggressive. It would be necessary to expend some serious effort to find a good plan and to realize it.

29... ♘e4 30. ♔a5!?

30. ♗f3 This looks more natural, but White follows his plan instead.

30... ♘d6 31. ♔b6 ♖c6+?!

31... ♗e5!? This would have been a better defensive plan. The idea is to prevent an infiltration with ♔a7. 32. ♗xg5+ f6 33. ♗c1 ♖c6+

Position after: 33... ♖c6+

34. ♔a5 [or 34. ♔a7 ♔d7 with a further ...♔c7 may even be bad for White] 34... ♖c5+ 35. ♔a4 ♘e4 36. ♗e3 ♖b5 This would give Black better practical chances to hold.

32. ♔a7 ♖c7

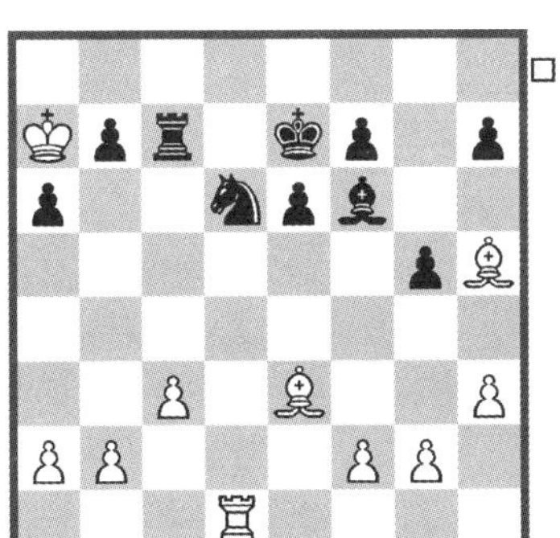

Position after: 32... ♖c7

33. ♗b6

33. ♗e2 Keeping the knight under control would probably have been better.
33... ♖c6 34. ♗a5 ♗e5?!

Now this doesn't make sense.

34... e5 Necessary instead to close the long light-squared diagonal.

35. ♗f3 ♖c5 36. ♗b4 ♖c7 37. ♔b6 ♖d7

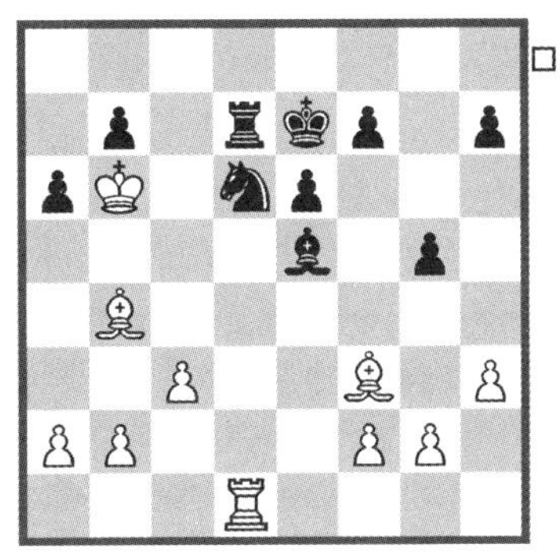

Position after: 37... ♖d7

38. ♖e1?!

Alternatively 38. ♗xd6+ or 38. c4 would have been more direct and thus better options.

38... f6?

38... ♔d8! A better defense missed by White. Now White is forced to go for the following line. 39. ♗xd6 ♗xd6 40. ♗xb7 Here Black can resist for a long time. 40... ♗c7+ 41. ♔xa6? ♖d6+ 42. ♔a7 f5! Now this would be unclear.

39. a4

After a series of energetic moves Black is hopeless.

39... ♔d8 40. ♗xd6

It finally happens.

40... ♖xd6+ 41. ♔xb7

The presence of opposite-colored bishops does not help Black. White is about to launch his queenside pawns with an easy win.

41... ♖d2 42. ♖d1!

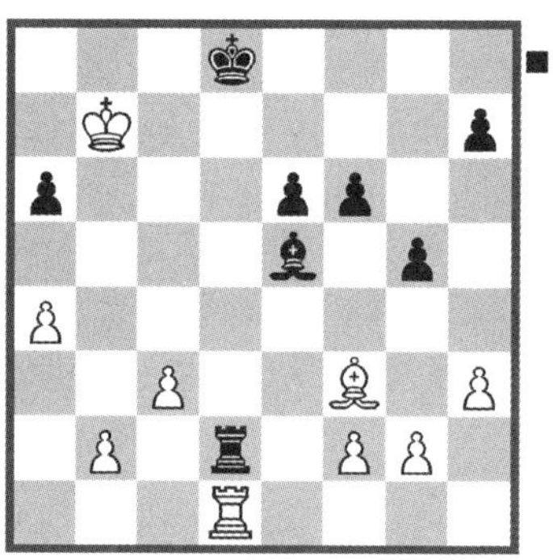

Position after: 42. ♖d1!

This would take place anyway.

42... ♖xd1 43. ♗xd1 a5 44. ♔b6 ♗c7+ 45. ♔c6 ♗f4 46. ♔b7 ♗e5

Black correctly keeps the focus on the c3-pawn to prevent any expansion.

47. ♗e2 ♗d6

47... f5 48. ♔c6 The threats are ♗c4 and then ♔b6.

48. g3 f5 49. ♔c6 ♗b8 50. ♗c4 e5 51. b4

Position after: 51. b4

51... ♗a7

51... axb4 52. cxb4 This would have been an easier win.

52. ♔b7 ♗xf2 53. bxa5

The quickest win.

53... ♗xg3 54. a6 ♗f2 55. ♗e6 f4 56. ♗d5 h5 57. ♗f3

1-0

Open Files

Of course, we must discuss endgames with major pieces (rooks!) on the board. Rook endgames arise more often than any others and it's clear that the importance of the open files increases in such cases. With fewer pieces on the board, infiltration will become easier and rook activity naturally becomes one of the key principles in such endgames.

However which file to take, when and where to invade, whether to trade rooks or not, whether to regain control of a file the opponent controls or to aim to control another file – these are all questions that may appear confusing, but this chapter (and indeed the whole book) will illuminate you with the answers.

Game 25

♙ Botvinnik, Mikhail
♟ Alekhine, Alexander
Netherlands 1938

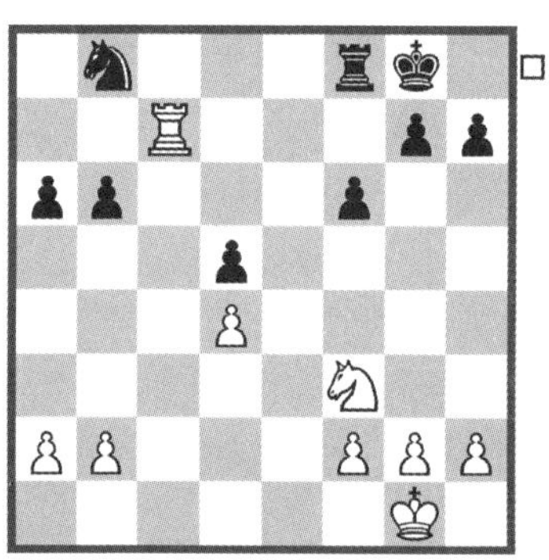

Traditionally, rooks are the pieces that come into the play last. This is why rook endgames are the most common in chess. And that is also why the importance of open (and semi-open) files grows with the reduction of material.

Our first example is a classical and unavoidable one – the famous clash between two greats from the past. Black's last move was 22... f6 – an excellent move which restricts the white knight and liberates the f7-spot for the rook; this will reduce the importance of White's control over the 7th rank.

23. ♔f1

23. ♖b7? ♖c8! 24. ♔f1 b5 This really looks to be a big achievement for Black. White cannot win without using his king and knight. It is time to activate them.

23... ♖f7 24. ♖c8+ ♖f8 25. ♖c3!

The rook temporarily goes to a "passive" position. Of course, even on the 3rd rank it can be very active, attacking the black queenside pawns to create some weaknesses! In actual fact, the rook would return to the 7th rank immediately if Black moves his knight or king. Black is in some kind of zugzwang and he decides to reduce the importance of the 7th rank by removing any targets after advancing the kingside pawns.

25... g5!

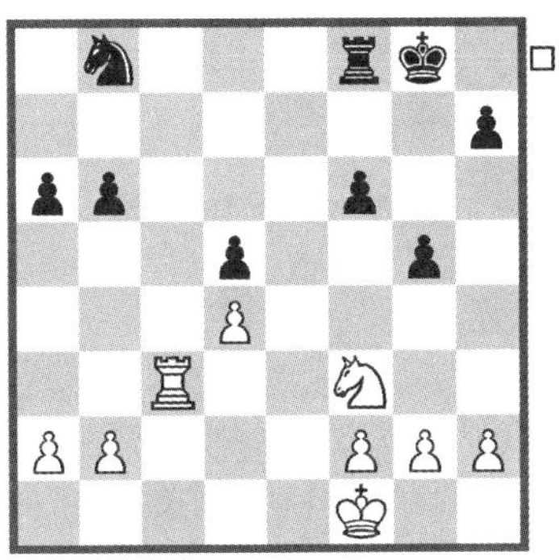

Position after: 25... g5!

An excellent move additionally reducing the importance of the 7th rank. Black's king aims for the good g6-spot and to remove the pawns from the 7th rank.

A) 25... ♘d7 This again allows 26. ♖c7.

B) 25... ♔f7 This also allows 26. ♖c7+.

26. ♘e1!

An excellent move. The knight can be placed on f5 via c2 and e3. Another possibility is to place it on b4.

26... h5 27. h4!!

After this deep strategic move, new weaknesses would inevitably arise in Black's camp. After eliminating the g5- pawn, the f4-square would be accessible for the white knight. If Black waits, an exchange on g5 will give White control over the e5-square. Indeed, this powerful pawn blow is connected with the activation of the knight!

27... ♘d7

A) 27... gxh4 28. ♘d3 White will place the knight on f4 leading to full domination.

B) 27... ♔f7 28. ♖c7+ ♔g6 29. hxg5 fxg5 30. ♖b7 b5 31. ♖b6+

Position after: 31. ♖b6+

31... ♔f5 32. f3 This sets up great problems for Black.

28. ♖c7 ♖f7 29. ♘f3!

A very typical maneuver by Botvinnik. Such moves became his trademark! He is ready to lose a tempo or even two to provoke an advance of the g-pawn which will create weaknesses.

29... g4 30. ♘e1 f5 31. ♘d3 f4

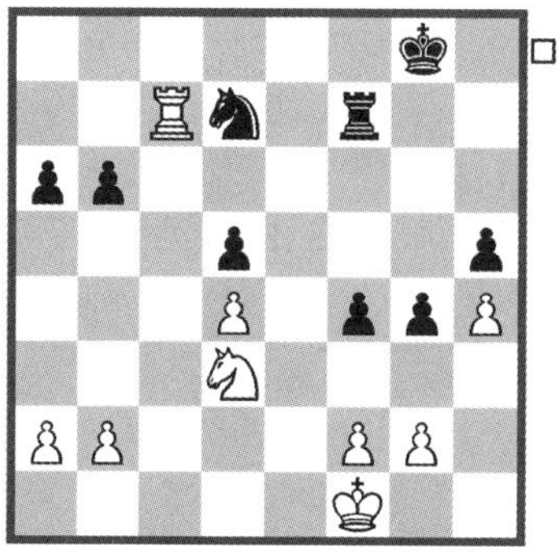

Position after: 31... f4

Black has prevented the installation of the knight on f4 but his pawns are so advanced and lack support from the pieces. The entire black army is over-extended and without harmony.

32. f3

Fixing the target on f4. Look how the black knight is restricted by the black pawns. Black is hopeless.

32. ♘b4 This wins material. Nevertheless there are still some chances for Black after the following. 32... ♘f6 33. ♘xa6

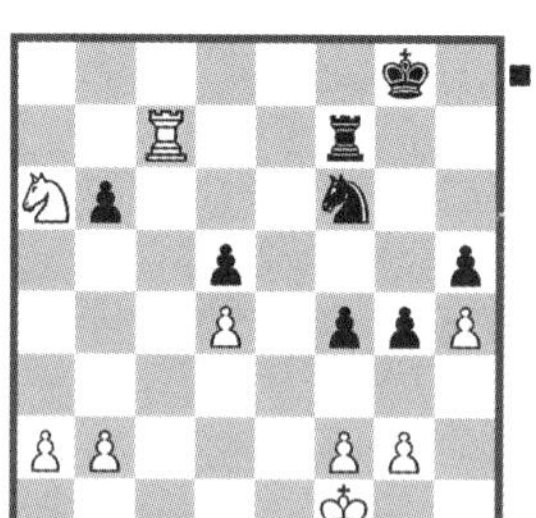

Position after: 33. ♘xa6

33... f3. White keeps both pieces on the board and plays without any rush.

32... gxf3 33. gxf3 a5

Taking control over the b4-square. What else?

34. a4

Fixing the target on b6.

34... ♔f8 35. ♖c6 ♔e7

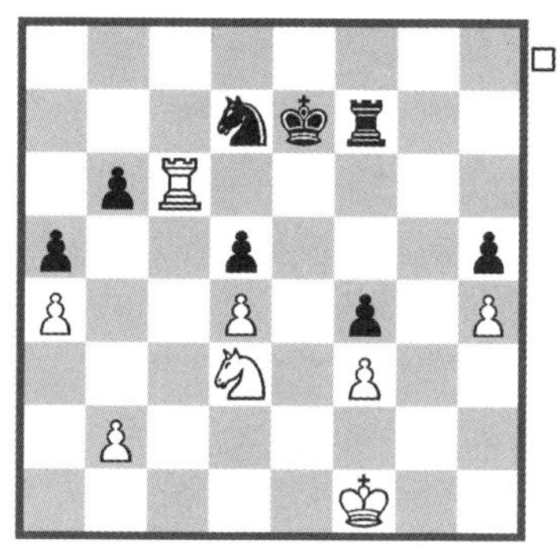

Position after: 35... ♔e7

Black's pieces are paralyzed. Both the knight and rook must protect the exposed pawns and this creates problems for the black king.

36. ♔f2 ♖f5

Black can do nothing, except to wait.

37. b3 ♔d8 38. ♔e2

The idea is to move the king to c4 and advance the b-pawn, destroying Black's queenside pawn structure.

38... ♘b8

Setting a trap.

39. ♖g6!

39. ♖xb6? ♔c7 Black has counterplay after 40...♘c6.

39... ♔c7

This move doesn't gain a tempo as after 39. ♖xb6?.

40. ♘e5 ♘a6

Position after: 40... ♘a6

41. ♖g7+

The conversion of the advantage is a matter of style.

41. ♖g5 This looks to lead to a quicker win. 41... ♖xg5? 42. hxg5 ♔d6 43. g6 ♔e7 44. g7

41... ♔c8 42. ♘c6 ♖f6 43. ♘e7+ ♔b8 44. ♘xd5

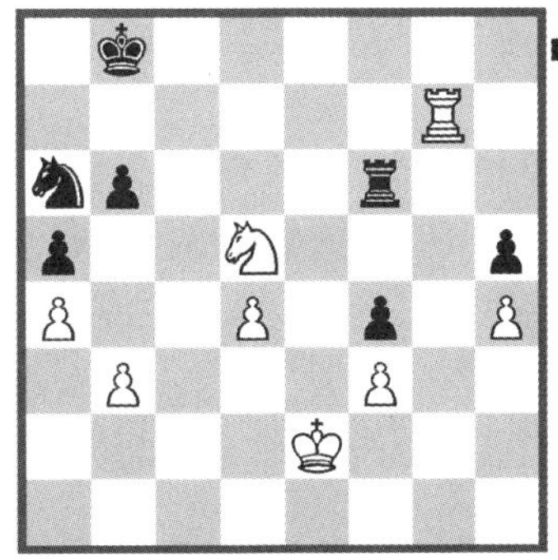

Position after: 44. ♘xd5

Look at the difference in the knights' activity in this game. Black's knight has achieved nothing while White's dances and creates miracles.

44... ♖d6 45. ♖g5 ♘b4 46. ♘xb4 axb4

The knights have now disappeared but White has both a material and positional advantage. The game is over.

47. ♖xh5

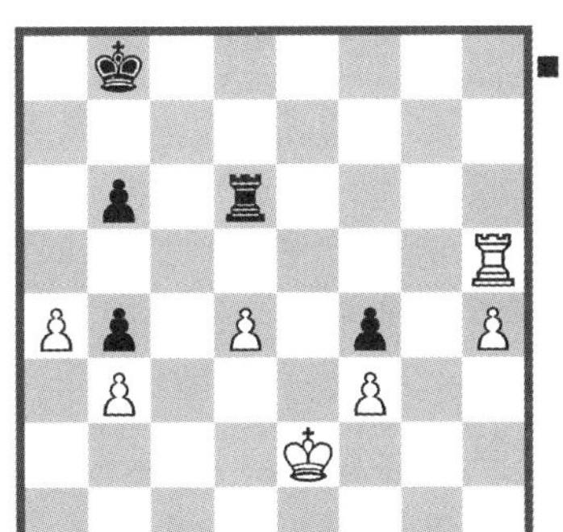

Position after: 47. ♖xh5

47... ♖c6

47... ♖xd4 48. ♖f5 ♔c7 49. h5 This

also wins easily.

48. ♖b5 ♔c7 49. ♖xb4 ♖h6 50. ♖b5 ♖xh4 51. ♔d3

Black resigned. Alekhine's words explain this struggle perfectly: "Of the 14 games I played in this tournament only once did I feel that my opponent outplayed me – it was the game with Botvinnik in round seven".

1-0

Game 26

♙ Kramnik, Vladimir (2770)
♟ Leko, Peter (2743)
Budapest 2001

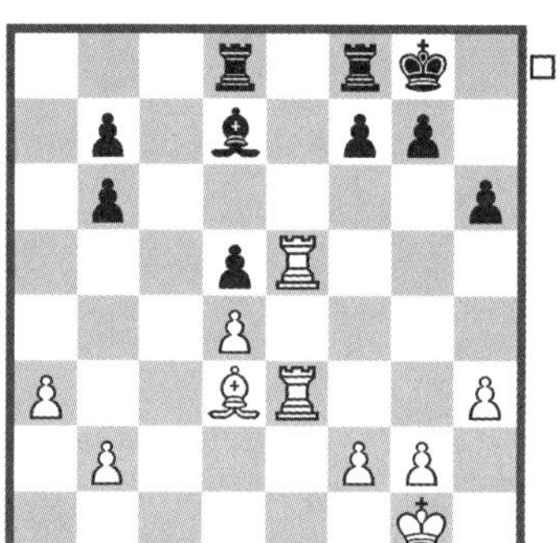

White enjoys a solid and lasting advantage, with the better bishop, better structure and just as importantly, stable control over the e-file.

23. ♗e2

Very fine play by Kramnik. Before launching his kingside armada he opens up the third rank for a potential attack.

23. ♖xd5 Of course, this would be a huge mistake because after 23... ♗c6 Black gets out of the problems.

23... ♗e6 24. f4

White follows his main plan.

24. ♖b3 This gives nothing because of the simple 24... ♖d6.

24... g6 25. ♗d3

With the idea of f5.

25... ♗c8 26. ♖e7

Before any pawn action it is good to have the pieces on their optimal positions.

26. f5 ♔g7! [26... f6? 27. ♖e7 g5

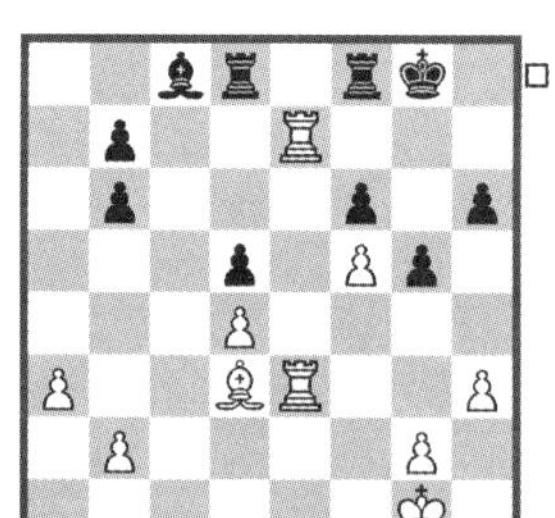

Position after: 27... g5

28. ♗b5!+–]

26... ♔g7

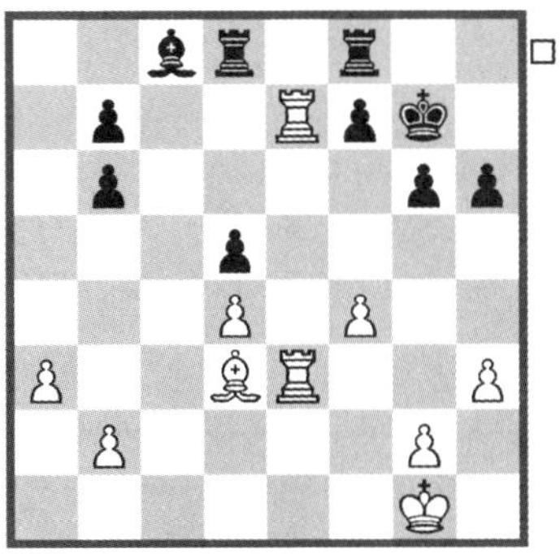

Position after: 26... ♔g7

26... ♖d7 This gives nothing in view of the waiting and improving move 27. g4.

27. ♗b5!

Black's pieces are paralyzed.

27... ♔f6 28. ♖c7 ♖d6 29. ♖ec3 ♖dd8 30. ♖e3

Don't rush!

30... ♖d6 31. a4?!

Fixing may be good. However it is not so important.

31. ♔f2 More natural and better.

31... ♖dd8 32. ♔f2 ♖d6 33. g4 ♖dd8 34. ♔g3 g5

(see diagram next column)

Otherwise White will play h4 with g5.

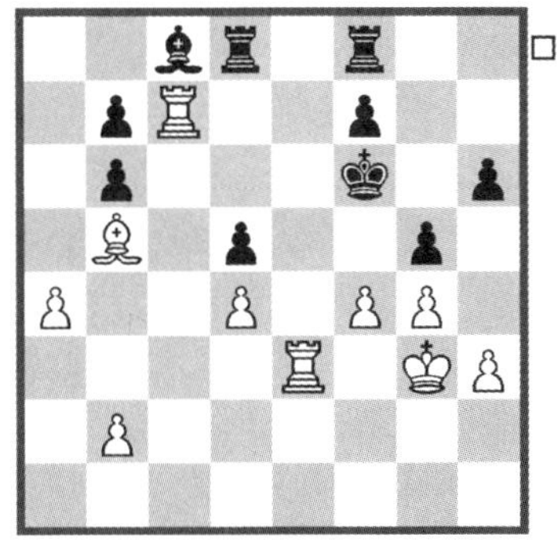

Position after: 34... g5

35. f5

Locking in the black bishop forever.

35... h5 36. ♖ee7 hxg4 37. hxg4 ♔g7 38. ♔f3 ♔f6

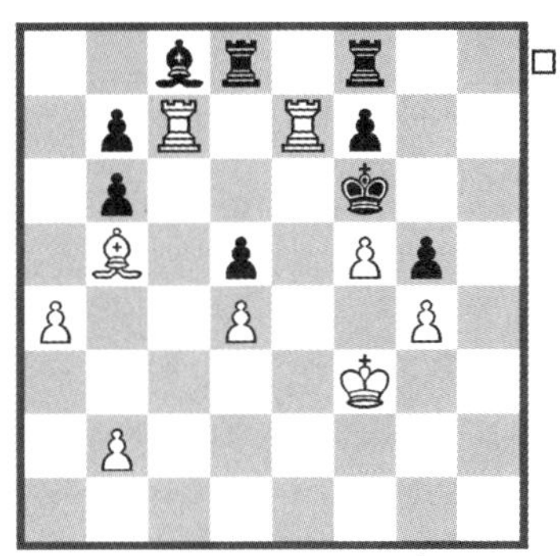

Position after: 38... ♔f6

Ruling the file has led to full paralysis of the opponent's troops – not the only example that confirms the principle.

39. ♔e3

White's king itself would decide the game.

39... ♔g7 40. ♔d3 ♔f6 41. ♔c3 ♔g7 42. ♔b4 ♔f6

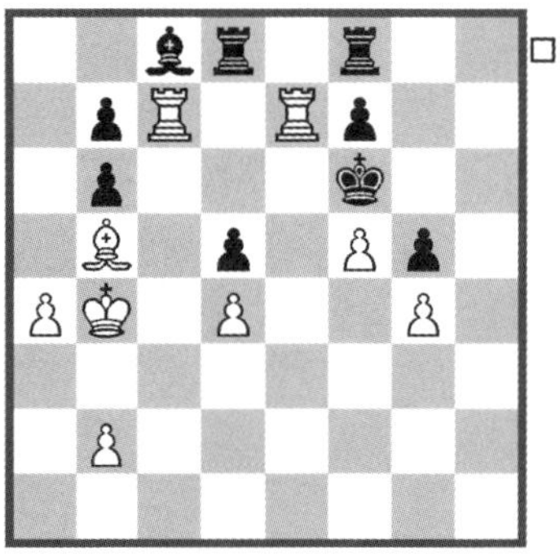

Position after: 42... ♔f6

43. ♔a3

43. a5 bxa5+ 44. ♔xa5 This is winning but the played move is more precise.

43... ♔g7 44. b4 ♔f6 45. a5 bxa5 46. bxa5 ♔g7 47. ♔b4

Now with the pawn already on a5 White invades with the king.

47... ♔f6 48. ♔c5 ♔g7 49. ♗e2

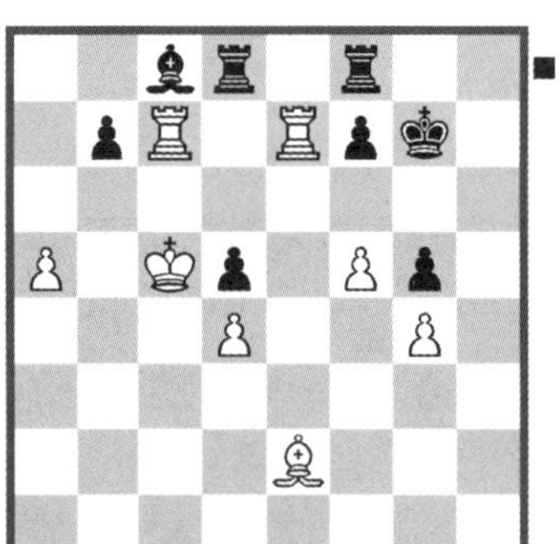

Position after: 49. ♗e2

49... ♖de8 50. ♖xe8 ♖xe8 51. ♗f3

1-0

Game 27

♙ Petrosian, Tigran V
♟ Portisch, Lajos
🌍 Palma de Mallorca 1974

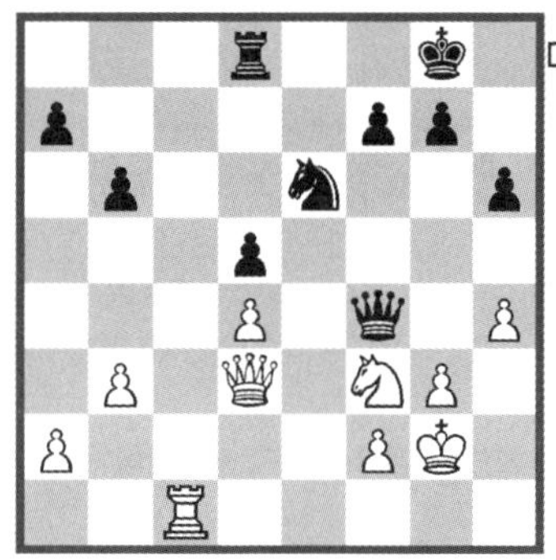

From the point of view of the competition, this was a very important moment in the entire match. Winning this game at the moment when the match was balanced resulted in Petrosian advancing to the semi-final of the Candidates tournament. Portisch, after winning 2 of the last 3 games in the match, probably wanted to exploit his opponent's vulnerable state and tested his fate with the ridiculous 21... ♕f6-f4, instead of the correct 21... g6, so as to hold a worse position. Who could predict Petrosian's fabulous move, completely shocking his rival and bringing the win in the game and the entire match!

22. gxf4!!

What the hell, my goodness!

22... ♘xf4+ 23. ♔g3 ♘xd3 24. ♖c3

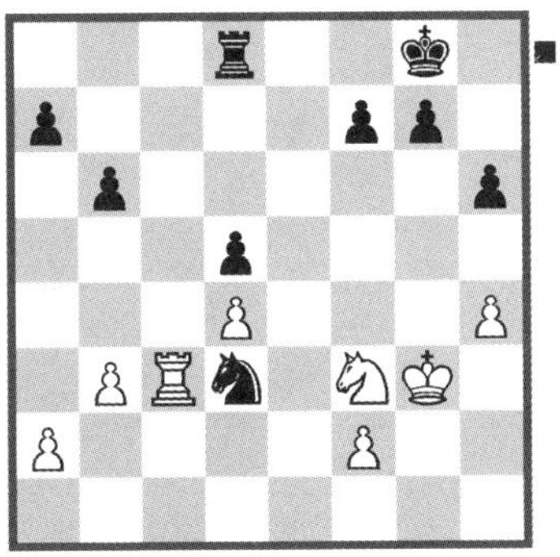

Position after: 24. ♖c3

White is a pawn down and he has a damaged pawn structure. But he has an active king, and full control over the c-file – it's more important! Black is in big trouble.

24... ♘b4!

24... ♘b2? This was later wrongly suggested as better. White has the following line. 25. ♘e5 ♖e8 26. ♖c7

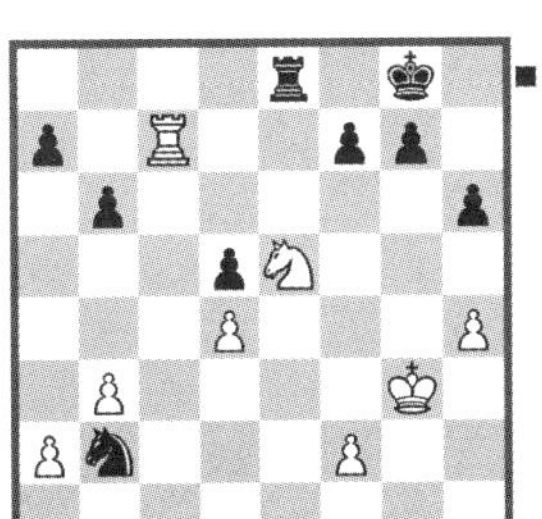

Position after: 26. ♖c7

A) 26... f6 27. ♘c6 ♘d3 [27... ♖e1 28. ♘e7++–] 28. ♖xa7 White must be winning.

B) 26... a5 27. h5 Black cannot find any kind of counterplay.

25. a3 ♘a6

Nevertheless this looks to be a better defense. However, with such a bad knight, the extra pawn means nothing.

26. b4!

Position after: 26. b4!

26... ♘b8?!

A) 26... ♖d7?! 27. ♖c8+ ♔h7 28. b5 ♘c7 29. ♘e5

Position after: 29. ♘e5

29... ♖e7 30. ♘c6 ♖d7 31. a4 Black is hopeless.

B) 26... ♔h7!? 27. b5 ♘b8 28. ♖c7 a6 [28... ♖d7 29. ♖c8 ♖b7 This is dominating as shown by Petrosian.] 29. bxa6 ♘xa6 30. ♖xf7 This is difficult to hold.

C) 26... h5! 27. ♘e5 f6 28. ♘c6 ♖d7 29. b5 ♘c7

Position after: 29... ♘c7

This may look to be a good defensive try, but White is dominant after the following. 30. ♘xa7 ♘e6 31. ♖c8+ ♔h7 32. ♘c6

27. ♖c7 a5

Reducing the material must be a good idea.

27... a6 28. ♘e5+–

28. b5

Of course, we don't reduce the number of pawns.

28... ♘d7 29. ♔f4

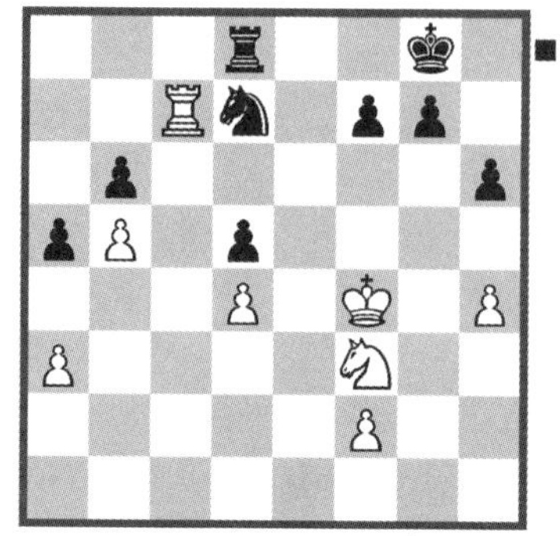

Position after: 29. ♔f4

29... h5

A) 29... f6 30. h5+–

B) 29... ♘f8!? 30. ♖c6

Position after: 30. ♖c6

30... ♖e8 [30... ♘e6+ 31. ♔e5!+–] 31. ♖xb6 This must be winning.

30. ♘e5!

Perhaps Portisch missed this move.

30... ♘f8

30... ♘xe5 31. ♔xe5+–

31. ♖b7 f6 32. ♘c6

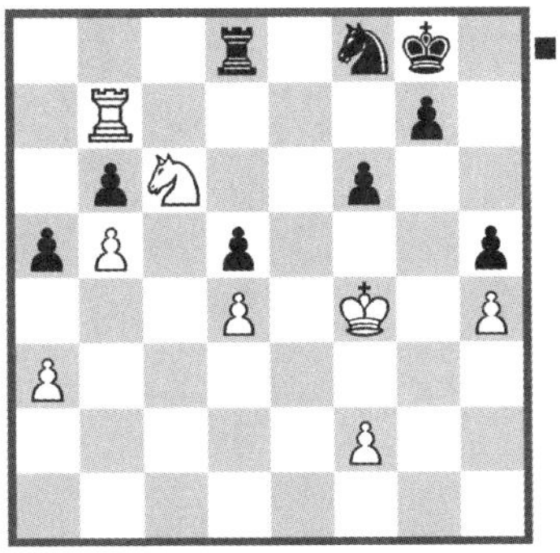

Position after: 32. ♘c6

32... ♘g6+

32... ♖e8 This is the last try here. 33. ♔g3! ♖e2 34. ♘e7+! However this will lead to a win in any case.

33. ♔g3 ♖d6 34. ♖xb6 ♖e6 35. ♖b8+ ♘f8 36. ♖a8 ♖e1 37. ♘d8 ♔h7 38. b6

Position after: 38. b6

38... ♖b1 39. b7 ♘d7 40. ♖xa5

Black resigned.

1-0

Game 28

♙ Alapin, Simon
♟ Rubinstein, Akiba
Prague 1908

White's attack on the kingside has missed its mark and as a result time has been wasted with weaknesses created. Black has a harmonious development with chances to use the soon-to-be opened d-file and semi-opened a-file for his initiative.

17... ♖fd8 18. ♖f2

Covering the 2nd rank.

18. ♖fd1 b5

18... ♖d7

Black rather doubles first on the d-file before capturing. Very often the threat is more dangerous than the execution!

A) 18... dxe4 19. dxe4 ♖d3 20. ♘c2 This doesn't give much to Black.

B) 18... b5! This would also have been very good. In such positions it is very important and useful to advance the doubled pawn to keep the flexibility of the pawn structure.

19. ♘c2 ♖ad8 20. ♖e1 dxe4 21. dxe4

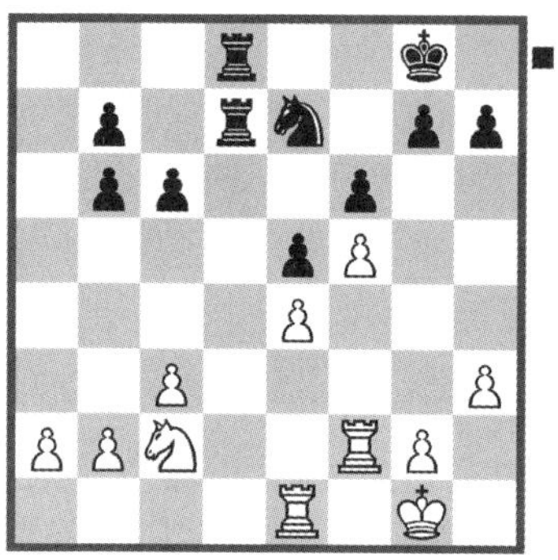

Position after: 21. dxe4

21... ♘c8?

21... b5! Precise – before White moves a4, this pawn must be advanced first.

22. ♖fe2

22. a4! This was better, stopping Black's b-pawns.

22... b5!

Black's knight eyes the squares a4 and c4.

23. ♘a1

23. ♔f2 ♘b6 24. b3 This looks to be more resistant.

23... ♘b6 24. ♘b3 ♘a4!

A much better option for the knight. Not only does it control the c5-square, but it also targets both the white pawns and cannot be attacked because the c3-pawn would fall. Furthermore the path for the c6-pawn is opened.

25. ♔f2 c5!

Kicking away the white knight; the black knight would be transferred to c5, attacking the e4-pawn and threatening to jump to d3.

26. ♖c2

Position after: 26. ♖c2

White's pieces are cramped and focused on the defense. Black has a strong hold of the d-file, the knight is on its optimal position – however, there is still nothing concrete. This is why Akiba decides to exploit the "principle of two weaknesses". The point is that the side having more space and the more active pieces would have the better "communication lines". If the opponent has one weakness, it is important to create another weakness on the opposite part of the board. Then by simultaneously attacking both of them, one will finally fall due to our better communication lines; the opponent would not be able to transfer defenses as quickly as we would deliver attacks. In this game White takes care of the d-file – his pieces must cover the infiltration squares. Rubinstein felt that he must open another front!

26... g6! 27. fxg6 hxg6 28. ♘c1 c4! 29. ♔e3 ♔f7

A very fine move. White cannot find a reasonable plan and it is extremely uncomfortable to watch the opponent improve their position with every move.

30. ♖f1 ♖d1

Black decides that it is the right moment to invade.

31. ♖xd1 ♖xd1 32. ♔e2

Position after: 32. ♔e2

32... ♖d7

Keeping the rook on the 1st rank was also good, but Black rather controls the d-file. White cannot oppose it.

33. ♔e3 ♘c5 34. b3 ♔e6 35. bxc4 bxc4

Black is perfectly centralized. The king is able to protect the knight, so the rook can again infiltrate to d1.

36. ♖b2 ♖d1

The game is over. White will soon face a zugzwang. He cannot protect so many weak pawns.

37. ♖b6+ ♔d7 38. ♘e2 ♔c7!

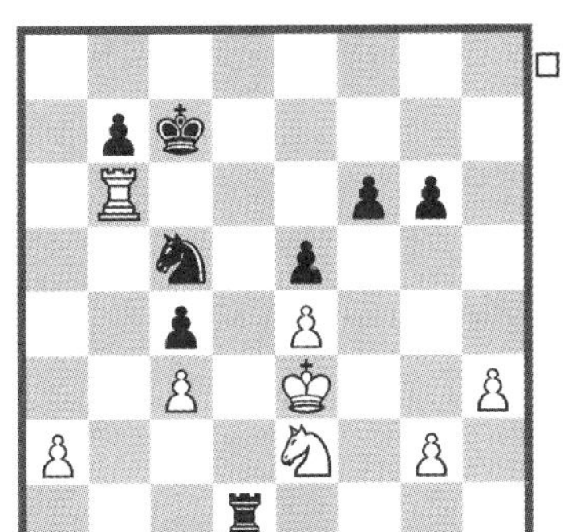

Position after: 38... ♔c7!

Tactics serve strategy!

39. ♖b4

39. ♖xf6 ♖d3+ 40. ♔f2 ♘xe4+

39... ♖d3+ 40. ♔f2 ♘xe4+ 41. ♔e1 ♘d6

Black's knight dances, destroying the white pawns at the same time. The optimally centralized black troops easily break every sign of White's resistance.

42. ♖a4 ♔c6

Not forgetting even the king!

43. ♖a8 ♔d5 44. h4 ♘f5 45. ♖f8

Position after: 45. ♖f8

45... ♘e3

Once again, some small and funny tactics. White's knight looks like a policeman on a crossroad. There is significant traffic around it.

46. ♖g8

46. ♖xf6 ♖d1+ 47. ♔f2 ♘g4+

46... ♘xg2+ 47. ♔f2 ♘xh4 48. ♖d8+ ♔e4 49. ♘g3+ ♔f4 50. ♘e2+ ♔g4 51. ♖c8 ♖f3+

0-1

Game 29

♙ Nimzowitsch, Aron
♟ Tarrasch, Siegbert
Breslau 1925

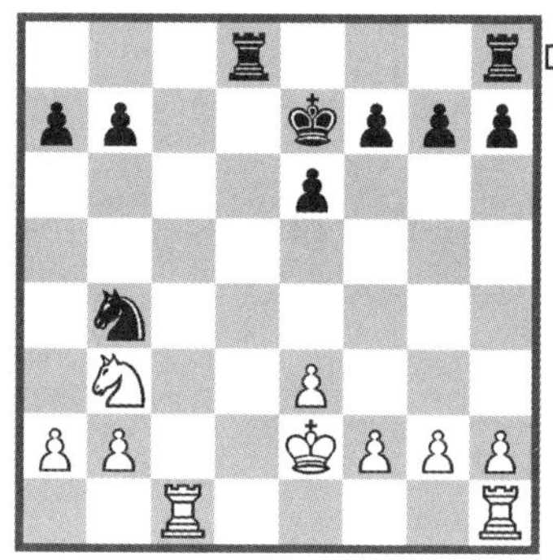

Here is a clash of the titans from the beginning of the last century between eternal opponents. Black is in an uncomfortable situation. White threatens to penetrate to the 7th rank. On the other hand, Black has nothing on his d-file. Black must play very precisely.

18. ♖c4!

From this moment the reader can enjoy Nimzowitsch's patient and brilliant realization of a small advantage.

18... ♘a6?

A) 18... ♘c6 19. ♖hc1 The idea is to play ♘c5 to support White's initiative.

B) 18... ♘d5 19. ♖hc1 This is still preferred for White, but these lines look to be the lesser evil.

19. ♖hc1

Now the c7-square is covered but the black knight will be out of play for a long time.

19... ♖d7

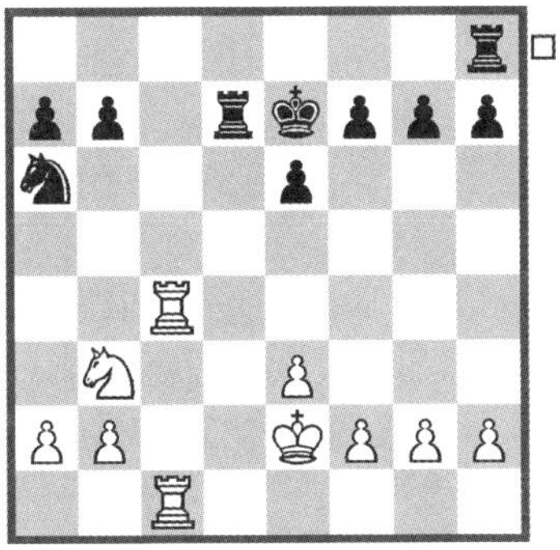

Position after: 19... ♖d7

20. f4!

Impressively played. This move secures the knight's future position on d4. Furthermore the white king gets a perfectly safe and active position on f3, with even a possible plan of expanding on the kingside.

20... ♖hd8 21. ♘d4 f6

Black wants to attack the white knight and penetrate to the 2nd rank if possible. Of course, White can prevent this by moving the knight to f3 immediately or after being attacked. Before any action in the center or the kingside White would rather lock out the black knight using the queenside pawns. His next move patiently leads to this goal.

22. a4!

Nimzowitsch would rather avoid the move 22. b4 after which 22... b5!? can lead to some complications. Although these must be in White's favor, there is no reason to complicate. In positions where you dominate and the opponent is out of real counterplay, it is always good advice to play patiently and go for action after eliminating counterplay possibilities.

22... e5 23. fxe5 fxe5 24. ♘f3! ♔e6

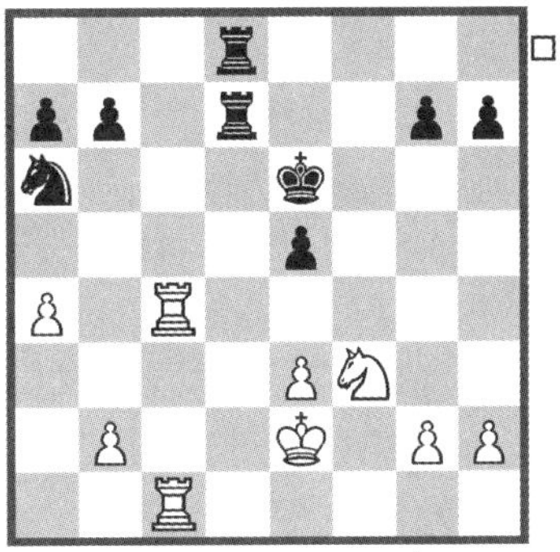

Position after: 24... ♔e6

It looks like Black has consolidated. However, this is an illusion. His rooks are not threatening anything on the d-file. White's king can easily meet any danger even in the center. The main problem is Black's knight which is misplaced. On other hand, the white knight is perfectly placed. It keeps control over the d2-square, attacks the isolated pawn on e5 and is ready to jump with a fork to g5.

25. b4 b6 26. ♖1c2!

Very useful prophylaxis.

26... h6

27. h4!

Before any direct action White wants to collect as many advantages as possible. His last move fixes Black's pawn structure on the kingside. Thus there are more pawn targets available for attack there. Also, placing a pawn on g5 enables White to use more easily the g5 and even f5-squares, which can be used by the white rook and knight afterwards.

27... ♖d6 28. h5! ♖d5 29. ♖g4

Here we are! Black's position now suddenly collapses. White's rook will simultaneously disturb the black king and pawns using the c- and g-files.

29... ♖5d7

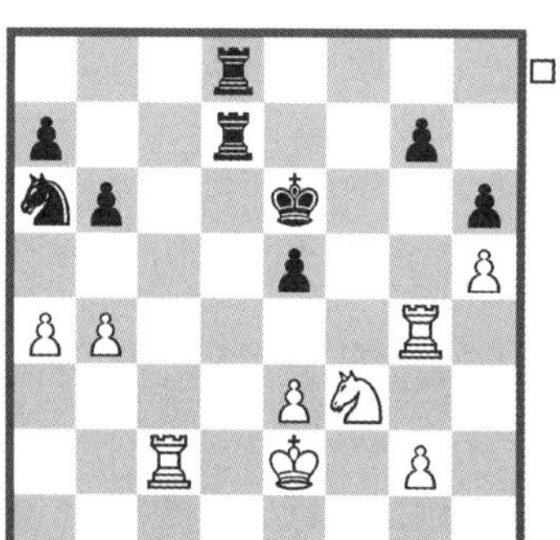

Position after: 29... ♖5d7

30. ♖c6+

30. ♖g6+ More precise.

30... ♖d6

A) 30... ♔f5? 31. ♖cg6+– Mate will follow soon.

B) 30... ♔d5 This was correct and White should go for repetition after 31. ♖c1 ♔e6.

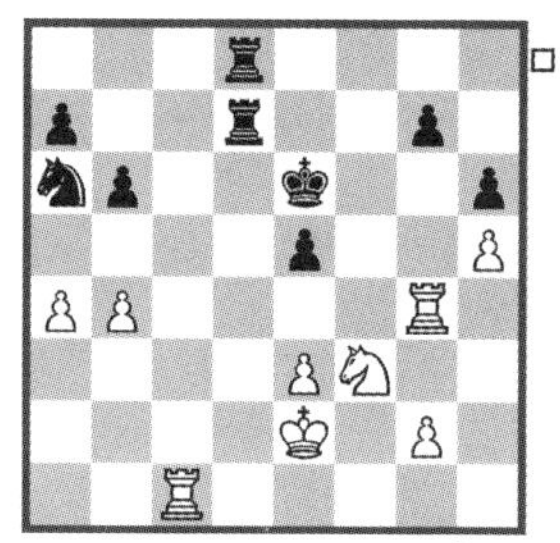

Position after: 31... ♔e6

Here 32. ♖g6+ wins.

31. ♖g6+ ♔e7

31... ♔d5 32. ♖cxd6+ ♖xd6 33. e4+! ♔c6 34. b5+

32. ♖xg7+ ♔f8 33. ♖xd6 ♖xd6 34. ♖xa7 ♘xb4 35. ♘xe5

Position after: 35. ♘xe5

The situation has stabilized. White has a completely winning position. Not only does he have two extra pawns, but the white pieces also dominate. White's conversion is impressive.

35... ♖e6+– 36. ♘g6+ ♔g8! 37. ♘e7+ ♔f8 38. ♘f5 ♘d5 39. g4

Position after: 39. g4

White has consolidated the kingside position with the super knight's maneuver. It protects the pawn on e3 now and attacks the weak pawn on h6. The game is over.

39... ♘f4+ 40. ♔f3 ♘d3 41. ♖a8+! ♔f7 42. ♖h8 ♘c5 43. ♖h7+

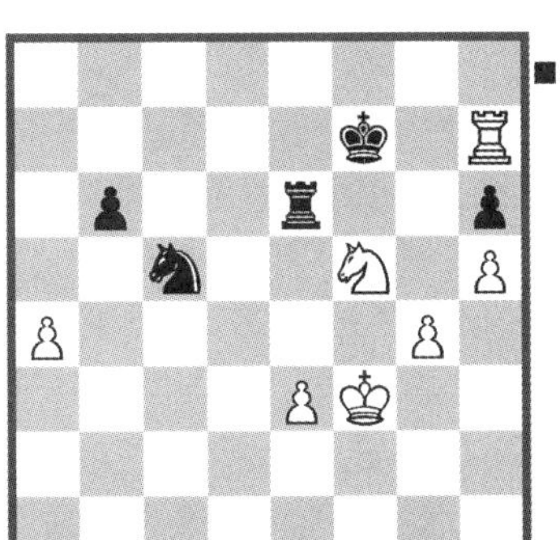

Position after: 43. ♖h7+

43... ♔g8

43... ♔f8 44. ♘xh6

44. ♖xh6 ♖xh6 45. ♘xh6+ ♔f8 46. ♘f5 ♘xa4

White's pawns are much faster. The rest of the game doesn't require any comment.

47. h6 ♔g8 48. g5 ♔h7 49. ♔g4 ♘c5 50. ♔h5 ♘e6 51. g6+ ♔g8 52. h7+ ♔h8 53. ♔h6

1-0

Game 30

♙	Andersson, Ulf	(2560)
♟	Robatsch, Karl	(2435)
🌍	Munich 1979	

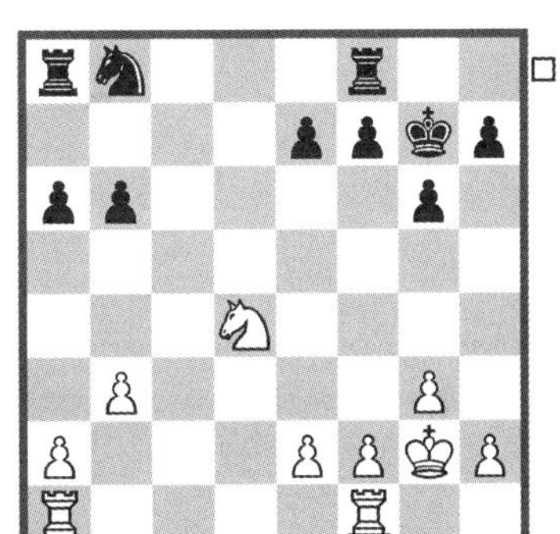

Now I highly recommend switching to the magnificent opus of one of the finest strategists ever and one of my life-long mentors: Ulf Andersson. He achieved the peak of his career in 1984

reaching no.4 in the world's rating list. However his legacy is much larger –he was the unsurpassed master in handling rook endgames, those against a d5 isolated pawn and especially those that arose from the Catalan. No one in chess history was able to perform such miracles on the board using a rook and knight combination. Also, Ulf's games are the initial reasons why I believe that: "A rook and knight are NOT WORSE than a rook and bishop"!

I am sure such a strong statement may cause shock and outrage, but looking in my database for games to include in my books on "the bishop versus the knight" I saw that in 55% of cases the rook and knight prevail. All this is thanks to Ulf! I think it is time now to present one of Ulf's masterpieces on our topic of the open file, as a personal homage to my mentor.

That's a typical good Catalan endgame for White. If it doesn't seem too scary for Black at first sight, seemingly, it's "just a bit passive". But if you give this position to a player with a good technique with White, he would win most of the time.

16. ♖ac1 ♖a7 17. ♖c2

Not only doubling but at the same time controlling the 2nd rank.

17... ♖d8 18. e3

Position after: 18. e3

18... e5?!

This is the first sign of Black's impatience. Patience is simply vital in such situations.

18... a5!? This looks more logical, to somehow set the knight on c5, but now the b5-spot will be weakened.

19. ♘f3 f6

Position after: 19... f6

19... e4 This looks optically bad due to 20. ♘d4.

20. g4!

A typical approach. White intends to play on both wings. Black must guard on the queenside without anything specific to do and must now deal with the g5-advance.

20... ♖d6

A) 20... h6 21. h4 g5

Position after: 21... g5

22. h5! White will transfer the knight to f5 and eventually win.

B) 20... g5 21. h4 This does not change anything from the previously mentioned line.

21. ♖fc1 ♘d7

Position after: 21... ♘d7

21... a5 A better defense, but in any case it looks hopeless for Black after the following. 22. ♘d2 f5 23. ♘c4 ♖e6 24. gxf5 gxf5 25. ♖d1

22. ♖c6

Now it is possible and timely to invade.

22... ♖xc6 23. ♖xc6 ♔f7

23... ♖b7 24. ♘d2 ♔f7 25. ♘e4 ♔e7 This will transpose.

24. ♘d2 ♔e7 25. ♘e4 ♖b7 26. b4

26. h4 Another way to win.

26... ♖b8

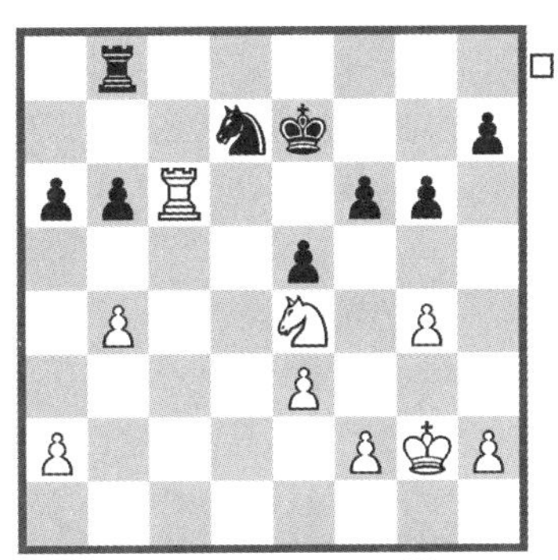

Position after: 26... ♖b8

27. ♘c3 f5 28. ♘d5+ ♔f7 29. ♔g3 h5

An act of desperation.

30. gxf5 gxf5 31. ♖d6 ♖b7 32. ♔h4 ♔g7 33. ♔xh5

1-0

Game 31

♙ Andersson, Ulf (2605)
♟ Gheorghiu, Florin (2550)
Moscow 1982

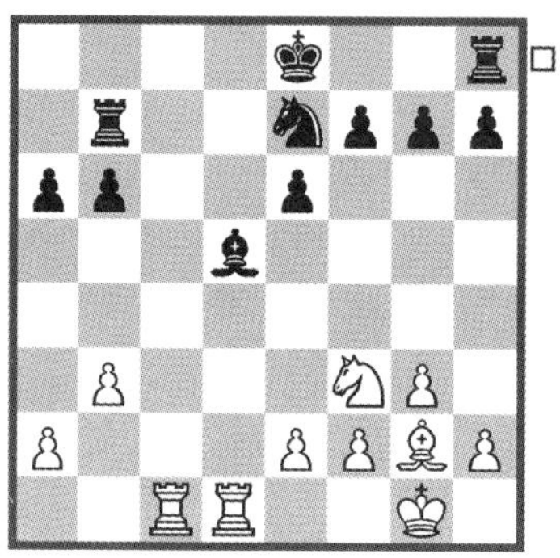

Here is another Catalan masterpiece. White is much better in this example. Both the open files are under his control. However penetration is not currently possible. Thus the next move is clear.

18. ♘e5! ♗xg2

18... f6 19. e4!

Position after: 19. e4!

19... ♗xb3 [19... fxe5 20. exd5] 20. axb3 fxe5 21. ♖d6 In both cases Black's position is in ruins.

19. ♔xg2 0-0

If Black must make such an anti-centralizing move then his position must be very bad.

20. ♖d6

White invades.

20... h6

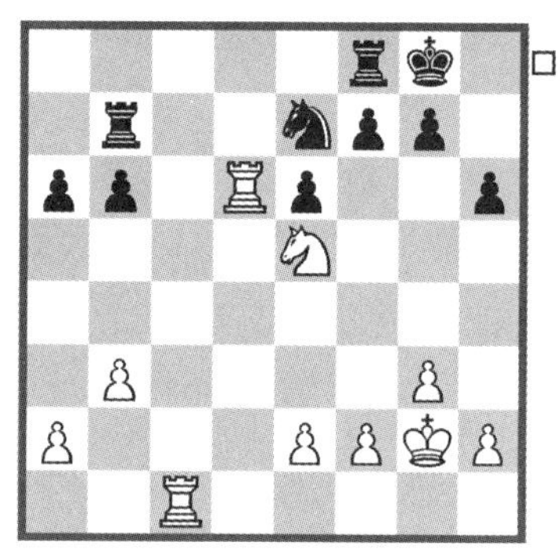

Position after: 20... h6

20... g5 Better, to prevent White's possible expansion and to make space for the king; however after 21. e4 Black's position is awful.

21. e4!

Before activating the king White restricts the black knight.

21... ♖e8 22. ♔f3 ♖a8 23. ♔e3 a5 24. ♖cd1 b5

Black can do nothing on the queenside. While he is "organizing" these "activities" White has organized a definite penetration.

25. ♖d8+ ♖xd8 26. ♖xd8+ ♔h7 27. ♘xf7

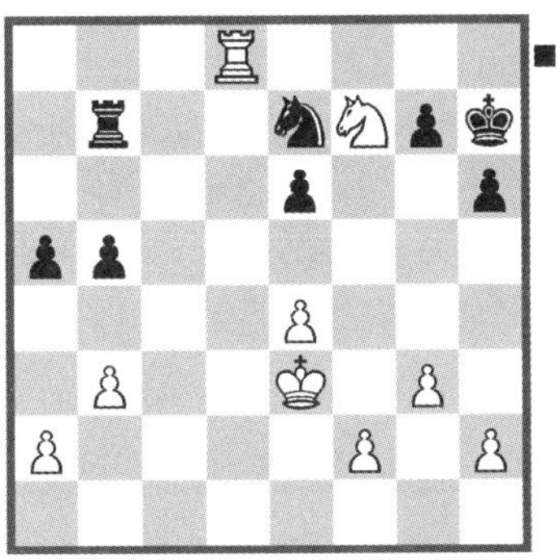

Position after: 27. ♘xf7

The game is over.

27... ♘c6 28. ♖c8 ♘b4 29. ♖h8+

White works on mating the opponent.

29... ♔g6 30. ♘e5+ ♔f6 31. f4 ♔e7 32. ♖g8 ♔d6 33. ♖d8+ ♔e7 34. ♖a8 ♘xa2 35. ♖xa5 ♘c3

Position after: 35... ♘c3

Black has lost the last chance for counterplay. The rest needs no comment.

36. ♔d3 b4 37. ♖a6 ♘b5 38. ♘c6+ ♔d7 39. ♘d4 ♘xd4 40. ♔xd4 ♔e7 41. g4

1-0

Game 32

♙ Andersson, Ulf (2560)
♟ Tempone, Marcelo
Buenos Aires 1979

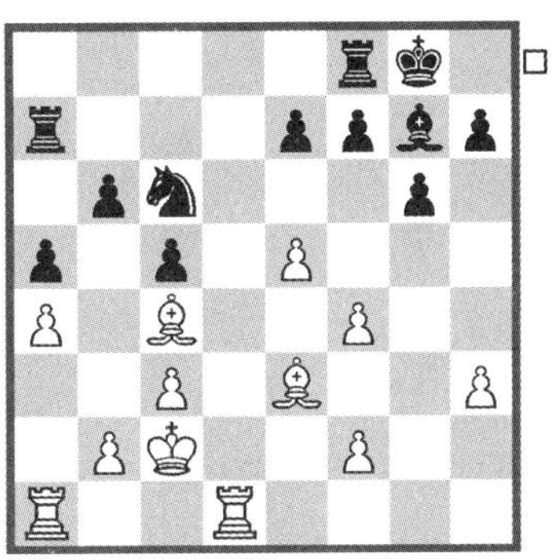

Here the domination on the file together with White's active king, powerful bishop pair and desperately weak light-squared complex decides the game. White's damaged structure is an absolutely irrelevant positional factor – the game will be quickly ended on another side.

18. ♖d2

Simply preparing to double.

18... e6 19. ♖ad1 ♖c8 20. ♔b3

Before impact, activate all your troops.

20... ♗f8 21. ♗b5 ♖cc7

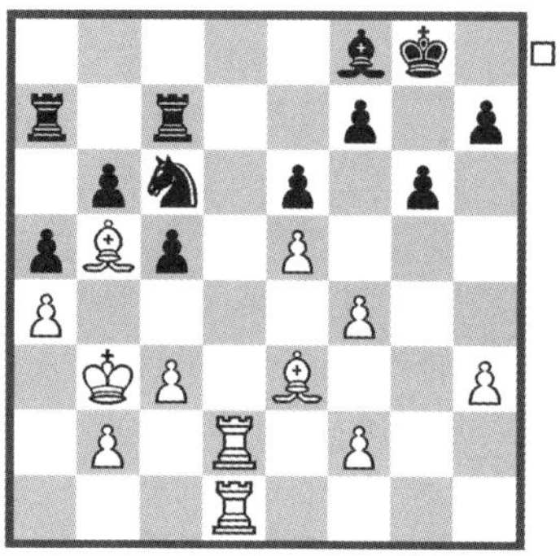

Position after: 21... ♖cc7

22. ♗xc6

The simplest.

22... ♖xc6 23. ♔c4 ♗e7 24. ♖d7 ♖cc7 25. ♖xc7 ♖xc7 26. ♔b5 ♖c8 27. ♖d7 ♔f8 28. ♔xb6

Position after: 28. ♔xb6

28... ♔e8 29. ♖b7 ♗d8+ 30. ♔b5 c4 31. ♗c5
1-0

Game 33

♙ Andersson, Ulf (2635)
♟ Hulak, Krunoslav (2515)
Wijk aan Zee 1983

This is a slightly different endgame with major pieces on the board. Nevertheless it is not a problem for Andersson to realize a huge positional advantage, even without his famous knight.

24. ♕c3

Clearly gaining full control of the file.

24... ♖xc4 25. ♕xc4 ♔f7 26. h3

Position after: 26. h3

With control on the file it is time for pawn play. White plays on the side where there are more possibilities – a logical approach.

26... f5?

Contrary to Nimzowitsch's principle of gradually improving in passive positions.

26... h5 This was necessary instead.

27. ♖c3

Predicting that there will be a job on the f-file Andersson exploits Black's last bad move.

27... fxe4?

A good move, played at the wrong moment. Black wants to get counterplay against the isolated d5-pawn, but this weakens his king. Furthermore, White would be able to use the majority on the kingside to create an outside passer. Black is already lost.

27... ♔g8 28. exf5 ♕xf5 29. ♖f3

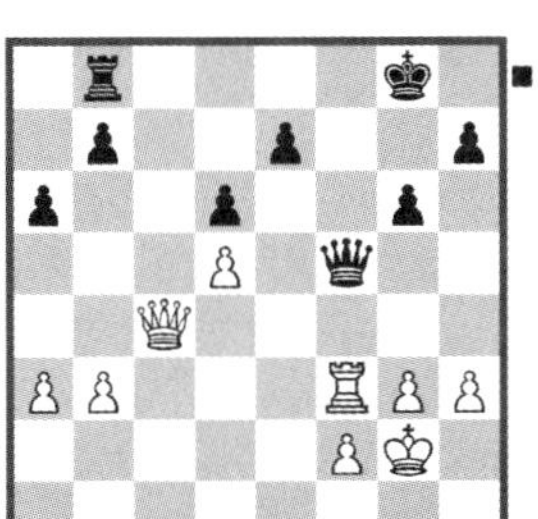

Position after: 29. ♖f3

29... ♕e5 30. ♖e3 This gives White a much better game.

28. ♕xe4 ♖f8

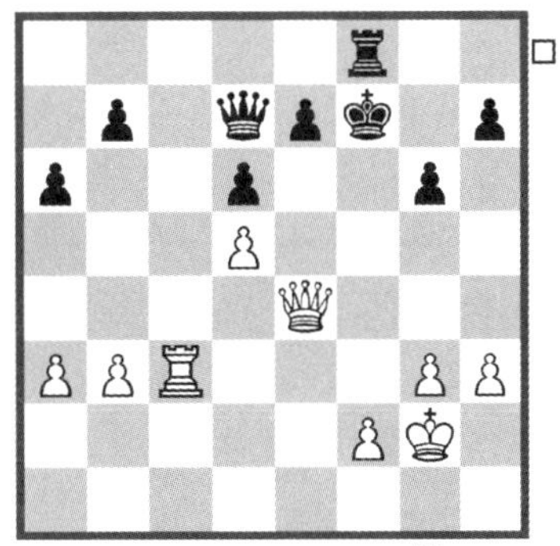

Position after: 28... ♖f8

29. a4!

Restricting Black on the queenside. Black must take care of both flanks which is practically impossible.

29... ♔g7 30. g4

Now restricting on the kingside. White tightens the noose around the black queen's neck.

30... ♖f6 31. ♕d4

Eyeing both flanks.

31... g5 32. f4 h6

(see diagram next page)

Position after: 32... h6

33. f5

The most methodical win.

33... ♕d8 34. ♕b4 ♖f7 35. ♖c4

"Don't rush!"

35... ♔h7 36. ♕c3 ♕g8 37. ♖c7 b5

Position after: 37... b5

38. axb5

38. a5 More methodical but it is a matter of style.

38... axb5 39. ♕d3 ♔h8 40. ♕xb5 ♕a8 41. ♕c4 ♕a2+ 42. ♕c2 ♕a6

After the king is secured it is time to advance.

43. b4 ♔g8 44. ♕e4 ♕a2+ 45. ♖c2 ♕b3

Position after: 45... ♕b3

46. b5! h5

If 46... ♕xb5 47. ♕e6 ends the game.

47. ♕c4 ♕b1 48. ♕e4 ♕b3 49. gxh5 ♔g7 50. f6+

Black resigned.

1-0

Game 34

♙	Andersson, Ulf	(2590)
♟	Limp, Eduardo Thelio	(2275)
🌍	Rio de Janeiro 1985	

White is evidently better. Black has wasted time in the opening, leading to a drastic difference in the pieces' activity. He is simply unable to finish the development of his queenside troops properly. Furthermore, his "developed" pieces (the kingside rook and knight) are awful. White's clear plan is to prevent Black's liberation, at the same time seizing the initiative. First it is time to double up so as to secure domination of the file and not allow Black to fight for it.

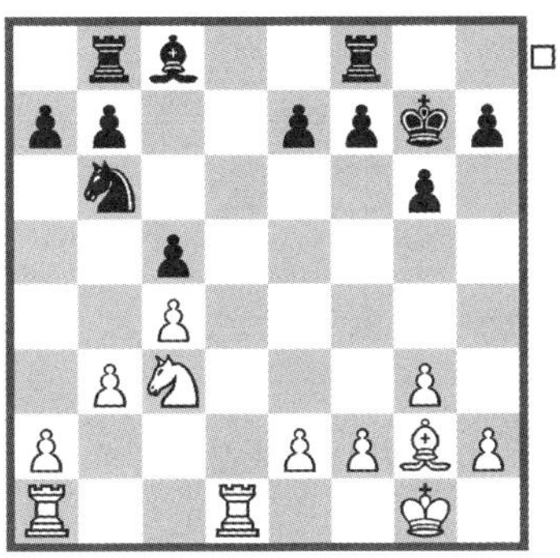

16. ♖d2 ♘a8

Trying at least to eliminate pressure from the b7-pawn.

17. ♖ad1 ♘c7 18. f4!?

White gains space and prepares ♔f2-♔e3.

18... ♗e6 19. ♘e4

Forcing b6, after which c6 will be weak. Another idea is ♘g5 and eliminating the piece controlling d7.

Position after: 19. ♘e4

19... b6 20. ♘g5 a5

Removing the pawns from the 7th rank.

21. ♔f2

21. ♘xe6+ ♘xe6 22. ♖d7 ♖fd8 This gives White nothing.

21... ♗c8 22. ♗c6

A typical "Andersson" move. There are no actual threats. Andersson simply wants to underline White's domination of the board. The move has great psychological effect.

22... f6?!

22... ♘e6 23. ♘xe6+ ♗xe6 24. ♗d7 After this line, the point of ♗c6 is clear. White eliminates ♗e6 and prepares infiltration with ♖d7.

23. ♘e4!

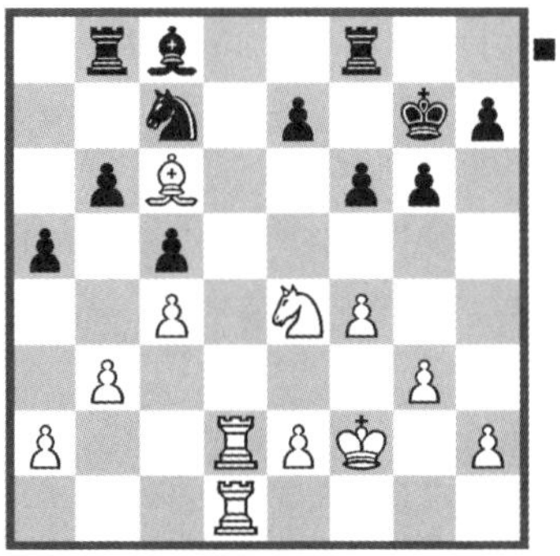

Position after: 23. ♘e4!

23... ♘e6 24. e3 ♔f7 25. g4

White even gains space on the kingside. Andersson's style is perfect. After some "slow" moves he makes an active one. Such playing rhythm is very dangerous for the opponent.

25... ♗b7?

And Black's defense collapses. Now White's rooks invade the 7th rank.

26. ♗xb7 ♖xb7 27. ♖d7 ♖xd7 28. ♖xd7 ♖b8

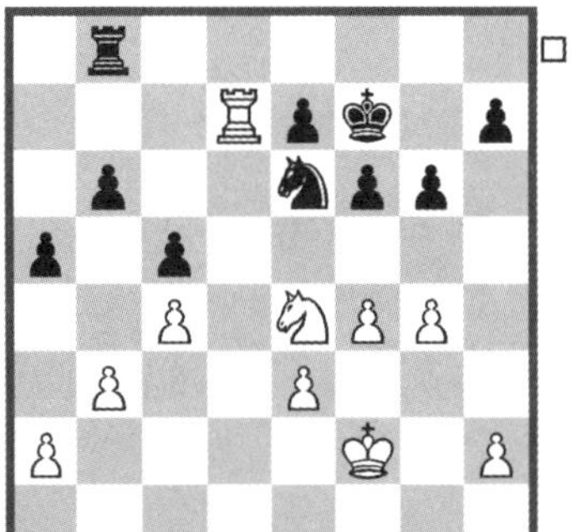

Position after: 28... ♖b8

The position is hopeless for Black. White's rook and knight dominate. Black is out of any counterplay. There are so many squares available for White's knight, but not one for Black's. Even White's king can take part in the attack.

29. ♘c3 ♘f8 30. ♖a7 ♔e8 31. ♘d5 ♘d7 32. ♘c7+ ♔d8

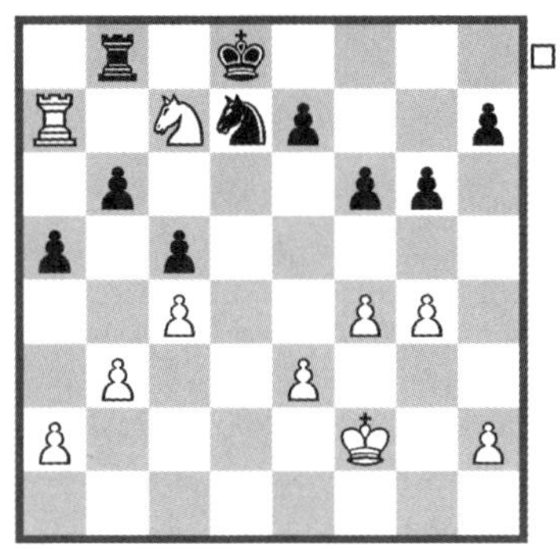

Position after: 32... ♔d8

33. ♔e2

Black is fully paralyzed and there is no reason to rush. By choosing a slow rhythm the opponent will get a chance to make mistakes, and help us to realize the advantage. Furthermore at any given moment the rhythm can be changed. At this point, it is vital to patiently activate all the pieces – so let's activate the king! Yes, the king gets ready for a long journey – the target is the c6-square!

33... ♔c8?

33... ♖c8 More resistant, but the result is indisputable.

34. ♘a6! ♖b7 35. ♖a8+ ♖b8 36. ♘xb8 ♘xb8 37. ♔f3

1-0

Game 35

♙ Andersson, Ulf (2630)
♟ Nijboer, Friso (2485)
Wijk aan Zee 1990

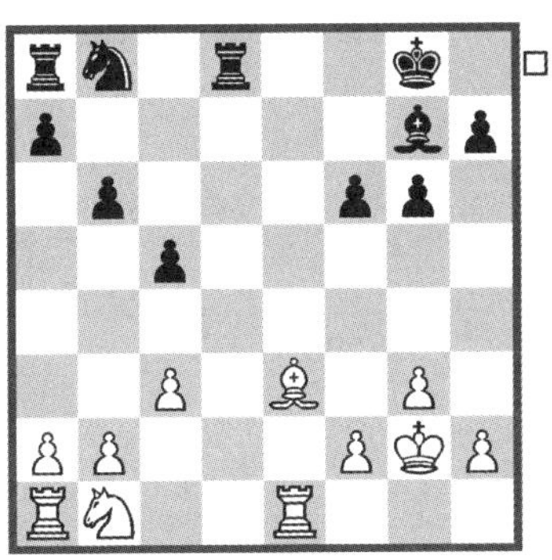

Is it possible for White to win this position? It really looks as if White's optical advantage is not specific. However let's allow the wizard to speak as White.

17. ♘a3!

The knight goes to the dream c4-spot, from where it will supervise the entire board.

17... ♘c6 18. ♘c4 ♗f8

Trying to get control over the important d6- and e7-squares.

19. a4

This pawn simply belongs here. Not only does it secure the knight, but White can also play a5 at some moment as well.

19... ♘e7?

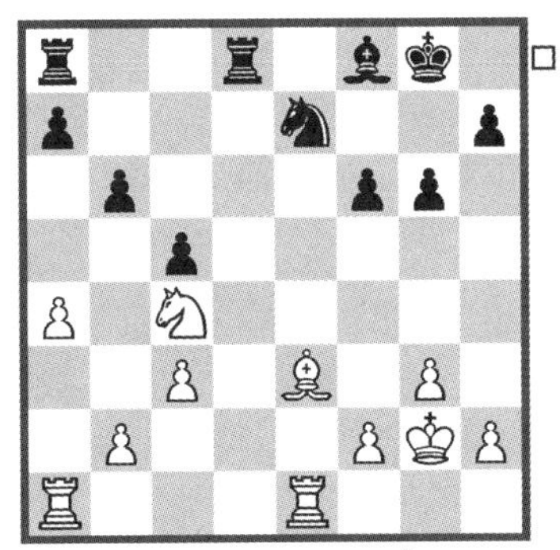

Position after: 19... ♘e7?

Black's last move is a bad idea.

19... ♔f7 This would have been normal instead, keeping all the squares covered.

20. ♗h6

What a superb solution. Of course, White's dream is a rook endgame with a knight against a bishop, but that is impossible to get. Instead, Andersson observes that the black bishop is the main defender and with rooks and knights on the board there is no harmony in Black's army.

20... ♘f5 21. ♗xf8 ♔xf8 22. ♖e6 ♔f7?

22... ♖e8! Shockingly this was the correct defense. 23. ♖ae1 [23. ♖xf6+ ♔e7 24. ♖c6

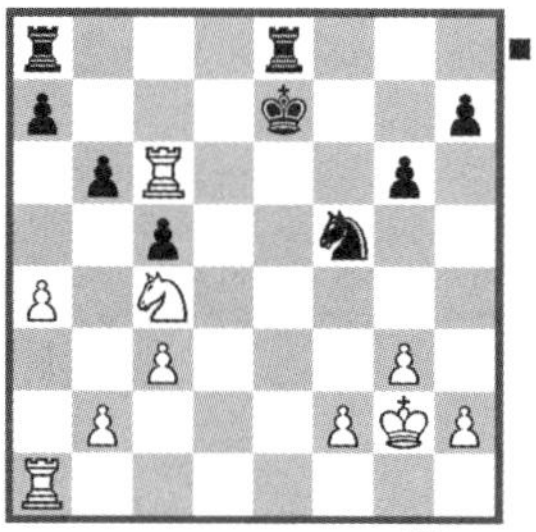

Position after: 24. ♖c6

24... ♔d7 This would give only a draw.] 23... ♔f7 24. ♖xe8 ♖xe8 25. ♖d1 ♔e7 Now this just looks better for White.

23. ♖c6 ♖d7 24. ♖e1 ♘e7 25. ♖ce6

Now the white rooks are safe from exchanges.

25... ♘d5

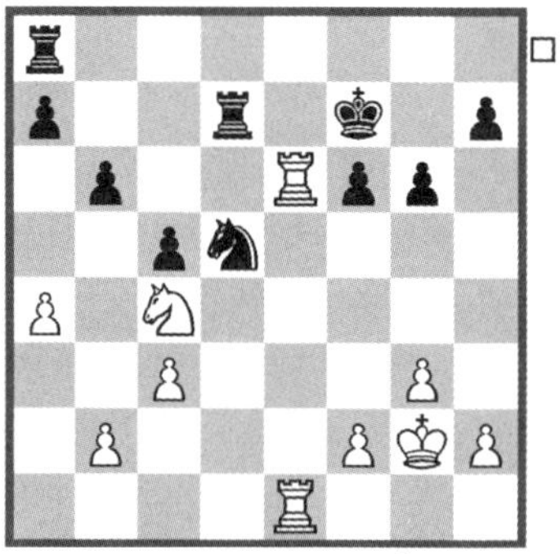

Position after: 25... ♘d5

26. a5?!

Strategically a natural move, but not the best one.

26. ♘d6+ ♔f8 27. ♖d1! White would win on the spot.

26... ♖b8 27. axb6 axb6 28. ♘d6+ ♔f8 29. c4 ♘c7 30. ♖xf6+ ♔g7 31. ♘e4

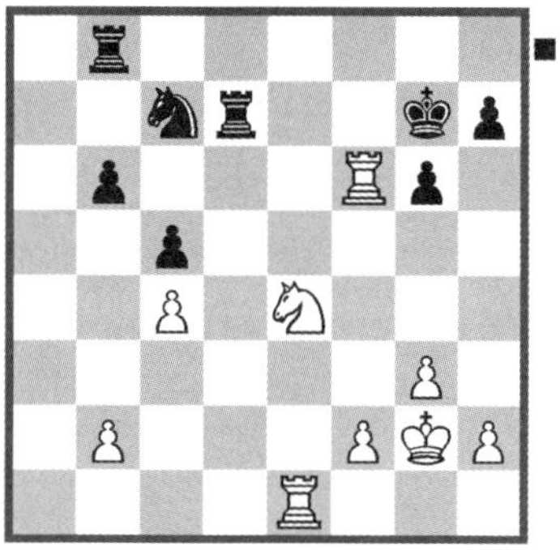

Position after: 31. ♘e4

White has obtained the pawn, keeping all the pluses. The game is decided.

31... ♖e7 32. ♖f3?!

Another mistake.

32. ♖c6 Evidently by far the best move.

32... b5 33. b3 bxc4 34. bxc4 ♖b4 35. ♖c3 ♘e8?

(see diagram next page)

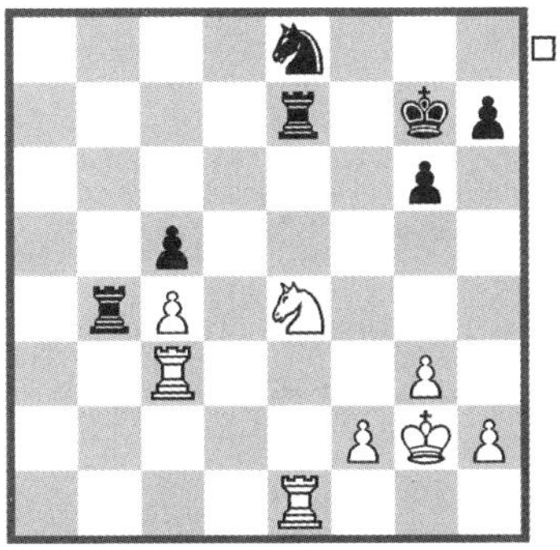

Position after: 35... ♘e8?

35... ♘a8! This was better. 36. f3 ♘b6 37. ♖ec1 ♘a4 White must still work to convert. Now this would be difficult to accomplish.

36. ♖ee3

Cementing the position and avoiding all tactics.

36... ♖c7 37. ♘g5

The knight becomes dominant now.

37... ♖c8 38. h4

Position after: 38. h4

38... h6 39. ♘e6+ ♔f6 40. ♘f4 ♔f7 41. ♖f3 ♖b7 42. ♖ce3 ♘d6 43. ♘xg6+

1-0

Game 36

♙ Maric, Rudolf
♟ Petrosian, Tigran V
🌍 Vinkovci 1970

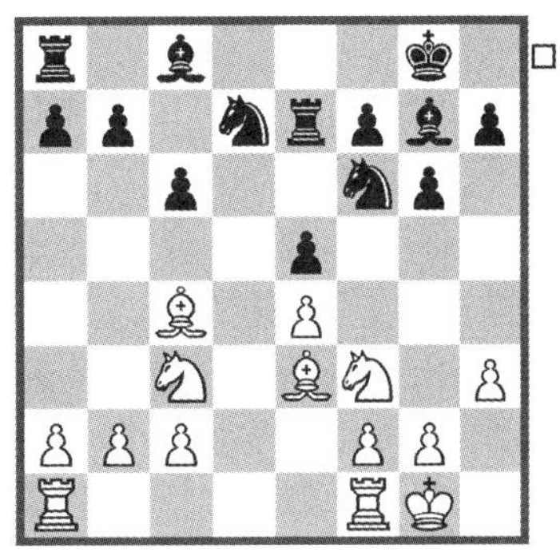

It is time to present another mentor of mine, but this time playing poorly, to conclude this chapter with a remarkable example. Iron Tigran has allowed some serious imprecisions probably by trusting to his routines, and achieved this hopeless situation as Black. He probably underestimated the strong master Maric who taught him (and the entire chess world) a remarkable lesson.

13. a4

An absolutely necessary move, not only to prevent ...b5, but also to fix the target on a7 with a5.

13... b6

13... a5 This looks to be necessary, but White will keep his domination with 14. ♖fd1 transferring the f3-knight to the g5- or c4-spot for instance.

14. ♖fd1

Occupying the file.

14... ♗b7 15. ♖d6 a6

Still preparing ...b5. Alas, there is nothing to get from it.

16. ♖ad1 b5 17. ♗b3 h6

Position after: 17... h6

White has achieved the maximum. His pieces are on optimal places. Thus it is time for pawn action.

18. g4!

Black is unable to prevent ♘g5.

18... ♖c8

18... g5 This gives nothing in view of the simple 19. h4.

19. g5 hxg5 20. ♘xg5 ♖c7

Black has overextended his defensive lines which are about to collapse.

21. a5!

Again a brilliant move eliminating the barricades on the d-file and threatening ♗b6.

21... ♔f8

Black blunders in a lost position, allowing beautiful tactics.

22. ♗xf7!

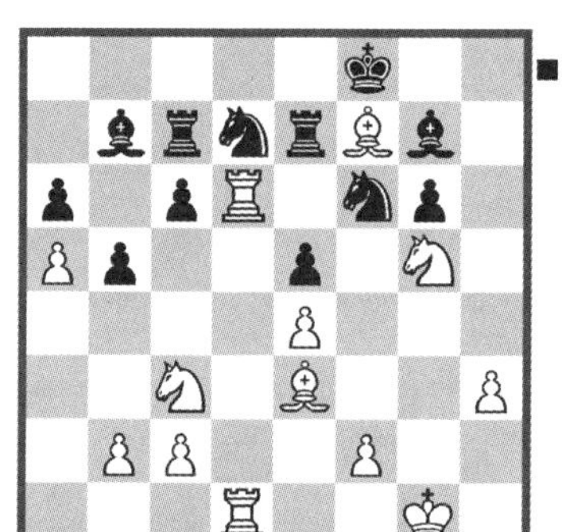

Position after: 22. ♗xf7!

22... ♖xf7 23. ♘e6+ ♔g8 24. ♘xc7 ♗f8 25. ♘e8! ♔h7 26. ♖xd7!

Another terrible strike. *Finis opus coronat.* Black resigned.

1-0

The Bishop Pair

Similar to the previous chapter, a series of exchanges in the middlegame that transfers the game to the endgame would likely cause the position to be opened, which will favor the side having the bishop pair.

There are some principles related to exploiting the advantage of the bishop pair, such as setting the pawn on the color of the opposite-colored bishop and gaining space, which refer more to the middlegame; while in the endgame another principle becomes widely implemented – the ability at a good moment to trade one of the bishops in order to simplify any conversion! Of course, there are also positions where the bishop pair is simply inferior in the endgame and these are explored here too.

Game 37

♙ Kortschnoj, Viktor Lvovich
♟ Matanovic, Aleksandar
Palma de Mallorca 1968

It is clear that the bishop pair is dominating in this open position. However there are some exceptions. Every master knows how to predict the arising endgame and if necessary to modify the pawn structure to make it good (or bad for their opponent). This chapter will demystify all the principles regarding the bishop pair in the endgame. Our first example is a classical one. White is absolutely winning because his bishop pair dominates here. In addition Black has weak pawns on the queenside and suffers without space. White instructively first activates the king.

32. ♔f2 g6

Setting up a barrier on the kingside and waiting for any advance to block the position. Alas, White may easily invade.

33. e5

The win is a matter of style. "Viktor the Terrible" usually prefers direct play. The following alternatives would be more methodical options.

A) 33. a4 Liberating the bishop.

B) 33. ♔e3 Centralizing the king.

33... fxe5 34. ♗xg6 exf4 35. gxf4

Position after: 35. gxf4

White is not afraid of radically trading pawn material. The position is open enough now.

35... e5 36. ♔f3 ♔e6 37. a4

Now it is necessary.

37... ♔d5 38. h4

White predicts that the h6-pawn may fall soon and thus wants to have the potential passer advanced – a very sensible and vital approach.

38... ♔e6 39. ♗c2 ♘f5 40. ♗b3+

(see diagram next column)

Position after: 40. ♗b3+

40... ♔f6 41. fxe5+

The pawn would be traded sooner or later.

41... ♘xe5+ 42. ♔e4 ♘xh4

Black took the dangerous h-pawn, but it won't be enough to reach equality. The next move leads to a deadly pin.

43. ♗c3 ♘hg6 44. ♗d4

Position after: 44. ♗d4

Finally the weak pawns on the queenside will fall.

44... h5 45. ♗xb6 ♘d7 46. ♗d4+ ♔e7

Black has a chance to eliminate White's remaining pawns. However there is a clear problem: the endgame with the bishop pair against the knights is simply winning.

47. a5!

Position after: 47. a5!

47... h4 48. ♗d5

White's bishops powerfully target the queenside and help the pawns to promote.

48... h3 49. ♗xb7 ♔d6 50. ♗g1 ♘c5+ 51. ♔f3 ♘e5+ 52. ♔g3 h2

Position after: 52... h2

53. ♔xh2 ♘xb7 54. a6 ♘f3+ 55. ♔h1

A famous diagram with a famous motif. The "fianchettoed" knight is unable to stop the passer on the edge. Black resigned.

1-0

Game 38

♙	Ye, Rongguang	(2480)
♟	Nunn, John DM	(2575)
🌍	Luzern 1989	

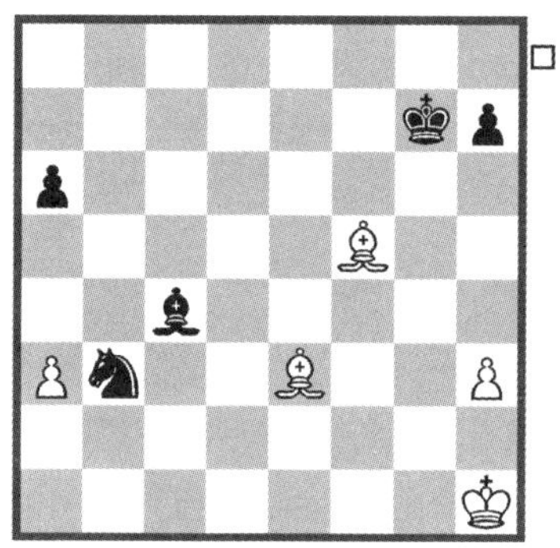

Here is a less drastic situation than in the previous example. The presence of the bishop gives Black the chance to organize a barrier – a typical defensive method with this material balance. However the most important factor giving Black chances for a draw is the reduced pawn material – all Black needs to do is to give away the knight for both pawns. Of course in addition, there are chances to transfer the endgame to a theoretical opposite-colored bishops endgame or an endgame with a bad bishop.

41. ♔g2

The first stage is to activate the king.

41... ♗d5+ 42. ♔g3 ♘a5

Black wants to set up a barrier with the knight on c4.

43. ♗d4+ ♔g8 44. ♔f4 ♘c4 45. ♗c5 ♔g7

Position after: 45... ♔g7

46. h4

White wants to use this pawn to attack the opponent's king.

46... ♔g8 47. ♔g5!

This is the only path the king may use to invade.

47... ♘e5 48. ♔f6 ♘f3

48... ♘c6 49. ♗d3! [49. ♗e6+? This is not good enough. 49... ♗xe6 50. ♔xe6 ♘a5 This should lead to a draw. Black will wait for the white king to go toward the a-pawn to transfer his king toward a8, with a draw after the knight captures the h-pawn.] 49... a5

Position after: 49... a5

50. ♗b6 The black a-pawn is in danger. Then the position with the opposite-colored bishops should be winning for White because of his active king. Sacrificing the black bishop for the a-pawn would lead to defeat.

49. ♗f2!

Precise! White's king has made progress, so there is no need to advance the h-pawn any further. With the pawn on h6 White would not be able to convert the position with the extra dark-squared bishop.

49... ♗b3 50. ♗g4 ♗d5

(see diagram next page)

Position after: 50... ♗d5

51. a4

Advancing the pawn is an improvement. When the a6-pawn falls it will be closer to promotion.

51... ♘d2 52. ♗e1 ♘f3 53. ♗g3

The "don't rush" principle in action.

53... ♘d2 54. a5 ♗c4 55. ♗e1 ♘b3 56. ♗c3 ♘c5 57. ♔e5 ♘b3

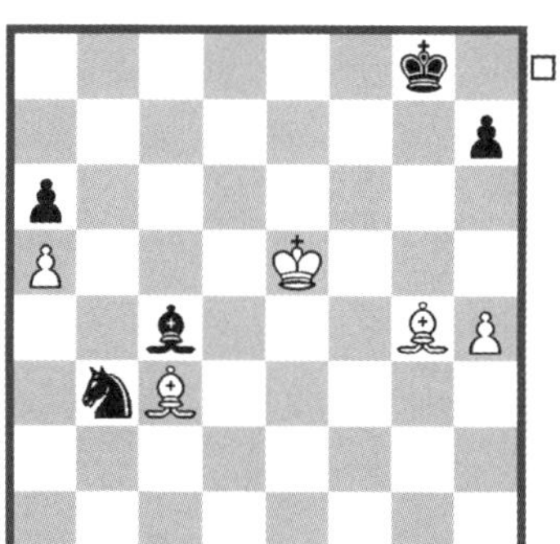

Position after: 57... ♘b3

Black's minor pieces are safe. However the a6-pawn is in danger.

58. ♔d6 ♔f7 59. ♗h5+ ♔g8 60. ♔c6 ♔f8 61. ♗b4+

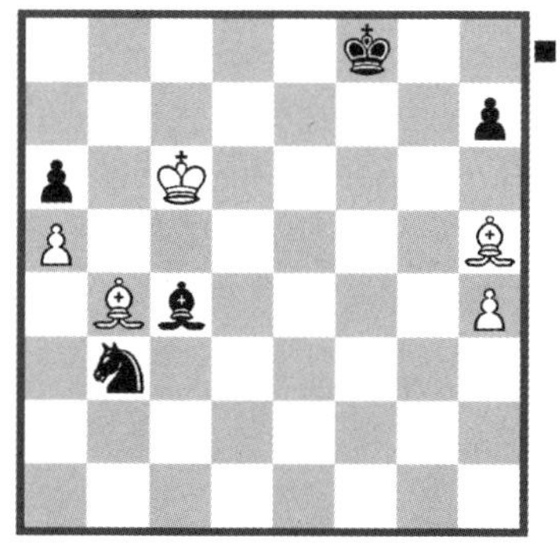

Position after: 61. ♗b4+

61... ♔g7 62. ♔b6 ♔f6 63. ♗g4 ♘c1 64. ♗c8 ♘d3 65. ♗a3

Black resigned.

1-0

Game 39

♙ Hort, Vlastimil
♟ Ciocaltea, Victor
Budapest 1973

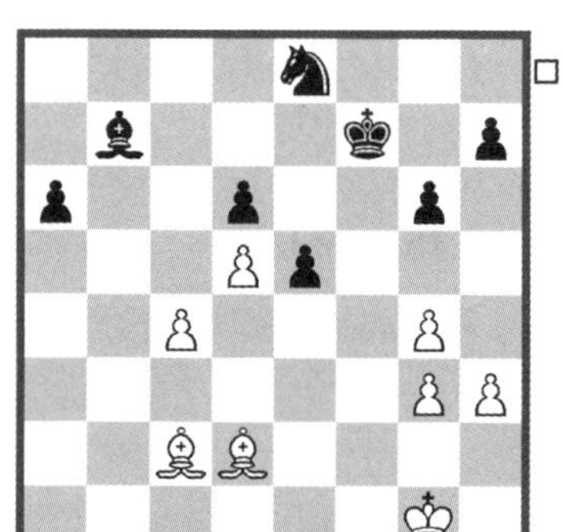

In this example it may appear that White has a problem because his majority on the kingside is useless and Black has an extra passer. In actual fact, to the contrary, Black is desperately lost. After White's next powerful move Black is unable to activate his knight.

32. g5!

Paralyzing the knight. White achieves one more goal – he fixes the black kingside pawns which may be under attack after White's h4-h5 advance.

32... ♗c8

32... ♘g7 33. g4 Keeping the knight locked in.

33. g4 ♗d7

After fixing the structure White goes for the natural phase in the endgame – centralizing the king.

34. ♔f2 ♔e7 35. ♗a5

Controlling the c7- and d8-squares. Black is paralyzed.

35... ♗c8 36. ♔e3 ♗d7

(see diagram next column)

As he is dead paralyzed, Black can only wait.

Position after: 36... ♗d7

37. ♗b6 ♗c8 38. ♔e4 ♗d7 39. ♗b3 ♗c8

With all the pieces placed on their best spots White finally creates a passer with his next move.

40. c5 ♗d7 41. c6

Position after: 41. c6

This move even locks in the bishop.

41... ♗c8 42. ♗c4 ♘g7 43. ♔d3 ♘e8 44. ♔c3

Black can do nothing against the white king's march toward a5. Black resigned.
1-0

Game 40

♙ Sadvakasov, Darmen (2585)
♟ Kramnik, Vladimir (2797)
Astana 2001

Our next example is from top level praxis. The former world champion Kramnik is better with the black pieces here. The problem is the structure on the queenside but the bishop pair should still prevail.

30... f5!

Not only launching the majority, and restricting the white bishop, but also opening up the diagonal for the black king.

31. c4?

White immediately errs. It is wrong to advance this pawn so much, giving Black the chance to use the d4-spot.

31. a3 ♔f7 32. b4 This alternative, followed by setting the pawns on the dark squares supporting a barrier, would have been a better choice. It would be extremely difficult (if in fact even actually possible at all) for Black to make progress.

31... ♔f7 32. c5

Now White's idea is clear – to fix the target on c5.

32... a5?!

I would rather suggest direct action on the kingside. Reducing the pawn material must be in White's favor.

32... g5 More methodical and logical.

33. a3 ♔e6 34. b4 axb4 35. axb4 ♔e5 36. ♔e3

Position after: 36. ♔e3

Both sides have improved their armies. Black wants to remove the white king so as to invade somehow.

36... ♗g5+ 37. ♔d3 ♗a6+ 38. ♔c2?!

Not bad.

38. ♔c3 This is simpler. 38... ♗b5 39. ♘b6 This gives Black nothing, as can be seen in the following instance. 39... f4?! 40. ♘d7+ ♔e6 [40... ♔f5 41. g4+! ♔e6 42. ♘b8±] 41. ♘b8 fxg3 42. hxg3 ♗f6+ 43. ♔b3

Position after: 43. ♔b3

Here 43... h5! is the only move leading to a balanced game. [43... ♗e5? 44. ♘xc6 ♗xc6 45. ♗xc6 ♗xg3 46. b5+–]

38... ♔d4

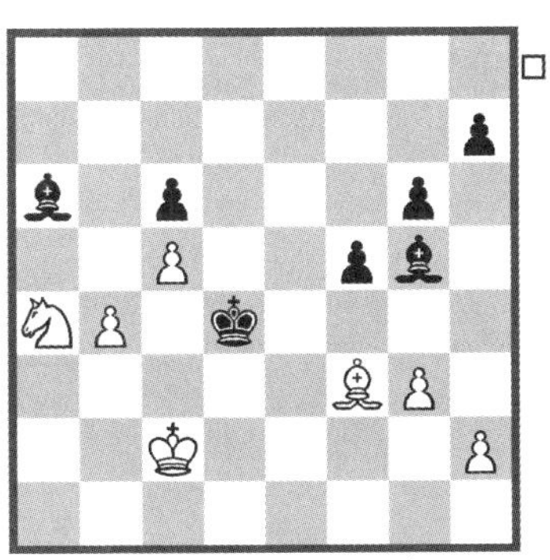

Position after: 38... ♔d4

39. ♘c3?

The final mistake, perhaps made in time trouble. In any case it is hard to explain.

39. ♗xc6 This move should have been played automatically. 39... ♔c4 40. ♘b6+ ♔xb4 41. ♘d7 White has ideas of ♘f8 or to move the bishop back with an upcoming c6. White risks nothing.

39... ♗d3+! 40. ♔b3 ♗c4+

Repetition probably due to zeitnot.

41. ♔c2 ♗d3+ 42. ♔b3 ♗d2

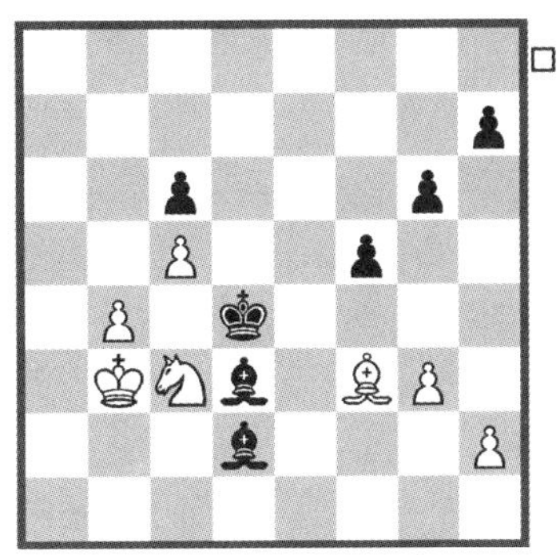

Position after: 42... ♗d2

The bishop pair is a pair of bosses. Together with the king there is a deadly attack.

43. ♘d1

43. ♘e2+ This would not have helped. Black just responds as follows. 43... ♔e3 44. ♘f4 ♗e4! Black wins.

43... ♗e4

A very important ability of the bishop pair is to exchange one of the bishops for the opponent's knight or bishop.

44. ♗e2 ♗d5+ 45. ♔a4

After driving the white king far from the battlefield Black strikes.

45... g5 46. b5

Position after: 46. b5

An act of desperation.

46... ♔xc5! 47. bxc6 ♗xc6+ 48. ♔b3 ♔d4 49. ♗f1 ♗e1 50. ♗e2 g4!

Position after: 50... g4!

51. ♗a6 h5 52. ♔c2 ♗e4+ 53. ♔c1 ♗f3 54. ♗c8 f4 55. gxf4 h4 56. f5 g3 57. hxg3 hxg3

0-1

Game 41

♙ Gheorghiu, Florin
♟ Olafsson, Fridrik
Athens 1969

White's next move is an excellent practical decision. Every true master would play this move automatically, even before ♔f2. It is good to set the pawns on the color of the opponent's bishop and gain space – two very important principles when playing with the advantage of a bishop pair.

22. g4!

22. e4? But not this move because of the following. 22... f5! 23. ♗d3 ♗b7 Black dominates on the d5-square with chances which are not worse.

22... ♗b7 23. ♔f2 f5

Black constantly fights against the e4 advance.

24. h3

White keeps the tension. It would be in his favor if Black took first.

24... ♔f7 25. ♗d3 ♗d5 26. ♗c3!

Position after: 26. ♗c3!

With the idea of activating the bishop via the g3-square.

26... ♗b7?

Black starts to wander. It would be better to organize a defensive set-up on the kingside.

26... g5!? I think this would make sense.

27. ♗e1 ♗d5

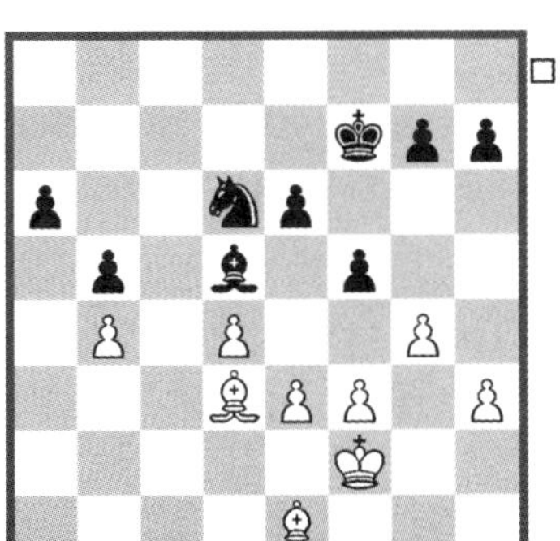

Position after: 27... ♗d5

Black persistently wastes time.

28. ♔g2?!

A) 28. ♔e2? fxg4 [28... ♗c4? 29. ♗g3 White wins after creating two connected passers.] 29. hxg4 ♗c4 Black will survive.

B) 28. gxf5! exf5 29. ♔e2 It looks impossible for Black to hold after ♗g3 with the upcoming e4 sooner or later.

28... ♗c4 29. ♗c2 ♗d5 30. gxf5 exf5

Black takes with the pawn to stop e4. But after preparation White should be able to create two connected passers.

31. ♗g3 ♘c4 32. ♔f2 ♘d2

Position after: 32... ♘d2

Black must complicate.

33. ♗xf5 ♗xf3 34. ♗c8 ♗c6 35. ♗e5

35. ♗xa6?? ♘e4+–+

35... ♘e4+ 36. ♔e2 g5

Black has played well in the previous stage and does not care about the unimportant a6-pawn. The most important factor is that he has a firm blockade and an active kingside majority. Black should not lose.

37. ♗xa6 ♗d7?

Black collapses, probably in zeitnot.

37... ♘c3+ 38. ♔d2 ♘d5 39. ♗d6 ♔e6 40. ♗f8 ♔d7 This leads to a locked bishop on a6 and an obvious draw.

38. ♗b7

This bishop comes back to play and the game is over.

38... ♘f6 39. ♗g2 ♗f5 40. ♗xf6 ♔xf6 41. e4

Position after: 41. e4

41... ♗e6 42. ♔e3 ♗c4 43. ♗f3

Black resigned.

1-0

Game 42

♙ Bogdanovski, Vlatko (2435)
♟ Gicev, Blagoja (2336)
Skopje 2002

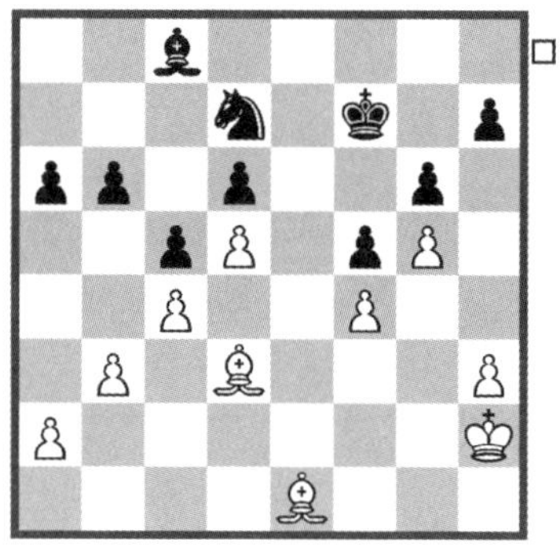

A bishop pair can dominate even in blocked positions – give the bishop one important diagonal and it will become good. On the other hand the opponent may face problems even in a blocked position if their bishop is bad and/or their knight does not have good and safe spots. Our next example perfectly illustrates this.

35. ♗c3

White activates the dark-squared bishop. The point is that the light-squared one is still useless.

35... ♗b7?!

35... a5 I would rather suggest this as the move which would be played by any true master automatically. The point is to stop b4 and to be ready to trade many pawns if White prepares the advance. Also, the knight can use the route b8-a6.

36. h4 ♗c8 37. h5 ♗b7 38. a3

Position after: 38. a3

38... ♗c8?

Even if the previous moves were not mistakes, this is a direct mistake.

38... a5 This was necessary instead.

39. h6?!

This is natural (capturing on g6 will create a weak pawn for Black – g6; now Black has both g6 and h7 as targets), but 39.b4 should have been preferred instead.

39... ♘b8 40. ♗f6 ♔e8 41. ♔g3 ♘d7 42. ♗c3 ♘f8?

Both sides have allowed many mutual mistakes, Black missed ...a5 and White missed b4. Finally, White has nothing else to do.

Position after: 42... ♘f8?

43. b4! ♗b7?

The final mistake.

43... ♔e7! This was necessary to protect the d6-pawn – so that after 44. a4 he would be able to respond with 44... cxb4!.

Position after: 44... cxb4!

45. ♗xb4 a5! A dead draw.

44. a4! ♗c8

44... ♘d7 This would not have helped because White has the following. 45. a5! bxa5 46. bxc5 ♘xc5 47. ♗xf5! Here you can see the point of the move 39.h6.

45. a5

Of course, Black is lost now.

45... bxa5 46. bxc5 dxc5 47. ♗xa5 ♔d7 48. ♗c3 ♔e7 49. ♔f2 ♔f7

Position after: 49... ♔f7

50. ♔e3

White's king goes to a5.

50... ♘d7 51. ♗a5 ♔e7 52. ♗c7 ♘f8 53. ♔d2 ♗d7 54. ♗c2 ♗e8 55. ♔c3 ♗d7 56. ♔b2 ♗e8 57. ♔a3 ♔d7 58. ♗b6 ♔d6 59. ♗a7 ♘d7 60. ♗a4

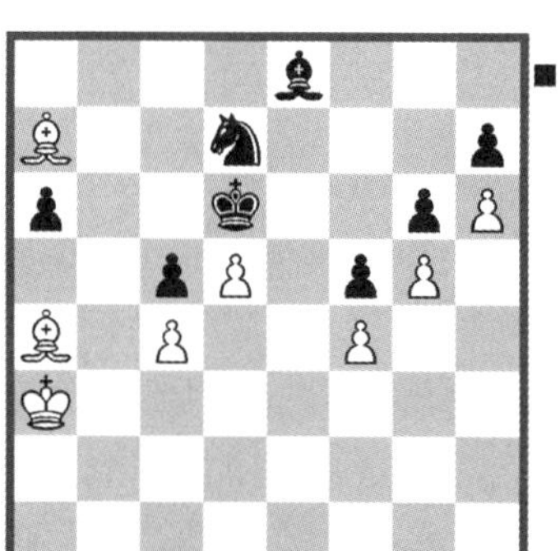

Position after: 60. ♗a4

It becomes clear that Black must not keep all the doors closed.

60... ♔c7 61. ♗xc5 ♗f7 62. ♗d4 ♔d6 63. ♔b4 a5+ 64. ♔b5 ♗g8 65. ♗b3 a4 66. c5+

1-0

Game 43

♙ Uhlmann, Wolfgang
♟ Andersson, Ulf
Skopje 1972

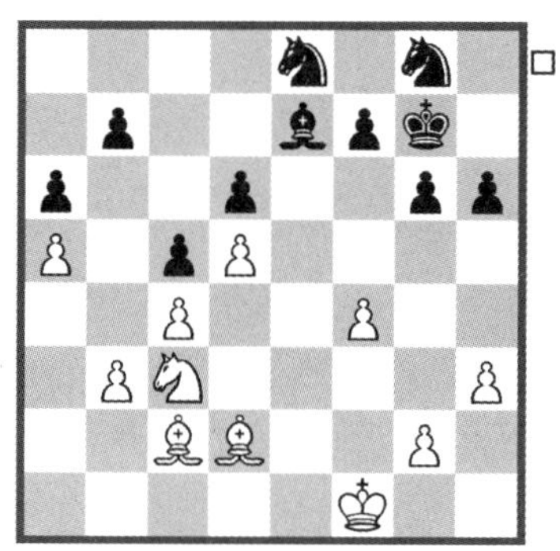

Let's continue with a similar King's Indian structure, but with more material on the board. Our next position is typical for many lines. Black is in big trouble. White's bishop pair is actually very good and there is a possibility of striking on the queenside with the idea to open up the position and to access the a6- and b7-pawns. All this is due to the well organized advance of the pawn to a5 – this pawn fixes the potential weaknesses on the light squares.

33. b4

33. g4 Another approach. The point might be firstly to accumulate slight advantages on the other side or even to strike there. We will see something similar in the next game where the strong German grandmaster Uhlmann is the victim instead of the executioner as in the current game – it appears that he may well have learned the lesson from two years earlier.

33... cxb4 34. ♘a4 ♘gf6

Black hurries to transfer the knight on d7 to cover the important b6- and c5-spots.

35. ♘b6

If 35. ♗xb4 then 35... ♘d7.

35... ♗d8 36. ♗xb4 ♗xb6

An excellent practical decision. Black must take the knight.

36... ♔f8? This will allow 37. ♘c8!.

Position after: 37. ♘c8!

37... ♗c7 38. g4 Leading to almost complete paralysis for Black.

37. axb6

Position after: 37. axb6

37... ♔f8?

A terrible mistake.

37... ♘d7! This was necessary. 38. ♗a4 ♘xb6 39. ♗xe8 ♔f8 Now this would lead to a draw.

38. c5

White takes his chance.

38... ♘d7?

Another mistake.

38... dxc5 39. ♗xc5+ ♔g8 40. ♗d4!

(see analysis diagram next page)

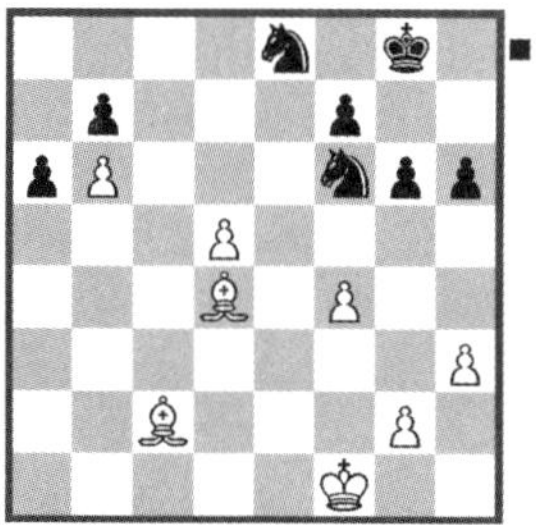

Position after: 40. ♗d4!

40... ♘xd5 41. ♗e4 ♘ef6 42. ♗f3 This is winning for White, but it would have been more resistant for Black.

39. c6! bxc6 40. b7 cxd5 41. ♗a4 ♘b8 42. ♗xe8 ♔xe8 43. ♗xd6

Black resigned.

1-0

Game 44

♙ Polugaevsky, Lev
♟ Uhlmann, Wolfgang
Amsterdam 1970

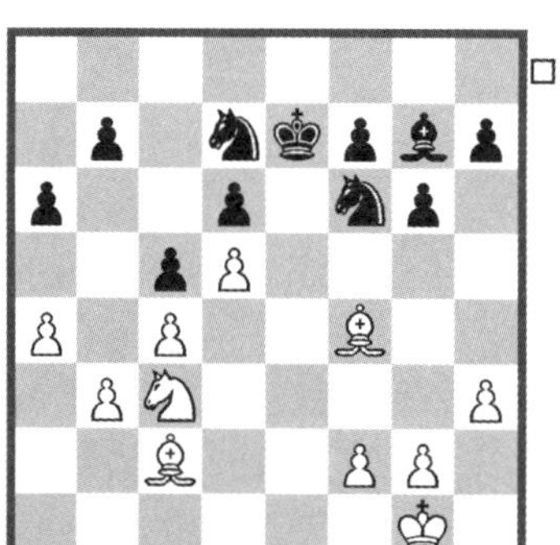

White is conventionally better due to his bishop pair advantage. A perceptive reader would already know that White should fix the targets on the color of the bishop that does not have an opponent. Thus the following is played.

24. a5! h5

I like this approach. Despite serious chances on the queenside White can organize a kingside expansion and Black wishes to deal with this. I think holding a waiting policy would offer less chances to resist.

25. ♗d2 ♘e8 26. g3

There is no need to rush. White prevents any potential fixing with ...h4.

26... ♗d4 27. ♔g2

The king goes toward the center and prepares for expansion.

27... ♘g7 28. f4 ♘f5?!

Position after: 28... ♘f5?!

Black sets a positional trap.

28... f5!? This deserves attention.

29. ♘d1

White avoids the trap.

29. ♗xf5 This can be met as follows. 29... ♗xc3! 30. ♗xc3 gxf5 Black is okay.

29... ♘h6 30. ♔f3 f5

Black goes for this now. Ossification of the position is the goal, together with the possibility of trading as many pawns as possible after White goes g4.

31. ♗d3 ♔d8 32. ♘e3 ♔e7

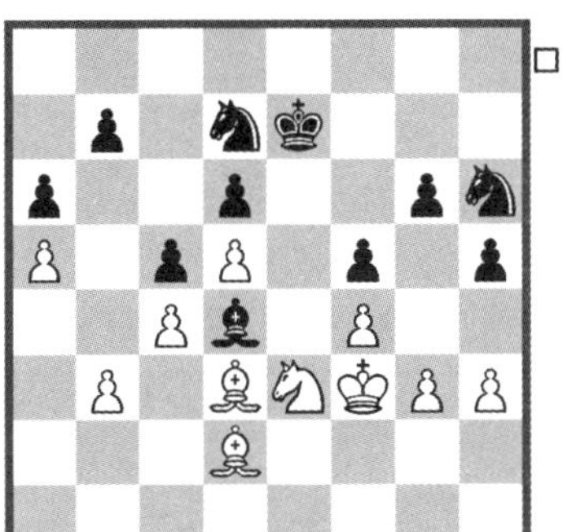

Position after: 32... ♔e7

33. ♘c2

33. ♘g2 This is the plan that White decided to accomplish later.

33... ♗b2 34. ♔e3 ♘f6 35. ♘e1

White finally moves the knight toward h4. The idea is to strike on g6 and advance g4.

35... ♗d4+ 36. ♔f3 ♗b2 37. ♘g2 ♘d7 38. ♘h4 ♔f6 39. ♔e3 ♘f7 40. ♗c2 ♗a1 41. ♔e2

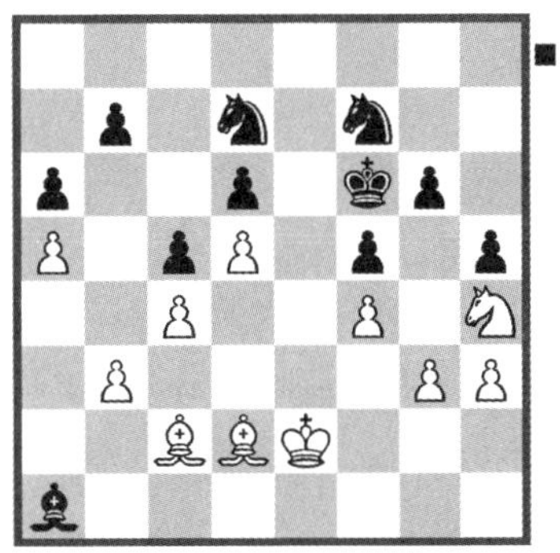

Position after: 41. ♔e2

41... ♗b2?!

The notorious move 41. Yes, the game was played with analog clocks, so probably the players, as usual, played one extra move after move 40.

41... ♘h6! This was simpler. Black must stop g4.

42. ♗e1

The last preparatory move.

42. g4 This was a reasonable option but Black still holds after the following. 42... hxg4 43. hxg4 fxg4 44. ♘xg6 ♘h6

Position after: 44... ♘h6

Now 45. ♗e1 will be met with 45... ♘f5.

42... ♗a1?

A decisive mistake.

The simple 42... ♘h6 would have stopped White's kingside activities. White would be forced probably to transfer play to the queenside where in any case Black has another knight guarding on d7.

43. g4! hxg4 44. hxg4 fxg4 45. ♘xg6

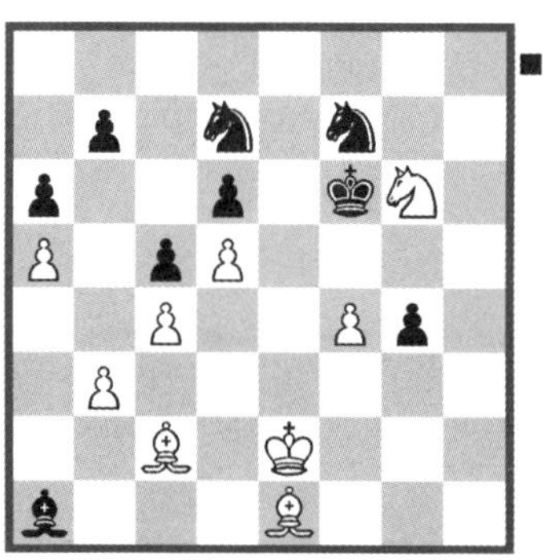

Position after: 45. ♘xg6

Now Black's position collapses.

45... ♔g7 46. ♘h4 ♔f8 47. ♗f5 ♘f6 48. ♗c8 ♘d8 49. ♘f5 ♘h5 50. ♗d2 ♗d4 51. ♘xd4

Black resigned.

1-0

Game 45

♙	Zlatanovic, Boroljub	(2371)
♟	Nestorovic, Dejan	(2340)
🌍	Kragujevac 2018	

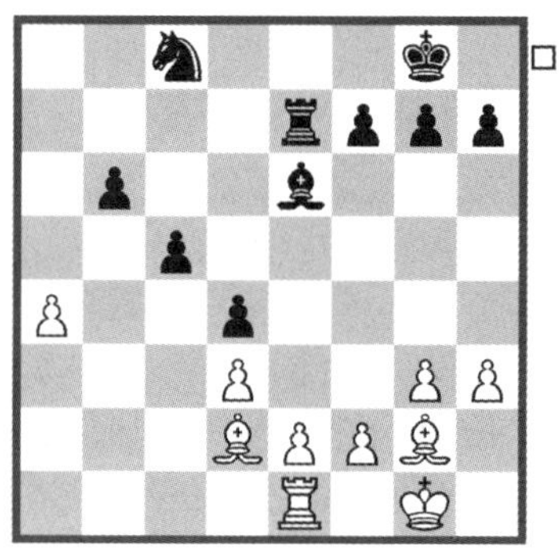

Let's now switch to more complex examples – ones with rooks on the board. Here White is better due to the bishop pair advantage, but Black's position is compact enough. If you don't know what should be the plan, think about the opponent's plan. Obviously, Black will play ...♖a7 with ...♗d7 and attack the weak a4-pawn. Thus, White must advance it.

27. a5! b5?

A terrible mistake. Black was close to time trouble and this fact makes the reaction stranger. The point is that Black's strong-looking queenside pawn armada is actually fragile and the a-passer is the more dangerous passer, supported by the powerful bishop pair and active rook.

27... bxa5 28. ♗xa5 ♖a7 Black would not risk a lot after this, with probably a draw as a result.

28. ♖c1 c4 29. ♗b4

After this it becomes clear that Black's majority is useless. Sooner or later e3 will crush Black's structure with an easy win.

29... ♖c7

30. e3

30. a6 This would win as well, of course.

30... dxe3 31. fxe3 f5

A random activity in time trouble. Black is hopeless anyway.

32. dxc4 bxc4 33. ♗c3!

(see diagram next column)

The rook goes to the b-file.

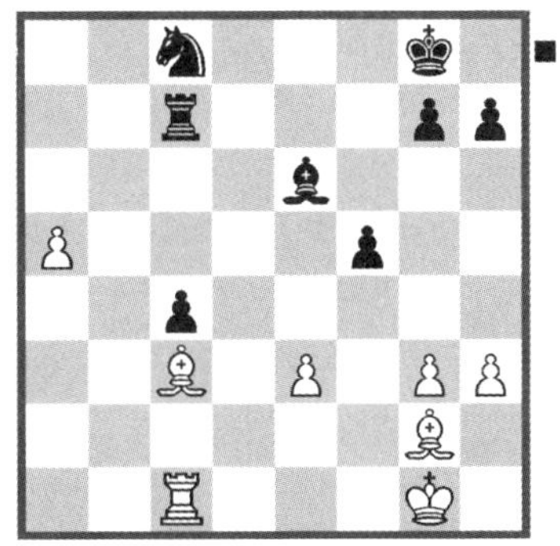

Position after: 33. ♗c3!

33... ♔f7 34. ♖b1 ♘e7 35. a6 ♗c8 36. ♖b7!

A final and beautiful touch! Black resigned.

1-0

Game 46

♙ Zlatanovic, Boroljub (2434)
♟ Mladenovic, Stefan (2181)
Paracin 2012

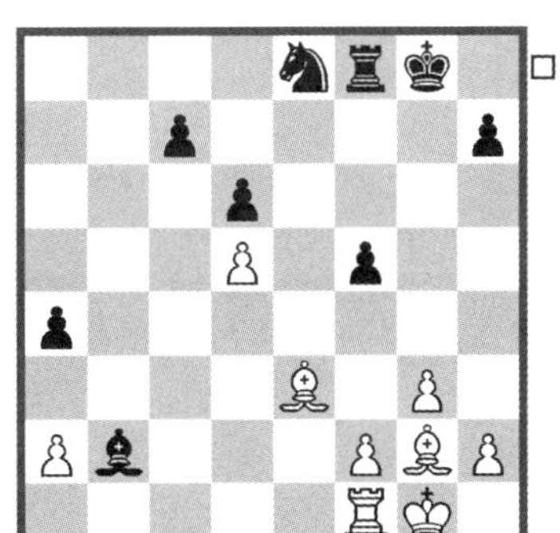

The material is equal and reduced and White is better due to the advantage of the bishop pair. After deeply analyzing the position it becomes clear that Black actually has a dangerous plan to target the white pawn on a2! His idea is to play ...a3 and transfer the knight to the queenside using the route ♘e8-f6-e4-c3. White must prevent this!

22. ♗h3!

And White did! The knight must change its route. The pawn on f5 is under attack so the direct above-mentioned threat is eliminated. Black has problems to reactivate his kingside pieces.

22... ♘g7 23. ♖d1

With the idea to place the rook on c2.

23... ♖b8

23... a3 24. ♖d3 The idea is 25 ♖b3 24... ♖b8 25. ♗d2 keeping a serious advantage.

24. ♗f1

The knight is deflected from its route and now the bishop prevents the move ...♖b5 in some lines.

24... ♖b4 25. ♖d2 ♗e5?!

(see diagram next column)

Black wants to set the rook on b2, but this would just help White to realize the advantage.

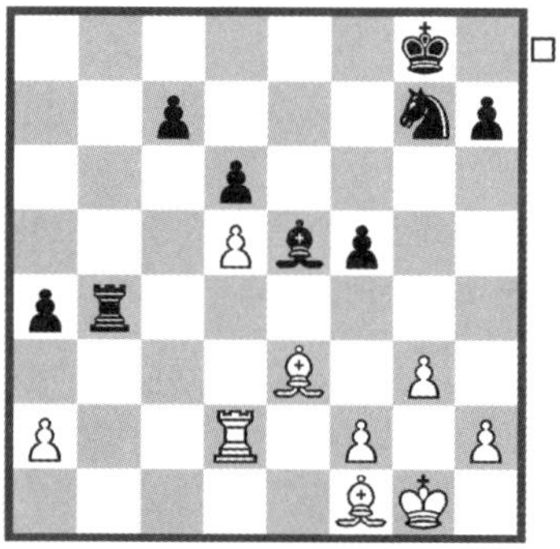

Position after: 25... ♗e5?!

26. ♖c2 ♖b2 27. ♖xb2 ♗xb2

After some fine maneuvers the a2-pawn is finally safe. After trading rooks Black is unable to find any active play. It is time for White to find the best places for his bishops and to centralize the king.

28. ♗b5!

This is a prelude to a very interesting set-up.

28... a3 29. ♗a7

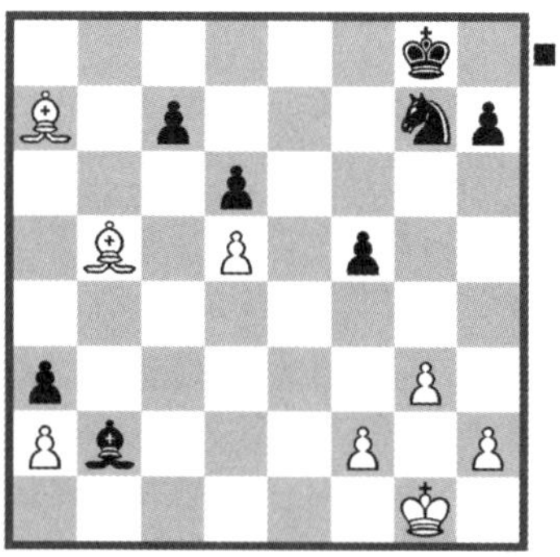

Position after: 29. ♗a7

29... ♗f6

29... ♗c3 This was a slightly better way to protect the pawn on c7, but now White's king goes toward the pawn on a3 and and gains a tempo on the bishop. 30. ♔f1 Black has big problems.

30. ♗b8 ♗d8 31. ♗d7 ♔f7 32. f4

Position after: 32. f4

A funny situation has arisen. Black can activate his king and knight without losing material only by playing ...♔g6 and ...♘h5; but then White exchanges the bishop for the knight after ♗e8 and probably gets a winning position due to there being so many fixed black pawns on its bishop's color.

32... ♘h5?!

Black goes for active play, but a tactic crushes his plans.

32... ♔e7 33. ♗c8 This gives nothing to Black after the following. 33... ♔f6 34. ♔f2 ♔g6 35. ♗d7

(see analysis diagram next column)

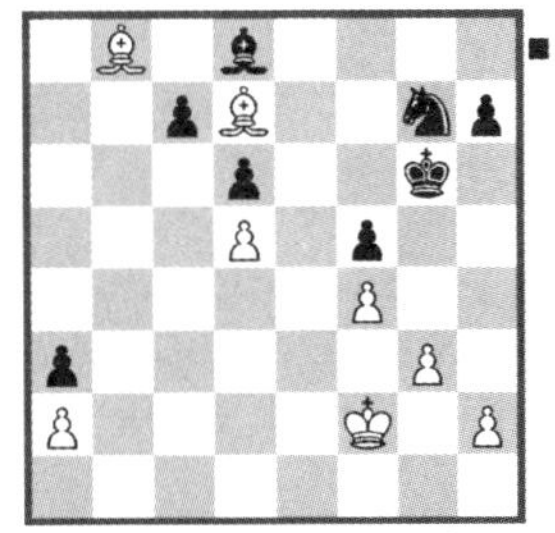

Position after: 35. ♗d7

White keeps the knight out of play. 35... ♘h5 36. ♗e8+ ♔h6 37. ♗xh5 ♔xh5 38. h3 As mentioned above this should be winning for White.

33. ♗xf5 ♘f6

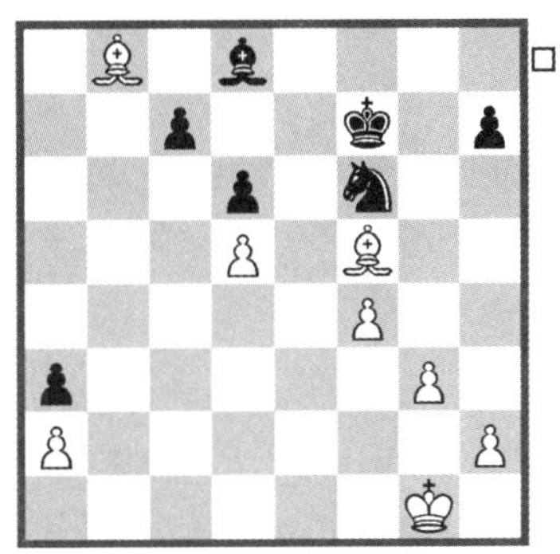

Position after: 33... ♘f6

34. ♗d3!

34. ♗e6+?? ♔e7 The knight gets the c3-square.

34... ♘xd5

White would play 35. ♗c4 anyway.

35. ♗c4+–

Black can get rid of the annoying pin only by allowing the doubling of his pawns. White is winning.

35... ♔e6 36. ♔f2 c6 37. ♗a7 ♔e7 38. ♗xd5 cxd5

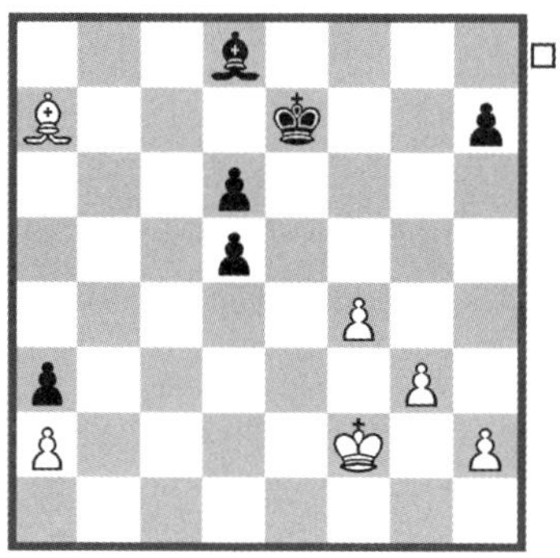

Position after: 38... cxd5

The rest is a matter of technique and comments are not needed.

39. g4 ♗a5 40. ♗d4 ♗b4 41. f5 ♗d2 42. ♔f3 ♗e1 43. g5 ♔f7 44. ♔g4 ♗d2 45. h4 ♗c1 46. h5 ♗b2 47. g6+ hxg6 48. hxg6+ ♔g8 49. ♗b6 ♔g7 50. ♗d8 ♗c1 51. ♗e7 d4

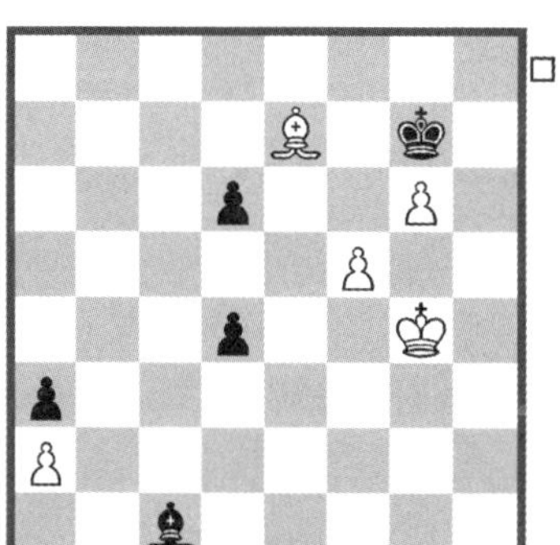

Position after: 51... d4

52. ♗xd6

52. ♔h5! This was winning in a few moves.

52... d3 53. ♗e5+ ♔f8 54. ♔f3 ♔g8 55. f6 ♗g5 56. f7+ ♔f8 57. ♗d6+ ♗e7 58. ♗xe7+ ♔xe7 59. ♔e3

Black resigned.

1-0

Game 47

♙ Zlatanovic, Boroljub (2378)
♟ Veljanoski, Andrej (1906)
Struga 2018

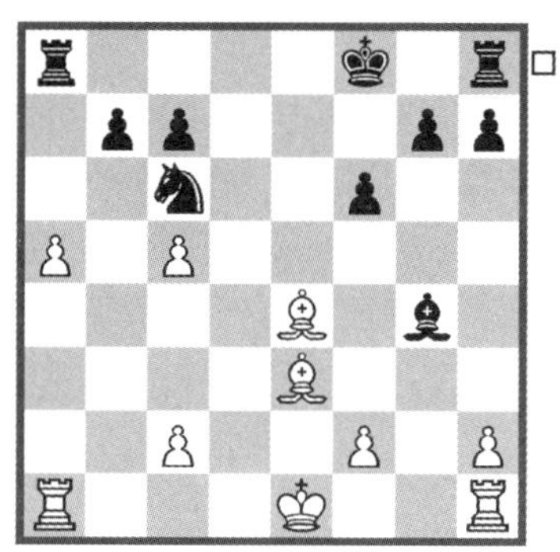

Although it may appear that White's damaged structure might be an important positional factor, White is actually winning. The powerful bishop pair together with the active rook will crush Black's queenside after the obvious blow.

24. a6! ♗d7

What else?

25. 0-0-0!

This is the fastest way to exploit the arising dangerous pawn on b7.

25... ♔e7 26. axb7 ♖a1+ 27. ♔d2!

There is beauty in this maneuver. The king goes to the queenside with castling and now comes back to the center.

27. ♔b2 ♖xd1 28. ♖xd1 ♖b8 This even looks holdable for Black.

27... ♖xd1+ 28. ♖xd1 ♖b8 29. ♖b1 ♘d8

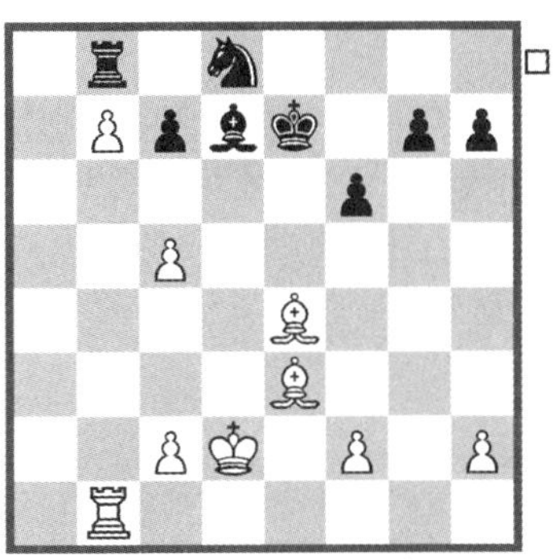

Position after: 29... ♘d8

30. ♗f4

By attacking the c7-pawn White reduces the pressure on the b7-passer and liberates the rook for the final maneuver.

30... ♘e6 31. ♗g3 ♔d8 32. ♖a1

There is no defense against ♖a8.

1-0

Game 48

♙ Topalov, Veselin (2700)
♟ Gelfand, Boris (2700)
Dos Hermanas 1996

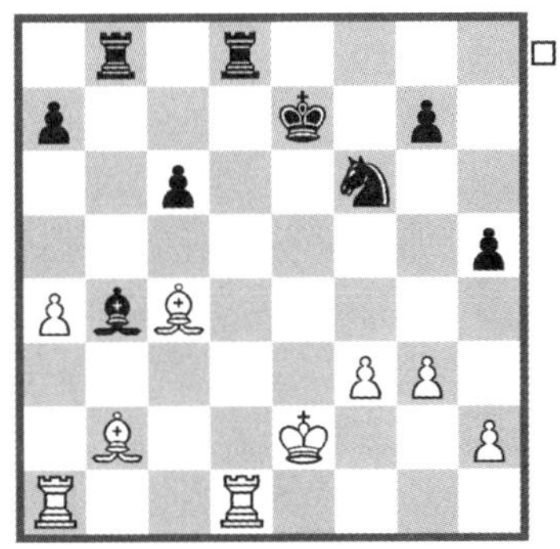

White is better due to the bishop pair advantage. The position is opened and the bishop pair should be the decisive factor.

21. ♖d4!?

White naturally wants to activate his pieces. The idea is to double the rooks. Black cannot simply capture the rook.

There was nothing wrong with 21. f4 – play on the side where you are stronger!

21... ♗a5?!

21... ♘d5!? This looks like a solid attempt to activate the pieces and perhaps force White to lose the advantage of the bishop pair. 22. ♖e4+ ♔f8 This gives Black enough active play with real chances to hold.

22. ♗a3+ ♔e8 23. ♖ad1 ♖xd4 24. ♖xd4 ♖b1 25. ♗d3

Threatening mate in one!

25... ♖e1+ 26. ♔f2

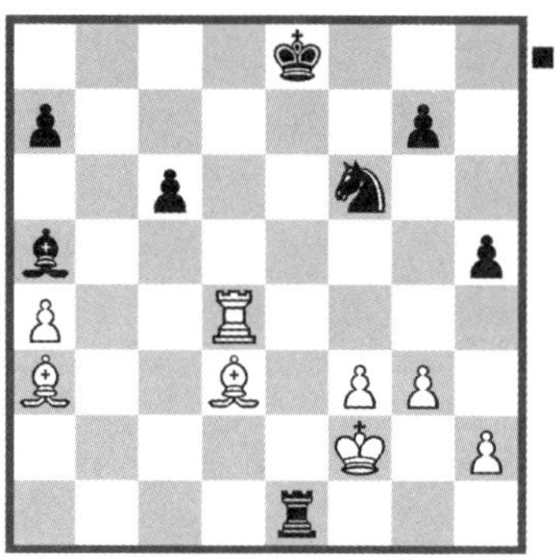

Position after: 26. ♔f2

26... ♔f7?

26... ♘d5! This was necessary here with the idea to bring the king closer to the queenside weaknesses. 27. ♗g6+ [27. ♗c5 ♖a1 28. ♗xa7 ♗b4 Black has some counter-chances.] 27... ♔d7 28. ♗xh5 ♖a1 29. ♗c5 ♗e1+

Position after: 29... ♗e1+

30. ♔e2 ♗c3 31. ♖e4 ♗f6 A forced line showing that White must work to convert.

27. ♗c5 ♖a1 28. ♗c4+ ♔e8 29. ♗d3 ♔f7 30. ♗xa7

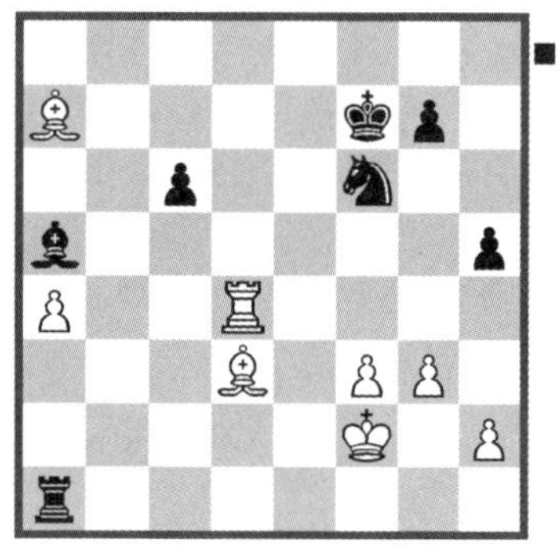

Position after: 30. ♗xa7

After some repetition probably due to time trouble White captured the pawn and Black has nothing in return.

30... ♖a2+ 31. ♔g1!

31. ♔e3?? ♗d2+ 32. ♔e2 ♗c3+–+

31... ♖a1+ 32. ♔g2 ♖a2+ 33. ♔h3 ♖a3 34. f4

White has precisely calculated that Black has nothing despite weakening the g4-square.

34... ♗e1 35. ♗c5 ♖c3 36. ♗c4+ ♔e8

(see diagram next page)

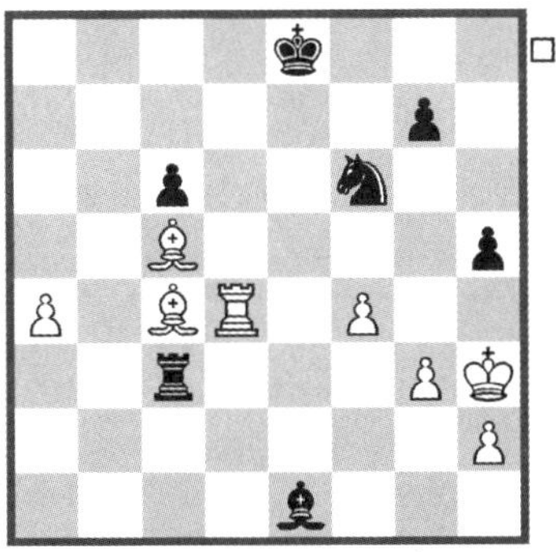

Position after: 36... ♔e8

37. ♗b4!

A final touch! Black is threatening ...♗f2.

37... ♖c1 38. ♗xe1 ♖xe1 39. a5 ♖a1 40. a6 ♔e7 41. ♖d2

After ♖a2 White wins trivially. Black resigned.

1-0

Game 49

♙	Ivanchuk, Vassily	(2729)
♟	Karjakin, Sergey	(2660)
🌍	Wijk aan Zee 2006	

White should be better here because of the presence of the bishop pair in the opened position. In order to make the bishop pair more influential White must open up the position more.

(see diagram next column)

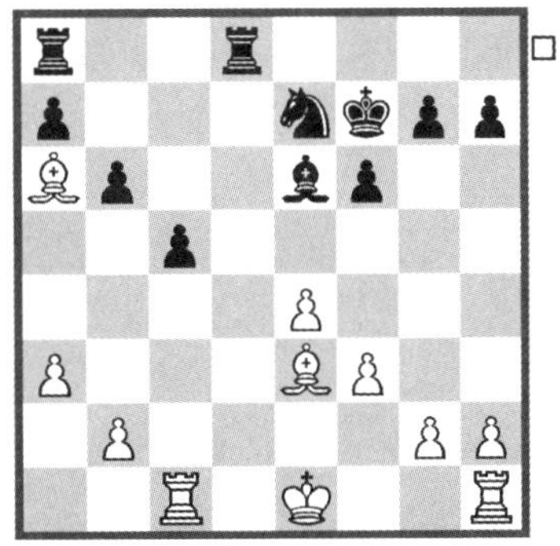

21. b4 cxb4 22. axb4 ♗c8

Black wants to eliminate the pressure.

23. ♗e2 ♗e6 24. ♔f2 ♖ac8 25. ♖a1 ♘c6

What else?

26. ♗a6 ♖b8

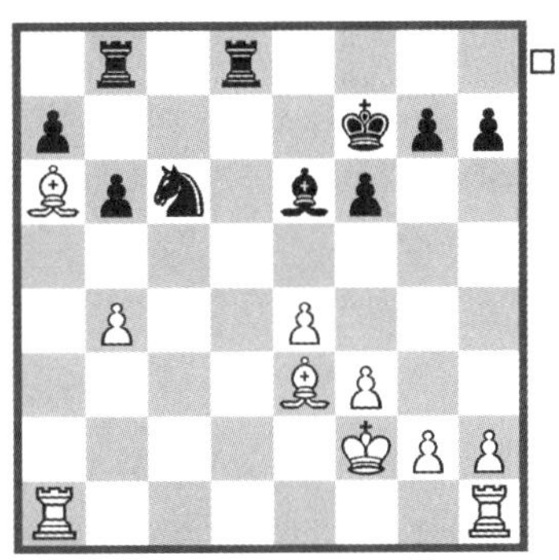

Position after: 26... ♖b8

27. ♗b5

Black's queenside is about to collapse.

27... ♘xb4 28. ♖xa7+ ♔g8 29. ♖e7 ♗f7 30. ♖a1

Doubling on the 7th rank is the ultimate goal.

30... ♖a8 31. ♖d7!

Tactics serve strategy.

31... ♖dc8 32. ♖xa8 ♖xa8 33. ♗xb6

Position after: 33. ♗xb6

Finally there is a material advantage. Nevertheless White is far from converting. All his pawns are on one side which drastically complicates his task.

33... h6 34. ♔g3 ♖c8 35. ♖d6 ♗e8 36. ♗e2 ♖c6

It may look like a significant improvement for Black. From one point of view, the white rook is more active. However the white king can become active now.

37. ♖xc6 ♘xc6

Black has managed to exchange the rooks, but nevertheless the bishop pair is dominant and Black's game looks lost.

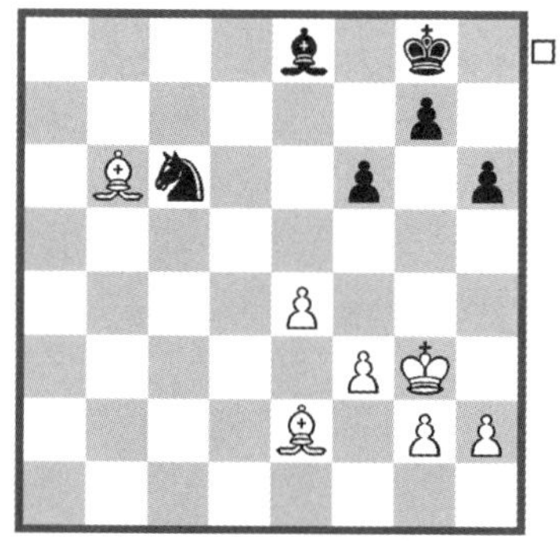

Position after: 37... ♘xc6

38. ♔f4 ♘e5 39. ♗c7 ♗d7 40. ♔e3

White avoids the primitive trap. The king goes toward d6 to support the future passed pawn on the e-file.

40. ♗xe5?? g5+ 41. ♔e3 fxe5=

40... ♔f8 41. ♔d4 ♘f7 42. ♗a5 ♘e5 43. ♗b4+ ♔e8 44. ♔c5 ♘g6 45. ♗d2 ♘e5 46. ♔d6 ♗a4

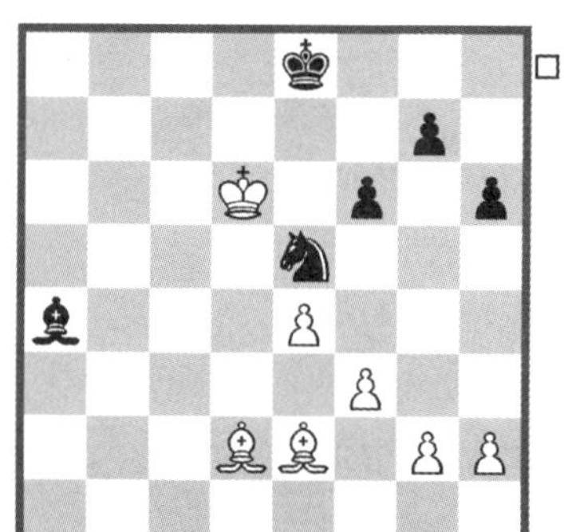

Position after: 46... ♗a4

47. f4

After some patient maneuvering White finally advances. It is good advice to only go for pawn action once the pieces are on their best spots.

47... ♘f7+ 48. ♔c7 ♗d7 49. ♗b4 ♗a4 50. ♗c4!

Setting Black in a zugzwang.

50... ♘h8 51. g3

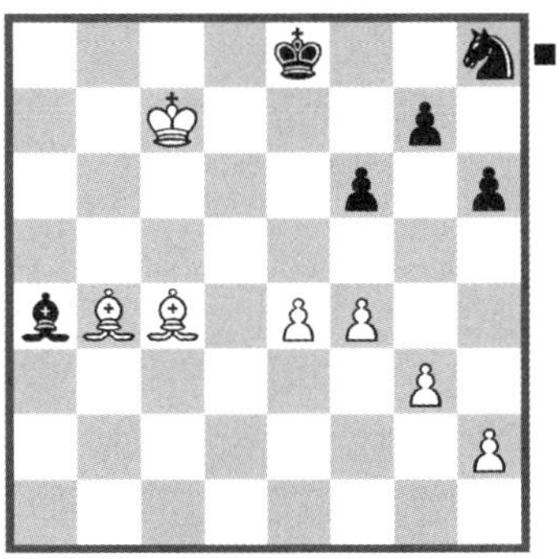

Position after: 51. g3

"Don't rush!"

51... ♘f7 52. h4 ♘h8 53. ♗d6 ♘g6 54. ♗e2 ♘h8 55. ♗c4 ♘g6 56. e5!

Finally, with all his pieces on their best spots White advances.

56... fxe5 57. fxe5 ♘e7 58. e6 g6 59. ♗c5 ♘f5 60. ♗d3 ♘e7 61. ♔d6!

(see diagram next column)

The king goes to f6.

Position after: 61. ♔d6!

61... h5 62. ♔e5 ♘f5 63. ♔f6 ♗c6 64. e7

1-0

Game 50

♙ Englisch, Berthold
♟ Steinitz, William
London 1883

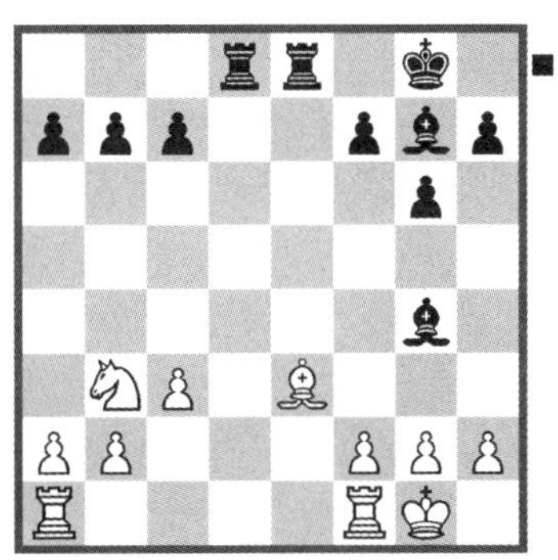

With an ultra-dominating bishop pair and active rooks Black is dominant here. Let's mention some principles and facts about play with the bishop pair advantage: the side having the bishop pair should open up the position (which has already been done here). Furthermore, they should aim to gain space, of course with care and without allowing the opponent to install a knight somewhere (in a hole). If the opponent has a bishop and knight it is useful before any direct action to set the pawns ON THE OPPONENT'S BISHOP'S COLOR – doing so would restrict both the opponent's minor pieces (as will become clear soon). Finally we must keep in mind the ability to trade one of our bishops for a bishop or knight with the idea to transform the endgame to a desired one.

17... b6!

Black restricts both the white minor pieces, taking away the a5- and c5-squares and preparing to gain space on the queenside.

18. h3 ♗e6 19. ♖fd1 c5!

Black restricts the white pieces further, taking away even the d4-square.

20. ♗g5 f6 21. ♗f4 ♔f7 22. f3

Position after: 22. f3

22... g5!

Black consistently gains space, setting his pawns on the dark squares.

23. ♖xd8 ♖xd8 24. ♗e3 h6

Preparing the next move.

25. ♖e1 f5!

Some pawns could be on the light squares. Black intends with ...f4 to gain more space. White prevents this.

26. f4

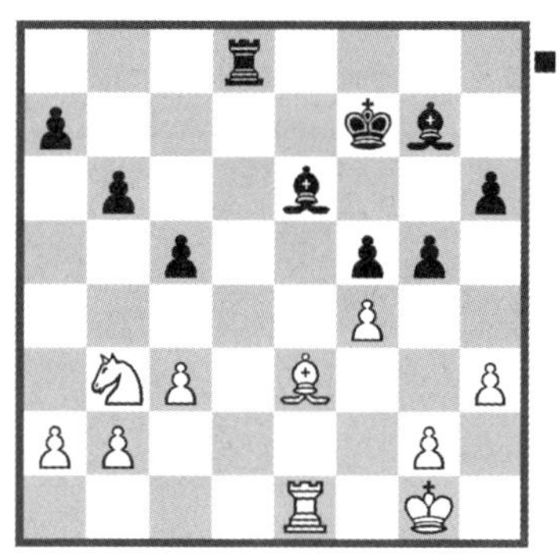

Position after: 26. f4

26... ♗f6

26... g4 This should have been preferred. It forces White to decide what to do with the h-pawn. The other benefit is that the black dark-squared bishop is not obliged to protect the pawn on g5. 27. hxg4 [27. h4 ♗f6 28. g3

(see analysis diagram next page)

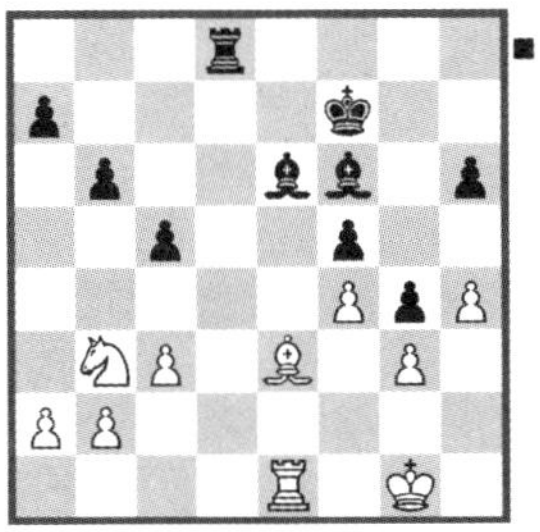

Position after: 28. g3

28... a5] 27...fxg4 Black would be ready to launch his h-pawn with a dangerous initiative on the kingside.

27. g3 a5! 28. ♘c1 a4! 29. a3 ♗c4!

Paralyzing the knight.

30. ♔f2

Black's pieces dominate, especially the bishop on c4. It looks like all his pieces are on their best spots and cannot be further improved. Well, isn't it time to use the pawns? Steinitz demonstrated a high-level performance in the rest of the game. He gave us a perfect example of the various possibilities when having the bishop pair advantage. Now it is time to see the final advantage – the ability to exchange one of the bishops!

30... gxf4!

I am sure that less than half of masters would have chosen this amazing solution.

31. ♗xf4 ♗g5!

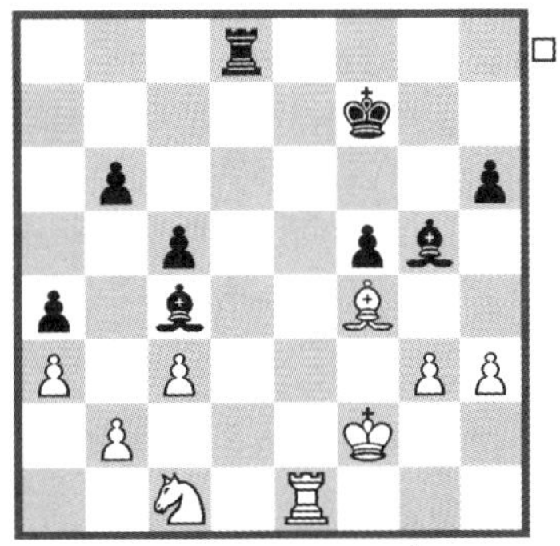

Position after: 31... ♗g5!

Eliminating the piece controlling the d2-square.

32. ♗xg5 hxg5 33. ♔e3

Re-establishing control over d2.

33... ♔f6

Black has various possibilities: threaten to penetrate via the d- or e-file, advance the f-pawn, or attack the h-pawn. White's position is hopeless.

34. h4 gxh4!

The correct move order.

A) 34... ♖e8+?! This is less methodical. However Black would win anyway after the following. 35. ♔f2 ♖xe1 36. hxg5+ ♔xg5 37. ♔xe1 ♔g4 38. ♔f2 ♔h3 39. ♔f3 ♔h2

Position after: 39... ♔h2

40. ♔f2 [40. ♔f4 ♔g2 41. ♔xf5 ♔f3!!] 40... b5 41. ♔f3 ♔g1

B) 34... f4+

Position after: 34... f4+

Obviously good. 35. ♔f3 [35. gxf4 gxh4–+] 35... gxh4 36. gxh4 [36. ♔xf4 h3; 36. gxf4 ♖d2] 36... ♔f5

35. gxh4 ♖e8+ 36. ♔f2 ♖xe1 37. ♔xe1 ♔e5!

(see diagram next column)

The point of the simplifications forced by Steinitz on move 30.

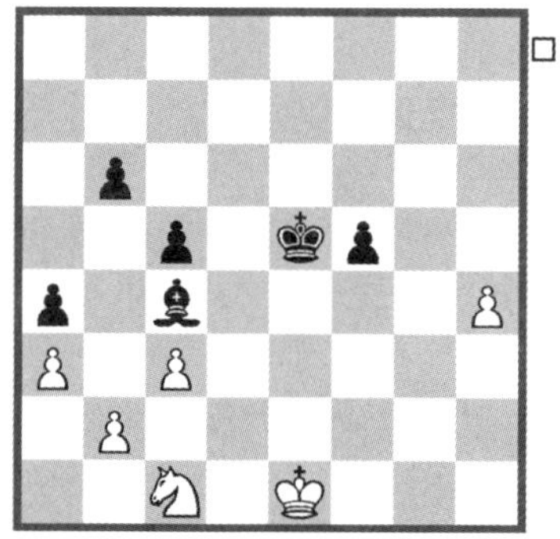

Position after: 37... ♔e5!

38. ♘e2 ♗xe2 39. ♔xe2 ♔f4 40. c4 ♔g4 41. ♔e3 f4+ 42. ♔e4 f3 43. ♔e3 ♔g3

White resigned.

0-1

Game 51

♙ Richter, Berthold
♟ Tarrasch, Siegbert
🌍 Nuremberg 1888

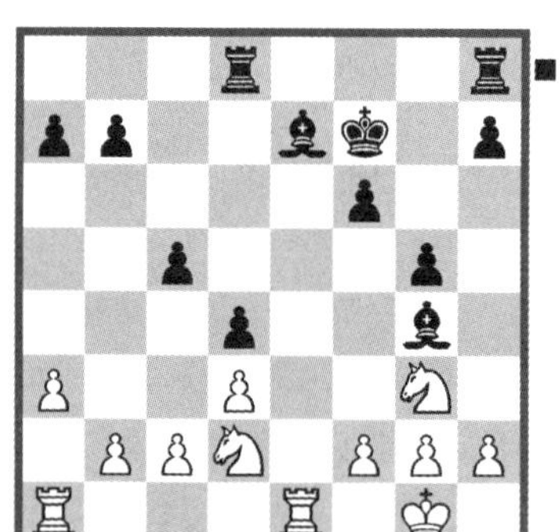

Black is better because the gained space is a serious addition here to the bishop pair advantage. However, the presence of many pawns on the board can be in the knight's favor. Black's play is instructive.

20... h5!

Black gains additional space on the kingside.

21. f3 ♗d7 22. ♖e2?

A very bad move. With such random play White must collapse.

22. a4! This was necessary. White must create some spots for knights. The last move would create one on c4. Black would have had to show very nice technique to convert this position into a win.

22... b5 23. ♖ae1 ♗f8 24. ♘ge4 ♖g8 25. ♘b3 ♖c8 26. ♘ed2

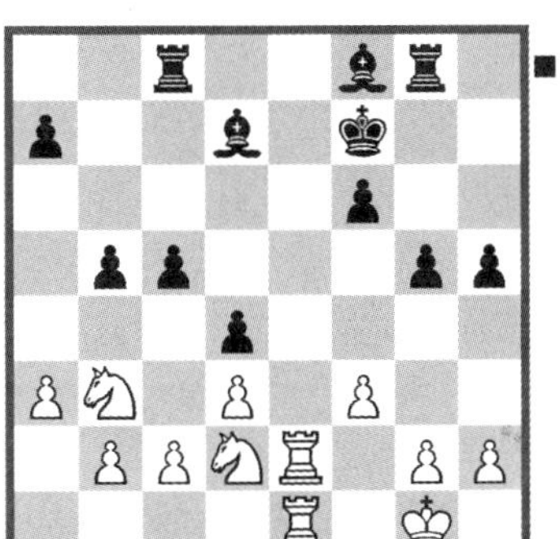

Position after: 26. ♘ed2

White tries to control c4 but it is too late.

26... ♗d6 27. ♘e4 ♗f8 28. ♘ed2

After a series of more or less normal moves Black goes for another advance, gaining new space.

28... f5?!

28... g4 This was more appropriate.

29. ♖e5?!

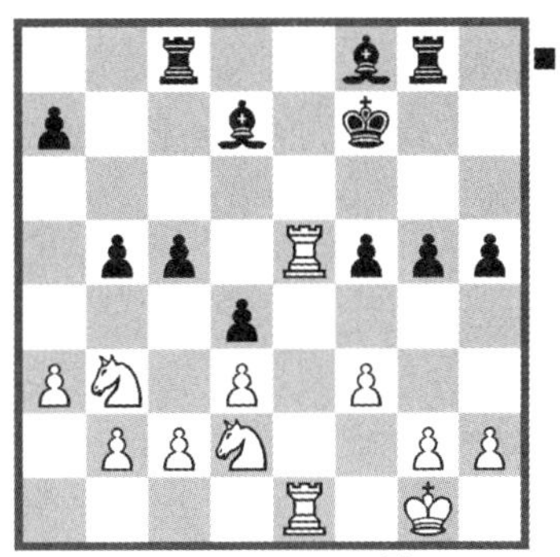

Position after: 29. ♖e5?!

29. a4! a6 [29... bxa4 30. ♘a5 White is relatively safe after getting control over the c4-square.] 30. axb5 axb5

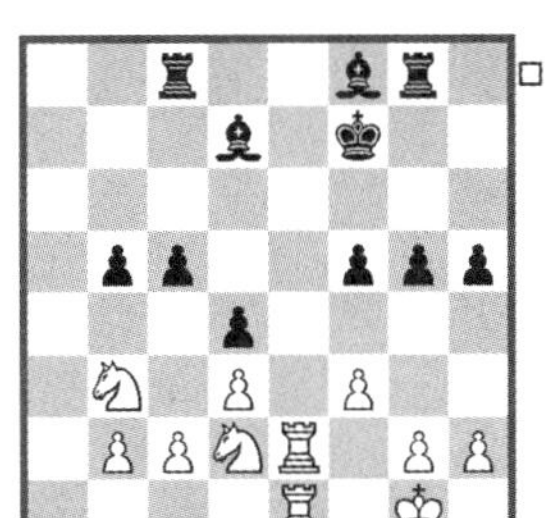

Position after: 30... axb5

31. g4! In order to gain control over e4. This would have been a better defensive decision.

29... ♗d6?

A serious mistake. White didn't make use of it to escape.

30. ♖5e2?

30. ♖d5! ♖g6 Now the following common maneuver looks completely safe for White. 31. a4 a6 32. axb5 axb5 33. g4

30... ♖a8 31. ♘a5

The knight can't stay here for very long.

31... ♖ab8 32. ♘ab3 h4

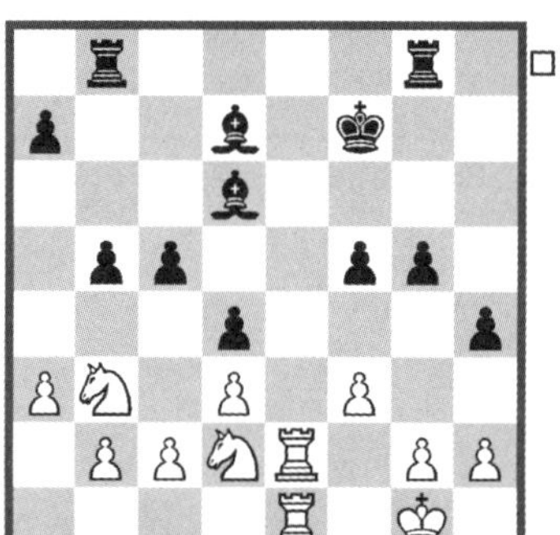

Position after: 32... h4

33. ♔h1 ♖g6 34. ♔g1 ♗e6 35. ♖f2 ♖a8 36. ♖fe2 a5 37. ♘b1 a4!

Finally Black kicks back the white cavalry and secures dominance over White's queenside.

38. ♘3d2 c4! 39. ♘f1 ♖c8 40. ♔h1 c3!

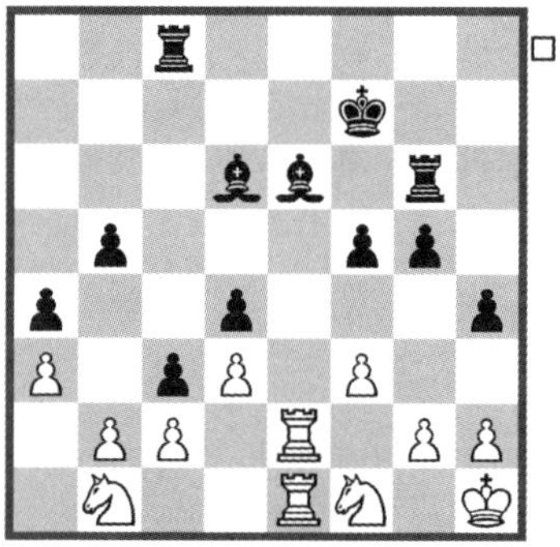

Position after: 40... c3!

Predictably, the a-passer will end the game.

41. bxc3 dxc3 42. ♘e3 b4 43. ♘c4 ♗xc4 44. dxc4 ♖xc4 45. ♖e3 bxa3 46. ♘xc3 ♗b4

0-1

Game 52

♙ Polugaevsky, Lev
♟ Ivkov, Borislav
Belgrade 1969

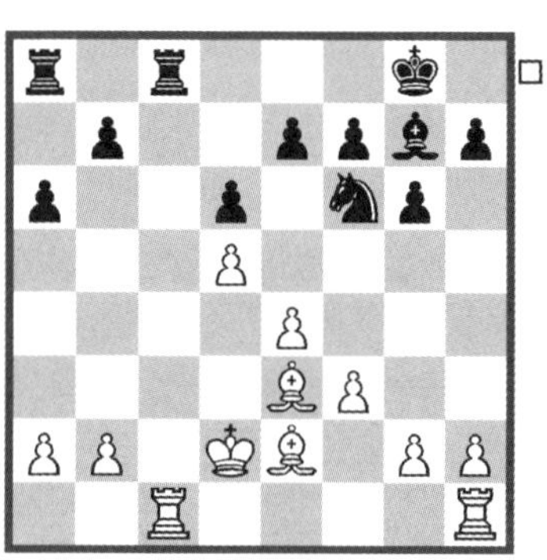

White is better due to the bishop pair and space advantage. Usually these two factors go together. Let's see an instructive conversion by the former super-star Lev Polugaevsky.

16. b4

With centralized pieces, development completed and his activated king White immediately launches his pawn attack on the queenside. In positions with the bishop pair advantage one very logical approach is to take up space.

16... ♔f8 17. a4 ♘d7 18. a5!

An excellent move which advanced players would play without calculating. – there is nothing to calculate. Having the bishop pair advantage it is useful to set the pawns on the opponent's bishop's color. By this set-up, the pawns would successfully restrict the activity of the opponent's bishop and knight. Furthermore, with this set-up, the opponent's pawns would be fixed on the color of our bishop. Thus, the pawns on a6 and b7 would be fixed and could later become weak.

18... ♗b2 19. ♖c2!

Gaining tempo.

19... ♖xc2+ 20. ♔xc2 ♗g7 21. ♔b3 ♖c8 22. ♗d2!

22. ♖c1 This is also good, but the played move is much better. The point is that Black cannot organize any special play and would have to deal mostly against White's regroupings. Thus, the rooks can be exchanged at any given moment. It is natural, incidentally, to keep as many pieces as possible on the board in positions where you have a space advantage.

22... ♗d4

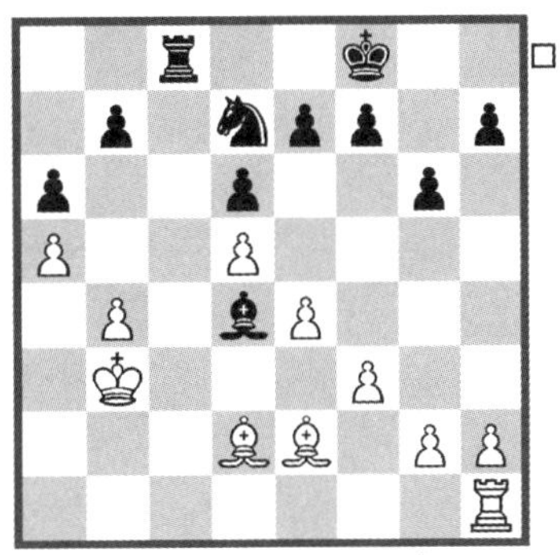

Position after: 22... ♗d4

In retrospect Black should have tried 22... e6 to try to change the character of the game. Of course opening up the position would favor White too, but as we will see, a waiting strategy is not a good option.

23. g4!

This pawn goes to g5! Black cannot prevent this fixing and his pieces will become more and more restricted.

23... ♔g7 24. g5 ♖c7 25. ♖d1 ♔f8 26. f4 ♗g7 27. ♗g4

The point of White's pawn set-up is evident. Black's pieces are cramped and it is no wonder that White would go on to win the game convincingly.

27... ♔e8 28. ♖f1!

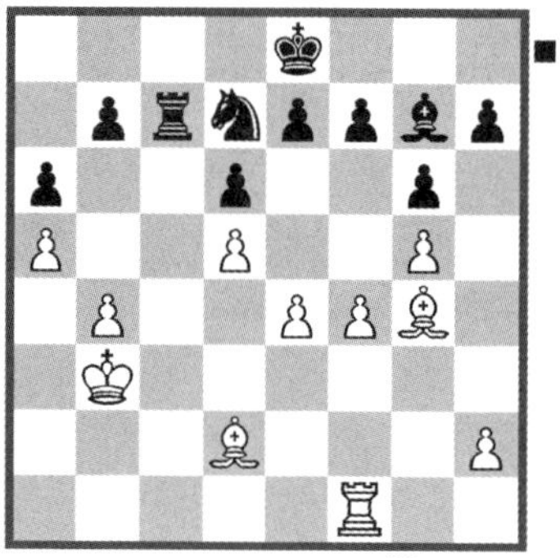

Position after: 28. ♖f1!

This rook acts as a submarine against the f7-pawn. It can be useful in the case of advancing either the e- or f-pawn.

28... ♗d4 29. h4

However since f7 is still protected, White improves further his chances on the kingside; even the h-pawn is joining the attack.

29... ♗g7 30. h5 ♗d4 31. ♖h1

The idea is to penetrate through the h-file.

31... ♗g7 32. ♖h3

White keeps improving his position. It is instructive to see how Polugaevsky sets up threats on various files and forces Black to play accurately.

32... ♔f8

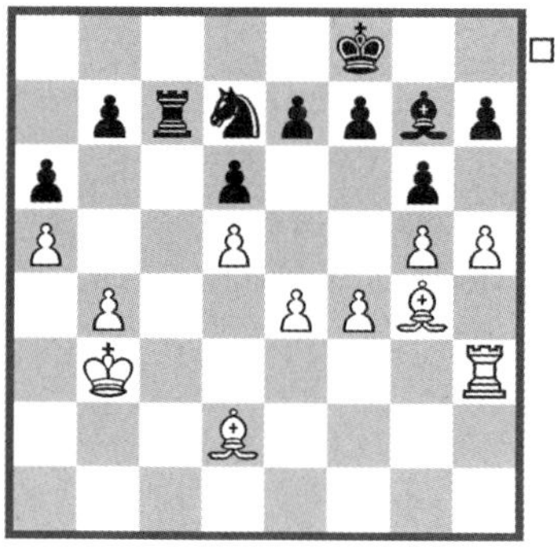

Position after: 32... ♔f8

Finally, Black makes a mistake.

32... ♘f8 This was a more precise move. However of course, it is not easy to find all the nuances during the game.

33. h6! ♗d4 34. ♖d3

34. ♗c3 ♗xc3 35. ♖xc3 ♖xc3+ 36. ♔xc3 ♔e8 37. ♔d4 ♔d8 38. e5 This also wins with the idea of 39. e6!.

34... ♗a7 35. ♗h3 ♗g1 36. ♗c3 ♔e8

(see diagram next page)

White sets the scene for a decisive strike.

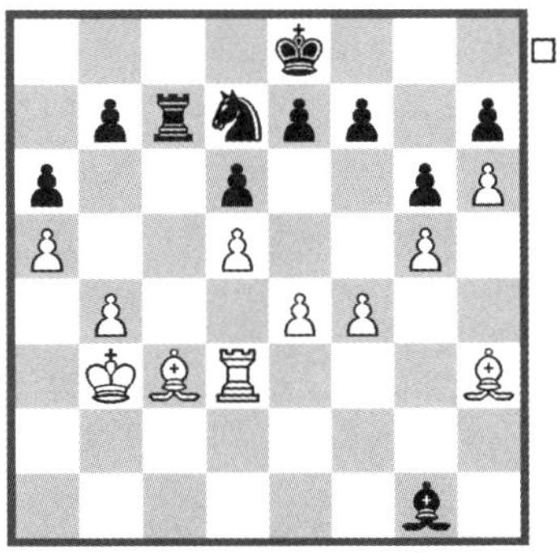

Position after: 36... ♔e8

37. e5! ♗h2

37... dxe5 38. fxe5 White has dangerous threats of advancing both the d- and e-pawns.

38. exd6 exd6 39. ♖e3+ ♔d8 40. ♖e4 ♗g1

Finally, at the end of the game the reader can see one more very important feature of the bishop pair advantage – the possibility to exchange one of the bishops for a knight or bishop in order to simplify the conversion.

41. ♗xd7

1-0

Game 53	

♙	Kramnik, Vladimir	(2625)
♟	Ulybin, Mikhail	(2570)
🌍	Chalkidiki 1992	

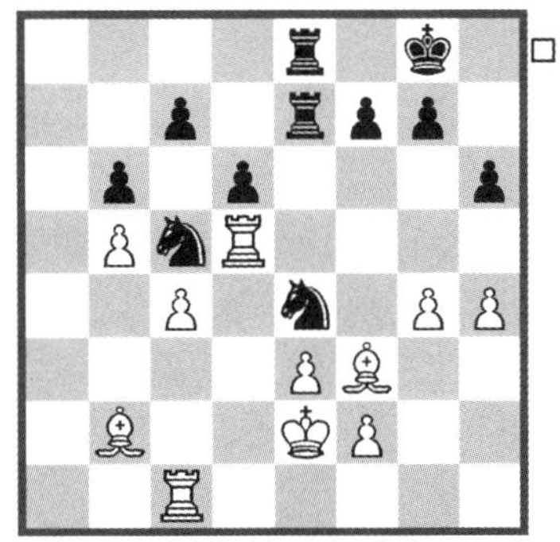

Although it may appear that Black is fine in our next position, he is in fact in big trouble. Here the c5-square is not significant: there is no action for the knight from there, while the white bishops are very active, and after the next move even the rook will dominate on the a-file.

33. ♖a1 ♘f6?!

Brave, but objectively Black does not have a good choice.

34. ♖dd1

There is no special reason to capture. Perhaps the bishop can be traded for the knight on c5, damaging Black's structure.

34. ♗xf6 This cannot be bad, of course. 34... gxf6 35. ♖a7 After this however, there is nothing direct that is apparent, although Black really looks hopeless.

34... ♘fe4 35. ♖a7 ♔f8

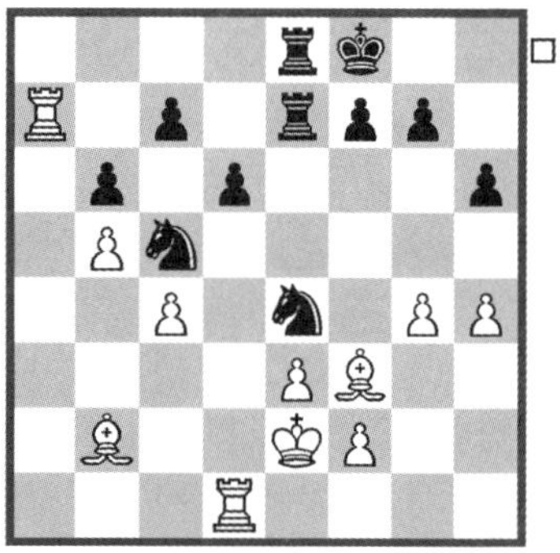

Position after: 35... ♔f8

36. g5!

Very inventive. An excellent move, with a brilliant idea behind it. After opening the h-file Black may have problems with it. Also, by capturing twice on g5 White gains access to the c6-square.

36... hxg5 37. hxg5 ♘xg5 38. ♗c6 ♖c8 39. ♖h1 ♔g8 40. ♖aa1!

The game would be decided on the kingside after this rook joins the attack.

40... ♘ce6

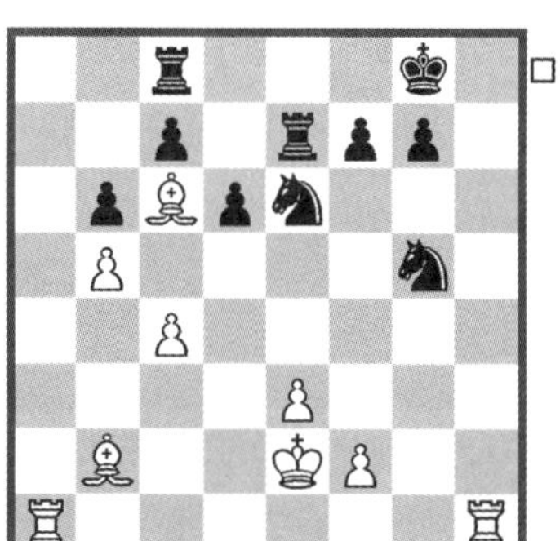

Position after: 40... ♘ce6

40... f6 41. ♗d5+ ♘f7 42. ♖ag1 ♔f8 43. ♗xf6!

41. ♖h4

Black's king is under fire from all of the white pieces. There is no defense against doubling on the h-file.

41... f6 42. ♖g1 ♔f7 43. ♗d5 ♔e8 44. ♖h8+ ♘f8 45. f4 ♘ge6

45... ♘gh7 This leads to a beautiful win after the simple 46. ♗g8+–.

46. ♔f3

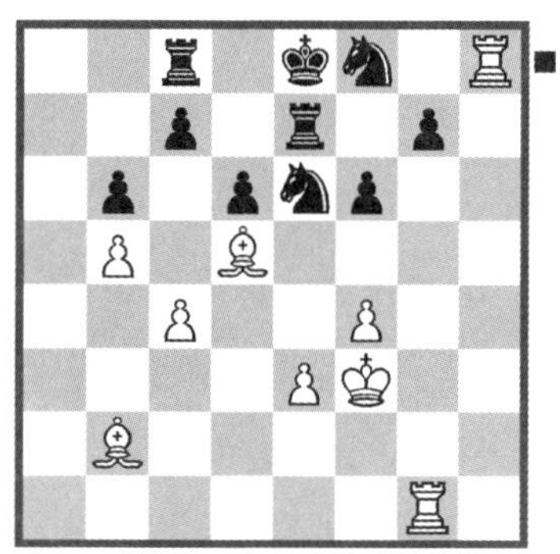

Position after: 46. ♔f3

46. ♗xe6 ♖xe6 47. ♖xg7+– This also wins.

46... f5

46... ♘c5 47. ♗xf6 gxf6 48. ♖xf8+ ♔xf8 49. ♖g8# Another beautiful win.

47. ♖g6! ♘c5 48. ♗xg7 ♖f7 49. ♗xf8

1-0

Game 54

♙ Carlsen, Magnus (2714)
♟ Adams, Michael (2729)
Khanty-Mansiysk 2007

White must be better due to the (potentially) strong bishop pair. The pair is not active at the moment, while the black cavalry is very active and stable! White must keep the bishop pair, waiting for a better situation later, or the advantage would disappear.

34. ♗e1! ♔e7 35. ♔g1!

Again Carlsen finds a powerful way to improve the position – the point of the previous move.

35... ♘b8 36. ♗f2 ♘d7 37. ♖e1+ ♔f8 38. ♖d1 ♔e7 39. ♖e1+ ♔f8

(see diagram next column)

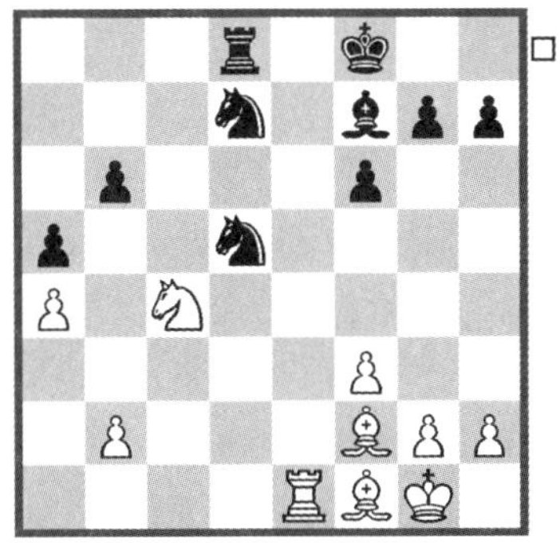

Position after: 39... ♔f8

40. ♘d6

After some repetition, probably due to zeitnot, White decides to act. Clearly, White has achieved much since the last diagram.

40... ♘e5

There is no good way to keep the bishop.

40... ♗g8 41. ♖d1 ♘e5 42. ♘c4

Position after: 42. ♘c4

42... ♘xc4 43. ♗xc4 This is very bad for Black.

41. ♘xf7

Of course. The bishop pair will dominate.

41... ♔xf7 42. ♖d1

The bishops are much stronger than the knights and in spite of the material equality White has a clear advantage.

42... ♔e7 43. f4 ♘g4 44. ♖e1+ ♔f8 45. ♗d4

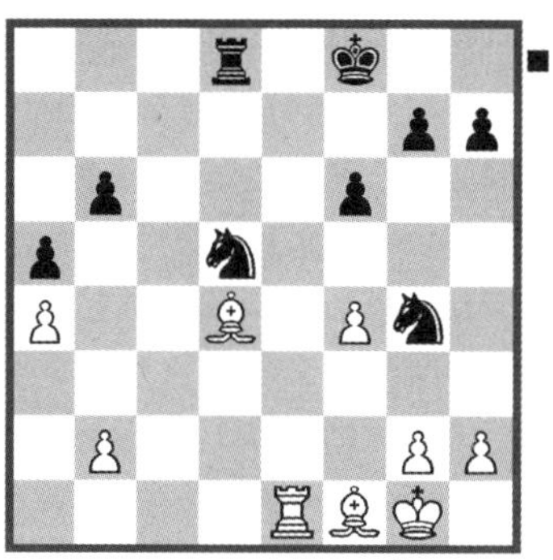

Position after: 45. ♗d4

45... ♖d6

Again taking on f4 loses. 45... ♘xf4 46. ♗xb6 ♖d5 47. b4! axb4 48. a5 The knights cannot fight against the marginal passed pawn.

46. h3

(see diagram next column)

Position after: 46. h3

46... ♘h6?!

Misplacing the knight makes White's task easier.

46... ♘xf4!? This would have been a solid option here. 47. ♖e4 ♘e6 48. ♖xe6 ♖xe6 49. hxg4± This is probably winning for White, but it is not easy to realize the advantage.

47. ♖d1 ♘f5 48. ♗f2 ♔e7 49. g4 ♘h6 50. f5 ♘f7

Position after: 50... ♘f7

51. ♗g2

Horwitz bishops in action!

51... ♘f4 52. ♖xd6 ♘xd6 53. ♗xb6 ♘c4 54. ♗c5+ ♔d7 55. ♗f1

Even stronger is the following. 55. b3 ♘xg2 56. ♔xg2 ♘d2 57. b4+–

55... ♘xb2 56. ♗b5+ ♔d8 57. ♗b6+ ♔e7 58. ♔h2+–

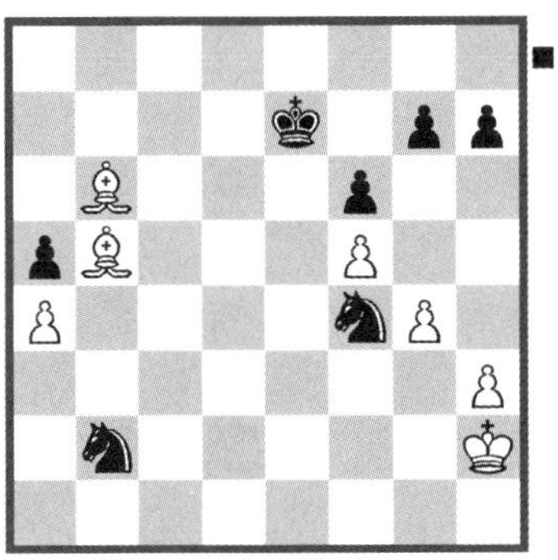

Position after: 58. ♔h2+–

58... ♘d5 59. ♗xa5 ♔d6 60. ♗d2 ♔c5 61. ♔g3 ♘c7 62. ♗e3+ ♔b4 63. ♗d2+ ♔c5 64. ♗c1 ♘c4

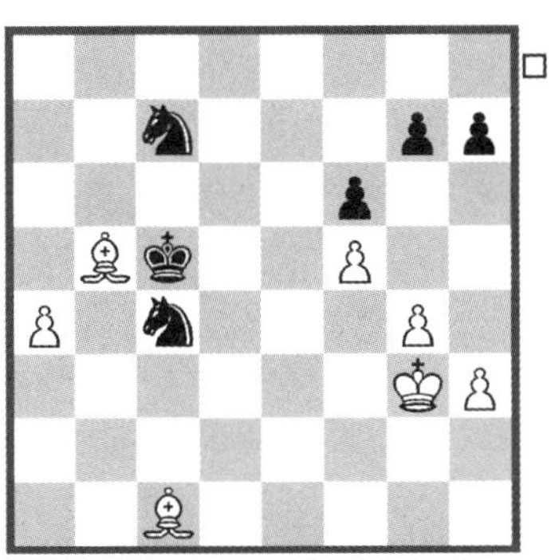

Position after: 64... ♘c4

65. ♗xc4

Simplifying in order to convert!

65... ♔xc4 66. ♗d2 ♘a6 67. a5 ♔b5 68. ♔f3 ♘c5 69. ♗c3 h6 70. ♔e3 ♔c4 71. ♗d4 ♘a6 72. ♔e4 ♘b4 73. h4 ♔b5 74. ♗c3 ♘a6 75. ♔d5 ♘c5 76. ♗d4 ♘d3 77. ♔e6

1-0

Game 55

♙ Portisch, Lajos (2600)
♟ Krasenkow, Michal (2605)
Jakarta 1996

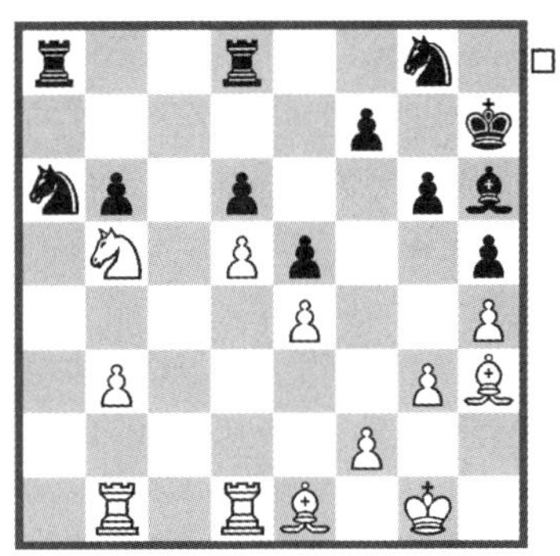

In our next example White is dominant, not only because of the good bishop pair. The black cavalry is awful, especially after White's next strong move.

27. b4! ♘f6 28. f3 ♘e8 29. ♗f2 ♖db8 30. ♗d7! ♘ac7 31. ♖a1

White cannot use the c-file, but actually the a-file is good enough.

31... ♖xa1 32. ♖xa1 ♗d2

A last attempt to become active.

33. ♘xc7 ♘xc7

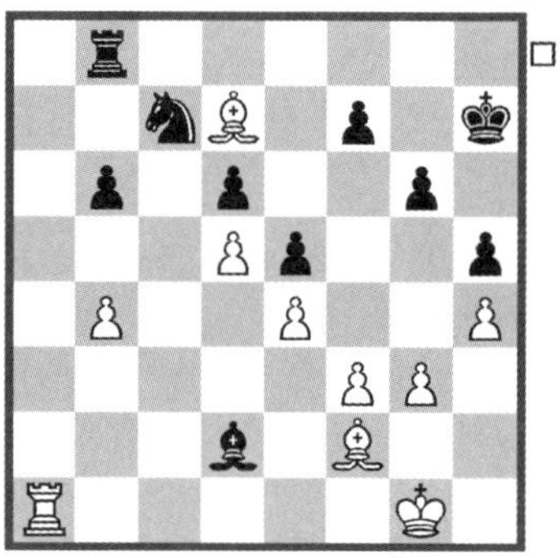

Position after: 33... ♘xc7

34. b5

White cements the position on the queenside. Even if Black installs the bishop on c5 it would be simply lost for him.

34... ♔g8 35. ♖a7 ♘e8 36. ♖a6

All roads lead to Rome.

36. ♗xe8 ♖xe8 37. ♖d7!

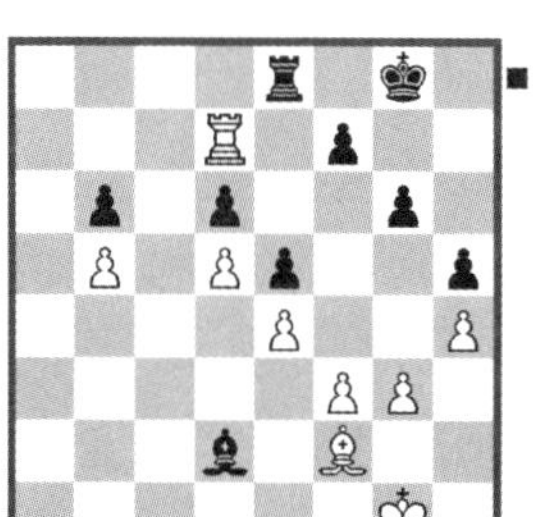

Position after: 37. ♖d7!

37... ♗b4 38. ♗xb6 ♖b8 39. ♖d8+ Another clear win.

36... ♘f6 37. ♗c6 ♗a5

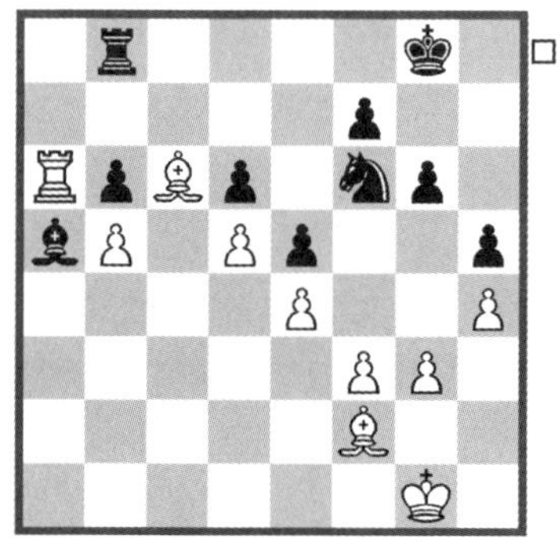

Position after: 37... ♗a5

38. ♔f1

The king itself moves to decide the result.

38. ♖xa5 bxa5 39. ♗a7 This is a winning method but in any case White can play calmly.

38... ♔f8 39. ♔e2 ♔e7 40. ♔d3 ♖c8 41. ♖a7+ ♔f8 42. ♔c4 ♖b8

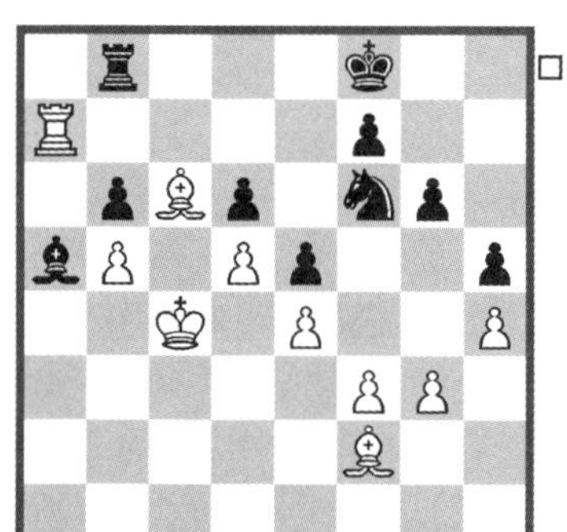

Position after: 42... ♖b8

43. ♔b3

The last moment to go for the following. 43. ♖xa5 bxa5 44. ♗a7+–

43... ♗d2 44. ♖a6 ♔e7 45. ♗xb6

The game is over and no further comments are necessary.

45... ♘d7 46. ♗f2 ♘c5+

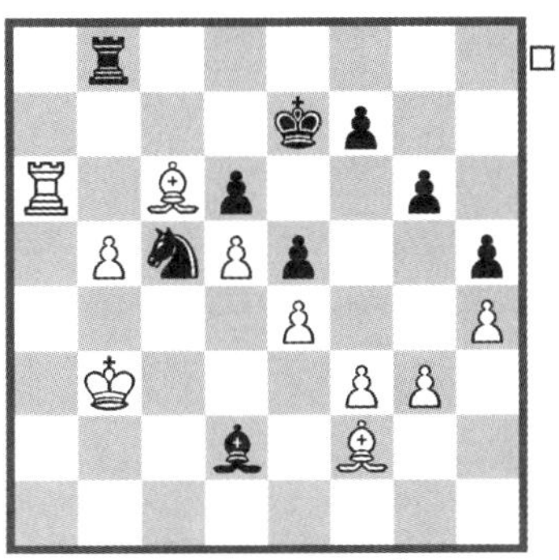

Position after: 46... ♘c5+

47. ♔c4 ♗h6 48. ♖a7+ ♔f6 49. ♖a3 ♗f8 50. ♗e3 ♔g7 51. ♖a7 ♔g8 52. ♗d2 f5 53. exf5 gxf5 54. ♗g5

Position after: 54. ♗g5

54... e4 55. fxe4 fxe4 56. ♗f4 ♘d3 57. ♗e3 ♘c5 58. ♖a8

1-0

Game 56

♙ Boleslavsky, Isaak
♟ Shcherbakov, Vitaly Sergeevich
Moscow 1942

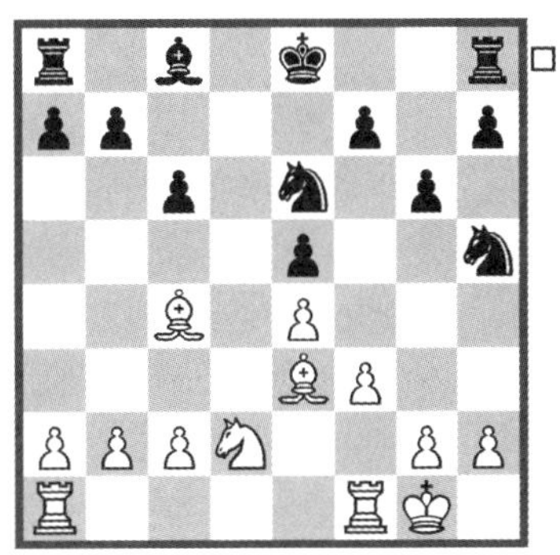

This position arose from the Philidor Defense after Black committed a serious mistake. Although it may look complex, Black is actually hopeless. The bishop pair dominates here and in particular, some of the dark squares (such as d6) in Black's camp can be easily exploited. White's first move is simple and amazing.

14. a4!

Not only eliminating the possibility of ...b5, but also after advancing that pawn to a5, Black's queenside would be paralyzed and the a7-pawn would be in danger. Don't forget – gain space when you have the bishop pair advantage!

14... ♔e7 15. ♖fd1 ♖d8

16. ♗a2

Vacating the c4-square for the knight.

16. a5 Clearly a good move.

16... f6 17. ♘c4 b6 18. ♖xd8 ♘xd8

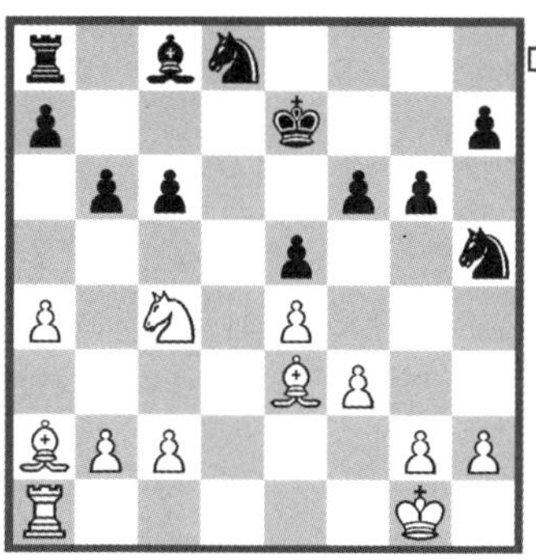

Position after: 18... ♘xd8

19. a5

Finally. This move hasn't lost its poison. Black must weaken his dark-squared complex.

19... ♗e6 20. ♗b3 ♗xc4 21. ♗xc4

White is strategically winning. His perfectly activated army, together with the commenced attack on the queenside will easily crush Black's defense. Black cannot counter because his pieces are either not activated or misplaced.

21... b5 22. ♗c5+ ♔e8 23. ♗g8

White wants if possible to provoke the creation of new weaknesses and gain tempi.

23... ♘b7 24. ♗f2 a6

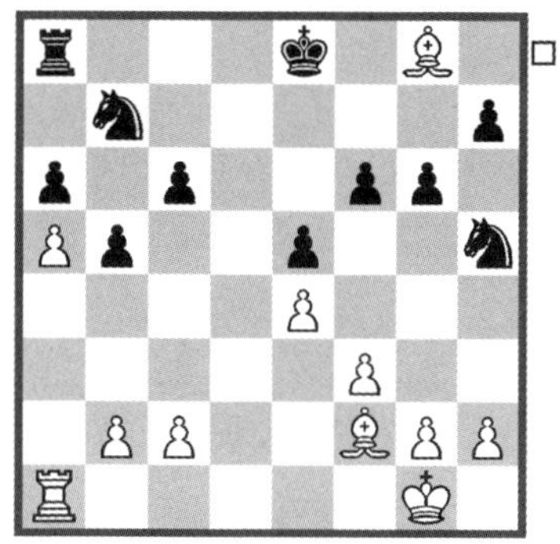

Position after: 24... a6

Black secures the queenside.

25. ♗b6!

This bishop would become a bone in the throat. The a5-pawn is safe now and Black is unable to place his rook on the open file.

25... ♔f8 26. ♗b3 ♔e7 27. g3 ♘g7 28. c4

Having the bishop pair, it is vital to open up the position. Black must wait.

28... ♖c8 29. ♖c1 b4

(see diagram next page)

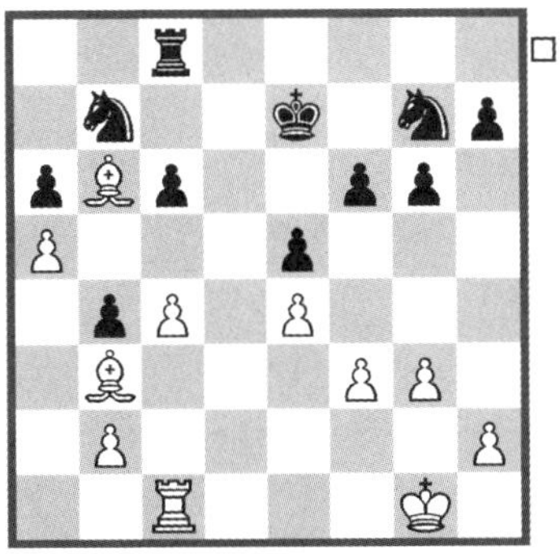

Position after: 29... b4

30. c5!

Excellent! White voluntarily leaves the bishop on b6 "out of play". However after White's next move, the black rook will be out of play also, fixed to protecting the pawn on a6.

30... ♘d8 31. ♗c4 ♖a8

The pawn on b4 is practically lost. For the rest of the game the white rook and bishop on c4 will play against the two knights. White is winning.

32. ♔f2

The first phase is the centralization of the king.

32... ♘de6 33. ♔e3 ♘d4

(see diagram next column)

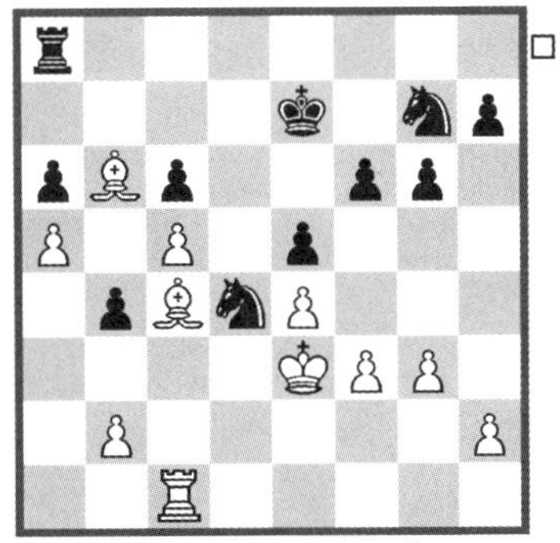

Position after: 33... ♘d4

34. f4

The second phase is the opening of the position on the kingside – the white rook needs a file to infiltrate.

34... ♘ge6 35. ♖f1 ♘c2+ 36. ♔d3 ♘cd4 37. f5 gxf5 38. exf5

Black is unable to prevent the advance of White's kingside pawn phalanx.

38... ♘g7 39. ♔e4 ♘e8 40. g4 ♘c2

Black's knight wanders.

41. ♖f2 ♘d4 42. g5 ♘b5

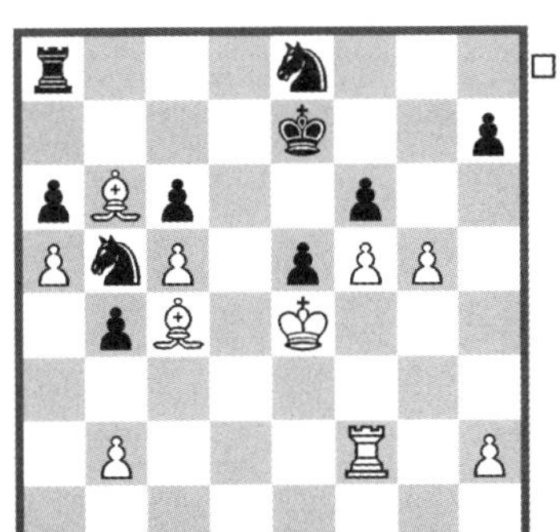

Position after: 42... ♘b5

43. ♗xb5

Now the bishop can even be exchanged. As a result a dangerous passed pawn will appear.

43... axb5 44. h4 ♔f7 45. ♖d2 ♔e7 46. b3

Patiently. There is no reason to rush. Black is hopeless.

46... ♖b8 47. a6

Using the moment to advance.

47... ♖c8 48. a7 ♖a8 49. ♖d8

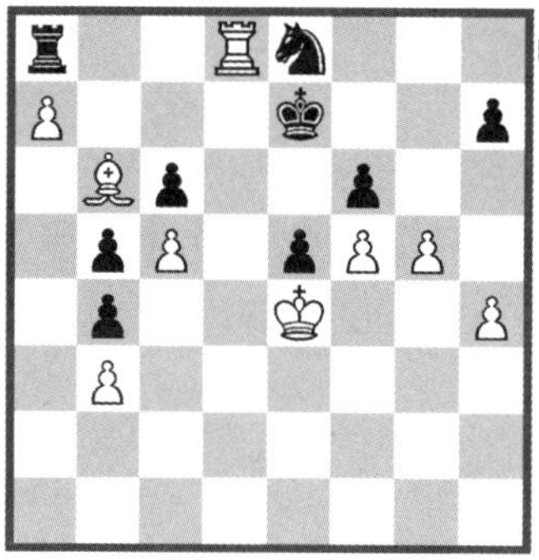

Position after: 49. ♖d8

The tactics come to an end to serve a fine strategy.

49... ♘c7 50. ♗xc7 ♖xa7 51. gxf6+

Black resigned.

1-0

Game 57

♙ Klavins, Janis
♟ Ragozin, Viacheslav
Riga 1952

Let's now see some examples where the bishop pair is a handicap for the player. And let's start with some simple examples.

Our first example is trivial but still a brutal demonstration of how having the bishop pair can be a handicap in a blocked position. The bishop pair is so restricted here. Although it may appear that Black does not have routes to invade with his king in order to convert, in actual fact, the win is trivial.

27... ♗c1!

Before the knight comes to f4, the bishop goes into the enemy's territory.

28. ♗d1 ♘f4

All the white pieces are locked in. It is almost impossible to find any other game where a bishop pair is more restricted and more sad. The game is over. All Black needs to do is to improve his king. The plan is, with the king on h3, to play ...♘d3.

29. ♗c2 f6 30. ♔f1 ♔f7 31. ♗d1 ♔g6 32. ♗c2 ♔g5 33. ♗b1 ♔h4 34. ♗c2 ♔h3 35. ♔g1

Position after: 35. ♔g1

35... h6

Black decides not to rush. Everything wins.

35... ♘d3–+

36. ♗b1 h5 37. ♗c2 ♘d3 38. ♔f1 ♔xh2 39. ♔e2 ♔g2 40. ♗xd3 cxd3+

0-1

Game 58

♙ Shamkovich, Leonid (2390)
♟ Benjamin, Joel (2570)
Las Vegas 1995

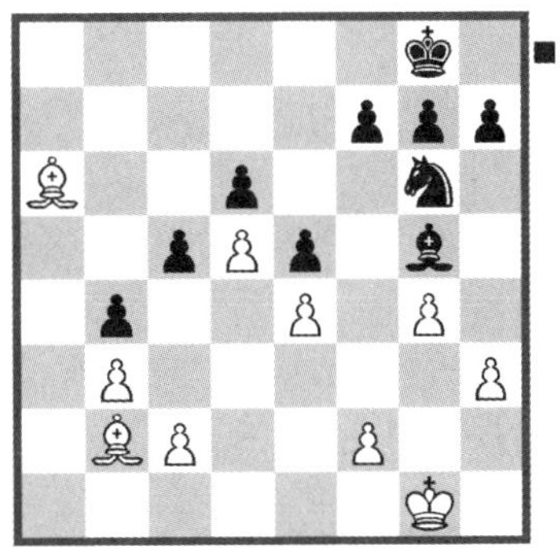

This next example is reminiscent of the previous one. It is also trivial – there is brutal domination by Black's minor pieces. However, the white light-squared bishop has its freedom and that complicates any realization of the advantage. However in any case, White cannot do anything after Black naturally infiltrates with his minor pieces.

28... ♗d2 29. ♔g2 ♘f4+ 30. ♔g3 g6

Black makes space for the king. He would try to open up the position on the kingside. Such opening up would not be in White's favor. On the contrary, White practically plays without his dark-squared bishop. Even if it gets exchanged for its counterpart, White would achieve nothing – furthermore, this would lead to a desperately poor endgame for him.

31. h4?!

In theory, it is good to set the pawns on the same colored squares as that of the opponent's bishop, but this time it is bad. It is better to wait.

31... ♔f8 32. ♔f3 ♔e7 33. ♗c4 ♔f6

Position after: 33... ♔f6

34. g5+?

This is already a major mistake. It is strange that such an experienced player should make such an elementary mistake. After this Black will easily create a passed pawn on the h-file while at the same time White's backward f2-pawn would be useless.

34. ♗f1 This would have been natural, with waiting.

34... ♔g7 35. ♔g4 f6! 36. ♗b5 ♔f7 37. ♗c4 ♔g7

(see diagram next column)

Position after: 37... ♔g7

Black does not rush.

38. ♗b5 ♘g2! 39. gxf6+ ♔xf6 40. h5

Otherwise, Black would play ...h5 anyway with ...g5 and the same position will arise.

40... ♘f4 41. hxg6 h5+

But not, of course 41... hxg6??=.

42. ♔h4 ♔xg6 43. ♗e8+ ♔h6

Black is practically a pawn up.

44. ♗f7

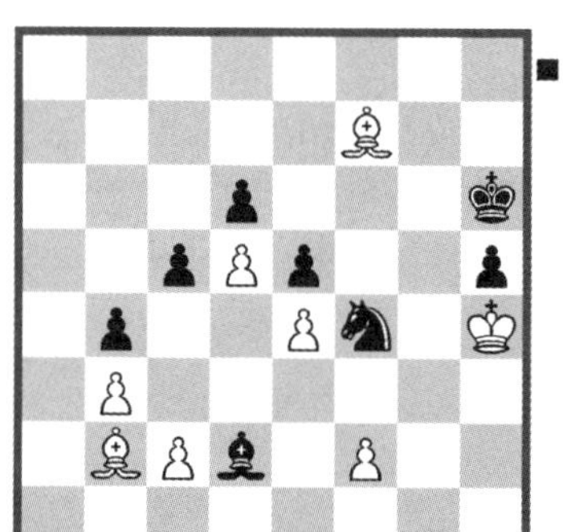

Position after: 44. ♗f7

44... ♘g6+?!

Such a strange move.

44... ♘g2+! 45. ♔g3 ♘e1 This would have been the correct way to convert the advantage into a win.

45. ♔g3

45. ♗xg6? ♔xg6 This is hopeless for White. Black can play the pawn endgame with an outside passer.

45... ♔g5 46. ♔f3 ♘f4 47. ♗e8 h4

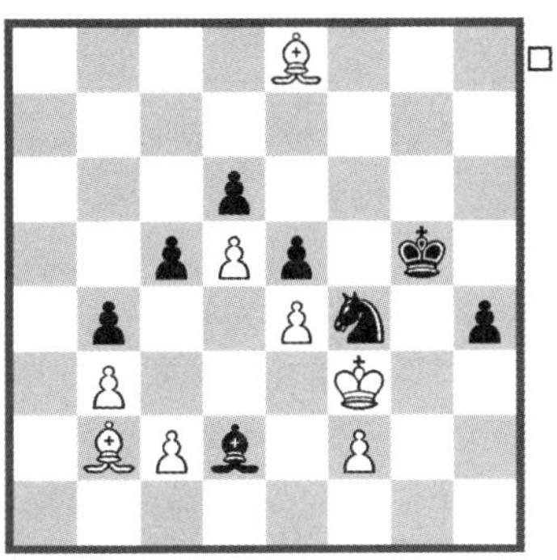

Position after: 47... h4

48. ♗b5

48. ♗d7 This would have led to a beautiful win for Black after the following. 48... h3 49. ♔g3 ♘e2+ 50. ♔xh3 ♗c3 51. ♗xc3 bxc3

48... ♘h5 49. ♗f1 ♘f6 50. ♗h3 ♗f4 51. ♗e6

It may look as if White is ok and the h-passer is stopped. However Black still plays with two pieces versus one.

51... ♔h5 52. ♗f7+ ♔h6 53. ♗e6

Position after: 53. ♗e6

53. c3 This brings nothing. Black should not react on the queenside. 53... h3 Black has an easy win.

53... ♘h7

This move leads to a win.

54. ♗f5 ♘g5+ 55. ♔g2 ♗d2 56. f3 ♔g7 57. ♗g4 ♔f7 58. ♔f2 h3

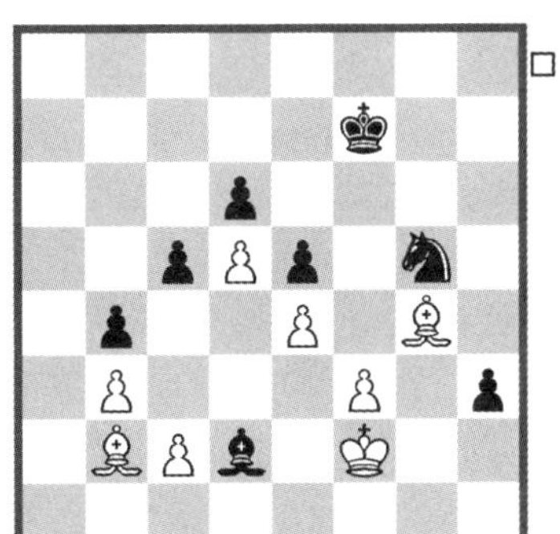

Position after: 58... h3

59. ♔g3 ♗f4+ 60. ♔f2 ♔g6 61. ♔f1 ♔h6 62. ♔f2 h2 63. ♔g2 ♘h7

The knight liberates the g5-square for the king.

64. c4 ♔g5 65. ♗f5 ♘f6 66. ♗e6 ♔h5

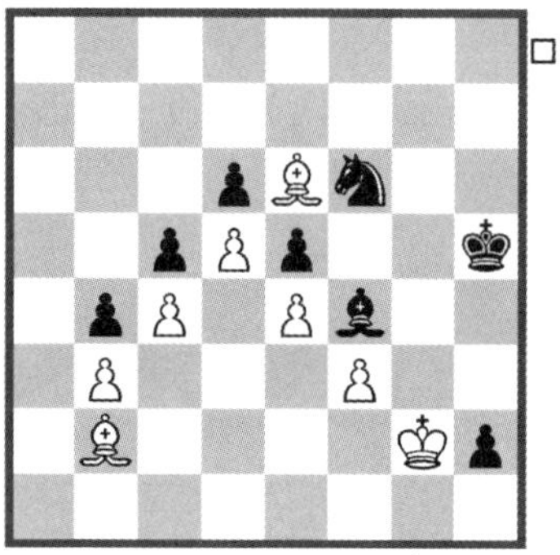

Position after: 66... ♔h5

67. ♗f5 ♔h4 68. ♗e6 ♘h7

The knight uses the route ...♘g5-h3-f2 and Black wins. White resigned.
0-1

Game 59

♙	Torre, Eugenio	(2523)
♟	Nielsen, Peter Heine	(2620)
🌍	Bled 2002	

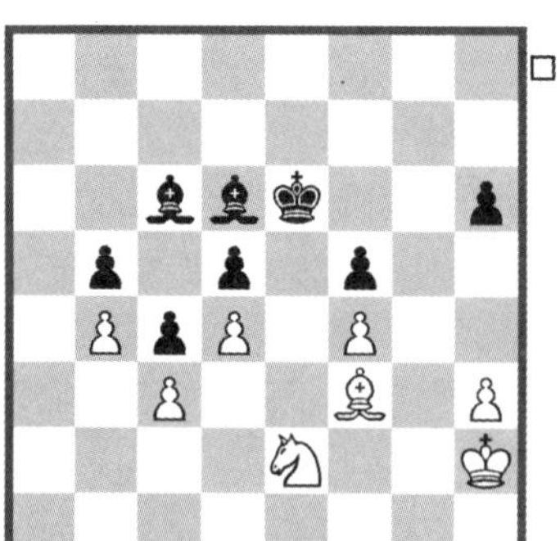

White is dominant here and is actually strategically winning. It may look like a fortress, but it isn't. However analyzing the position more deeply you will see that Black has problems defending his pawns. White has a clear plan: the bishop goes to h5, the knight to e5 (or e3) and the king will aim to invade via h4. Let's see this on the board.

52. ♗h5 ♗e7 53. ♔g3

Preventing ...♗h4.

53... ♗f6 54. ♘g1 ♔e7 55. ♗g6 ♗d7 56. ♘f3 ♔f8

Black defends well.

57. ♘e5

Position after: 57. ♘e5

57... ♗e6

A) 57... ♗xe5 58. fxe5 This is just lost for Black.

B) 57... ♗c8 Another defensive move.

58. ♘f3

Installing the knight on e5 gives nothing. Thus the knight goes to e3.

58... ♗d7

58... ♔e7 59. ♘h4! ♔f8 60. ♘xf5 ♗xf5 61. ♗xf5 ♔e7

Position after: 61... ♔e7

62. ♗c8 ♔d6 63. ♔g4 This is lost for Black.

59. ♘e1 ♔g7 60. ♗h5 ♔f8 61. ♘c2

Position after: 61. ♘c2

The knight gets the e3-spot and one pawn falls.

61... ♗e6

61... ♗d8!? 62. ♘e3 ♔g7 63. ♘xd5 ♗c6 This is a better way for Black to hold. Black should actually keep the f5-pawn with the idea of maintaining a barrier. However a pawn is a pawn, and the game is lost for him.

62. ♘e3 ♔e7 63. ♗g6 ♗g7 64. ♗xf5 ♗f7 65. ♗c8 ♗f8 66. ♗a6

1-0

Game 60

♙ Suba, Mihai (2500)
♟ Smyslov, Vassily V (2565)
Las Palmas 1982

Let's now switch to positions with some major pieces on the board: first with queens. In our next example the bishop pair is definitely not an advantage. However, White is not in any difficulties. His bishop pair is active enough. Black is on the move and he goes for a typical approach for the side playing with the bishop and knight versus the bishop pair – to set his pawns on the same colored squares as the bishop's color, then to exchange the bishops of the same color and to dominate with the knight over the remaining bad bishop. Often masters worldwide have demonstrated this logic and the power of this plan. Thus, Black's next move is natural.

38... c4 39. d4??

And this is a terrible mistake! The passed pawn is absolutely worthless. Much more important is the fact that the white bishops are stuck now.

39. g3 This waiting move is a much better option. 39... cxd3 40. ♗xd3 The position is balanced. White has a slightly damaged pawn structure but the bishop pair works well.

39... a5

Of course. There is nothing that White can do against Black's majority on the queenside. Launching the majority together with the above-mentioned concept will bring an easy win.

40. ♕b2 ♘c7

I like this multi-purpose move. Black directs the knight to the desired spot on d5 or e4, or as happened in the game, to b5.

41. ♗c1

Position after: 41. ♗c1

41... ♘b5

A) 41... ♗e4 Another natural move, liberating the d5-square.

B) 41... ♔d7 42. ♕a3 ♘e8 43. ♕f8 ♕f6 Also excellent. Black will direct the knight to e4.

42. ♕c2 ♔f6

42... ♘d6 Why not this?

43. ♔g1 ♗e4 44. ♕f2?!

Position after: 44. ♕f2?!

White is in a horrible situation and goes for bluffs and tricks.

44... ♔f7!?

Black has decided to avoid any complications. From a method point of view he was right. He later converted smoothly, so this decision was correct.

44... ♘xc3 This should have been played. 45. d5 [45. ♗b2 ♘d5–+] 45... ♘xd5 46. ♕d4+

Position after: 46. ♕d4+

46... ♔g6 47. ♗xc4 ♘f6 This is winning for Black.

45. ♗d2 ♘d6 46. ♕h4 h6 47. ♕h5+ ♔g8 48. ♕g6

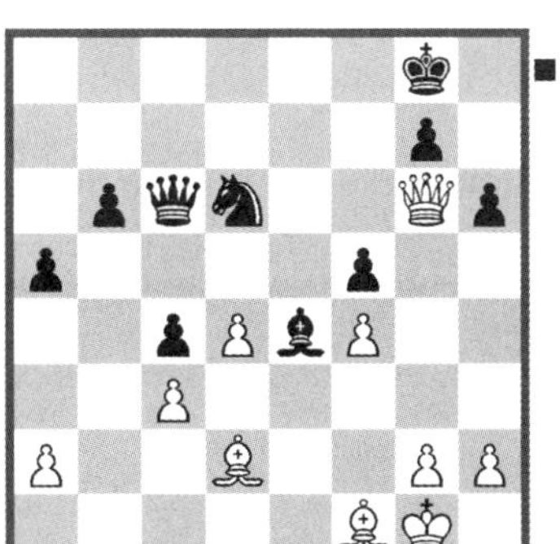

Position after: 48. ♕g6

This is the maximum that White can achieve. However, a queen without any support from the bishops can deliver zero threat.

48... ♗d5 49. ♗e1 ♗f7 50. ♕g3 ♕e4

Black has invaded and the game is over.

51. ♕h4 ♔h7

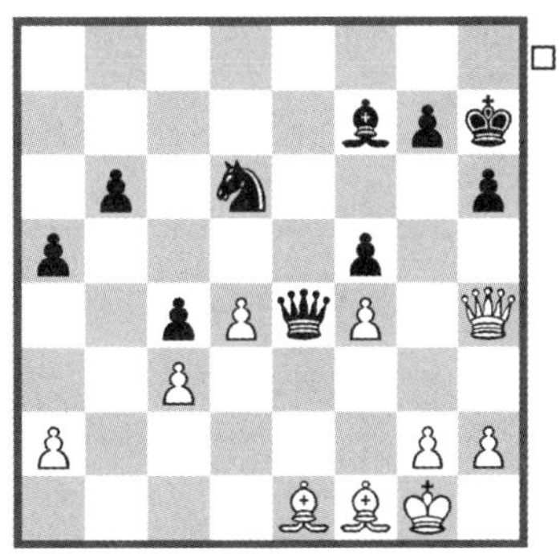

Position after: 51... ♔h7

52. ♗f2

52. ♕d8 ♕xe1 53. ♕xd6 ♕e3+ 54. ♔h1 ♕f2 A pretty line underlining the problems White had with his bishops.

52... ♗d5 53. ♕d8 ♘b5 54. ♕xb6 ♘xc3 55. ♕xa5 ♘e2+ 56. ♗xe2 ♕xg2#

Ending in the manner of a gentleman.

0-1

Game 61

♙ Sethuraman, SP. (2545)
♟ Romanov, Evgeny (2606)
Moscow 2011

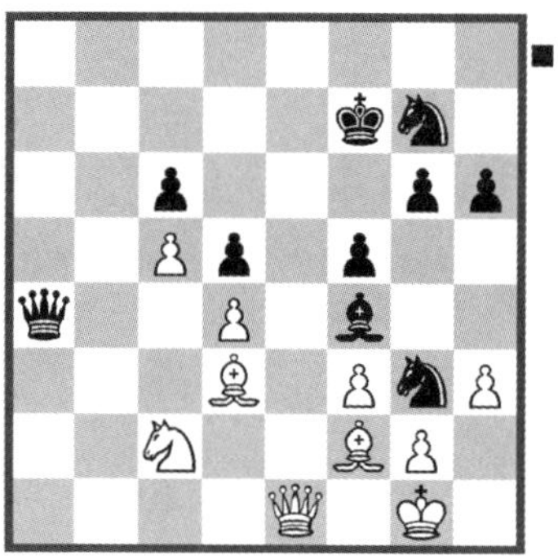

The situation is unclear in our next example. White has his queenside pawns "properly" placed and despite the fact that the position is blocked, the weakness of the c6-pawn is a compensating factor. Nonetheless I would rather choose the black pieces due to the dark-squared holes on the kingside.

41... ♘3h5 42. ♕b4

A normal move driving the black queen back to passivity.

42. g4 However this move, with the idea of levelling the problems with the g3-square is also good. Now it is about equal after the following. 42... fxg4 43. fxg4 ♘f6 44. ♕b4

42... ♕a8 43. ♕b6 ♘e6

Getting ready to protect c6 from d8 and attacking d4 at the same time.

44. ♗a6

After this move it may look as if Black is in trouble because his queen is stuck in the corner. However, it actually gives Black the chance to force a trade of queens.

44. ♘b4 This would practically force the following. 44... ♕a1+ 45. ♗f1 ♘g3 46. ♗xg3 ♗xg3

Position after: 46... ♗xg3

47. ♘xc6 ♘xd4 A draw results.

44... ♗c7

Black simply played this forcing the following.

45. ♕b7 ♕xb7 46. ♗xb7 ♘d8 47. ♗c8

(see diagram next page)

Despite the fact that White looks more active, it is actually Black that is without problems and who has the prospects to search for more than a draw.

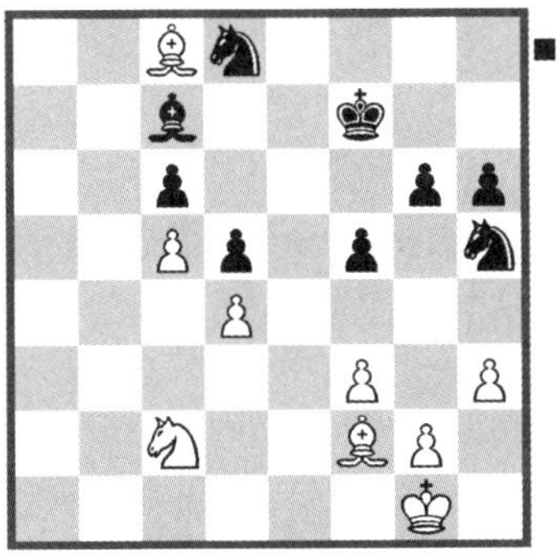

Position after: 47. ♗c8

47... ♗a5 48. ♔f1

A normal move, but I would have gone for something else.

48. ♗e1 This is safer and should be better and now White is okay after the following. 48... ♗xe1 49. ♘xe1 The bishop neutralizes the black knight that is controlling the important e6-square.

48... ♘g7 49. ♘e1?!

This doesn't spoil anything but gives Black the chance to make something out of nothing.

49. ♗e1 Again this would have been my choice. 49... ♗xe1 50. ♔xe1 ♘ge6

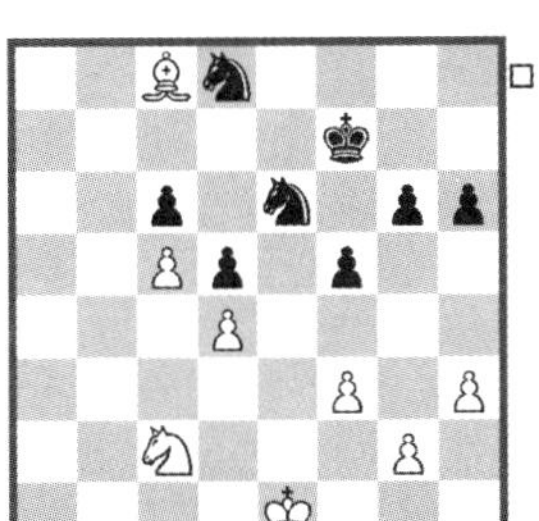

Position after: 50... ♘ge6

51. ♗xe6+ ♘xe6 This gives full equality.

49... ♗xe1! 50. ♔xe1 f4

Suddenly White has problems, though to be fair there is still nothing concrete.

51. ♔d2 ♔e7

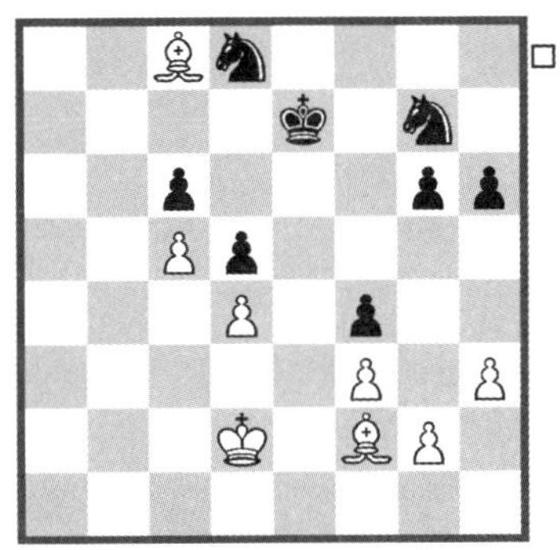

Position after: 51... ♔e7

52. ♗h4+?!

Wasting time.

52. ♗a6 Placing the bishop on d3 would have been a better option.

52... g5 53. ♗f2 ♘de6

54. ♗a6?

Now this misses the mark.

A) 54. ♗xe6!? This would have been a better option.

B) 54. h4! Reducing the pawn material is the best. 54... ♘f5 55. hxg5 hxg5

Position after: 55... hxg5

56. ♔c3 White is now safe.

54... ♘f5

Black's cavalry is on their best spots and White must play very precisely.

55. ♔c3

Position after: 55. ♔c3

55... h5?

55... ♘e3!! 56. ♗xe3 fxe3 57. g3 h5! This would have given Black a decisive advantage after, for instance

(see diagram next column)

Position after: 57... h5!

58. ♔d3 e2!.

56. ♗d3?

56. ♗f1! This would have eliminated the threat of ...♘e3.

56... ♘e3!

Finally, Black jumps and wins!

57. ♔d2

57. ♗xe3 fxe3 The knight comes to f4 with a win.

57... ♘xd4 58. ♗xe3 fxe3+ 59. ♔xe3 ♘e6 60. g3

Position after: 60. g3

60... ♔f6?

60... ♘xc5 Why not this?

61. ♗e2?

White misses a chance.

61. h4!! A fixing! 61... gxh4 62. gxh4 ♘xc5 63. ♗e2 ♘e6 64. f4 ♘g7 65. ♔d4 ♔f5 66. ♔c5 This will surprisingly lead to a draw!

61... ♔f5 62. ♗d3+ ♔f6 63. f4 gxf4+ 64. gxf4

Position after: 64. gxf4

64... d4+?!

64... h4! Instead, this move with fixing would have been more methodical.

65. ♔d2 ♘xc5 66. ♗e2 h4 67. ♗f3 ♔f5 68. ♗xc6

(see diagram next column)

Position after: 68. ♗xc6

68... ♔xf4 69. ♗g2 ♔g3 70. ♗f1 ♔f2 71. ♗e2 ♘b3+ 72. ♔d1 ♔e3 73. ♗c4 ♘c5

0-1

Game 62

♙ Nezhmetdinov, Rashid
♟ Luik, Helmuth
Kharkov 1958

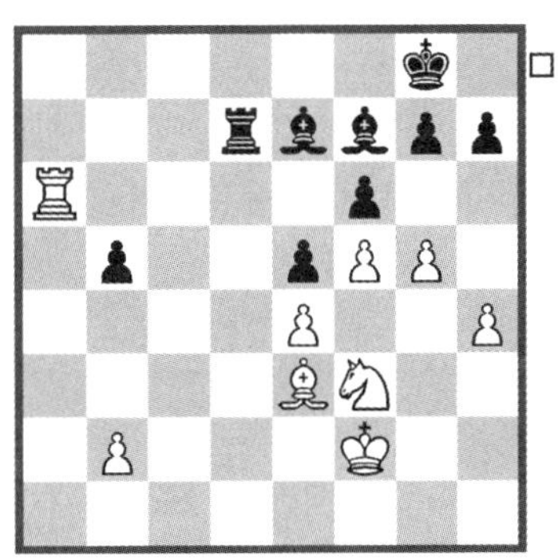

Although it may appear that Black is okay, there is an amazing hidden tactical resource for White to prove that the bishop pair is inferior here. White has a threatening formation on the kingside, but nevertheless everything is stable in Black's camp. Thus White must try to organize something on the kingside.

27. b4!

Not a big deal for Nezhmetdinov to find this. White intends to install the bishop on c5.

27... ♗e8?

Black collapses immediately.

A) 27... ♗xb4?? 28. ♖a8++–

B) 27... ♗h5! 28. ♗c5 ♔f7 This leads to a position where Black should hold.

28. ♗c5 ♔f7

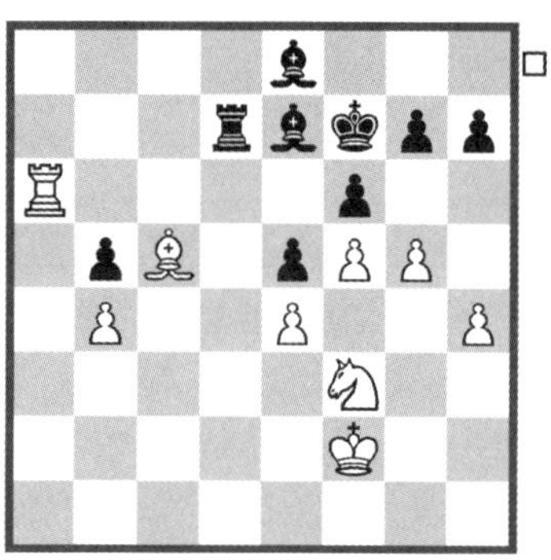

Position after: 28... ♔f7

29. g6+!!

Amazing shot that was not missed by the great combinatory player.

29... hxg6 30. fxg6+ ♔f8 31. h5

Now the game is decided; the knight comes to f5 and Black is just unable to organize anything.

31... ♗xc5+ 32. bxc5 ♖c7 33. ♖a8 ♖xc5 34. h6?

A mistake!

34. ♘h4 Installing the knight on f5 before h6 would have led to an easy win.

34... gxh6 35. ♘h4

Position after: 35. ♘h4

35... ♖c6?

35... ♖c2+ 36. ♔f3 ♖c3+ 37. ♔g4 [37. ♔e2? ♖g3!] 37... h5+! 38. ♔xh5 [38. ♔f5?? ♔e7 39. g7 ♖g3 Black even wins!] 38... ♖g3 This was a hidden possibility to hold.

36. ♘f5 ♖e6 37. ♖b8 h5 38. ♔g3 b4 39. ♔h4

(see diagram next page)

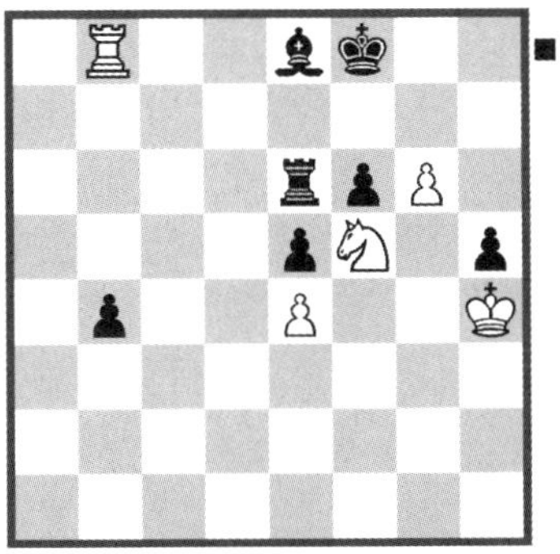

Position after: 39. ♔h4

39... b3 40. ♔xh5 b2 41. ♔h6 ♔g8 42. ♖xb2

1-0

Game 63

♙ Pflichthofer, Peter
♟ Riefner, Edwin (2230)
Germany 1990

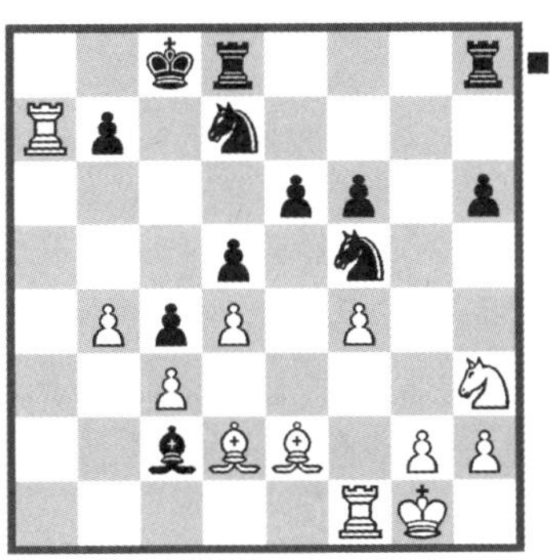

In this, unfortunately forgotten, game White is in big trouble. His bishops are not working at all. With his next move Black occupies the e4-square.

19... ♘d6! 20. ♗g4?

White plays without a plan. Step-by-step Black convincingly increases his undisputed advantage.

20... f5!

20... ♗f5 This would also have been good, but Black had another idea.

21. ♗f3 ♘f6 22. ♖c1 ♗e4

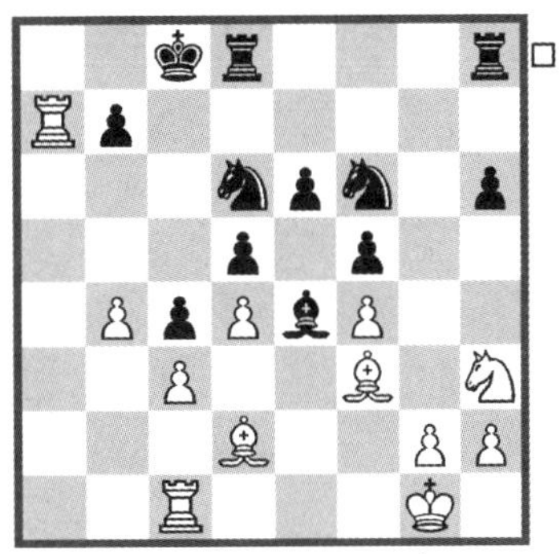

Position after: 22... ♗e4

23. ♖a8+?

A bad plan which at least loses time.

23... ♔c7 24. ♖xd8?

And this is already a big mistake. Only if there are four rooks can White hope for some counterplay.

24... ♖xd8 25. ♖a1

This rook has only a defensive role on the a-file.

25... ♖g8!

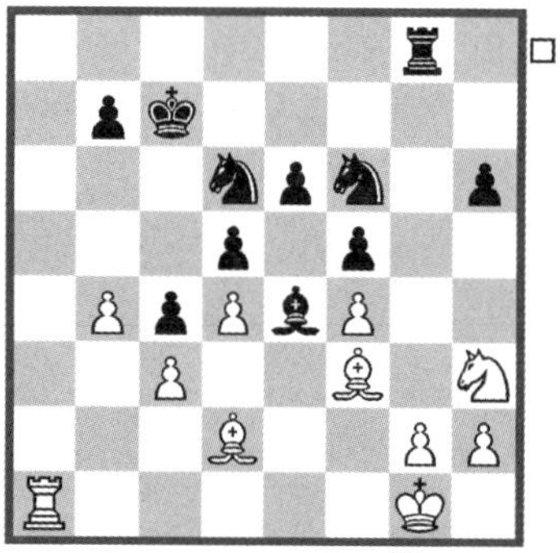

Position after: 25... ♖g8!

25... ♗xf3? 26. gxf3 Clearly Black cannot make progress – the e4-square has been taken away.

26. ♗xe4?

The game is over now. Black simply attacks the c3-pawn with both knights and White must leave the a-file.

26. ♔f2! ♘g4+!

A) 27. ♗xg4? fxg4!! Far better than the other capturing. 28. ♘g1 ♗d3! After this Black would at some moment exchange his bishop for the knight and dominate thereafter. The winning plan would be simple: exchange the rooks and penetrate with the king either via the a4-square or via the just-vacated f5-square! That is the point of capturing on g4 with the f-pawn – both routes would be opened for the black king and the white knight would be paralyzed and finally be exchanged.

B) 27. ♔g1! Black can now penetrate as follows. 27... ♗xf3 28. gxf3 ♘e5+ 29. ♔f2 ♘d3+ 30. ♔f1 However nothing concrete would be visible. Black would be forced to find some other way to crash through White's defense.

26... ♘fxe4–+

Now Black just easily wins – see the introductory note to the previous game regarding Black's plan. The same plan is implemented by Black in this game.

27. ♗e1 ♘b5 28. ♖c1 ♖a8 29. ♘f2 ♖a3

Everything is clear.

30. ♘xe4

Position after: 30. ♘xe4

30... dxe4

30... fxe4 This is, of course, very bad. White has counter-chances after 31. g4.

31. ♖c2 ♔c6 32. ♔f2 ♘c7!

A final regrouping! The knight would attack both pawns on c3 and f4 and control the blockading e3-square. Black's king would penetrate via a4.

33. ♔e2 ♘d5 34. ♗d2 ♔b5 35. h3 h5 36. ♔f2

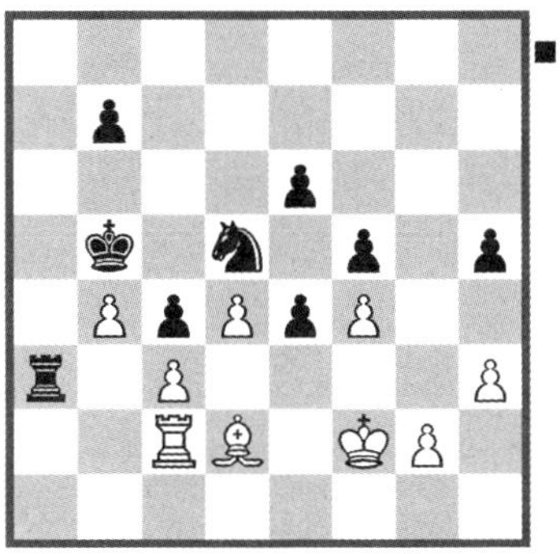

Position after: 36. ♔f2

36... e3+

A powerful demonstration with some tactics.

36... ♔a4 This also wins easily.

37. ♗xe3 ♖xc3 38. ♖xc3 ♘xc3 39. ♔g3 ♘d5!

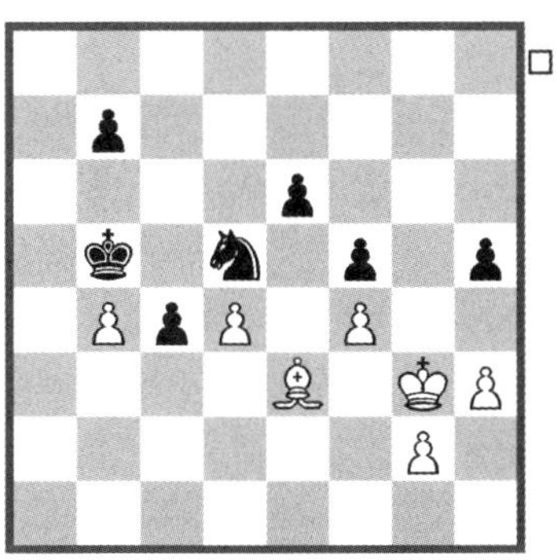

Position after: 39... ♘d5!

40. ♗c1 ♔xb4

Black has calculated precisely that White's counterplay would not be quick enough.

41. ♔h4 ♔b3 42. ♔xh5 ♔c2 43. ♗a3 ♘xf4+ 44. ♔g5 ♘xg2

White finally resigned.

0-1

Game 64

♙	Zlatanovic, Boroljub	(2393)
♟	Andreev, Sasho	(2191)
🌍	Plovdiv 2015	

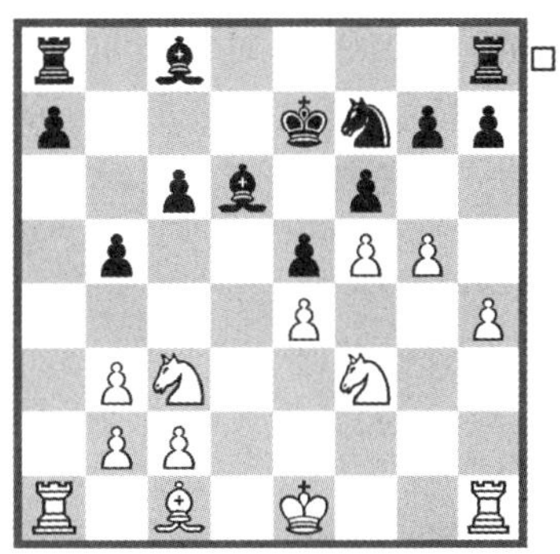

After a strangely played opening both players have reached this situation on the board. I correctly evaluated that Black's bishop pair is useless and that I can play on both wings. On the kingside I can attack his base on f6, while on the queenside I can use the a-file and weakness of the c5-spot for both strategic and tactical operations. The game continued as follows.

15. h5

Clearly the idea is to play h6 creating a passed f5-pawn.

15... h6?!

Let's not blame Black for this move because this reaction is natural – he keeps the pawn on f6 and gets ready to install his knight on g5.

15... ♗c5! Playing this to prevent both ♗e3 and ♖g1 would have been better. Nevertheless after 16. ♔e2! (with the idea of ♗e3) White is much better. [16. h6!? This is not as good because of 16... g6! with an unclear position.]

16. g6

I would gain nothing from installing my knight there – it would simply be misplaced after the following. 16. gxf6+ gxf6 17. ♘h4 ♖d8 18. ♘g6+ ♔e8

16... ♘g5

16... ♘d8 This was better. The played move eventually allows White to create a strong g-passer. 17. ♗e3 This leads to domination. I was pretty sure that at some moment a sacrifice on h6 would end the game.

17. ♘xg5 fxg5 18. ♗e3 a6

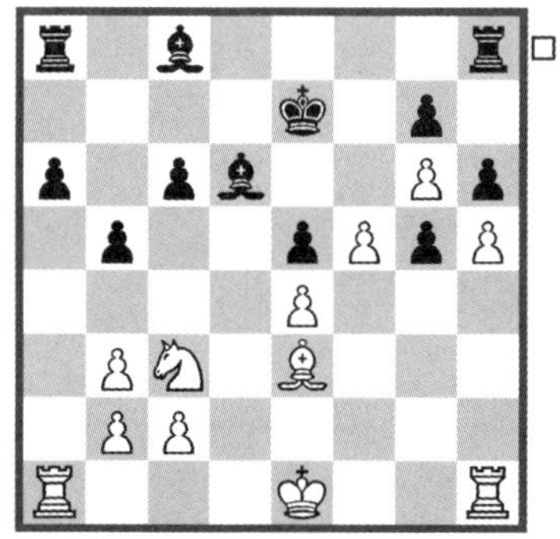

Position after: 18... a6

Everything loses.

19. 0-0-0 ♗d7 20. ♖h2

Black shocked me with resignation. To be fair his position is lost. 20. ♖h2 ♖ad8 21. ♖hd2

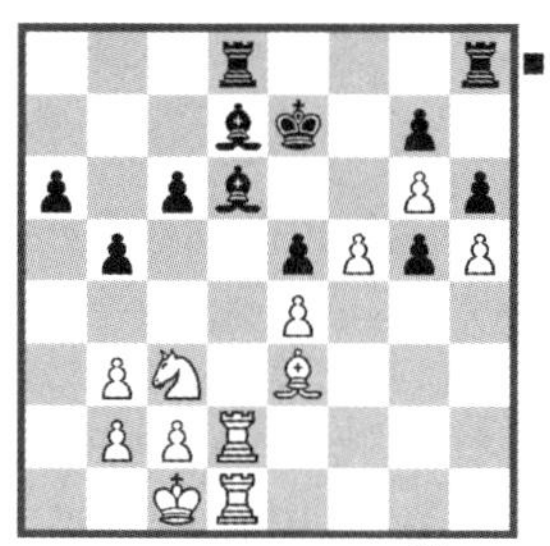

Position after: 21. ♖hd2

21... ♗c7 [21... ♗c8 22. ♖xd6 ♖xd6 23. ♗c5+–; 21... ♗b4 22. ♗b6+–] 22. ♗c5+ ♔e8 23. ♖f1 This leaves Black in a hopeless situation because White transfers his knight to g4, or plays f6 without this.

1-0

Game 65

♙ Magerramov, Elmar S (2565)
♟ Kohlweyer, Bernd (2420)
Bad Woerishofen 1993

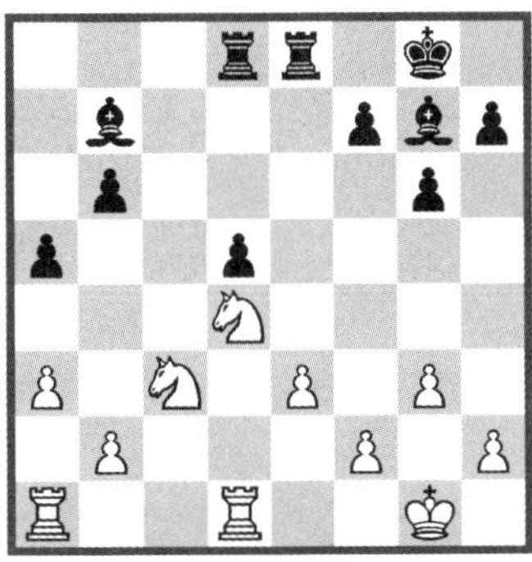

Let's conclude the chapter with a typical example. This could be analyzed in the chapter "Pawn Weaknesses", but the more significant fact here is that the bishop pair is simply bad. The dark-squared bishop has a nice diagonal but its attack on the d4-spot is irrelevant. White dominates on the key squares and with his next move goes for the initiative on Black's weakened queenside.

27. ♘a4!

This move deflects the black rook from the 8th rank, so White can firmly occupy the c-file.

27... ♖d6 28. ♖ac1 ♖c8

28... ♖e7!? This looks like a reasonable alternative. The idea is to control all the infiltration squares on the c-file before regrouping. White can build his initiative with, for instance, 29. ♖d2 and ♖dc2 next.

29. ♖xc8+ ♗xc8

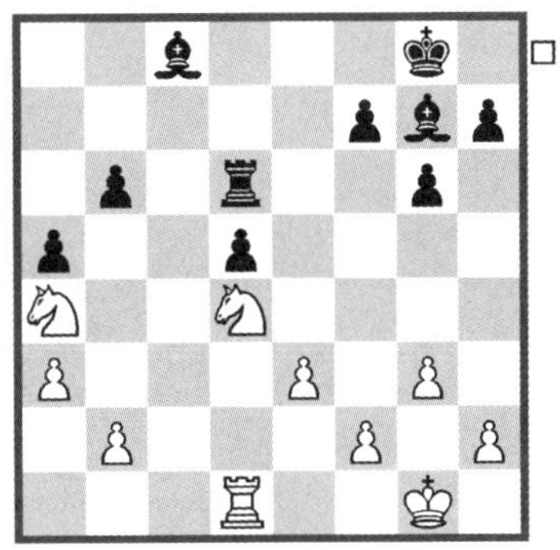

Position after: 29... ♗xc8

30. ♘b5

30. ♖c1?! This does not look as good because after 30... ♗g4 Black threatens to take on d4 with the rook infiltrating.

30... ♖d8 31. ♘d4

There is no need to rush.

31... ♖d6 32. f3

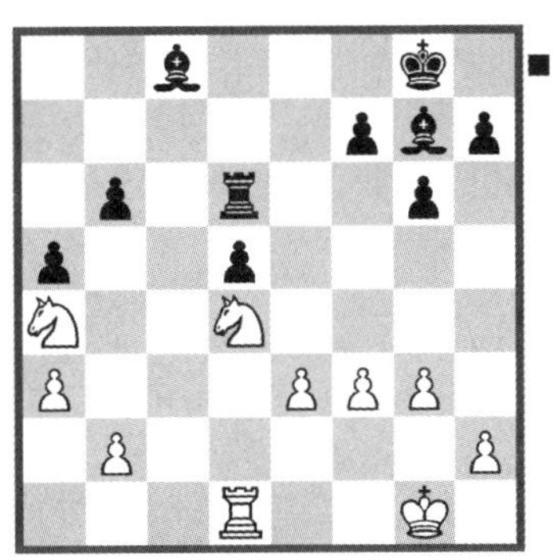

Position after: 32. f3

A typical approach. White brings the king closer to the center and eliminates potentially the annoying possibility of ...♗g4. The weakening of the e3-pawn is irrelevant.

32... ♗d7 33. ♘c3 h5 34. ♔f2 ♔f8 35. ♔e2

The idea is to control the d4-square with the king, of course, so as to be ready to recapture with the king on d4 after the rook comes to c1 and to eliminate any possibility of ...d4 after the knight leaves d4.

35... ♗c8!

A good response. The bishop belongs on a6.

36. b4!

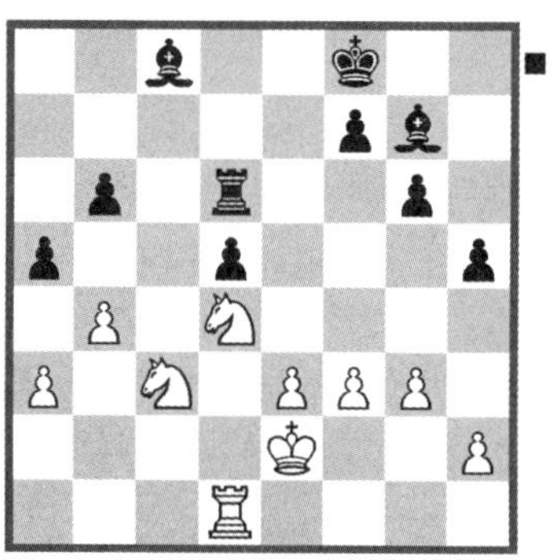

Position after: 36. b4!

White's counters are also classy. After the pawn comes to b5 the king will be safe on d3. There are also benefits of gaining control over c6 and fixing the pawn on b6 and the rook on d6 due to the threat of ♘a4.

36... axb4 37. axb4 ♗a6+

A clear mistake. Black provokes something that White intends to do anyway.

A) After the pawn material has been reduced on the queenside, the shocking 37... ♗xd4!? should be considered as an option. 38. ♖xd4 ♗e6

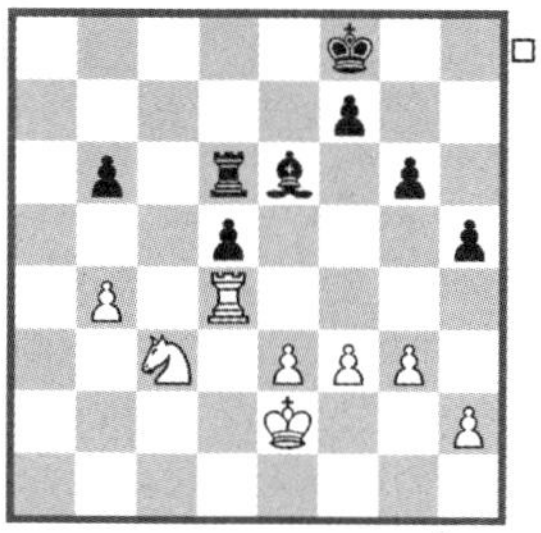

Position after: 38... ♗e6

39. b5 [39. e4 ♖c6 This gives nothing to White.] 39... ♔e7 This looks holdable for Black. However it is very difficult to go for this line in practical play and Black was right not to choose it.

B) 37... ♗h3 However this neutral move deserves serious consideration.

38. b5 ♗b7 39. ♖a1

Suddenly Black has problems that are more serious than White's frontal attack on the d5-pawn.

39... ♗f6 40. ♔d3 ♖d7 41. ♘a4

A) 41. ♖a7 This can be met as follows. 41... ♗d8 Now 42. ♘xd5 gives nothing in view of the calm 42... ♔e8!.

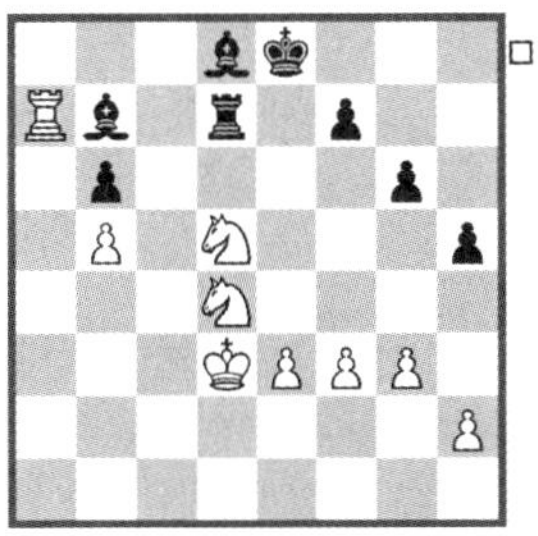

Position after: 42... ♔e8!

A forced line can be as follows. 43. e4 ♗xd5 44. ♖xd7 ♗xe4+ 45. ♔xe4 ♔xd7 White is unable to create another weakness on the kingside with a probable draw as the result.

B) 41. f4! Waiting before moving on the queenside was better. There will be annoying ideas of h3 and g4-g5 with a dangerous fixing.

41... ♗d8 42. ♖c1

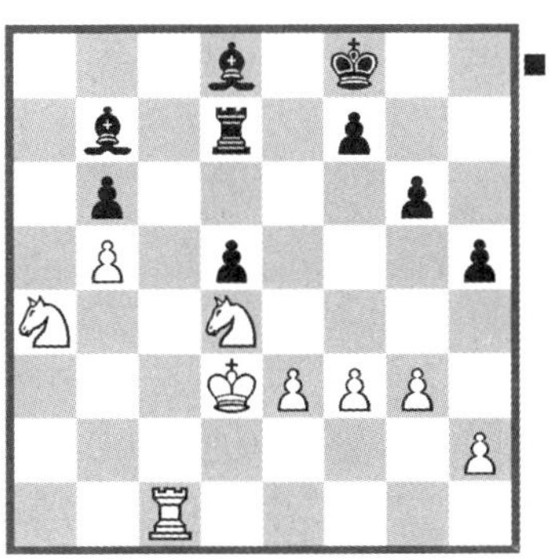

Position after: 42. ♖c1

42... ♗c7?

Clearly Black was not ready to play 42... ♖c7! reducing White's attacking potential.

43. ♘c6!

Now this knight is a real "bone in the throat".

43... f6 44. f4!

Instructive – restricting the black bishop and making the d4-spot comfortable for the king.

44... ♔f7 45. ♔d4 ♔e6

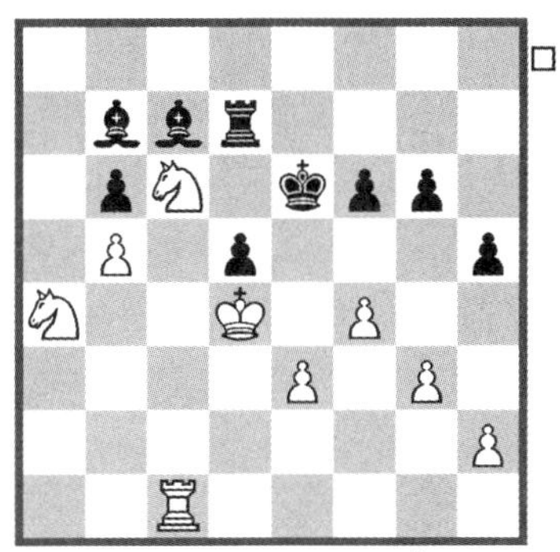

Position after: 45... ♔e6

46. h3

Now White prepares g4.

46... ♖h7?!

This prophylaxis does not work.

46... f5!? An ugly but drastic move to prevent g4.

47. ♘c3! ♖d7 48. g4 hxg4

Otherwise there are good options of gxh5 or f5.

49. hxg4 ♗d6 50. ♘a4!?

Again paralyzing the black pieces.

50. ♔d3! Liberating the d4-spot for the knight looks to be the best. 50... ♗c5 51. ♘d4+ ♗xd4

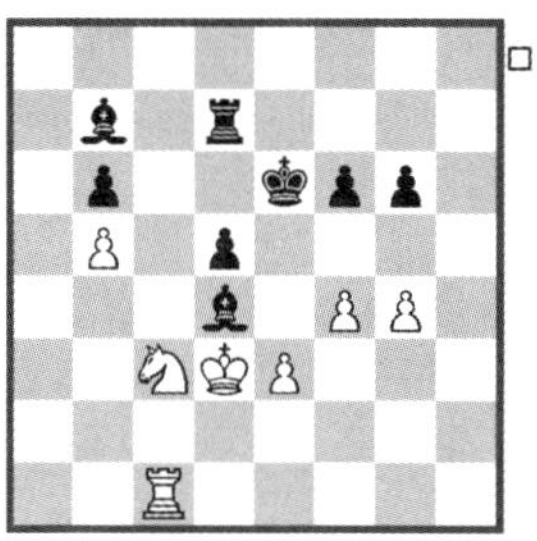

Position after: 51... ♗xd4

What else? 52. exd4! This looks lost for Black.

50... ♗c7

(see diagram next column)

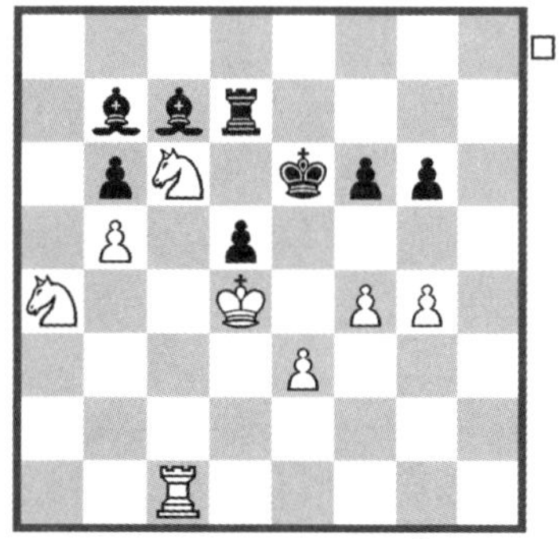

Position after: 50... ♗c7

51. ♖h1

Finally White has found the file on which to invade.

51... ♖g7?

51... ♗xc6! 52. bxc6 ♖d6 The last chance to hold where after 53. ♖c1 ♔f7 there is no obvious plan for White to improve.

52. ♘c3 ♖d7 53. ♖h6 ♖g7 54. ♘xd5 ♖d7 55. f5+

1-0

Activity & Harmony

Everyone knows that from the very beginning of the game, activity must be the focus. However more advanced players know that activity alone is not enough – even active pieces may be simply bad. In short, the pieces must collaborate. Now we get the concept of harmony! Yes, even in the endgame, take care with harmony! It is especially in endgames where there are few pawns on the board that the importance of activity (and harmony, of course) increases.

Moreover, even in closed positions, activity is essential; if you have activity in blocked situations, then it is probable that the opponent is without activity! Just imagine if there is an endgame with pawns on both flanks (for instance, with mutual majorities) – it is clear that activity and harmony will be the ultimate principles, because the pieces must control both flanks at the same time (or support your majority and stop the opponent's).

Game 66

♙ Van der Sterren, Paul (2605)
♟ Glek, Igor Vladimirovich (2615)
Germany 1995

This chapter is dedicated to the very important principles of activity and harmony. As you know from advice related to the opening and middlegame it is not good enough to just set your pieces on active spots. No, they must also work from these spots; but even this is not enough – the pieces must collaborate. They need to move in unity toward some task. A few further examples will explain this in detail – the importance of harmony is not diminished in the endgame!

Our first example is the simplest one. Black is on the move and the ultra-active rook alone cannot do anything – the bishop's support is essential, the quicker the better. Now, it is not difficult to find a solution.

25... c5!

Contrary to the principles related to setting the pawns on the proper color in a bishops' endgame. However with this move Black secures the d4-spot for the bishop and restricts the white rook.

26. h3

26. g3 This may look precise, but the second rank would be dangerous if opened.

26... ♗d4 27. b4

White naturally wants to undermine the position of the black bishop.

27. a4 A calm defense and probably a better option. After 27... h5 Black dominates with nothing concrete apparent.

27... ♔f8

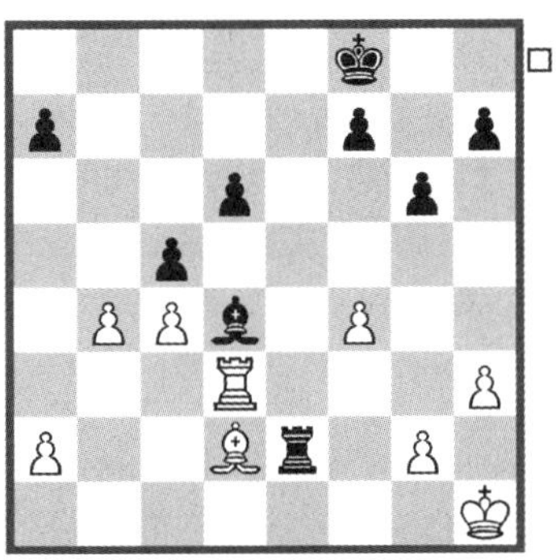

Position after: 27... ♔f8

Of course, Black ignores White's expansion.

28. b5

There is nothing better.

28... ♔e7

Black intends to simply win the game after ...♔e6 and ...d5.

29. f5 d5

Black goes for this anyway. White is completely lost.

30. fxg6

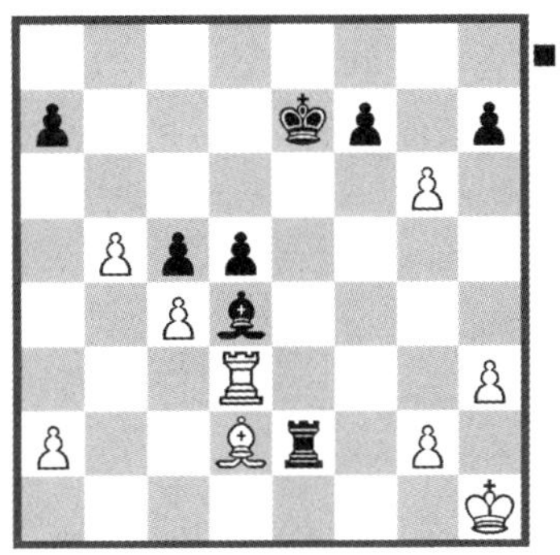

Position after: 30. fxg6

30... hxg6

30... fxg6 This is optically even better, of course.

31. ♗f4 dxc4

The rest is a matter of technique.

32. ♖a3 ♖b2 33. ♖xa7+ ♔f6 34. h4 ♖xb5

(see diagram next page)

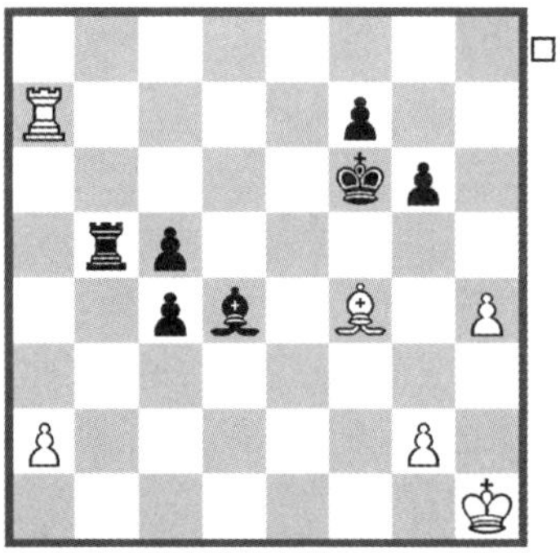

Position after: 34... ♖xb5

35. ♗g5+ ♔g7 36. a4 ♖b1+ 37. ♔h2 c3

0-1

Game 67

♙ Georgiev, Kiril (2592)
♟ Drygalov, Andrey (2495)
Chess.com 2020

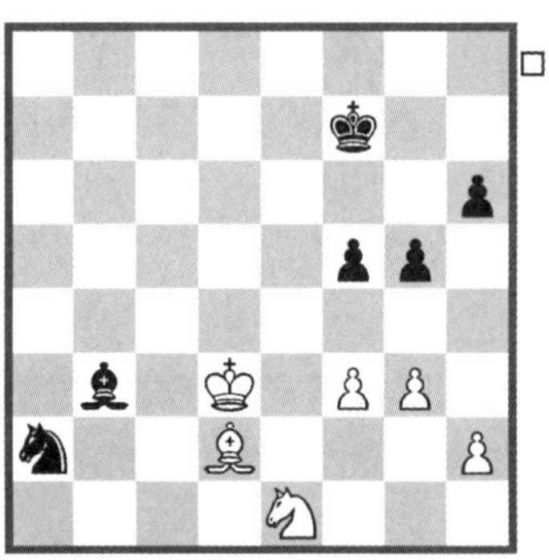

A very interesting situation. Black plays practically without the knight, but White cannot simply take it physically. The plan to convert is to organize an attack on Black's kingside using an extra piece. This would not be difficult for such a great maestro as Kiril Georgiev. It is very important that Black must not trade his bishop for the white knight.

46. ♔d4 ♔f6 47. ♘d3 ♗d1 48. f4

Necessary.

48... ♗e2 49. ♘e5 gxf4

What else? This is essential at some point.

50. gxf4 ♔e6

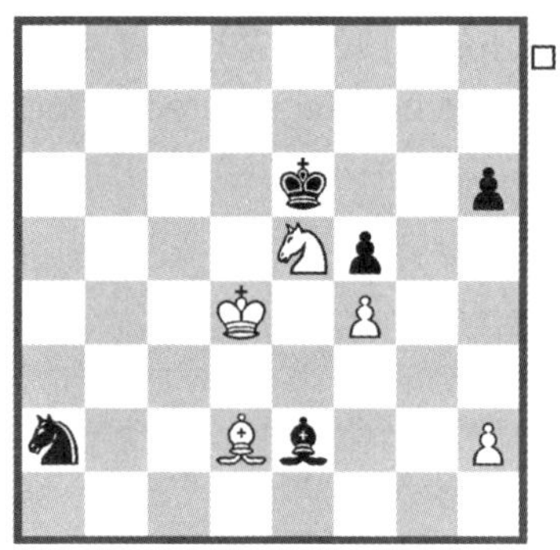

Position after: 50... ♔e6

51. ♔c5

White's plan is to collect the f5-pawn with the knight and king. With some checks White will easily drive the black king back.

51... ♗d1 52. ♘c6 ♔f6 53. ♘d4

Paralyzing the black bishop slightly, controlling the e6-square and attacking the f5-pawn.

53... ♔g6 54. ♔d6 ♗g4

Counter-attacking with 54... ♔h5 gives nothing in view of the following. 55. ♘xf5 ♔g4 56. ♘xh6+ ♔h3 57. f5 ♔xh2 58. f6

Position after: 58. f6

58... ♗h5 59. ♘f5 ♔h3 60. ♘d4 ♔g4 61. ♔e6 White wins after f7 and going back to capture the knight. Black's king faces a barrier!

55. ♔e5 ♗h3 56. ♔e6 ♗g4

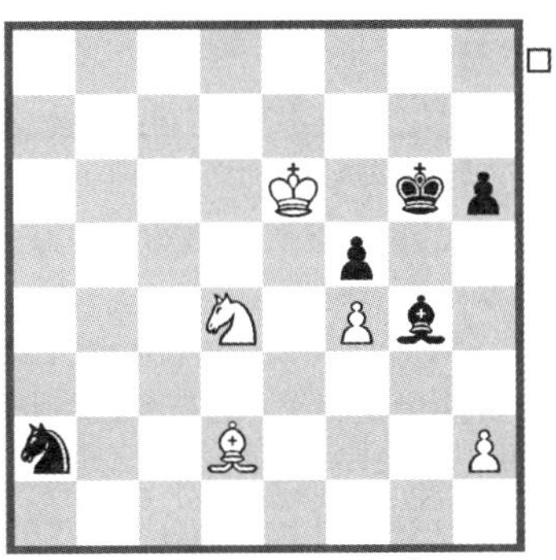

Position after: 56... ♗g4

57. ♘c6

The knight goes to e7 and the f-pawn falls.

57... ♗h3 58. ♘e7+ ♔h5 59. ♔f6 ♔g4 60. ♘xf5 ♔f3 61. ♘g3

Position after: 61. ♘g3

Again a barrier!

61... h5 62. ♘xh5

62. ♔g5! This was also possible and even more methodical.

62... ♔e2 63. ♗a5 ♘c1

Black's knight is active again, but White easily wins with two extra pawns.

64. ♔g5 ♘d3 65. f5 ♔f3 66. ♗c7 ♘c5 67. ♘f4 ♗f1

Position after: 67... ♗f1

68. h4

Georgiev attacks with all his forces, reminding his opponent that there are two extra passed pawns.

68... ♗c4 69. h5 ♗g8 70. ♔g6 ♘e4 71. f6 ♔g4 72. h6 ♘g5 73. ♔g7

Position after: 73. ♔g7

A beautiful position.

73... ♗c4 74. h7 ♘xh7 75. ♔xh7 ♔f5 76. ♔g7 ♗b3 77. ♘e2 ♗c4 78. ♘d4+ ♔e4 79. ♘b5 ♗b3 80. ♔f8 ♔d3 81. ♔e7

Position after: 81. ♔e7

81... ♔e4 82. ♘d6+ ♔f4 83. ♘c4+

White saves energy by winning in style, avoiding an endgame with the extra knight and bishop. Black resigned.

1-0

Game 68

♙	Georgiev, Kiril	(2591)
♟	Markovic, Zoran S	(2334)
🌍	Veliko Gradiste 2019	

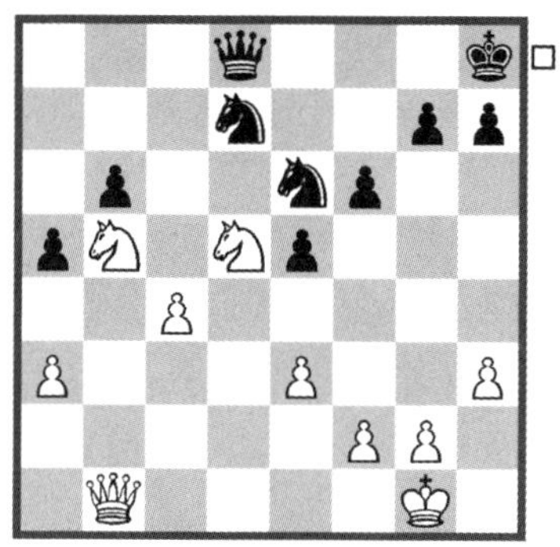

The next example is also from Georgiev's praxis. Generally, he is a very good choice to learn about harmony. On this next diagram White has the more active pieces. Black's more compact structure does not compensate for it. White should make his queen more active and the solution is not difficult.

35. ♘bc3 ♘ec5 36. ♕b5 h6

Black can only "sit and wait"... for now. He must be accurate to seek chances to somehow reactivate his pieces.

37. ♕c6 ♕b8

37... e4!

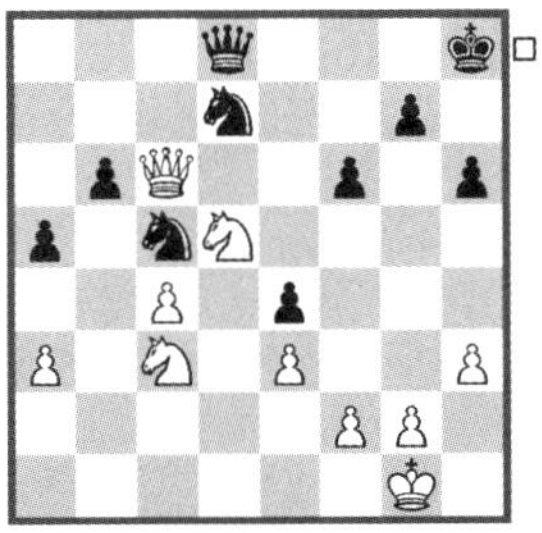

Position after: 37... e4!

38. ♘b5 [38. ♕d6 ♘b7 39. ♕e6 ♘bc5 White has nothing special.] 38... ♘e5 39. ♕xb6 ♕xb6 40. ♘xb6 ♔g8 This would give Black some chances (to be fair, mostly practical ones) to survive.

38. ♘b5

38. ♘a4! This would have been a crushing move!

38... ♔h7

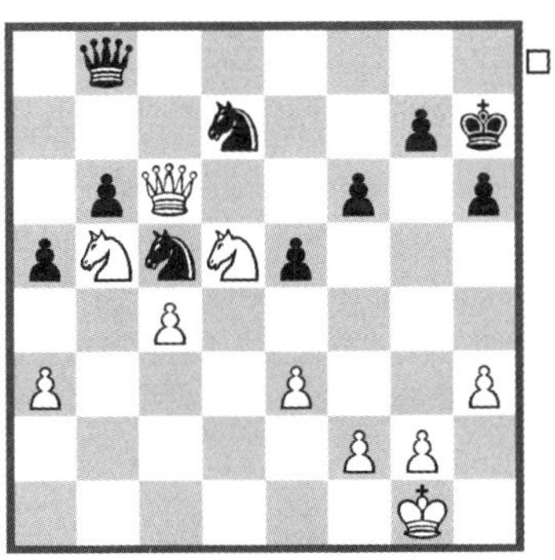

Position after: 38... ♔h7

38... e4 This was once again needed to give the knight access to the e5-spot.

39. ♘bc7

39. ♘d6 This looks more logical. Georgiev wanted instead to keep this square for the queen.

39... ♔h8 40. ♕d6 ♔h7 41. ♕e7

White's queen is in a dangerous position and Black decides to trade it.

41... ♕f8 42. ♕xf8 ♘xf8 43. ♘xb6 ♔g6

Position after: 43... ♔g6

White has gained a pawn, but at the price of reducing his attacking potential. Black has reactivated his pieces and also has practical chances to hold – it is easy to blunder with so many knights on the board.

44. ♔f1

The first phase is to centralize the king.

44... ♔f7 45. ♘bd5 ♘fe6 46. ♘b5

This is a matter of style. White can aim to exchange at any given moment.

46... ♔e8 47. ♔e2 ♔d7 48. f3

Position after: 48. f3

Restricting the black cavalry.

48... ♔c6 49. ♔d2 ♘a4 50. ♔c2 ♔d7 51. ♘bc3

Sooner or later this will happen.

51... ♘xc3 52. ♔xc3 ♔d6 53. ♔d3 ♘c5+ 54. ♔c2

Position after: 54. ♔c2

In such situations it is very good advice to implement the "don't rush" principle.

54... ♔d7 55. ♘c3 ♔c6

56. ♘e2

56. ♘e4?? ♘xe4! You should observe for yourself that this is a draw. White's king cannot invade Black's camp after 57. fxe4 a4!.

56... ♘e6

Position after: 56... ♘e6

57. ♘c1

White dances with the knight, trying to confuse the opponent or to eventually make progress. Of course, the kingside pawn play is on the agenda, but there is no need to rush.

57... ♔c5 58. ♔c3 ♔c6 59. ♘b3 ♔b6 60. ♘c1 ♔c6 61. ♘d3 ♔b6 62. ♔b3 ♔c6 63. ♔c3 ♔b6 64. ♔d2 h5

(see diagram next page)

Black wants to give concrete character to the position.

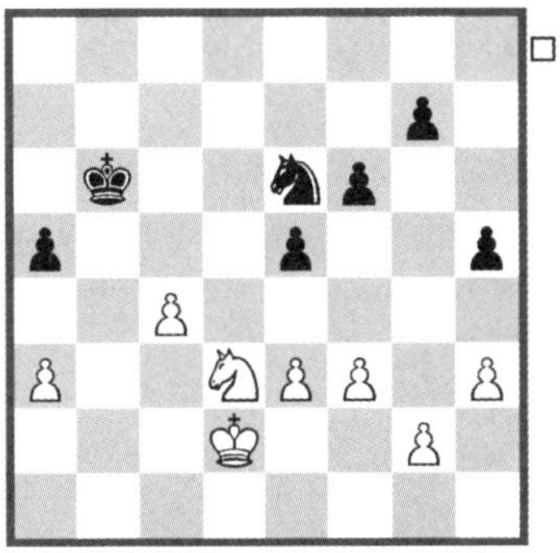

Position after: 64... h5

65. h4

There is no need to allow Black to gain a lot of space.

65... ♔c6 66. ♘f2 ♘c5 67. ♔c2 ♔b6 68. g4?!

A natural-looking move, but it is actually a serious imprecision.

68. ♘h1 The idea is to provoke weaknesses in the opponent's camp – this would have been a more appropriate move.

68... hxg4?

68... e4! The move missed by both players. Now, for instance, material could be reduced in a way that is favorable for Black.

(see diagram next column)

Position after: 68... e4!

69. fxe4 [69. ♘xe4?? This even loses after the following. 69... ♘xe4 70. fxe4 hxg4; 69. gxh5 exf3 This should not be seriously considered.] 69... hxg4

69. ♘xg4?

69. fxg4 Correct; the idea is to transfer the knight to f5. The point is, of course, if possible to provoke ...g6 and win after creating a passed h-pawn.

69... ♘e6?

69... e4! 70. f4 ♘b7 After installing a knight on f5 Black would be out of difficulties.

70. ♔d3 ♘c5+ 71. ♔d2

Position after: 71. ♔d2

71... ♘e6?

71... e4! A well-known defensive resource.

72. ♘f2 ♔c6 73. ♘e4 f5

Black decides not to wait. Alas, the right moments for direct play are gone.

74. ♘f2 ♘c5 75. ♘d3 ♘d7 76. f4

White simplifies the position and opens some paths for the king.

76... exf4

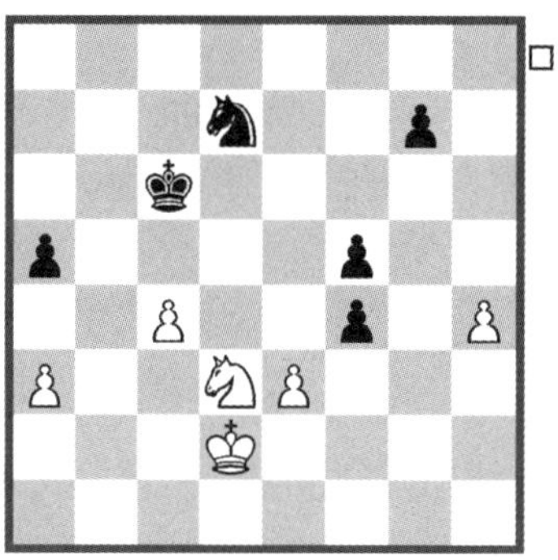

Position after: 76... exf4

76... e4 77. ♘e5++–

77. ♘xf4

77. exf4 Renewing the threat of ♘e5 would have been better.

77... ♘e5 78. ♔c3 g6

It looks like Black's position is impregnable now.

79. ♔b3

Georgiev tries to invade with the king via the a4-square.

79... ♔c5?

79... ♔d6! Now 80. ♔a4 gives nothing in view of 80... ♘xc4.

Position after: 80. ♔a4

81. ♘xg6 ♔e6 The king will take care of the passed h-pawn with a draw. Such regroupings can be easily missed in a practical game of chess due to the long-term pressure, defense and suffering.

80. ♔a4 ♔b6 81. c5+

Position after: 81. c5+

White tries with his last chance.

81... ♔xc5 82. ♔xa5 ♘c4+ 83. ♔a4 ♘xe3?

The final and fatal mistake which can be understood because of the tendency to reduce the pawn material. This time, however, it would have been better for Black not to follow the famous principle.

83... ♘e5 84. ♔b3 ♔b5! 85. ♔c3 ♔a4 This is holdable because the white king cannot use the d4-square.

84. ♘xg6 ♘g4 85. h5 ♔c4 86. ♔a5 ♔c5 87. a4 ♘h6 88. ♔a6 ♔c6 89. a5

Position after: 89. a5

We are closer and closer to the finale.

89... ♘g8 90. ♘f4 ♔c5

90... ♘h6 91. ♔a7 ♔c7 92. a6 ♘g8 93. ♘e6+ ♔c6 94. ♔b8+–

91. ♘g6 ♔c6 92. ♔a7 ♔c7 93. a6 f4

(see diagram next column)

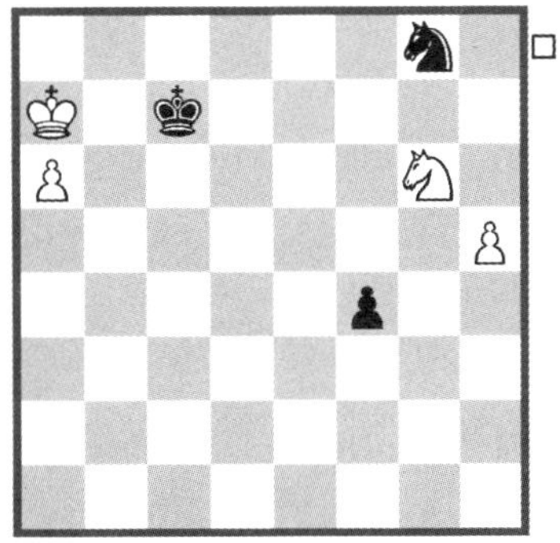

Position after: 93... f4

94. ♘xf4 ♘e7 95. ♘e6+ ♔d6 96. h6

Black resigned. A very tense game and a real roller-coaster.

1-0

Game 69

♙	Tate, Alan	(2308)
♟	Georgiev, Kiril	(2588)
🌍	Heraklion 2019	

On this diagram Black is completely winning. The diagnosis is crystal clear from the brutal invasion by the rooks and the better knight.

44... ♖b1

Attacking the b2-pawn and making space for another rook.

45. ♖dd2 ♖c4 46. ♗h3 ♔g7 47. ♗g2 ♘d7

A very good maneuver. The knight cannot obtain the g4-spot, but goes to c5. From there it will both protect the a4-pawn and attack the e4-pawn.

48. ♔f2 ♘c5 49. ♗f3 ♖cc1 50. ♗g2

Position after: 50. ♗g2

Black has all his pieces optimally active. In such situations, it is usually good to go for pawn action.

50... g5 51. hxg5 ♔g6 52. ♔e3 ♖g1

Paralyzing the white army.

53. ♗f3 ♖xg3 54. ♖h2 ♖f1

A demonstration of power.

55. ♖df2 ♖fg1 56. ♔d2 ♖xg5

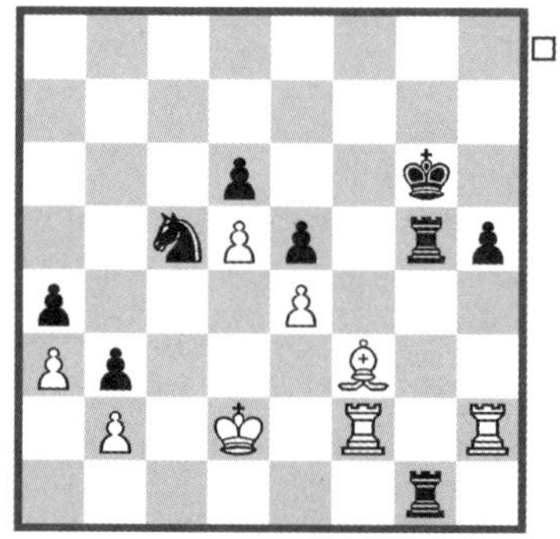
Position after: 56... ♖xg5

57. ♖h4 ♖b1 58. ♔e3 ♖g3

The rook has done its job and goes again to the active g3-spot.

59. ♖fh2 ♖f1 60. ♖f2 ♖xf2

Position after: 60... ♖xf2

Now Black has nothing against the exchange.

61. ♔xf2 ♖g5 62. ♗e2 ♔f6 63. ♔e3 ♖g1 64. ♗xh5 ♖e1+ 65. ♗e2 ♖b1

(see diagram next page)

The game is over.

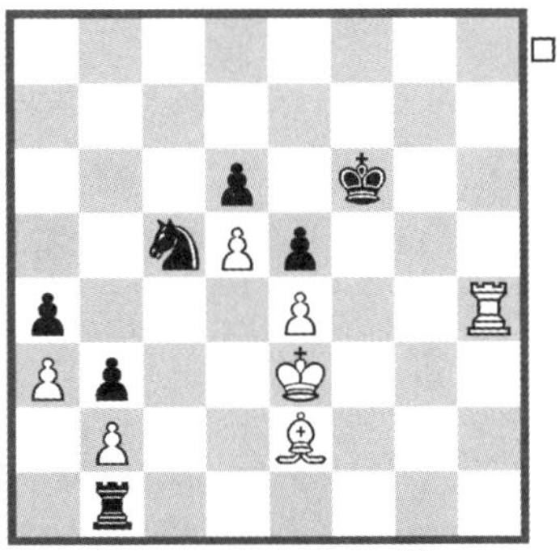

Position after: 65... ♖b1

66. ♖h6+ ♔e7 67. ♖h7+ ♔d8 68. ♖h8+ ♔c7 69. ♗b5 ♖xb2 70. ♗c6

Position after: 70. ♗c6

70... ♖a2 71. ♖h1

White resigned. A flawless and smooth conversion of the advantage.

0-1

Game 70

♙	Miles, Anthony John	(2220)
♟	Byrne, Robert Eugene	(2530)
🌍	Reykjavik 1980	

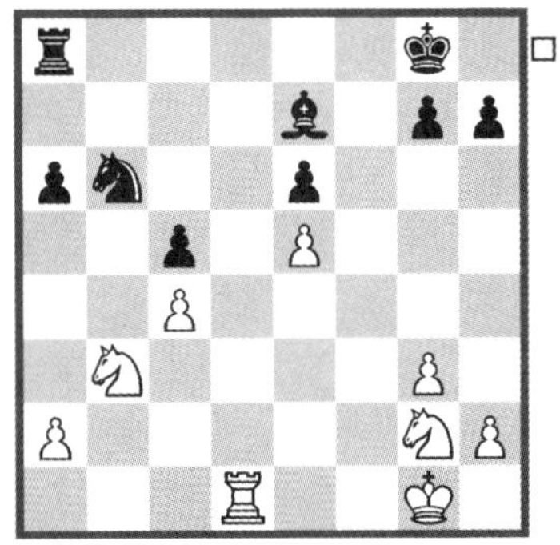

White is better here because Black has problems with his bishop. The pairs of separated pawns on the c- and e-files are set in White's favor. White can more easily occupy the key squares and find spots for his knights.

31. ♘a5!

The knight covers the c4-square from a safe and active spot.

31... ♗f8 32. ♘f4

Now another knight joins in the active play.

32... ♖e8 33. ♔f2

The king goes to the center. Before any action, this is advisable.

33... g5

Black wants to release pressure from e6 and to activate the king and rook.

34. ♘h5 ♗e7 35. ♔e3 ♔f7 36. ♖f1+ ♔g6

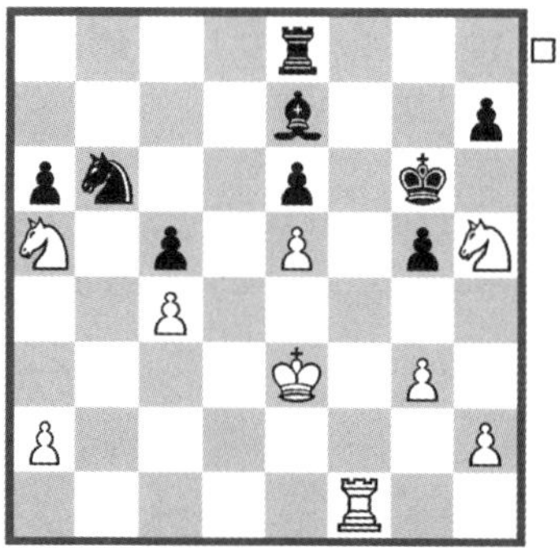

Position after: 36... ♔g6

37. g4

With this move White tightens the loop around the black king and restricts the bishop more.

37... h6 38. ♖b1 ♗d8 39. ♔e4 ♗c7?!

39... ♖f8! This was needed to get control back over the file. 40. ♘c6 ♗c7 41. ♘f6

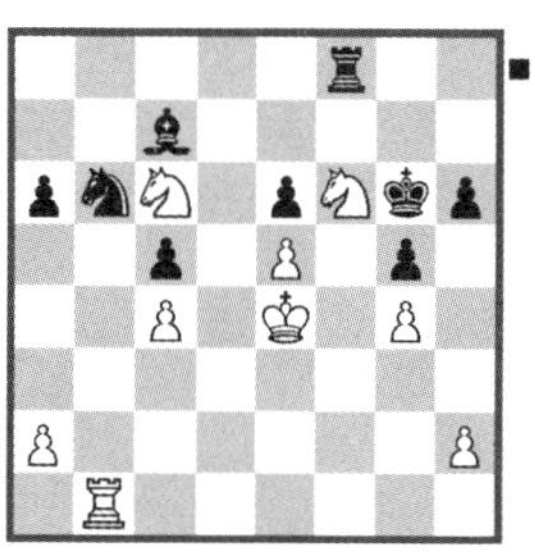

Position after: 41. ♘f6

Now this looks to be the only way for White to maintain the initiative. 41... ♘xc4 However this calm move is actually okay for Black although it looks bad. 42. ♖c1 ♘b2 43. ♖xc5 ♖f7

40. ♖f1

Position after: 40. ♖f1

40... ♗d8?

The wrong way to control f6.

40... ♘d7! 41. ♘c6 ♖f8

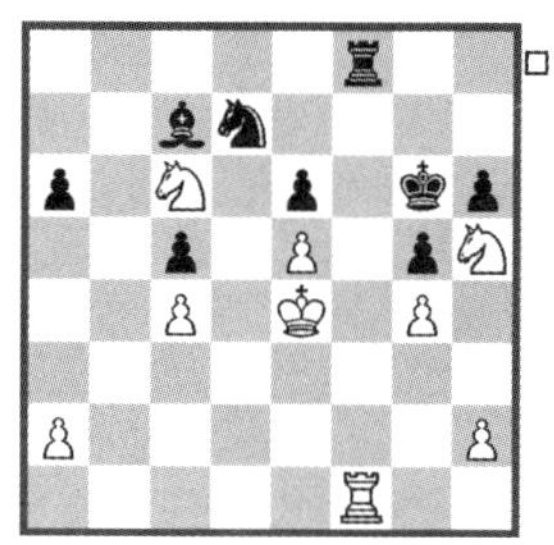

Position after: 41... ♖f8

42. ♖xf8 [42. ♖d1 ♘b6 White has nothing.] 42... ♘xf8 43. ♘f6 ♔f7 White keeps his plus, but without rooks there are no threats. There is nothing apparent that is concrete for White.

41. ♖f3 ♗e7 42. ♖b3

White's rook acts against the weaknesses on both flanks. There is no need to rush.

42... ♗d8 43. ♘c6 ♗c7 44. ♖f3 ♘d7

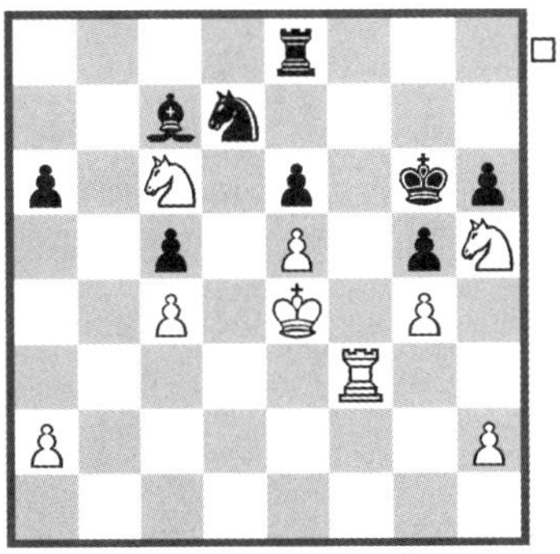

Position after: 44... ♘d7

Black played this move too late. The knight is already on c6.

45. a4 ♖f8 46. ♘e7+

46. ♖d3 ♘b6 47. a5 ♘xc4 48. ♖d7 A more direct way to convert here.

46... ♔h7 47. ♖xf8 ♘xf8 48. ♘f6+ ♔g7 49. ♘e8+

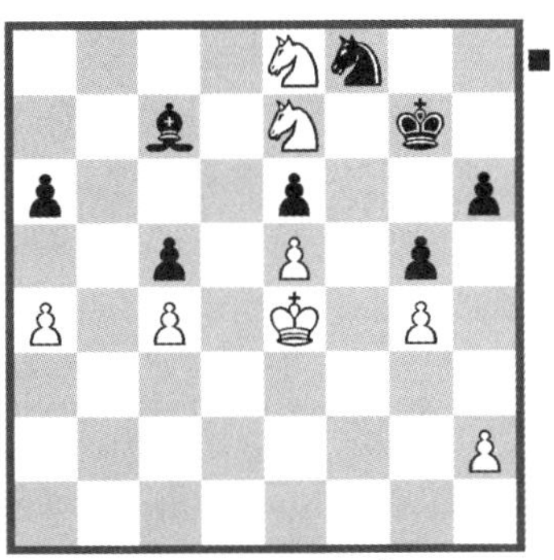

Position after: 49. ♘e8+

This fork simplifies the position and wins easily.

49... ♔f7 50. ♘xc7 ♔xe7 51. ♘xa6 ♘d7 52. ♘c7 ♘b6 53. a5

White has calculated that the advance would lead to a win.

53... ♘xc4 54. a6 ♔d7 55. a7 ♘b6 56. a8=♕ ♘xa8 57. ♘xa8 ♔c6 58. ♔d3

Position after: 58. ♔d3

58... ♔d5

58... ♔b7 59. ♔c4 ♔xa8 60. ♔xc5+–

59. ♘b6+ ♔xe5 60. ♔e3 ♔d6 61. ♔e4 ♔c6 62. ♘c4 ♔b5 63. ♘d2

Position after: 63. ♘d2

The knight stays far from the black king and the white king's march ends the game.

63... ♔b4 64. ♔e5 c4 65. ♘xc4 ♔xc4 66. ♔xe6

1-0

Game 71

♙ Zlatanovic, Boroljub (2412)
♟ Antic, Nenad (2030)
🌍 Kragujevac 2013

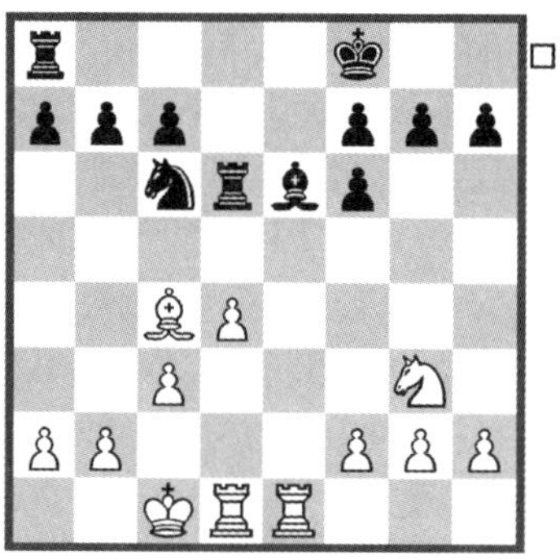

This is a fragment from one of my games. White is strategically winning because of Black's sterile majority – he is practically a pawn up! But how to convert? Advancing with a fork is tempting, but is it winning?

16. d5!

White has precisely calculated that this move works. Now it must be played, because the a2-pawn is under attack.

16... ♘a5 17. dxe6 ♖xd1+ 18. ♔xd1 ♘xc4 19. e7+! ♔e8 20. ♘h5 ♔d7 21. ♘xg7 ♘d6

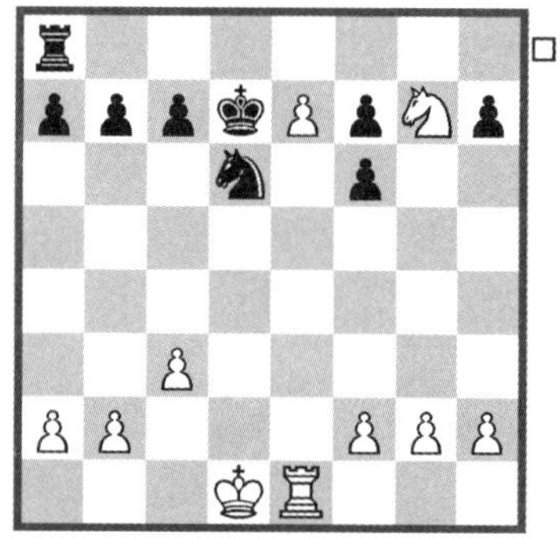

Position after: 21... ♘d6

After a series of forced moves the situation has stabilized. Was White right to go for this line? It looks like the passer is in danger and after taking it back Black will have some chances to hold.

22. ♘h5! ♘e8 23. ♔c2 a5

This was Black's idea – the rook goes to the e6-square. However with some tactics, White refutes all the threats to level the game.

24. ♘g3 ♖a6 25. ♘e4

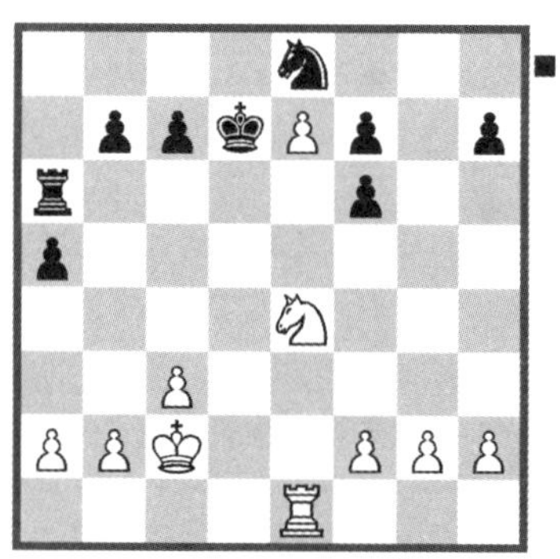

Position after: 25. ♘e4

This prevents the move ...♖e6, at the same time keeping the pawn safe.

25... ♖c6

A) 25... ♔xe7? 26. ♘c5++–

B) 25... ♖e6? 26. ♘c5++–

26. f4

The point will be clear soon.

26... b6 27. f5 ♘g7 28. g4 ♔xe7

Black has taken a pawn. So why did White go for this line?

29. a4!

The point. Black's rook is trapped. White plans to attack the rook with his king.

29... ♔f8 30. ♔d3 ♘e8

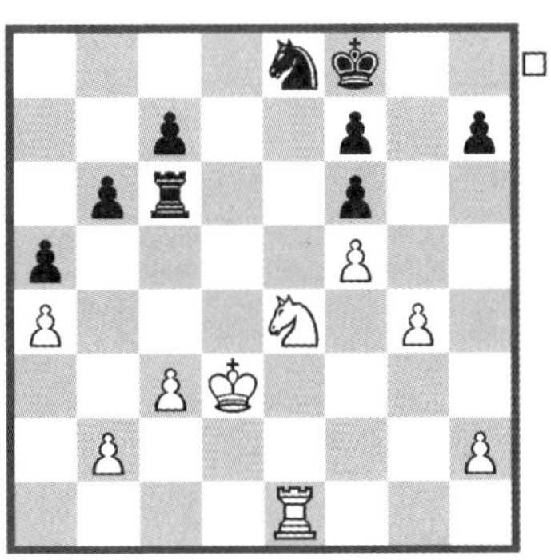

Position after: 30... ♘e8

31. b4

31. ♔d4 This wins too.

31... axb4 32. cxb4 b5 33. a5 ♘d6 34. ♘xf6

Black's position is collapsing and he resigned.

1-0

Game 72

♙ Gligoric, Svetozar
♟ Kramer, Haije J
🌍 Amsterdam 1950

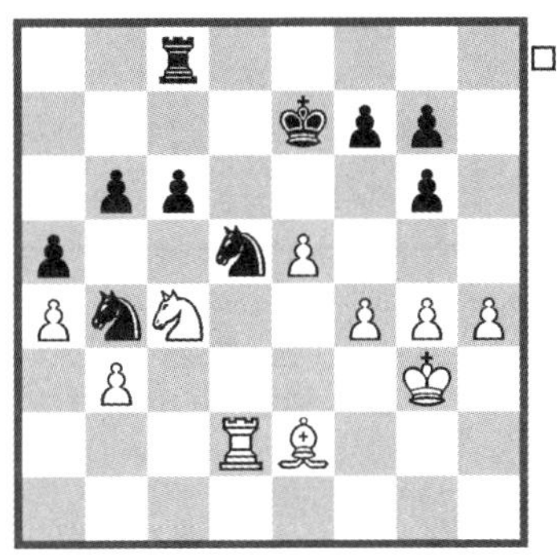

Here White evidently stands better. Black's cavalry is somewhat cramped and with his next move White practically paralyzes it.

37. ♗f3

Now neither of the black knights can move.

37... ♖d8 38. f5!

Gligoric plays directly. With his pieces on their best spots this is the logical way to proceed.

38. h5 Another good, but less methodical move.

38... gxf5 39. gxf5 ♖h8 40. h5 ♖d8 41. h6!

Again, concrete play by Gligoric.

41... gxh6 42. f6+ ♔d7 43. ♗h5

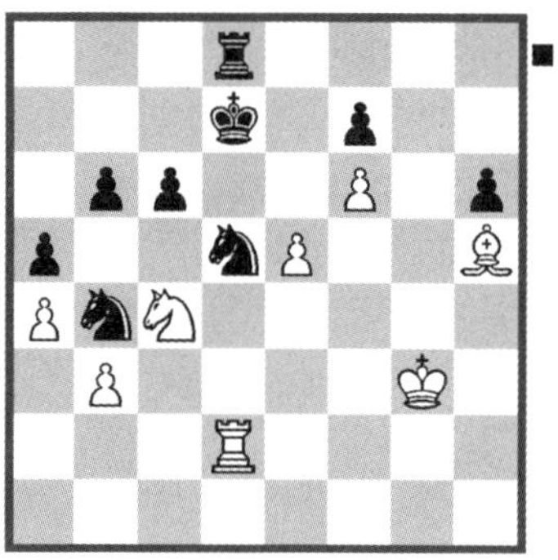

Position after: 43. ♗h5

43... ♖g8+

43... ♔e6 This would have led to a fine mate after 44. ♗g4#.

44. ♔f3

The bishop does not need this spot anymore.

44... ♔e6

Black decides that he would rather give the exchange away.

44... ♖f8 45. ♘xb6++–

45. ♗g4+ ♖xg4 46. ♔xg4 b5 47. ♘xa5 bxa4 48. bxa4 ♔xe5

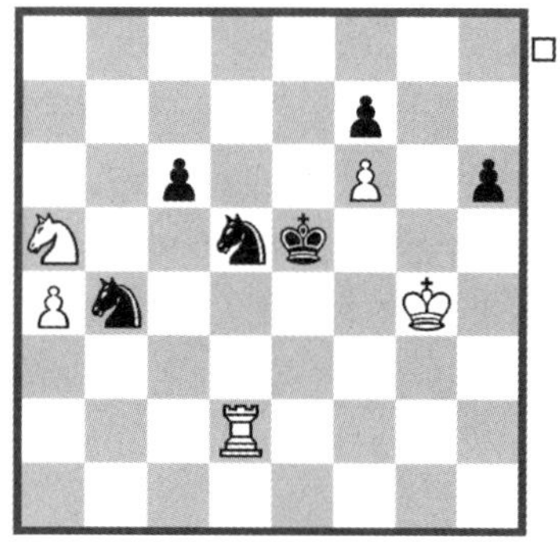

Position after: 48... ♔xe5

The storm has passed. In such situations usually the first task is to re-establish centralization, coordination and harmony.

49. ♘c4+ ♔xf6 50. ♖h2

There is nothing wrong with 50. a5.

50... ♔g6 51. ♘e5+

The two pawns here cannot compensate for the exchange. White's passer, supported by such active pieces, will decide the result.

51... ♔g7 52. ♔f5 f6 53. ♘c4 ♔f7

(see diagram next page)

It is impossible to give good advice here. Black moves his king toward the white passer.

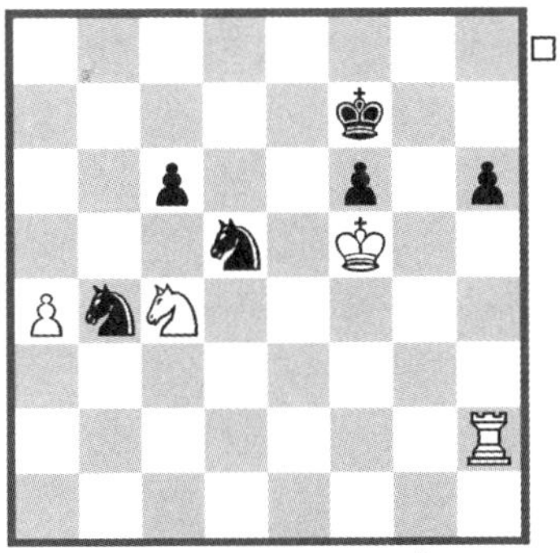

Position after: 53... ♔f7

54. ♖xh6 ♘e7+ 55. ♔e4 ♔e6 56. ♘e3?!

56. ♖h5! The precise move order.

56... c5?!

56... ♔d6 A better way to resist.

57. ♖h5

Position after: 57. ♖h5

57... f5+

57... ♔d6 58. ♘f5++–

58. ♘xf5 ♘ed5 59. ♘g7+ ♔d6 60. ♖h6+ ♔c7 61. ♘e6+ ♔b8 62. ♘xc5

Position after: 62. ♘xc5

Black has lost all his pawns. The game is over.

62... ♔a7 63. ♔d4 ♘c7 64. ♖h7 ♔b8 65. ♔c4 ♘c6 66. ♖h6

White will trade the knight. Black resigned.

1-0

Game 73

♙ Alekhine, Alexander
♟ Teichmann, Richard
Berlin 1921

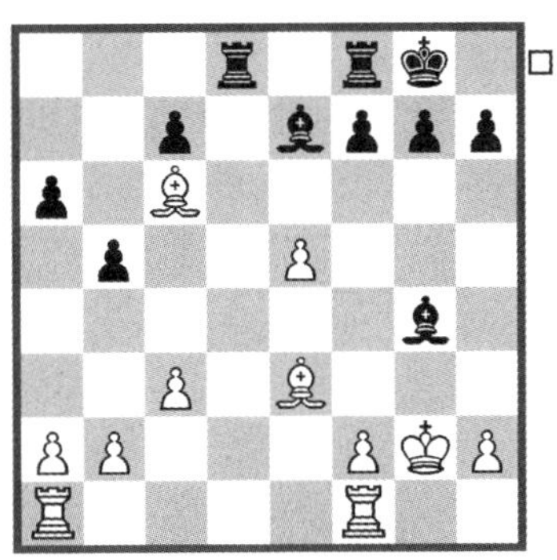

White is better. He has the better structure. Naturally, White should activate his pieces and in the process exploit the weaknesses. Alekhine finds a direct approach. He activates the rook even without moving it and starts attacking immediately.

17. a4!

White strikes first. Due to the superior activity of the bishop on c6 Black cannot use the rooks properly and White doesn't waste time going for a direct attack. However, Black's reaction is also classy.

17... f6!

The fearless attacker Teichmann never liked to defend. He always pretended to go for the attack... or counter-attack.

17... b4 This would keep the a-file closed, but the pawn structure would be ruined. 18. cxb4 ♗xb4 19. ♖ac1 This must be preferable for White.

18. axb5

Suddenly, the white king would be in trouble if White captures on f6. 18. exf6? ♖xf6 This is unpleasant with the idea of ...♖g6.

18... axb5 19. ♗xb5 fxe5 20. ♗c4+

(see diagram next column)

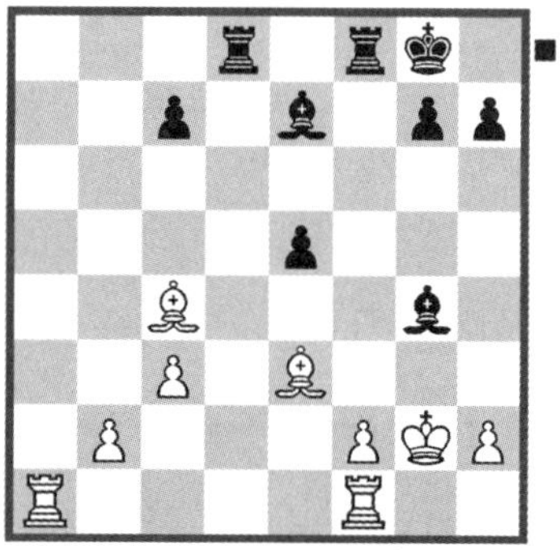

Position after: 20. ♗c4+

Keeping the king as far as possible from the center and removing the bishop from the b-file, making the move ...♖b8 useless.

20... ♔h8 21. f3 ♗h5 22. ♖a5

White has managed to trade his weak e5-pawn against Black's queenside – all the weak pawns are gone. Several new weak pawns have been created: c7, e5, f3. With his last move White attacks the pawn on e5 and is ready to play ♗c5 at some point, securing the perfect place for the rook. However it is Black's turn and he immediately notes that White also has weaknesses.

22... ♖d1! 23. ♗d5!

An exclamation mark is given because this was the only chance for White to play for a win. Furthermore the idea is that even if it was not enough to win the game, it is still amazing. Not many players would have found this possibility – Alekhine finds one of the most beautiful ideas ever.

A) 23. ♖xd1 ♗xf3+ 24. ♔g1 ♗xd1 25. ♖xe5 ♗d6 This would not have satisfied White – Alekhine definitely wanted more than a draw.

B) 23. ♖xe5 ♖xf1 24. ♔xf1 ♖xf3+

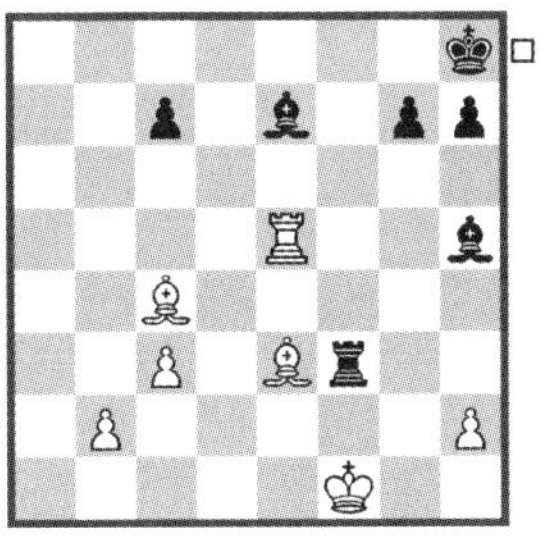

Position after: 24... ♖xf3+

25. ♔g2 ♗d6 This is also drawish.

23... ♖xf1 24. ♔xf1 ♗xf3 25. ♗xf3 ♖xf3+ 26. ♔e2 ♖f8

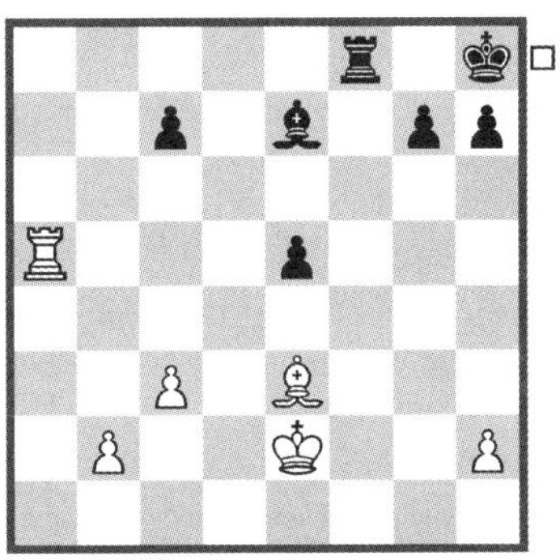

Position after: 26... ♖f8

27. ♔d3!

What a miracle! What is the point? The point is that the pawn on e5 simply blocks the black bishop, causing a mess in Black's camp. The rest of the game confirms Alekhine's idea. White simply wants to set his king on e4, and after establishing control over the entire center, to advance the queenside pawns. It is, by the way, important that the white bishop is dark-squared, so that the endgame with the bishop and h-pawn is winning – Black cannot simply sacrifice his bishop to eliminate the white queenside pawns.

27. ♖xe5 ♗d6 28. ♖h5 g6 Centralizing the black king would give Black an easy draw.

27... ♔g8?!

27... e4+ This was better, although White benefits by capturing the pawn back, at the same time centralizing his king. 28. ♔xe4 ♗d6 29. h3 After this White is better, but Black is probably able to hold without particular problems.

28. ♔e4

Position after: 28. ♔e4

28... ♖b8?

A bad move. Black cannot stop the white pawns by keeping the rook in front of them. White's centralized army easily supports the pawn majority. It would have been better to continue with the king's centralization.

28... ♔f7!

29. b4 ♔f7 30. b5 ♔e6 31. c4

Everything is going smoothly. Evidently Black's counter-action on the kingside is late and he must take care with the queenside.

31... ♔d7 32. ♖a7 ♗d6?

This is the final mistake and the position is lost.

32... ♔d6 This was much better instead, with a more resistant defense. A draw should be the expected result.

33. ♔d5

White could also have won with 33. b6, using the moment to advance this pawn due to the pin.

33... e4 34. b6!

(see diagram next column)

Of course, the pawn on e4 is not important.

Position after: 34. b6!

34... ♖f8 35. c5 ♖f5+ 36. ♔c4

Black resigned.

1-0

Game 74

♙	Karpov, Anatoly	(2710)
♟	Sokolov, Andrei	(2645)
🌍	Linares 1987	

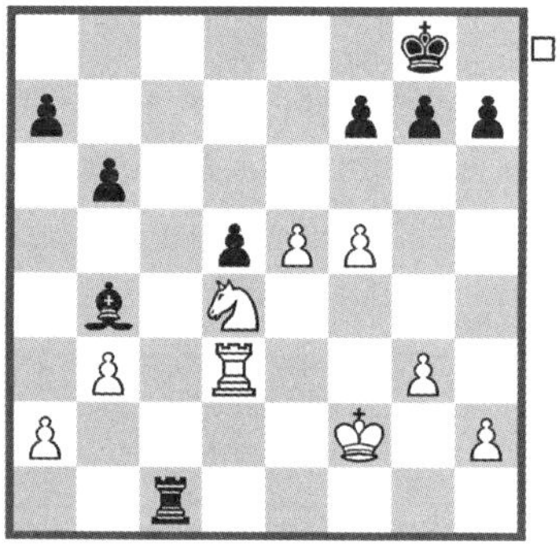

In this position White is slightly better due to his influential knight and more compact structure. Of course White has better harmony – his pieces collaborate perfectly, together controlling a wide spectrum of central squares. There is a space advantage as well, which White underlines with his next move.

28. g4 ♔f8 29. ♔f3 ♖f1+ 30. ♔g3 ♖c1 31. ♔f4 h6

Black decides to fight against White's activity and expansion.

32. h4

Continuing to expand, of course.

32... ♔e8 33. ♘f3

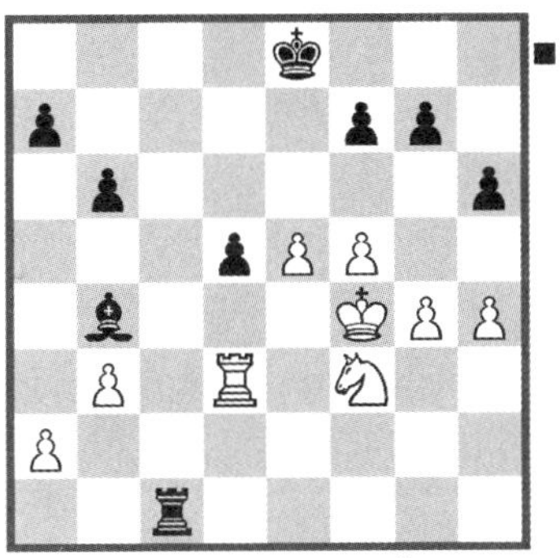

Position after: 33. ♘f3

33... ♖c2

33... ♖c5 This looks more logical. 34. g5 Keeping the advantage for White.

34. a4

Of course, White declines the exchange of pawns – the pawn on d5 is a weak one.

34... ♖b2 35. ♘d4 ♗e7 36. h5

Karpov instructively fixes the black pawns on the bishop's color.

36... a6

Position after: 36... a6

37. ♔f3!

This is a typical Karpov move. The king belongs on a light square, at the same time the f4-square is liberated for the knight.

37... ♗c5 38. ♘e2 d4 39. ♘f4 ♔d7 40. e6+!

Not often do we see Karpov playing direct chess.

40... ♔e8

40... fxe6 41. ♘xe6 This leads to the loss of the g7-pawn.

41. ♔e4

It is time to activate the king.

41... a5

Position after: 41... a5

Voluntarily setting the pawn on a dark square, but eliminating the threat of White's strike with a5.

42. ♖f3 ♖b1 43. ♘d5 ♖g1

It looks like Black has achieved a lot. However White found a nice tactic.

44. ♔d3! ♖xg4?

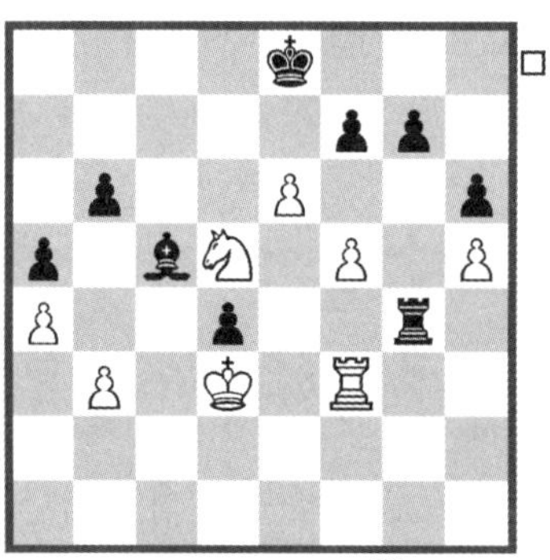

Position after: 44... ♖xg4?

A) 44... ♖d1+ This was a better option. 45. ♔c4 ♖c1+ 46. ♔b5

Position after: 46. ♔b5

46... ♖e1 Black can still fight.

B) 44... ♔f8 This would also have been better, although 45. ♖f4 keeps a big advantage.

45. f6!

This was probably missed by Black.

45... ♗d6

Alternatively 45... fxe6 46. f7+ ♔d7 [46... ♔f8 47. ♘c7] 47. ♘xb6+ followed by 48. ♘c4 looks winning.

46. ♘xb6 ♖g5 47. fxg7

White finally simplifies the position by transferring to a winning endgame.

47... ♖xg7 48. ♘c4 ♗b4 49. exf7+ ♖xf7 50. ♖xf7 ♔xf7

(see diagram next page)

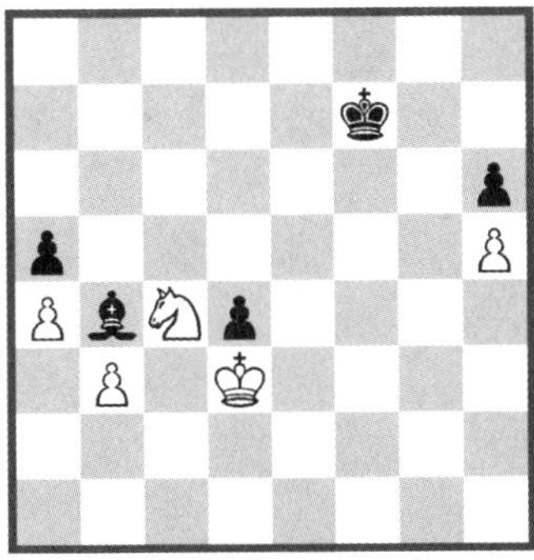

Position after: 50... ♔xf7

51. ♘e5+!

Further proof that Karpov's endgame technique must often be analyzed.

51... ♔f6 52. ♘c6 ♗e1 53. ♘xd4

The endgame is technically winning for White, but some technical issues are still present.

53... ♗b4 54. ♘c6 ♗e1 55. ♔e2 ♗c3 56. ♔d3 ♗e1

Position after: 56... ♗e1

57. ♔c4

Finally Karpov goes for the win. He has calculated precisely.

57... ♔g5 58. ♘xa5! ♗xa5 59. b4 ♗d8 60. a5 ♔xh5 61. ♔b5 ♗g5 62. a6

Position after: 62. a6

62... ♗e3 63. ♔c6

1-0

Game 75

♙	Petrosian, Tigran V	(2605)
♟	Ivkov, Borislav	(2480)
	Bugojno 1982	

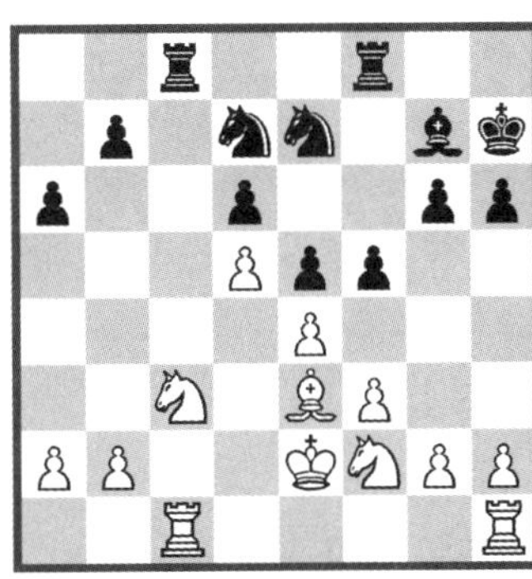

White is better due to the gained space and the conventionally better bishop. Petrosian rationally opts for simplifications – his rooks are not better, but his minor pieces are! He uses a fine maneuver in the manner of Karpov.

19. ♘b1!

The knight would not find happiness on a4, thus it goes via a3 to c4. Black's reaction ...b5 would be a serious weakening.

19... ♖xc1 20. ♖xc1 ♖c8

Generally the side suffering with space problems should reduce their material.

21. ♘a3 ♖xc1 22. ♗xc1 h5

Black's response is logical – he wants to activate his worst piece.

22... b5 This would weaken the a6-pawn and c6-squares which can be exploited with 23. ♘c2 followed by ♘b4.

23. ♘c4 ♘c8

A good defensive position for the knight.

24. ♗d2 ♗f6

(see diagram next column)

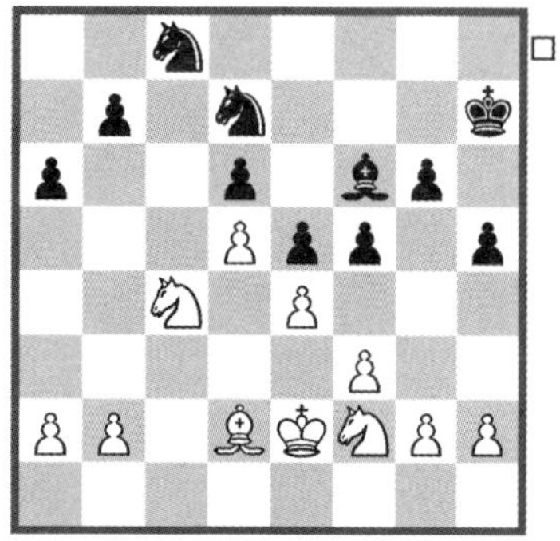

Position after: 24... ♗f6

25. ♘a5!

White provokes new light-squared weaknesses and further restricts the black cavalry.

25... b6 26. ♘c6 ♔g7 27. ♗e3 ♔f7 28. ♘d3 ♔e8 29. a4 ♗d8

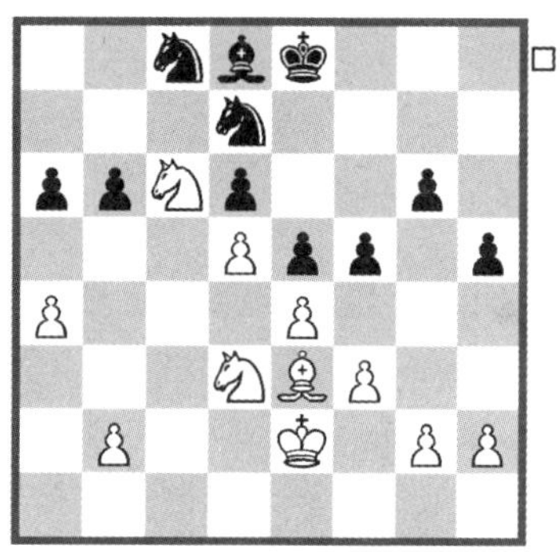

Position after: 29... ♗d8

30. ♘db4

White creates new weaknesses in Black's camp and the game is practically over.

30... a5 31. ♘a2 f4

An act of desperation. Black wants to focus all his defensive resources on the queenside. Alas, the kingside will not be firmly closed – White would be able to capitalize even there.

32. ♗f2 g5 33. ♔d3

The king itself joins in the devastating attack. All the pieces, including the king, should collaborate in the endgame.

33... ♘f8 34. h3 ♘g6 35. ♘c3 ♗f6 36. ♔c4

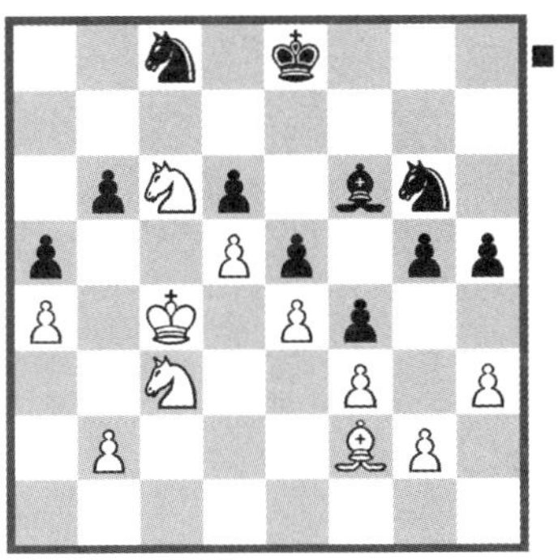

Position after: 36. ♔c4

36... ♔d7 37. ♔b5 ♔c7 38. ♔a6 g4

Desperation.

39. hxg4 hxg4 40. fxg4 ♗h4

(see diagram next column)

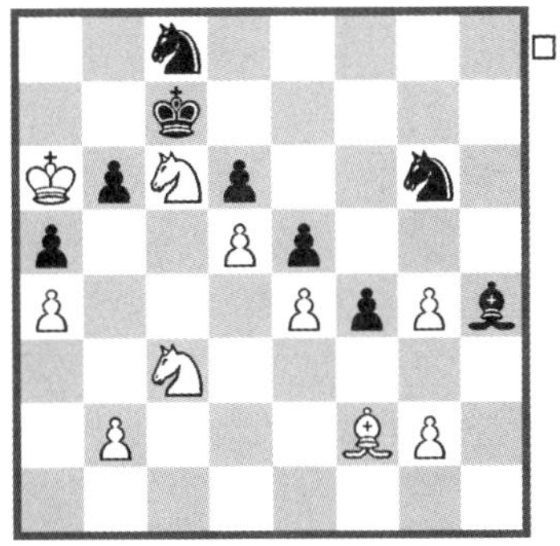

Position after: 40... ♗h4

41. ♘d1

White simplifies the position leading the game toward an inevitable zugzwang.

41. ♗g1 This would also have been winning.

41... ♗xf2 42. ♘xf2 ♘ce7 43. ♘xe7 ♘xe7 44. g5

Position after: 44. g5

44... ♘g6 45. ♘g4 ♘h4 46. ♔a7 ♘g6 47. ♘h2 ♘h4 48. ♘f3 ♘g6 49. b3 ♘f8

1-0

Game 76

♙ Gonzales, R.
♟ Delchev, A.
Spain 2009

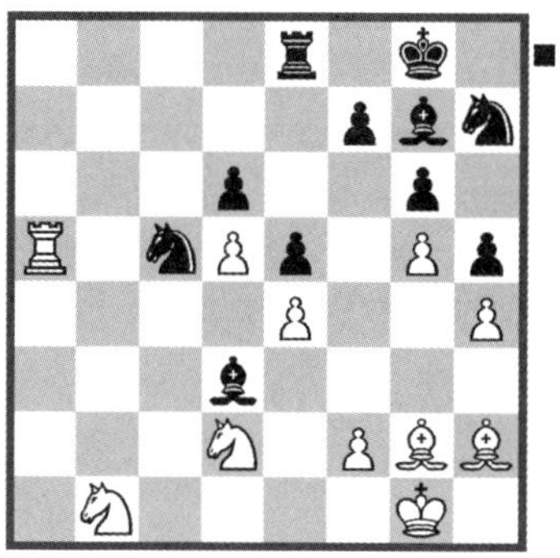

One may say that this is a boring position and a dead draw. Analyzing it more deeply, it will become apparent that White lacks harmony. The bishops are poorly placed and not targeting anything important. Black, with better pieces, should opt for active play. In any case, all the pawns are on one side which drastically improves White's chances for a draw.

30... f6!

An excellent move. Black creates a significant advantage on the kingside – the passed pawn on the h-file. He is not afraid to reduce the pawn material.

31. gxf6 ♗xf6

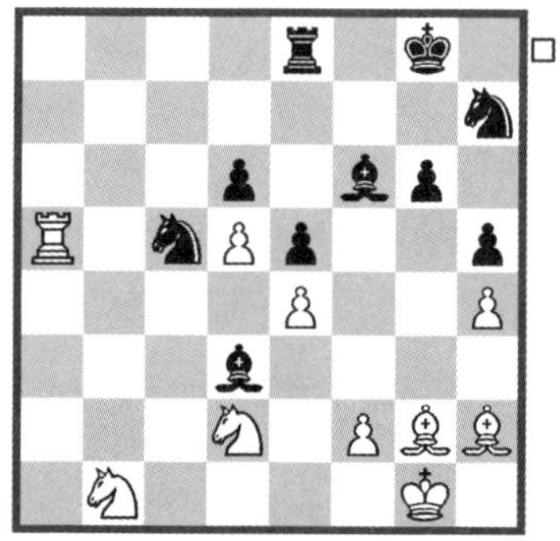

Position after: 31... ♗xf6

32. ♗g3?

32. ♘a3! This would have been better, with the idea to activate his pieces at any cost – an engine move. However it is probably hard to find. 32... ♗xh4 33. ♘ac4 ♗e7 34. ♗xe5! Now this would have given White enough compensation and activity with a draw as the most probable result. However White was not ready to take drastic measures.

32... g5 33. f3

33. hxg5 ♗xg5 This does not change anything. Black dominates.

33... ♖b8 34. ♘c3 gxh4 35. ♗f2 ♗g5

(see diagram next page)

Surprisingly, Black is already winning. White's pieces are hidden behind the pawn wall with no activity.

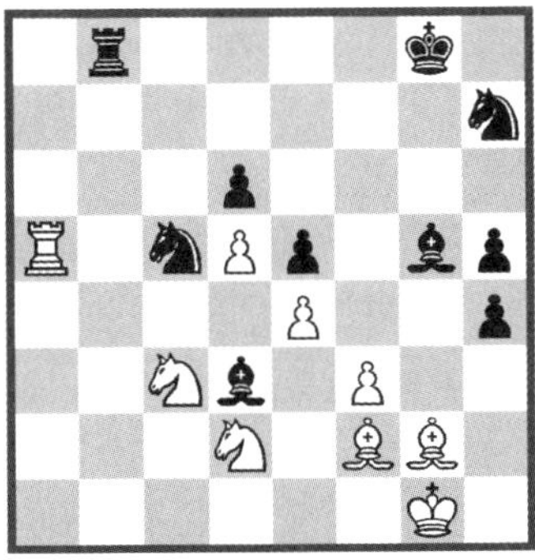

Position after: 35... ♗g5

36. ♘f1 ♘b3 37. ♖a3 ♘d4 38. ♘h2

White must not take the knight.

38... ♖c8 39. ♘a2 ♘e2+

Position after: 39... ♘e2+

White's position is tragicomical.

40. ♔h1 ♗b1 41. ♗f1 ♘g3+ 42. ♔g2 ♗d2

Getting another knight ready to join the attack via the liberated g5-square.

43. ♗d3

This exchange will not help White.

43... ♗xd3 44. ♖xd3 ♖c2

Position after: 44... ♖c2

A decisive invasion.

45. ♖xd2 ♖xd2 46. ♘b4 ♘f8 47. ♘f1 ♘xf1 48. ♔xf1 h3 49. ♘c6 h2 50. ♘e7+ ♔f7

0-1

Game 77

♙	Delchev, Aleksander	(2600)
♟	Lehnert, Michael	(2025)
🌍	Lugano 2007	

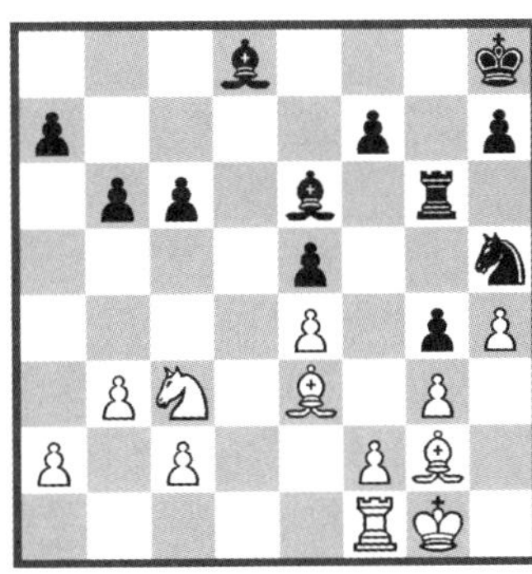

The next example is from the praxis of a strong Bulgarian grandmaster. Black's pieces (rook and knight) are stuck on the kingside and White immediately uses this fact to strike on the opposite side.

26. a4!

An excellent and logical decision. There is a clear threat to crush Black's queenside structure.

26... ♘f6

Black relocates his pieces.

26... a5 This should have been preferred. However, White can continue to press strongly after the following. 27. ♖d1 ♗c7 28. ♗f1! The idea is ♗c4.

27. a5 ♘d7 28. axb6 axb6

It appears that the rook could not be relocated quickly. White invades.

29. ♖a1 h5 30. ♖a7 ♖g8 31. ♘a2?!

Position after: 31. ♘a2?!

An imprecise move which wastes time.

31. ♗f1 Correct, with the idea of the above-mentioned ♗c4.

31... c5?

31... ♗e7! This prevents ♘b4 and opens up the 8th rank for the rook. White would have serious problems to convert.

32. ♘c3?!

32. ♗b5! ♘b8 33. ♗b5+- This is better instead.

32... f5?

An act of desperation.

32... ♘b8 This would prolong resistance. However after 33. ♘d5 I think the result would be the same.

33. exf5 ♗xf5 34. ♗e4! ♗xe4 35. ♘xe4 ♘b8 36. c3

Position after: 36. c3

A very fine move "in advance".

36... ♘c6 37. ♖d7 ♘b8 38. ♖f7 ♖e8 39. ♘d6

Black resigned. Heavy material loss is inevitable.

1-0

Game 78

♙ Smeets, Jan (2632)
♟ Beliavsky, Alexander G (2662)
Amsterdam 2009

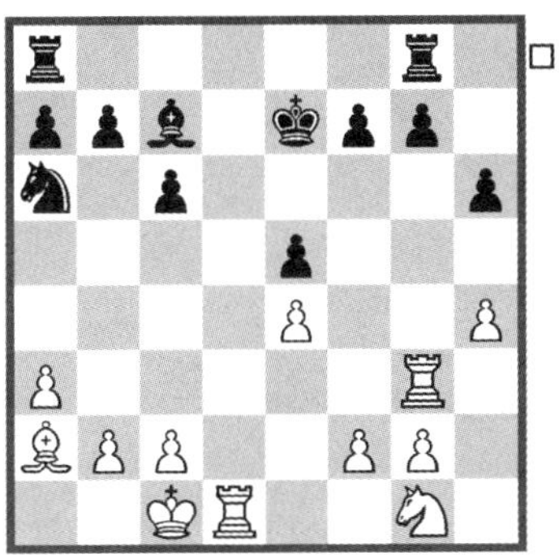

White is evidently better because of his better-placed pieces. Perhaps it is not obvious at the moment, but the white bishop is much better than its counterpart – a very important and often key factor in positions with opposite-colored bishops. White's bishop collaborates better with the other pieces and can present more threats than Black's. In particular, after White's next excellent move the black minor pieces become worse.

18. b4!

An excellent move which every true master would make automatically. Black's knight and bishop are restricted now. The knight would remain out of play until the end.

18... g6 19. ♘f3

Preparing h5 with a possible ♘h4. Furthermore, the knight can be used on the queenside.

19... ♖ad8

Black wants to trade White's "active" rook. In actual fact, the active rook is on the other side.

20. ♖xd8 ♖xd8 21. h5!

Crushing Black's kingside.

21... g5

21... gxh5 This is met with the following. 22. ♖g7 ♖f8 23. ♖h7 Black's kingside is about to collapse.

22. ♘d2

22. ♘h2! A precise way to reactivate the knight. This can be done via g4 with tempo. Furthermore, the maneuver ♖f3-f6 may also take place.

22... ♗b6

22... ♖f8 This was better, with the idea after 23.♖f3 to have g4!.

23. ♖f3

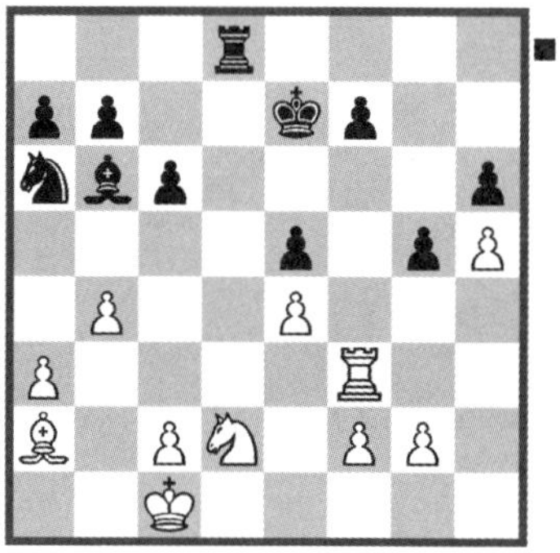

Position after: 23. ♖f3

Not only defending the pawn but also liberating the g3-spot for the knight. White's rook is an active one!

23... f6 24. ♘f1 g4

Black is already lost and he tries to change the character of the game. Alas, there is nothing that he can do.

25. ♖g3 ♗xf2 26. ♖xg4 ♖d7 27. ♖g7+!

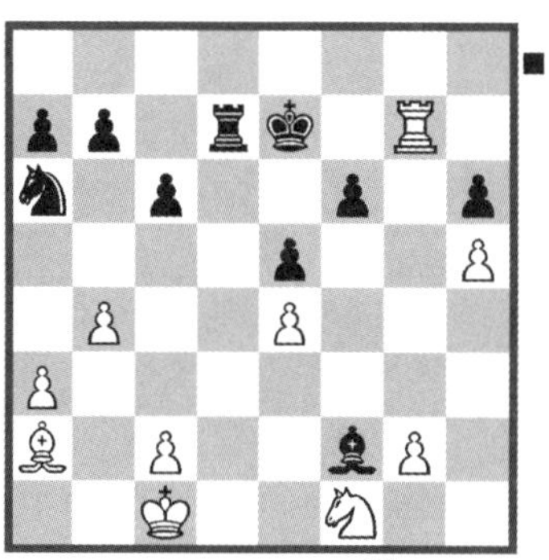

Position after: 27. ♖g7+!

27... ♔d8 28. ♖g6 ♗h4 29. ♔b2 ♗g5 30. ♘h2

Alternatively 30. ♘g3 with ♘f5 is good too, of course.

30... ♖d1

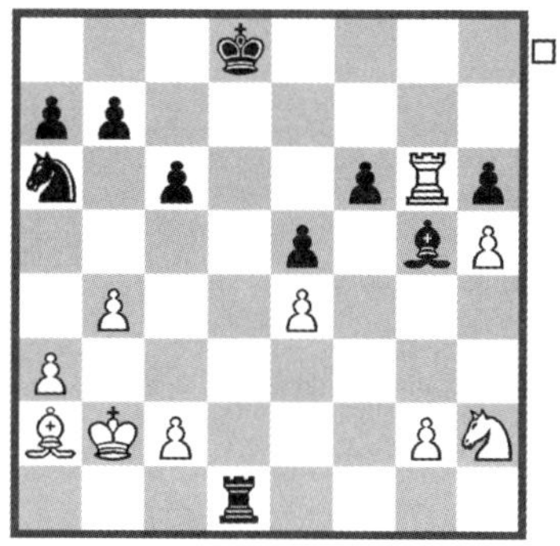

Position after: 30... ♖d1

31. ♘g4?

31. ♗e6 Necessary.

31... ♗c1+ 32. ♔b3

Now the white bishop is closed in and Black has got enough activity.

32... ♖e1 33. ♘xh6 ♖e3+ 34. c3 ♖e2!

(see diagram next page)

White's king is in trouble.

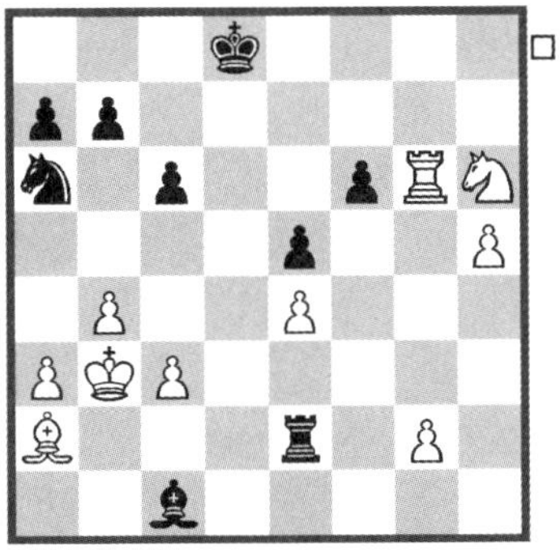

Position after: 34... ♖e2!

35. ♖g8+ ♔c7 36. ♖g7+ ♔b6 37. ♘f5 ♘c7?

A fatal mistake.

A) 37... ♘c5+!! Perhaps in time trouble Black missed this powerful move.

Position after: 37... ♘c5+!!

38. bxc5+ [38. ♔c4?? ♖xe4+–+] 38... ♔xc5 This leads to a draw after the inevitable ...♖b2. You may find the possible continuations yourself to be sure of the draw.

B) 37... ♖b2+?? 38. ♔c4 ♖xa2 39. ♘d6+–

38. ♘d6

38. a4

Position after: 38. a4

This would also give the win after, for instance, the following line. 38... ♖b2+ [38... ♘e6 39. a5+ ♔a6 40. ♖e7+–] 39. ♔c4 ♖xa2 40. a5+ ♔a6 41. ♖xc7

38... ♘b5

38... ♖b2+ 39. ♔c4 ♘b5

Position after: 39... ♘b5

This loses after the following. 40. ♖xb7+ ♔a6 41. ♖xb5 cxb5+ 42. ♔c5 ♖xa2 43. ♔c6! White has a study win after ♘xb5.

39. ♘c4+ ♔a6 40. ♗b1

1-0

Game 79

♙ Smyslov, Vassily V
♟ Polugaevsky, Lev
Palma de Mallorca 1970

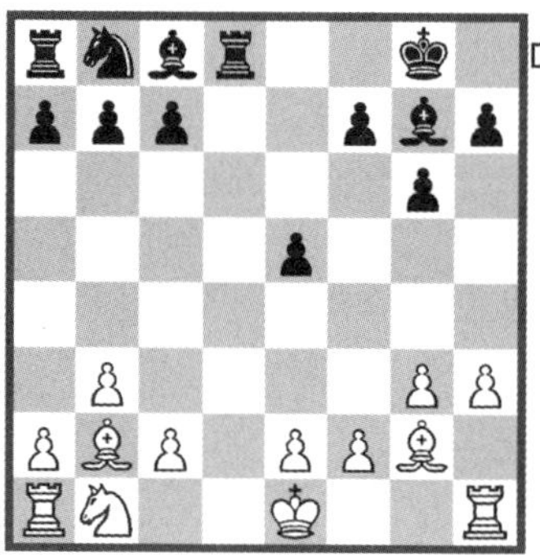

It may appear that Black is without problems, but Smyslov managed to demonstrate that White is actually dominating. Black cannot easily activate the queenside pieces due to pressure on the b7-spot and is forced sooner or later to play ...c6. This is why White does not go on to place his knight on c3 where it would be restricted and block the bishop.

11. ♘d2!

The knight aims for the c4- or e4-squares. At the same time White prepares to long castle – the fastest way to activate his rooks.

11... ♘d7

A) 11... ♘c6 This is less flexible and allows White to capture it with a huge advantage.

B) 11... ♘a6 This also has its logic but White is undisputedly much better after the following. 12. 0-0-0 c6 13. ♘c4

12. 0-0-0 ♖e8

12... ♘f8 13. ♘c4

13. ♘c4 ♘b6

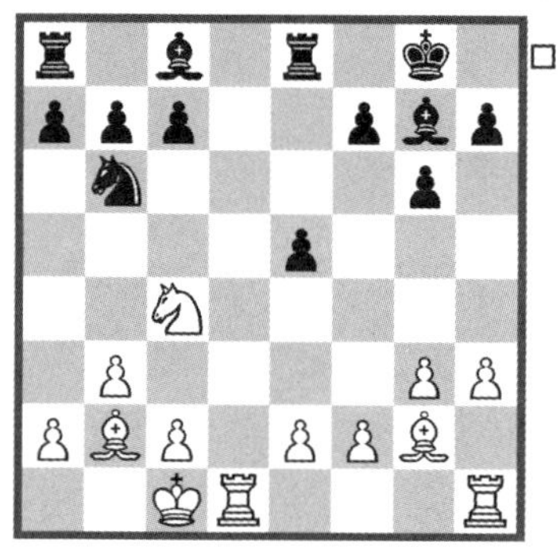

Position after: 13... ♘b6

14. ♘a5

The knight from here puts strong pressure on Black's queenside. A similar approach will be seen in the next two games. At the same time Tarrasch's quote about the bad knight on b6 will be proven.

14... ♖b8 15. ♖d2 c6

Black prepares to activate the c8-bishop, but after White's next move there is nothing that Black can do with it.

16. ♖hd1 f6

Preparing to centralize the king.

17. ♖d8

Clearly infiltrating.

17... ♔f7 18. ♖xe8 ♔xe8 19. ♗a3

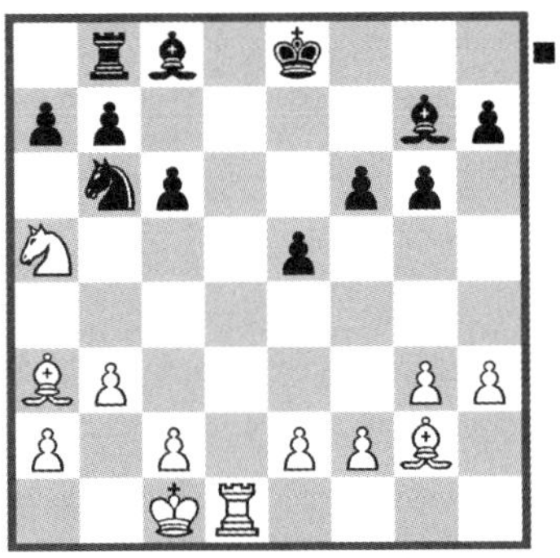

Position after: 19. ♗a3

19... ♘d5

An act of desperation. Black wants to reduce the activity of the white pieces by giving up a pawn.

19... ♗e6 This loses after 20. ♗d6.

20. ♗d6 ♖a8 21. c4 ♘e7 22. ♗c7 f5

22... ♗e6 This is not the lesser evil. 23. ♘xb7 Black is dead lost without a pawn together with his badly-placed pieces and a damaged queenside structure.

23. ♖d8+ ♔f7

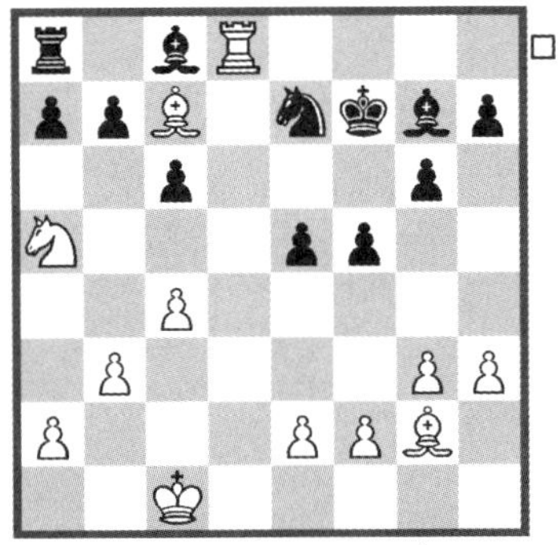

Position after: 23... ♔f7

24. c5

White prevents any possibility of playing ...b6 and opens the route for the knight toward d6. With such passive pieces Black is hopeless.

24... ♘d5 25. ♗d6 ♗f6 26. ♖f8+ ♔g7

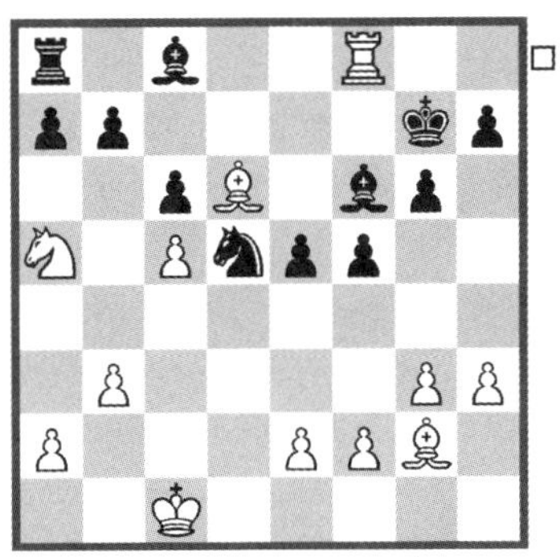

Position after: 26... ♔g7

27. ♘c4?!

27. ♗xd5 cxd5 28. b4 This would have led to a direct win. Black is unable to oppose the crushing attack on the queenside.

27... e4

Black closes the diagonal.

28. f3

... But only for a moment.

28... exf3 29. ♗xf3 ♗g5+ 30. ♔d1

The king goes to the safe zone. The loss of the a2-pawn is irrelevant.

30... ♘c3+ 31. ♔e1 ♘b5

31... ♘xa2 32. ♘e5+–

32. ♖e8 ♔f7 33. ♖h8 ♗f6

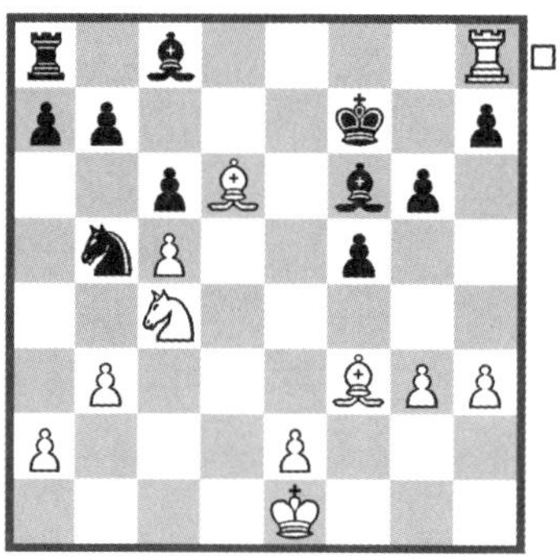

Position after: 33... ♗f6

34. ♘e5+!

34. ♖xh7+?? ♔g8

34... ♔g7 35. ♖e8 h5 36. e3

There is no reason to rush anywhere.

36... ♘c3 37. ♘xc6! bxc6 38. ♗xc6 ♗b7 39. ♖xa8 ♗xc6 40. ♖xa7+

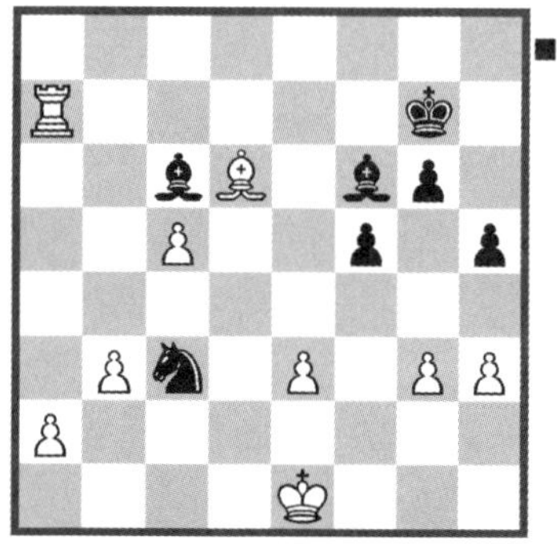

Position after: 40. ♖xa7+

40... ♔g8 41. ♖a6 ♗d5 42. c6 ♘e4 43. c7 ♗b7 44. ♖a8+ ♔f7 45. ♗b4

Black resigned.

1-0

Game 80

♙	Eingorn, Vereslav S	(2470)
♟	Dolmatov, Sergey	(2535)
🌍	Tashkent 1980	

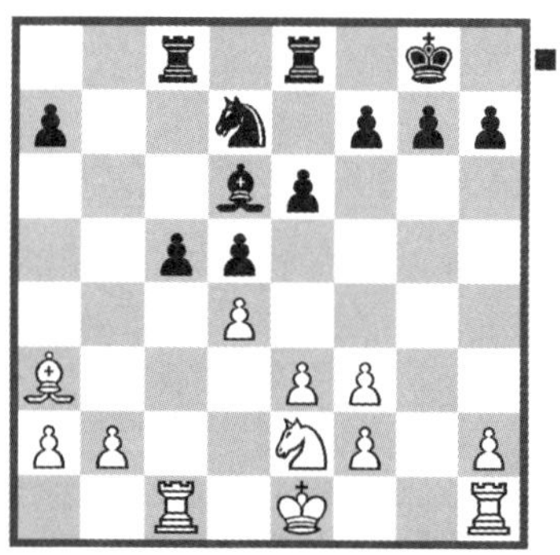

There is an interesting situation on this diagram. Black has better development; White's king is still in the center, but there will be no comfort. Black's current queenside action is stopped due to the pinned c5-pawn. Black definitely needs to find a way to capitalize on his better development. It is time to go for the initiative, as follows.

17... e5! 18. dxc5

A) 18. dxe5? ♘xe5 Black will dominate thanks to the attack on the d3- and f3-squares.

B) 18. 0-0 Black has the following. 18... exd4 19. ♘xd4 ♗f8 20. ♘b3 c4 Black has some initiative.

18... ♗xc5 19. ♗xc5 ♘xc5 20. ♔d2

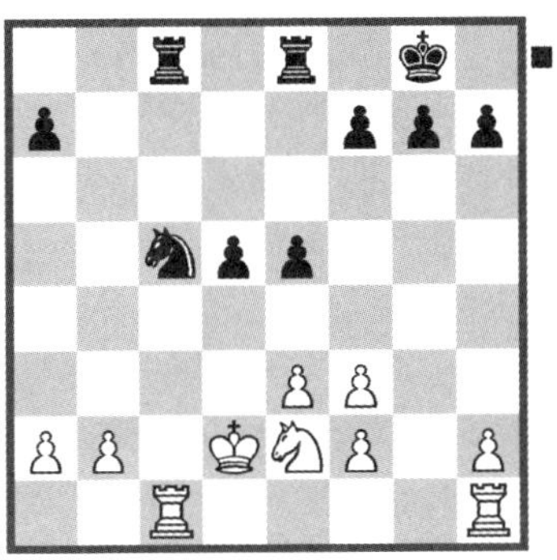

Position after: 20. ♔d2

20... e4!?

Consistently striving to gain the initiative. Black bravely secures the d3-spot for the knight, allowing the d4-spot for its white counterpart.

21. ♘d4 ♘d3 22. ♖xc8 ♖xc8 23. ♔e2

(see diagram next column)

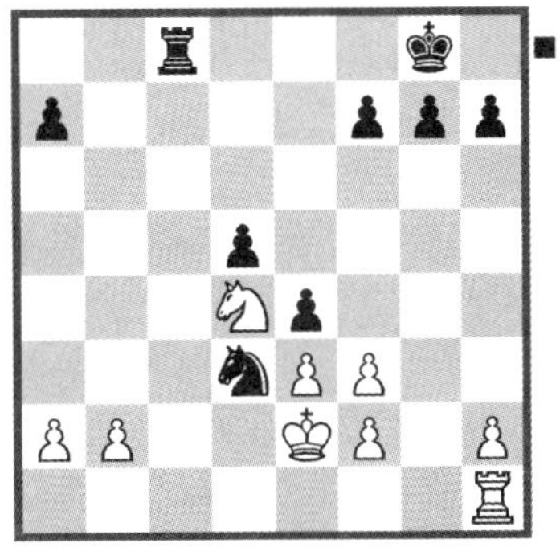

Position after: 23. ♔e2

Also deserving serious attention is the following line. 23. f4!? ♘xf2 24. ♖b1 The queenside pawns are directly advancing.

23... g6?!

23... ♘xb2 24. ♖b1 ♘a4 25. ♖b7 ♘c3+ This would give winning chances.

24. fxe4 dxe4 25. ♖b1

25. b3!? A serious alternative, with the idea to keep the rook active.

25... f5 26. h4 ♔g7

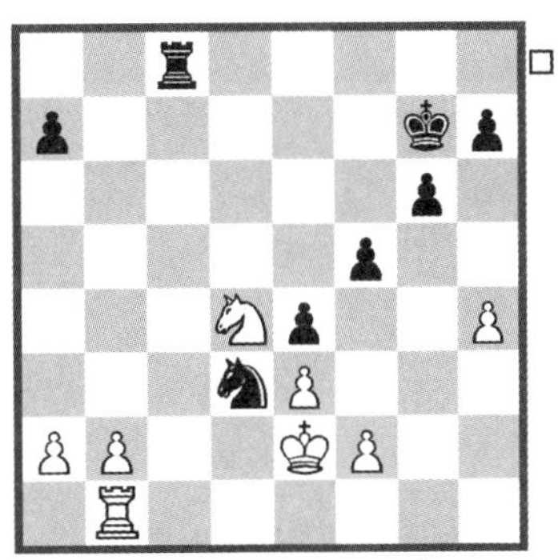

Position after: 26... ♔g7

27. f4?

A mistake. This natural-looking move leads to a lost endgame.

27. a4 It was better to launch the majority.

27... ♔h6!

I think White simply missed this possibility.

28. ♔d2 ♔h5 29. b4

Too late and too slow.

29... ♔xh4 30. ♖h1+ ♔g3 31. ♖xh7 ♘xb4 32. ♖g7

Position after: 32. ♖g7

The observer may come to the conclusion that White is almost ok. However Black's next powerful response refutes that observation.

32... ♔f2! 33. ♖xg6 ♖d8!

Black finds an amazing tactical possibility to end the game. Tactics often serve strategy: play healthy and logical moves and you can expect tactical help.

34. ♖h6 ♖xd4+! 35. exd4 e3+ 36. ♔c3 ♘d5+ 37. ♔c4 ♘xf4 38. d5

Position after: 38. d5

White's counterplay is too slow and Black easily finishes the job.

38... e2 39. ♖h1 e1=♕ 40. ♖xe1 ♔xe1 41. d6 ♔d2 42. ♔d4 ♘e6+

Position after: 42... ♘e6+

43. ♔e5 ♘c5 44. ♔xf5 ♔c3 45. ♔f6 a5 46. ♔e5 a4 47. ♔d5 ♘d7

0-1

6

Space Advantage

First I wish to remind you about a fact related to the middlegame. If you have "more space" that still does not mean that you have a "space advantage" – you will have a space advantage only when your opponent suffers with lack of space, when his pieces hinder each other.

As regards the endgame, you can come to the conclusion yourself – because of the reduced piece and pawn material there are fewer chances to obtain a position with a "space advantage" for one side.

Other principles are valid in the same way as for middlegames: having a space advantage will give you a comfortable situation to play on both wings, probably without any rush; if you have a space advantage you should generally avoid reducing material, etc. Everything will become clear after this chapter.

Game 81

♙ Ceasarjulius (2286)
♟ Zlatanovic, Boroljub (2348)
Playchess 2015

Black is absolutely dominant due to his space advantage and safer pawn structure. The pawns on the queenside are fixed in Black's favor and White has a problem with his c4-pawn. However, the pawns on the kingside are fixed in White's favor.

The key for Black to access the position here is to advance the kingside pawns – Black will break the blockade and unfix the pawns. White is unable to oppose this plan. Although this was an internet blitz game, one should still follow strategic concepts and principles.

32... ♗e6 33. ♘b2 g5!

Before White plays h4 this move should be played first.

34. ♔d2 ♔f6 35. h3

Position after: 35. h3

35... f4!

With a fully active army it is time to strike. White has an unpleasant dilemma: to allow the strong ...f4-f3 or to unfix the kingside pawns and unleash the great kinetic energy of the black phalanx.

36. ♔c3

36. exf4 gxf4 This is also hopeless for White. Can you work out the winning plan for Black?

36... f3! 37. ♗f1 fxg2 38. ♗xg2 ♗f5

Black's next phase is obvious – advance the pawn to h4 and then ...g4 would create a dangerous h-passer. The game is already over.

39. a5 h5 40. axb6 axb6 41. ♘a4 ♘d7 42. ♔b3

There is nothing that White can achieve on the queenside.

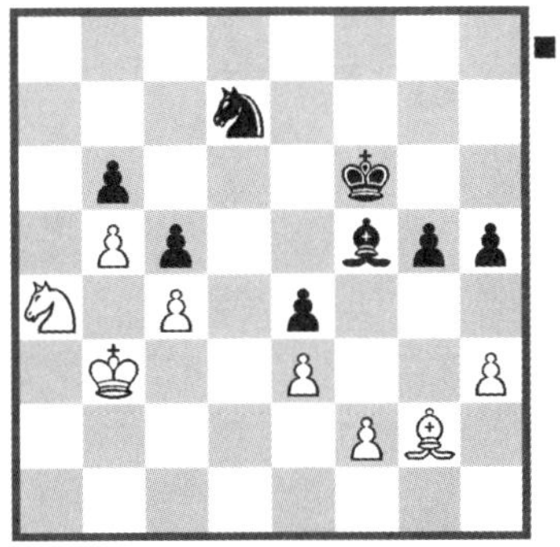

Position after: 42. ♔b3

42... ♔e5 43. ♘c3 h4 44. ♘d5 g4

Smoothly following a simple plan.

45. hxg4 ♗xg4 46. ♘c3 ♗f5 47. ♘d5 h3 48. ♗h1 h2 49. ♘f4

Position after: 49. ♘f4

49... ♗g4

The bishop comes to f3 and White should resign.

50. ♔c3 ♗f3 51. ♘g2 ♘f6 52. ♔d2 ♘g4 53. ♔e1 ♔f6 54. ♔f1 ♘e5

0-1

Game 82

♙ Tikhomirova
♟ Morozova
Kiev 1966

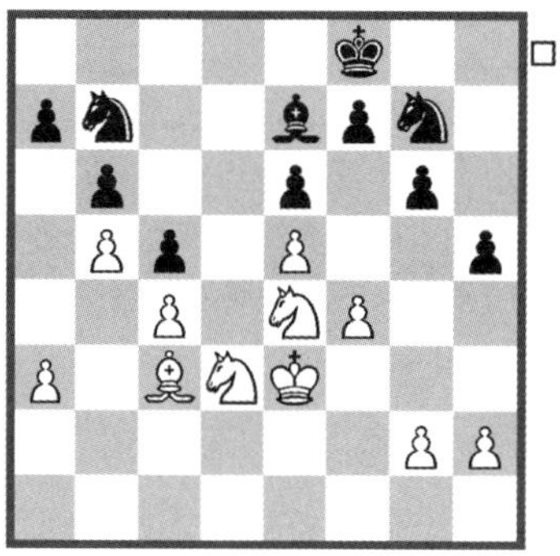

The first stage is clear – White should advance the a-pawn. As a coach, I love this game. This is one more reason why you should study games that are not often published or those of less well-known players.

In this multi-piece endgame with an opened d-file and fixed pawns on c4 and e5 against c5 and e6, White has a clear advantage here. There are not many options for Black against an expansion on the kingside. The advance ...f6 usually simply leads to positions with White's outside passer on the kingside. At the same time, Black's action on the queenside is never dangerous – it is not based on a space advantage!

1. ♘c1 ♘f5+ 2. ♔d3 ♔e8 3. a4 ♔d7 4. ♘b3 ♘h4 5. g3 ♘f5 6. a5 ♘d8

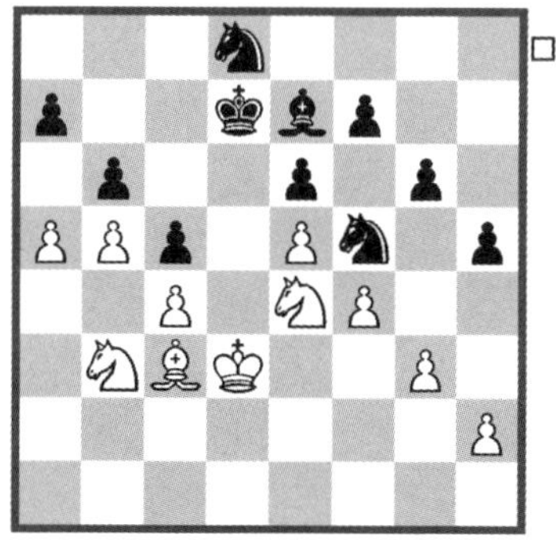

Position after: 6... ♘d8

7. a6!

Excellent. Capturing instead will create only one target – on b6. Now there are two targets – both a7 and b6; another reason is that the d8-knight is paralyzed now. The game is already over.

7... ♔c7 8. ♘bd2

Now White switches to the kingside. Expanding there and opening the position will leave Black with a much worse bishop.

8... ♔b8 9. ♘f6!

One of the many approaches here. The knight vacates e4 for its colleague.

9... ♘h6

9... ♗xf6 10. exf6 ♔c8 11. ♗e5 Black is hopeless. The sole active knight will be driven back with an easy win on the kingside utilizing all the troops.

10. ♘de4 ♔c7 11. ♘e8+

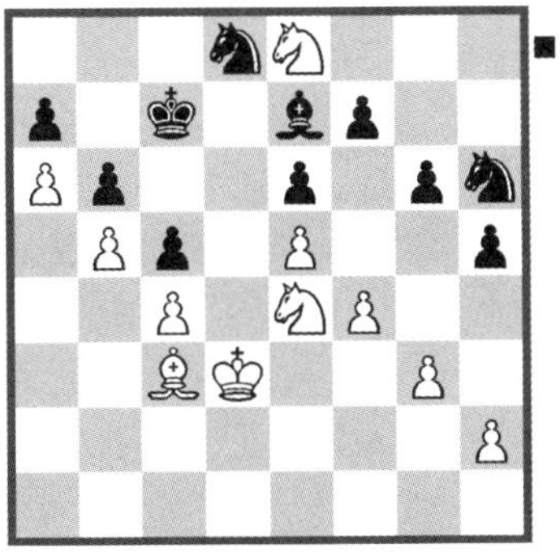

Position after: 11. ♘e8+

White's cavalry enjoys its invasion of Black's camp.

11... ♔d7 12. ♘4f6+ ♗xf6

Black has managed to force White's recapture with the knight. However that would not help him. He is simply a piece down.

13. ♘xf6+ ♔c7 14. h3 ♘f5 15. g4 hxg4 16. hxg4 ♘e7 17. ♘e4 ♔b8 18. ♗e1 ♘g8 19. ♗h4

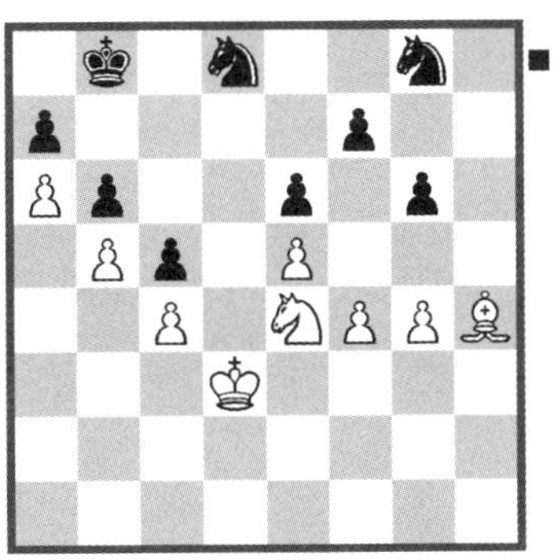

Position after: 19. ♗h4

19... ♔c7 20. ♔e3 ♔d7 21. ♔f3 ♔c7 22. ♘d6 f5

Position after: 22... f5

23. gxf5

Not a mistake, but it is an error in terms of method.

23. ♗g5 More principled. After the king goes deeper into the kingside White can decide whether to take or not.

23... gxf5

23... exf5 Optically better, but it does not change anything.

24. ♗g5 ♔d7 25. ♔g3

Position after: 25. ♔g3

The king invades. The game is over.

25... ♘e7 26. ♔h4 ♘g6+ 27. ♔h5 ♘e7 28. ♗xe7 ♔xe7 29. ♔g6

Black resigned. An absolutely brilliant endgame from the very first move.

1-0

Game 83

♙ Zlatanovic, Boroljub (2421)
♟ ChristophS (2237)
Playchess 2021

White is clearly better due to his evident space advantage. Moreover, the white bishop is better and so is the knight. The plan is also apparent – to aim for g5 and try to create a breakthrough on the kingside.

30. ♗c1 ♗c8 31. ♔g3 ♗d7 32. ♘d1

The knight goes toward a better spot – this could be g4 or g5.

32... ♘c7 33. ♘f2 ♘a6

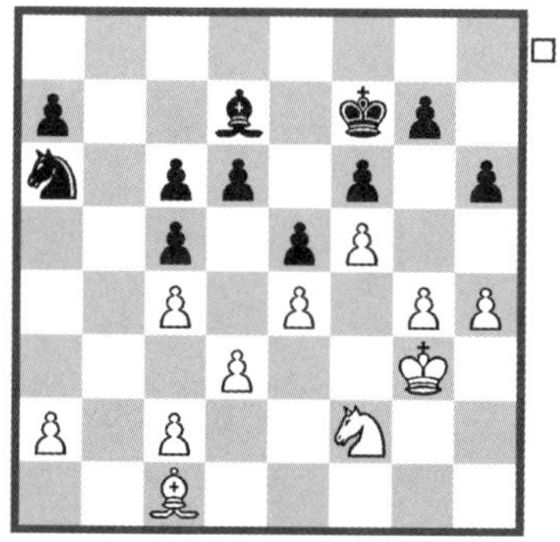

Position after: 33... ♘a6

34. a3

There is no need to rush. Black's knight must stay out of play.

34. ♗d2? ♘b4 35. ♗xb4 cxb4 This gives White nothing, of course.

34... ♘c7 35. g5?!

It is clear that sooner or later this must be played, but probably some preparation would have been better. This was a blitz game and I could not find any promising preparing maneuver.

35. ♗d2 Instead this should have been preferred – perhaps even with ♘h3 afterwards to prepare g5 and recapture with check.

35... d5??

A decisive mistake. Black must reduce the pawn material and gain some space on the kingside.

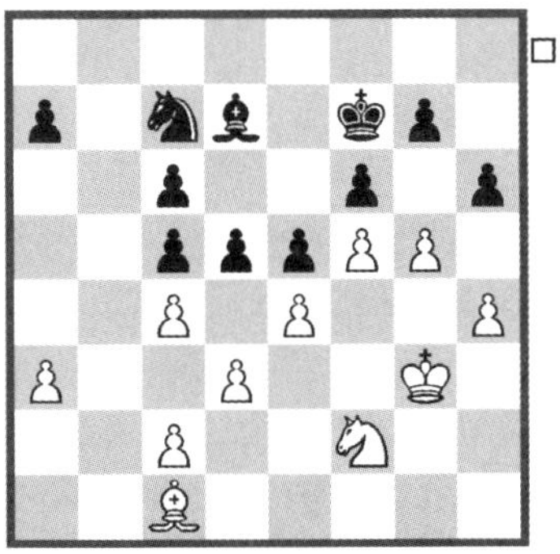

Position after: 35... d5??

A) 35... h5? 36. g6+ The h5-pawn falls with a decisive advantage.

B) 35... hxg5 36. hxg5 g6 This would give Black a safe position. His bishop would also start working.

36. g6+!

I think this is even better than capturing the pawn for free. Now the sacrifice on h6 becomes inevitable and the game is over.

36. gxh6 gxh6 37. ♗xh6 d4 White would still need to work to convert.

36... ♔f8 37. ♔g4 dxc4

38. ♗e3

38. dxc4 This also wins, but I preferred to invade with the bishop.

38... cxd3 39. ♗xc5+ ♔e8 40. cxd3 ♘b5 41. ♔h5

(see diagram next column)

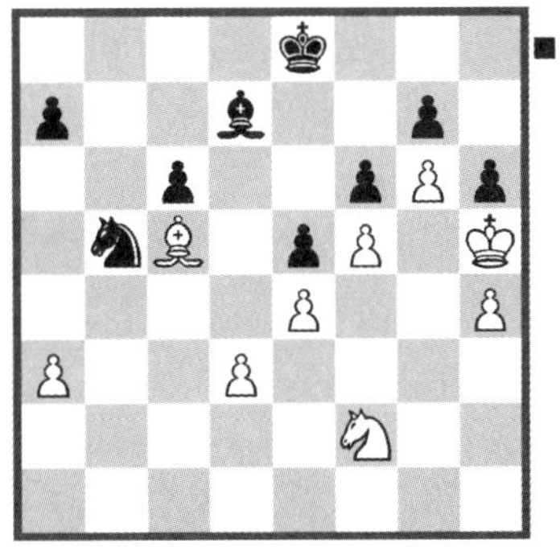

Position after: 41. ♔h5

The powerful bishop paralyzes the entire black army. The rest is trivial.

41... a6 42. ♘g4 ♘c3 43. ♘xf6+ ♔d8 44. ♘xd7 ♔xd7 45. f6 ♘e2 46. fxg7 ♘f4+ 47. ♔xh6

1-0

Game 84

♙ Gelfand, Boris (2693)
♟ Campora, Daniel Hugo (2549)
Izmir 2004

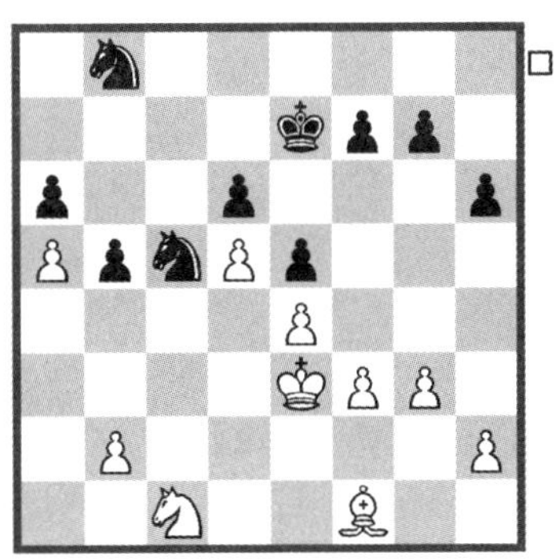

White is apparently better. Black may have problems with the targeted queenside pawns and with his lack of space.

32. b4

White must opt for this. Sooner or later Black may force it with ...♘b7. However White would keep enough resources on the kingside to make a breakthrough.

32... ♘cd7 33. ♗h3 ♘f6 34. ♘d3

Position after: 34. ♘d3

34... ♘e8?!

Black wants to set the knight on c7 and wait. This, however, does not look to be the best defense.

34... ♘bd7 Natural.

35. f4 f6

A sad necessity. Now the black cavalry is restricted.

36. ♗c8 ♘c7 37. ♔f3 ♔d8 38. ♗f5

White has occupied the light squares on the kingside and is ready to infiltrate with his king.

38... ♘d7 39. h4 ♘f8

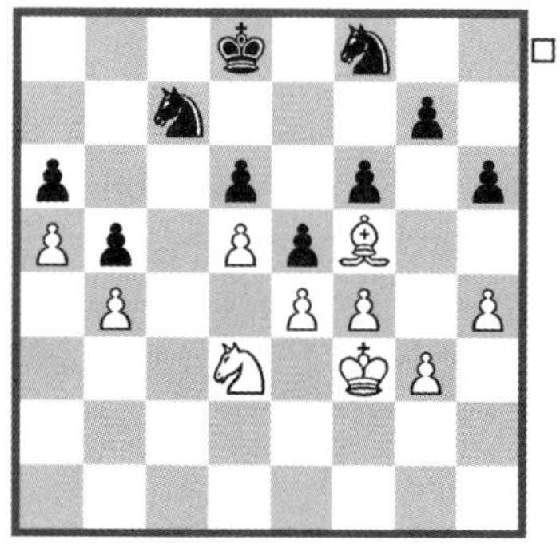

Position after: 39... ♘f8

40. h5 ♘e8 41. ♘f2!

The knight aims for the f5-square. White must organize this, whereas Black is unable to organize anything. His pieces are horribly cramped.

41... ♘c7 42. ♘d1 ♘e8 43. ♘e3 ♘c7 44. ♗h3 ♘e8 45. ♗f5 ♘c7

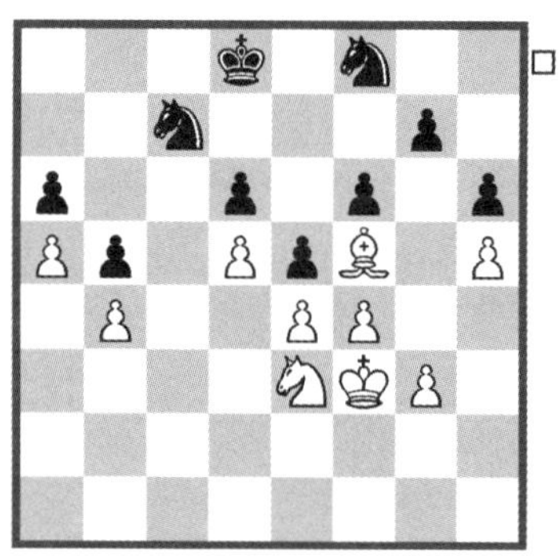

Position after: 45... ♘c7

46. ♗g6! ♘xg6 47. hxg6 ♘e8 48. ♘f5

A kind of zugzwang. The king is going to h5 and a sacrifice ends the game – a brutal consequence of the gained space.

48... ♔d7 49. ♔g4 ♔d8 50. ♔h5 ♔d7 51. ♘xg7

Position after: 51. ♘xg7

51... ♘xg7+ 52. ♔xh6 f5 53. ♔xg7 fxe4 54. ♔f7 e3 55. g7 e2 56. g8=♕ e1=♕ 57. ♕e8+

1-0

Game 85

♙ Geller, Efim P
♟ Hort, Vlastimil
🌍 Skopje 1968

The position may look to be dead drawish but this is an illusion. White is clearly better due to his space advantage and better bishop. Black has more pawns fixed on his bishop's color and must deal with White's initiative on the kingside. White intends after some preparation to launch his kingside pawns.

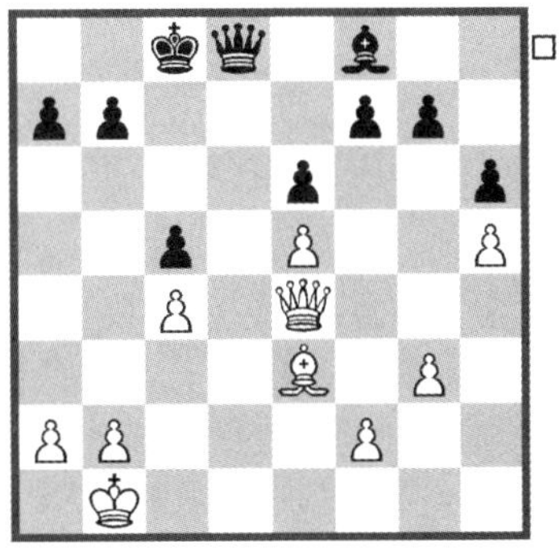

24. ♔c2

The king gains control over the d3-square to liberate the queen.

24... ♕a5 25. a3 ♕a4+ 26. ♔c1 ♔c7 27. ♕f4 ♕d7 28. b3!

An excellent prophylactic move. Black's queen can no longer reach a4. White's king comes to c2 and the threat of ♕e4-h7 would be very dangerous.

28... ♔d8 29. ♔c2 ♔e8 30. ♕e4 ♗e7

White delays the move ♕h7 because Black's kingside is well-protected. Instead, White launches his powerful kingside phalanx.

31. g4 ♕c7 32. f4 ♗h4

White has the possibility to advance f5 with the idea of f6! Another good move is g5 with the idea of gxh6. Nevertheless White makes no decision yet, first improving his king.

Position after: 32... ♗h4

33. ♔d3

A) 33. g5 hxg5 34. fxg5 ♗g3 35. ♗f4 ♗xf4 36. ♕xf4 ♕c6 It would be difficult to convert this, despite the better position.

B) 33. f5 ♗g3 34. fxe6 fxe6 35. ♕g6+

Position after: 35. ♕g6+

35... ♔f8 [35... ♕f7 36. ♕xf7+ ♔xf7 37. ♗xc5 ♗xe5 This is much better for White – his badly-placed pawn on e5 has disappeared, while Black remains with the same weaknesses on the kingside.] 36. ♕xe6 ♗xe5 Clearly much better for White, but White wanted to achieve the same position with an activated king.

33... b6?

Clearly a bad move weakening the light-squared complex.

34. f5 ♗g3

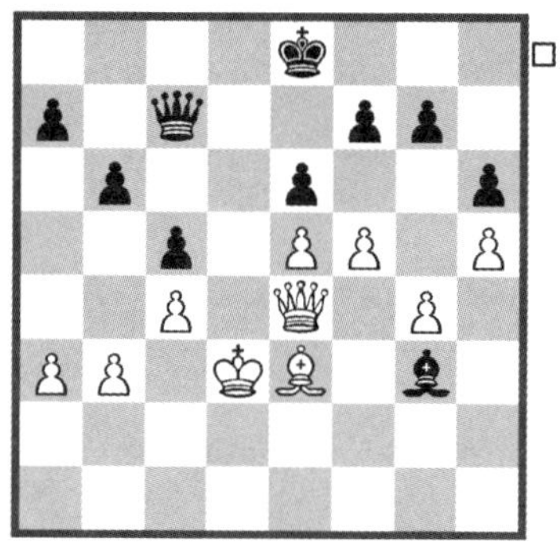

Position after: 34... ♗g3

35. fxe6?

35. ♕a8+! ♕d8+ [35... ♔e7 36. f6+!

Position after: 36. f6+!

36... gxf6 37. ♗xh6!+–] 36. ♕xd8+ ♔xd8 37. ♔e4 This is winning for White, but White followed the abovementioned plan of forcing the win with f5-f6.

35... fxe6 36. ♕g6+ ♔f8??

36... ♕f7! This is good here. 37. ♕xf7+ ♔xf7 38. ♔e4 Black has chances to hold the position – White still has a weak pawn on e5.

37. ♕xe6 ♗xe5

Position after: 37... ♗xe5

White's queen is placed perfectly. Black cannot disturb the white king with checks and his king directly joins the attack!

38. ♔e4! ♗h2 39. ♔f5 ♗g3 40. ♗d2 ♗h2 41. ♗e3

Probably in time trouble. White decided to repeat moves before making a decision.

(see diagram next column)

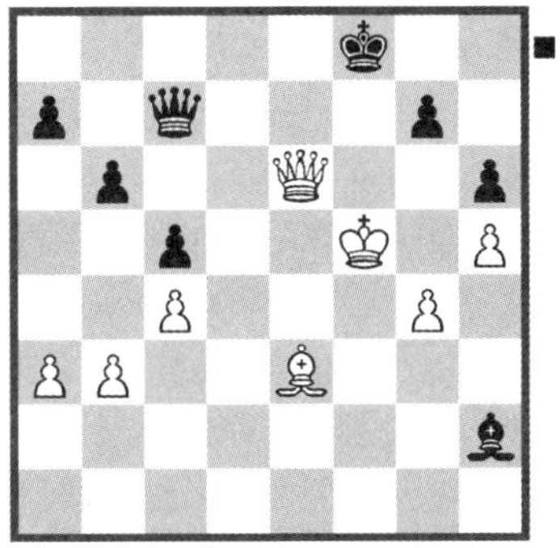

Position after: 41. ♗e3

41... ♕f7+

Black resigned here.

41... ♕f7+ 42. ♕xf7+ ♔xf7 43. ♗d2 White follows with ♗c3 leading to an easy win after transferring the king to the queenside with ♔e4-d5-c6-b7. Black is hopeless. You can check the various lines for yourself.

1-0

Game 86

♙	Mehmed, Elif	(2165)
♟	Zlatanovic, Boroljub	(2377)
🌍	Paracin 2020	

White is evidently better due to her space advantage and Black already has problems. Black does not have control over the key c5-square and sooner or later White will prove it has great impact. I played the move in the game because I needed to win in the last round to finish first. Overestimating my chances without any objectivity I well-deserved this brutal defeat.

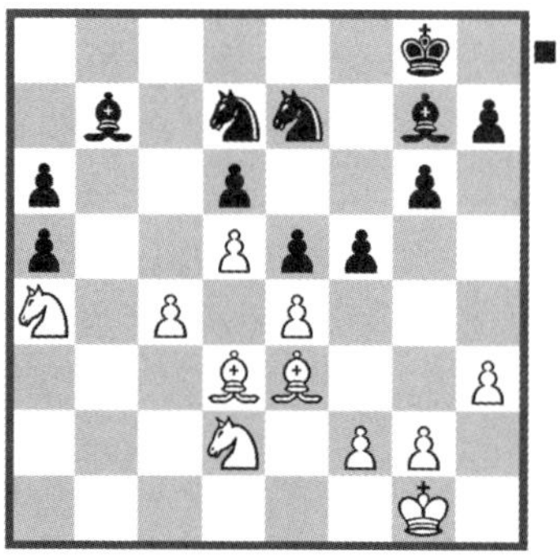

26... fxe4?

This move makes White's task much easier.

Here I saw the following variation. 26... f4! 27. ♗b6 ♘xb6 28. ♘xb6 ♘c8 29. ♘a4 ♗f6

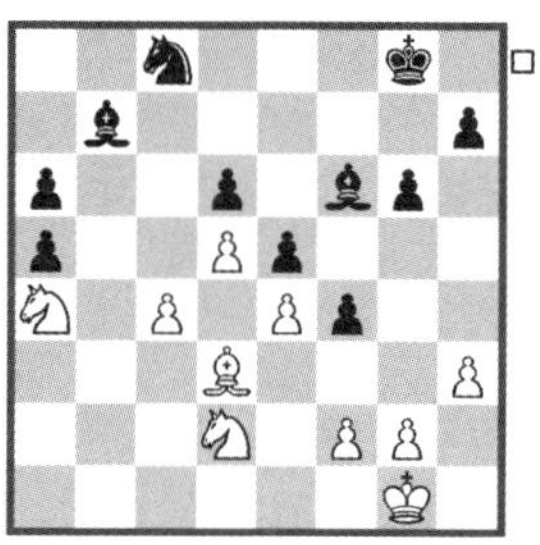
Position after: 29... ♗f6

30. ♘b3?! [30. c5! However this is much stronger. 30... dxc5 31. ♘xc5 ♘d6 32. ♘c4! Now this should win the game.] 30... ♗d8 31. c5 dxc5 32. ♘bxc5 ♘d6

(see analysis diagram next column)

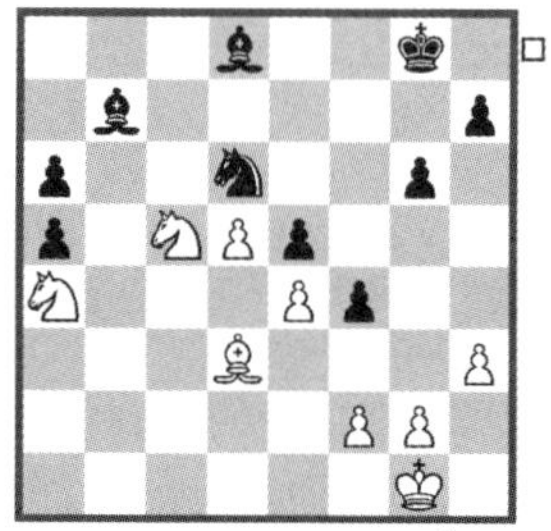
Position after: 32... ♘d6

33. ♘xb7 ♘xb7 34. ♗xa6 ♘d6 This would have led to a safe and solid endgame for me.

27. ♘xe4 ♘c8 28. ♗d2 ♗f8 29. ♗xa5 ♗e7 30. ♗e2!

Position after: 30. ♗e2!

The bishop joins the attack decisively.

30... ♔f7

30... ♘f6 This move, as planned earlier, does not achieve anything because of the simple 31. ♘ac3.

31. ♗g4 ♔e8 32. ♗c7 ♗f8 33. ♗e6

A picturesque position. Clearly, White is winning and Black's "strategy" has failed – compliments to my young and talented opponent. Her smooth technique produced an excellent example for our topic!

33... ♗e7 34. ♔f1

White should not forget about the king.

34... a5

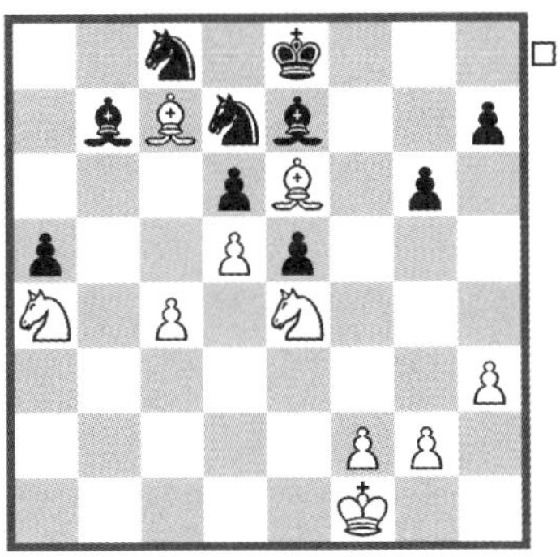

Position after: 34... a5

An act of desperation.

35. ♔e2 ♗a6 36. ♔d3 ♗f8 37. ♗xa5 ♔e7 38. ♗c7 ♗h6

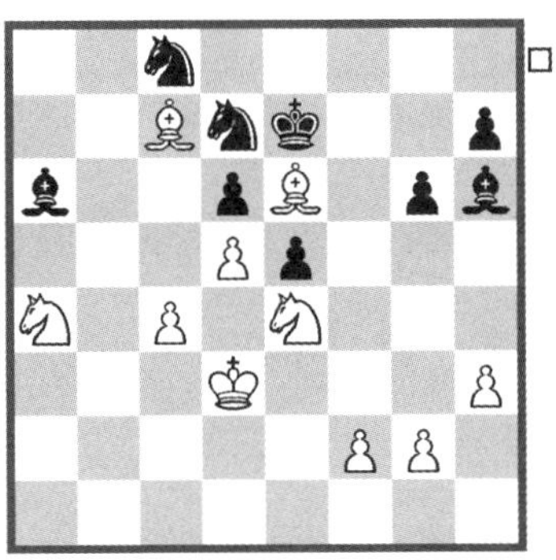

Position after: 38... ♗h6

38... ♘f6 39. ♗xc8 ♗xc8 40. ♗xd6++–

39. ♗a5!

The bishop goes to a better place to attack the d6-weakness.

39... ♗f8 40. ♗b4 ♔e8 41. ♔c3 ♘db6

Position after: 41... ♘db6

Capitulation.

42. ♘xb6 ♘xb6 43. ♗xd6 ♗xd6 44. ♘xd6+ ♔e7 45. c5 ♘a4+ 46. ♔b4 ♘b2 47. ♘e4 ♗f1 48. g3 ♗g2 49. ♔c3 ♘a4+ 50. ♔b3

Black finally resigned. Probably the only defeat in my life that I accepted with a smile. I knew at that moment that it would be a perfect example for this book!

1-0

Game 87

♙ Kramnik, Vladimir (2770)
♟ Polgar, Judit (2670)
Dortmund 1997

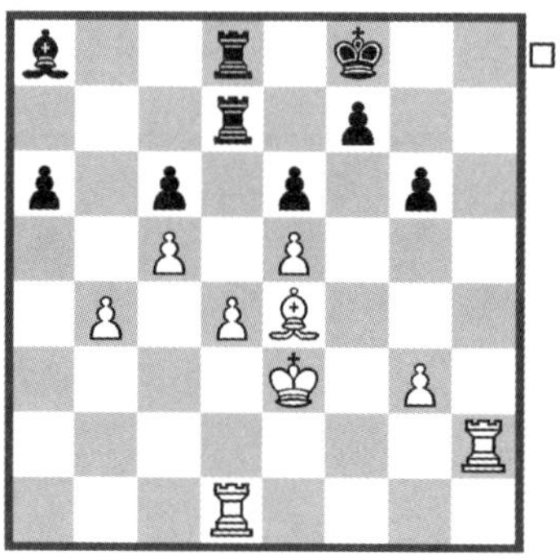

White's domination is apparent here, with a much better bishop, and also better prospects for the rooks.

35. ♖f1!

35. ♖h8+ ♔g7 36. ♖xd8 ♖xd8 37. ♖a1

Position after: 37. ♖a1

37... ♗b7 38. ♗d3 This would have given White less. There is no reason to trade a couple of rooks. White can aim for that at any given moment.

35... ♖xd4

What else?

35... ♔g7 36. ♖fh1 ♖xd4 37. ♖h7+

Position after: 37. ♖h7+

37... ♔f8 38. ♗xg6! Crushing.

36. ♖h7

Position after: 36. ♖h7

36... ♖8d7

36... ♖xb4 37. ♖fxf7++–

37. ♖h8+ ♔e7 38. ♖xa8 ♖xb4 39. ♗xc6 ♖b3+ 40. ♔f2 ♖d2+ 41. ♔e1

1-0

Game 88

♙ Acevedo, Armando
♟ Fischer, Robert James
Siegen 1970

With such an awful bishop and weak light squares White is desperately lost.

37... ♖a1

Fischer naturally keeps the rooks.

38. ♗e1 ♔d7 39. ♗d2 ♔c6 40. ♗e1 ♘a3 41. ♔d2 ♔b5

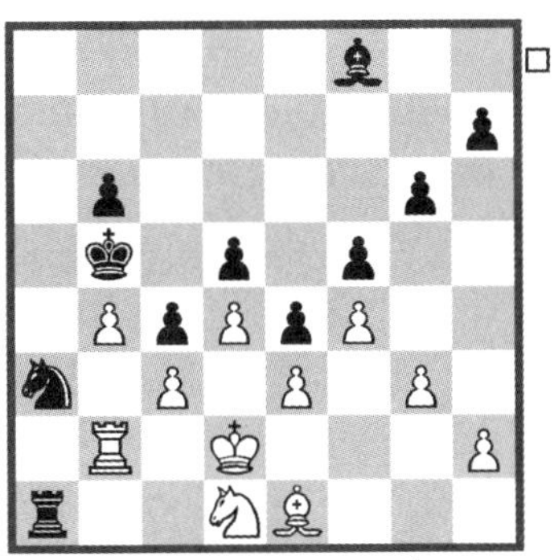

Position after: 41... ♔b5

42. ♗f2 ♔a4 43. ♗e1 ♗e7 44. ♗f2 ♘b5

The knight has opened the door to his majesty and returns to b5 to serve again.

45. ♔c2 ♔a3 46. ♖b1 ♖a2+ 47. ♖b2 ♘xc3

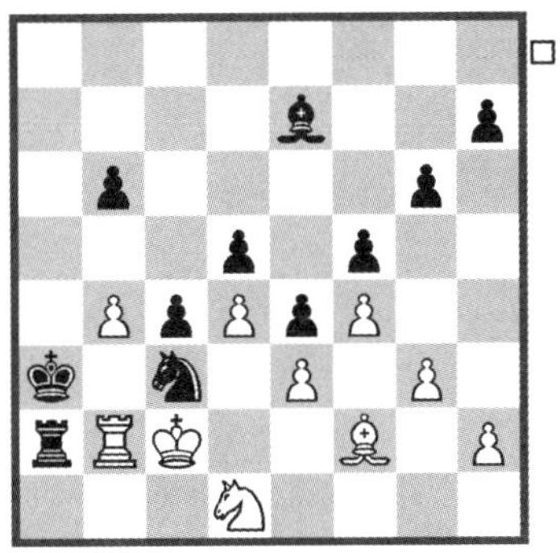

Position after: 47... ♘xc3

48. ♔xc3 ♖a1

White resigned. No comments are needed as everything is crystal clear.

0-1

Game 89

♙	Djuric, Stefan	(2500)
♟	Jussupow, Artur	(2570)
	Sarajevo 1984	

Black naturally gains more space and fixes more white pawns on the bishop's color. I like this approach.

30... g4 31. ♘g1

Necessary, in order to cover the e2-square.

A) 31. ♘e1? ♖e2–+

B) 31. ♘h2? ♗xg3!–+

C) 31. ♘h4?! ♘xh4+ This is much better for Black.

31... h5 32. a4

The correct decision. White cannot simply sit and wait.

32... h4

Black however continues attacking on the kingside. White must play very precisely because Black's attack is more dangerous since it is connected with an attack on the king.

33. axb5?

A serious mistake.

33. gxh4! ♘xh4+ 34. ♔f1 White is passive but okay. Black would have been forced to deal with the queenside because there is nothing apparent on the kingside.

33... hxg3

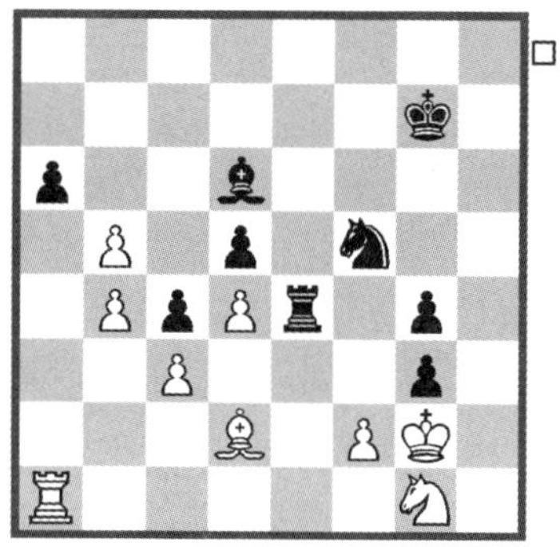

Position after: 33... hxg3

34. fxg3

34. bxa6?? ♘h4+! It is mate on the next move.

34... axb5 35. ♖a5 ♘xg3 36. ♖xb5

It really looks like Black must have something good on the kingside. White's rook is stuck on the queenside and Black should act quickly. In terrific time trouble the great maestro Jussupow nevertheless found an inventive regrouping, giving him winning chances.

36... ♖e8! 37. ♖xd5 ♘e4

The knight defends the bishop which secures the knight and prohibits ♖e5. As a result Black will manage to transfer the rook via h8 to h2!

38. ♗e1 ♖h8

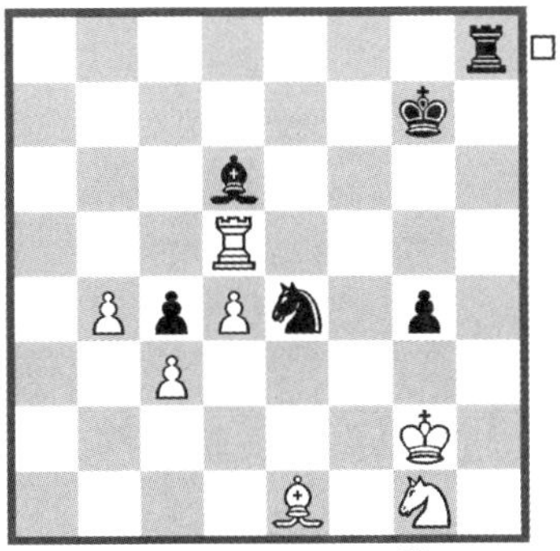

Position after: 38... ♖h8

39. ♔f1?

39. ♖a5! This is better. 39... ♖h2+ 40. ♔f1 This still gives nothing apparent to Black, although it looks horrible for White.

39... ♖h2?

39... ♖h1! This is better. In comparison to the above-mentioned line Black is a tempo up. 40. ♔g2 ♖h2+ 41. ♔f1 ♖b2 Now Black wins due to the threat of ...g3-g2.

40. b5?

The curse of move 40.

40. ♖a5 This would have transposed to the above-mentioned line with some chances to hold.

40... ♖b2 41. ♘e2 ♖b1

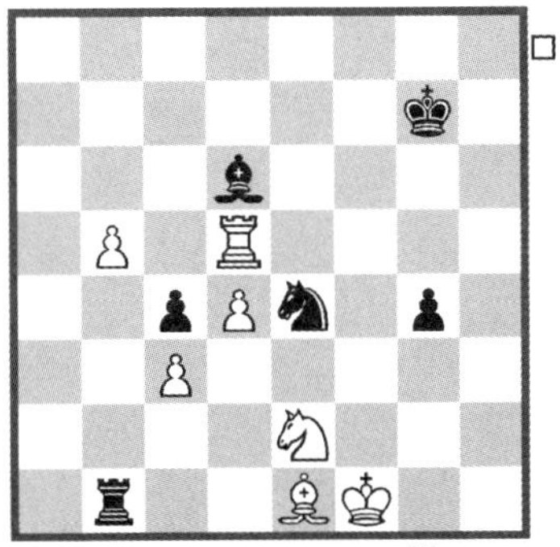

Position after: 41... ♖b1

White is fatally pinned and in zugzwang.

42. b6

A necessity.

42. ♖h5 ♗g3!–+

42... ♖xb6 43. ♗h4 ♖b1+ 44. ♔g2 ♖b2 45. ♔f1 ♔g6

Black controls everything.

46. ♖a5 g3 47. ♖a8 ♔h5 48. ♗xg3

Position after: 48. ♗xg3

48... ♘xg3+ 49. ♘xg3+ ♗xg3

The rest is not complicated. White must not take the c4-pawn because of the mating threats.

50. ♖c8 ♔g4 51. ♖xc4

Played anyway.

51... ♔f3 52. ♖b4 ♖h2

Position after: 52... ♖h2

Now the c3-pawn helps Black to convert. If a game is perfectly played strategically, tactics will come in at some point to serve the player.

53. ♔g1 ♖h8 54. ♖b2 ♖e8

0-1

Game 90

♙ Gelfand, Boris (2673)
♟ Anisimov, Pavel (2533)
St Petersburg 2018

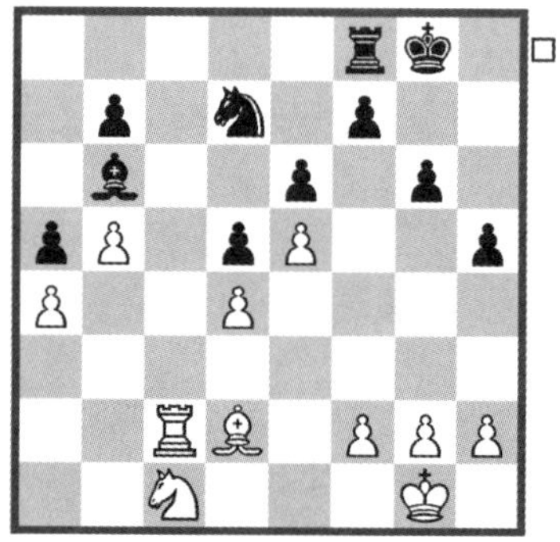

An interesting endgame may occur after many openings. Here White dominates on a file which is currently neutralized. Both bishops are "both good and bad", but nevertheless White should stand stronger. However the key factor is White's space advantage. There is nothing that Black can do to stop White's kingside expanding.

28. ♘b3 ♖a8

28... f6?! This looks ugly, but I would rather have tried it. Waiting would have been no good, not least for psychological reasons.

29. ♗g5! ♔f8 30. ♔f1

Centralization of the king before anything else.

30... ♔e8 31. ♔e2 ♗d8

What else?

32. ♗xd8 ♔xd8

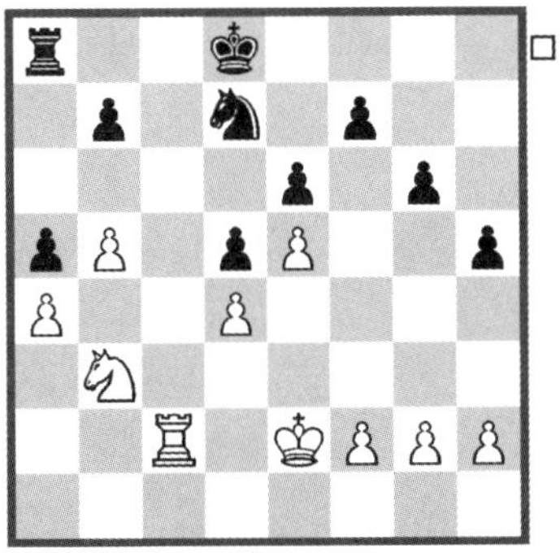

Position after: 32... ♔xd8

Black aims with ...b6 and ...♖c8 to transfer the game to a worse but perhaps holdable knight endgame. Gelfand simply but brilliantly converts. Now trading rooks would lead to a lost pawn endgame – White would create an outside passer on the h-file with an easy win.

33. ♘c5! ♘xc5 34. ♖xc5 ♔d7

34... ♖c8 35. ♖xc8+ ♔xc8 36. ♔e3

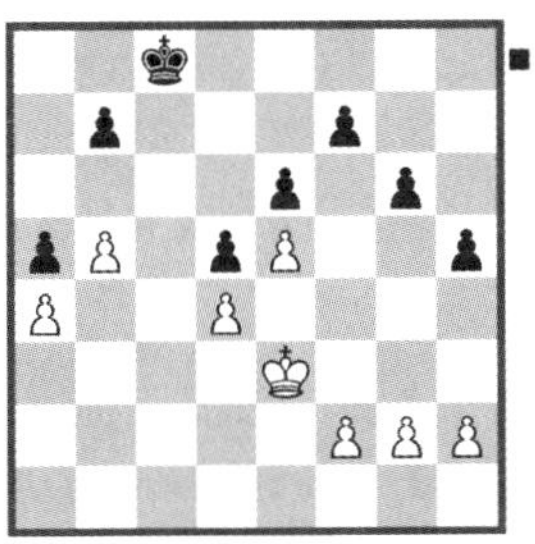

Position after: 36. ♔e3

36... ♔d7 [36... g5 37. f4 g4 38. f5+–] 37. ♔f4 ♔e7 38. ♔g5 ♔e8 39. h4 White wins after f3 and g4.

35. h4!

After fixing, the white king will invade on the kingside.

35... ♖g8 36. g3

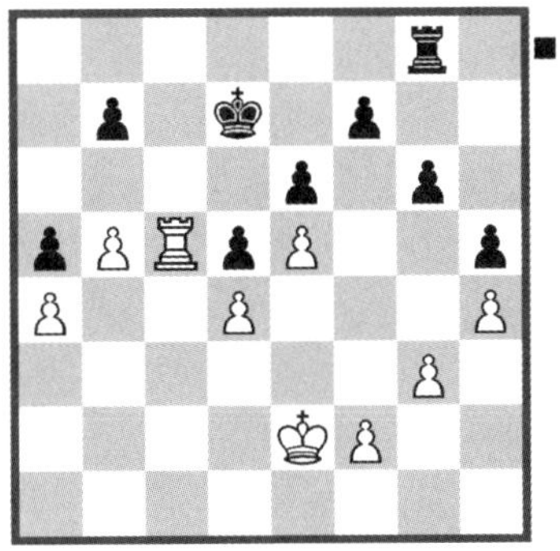

Position after: 36. g3

36... ♖a8

36... g5 37. hxg5 ♖xg5 38. b6+–

37. ♔e3 ♖f8

Necessary. Sooner or later Black must play this, although there is nothing to be gained thereafter.

38. f3 f6 39. exf6 ♔d6 40. b6

Gaining access to the b7-pawn. Black is lost.

40... ♖xf6 41. ♖c7 e5 42. dxe5+ ♔xe5 43. ♖xb7

(see diagram next page)

The rest is just a matter of technique – not an issue for Gelfand.

Position after: 43. ♖xb7

43... d4+ 44. ♔e2 ♔d5 45. ♖d7+ ♔c4 46. b7 ♖b6 47. ♖c7+

Position after: 47. ♖c7+

47... ♔d5

47... ♔b3 This should have been tested. 48. g4! Now only this move is the right way to win. This was Gelfand's next move in the game. I have no doubt that he would have played it if this subline had arisen.

48. g4 hxg4 49. fxg4 ♔e4 50. ♖e7+ ♔f4 51. h5 gxh5 52. gxh5 ♔g5 53. ♖e5+

The rook comes to b5. Black resigned.

1-0

Game 91

♙ Karpov, Anatoly
♟ Smith, Kenneth Ray
San Antonio 1972

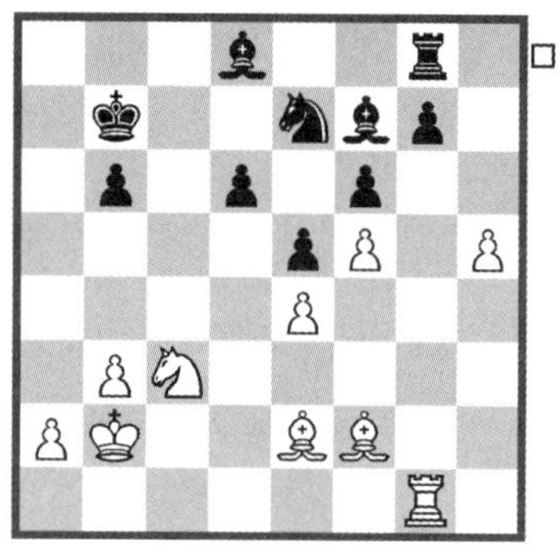

Karpov was always a great master in capitalizing on his space advantage. Let's remind ourselves of some of his masterpieces, such as his game versus Andersson (Stockholm, 1969), Gligoric (San Antonio, 1972) and especially Unzicker (Nice, 1974). Here we will analyze two other examples. It is more or less trivial to suggest a plan for him in our first example. White is strategically winning – Black has many weak pawns and problems with space. In particular, his dark-squared bishop is bad – so, let's trade the light-squared bishops!

43. ♗c4

So simple. There are also other good plans.

43. ♘b5 Clearly this is also winning.

43... ♗xc4 44. bxc4

With such a bad bishop, weak light squares and such a lack of space Black is hopeless. White has many ways to convert.

44... ♖h8 45. ♖h1

This is more methodical than capturing on g7.

45... ♔c6 46. ♔b3 ♖h7 47. ♗e3 ♖h8 48. ♔b4

Before any action, the king becomes active first.

48... ♖h7

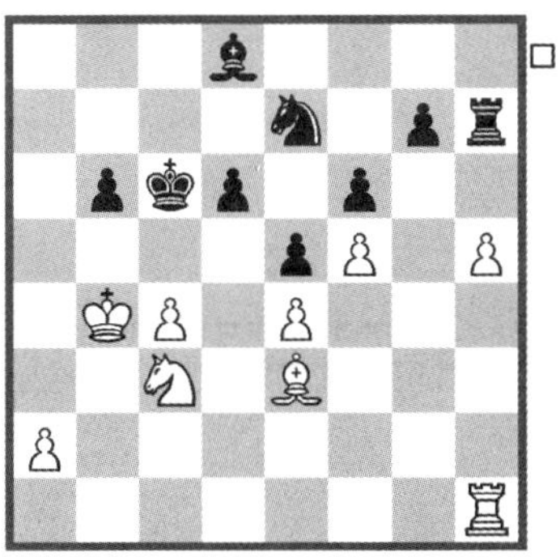

Position after: 48... ♖h7

49. ♘d5

This is the simplest. After the trades the white king goes ahead.

49... ♘xd5+

49... ♘c8 50. h6 gxh6 51. ♖xh6

Position after: 51. ♖xh6

51... ♖xh6 52. ♗xh6 This may soon lead to zugzwang.

50. cxd5+ ♔b7 51. ♔b5 ♗c7 52. a4

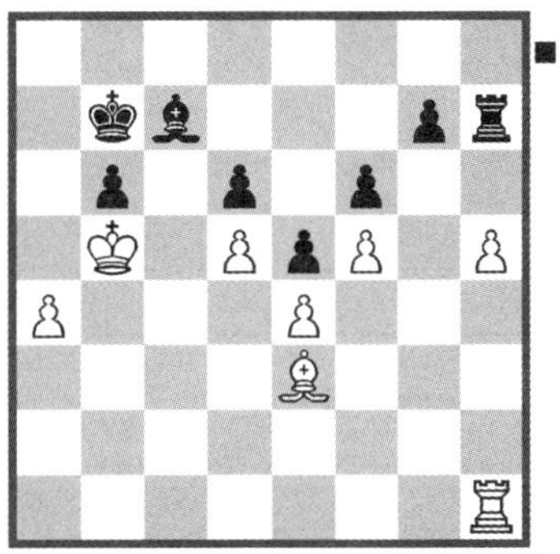

Position after: 52. a4

All the white pieces are on the light squares – a triumph of harmony and simplicity.

52... ♖h8 53. ♗d2 ♖h7 54. ♗b4 ♖h8 55. ♖g1!

With the bishop attacking the d6-pawn, this is an efficient and simple method to convert.

55... ♖h7

55... ♖xh5 56. ♖xg7 The d6-pawn falls.

56. ♖g6 ♗b8 57. h6!

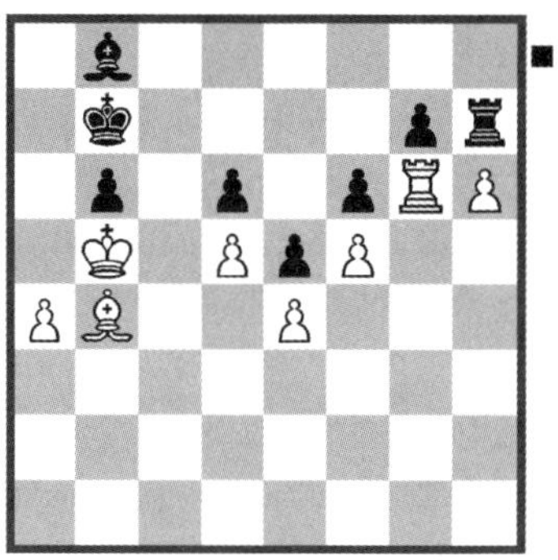

Position after: 57. h6!

57... gxh6 58. ♖xf6 h5 59. ♗xd6

Karpov has calculated precisely that the black h-passer is not dangerous.

59... ♗xd6 60. ♖xd6 h4 61. ♖xb6+ ♔a7 62. ♖g6 h3 63. ♖g1

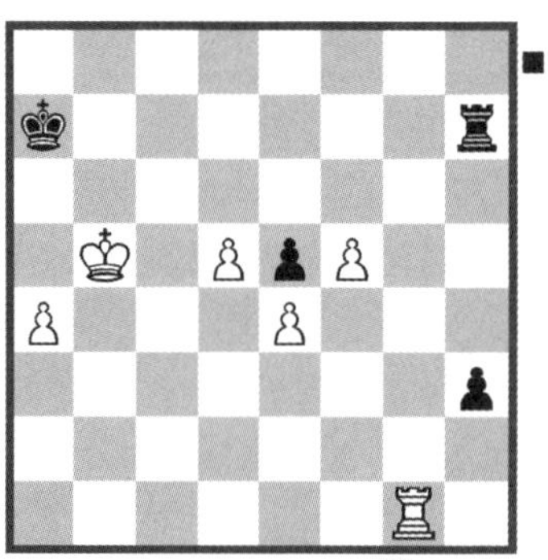

Position after: 63. ♖g1

63... ♖h4

63... h2 64. ♖h1 ♔b7 65. ♔c5 ♔c7 66. d6+ ♔d7 67. ♔d5 Black is just lost.

64. ♖g7+ ♔a8 65. f6 ♖f4 66. f7 h2 67. ♖h7 ♖xf7 68. ♖xh2 ♖f4 69. d6 ♖xe4 70. ♖h8+

Black resigned. I cannot remember a simpler and more brutal example in this topic.

1-0

Game 92

♙ Karpov, Anatoly
♟ Wirthensohn, Heinz
Skopje 1972

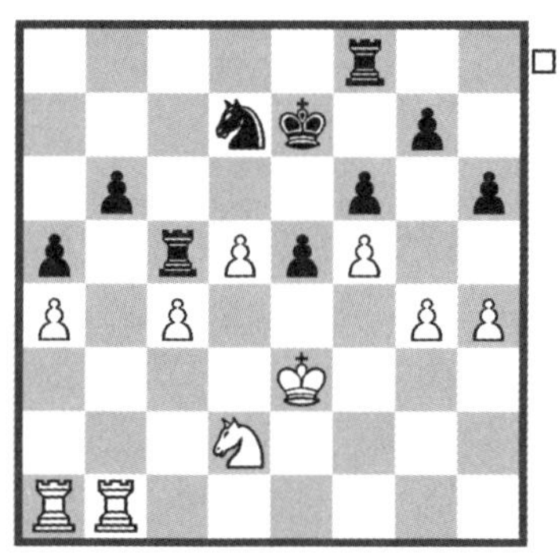

White is apparently better due to his space advantage. However, I would also like to point to the fact that White has a better knight. Well, it inevitably goes to its best (by far) spot on e4, while the best spot for the black knight on d6 is unattainable for Black.

31. ♖g1

Intending g5 at some opportune moment.

31... ♖cc8

Perhaps threatening to direct the knight to the d6-square via c5 and b7.

32. ♖ab1!

No way.

32... ♖b8 33. ♘e4! ♖bc8

33... ♘c5 34. ♖b5! ♘xa4 35. ♖a1 ♘c5 36. ♘xc5 bxc5 37. ♖axa5 This is hopeless for Black.

34. ♖gc1

Karpov reasonably switches to the queenside.

34... ♖fe8 35. ♖b5 ♖ed8 36. ♔d3

Total harmony. Black is hopeless against ♖cb1 and c5. Furthermore, White can play on the kingside too with g5. Playing on both flanks is not possible for Black.

36... ♔f8

(see diagram next column)

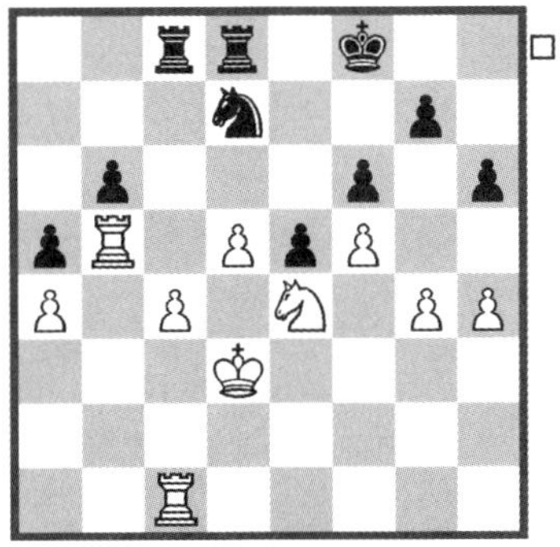

Position after: 36... ♔f8

37. g5

With the black rook stuck on the eighth rank, this is reasonable.

37. ♖cb1 This would also win.

37... hxg5 38. hxg5 ♔e7 39. ♖g1 ♖h8 40. gxf6+ gxf6 41. ♖g7+ ♔d8

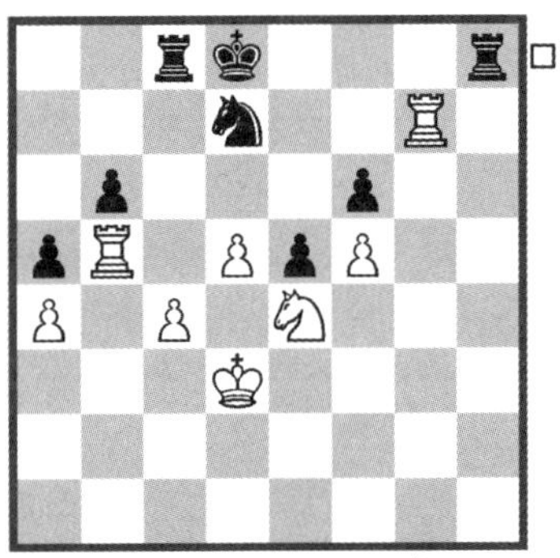

Position after: 41... ♔d8

42. ♘d6?

A serious mistake. Probably Karpov did not see the defense based on tactics.

42. d6! Threatening c5. 42... ♖h3+ 43. ♔e2 This wins easily.

42... ♖h3+?

Black immediately collapses at the moment when he has some chances.

42... ♘c5+ 43. ♔e3 ♖c7 The best defense. Now the following would give Black some practical chances to survive. 44. ♘f7+!

Position after: 44. ♘f7+!

44... ♔e8 45. ♘xh8 ♖xg7 46. ♖xb6 ♖g4

43. ♔e2 ♖h2+

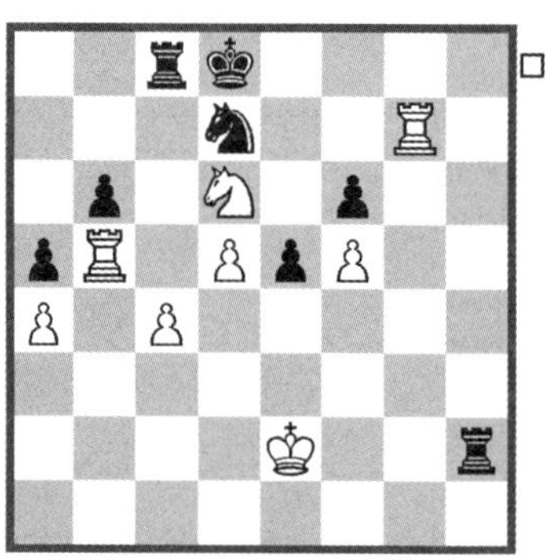

Position after: 43... ♖h2+

44. ♔e3

44. ♔e3 ♖c7 45. ♖g8+ ♔e7 46. ♖e8+ ♔xd6 47. ♖e6# A very beautiful mate.

1-0

Game 93

♙	Stojanovic, Dalibor	(2469)
♟	Delchev, Aleksander	(2635)
🌍	Novi Sad 2009	

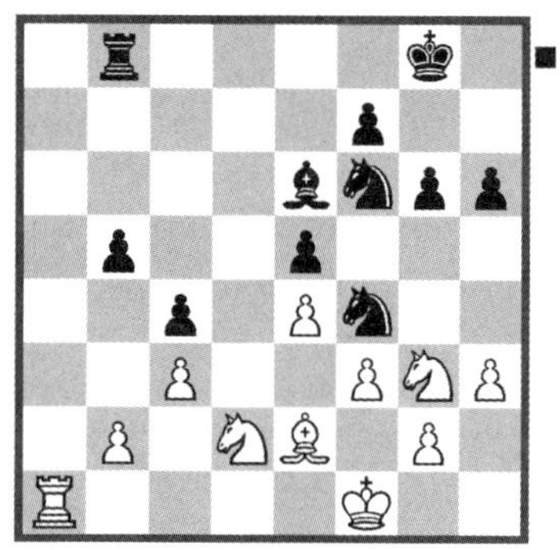

We see a similar structure on our next diagram. The pawns on the c- and e- files are fixed with an open d-file; and again the space advantage has a key role. Furthermore, White has no harmony in his camp and he is unable to organize anything. In particular the bishop and g3-knight are bad pieces. Black logically transfers his troops toward the queenside. The knight belongs on c5.

25... ♘d7 26. ♘h1

This maneuver makes sense. The final target for this knight should be e3.

26... ♘c5 27. ♘f2 ♘a4?!

27... ♖d8! 28. ♖d1 [28. ♘b1 ♘b3 29. ♖a7 ♘d2+

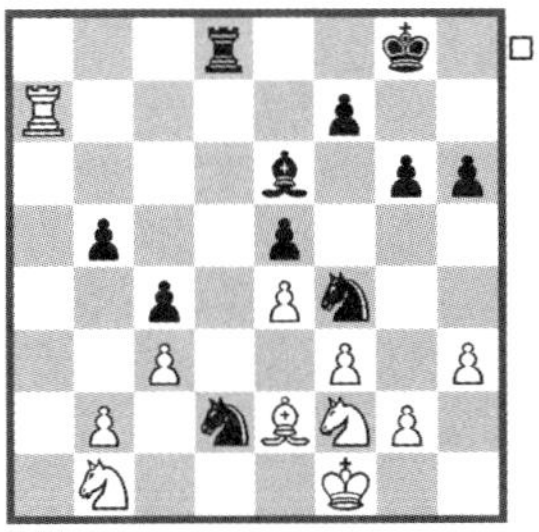

Position after: 29... ♘d2+

30. ♘xd2 ♖xd2 This wins easily.] 28... ♖a8 This would be winning after getting control over the a-file.

28. ♖a2 ♖d8 29. ♘b1

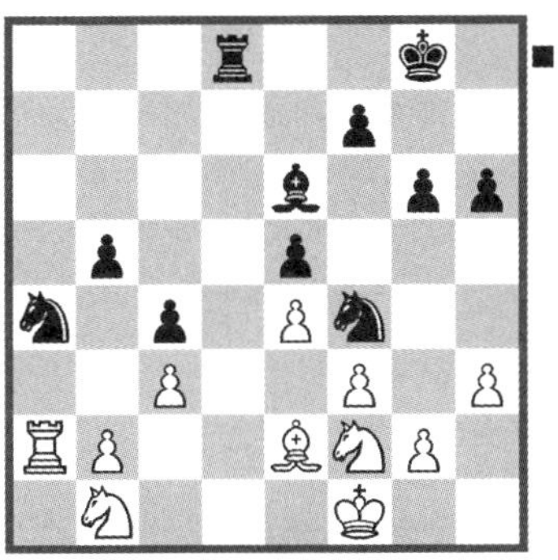

Position after: 29. ♘b1

29... ♘d3?

Delchev misses the opportunity to capitalize on the opposite flank with 29... f5!? because White must not take it. 30. exf5 ♗xf5 Black's advantage increases.

30. ♗xd3??

A terrible inconceivable mistake.

30. b4! This would have cancelled all Black's advantages, giving White a holdable endgame. Now 30... cxb3?? could even lose the game after 31. ♖d2.

30... cxd3 31. b3 ♗xb3 32. ♖d2 ♘c5

A clear pawn up and a completely winning position for Black.

33. ♘g4

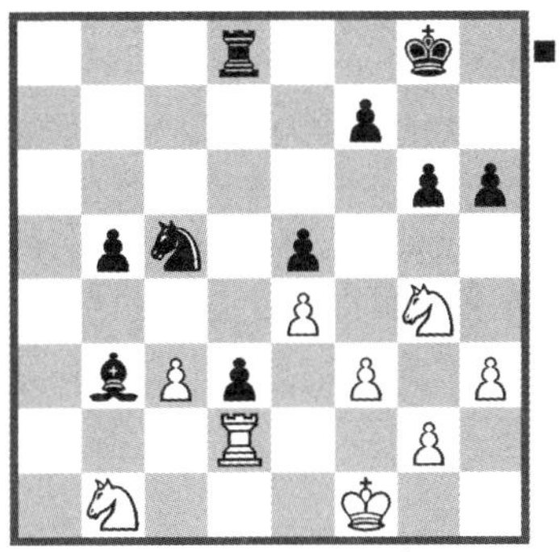

Position after: 33. ♘g4

33... ♗c2 34. ♘a3 ♘b3 35. ♔e1 ♘xd2 36. ♔xd2 ♖a8 37. ♘xb5 ♖a2 38. c4 ♗b1+ 39. ♔c1 ♖xg2 40. ♔xb1 ♖g1+

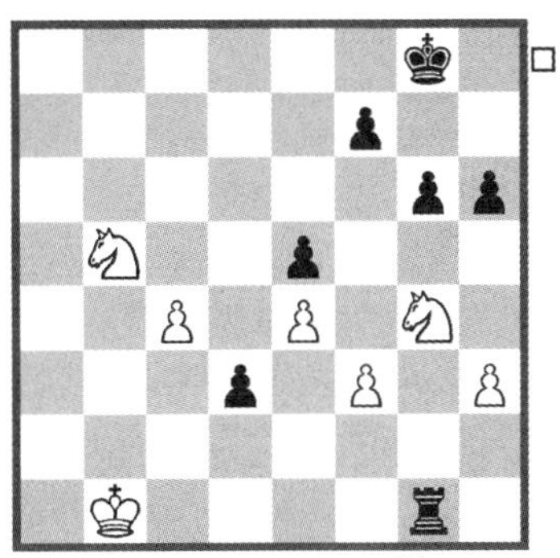

Position after: 40... ♖g1+

41. ♔b2 d2 42. ♘c3 d1=♕ 43. ♘xd1 ♖xd1

After a sequence of forced moves Black is winning. Converting is not an issue for a player with Delchev's knowledge.

44. ♘xe5 ♔f8

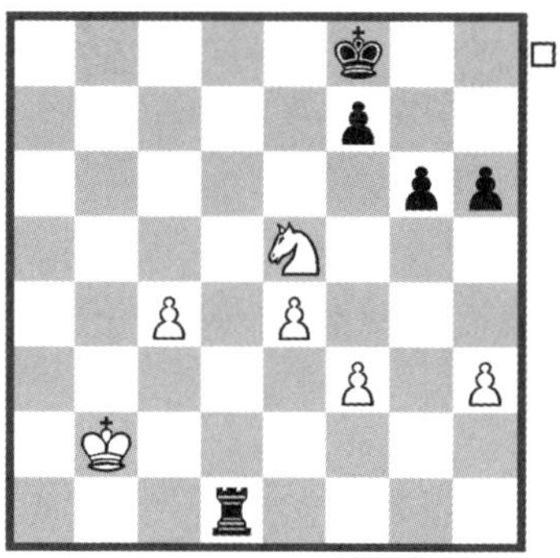

Position after: 44... ♔f8

The king is needed to win the game.

45. c5 ♔e7 46. ♔c2 ♖a1 47. ♔d3 ♔e6 48. ♔d4 ♖d1+ 49. ♘d3 g5!

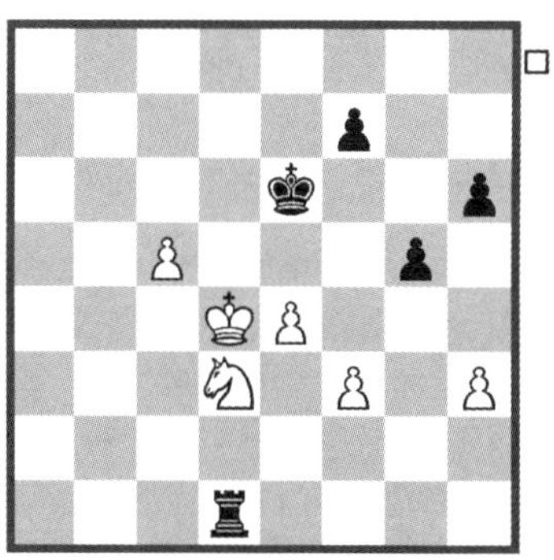

Position after: 49... g5!

50. e5 ♔d7 51. ♔c4 ♖f1 52. ♘b4 ♖xf3 53. c6+ ♔c7 54. ♔c5 ♖c3+ 0-1

Game 94

♙ Topalov, Veselin (2735)
♟ Ivanchuk, Vassily (2716)
Monte Carlo 2004

White is obviously better due to his space advantage. Even if Black is "formally better", his bishop is not better, so Black does not have any plus to oppose White's gained space. With his next move White gains new space, at the same time placing the e5-pawn far from the rest of phalanx.

29. g5!

It is always good to advance the upper doubled pawn which will result in new possibilities to advance.

29... ♘g7

Reasonably setting the knight on e6.

30. ♘f1

White himself regroups logically – the knight belongs on g4.

30... ♘e6 31. ♘h2 ♗e7 32. g3

White prepares f4 at some point. This may help Black to get rid of one weakness, but on the other hand new space would be gained for White. Of course, White should not rush with f4. Thus the played move will first prevent ...♘f4. White will try to attack e5 with all his troops – f4 can be on the agenda later, but first, White should try to make progress with his pieces.

32... ♗d8 33. ♘b3

Step-by-step White focuses all his pieces on the e5-pawn. This forces Black to play ...f6 and to add a new defense to e5. However ...f6 would crush Black's structure and weaken his king's position.

33... ♘b8 34. ♘f3

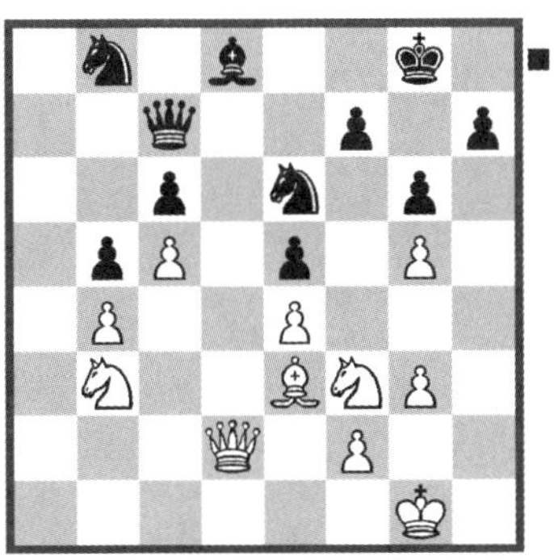

Position after: 34. ♘f3

Still there, to keep g5 protected and to liberate the queen.

34... ♗e7 35. ♘c1 ♘d7 36. ♘d3 ♗f8 37. ♕a2

There will be time later to attack the pawn from a1 or b2. More importantly, there is a threat of invading via the a-file.

37... ♗g7 38. ♕a8+ ♘df8 39. ♔g2

Don't rush!

39... f6

What else is there to do? White will simply transfer his bishop to b2, or play ♕a1.

40. gxf6 ♗xf6 41. ♗h6 ♔f7

Position after: 41... ♔f7

There are nice tactics after this move, but Black is lost anyway.

42. ♗xf8 ♘xf8 43. ♕xc6

1-0

Game 95

♙ Szabo, Laszlo
♟ Benko, Pal C
San Feliu de Guixols 1975

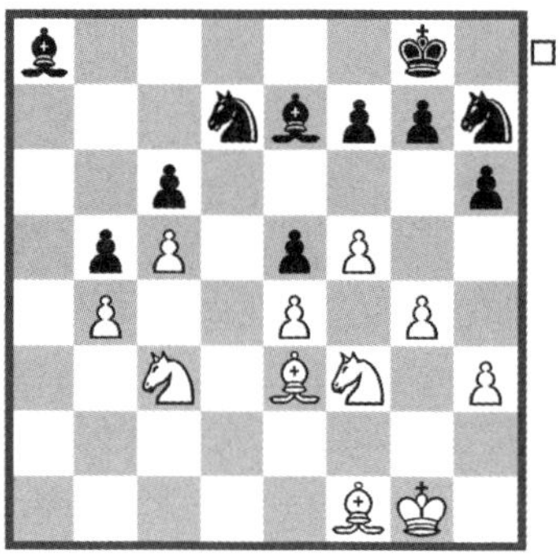

In our next endgame there is a similar structure. Again space advantage is the key factor. This time it is already decisive. With such a difference between both sides' piece activity (especially the light-squared bishops) Black is hopeless.

29. h4!

Why not? The pieces are on good spots, and the king is not needed. This move prevents a possible ...♘g5 or ...♗g5 which would make Black's task easier.

29... ♔f8 30. g5 hxg5 31. hxg5 ♔e8 32. ♘e2

The knight goes to the kingside. This is the area where progress is planned.

32. ♔f2 Of course, there is nothing wrong in activating the king first. That would be more methodical, but it is a matter of style.

32... ♘hf8

White's advantage is tremendous. However, how to make progress? Benko chooses a very beautiful plan based on gaining new space. He wants to provoke ...f6 after attacking e5.

33. ♘c1

33. ♘g3 This move, with the idea of ♘h5 does not spoil anything but is less logical.

33... ♗d8 34. ♘d3 f6

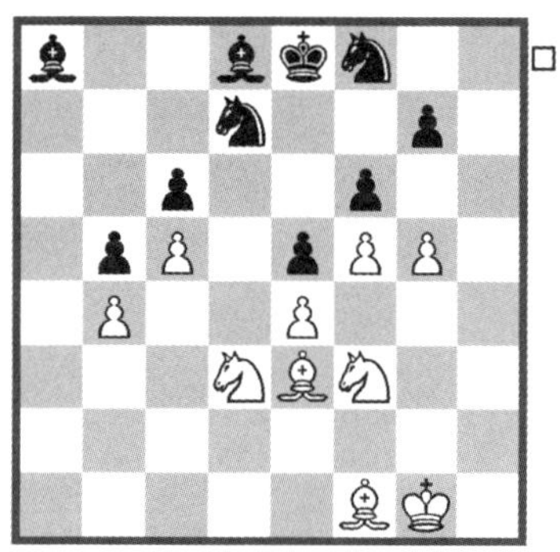

Position after: 34... f6

34... ♗c7 This can be met with 35. ♗c1, soon forcing Black's ...f6.

35. g6!

White does not care about blocking up the position too much. After the bishop comes to the a2-g8 diagonal a sacrifice will end the game.

35... ♘b8 36. ♗e2 ♘fd7 37. ♗d1 ♗e7 38. ♗b3 ♗f8 39. ♗f7+ ♔d8 40. ♘d2 ♗b7 41. ♔f2

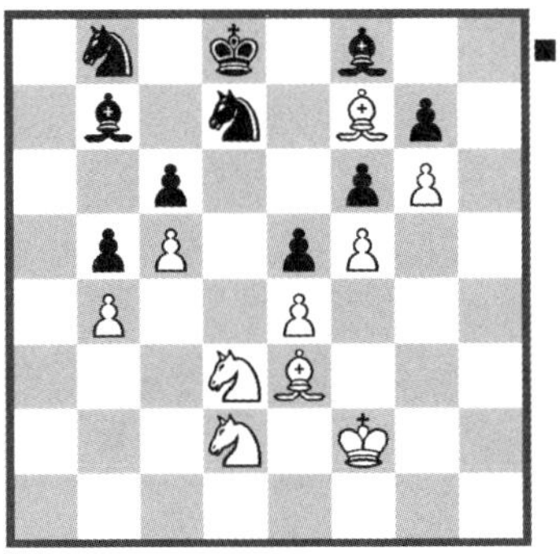

Position after: 41. ♔f2

The king goes to c3 to protect b4 and to liberate the minor pieces.

41... ♘a6 42. ♘b3 ♘ab8 43. ♔e2 ♘a6 44. ♔d2 ♘c7 45. ♔c3 ♘a6 46. ♘d2 ♘ab8 47. ♘f1 ♘a6 48. ♘g3 ♘c7 49. ♘h5

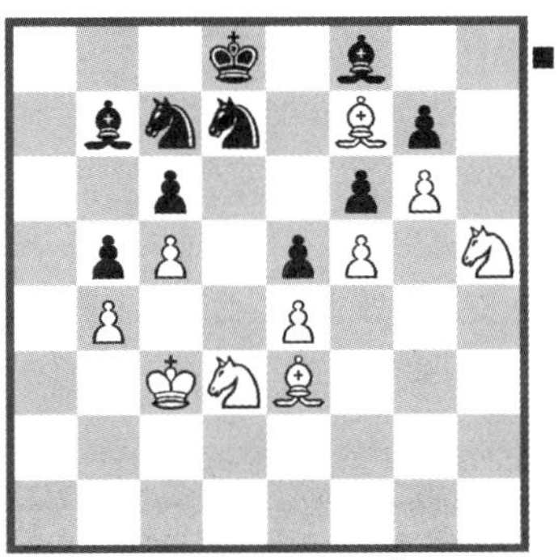

Position after: 49. ♘h5

49... ♔e7 50. ♘f2 ♗c8 51. ♘g4 ♗b7 52. ♗f2 ♗a8 53. ♗h4 ♘a6 54. ♗e6 ♘ab8

(see diagram next column)

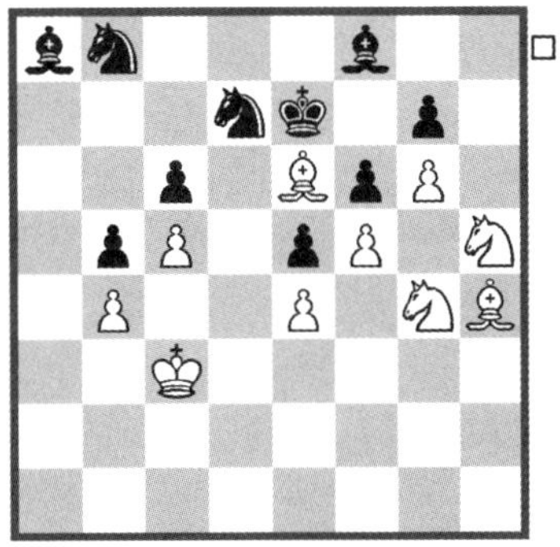

Position after: 54... ♘ab8

White tried for a sacrifice on f6, but Black protects the knight with the other knight to support the f6-spot. That is why White now directs his pieces toward the e5-pawn.

55. ♘g3 ♗b7 56. ♘f1 ♔e8 57. ♘d2 ♔d8 58. ♘f3 ♔c7 59. ♗g3 ♔d8

Position after: 59... ♔d8

60. ♘fxe5!

Black could not prevent this sacrifice. White will win easily by exploiting Black's horribly placed pieces.

60... fxe5 61. ♘xe5 ♘xe5 62. ♗xe5 ♘d7 63. ♗d6!

Necessary for White, but not difficult to find.

63... ♗xd6

What else?

64. cxd6 ♗c8 65. ♗xd7

Position after: 65. ♗xd7

A simplification. It is game over.

65... ♗xd7 66. ♔d3 ♔e8 67. ♔d4 ♔f8 68. ♔c5 ♔e8 69. ♔b6 ♔d8 70. ♔b7

Position after: 70. ♔b7

70... ♗c8+

70... c5 71. bxc5 b4 72. f6+–

71. ♔xc6 ♗d7+ 72. ♔d5 ♔e8 73. ♔e5 ♗c6 74. ♔f4 ♔f8 75. e5

Position after: 75. e5

75... ♗d5 76. e6 ♗b3 77. ♔e5

Black resigned. A simple but amazing endgame performance.

1-0

Game 96

♙ Kasparov, Garry (2595)
♟ Torre, Eugenio (2520)
Baku 1980

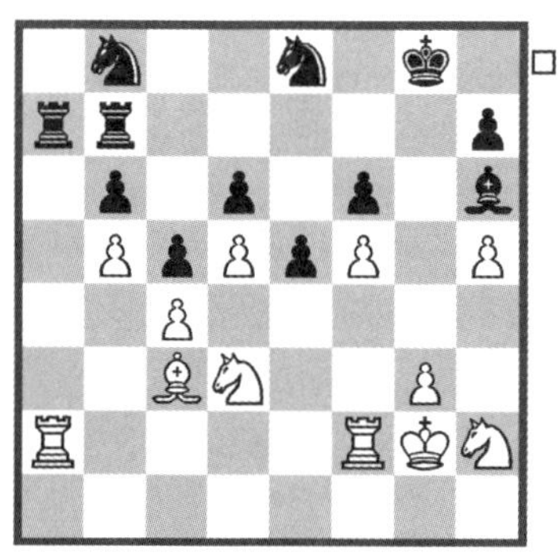

Here White has enough space to paralyze Black's cavalry. Black's knights each have three (only!) available squares and the endgame is simply lost for him. With his next maneuver Kasparov first opts for prophylaxis, preventing Black from obtaining control over the g5-square.

42. ♘g4! ♗g5 43. h6!

This is the point! If White allows ...h6 Black will get some relief; even the b8-knight could get some fresh air via the h7-square.

43... ♖e7 44. ♖fe2

Methodical – there is no need to rush.

44... ♔f7 45. ♘df2

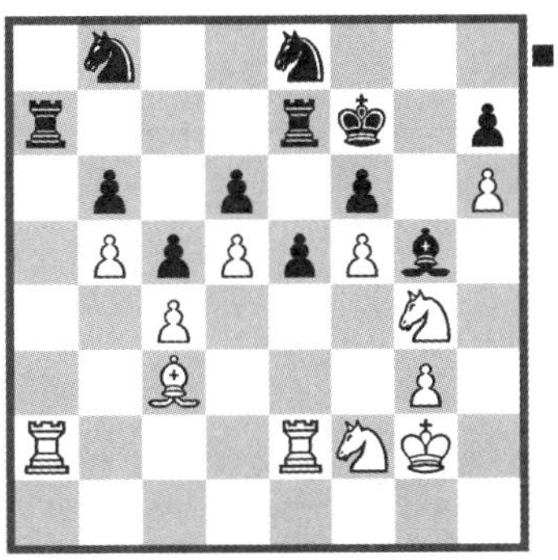

Position after: 45. ♘df2

First, it is time to install the knight on e4. Paralysis above all!

45... ♗c1 46. ♘e4 ♖ed7 47. ♔f3 ♔e7 48. ♖xa7

This leads to a simplification with near-collapse for Black.

48... ♖xa7 49. ♖e1 ♗g5 50. ♘xg5 fxg5

Position after: 50... fxg5

51. ♘xe5!

Some fine tactics easily end the game.

51... dxe5

51... ♖a3 52. ♘c6++–

52. ♗xe5 ♘d6 53. f6+ ♔d7 54. ♗xd6 ♔xd6 55. ♖e6+

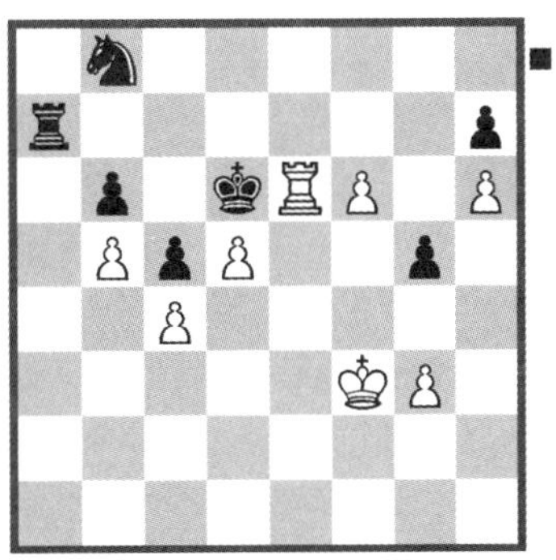

Position after: 55. ♖e6+

55... ♔c7 56. f7 ♖a1 57. ♔e2

Black resigned. A brutal example that explains Black's problems with lack of space.

57. ♔e2 ♘d7 58. d6+ ♔c8 59. ♖e8+ ♔b7 60. ♖e7 This wins on the spot.

1-0

Game 97

♙ Andersson, Ulf (2600)
♟ Sokolov, Andrei (2645)
Bilbao 1987

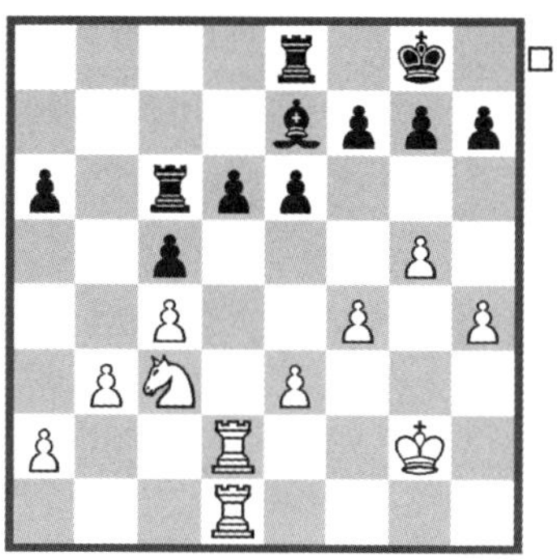

Evidently White is better in this next position. All his pieces, including the king, are better placed, and there is also a space advantage – a very important factor. Take a look at Andersson's straightforward play and superb technique.

25. ♘e4

Directly attacking the target on d6 and paralyzing Black.

25... ♖d8 26. ♔f3

The king becomes active.

26... ♔f8

Black also tries to get his king active.

27. ♔g4 ♔e8 28. f5!

With all the pieces set on their best places, it is time for pawn action.

28... exf5+ 29. ♔xf5 ♔f8 30. ♔g4

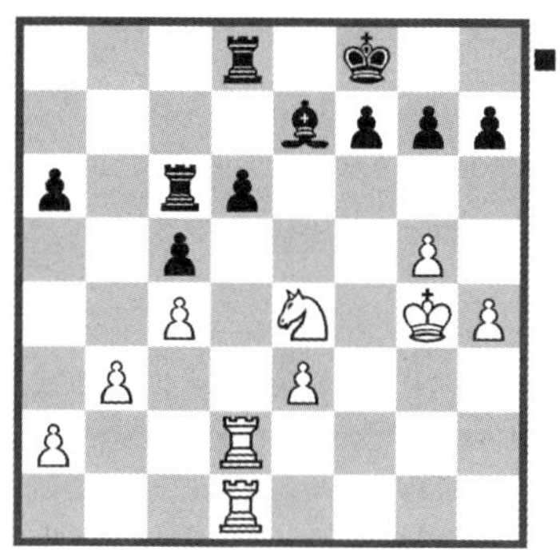

Position after: 30. ♔g4

The king returns to open the f-file for the rooks.

30... ♔e8 31. ♖f1 ♖d7 32. h5 ♗d8 33. ♖fd1 ♗e7 34. ♘c3

The knight dances in various directions and sets up numerous threats. It is time to transfer it to d5.

34... ♖cc7 35. ♘d5 ♖b7 36. ♖f1

(see diagram next page)

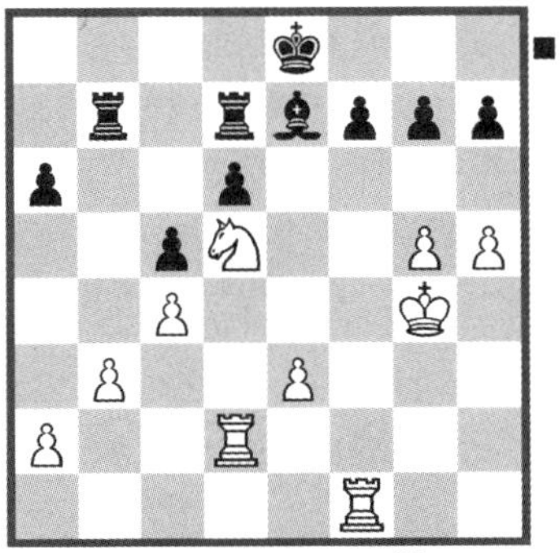

Position after: 36. ♖f1

White logically chooses f7 for his attack.

36... ♗d8 37. ♖df2 ♔f8 38. g6

A final strike crushing Black's defense.

38... h6 39. ♖xf7+ ♖xf7 40. ♖xf7+ ♖xf7 41. gxf7 ♔xf7 42. ♔f5

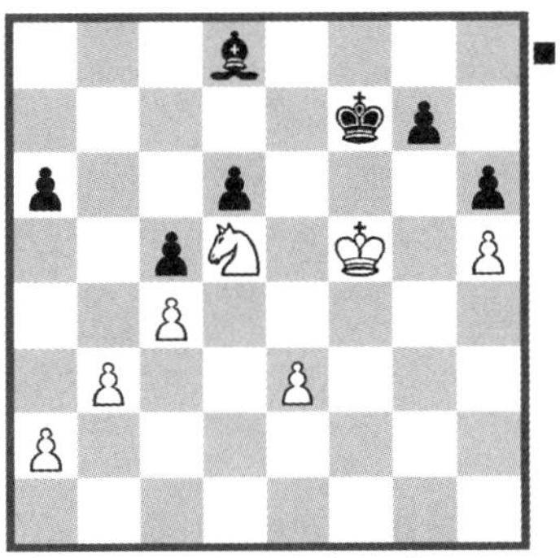

Position after: 42. ♔f5

The endgame is simply lost for Black.

42... ♗h4

42... a5 43. e4 Preparing e5.

43. b4 cxb4 44. ♘xb4 a5 45. ♘d3 ♗d8 46. e4

Black cannot use his majority. White will finally create a passed pawn.

46... ♗b6 47. a4

"Don't rush". Fixing comes first.

47... ♔e7 48. ♘f4 ♗d4 49. ♘e6 ♗c3

Position after: 49... ♗c3

50. c5

Finally.

50... dxc5 51. ♘xc5 ♔d6 52. ♘d3 ♗a1 53. e5+ ♔d5 54. ♘f4+ ♔c4 55. e6 ♗f6 56. ♘g6

Black resigned.

1-0

Game 98

♙ Kramnik, Vladimir (2740)
♟ Illescas Cordoba, Miguel (2635)
Dos Hermanas 1997

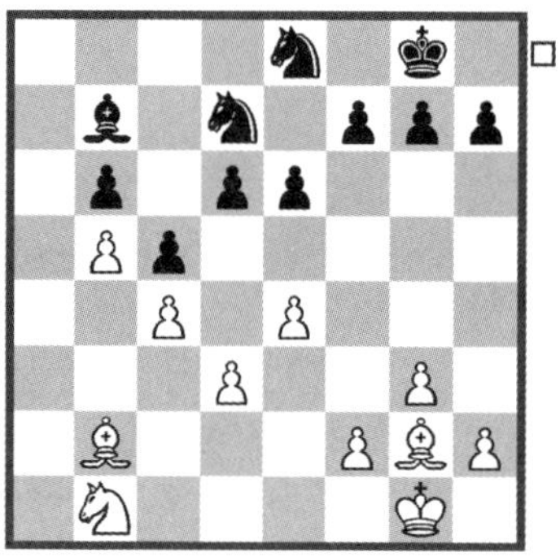

A very interesting and complex endgame. Kramnik convincingly went for it; he was sure that the bishop pair together with his space advantage were enough to secure the win.

23. f4

White's task is clear. He plans to grab as much space as possible – this is a natural approach for the side enjoying the bishop pair. However, it is vital not to create holes for the opponent's knight.

23... f6 24. ♘c3 ♔f7 25. ♘a4

Kramnik intends to open up the position slightly by pushing d4. The point is that Black must not take and White will get time to advance the pawn to d5! At the same time it stops Black's d7-knight, which is not dangerous at the moment. However, there was no reason to avoid 25. g4.

25... ♔e7 26. d4 ♔d8 27. d5

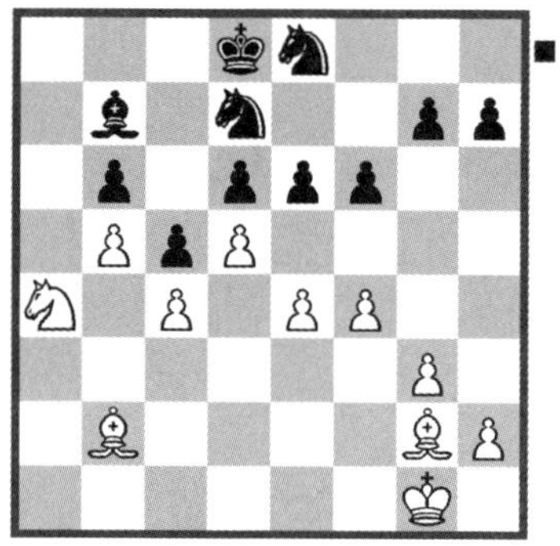

Position after: 27. d5

27... exd5

27... ♘c7 Waiting also loses after, for instance 28. h4 with an attack on the kingside. Black can do nothing. If the e6-pawn moves, it will cost him the b6-pawn.

28. exd5 ♘c7 29. ♗h3 ♘a8

This is the passive defense plan that Black had in mind. Now, Kramnik improves his position on the opposite side.

30. ♗e6! ♘f8 31. f5!

Position after: 31. f5!

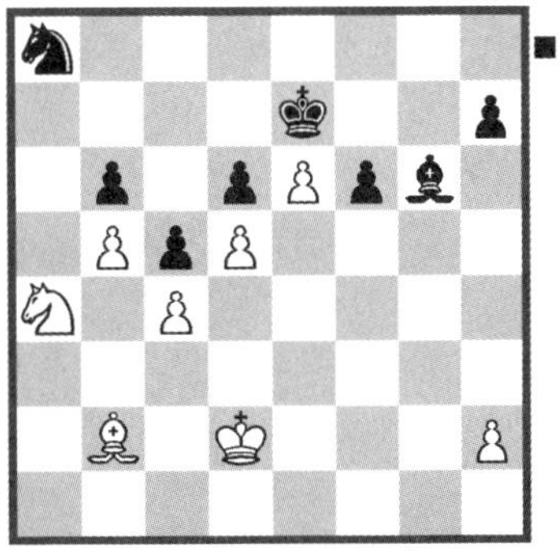

Position after: 38. ♔d2

31... ♗c8

31... ♘xe6 32. fxe6 This is tragicomical for Black.

32. ♔f2 ♗d7

32... ♗xe6 33. dxe6 White follows with transferring the bishop to f4 and the knight to e4 or d5, with an expansion on the kingside; Black is dead lost.

33. g4 ♔e7 34. g5

34. h4 This is not wrong, of course; it is a matter of style.

34... ♘xe6

A sad necessity and the best practical chance. Black wants to somehow attack the white pawns with his bishop.

35. fxe6 ♗e8 36. gxf6+ gxf6 37. ♔e3 ♗g6 38. ♔d2

A prelude to a patient regrouping.

38... ♗e4 39. ♗c1 ♗g2 40. ♔c3 ♗f1 41. ♗h6?!

Strange and unnecessary prophylaxis.

41. ♘b2 This is much better.

41... ♗g2 42. ♗f4 ♗f1 43. ♘b2 ♘c7 44. ♘d1 ♗g2 45. ♘e3 ♗e4

Position after: 45... ♗e4

Black must prevent ♘f5. White has activated his pieces, but a new regrouping is still required. White needs his king on the kingside to prepare ♘f5.

46. ♗h6 ♘e8 47. ♔d2 ♘c7 48. ♔e2 ♘e8 49. ♔f2 ♘c7 50. ♔g3 ♗d3 51. ♔g4 ♘e8 52. ♔f4 ♗b1 53. ♘f5+

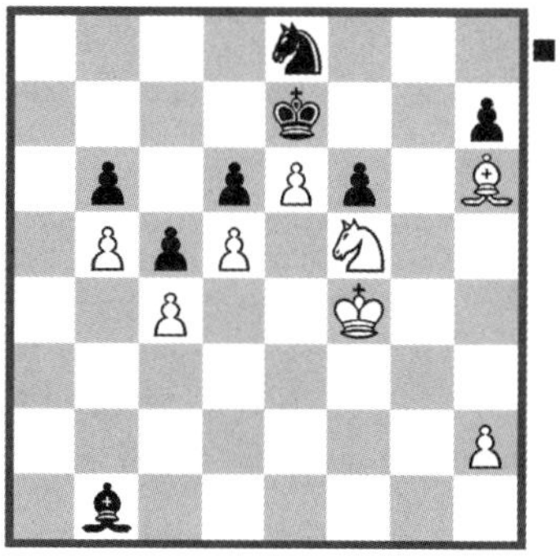

Position after: 53. ♘f5+

53... ♔d8

53... ♗xf5 54. ♔xf5 ♘c7 [54... ♔d8 55. ♗f8 ♔c7 56. ♗e7 White wins.] 55. ♗g7 ♘e8 56. ♗h8 A beautiful zugzwang.

54. ♗f8 ♗d3 55. ♗e7+ ♔c7

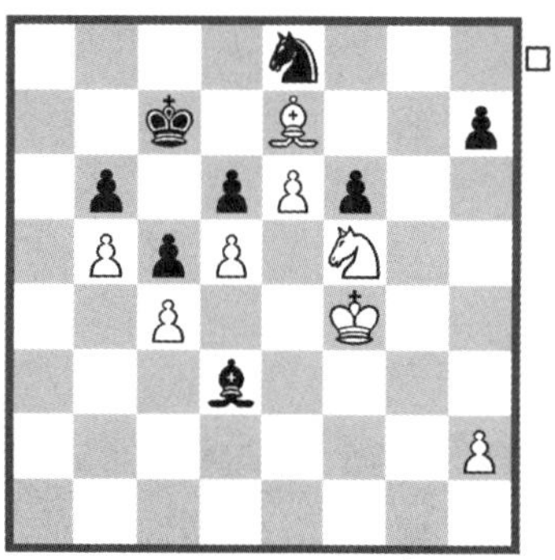

Position after: 55... ♔c7

White has achieved much by setting the bishop on e7. Now the c4-pawn deserves attention.

56. ♘e3 ♔c8 57. ♔g4

The king itself would decide the game.

57... ♔c7 58. ♔h5 ♘g7+ 59. ♔h6 ♘e8 60. h4 ♔c8 61. h5 ♔c7

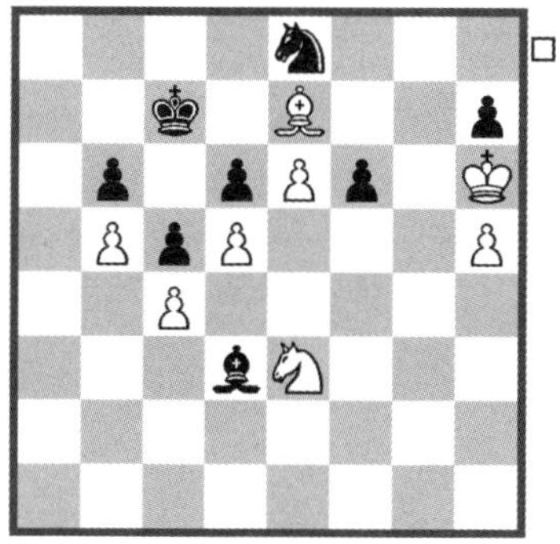

Position after: 61... ♔c7

62. ♘g2!

The only winning move which should have been the start of a very beautiful plan. However Kramnik mistakenly connected it with a bad idea.

62... ♔c8 63. ♘f4 ♗c2 64. ♗xf6?

A miscalculation which should have cost him the win.

64. ♘g6! Instead, this would have been the correct path. 64... hxg6 [64... ♗d3 65. ♔xh7 ♗xc4 66. ♘f4 This is hopeless for Black. White will play ♔g8 and simply advance the h-passer.] 65. hxg6 ♗d3 66. g7 ♘xg7 67. ♔xg7 ♗xc4 68. ♗xd6 ♗xd5 69. e7 ♔d7 70. ♔f8 White wins.

64... ♘xf6 65. ♔g7 ♘e8+ 66. ♔f7 ♘c7 67. e7

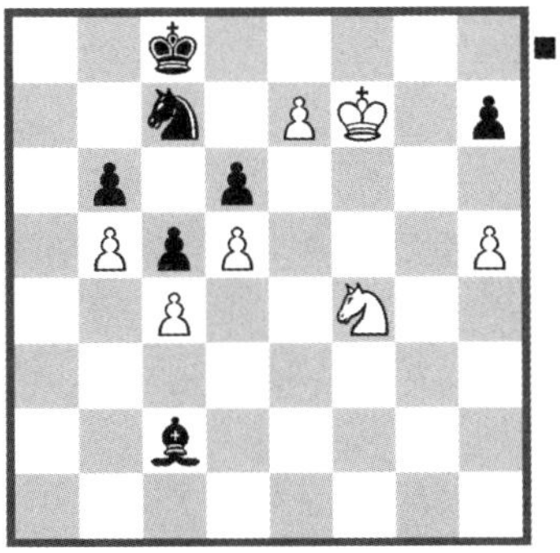

Position after: 67. e7

67... h6 68. ♘e6 ♗d1 69. ♔g6 ♘e8 70. ♘f8 ♗e2 71. ♔xh6 ♗xc4 72. ♔g6

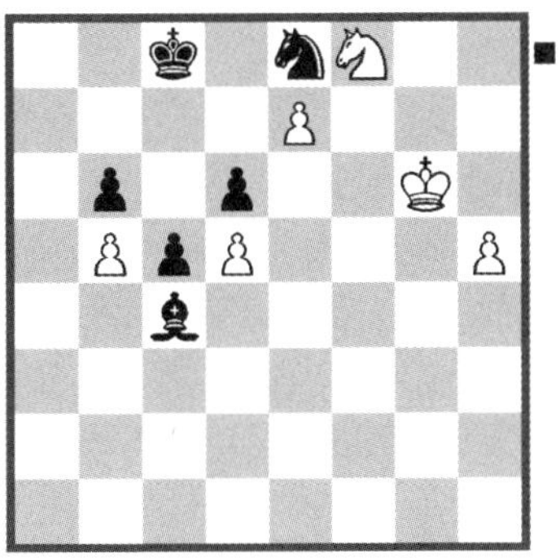

Position after: 72. ♔g6

The previous moves were obvious and forced. After a long struggle and much suffering Black makes a mistake.

72... ♗xd5?

72... ♗d3+! 73. ♔f7 c4 74. h6 c3 75. ♔xe8 c2 76. h7 c1=♕ [76... ♗xh7? 77. ♔f7+–] 77. h8=♕ ♗xb5+ 78. ♔f7 ♕f4+ This leads to a draw.

73. h6 c4?

A fatal mistake.

73... ♘c7! 74. ♘e6! ♗xe6 75. h7 ♔d7 76. h8=♕ ♔xe7 This leads to an unclear position which looks holdable for Black. Deeper engine analysis is required; we will not look any deeper into it.

74. h7 ♗e4+ 75. ♔f7 ♗xh7 76. ♔xe8

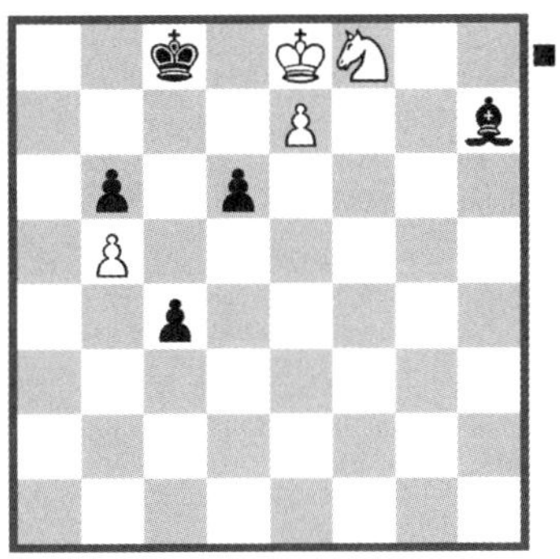

Position after: 76. ♔xe8

76... ♗g8 77. ♘d7! c3

Here Black resigned before seeing 78. ♔f8.

1-0

Key Squares

As it is for middlegames, it is essential even in endgames to establish firm control over key squares.

What are key squares? Generally they are squares that are safe from the opponent's attack and provide you with control over the whole board. In practice, for instance, these can be squares in front of the opponent's central pawn. Just remember the importance of the d4/d5-square in front of the isolated pawn! And it is equally essential to remember to over-control every key square.

By trading pieces on a key square we can deliver many different threats in various directions and this can crush the opponent's defense at any given moment! Its importance, exploitation and capitalization will be clear from this chapter.

Game 99

♙	Risteski, Emil	(2132)
♟	Zlatanovic, Boroljub	(2376)
🌍	Skopje 2019	

Our first example in this chapter will clearly demonstrate the power of occupying a key square. Here we will talk about the d5-square.

Black is dominant here because of three reasons: the aforementioned control over the d5-square, his better bishop (the set-up of pawns on d4 and d6 is clearly in Black's favor) and his powerful majority on the queenside; at the same time there is no danger from White's majority on the kingside. The first move is clear.

31... a5!

Fixing the target on b3. Any advance of this pawn will lead to the creation of a dangerous black passer.

31... ♗d5 32. b4

A) 32... ♔f7 33. ♗c3 ♔e6 34. ♘d1

Position after: 34. ♘d1

34... ♔d7 [34... ♘f5 35. g4 ♘h4 36. f4] 35. ♘e3

B) 32... a5 33. bxa5 bxa5 34. ♘e4

32. ♘e4 ♗d5

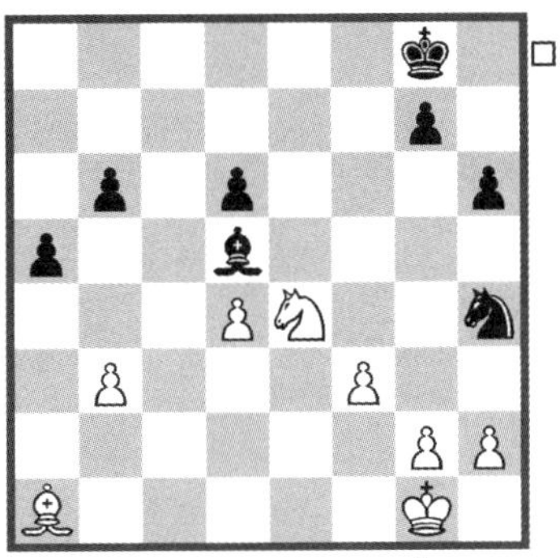

Position after: 32... ♗d5

33. ♘d2

33. ♘xd6!? This is optically unsatisfactory, but it would have been perhaps the last chance for White to resist. 33... ♗xb3 34. ♔f2 White would keep practical chances to hold.

33... ♔f7 34. ♔f2 ♔e6 35. g3 ♘f5 36. ♔e2 b5

Fully constricting White's position.

37. ♗c3!

Position after: 37. ♗c3!

There is no special benefit from this move, but White gives Black a chance to make a mistake if he chose a natural move.

37... b4!

Squeezing further.

Instead the natural 37... a4? is wrong and would lose a huge part of the advantage. 38. bxa4 bxa4 39. ♗b2 White would gain some space and converting would be an almost impossible mission.

38. ♗b2 ♗b7?

Black underestimates the possibility of d5.

A) 38... ♔d7 This is better, with the idea of ...♔c6-b5 and ...a4.

B) 38... g6! Also good, with the same idea.

39. g4 ♘e7

Position after: 39... ♘e7

40. ♔d3?

White misses the possibility to reduce material and activate his pieces, and as a result is inevitably lost.

40. d5+! ♔f7 This appears as winning for Black, but it is an illusion: 41. ♘c4 results in equality.

40... ♗a6+ 41. ♔e4 ♘d5!

Black kicks the white king back of course, not advancing the d-pawn. One characteristic of domination on a key square is the frequent swapping of pieces on it. This would produce various threats in different directions. Every piece with any contact with a key square would gain new strength.

41... d5+? 42. ♔e3 The black king and knight would lose the excellent spot on d5.

42. f4 ♘f6+ 43. ♔f3 ♔d5!

See the previous note!

43... ♗d3? 44. d5+ ♔xd5 45. f5 This gives White surprising counterplay.

44. g5

Position after: 44. g5

44... ♘g8!

if you do not know where to retreat to, simply imagine where you would like to have your knight. Of course, the desired spot is f5.

44... hxg5 45. fxg5 ♘h5 46. ♔e3 g6 47. ♘e4

45. ♘e4

45. gxh6 ♘xh6

45... ♗d3 46. ♘d2

White suffers with no space. Black controls all the important parts of the board.

46... ♘e7 47. ♔e3

Position after: 47. ♔e3

47... ♗b5

47... ♗c2 This also wins easily.

48. h4

Desperation in a lost position.

48. ♔f3 h5 49. ♔e3 ♘f5+–+

48... ♘f5+ 49. ♔f3 h5! 50. ♘c4 ♘xh4+ 51. ♔e3 ♘f5+ 52. ♔d3 a4

White resigned.

0-1

Game 100

♙ Pogonina, Natalija (2484)
♟ Bodnaruk, Anastasia (2463)
Novosibirsk 2016

In our next example White is winning. There is a huge difference between the pieces' activity and even more importantly, there are plenty of weak squares in Black's queenside, which are already under White's control.

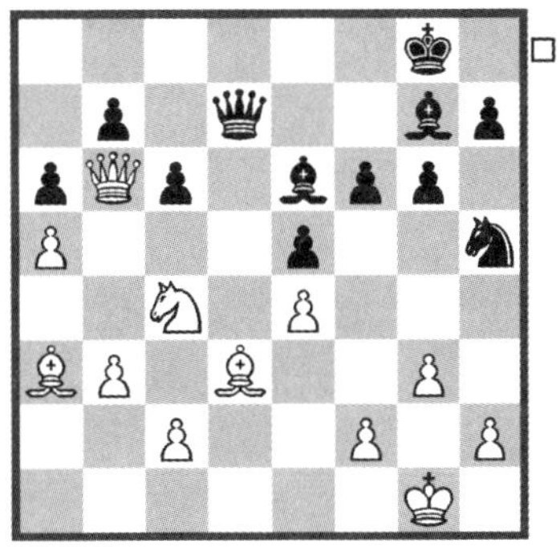

26. ♕a7

After this move White tightens the noose, setting up indefensible threats to the b7-pawn.

26... h6

With a lack of good moves Black opts for bad ones.

27. ♕b8+ ♕c8

Reducing material here just simplifies White's task.

27... ♔h7 28. ♘d6 White wins the b7-pawn and the game.

28. ♕xc8+ ♗xc8

(see diagram next page)

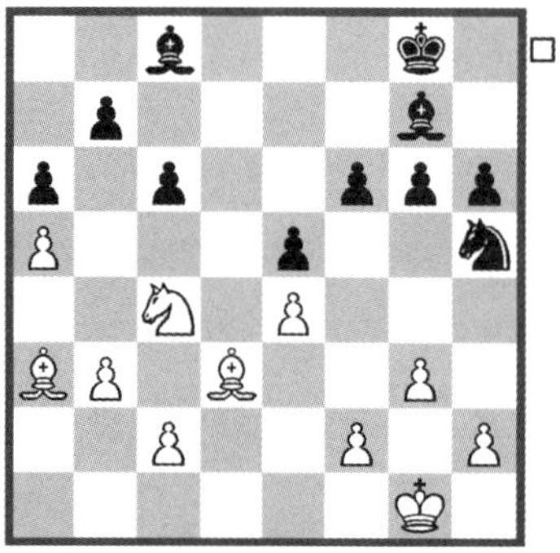

Position after: 28... ♗xc8

29. ♗c5

This move secures the bishop and ♘d6 would end the game afterwards.

29. ♘d6? This is bad due to 29... ♗f8!.

29... f5

It is too late for any counterplay.

29... ♗f8 30. ♗xf8 ♔xf8 31. ♘d6+–

30. exf5gxf5 31. b4 e4 32. ♗e2 ♘f6

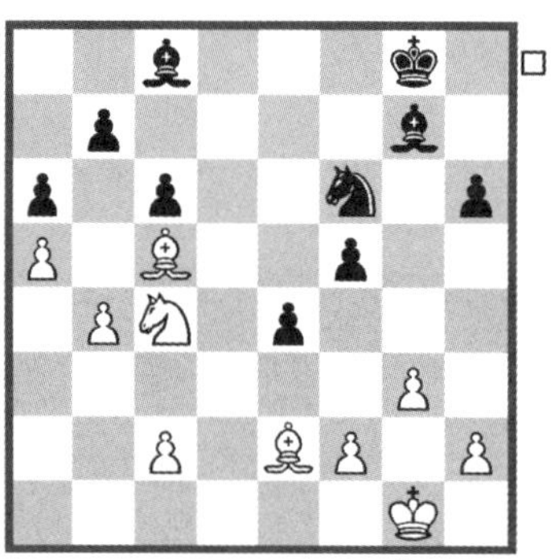

Position after: 32... ♘f6

33. ♘d6

Finally. Now the game is over.

33... ♗d7 34. ♘xb7 ♘d5 35. ♘d6 ♘c7 36. ♗b6 ♘b5

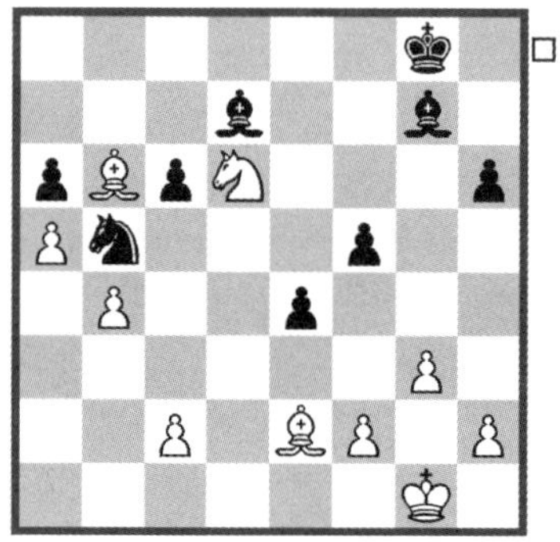

Position after: 36... ♘b5

37. ♘xb5

37. ♗c4+ ♔h7 [37... ♔f8 38. ♗c5!] 38. ♘xb5 cxb5 39. ♗d5+–

37... cxb5 38. c4

White's majority is unstoppable.

38... ♗f8 39. cxb5 ♗xb4 40. bxa6 ♗c6

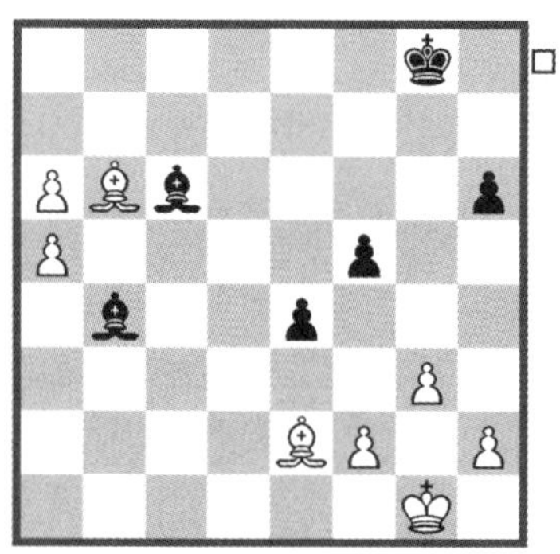

Position after: 40... ♗c6

41. ♗c4+

Directing the bishop to b7 will win instantly.

41... ♔g7 42. ♗e6 ♔f6 43. ♗c8 ♔e5 44. a7 ♔d6 45. a6

1-0

Game 101

♙ Mickovic, Slavisa (2132)
♟ Zlatanovic, Boroljub (2371)
Paracin 2016

This position does not look dangerous for White, but in any case I think Black should be preferred. It's not only because a queen & knight are supposed to work better together than a queen & bishop (as Capablanca already explained a long time ago). The point is that White cannot effectively use the bishop and he already has some problems with harmony. On the other hand Black has some infiltration ideas for both the queen and knights, as will soon become apparent.

28... ♕e6

Keeping the attack on the knight and intending to land on a2 with some threats.

29. f3?

Not an obvious mistake, especially according to the engine. However, from a human point of view, White must refrain from weakening the dark-squared complex – it seems that White may have missed Black's strong response on move 31.

29. ♘d2 This looks passive, but White has no problems after the following. 29... ♕a2 30. ♘c4 A solid response.

29... b5!

Black must liberate the queen from the defense of the e5-pawn.

30. ♘a3 c6 31. b4

Position after: 31. b4

31... ♕e7!

The only move supporting the initiative. The queen liberates the e6-square for the knight, at the same time making it safe. Also, it is very important to have the queen on a dark square; from e7 it may also have some influence on the a7-square.

32. ♔h2 ♘e6 33. ♘b1?

Now I agree with the engine that this is too slow.

33. ♕d2 This is simply necessary. White fights for the kingside dark-squared complex and prepares c4, which will liberate his troops.

33... ♘h5

After this move the game is strategically over. White is unable to control all the strong posts for the black pieces on f4, g3, g5 and h4. All Black needs to do is to find the optimal set-up on the kingside.

34. ♗f1 ♕h4

Preventing ♕f2. Black's queen goes to g3 and soon White will be hopeless against so many threats.

35. ♕d2 ♘g5 36. ♕e3 ♕g3+

(see diagram next column)

Everything is going smoothly.

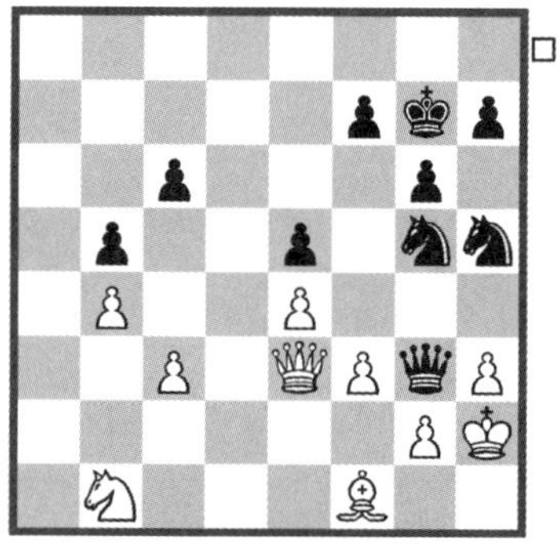

Position after: 36... ♕g3+

37. ♔h1 ♘f4

There is a threat of ...♘fxh3.

38. ♘d2

A picturesque position of a zugzwang! The surprisingly strong control of the important squares has led to a zugzwang! And this was not by accident! Remember this statement.

38... f6

Black secures the e5-pawn with the idea of avoiding play related to ♕c5 and a potential perpetual. The plan is to escape with the king to h6.

39. ♕a7+ ♔h6 40. ♕e3 ♔h5 41. c4

(see diagram next page)

White is forced to do this.

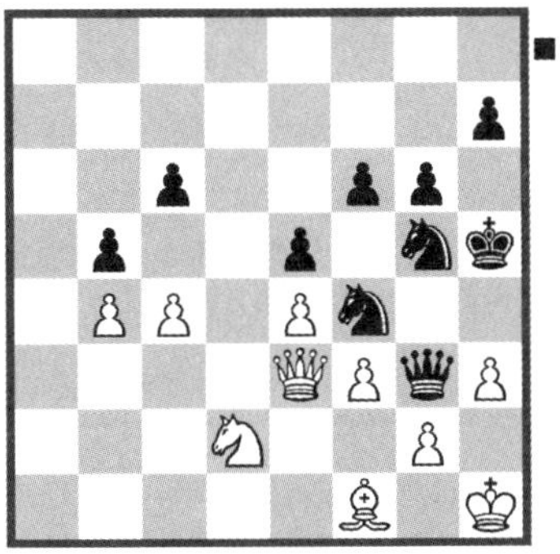

Position after: 41. c4

41... bxc4 42. ♘xc4 ♘fxh3 43. ♗e2 ♕e1+ 44. ♔h2 ♘f4

0-1

Game 102

♙ Sahil, Tickoo (2164)
♟ Zlatanovic, Boroljub (2404)
Serbia 2016

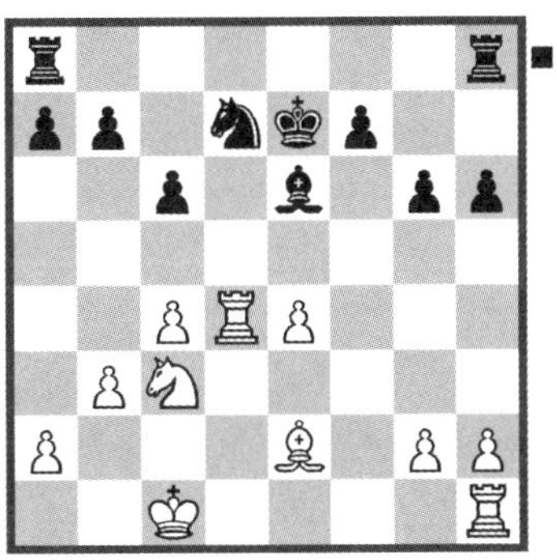

Black clearly dominates due to his domination of the e5-square. Unsurprisingly the draw offer was declined with ease.

17... ♘e5 18. ♖hd1 ♖hd8?!

Although this would lead to the direct use of the e5-spot, nevertheless the rooks should have been kept on the board.

18... g5!? This would have made more sense, with kingside play.

19. ♖xd8 ♖xd8 20. ♖xd8 ♔xd8

Position after: 20... ♔xd8

21. ♔d2?

21. c5 This was necessary here, proving Black was wrong to trade rooks.

21... c5!

Black accumulates new pluses. Fixing the white pawns on the bishop's color is one of the benefits. The weakening of the d5-square does not distract Black at all.

22. ♗f3 ♔e7 23. ♔e3 a6

Securing the spot on the d6-square for the king and preparing the potential thrust ...b5.

24. h4?!

Carelessly advancing the pawn on the edge may give the opponent a chance to create an outside passer!

24. g3 This would have been my choice here. White should direct his knight to d3 and after a potential trade, it should be holdable.

24... ♔d6 25. ♔f4

Position after: 25. ♔f4

25... f6!

Strengthening the e5-spot and preparing ...g5.

26. ♔e3 g5 27. hxg5?

This helps Black to play without risk on both flanks.

27. g3 gxh4 28. gxh4 ♘xf3 29. ♔xf3 ♔e5

(see diagram next column)

Position after: 29... ♔e5

30. ♔e3 ♗d7 31. ♘e2 f5! This should lead to Black's infiltration.

27... fxg5 28. ♘d5 ♗f7

Black carefully prepares the advance of the kingside majority.

29. ♘b6 h5 30. ♘c8+ ♔e6 31. ♘b6

Position after: 31. ♘b6

The knight wanders. White plays without a plan. To be fair it is hard to find anything better.

31... h4!

31... ♘xf3 This move now (or on previous moves) was also possible, but

Black did not want to give up the beautiful knight for the poor bishop.

32. ♗e2 ♗e8 33. ♘d5 ♗d7

The bishop is now on a good diagonal to support any further advance of the majority. White's pieces are completely worthless.

34. b4

White decides in panic to change the rhythm of play, in fear of Black's growing kingside initiative.

34... cxb4 35. ♘xb4 a5

Position after: 35... a5

Setting the queenside pawns on the dark squares in order to occupy the c5-spot in the future.

36. ♘c2 b6 37. ♘d4+ ♔d6 38. ♔d2 ♗e6 39. ♔c3 g4 40. ♘f5+

(see diagram next column)

Capitulation.

Position after: 40. ♘f5+

40... ♗xf5 41. exf5 g3 42. ♗f1 ♘g4 43. ♔d3 ♔e5 44. f6 ♘xf6 45. ♔e3 ♘g4+ 46. ♔d2 ♔f4 47. ♔d3 ♘e3 48. ♔e2 ♘xc4

White resigned.

0-1

Game 103

♙	LionGrandMaster	(2454)
♟	Zlatanovic, Boroljub	(2417)
🌍	Playchess 2013	

Black is dominant, in a similar way to the previous game. Here it is more evident due to White's horrible bishop. Black has a powerful cavalry and should convert without problem. However, this was a blitz internet game and inaccuracies are expected.

20... ♘f7

Black aims with the knight to first occupy the most important blockading spot on e5.

21. a3?!

Trying to set some pawns on the dark squares and obtain space, but missing the mark. This will only produce weaknesses. On the other hand, to be fair, it is difficult to suggest anything better – a logical consequence of the opponent's domination of the square in front of the isolated pawn.

21... ♘e5 22. b3 ♘c5 23. ♔c2

23. b4 ♘cd3! 24. ♖e3 a5! This leaves Black's position in ruins.

23... a5

A very important move when you have the knight on c5 between the pawns on c4 and c6.

24. ♗g2

(see diagram next column)

Position after: 24. ♗g2

24. b4? axb4 25. axb4 ♘cd3–+

24... h5 25. h3?

However this is even worse.

25. h4 This weakens the g4-square. For instance, White is hopeless after the following. 25... ♖xd1 26. ♖xd1 ♘g4

25... h4! 26. g4

26. gxh4 ♖h8–+

26... ♘e6 27. ♘e2 g5!?

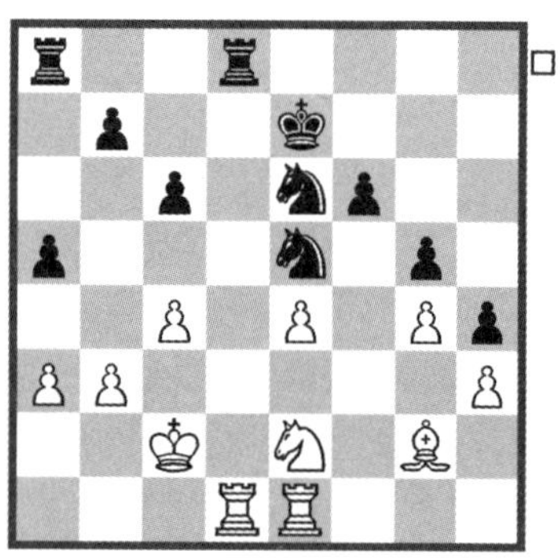

Position after: 27... g5!?

Perhaps Black should keep g5 for the knight. In any case, I felt that my position was trivially won and decided to constrict White further.

28. ♖xd8

Simplifications would not help White.

28... ♖xd8 29. ♖d1? ♖xd1 30. ♔xd1 a4!

Eliminating any doubt about the result.

31. ♔c2 axb3+ 32. ♔xb3 ♔d6 33. ♔b4

Position after: 33. ♔b4

33... ♘d3+

33... ♘f4 Another way to convert. The played move is nevertheless more precise because it exchanges the correct knight and does not allow White to play c5.

34. ♔c3 ♘df4 35. ♘xf4 gxf4!

(see diagram next column)

Position after: 35... gxf4!

36. ♔b4 ♘g5 37. c5+

White goes for some counterplay. Alas, there is nothing.

37... ♔e5 38. ♔a5 f3 39. ♗f1 ♘xe4 40. ♔b6 ♔d5 41. ♔xb7 ♘xc5+ 42. ♔b6 ♘b3 43. a4

Position after: 43. a4

43... c5??

A horrible mistake in time trouble.

43... ♘d2! 44. a5 [44. ♗d3 ♔d4–+] 44... ♘xf1 45. a6

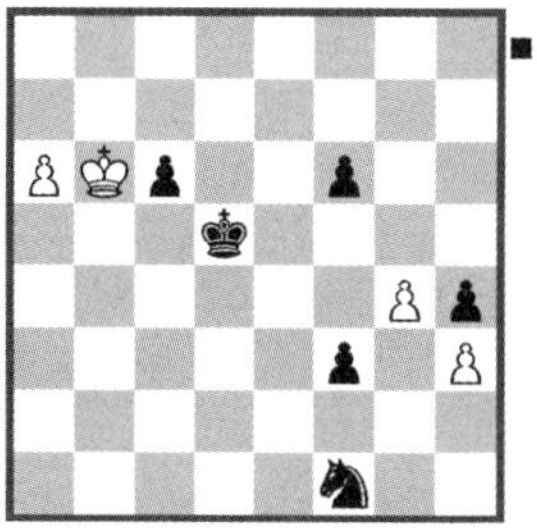

Position after: 45. a6

45... ♘d2 46. a7 f2 47. a8=♕ ♘c4+ This wins and was not difficult to find.

44. ♔b5??

44. a5 ♘xa5 45. ♔xa5 ♔d4 46. ♔b5 ♔e3 47. ♔xc5 ♔f2 48. ♗a6 ♔g2 49. ♔d4 f2 [49... ♔xh3 50. ♔e3 ♔xg4 51. ♗b7=] 50. ♔e4 f1=♕ 51. ♗xf1+ ♔xf1 52. ♔f5 ♔g2 53. ♔xf6 ♔xh3 A draw results.

44... ♘d4+ 45. ♔b6 c4 46. a5 c3 47. a6 c2

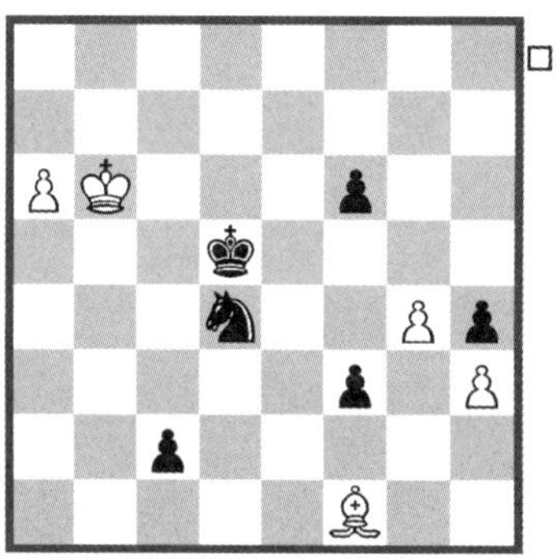

Position after: 47... c2

48. a7 c1=♕ 49. a8=♕+ ♕c6+ 50. ♕xc6+ ♘xc6

0-1

Game 104

♙ Geller, Efim P
♟ Bertok, Mario
Belgrade 1961

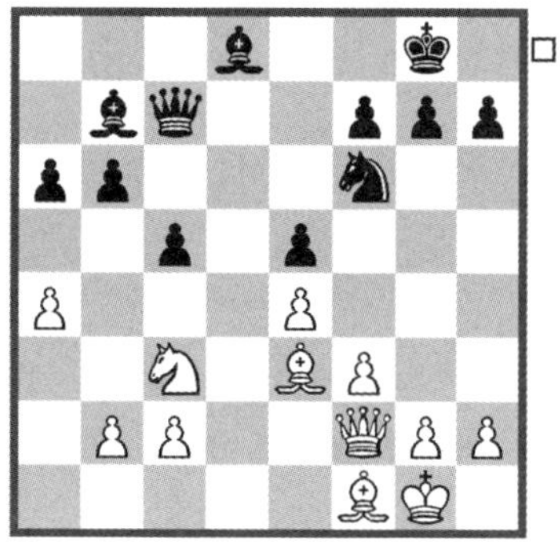

Everything is clear. White has a stable and big advantage. Perhaps it is not so obvious, but his domination on the light squares is the most important positional factor. Exchanging the rook did not help Black – White's advantages are apparent even without the rooks on the board.

19. ♗c4! ♗e7 20. ♕e2 ♕c8

20... a5 This is bad. Now even the b5-square would be added to the list of weaknesses.

21. ♕d3

Simply supporting the control over the important spots, fully in accord with Nimzowitsch's advice.

21... h6

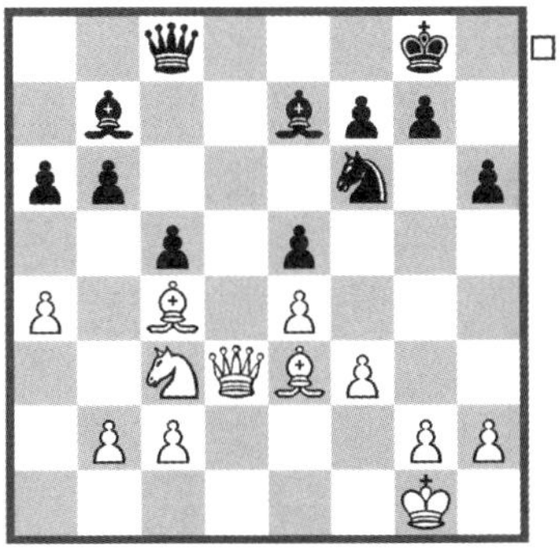

Position after: 21... h6

In return, Black prevents the maneuver ♗g5-f6 which would enhance White's domination of the d5-square.

22. ♔f1

Another instructive point: when there is an exchange of queens the king should be placed closer to the center. Moreover, the king from e1 (or e2) would control some infiltration squares on the d-file, giving freedom to the white queen. This point will become visible later.

22... ♗f8 23. ♔e1 ♗e7 24. ♗f2

The idea is to target the pawn on e5. Furthermore, it may be good to exchange the bishop for the knight on f6.

24... ♔f8

Black must wait. There is zero counterplay.

25. ♗g3 ♘d7 26. ♘d5

A brutal exploitation of the weakness. The point is that White can do it in a different way as well.

26. ♗d5 This is also natural, but the played move is better. White's light-squared bishop is better than Black's and if necessary, it can be exchanged at any given moment.

26... ♗g5

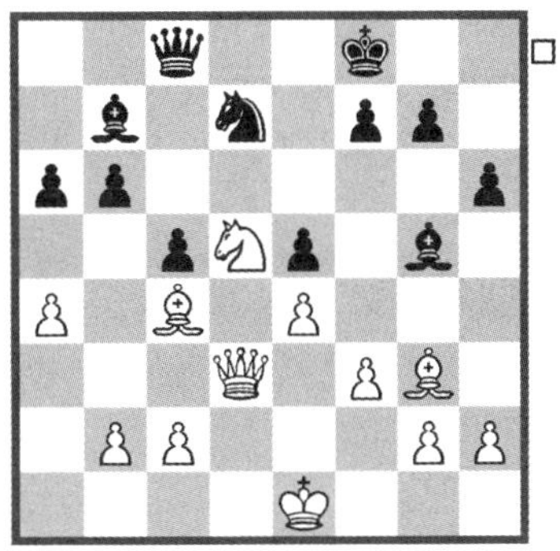

Position after: 26... ♗g5

27. ♗f2

Now targeting the pawns on b6 and c5 and preparing some possible tactical shots.

27. ♘xb6 ♘xb6 28. ♕d6+ ♔g8 29. ♕xb6 ♕d7 30. ♗d3 c4 31. ♗xc4 ♕d2+ 32. ♔f1 This is actually winning for White, but why complicate the task if the opponent is without any active play?

27... ♗d8 28. ♘e3

Both the queen and knight are targeting even d6 now.

28... ♗c7 29. ♘f5

Look at the position of Black's sad pieces – all of them are mostly restricted by the black pawns.

29... ♗b8 30. ♗h4 ♕c6 31. ♗d5 ♕c8

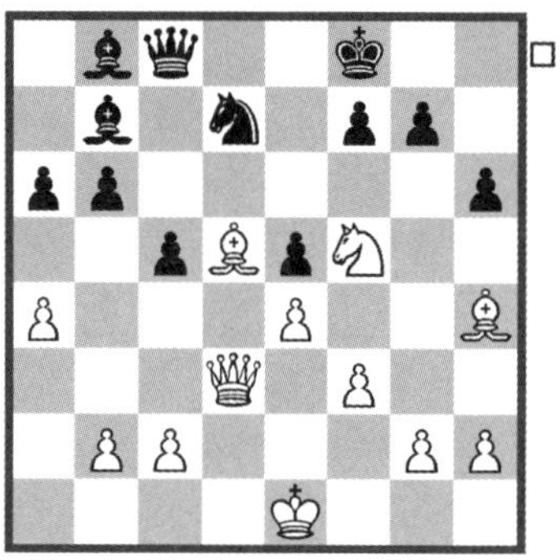

Position after: 31... ♕c8

32. ♗xf7!

Having perfectly led throughout the game, White deserves to finish it in style. Inevitably tactics now come in.

32... g5

32... ♔xf7 33. ♕c4+ ♔g6 [33... ♔f8 34. ♗e7+ ♔e8 35. ♕g8+] 34. ♘e7+

33. ♕c4 ♘f6

If 33... gxh4 34. ♕e6 Mating soon.

34. ♗f2 ♕c6 35. ♗g6 ♕d7 36. a5!

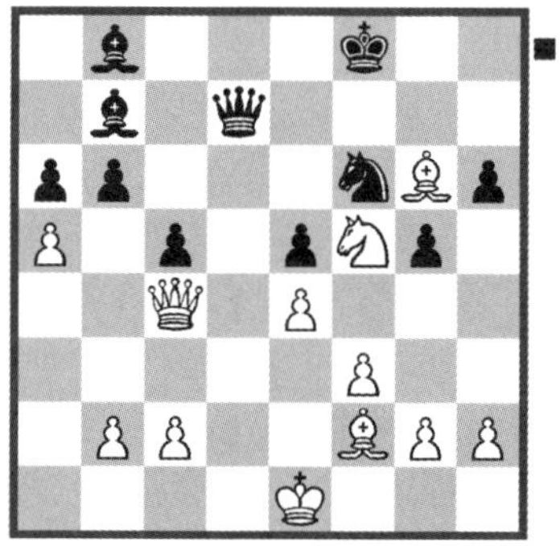

Position after: 36. a5!

Finally, even this blow happens. Black's position collapses after White has exploited all of Black's weaknesses.

36... ♗a7 37. axb6 ♗xb6 38. ♗xc5+ ♗xc5 39. ♕xc5+ ♔g8 40. ♕xe5

1-0

Game 105

♙ Petrosian, Tigran V
♟ Bannik, Anatolij
Riga 1958

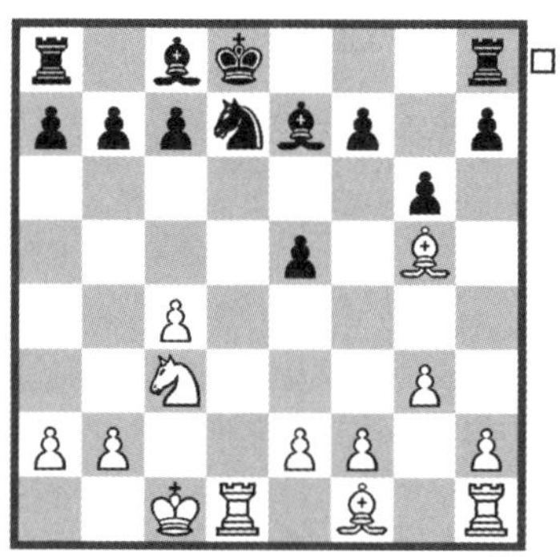

Black is clearly in difficulties. The weak squares in the center may be exploited by White with powerful jumps by his knight to the d5- or e4-squares. However, White must first solve the "exchange problem".

11. h4!

An amazing move. White uses the fact that the black pawn is already on g6. This would give impulse to White's attack on the h-file. Furthermore, Black must not capture on g5 because White would again dominate on the h-file and control the solid outposts on e4, f6 and h6.

11. ♗xe7+ This gives nothing. Black must play very precisely, but it appears that he is out of difficulties after the following. 11... ♔xe7 12. ♘d5+ ♔d8 13. ♗h3 f5 14. e4 c6

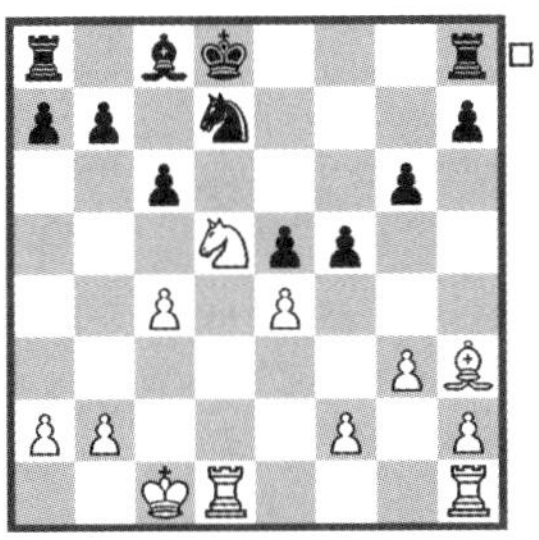

Position after: 14... c6

15. ♘e3 f4 16. ♗xd7 ♗xd7 17. ♘g4 ♖e8 18. ♘f6 ♖e7

11... f6

11... c6 12. ♘e4 h6 13. ♘d6 ♖h7 14. ♗xe7+

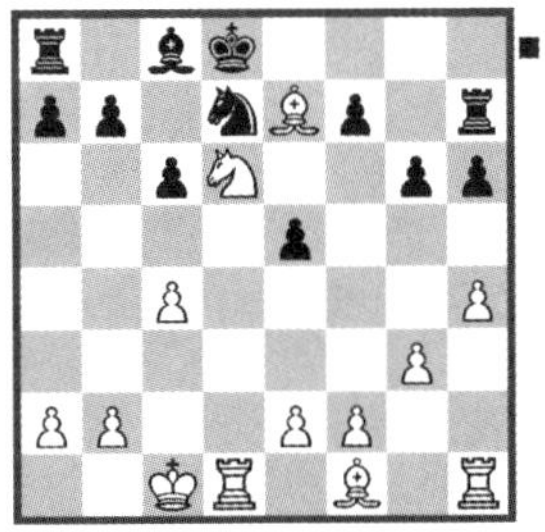

Position after: 14. ♗xe7+

14... ♔xe7 15. ♗h3 f5 16. e4 White is winning.

12. ♗e3

A perfect place for this bishop. Furthermore, White doesn't plan to advance the e-pawn; the bishop on f1 will be activated on g2 or h3.

12... c6 13. h5

Forcing Black's next move and creating new weaknesses.

13... g5 14. ♗h3 ♔c7 15. ♘e4

White's pieces are perfectly placed. After the obvious exchange of the light-squared bishops the e4- and f5-squares would come under White's control, giving him excellent winning chances.

15... ♘b6 16. ♗xc8 ♖axc8 17. b3

(see diagram next page)

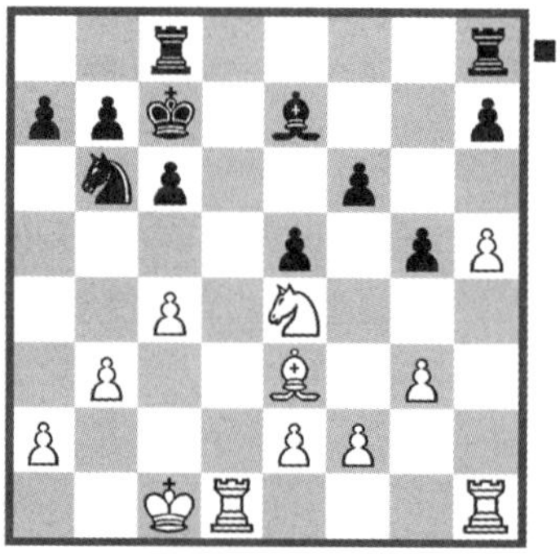

Position after: 17. b3

17... ♖cd8?!

A) 17... g4 This was suggested as better, although after Petrosian's plan of 18. h6 with the idea of 19. ♖h5 White keeps an edge.

B) 17... ♘d7 This was perhaps the best alternative although after 18. g4 White's advantage is undisputed.

Black's last move is natural – by reducing material he wants to reduce White's pressure, although it is very difficult to predict White's next brilliant move.

18. ♗c5!

What a surprise! Why exchange the good bishop for the bad one? The point is that the black bishop protects the pawn on f6 and controls the weak d6-square. Everything will become clear after seeing the entire game – the continuation confirms that Iron Tigran's idea was just brilliant.

18. ♗xb6+ axb6 19. g4 On the other hand this really looks perfect for White. Actually it is, but in his long analysis Petrosian showed that domination on the e4- and f5-squares and pressure on the weak f6-pawn would not guarantee a win in any future minor piece endgame. In fact all of the three above-named points should be counted as one weakness as they are close to each other. Petrosian explained that he would not have been able to create another weakness in Black's camp on the queenside and we should believe him. On the other hand, by choosing this paradoxical move in the game he convincingly proved that he was right. Let's see.

18... ♖xd1+

18... ♗xc5 This loses a pawn after the following. 19. ♘xc5 ♖he8 20. ♖xd8

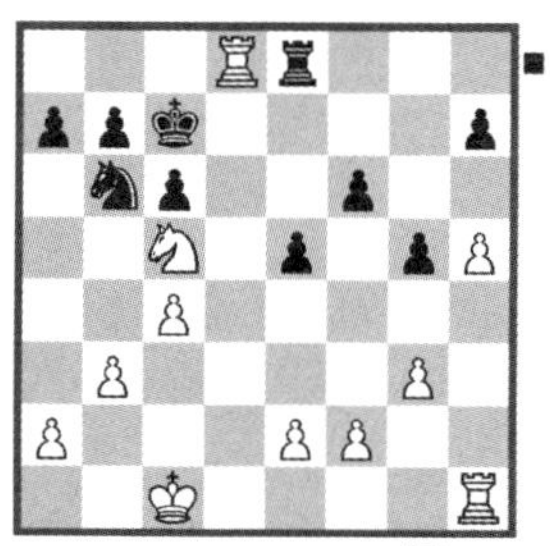

Position after: 20. ♖xd8

20... ♔xd8 [20... ♖xd8? 21. ♘e6+] 21. ♘xb7+

19. ♖xd1 ♗xc5 20. ♘xc5 ♖e8 21. ♘e4

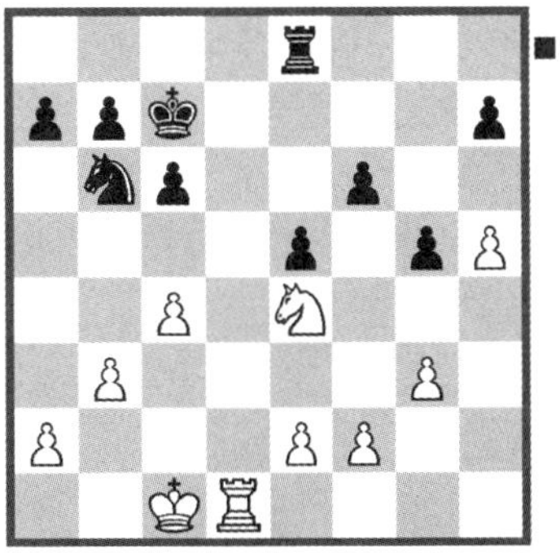

Position after: 21. ♘e4

Things have become clear – White uses the weak squares on c5, d5, e4, and f5 to create various threats. Black must play very carefully to avoid immediate collapse.

21... ♖e6

21... ♖f8 22. g4

Position after: 22. g4

22... ♘c8 [22... ♖f7 23. ♖d6] 23. ♘c5 ♖f7 24. ♘e6+

22. g4 a5

Played with the idea to exchange some pawns if White wants to launch a queenside expansion.

23. ♖d3!

It is time to remind ourselves of the words of the great genius José Raul Capablanca – that the third rank should be opened for rook maneuvers.

23... ♘d7 24. ♔c2 b6 25. ♖f3 ♔d8 26. a3

Preparing for queenside play.

26... c5

Black is forced to advance the c-pawn first. If he allows White to advance the pawns to b4 and c5 all the black pieces would be fully paralyzed. On the other hand, Black cannot play this move after White's move b4; if so then White again advances his b-pawn to b5 and the same thing (almost) would happen – Black would face paralysis.

27. ♔c3

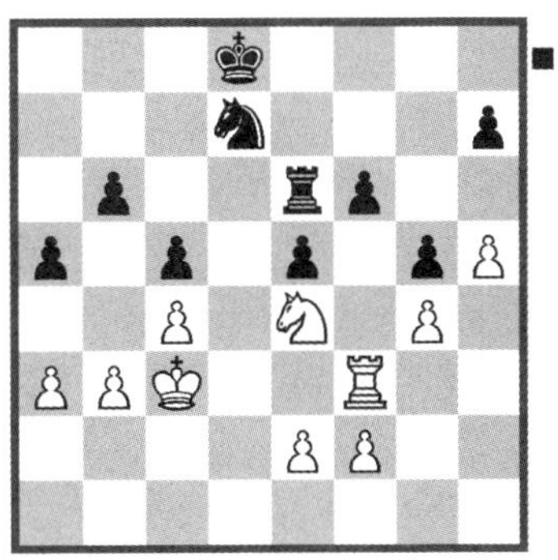

Position after: 27. ♔c3

27... ♔e7 28. ♖d3 ♖c6 29. ♖d5

Not such a dangerous move. It is more a demonstration of power following the important "don't rush!" principle.

29... ♘f8 30. ♘g3 ♘e6 31. ♘f5+ ♔e8 32. e3

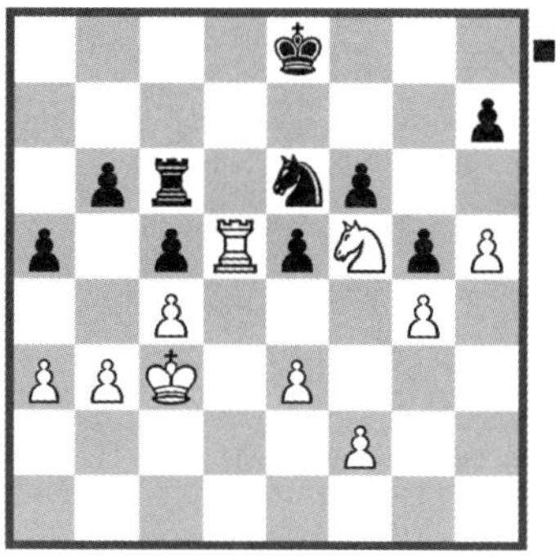

Position after: 32. e3

A sad destiny for the black knight – immediately after it obtains a chance to make an active jump, it is restricted again.

32... ♘c7

32... ♘d8 The idea is to place a knight on f7 and to control White's knight squares, or perhaps even to exchange it – this was correctly suggested as a better option, although it is not clear how Black can solve all his problems.

33. ♖d1 ♘e6 34. ♔d3 ♖c7 35. ♔e4 ♖c6 36. ♘d6+?!

A question mark is not given for this move because it would only delay the win. After a long journey, White will obtain almost the same position and find the win a little later. Perhaps due to time trouble Petrosian decided not to force play and instead waited for the next time control.

36. ♖d6! This easily wins. There are many weak squares being used by the white knight and the king simultaneously and these are fatal for Black. 36... ♖xd6 37. ♘xd6+ ♔d7

Position after: 37... ♔d7

38. ♘b5! White wins a pawn after setting the knight to d5 and the king to f5.

36... ♔e7 37. ♘f5+ ♔e8 38. ♘d6+ ♔e7 39. ♘f5+ ♔e8

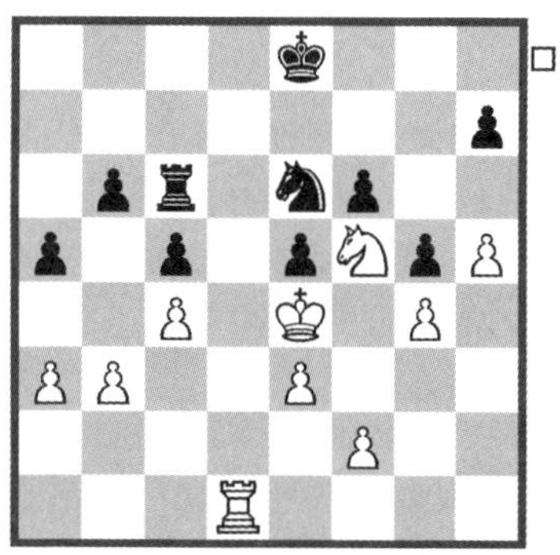

Position after: 39... ♔e8

A three-fold repetition – it is strange that Black did not claim a draw here!

40. a4?

The move is not objectively really bad, but I put a question mark because it's clearly against the spirit of the position. Such a move definitely blocks one side of the board and is not a good choice as a waiting move. Who knows, perhaps White needed to to open the position on the queenside in order to win the game?

40. ♖d2 This would have been a good choice as a neutral, waiting move.

40... ♘d8 41. ♘h6 ♘e6□

A) 41... ♖e6 42. ♔f5 ♖c6 43. ♘g8

B) 41... ♔e7 42. ♘g8+ ♔e8 43. ♔f5

C) 41... ♘b7 42. ♘g8 ♔f8 43. ♖d7!

42. ♘g8!

Missing the win several times; White must find only moves to crash through Black's defense or to get another chance as the one he missed on move 36.

42... ♘f8

42... ♔f7 43. ♖d7+! ♔xg8 44. ♔d5+–

43. ♖d2!

(see diagram next column)

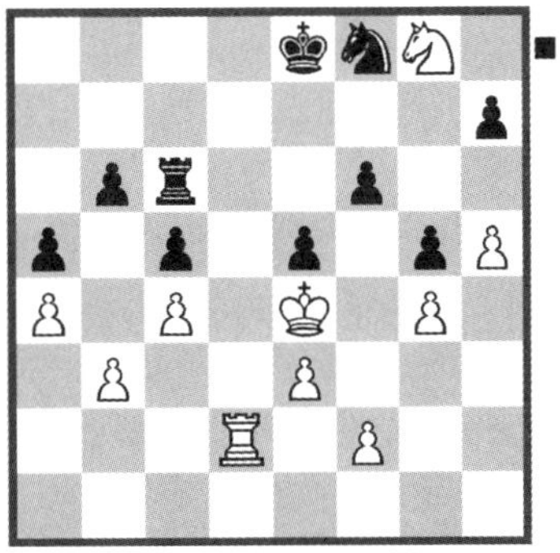

Position after: 43. ♖d2!

43. ♔f5? ♔f7 44. ♘h6+ ♔g7 45. ♖d8 ♘e6 46. ♖e8 ♘c7–+

43... ♔f7□

43... ♘d7 44. ♔f5 ♔d8 45. e4 ♔e8 46. f3 ♔d8 47. ♖xd7+! ♔xd7 48. ♘xf6++– Another interesting way to win the game.

44. ♘h6+ ♔e8 45. ♘f5 ♘e6

45... ♘d7 46. ♔d5

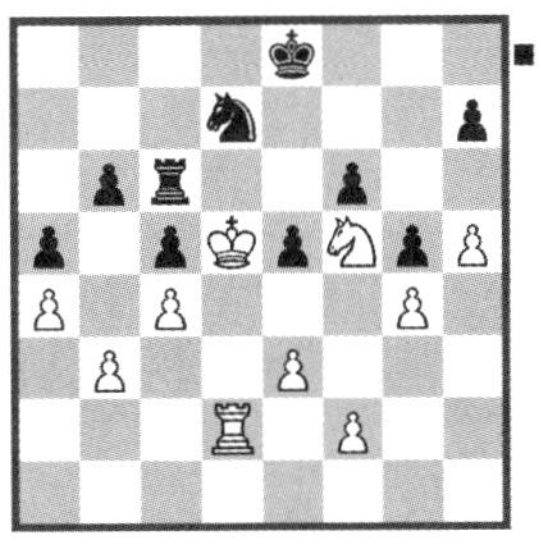

Position after: 46. ♔d5

46... ♘b8 [46... ♖c7 47. ♔e6] 47. ♖d1 ♔d7 48. ♔e4+ ♔e8 49. ♖d6 This also leads to an easy win.

46. ♖d6!

Finally, White goes for this winning move.

46... ♖xd6 47. ♘xd6+ ♔d7 48. ♘b5

Position after: 48. ♘b5

48... ♘g7

48... ♘f8 49. ♔f5 ♔e7 50. ♘c3 ♘d7 51. ♘d5+

Position after: 51. ♘d5+

51... ♔f7 52. e4 h6 53. f3! +- A very beautiful win. Now it is clear why it can be very important to have some reserve tempi in blocked positions. There is mutual zugzwang!

49. h6! ♘e8 50. ♔d5

Once again, zugzwang! You can be certain that White didn't win this game accidentally; the many zugzwang positions in this endgame are the result of White's full domination on the multitude of weak squares in Black's camp (b5, d5, d6, e4, f5).

50... f5

A desperate bluff. White easily combines a convincing conversion and beauty in the rest of the game.

51. ♔xe5 fxg4 52. ♘c3 ♔e7 53. ♘e4 ♔f7 54. ♔f5 g3 55. fxg3 g4 56. ♘g5+

Position after: 56. ♘g5+

56... ♔g8 57. ♔e6 ♘c7+ 58. ♔d7 ♘a6 59. e4 ♘b4 60. e5 ♘d3 61. e6

Such a typical game for Petrosian – a remarkable win with a convincing exploitation of his opponent's many weaknesses. Thanks to the mistake on the 36th move, we could explore the amazing beauty of this endgame, like some studies where we are presented with marvelous pictures of zugzwang.

1-0

Game 106

♙ Yudovich, Mikhail Mikhailovic
♟ Bondarevsky, Igor Tsakharovich
Tbilisi 1937

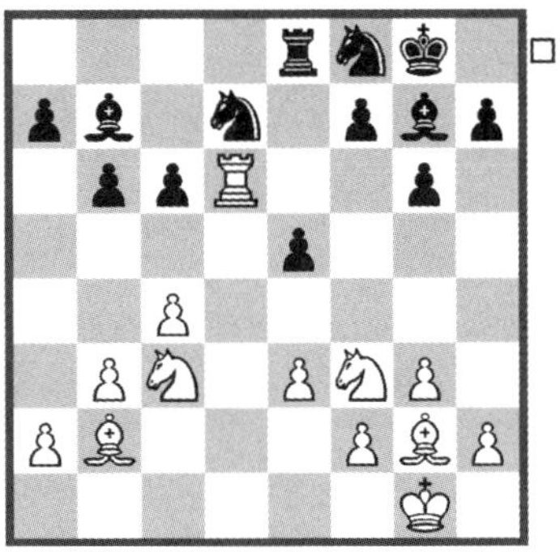

With his two bishops powerfully placed and the rook already deep inside the opponent's territory, White is clearly better. However it is necessary to bring new units into the attack and White redirects his cavalry with great impact.

20. ♘d2!

A brutal use of the important e4- and d6-squares.

20... ♖e6 21. ♘de4! f5

Black plays practically the best moves. If he can play ...e4 he would have excellent chances. However White prevents it!

22. ♖xe6 ♘xe6 23. ♘d6 ♗a8

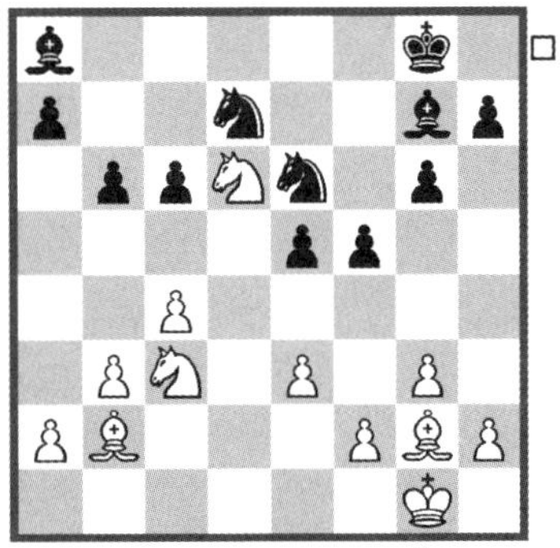

Position after: 23... ♗a8

24. e4!

White temporarily closes the long diagonal with idea to keep it opened! Furthermore, White strikes at the weak f5-pawn.

24... fxe4?

A horrible strategic mistake. This allows White to instantly activate all his pieces and at the same time create many weaknesses.

If Black advances, then the following is a nice forced line which is clearly in White's favor. 24... f4 25. ♗h3 ♘dc5 26. b4

Position after: 26. b4

26... ♘g5 27. bxc5 ♘xh3+ 28. ♔g2. Nevertheless this would have been the lesser evil for Black.

25. ♘cxe4 a5

The idea is to make this pawn safer.

26. ♘e8

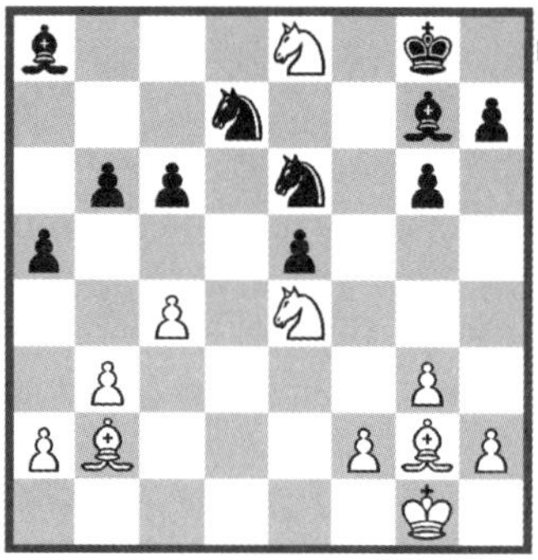

Position after: 26. ♘e8

There is nothing wrong with 26. ♗h3.

26... ♔f8

Black allows his bishop to be eliminated but nothing helps.

A) 26... ♗h8 27. ♗h3 ♔f7 28. ♘8d6+

Position after: 28. ♘8d6+

28... ♔e7 29. ♘c8+ ♔f7 30. f4+–

B) 26... ♗f8 27. ♘8f6+ ♘xf6 28. ♘xf6+ ♔f7 29. ♗xe5+–

27. ♘xg7 ♘xg7

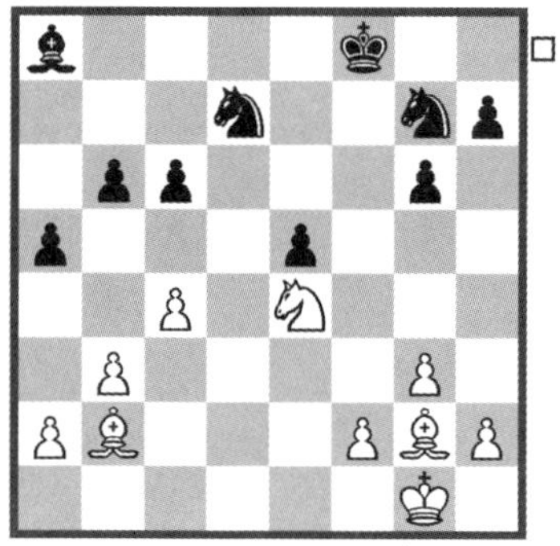

Position after: 27... ♘xg7

28. ♗a3+?!

28. ♘g5! h6 29. ♘f3 This would win directly.

28... ♔g8 29. ♘d6 ♘e6 30. ♘c8 ♔f7 31. ♘d6+ ♔f6 32. ♘e8+

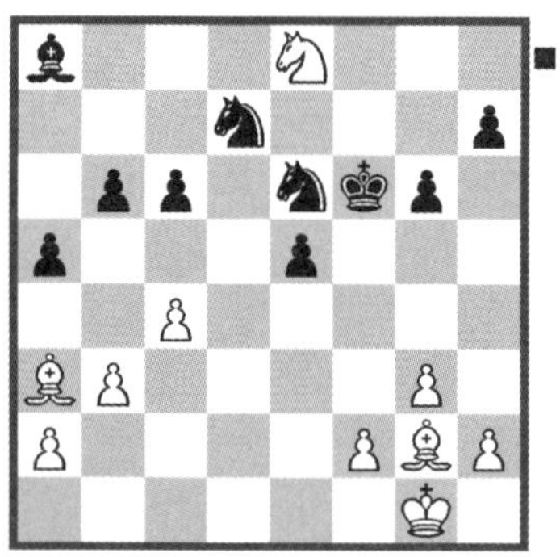

Position after: 32. ♘e8+

There is no need to rush. Black is unable to keep all his weaknesses under protection.

32... ♔f7 33. ♘d6+ ♔f6 34. ♘e4+ ♔f7 35. ♔f1?

However this is already too slow.

35. h4 This would have fixed Black's kingside pawns, and threatened ♘g5.

35... c5!?

Black improves his defensive chances with this. Anyway, White is much better.

36. ♘d6+ ♔e7 37. ♘c8+

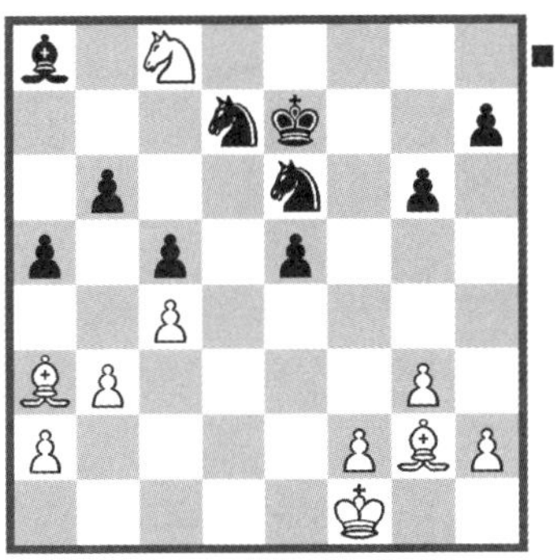

Position after: 37. ♘c8+

37... ♔d8 38. ♗xa8 ♔xc8 39. ♗c1 ♘d4 40. h4!

The correct approach comes late. Of course, White should have won earlier with his cavalry on the board exploiting the many weaknesses. But in any case, the bishop pair dominates.

40... ♘f6

40... ♘f8! This would have created a better defensive set-up. 41. ♗e4! White's attack on the kingside would be supported with ♗h6 and h5.

41. ♗g5 ♘e8 42. ♗d5!

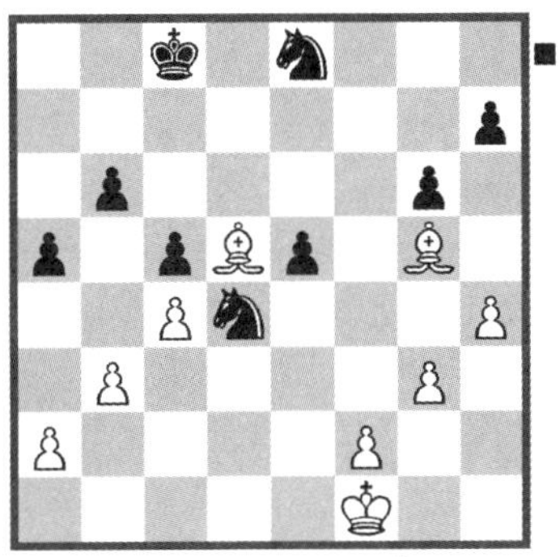

Position after: 42. ♗d5!

Black's queenside pawns are targets.

42... ♘d6 43. ♗g8 h5 44. ♗h7

A decisive material loss for Black is inevitable, despite his attempts to organize a counter-attack on the queenside.

44... a4 45. bxa4! ♘xc4 46. ♗xg6 ♘b2 47. ♗xh5 c4 48. ♗g4+

1-0

Game 107

♙ Minasian, Artashes (2590)
♟ Kharlov, Andrei (2600)
Linares 1999

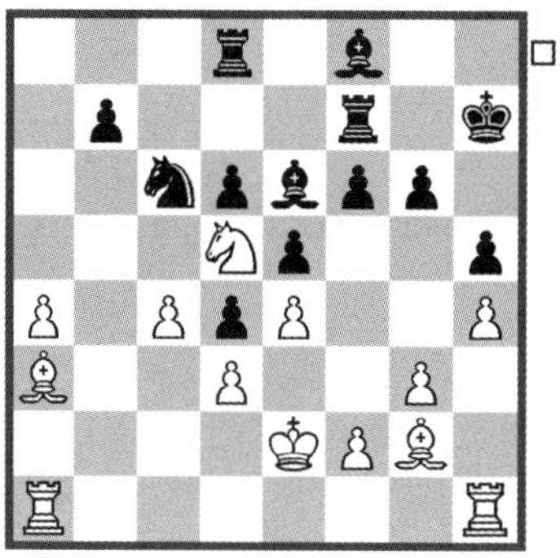

In this example White enjoys a stable and serious advantage. He has a better-mobilized army and direct and clear play on the queenside. Black can barely even find a logical plan. There is nothing for him to do on the kingside, while on the queenside he has problems with harmony. White first keeps his knight on the board.

24. ♘b6!

24. ♖hb1 This is also good, but the played move is logical and better.

24... ♘b8

24... f5 This does not achieve anything because White can ignore it with 25. ♖ab1!.

25. ♖ab1

Not 25. ♖hb1 because this rook may be needed on the f-file, or to prepare for the exchange ♗h3. The other rook has no job on the a-file.

25... ♘a6 26. ♖b5 ♘c5

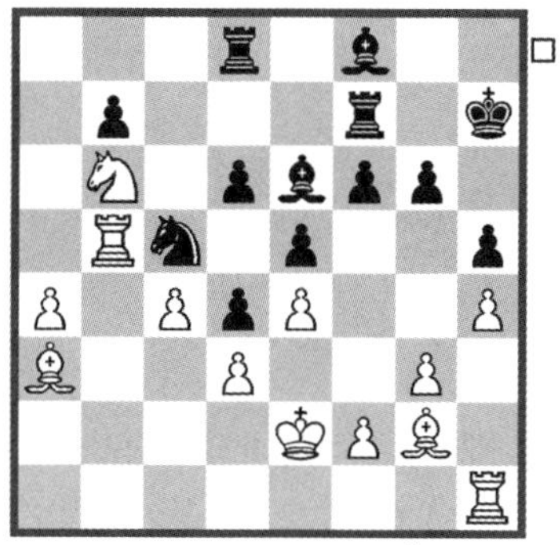

Position after: 26... ♘c5

It may look like an excellent decision for Black to transfer the knight here, but this is an illusion.

27. ♖hb1

Also a good option, but it still doesn't look direct.

27. ♗xc5 dxc5 28. ♗h3!

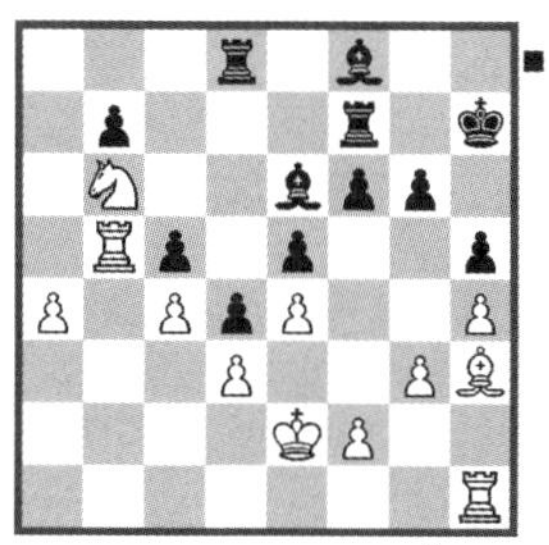

Position after: 28. ♗h3!

This gives White a decisive advantage after, for instance, the following line. 28... f5 29. ♖hb1 ♗d6 30. a5 Black would remain with his awful bishop pair.

27... ♔g7 28. ♖a5

28. a5 Regarded as good – preparing to eliminate the black knight with pressure on the b7-pawn.

28... ♖b8 29. ♖a7

There are no visible useful moves for Black.

29... ♖d8 30. a5 ♘a6

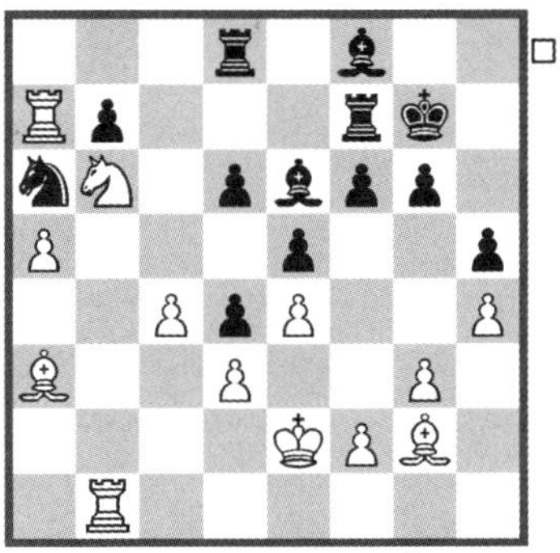

Position after: 30... ♘a6

31. ♘d5

After targeting so many crucial squares which allowed White to regroup, the knight goes back to d5, opening the b-file for action.

31... ♖dd7 32. ♖b6 ♗xd5 33. exd5! ♘c5 34. ♗xc5

The presence of opposite-colored bishops does not help Black.

34... dxc5 35. d6! ♗xd6 36. ♗d5 ♖fe7 37. a6!

Position after: 37. a6!

37... ♖e8

37... bxa6 38. ♖axa6 ♗c7 39. ♖xf6 This also loses.

38. ♖bxb7 ♖xb7 39. ♖xb7+

Black resigned.

1-0

Pawn Majority

Of course the natural goal of pawn play is the creation of a passed pawn and its promotion! However, this does not happen often!

The logical prerequisite to creating a passed pawn is to have a majority. Of course, with balanced material there would be majorities for both players, on different wings. Which majority is better? Well generally, it is clear that a 2:1 majority is "the best one". Not only because it can easily create a passer, but even more importantly, it is because of the fact that the passer will be a distant one – it should deflect the opponent's army (and king!) which would lead to progress and to gaining material on the opposite flank!

You may have already seen this approach a multitude of times. However what about other majorities? Is a 3:2 always better than a 4:3 majority? What about doubled pawns? What about exchanging pieces? Is it better to have more or fewer pieces kept on the board in a situation with mutual majorities? All these answers can be found in this chapter. And a lot of others besides!

Game 108

♙ Botvinnik, Mikhail
♟ Rabinovich, Ilya Leontievich
Leningrad 1934

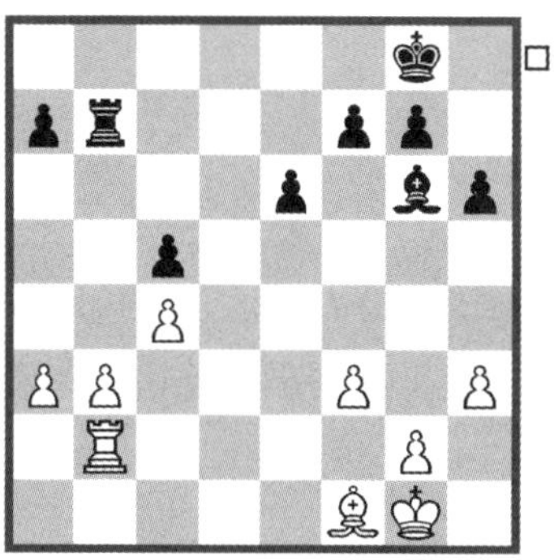

Let's start this chapter with a relatively simple example. White has the better majority – 3:2, which is usually better than 4:3. However the point is that Black has separated a- and c-pawns and it looks like the majority will soon transform to an even better version for White – 2:1.

35. b4

This should be played before ...a5.

35... ♔f8 36. ♔f2 ♔e7 37. ♔e3

37. b5 The idea is a4-a5. So this move should be generally played before Black can prevent it with his king.

37... ♔d7 38. ♗e2 ♔c7 39. b5

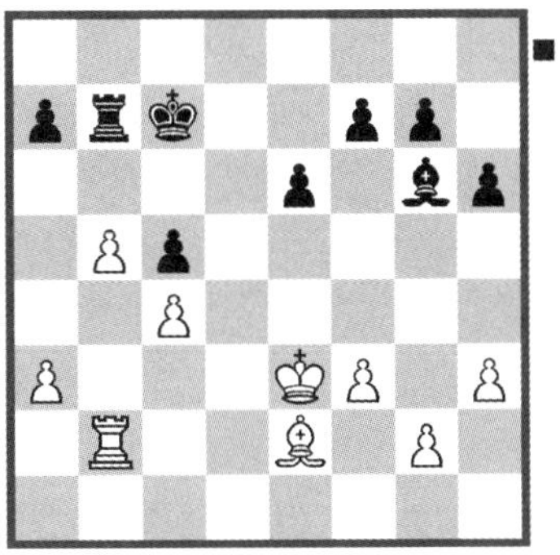

Position after: 39. b5

39... ♖b8

39... ♔b6 This is not good because of the following. 40. ♖d2 White invades. 40... ♔a5 41. ♖d6 ♔a4 42. ♔d2!

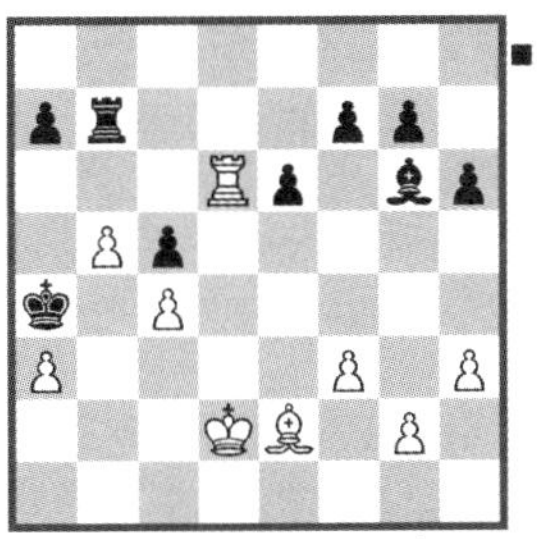

Position after: 42. ♔d2!

42... ♔b3 43. a4! White wins easily.

40. a4 f6

40... ♔b6 This again fails to 41. ♖d2!.

41. a5 e5

Black has set a barrier on the kingside, but White's queenside barrier is much more effective and dangerous. Black must deal with the persistent threat of b6, especially if it creates the a-passer.

42. ♖d2 ♗f7

Position after: 42... ♗f7

43. f4!?

White directly strikes at the barrier.

43. h4!? The idea of fixing with h5 and then opening the position is even better. Black must not capture on h5 because of ♖d5 with an easy win for White.

43... exf4+

Black must not allow his pawn to be isolated on e5 because ♔e4 will decide the game.

44. ♔xf4 ♖e8 45. ♗f3 ♗e6?

45... ♗xc4! Necessary. Black would get serious relief after the following. 46.

♖c2 ♗d3!

Position after: 46... ♗d3!

47. ♖xc5+ ♔b8 However, after 48. ♗c6 White will keep the advantage.

46. ♗c6 g5+ 47. ♔f3 ♖f8 48. ♗d5

After the black rook has left the e-file White can offer to trade the bishops without any chance for the opponent to obtain counterplay.

48... ♖d8

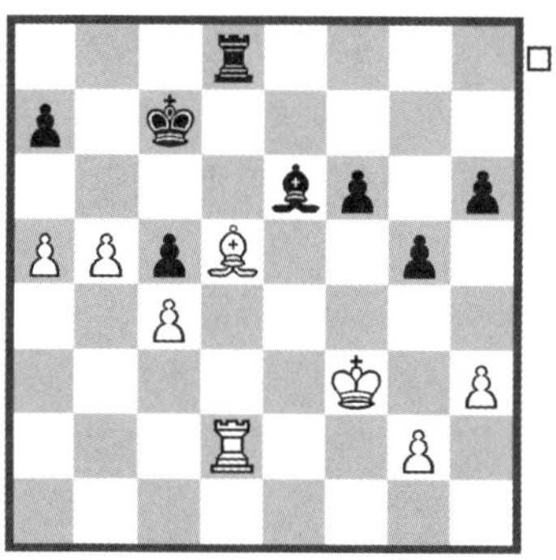

Position after: 48... ♖d8

49. ♔e3

White defends the rook.

49. ♔e4 This is also good, of course.

49... ♗c8

49... ♗xd5 50. ♖xd5!

Position after: 50. ♖xd5!

50... ♖xd5 51. cxd5 Let's remember the "rule of 7" (the “Cheron Rule”). White has two passers (after b6 the a-pawn will become a passer) on the 5th rank with two squares in-between, which leads to a win.

50. ♖a2

White prepares b6 with a6 with a win.

50. ♖b2 White follows with b6, winning directly.

50... ♗b7 51. ♖d2

There is no need to rush.

51... ♖e8+

Black declines a repetition.

52. ♔f2 ♖d8

(see diagram next page)

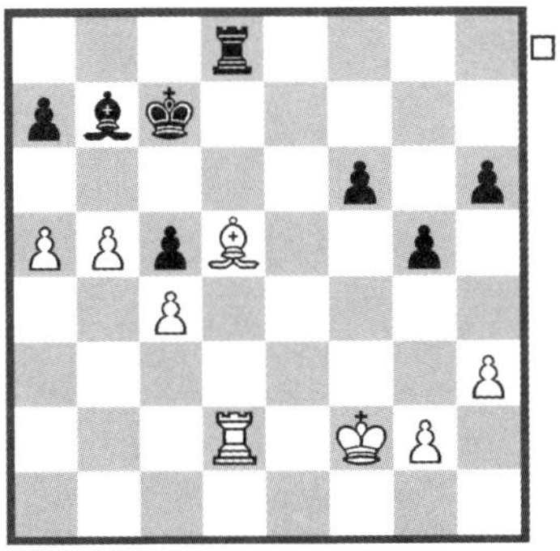

Position after: 52... ♖d8

53. g4

White fixes Black's kingside structure. After the bishops are gone this would be useful. The rook can go to f3 to attack the f6-pawn and the king gets the route f3-e4-f5 as well.

53... ♗c8 54. ♖d3 ♖f8 55. ♖e3! f5

A last attempt to get some play.

56. gxf5 ♖xf5+ 57. ♔g2

57. ♔g3 This is more methodical.

57... ♗d7

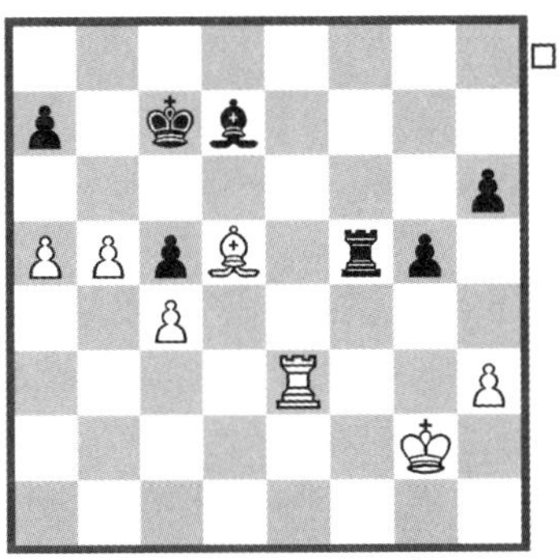

Position after: 57... ♗d7

58. b6+!

Finally, this break ends the resistance.

58... axb6 59. a6! ♔b8 60. ♖e7 ♔a7 61. ♗b7 ♗c6+ 62. ♗xc6+ ♔xa6 63. ♗e4

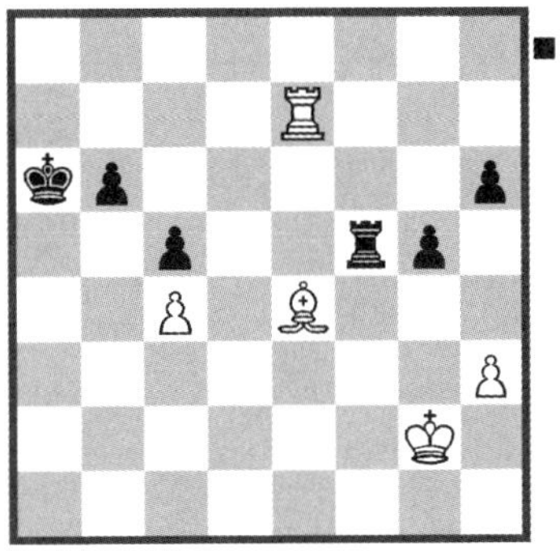

Position after: 63. ♗e4

It is time to resign.

63... ♖f4 64. ♗d3 ♖f6 65. ♗e2 ♔a5 66. ♔g3 ♔b4 67. ♖e3 ♖f4 68. ♖e6 ♔c3 69. ♖xb6 ♖e4 70. ♗f1 ♖f4 71. ♔g2 h5 72. ♖g6 g4 73. h4 ♔d2 74. ♖g5 g3 75. ♖xh5 ♖f2+ 76. ♔g1 ♖f4 77. ♖d5+

Black resigned.

1-0

Game 109

♙ Yates, Frederick Dewhurst
♟ Alekhine, Alexander
The Hague 1921

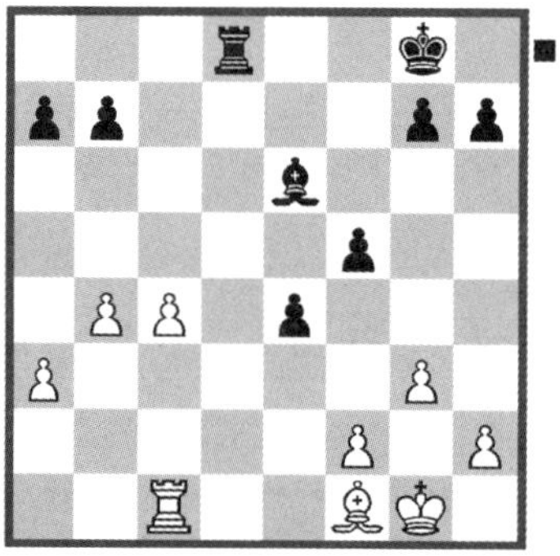

In our next example Black is better despite his formally "worse majority". Black dominates on the only open file and his pawns are more advanced – space is also a significant factor. In addition his king will be quicker to come to the center. This is the first task for Black.

26... ♔f7

26... ♖d2 This would achieve nothing. White would exploit the absence of Black's rook from its defensive position with 27. c5, with ideas of b5 and c6 and ♗c4 as well. The game would be equal.

27. c5 ♔f6 28. ♗c4

All moves have been natural. Perhaps Black's next move confused White.

28... ♗c8!?

Black keeps his "passive" bishop. However, he has an idea after preparing the natural ...f4 to install his bishop on the h3-square or the g4- and f3-squares. In any case, without bishops on the board there would not be any winning chances.

29. a4?!

29. h4! The side playing for a draw should exchange as many pawns as possible!

29... g5 30. b5 f4

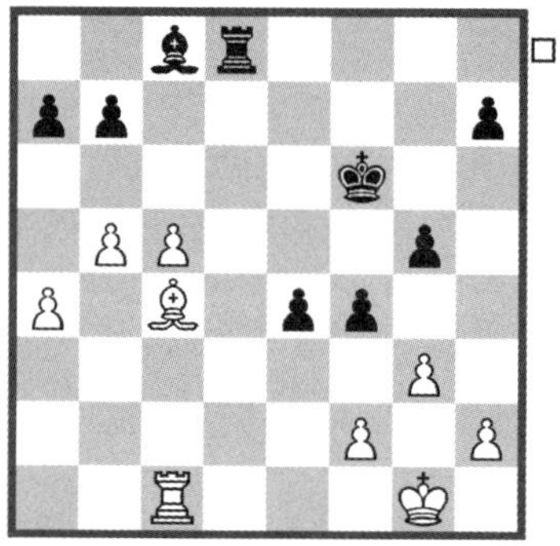

Position after: 30... f4

31. ♔f1?!

This must be bad. Now Black gets a strong initiative.

31. a5 This was better instead, with counter-chances on the queenside.

31... ♖d2 32. ♔e1 ♖b2

It becomes difficult for White to launch the majority. On the other hand Black has many possibilities on the kingside.

33. gxf4 gxf4

(see diagram next page)

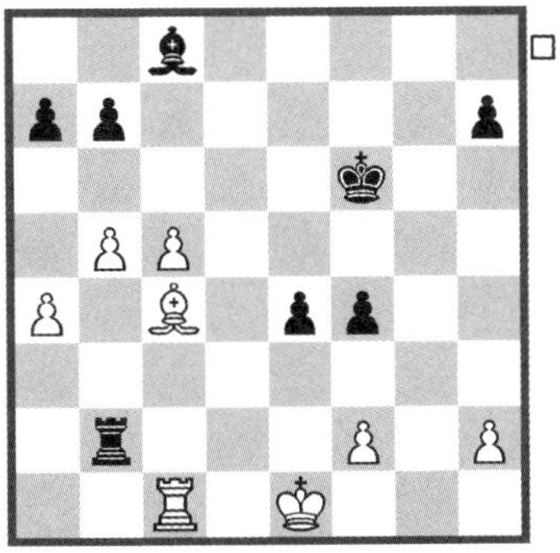

Position after: 33... gxf4

34. ♗e2

If 34. ♖d1 Black can respond, for instance, as follows. 34... ♖b4 35. ♖d6+ ♔e7 Black has a huge advantage.

34... ♔e5

Black's initiative looks dangerous.

35. c6! bxc6 36. ♖xc6?

A key mistake, although it looks very natural.

36. bxc6! This was necessary instead, although it looks ugly! 36... f3 37. ♗d1

Position after: 37. ♗d1

37... e3 38. ♖c2! This saves White in all lines!

36... ♗e6 37. ♗d1 ♖b1!

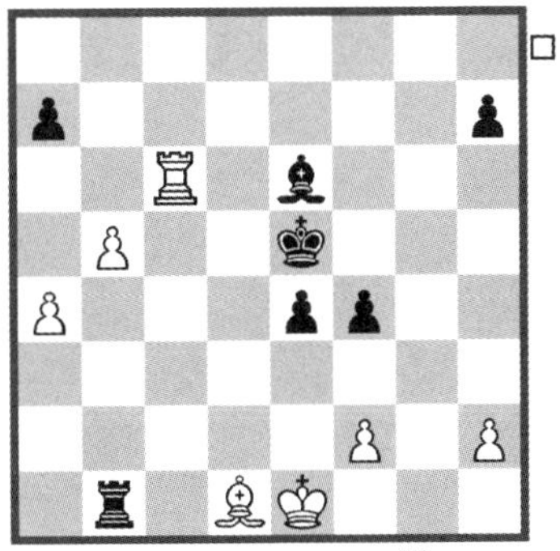

Position after: 37... ♖b1!

38. ♖c5+

There is already no escape.

A) 38. ♔e2 ♗g4+–+

B) 38. ♔d2 e3+ 39. fxe3 fxe3+–+

38... ♔d4 39. ♖c2 e3 40. fxe3+ fxe3 41. ♖c6

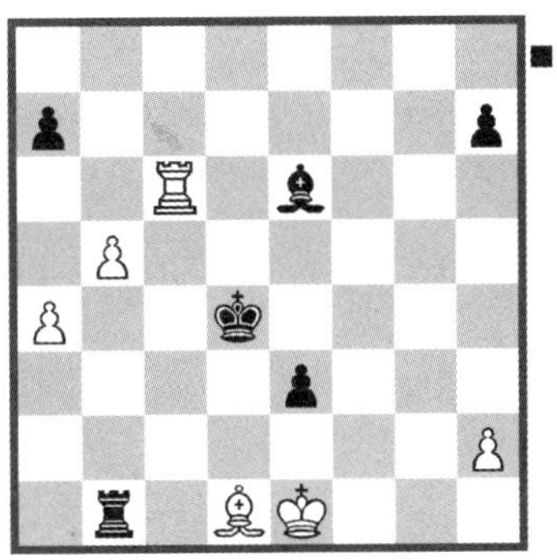

Position after: 41. ♖c6

41... ♗g4 42. ♖d6+ ♔e5 43. h3 ♗h5

The threat of ...e2 is unstoppable. White resigned.

0-1

Game 110

♙ Artemiev, Vladislav (2703)
♟ Yudin, Sergei (2525)
Cheliabinsk 2018

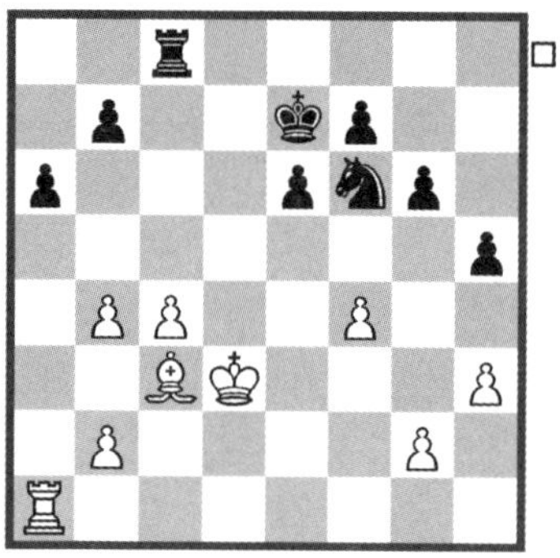

White is better due to pawns being present on both sides. In such situations the bishop will usually prevail. White's first task is to get rid of the doubled pawns and to liberate his majority. After getting rid of the doubled pawns, White's majority of 2:1 will become a key factor.

32. ♖a5! ♖d8+ 33. ♔e3 ♖c8 34. ♔d3

Don't rush!

34... ♖d8+ 35. ♗d4 ♘d7

(see diagram next column)

Position after: 35... ♘d7

36. ♔c3

The king is removed from the d-file.

36... ♔d6 37. b5

White follows the simplest plan.

37... axb5 38. ♖xb5 ♔c7 39. ♖a5 ♖e8 40. b4

The majority is activated. Black has been focused on defensive measures and his counterplay on the other side would come too late as a result.

40... f6 41. c5!

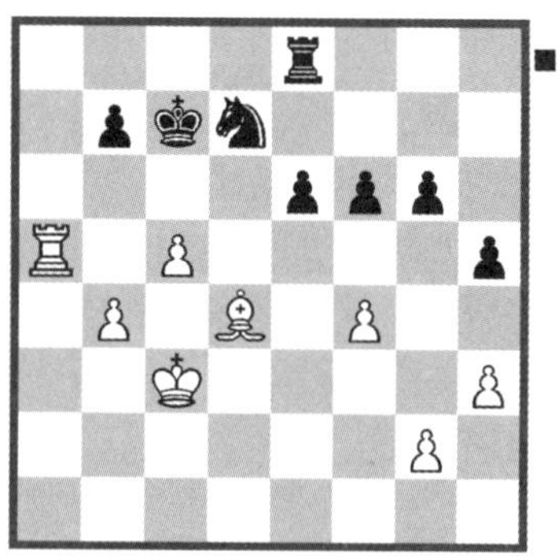

Position after: 41. c5!

White has perfectly calculated that he can close the rook's control of the 5th rank.

41... e5 42. fxe5 ♘xe5 43. b5

White's action looks dangerous! At the same time Black's knight has no action.

43... ♘d7?!

In a difficult position Black played an imprecise move.

43... ♔b8 This looks much better in order to prevent White's next move.

44. ♖a7!

Now Black's defense collapses.

44... ♘e5 45. c6

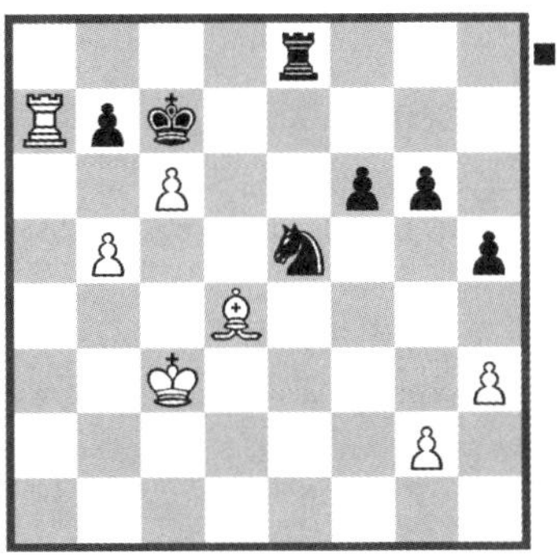

Position after: 45. c6

45... ♖b8 46. ♗xe5+ fxe5 47. ♖xb7+

Black resigned.

1-0

Game 111

♙ Smyslov, Vassily V
♟ Szabo, Laszlo
Hastings 1955

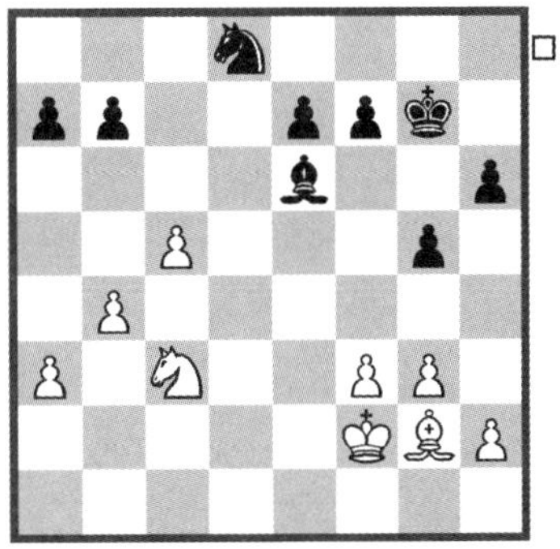

White is dominant although it may look as if Black is okay. White's queenside majority is the key positional factor here, especially after fixing the b7-pawn. Black cannot easily advance it to b6 because of c6, and even exchanging it would create the a-passer. With his next move White opens up the key diagonal and attacks b7.

30. f4! gxf4 31. gxf4 ♗b3 32. ♔e3

Note that Black can only create a passer on the e-file, and that's only rarely dangerous as it's easy to catch it – central passed pawns are almost always weak in the endgame. A central majority is nothing compared to a side majority.

32... ♔f6 33. b5

Straightforward play! Black is hopeless.

33... e5

Position after: 33... e5

Black's active play comes too late. White improves his position with a dose of tactics.

34. ♘e4+! ♔e6 35. c6! exf4+ 36. ♔xf4 bxc6 37. ♘c5+

It is game over.

37... ♔d6 38. ♘xb3 cxb5 39. h4

Position after: 39. h4

This pawn is destined to decide the game. Let's advance it!

39... ♘c6 40. ♗xc6 ♔xc6 41. ♔g4 b4 42. axb4 ♔b5 43. ♘d4+

1-0

Game 112

♙ Kristol
♟ Wu
Valetta 1980

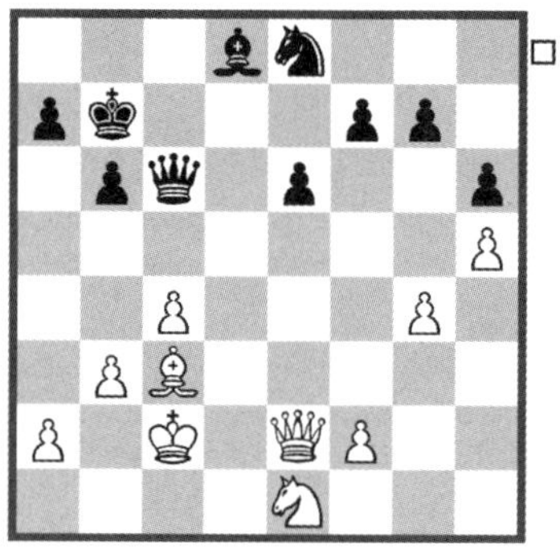

Here is a typical Caro-Kann endgame that illustrates Black's problems perfectly. White's h5-pawn creates a dangerous fix and is Black's main problem. On the other side White has no difficulties launching his majority. However, launching it may weaken the king's position, and thus White opts to trade queens – after this the white king would be safe and able to become active.

31. ♕f3 ♗f6

A very good defensive move. Black eliminates the pressure on the g7-pawn. White must keep the bishops – his better bishop is an important advantage.

32. ♗d2!

32. ♗xf6? ♘xf6 33. ♕xc6+ ♔xc6 34. f3

Position after: 34. f3

This keeps the better majority, but only momentarily. Black is not worse after 34... e5 followed by ...e4.

32... ♘d6 33. ♕xc6+ ♔xc6 34. f3?!

Position after: 34. f3?!

After 34. ♔d3!? perhaps White was afraid of 34... ♗h4.

34... b5?

The side playing for a draw should trade pawns, that is the correct approach. However here, this move is a serious mistake. Black simply transforms White's majority to 2:1, which is more dangerous, of course. Nevertheless, many pawns remain on the board.

34... ♗g5! 35. ♗b4 f5 This gives better defensive chances for Black.

35. cxb5+ ♘xb5 36. ♔d3 ♘d4 37. ♔e4 ♘b5 38. ♔d3

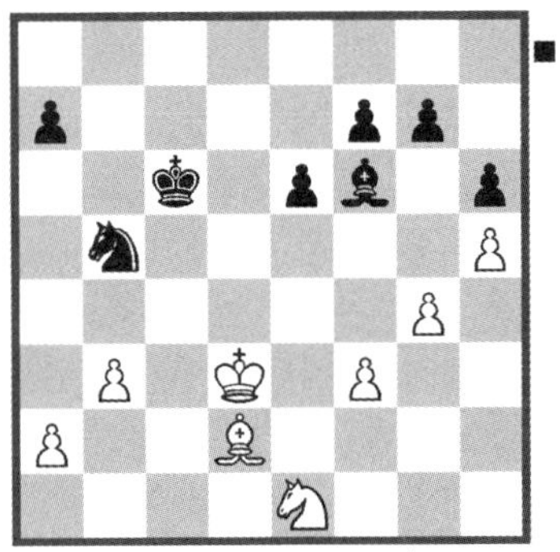

Position after: 38. ♔d3

White does not rush anywhere.

38... ♔d5 39. ♘c2 ♘d4 40. ♘e3+ ♔c6 41. ♔e4 ♘b5 42. ♘c4 ♘c7

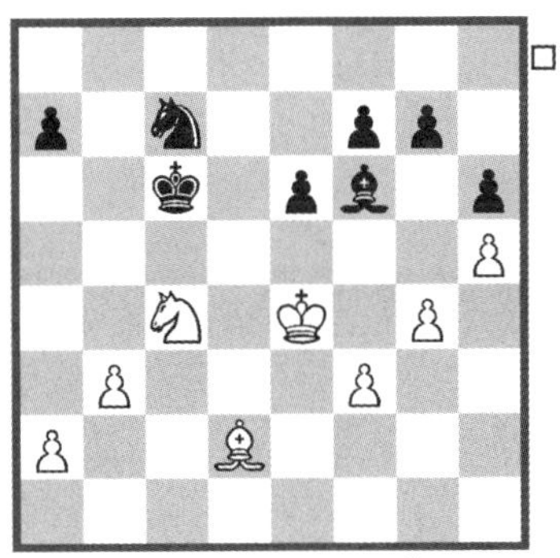

Position after: 42... ♘c7

42... ♘d6+ This would not help Black. 43. ♘xd6 ♔xd6 44. ♗f4+ ♔c5

[44... e5 45. ♗e3 a6 46. b4 White easily wins.] 45. ♗e5! Black is lost.

43. ♘e5+!

Simplification.

43... ♗xe5 44. ♔xe5 f6+

What else?

45. ♔e4 ♘e8 46. ♗b4!

Position after: 46. ♗b4!

46... ♔d7

46... ♘d6+ 47. ♗xd6 ♔xd6 48. b4 White easily wins due to his better majority!

47. ♗f8 a6 48. ♔d4

Black resigned. He is unable to prevent White's play on the queenside and invasion.

1-0

Game 113

♙ Gligoric, Svetozar
♟ Filip, Miroslav
Zagreb 1965

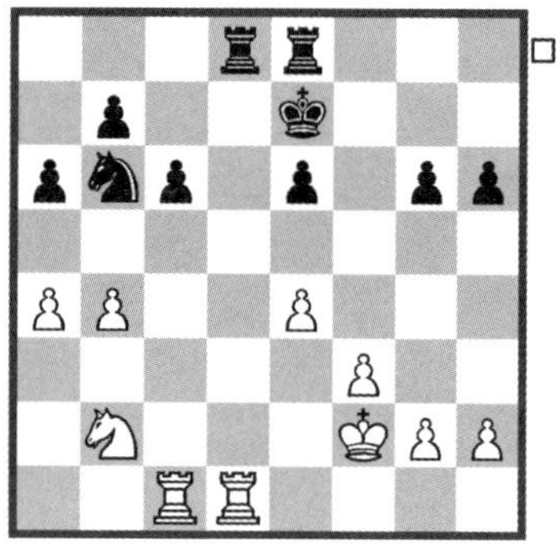

Black has a formally "better" majority. However it is an illusion. With his next move White reduces the mobility of Black's majority, achieving a strategically winning position.

28. a5! ♖xd1

28... ♘d7 This gives White some good alternatives. 29. ♘a4 [29. ♘c4; 29. ♘d3]

29. ♖xd1 ♘d7 30. ♘a4

White chose to set his knight on c5.

30... ♖f8

30... ♖b8 31. ♘c5 ♘f6 This would keep the knight on board, but Black would be paralyzed and dead lost.

31. ♘c5 ♘xc5 32. bxc5

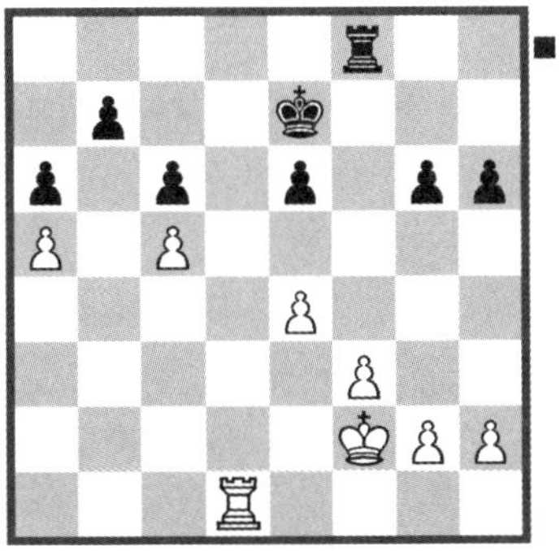

Position after: 32. bxc5

Black has got rid of the dangerous knight. Alas, his position is hopeless. White is practically a pawn up.

32... ♖f7 33. ♔e3 ♔f6 34. h4 h5 35. ♔f4! e5+

After provoking this move, the king retreats and White easily creates a passed pawn after g3 and f4. Do not rush in your games when the opponent is out of active moves.

36. ♔e3 ♔g7 37. g3 ♖e7 38. f4

Position after: 38. f4

There is nothing that Black can do. His rook cannot become active. The game is over.

38... exf4+ 39. gxf4 ♔f6 40. ♖d6+ ♔g7 41. e5 ♔f7 42. ♔e4 ♔g7 43. f5 gxf5+ 44. ♔xf5

Black resigned.

1-0

Game 114

♙ Levenfish, Grigory
♟ Flohr, Salo
Moscow 1936

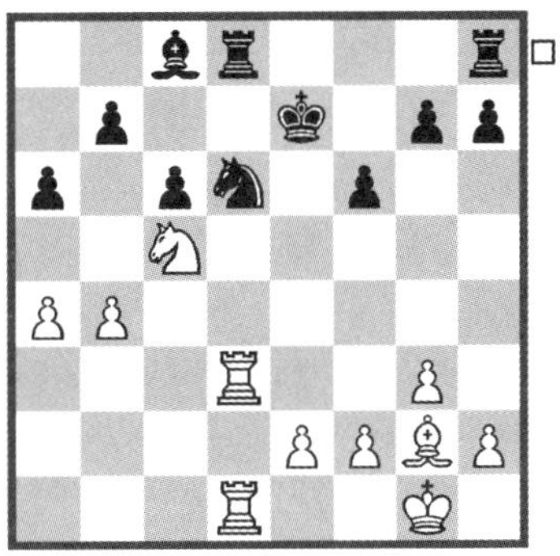

This position is similar to the previous one. At an appropriate moment White can play a5 paralyzing Black's queenside. Thus, White's majority is more valuable, giving him a clear edge. His better bishop is another reason to evaluate the position accordingly.

28. f4!

White rather opts for activating the king.

Alternatively, there is nothing wrong with playing 28. a5! immediately.

28... ♘c4

Trying to get rid of the annoying pressure on the d-file.

29. ♔f2

Let Black take first.

29... ♖xd3

What else? Black goes for the logical plan of reducing the number of pawns.

30. ♖xd3 ♖d8 31. ♖xd8 ♔xd8

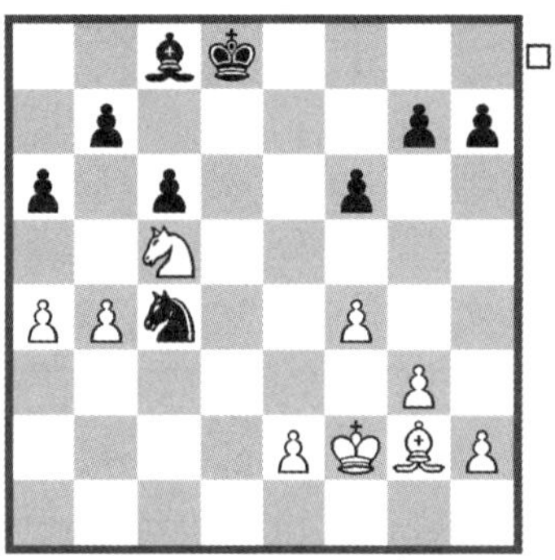

Position after: 31... ♔xd8

White has gained time and his pieces have become dangerously centralized.

32. ♗e4! h6 33. ♗d3?

White misses an interesting and strong possibility.

Instead 33. a5! here would have been better.

33... ♘b6?

A) 33... ♘d6? This may be met by the following. 34. a5!± ♔c7 35. e4 b6

Position after: 35... b6

36. axb6+ ♔xb6 37. ♔e3 Paralyzing.

B) 33... ♘b2! This should have been played. It looks strange, but Black should have given away the knight for the bishop. 34. a5 ♔c7 Now after this Black prepares ...b6. There is nothing concrete apparent for White. The game could have continued as follows. 35. ♔e3 b6! 36. ♘e4 ♘xd3

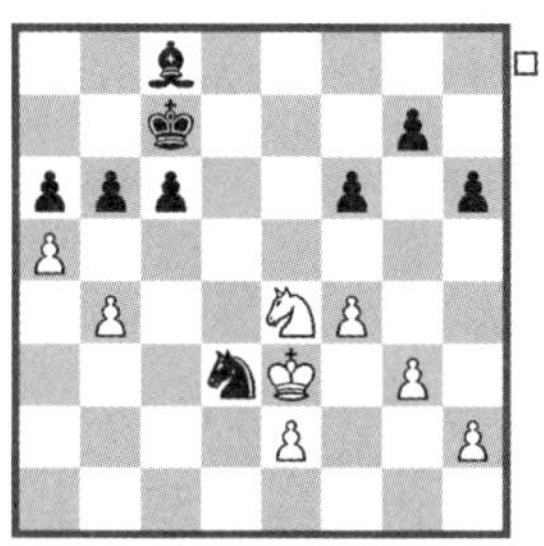

Position after: 36... ♘xd3

37. exd3 and after [37. ♔xd3?? This even loses after the following. 37... ♗f5! 38. ♔e3 ♗xe4 39. ♔xe4 c5] 37... ♗e6 There is nothing for White.

34. e4

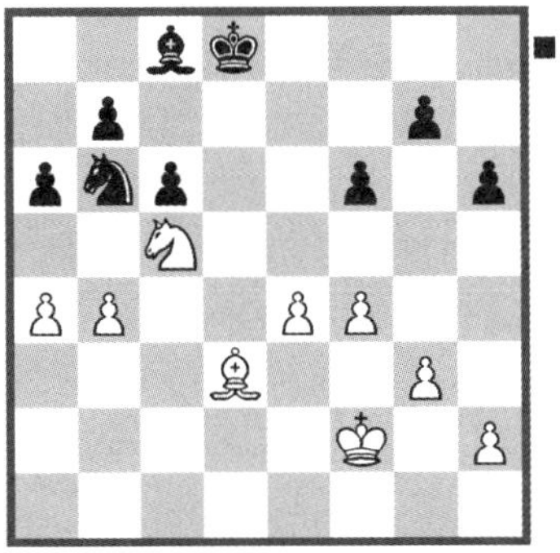

Position after: 34. e4

34... ♘a8?!

Black's knight wanders. Being unable to find a good plan, Black plays without one. It is unsurprising that White increases his advantage.

34... ♔e7 This would have been a better try with the idea of getting rid of ♘c5 after ...♘d7. In any case, White would be clearly better; Black would hope to set up a barrier and hold a much worse bishop endgame.

35. ♔e3 ♘c7 36. a5!

Finally.

36... ♔e7 37. ♗c4

(see diagram next column)

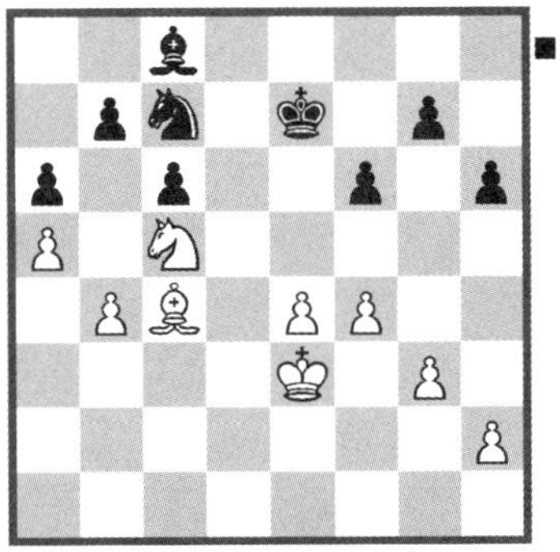

Position after: 37. ♗c4

37... ♔d6

37... ♘e6 38. ♗xe6 ♗xe6 39. ♘xe6 ♔xe6 40. ♔d4 This is lost for Black. He is unable to use his majority.

38. ♔d4 ♘e8 39. e5+ fxe5+ 40. fxe5+ ♔e7

Black's pieces are horribly placed. White instructively improves his position on another flank.

41. h4 ♘c7

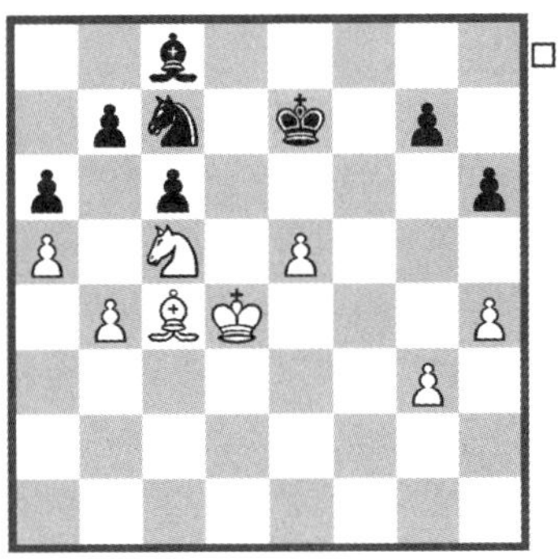

Position after: 41... ♘c7

42. ♘e4!

Targeting the d6-square and freeing the c5-square for the king.

42... ♗e6 43. ♘d6 ♗xc4 44. ♔xc4 ♔e6 45. ♘xb7

1-0

Game 115

♙ Zlatanovic, Boroljub
♟ Kahrovic, Mersid
Serbia rapid 2014

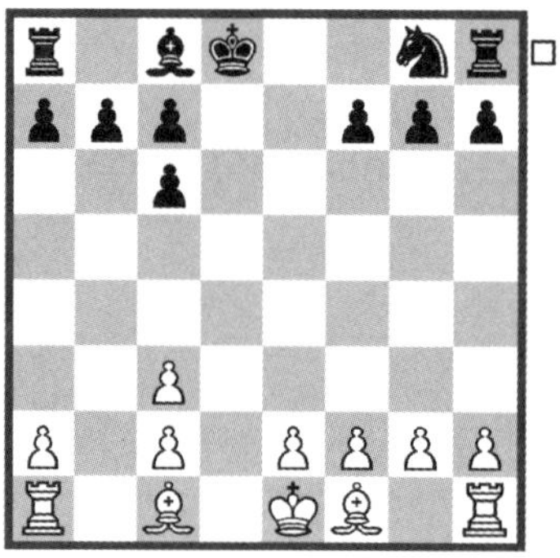

Here White has a powerful majority on the kingside and soon it will be supported by the bishop pair. From a deeper observation, you can see that Black lacks harmony, which is not compensated by White's damaged queenside pawn structure.

8. e4 ♗e6 9. ♗f4

An important move. White targets the c7-pawn preventing Black's mobilization.

9... ♘e7 10. 0-0-0+

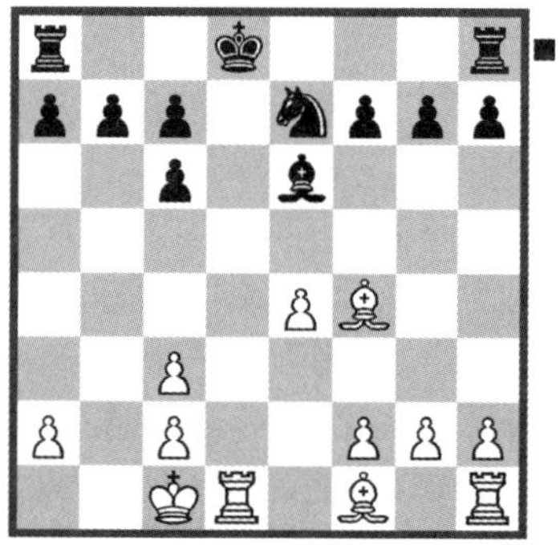

Position after: 10. 0-0-0+

10... ♔c8 11. a3

All the previous moves have been natural. White simply saves the a-pawn.

11... a5

In return Black tries to advance his majority. However there is nothing that can be achieved.

12. ♗e2 b6

12... b5 This weakens the c5-square.

13. ♖d2?!

Before any action on the kingside I wanted to double the rooks. This was a rapid game; perhaps in a classical game I would have opted for a more concrete approach.

13. g4! It would have been better to prevent ...h5.

13... a4?

The idea is to activate the rook on the fifth rank, but this can be deferred.

13... h5! This would have been good instead – Black would be fighting against White's advance.

14. ♖hd1 ♖a5 15. g4!

Position after: 15. g4!

White wants first to set his kingside pawns on the light squares. This would restrict both of his opponent's minor pieces.

15... f6?!

This simply allows White, after his next move, to gain even more space on the kingside.

15... g5!? After 16. ♗e3 ♘g6 White is better but it would be a long road to victory.

16. h4! ♘g6?

Black plays without a plan. With no real plan on the queenside he must deal with White's majority. After his careless move his position simply collapses.

16... g5 Playing this now gives nothing real to Black in view of the following. 17. hxg5 fxg5 18. ♗g3 White has a clear advantage, but nevertheless this would have been a better choice.

17. ♗g3 ♔b7 18. f4

White's phalanx is now unstoppable.

18... ♗c8 19. h5! ♘e7 20. ♖d8

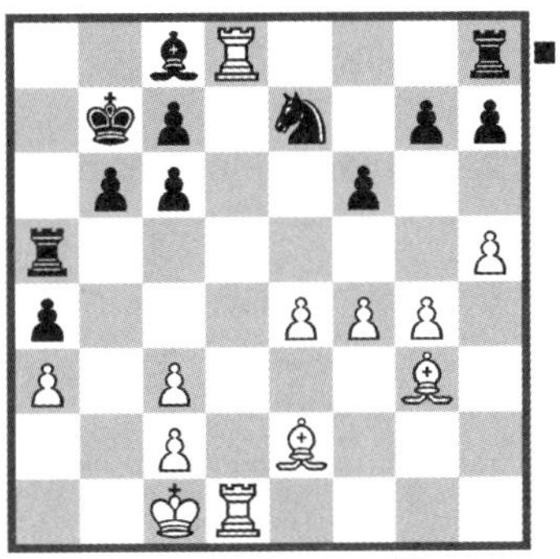

Position after: 20. ♖d8

The rook on the a5-square is out of play. White's rook simply destroys Black's kingside.

20... ♖g8 21. ♖xg8 ♘xg8 22. ♖d8 ♘h6 23. f5!

Locking out all the black pieces.

23... g6 24. ♖h8 gxf5 25. gxf5
1-0

Game 116

♙ Erenburg, Sergey (2512)
♟ Murariu, Andrei (2389)
Las Palmas 2003

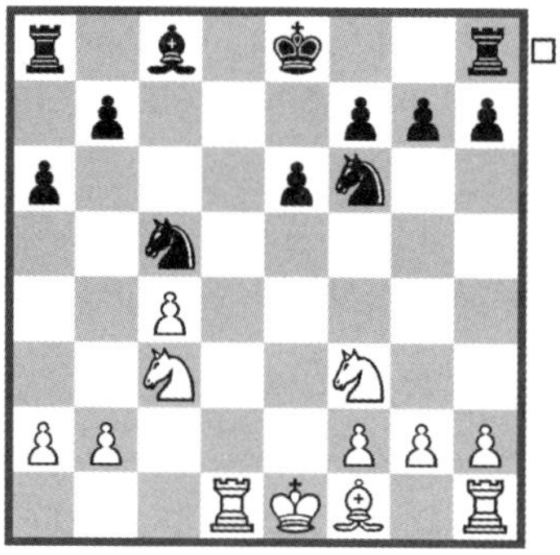

Here is a more complex example. White has many advantages: better development, more space and a better majority. However the advantage is not large. Black hasn't made a single bad move – he is ready to place his king on e7 and finish development soon. In such situations active play is extremely important.

12. b4!

White tries to prevent Black's natural development and cause some disharmony in Black's camp.

12... ♘fe4 13. ♘b1

Very interesting and actually a logical continuation. Black has a lack of space and White should keep the pieces. Furthermore, a few tempi can soon be gained after attacking the knight on e4.

13... ♘a4 14. ♖d4! ♘f6 15. ♗e2 ♔e7 16. ♔d2

Position after: 16. ♔d2

The king should be placed in the center and the kingside rook then comes to d1.

16... a5

Trying to activate the rook on the a-file and obtain some play.

17. a3 axb4 18. axb4 ♖d8 19. ♖xd8 ♔xd8 20. ♔c2 ♘b6 21. ♘c3 ♔e7 22. ♖d1

Position after: 22. ♖d1

After a series of natural moves Black loses his direction. This move is very strange – the pawn on f2 is actually untouchable.

22... ♘g4?

22... ♗d7 This was natural and a far better move.

23. h3! ♘f6 24. ♔b3 h6

It seems that Black has a deficit of good moves but some of them are apparent.

24... ♗d7 Why not?

25. ♘e5

White gradually improves all his pieces: the rook, then king and now it is time for the knight. Meanwhile, Black wastes time.

25... ♘bd7

Following a good strategy of reducing material in a worse position.

26. ♘xd7 ♗xd7

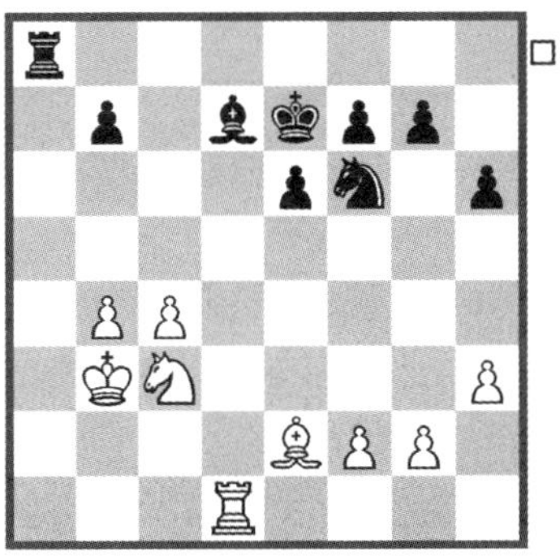

Position after: 26... ♗xd7

27. b5

White's advantage has become concrete: activity, space and of course, a better majority. Moreover, the black king is cut off from the queenside where a dangerous passed pawn will arise soon. *Summa summarum*, Black is lost. Here, White goes against Capablanca postulates on the majorities ("always advance the candidate pawn first"). But here it enables White to keep Black's pieces passive. The advance of the c-pawn would give away the c6- and d5-squares to the minor pieces. The point is that Black cannot prevent the creation of a passed pawn.

27. ♗f3 ♗c6 28. ♗xc6 bxc6 29. b5 This also looks good, but it is definitely not so dangerous for Black as the move played in the game.

27... b6?!

It is an illusion that Black can stop White's queenside pawns. White's majority cannot be stopped in this way. At the same time the b6-pawn becomes exposed.

Instead 27... ♗e8 with 28... ♘d7 would have been better but it should not affect the final result.

28. ♗f3 ♖b8 29. ♖a1

White organizes a total invasion.

29... ♗c8 30. ♖a7+ ♘d7 31. ♗c6

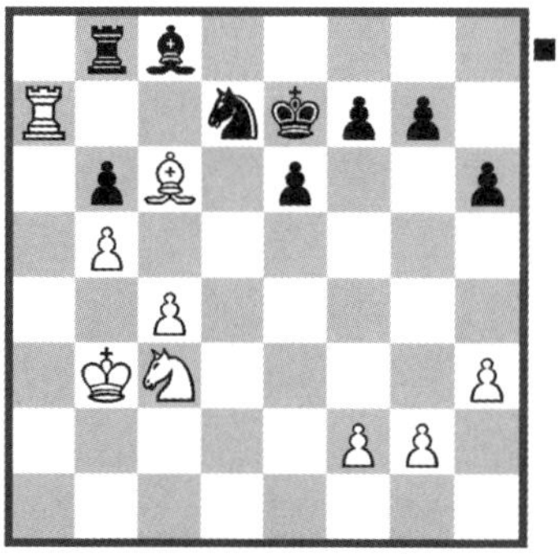

Position after: 31. ♗c6

Paralyzing Black's pieces; White opts to collect the pawn on b6. The rest is a matter of technique.

31... f5 32. ♘a4 ♔d6 33. ♗xd7

The simplest way to win.

33. ♔b4? ♘e5 White's mistake would give Black some chances.

33... ♗xd7 34. ♔b4

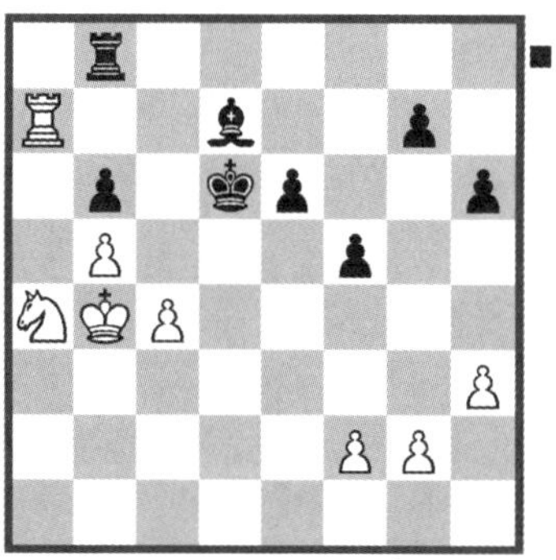

Position after: 34. ♔b4

The game is over.

34... ♔e7

34... ♗e8 35. ♘xb6 The tactics are serving the strategy.

35. ♖a6 e5 36. ♖xb6

White is a pawn up. He has two connected advanced pawns, so the rest is an easy job.

36... ♖d8 37. ♖b7 ♔f6 38. ♘c5 ♗e8 39. ♖c7

Black resigned.

1-0

Game 117

♙ Karpov, Anatoly (2725)
♟ Andersson, Ulf (2585)
Thessaloniki 1988

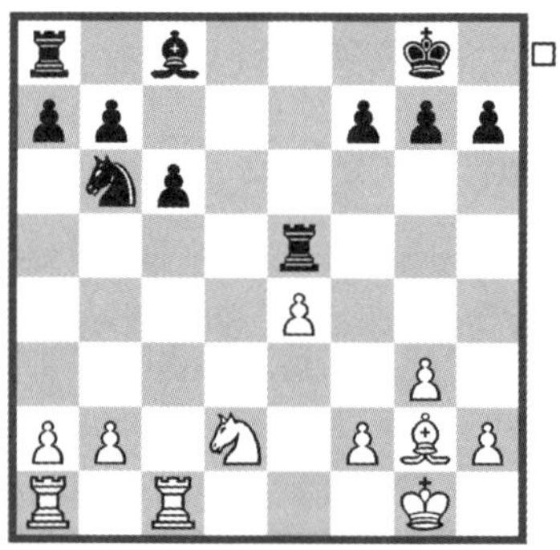

White is better here. His majority is mobile, his pieces are better placed and there will soon be control over the d-file.

17. f4

White launches the majority, gaining space.

17... ♖e7 18. a4?!

The great Karpov definitely had strong reasons for this move. But it later proved to be an inaccuracy, so he probably should have avoided playing it.

18. ♘b3 This would have been good, placing the knight immediately on c5.

18... a5

Logical. Black fixes the white pawn on the bishop's color. The problem is exposure of his pawn.

19. ♘b3 f6

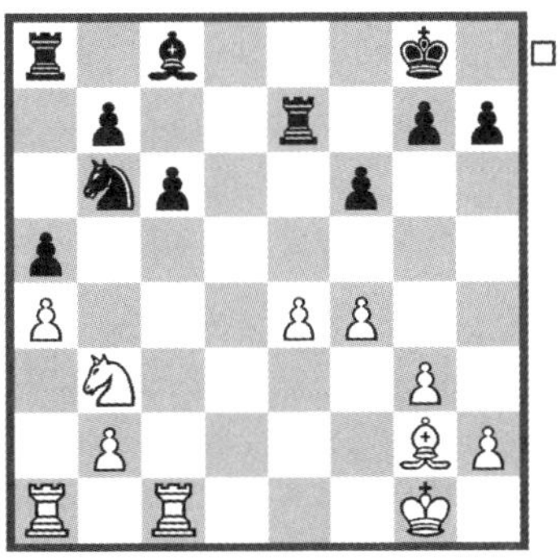

Position after: 19... f6

20. ♖a3?!

Karpov wants to play in style. After the knight comes to c5 the rook may go to b3.

20. ♖c5!? This will get a pawn. Perhaps Karpov did not like this move because of the following line. 20... ♗e6 21. ♘xa5 ♘d7 However here White has the advantage as follows. 22. ♘xb7

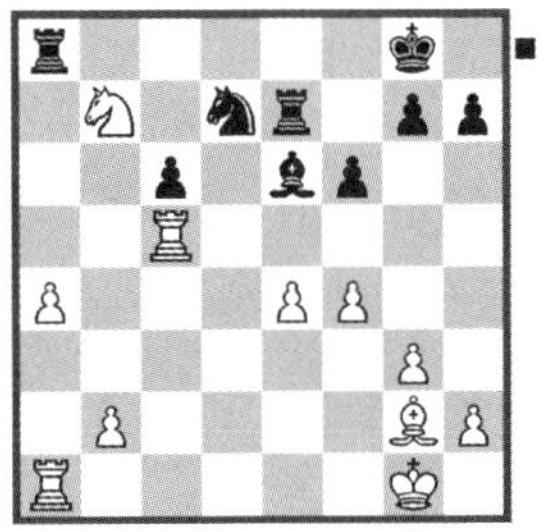

Position after: 22. ♘xb7

22... ♖b8 [22... ♘xc5 23. ♘xc5 This is dominant for White.] 23. ♖xc6 ♖xb7

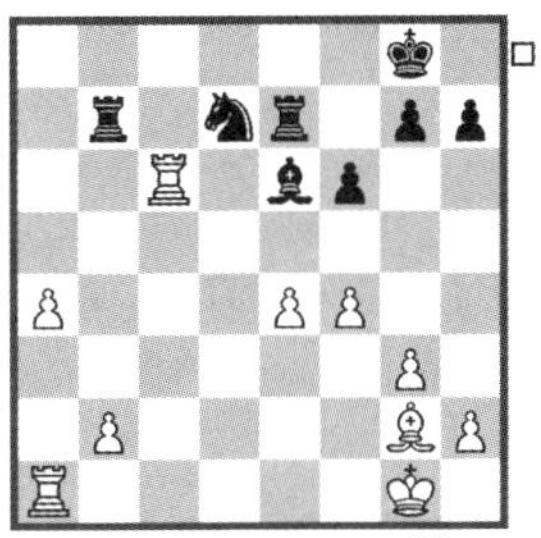

Position after: 23... ♖xb7

24. f5! ♗b3 25. ♖c8+ ♔f7 26. e5

20... ♗e6?

The start of a bad plan. The bishop does not belong on f7.

20... ♔f7 21. ♘c5 ♘d7! Black has a solid defense.

21. ♘c5 ♗f7 22. ♖d3

Now things are clear. Black cannot get rid of the dominant c5-knight and cannot oppose on the open file.

22... ♖ae8 23. ♗h3

Squeezing more and more.

23. h4 Playing this first looks even more logical.

23... ♘c8 24. ♗d7

One of Karpov's trademarks – he closes the file and will choose a good moment to re-open it, at the same time preventing ...b6.

24... ♖d8 25. ♖cd1

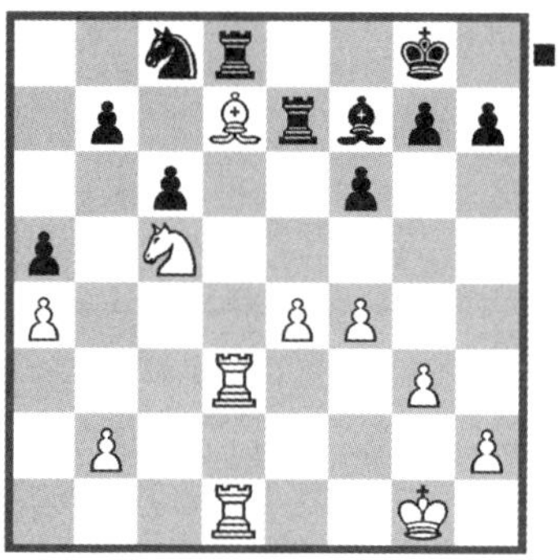

Position after: 25. ♖cd1

25... ♘b6

25... b6 This fails to 26. ♗xc6.

26. ♗g4 ♖xd3 27. ♖xd3 ♔f8

The situation has stabilized. White is dominant. Nevertheless Black's defense looks solid. However, it is not difficult for Karpov. The rest of the game is a typical masterclass.

28. ♖d8+ ♖e8 29. ♖d4 ♖b8?

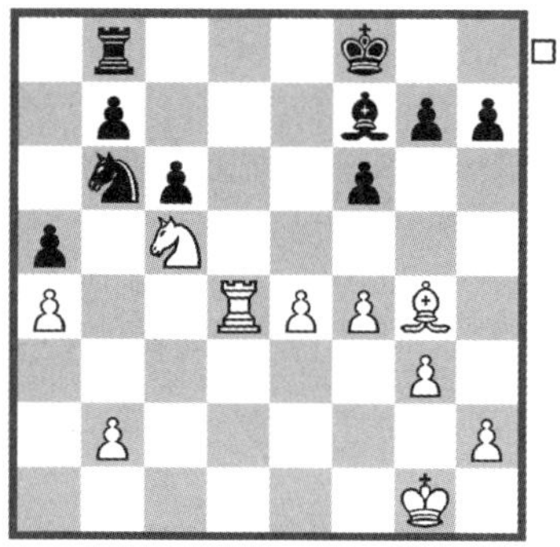

Position after: 29... ♖b8?

A mistake in a terrible position. However, it is not possible to suggest anything good here.

30. ♖d7! h5 31. ♗h3 ♔e8 32. ♖c7

The rook paralyzes the entire black army. Black goes desperate.

32... ♘a8 33. ♖xb7 ♖xb7 34. ♘xb7 ♘b6 35. ♘d6+!

A simplification at a good moment.

35... ♔e7 36. ♘xf7

(see diagram next page)

Position after: 36. ♘xf7

36... ♘xa4

36... ♔xf7 37. b3 This is just lost for Black.

37. ♘h8 ♘xb2 38. e5 a4

38... fxe5 39. ♘g6+ ♔f6 [39... ♔d6 40. fxe5+ The pawn goes on to queen.] 40. ♘xe5

Position after: 40. ♘xe5

40... a4 41. ♘xc6 White wins easily.

39. ♘g6+ ♔e8 40. ♗e6 ♘d3 41. ♗g8 fxe5 42. ♘xe5 ♘b4 43. ♘c4

(see diagram next column)

The rest is irrelevant.

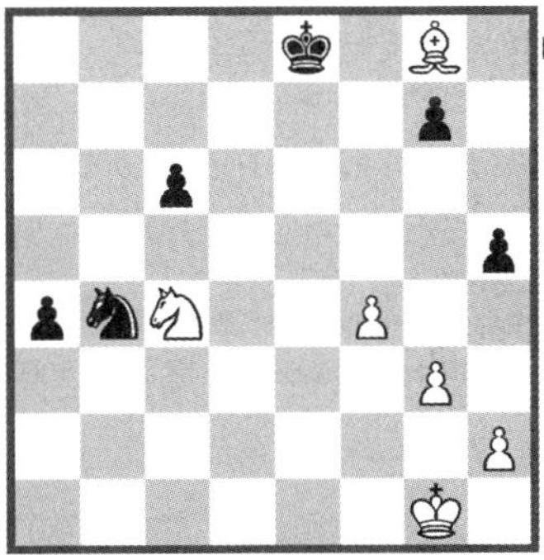

Position after: 43. ♘c4

43... h4 44. ♗h7 hxg3 45. hxg3 ♔e7 46. ♗e4 ♔f6 47. g4 ♔e6 48. ♔f2 ♘d5 49. ♔f3 ♘b4 50. g5 c5 51. f5+ ♔e7 52. ♔e3 ♔f8 53. ♔d2 ♔e7 54. ♔c3

1-0

Game 118

♙ Smyslov, Vassily V (2560)
♟ Gligoric, Svetozar (2560)
Moscow 1979

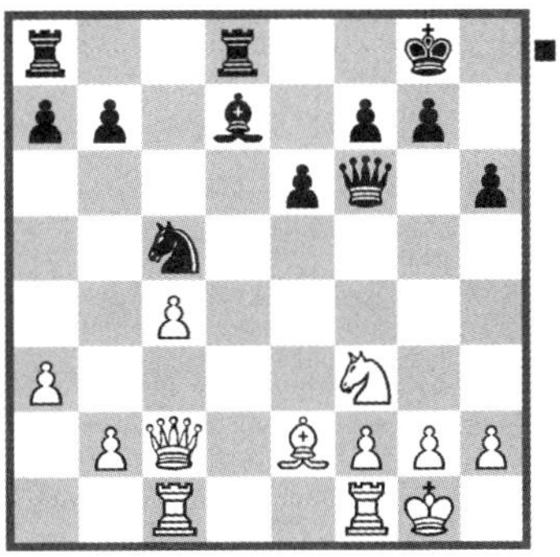

The position looks normal and balanced. However, it is very interesting and is actually dominating for Black! And yes, this is not the endgame yet.

The endgame will appear in a few moves but the game must be analyzed from here as it is extremely instructive.

16... ♗a4!

This is the point. With this move Black practically locks in White's queenside by blocking the majority and controlling the important d1-square. White is strategically lost!

17. ♕c3 ♕xc3 18. ♖xc3 ♗b3!

With a fully open position White is practically paralyzed.

19. ♖fc1 a5!

It is good to support the bishop by playing ...a5-a4, in order to liberate the knight from this task. Any possible action on the kingside can be deferred for now.

20. ♔f1 ♖a6 21. ♔e1 ♖ad6 22. ♖b1 a4 23. h3

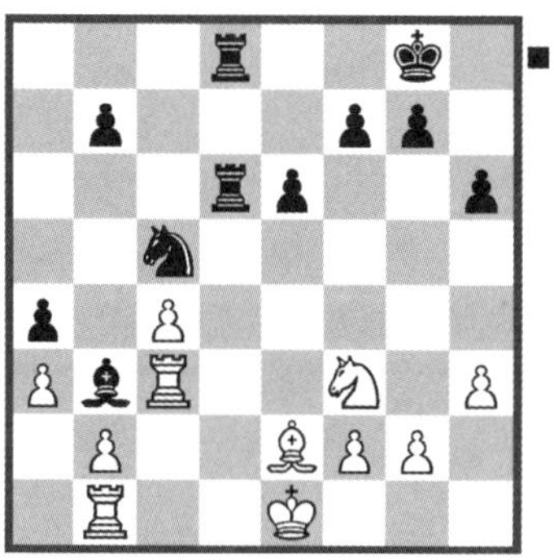

Position after: 23. h3

Black's pieces are active; it is time for the king.

23... f6 24. ♘h2 b6 25. ♘f1 ♔f7 26. f3

Now Black decides to launch his majority. The game is practically decided.

26... f5

Of course, this move is not methodical, but Black gives White "a chance" to fix with f4, and even severely weaken the e4-square.

27. ♘e3 g5 28. ♘c2 ♔f6

There is no reason to go for 28... ♗xc2.

29. ♘a1

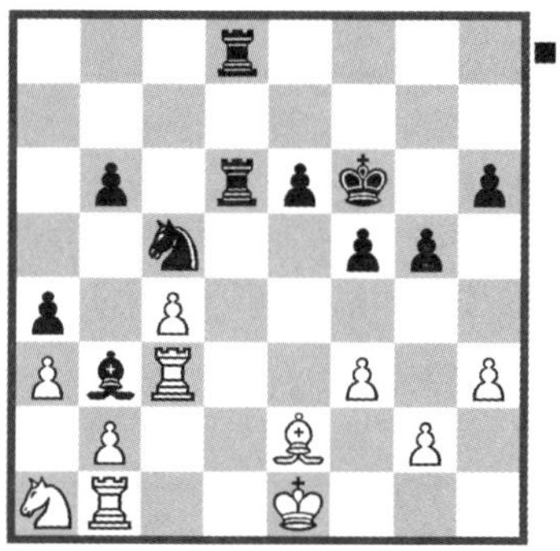

Position after: 29. ♘a1

White has performed some serious acrobatics to eliminate the monster b3-bishop. Alas, eliminating this bishop would not help White. Take a look at the white pieces – it is almost impossible to believe that they belong to the great Smyslov.

29... h5 30. ♘xb3 axb3

30... ♘xb3 This is also possible. 31. ♖d1 [31. ♗d1 ♘c5–+] 31... ♖xd1+

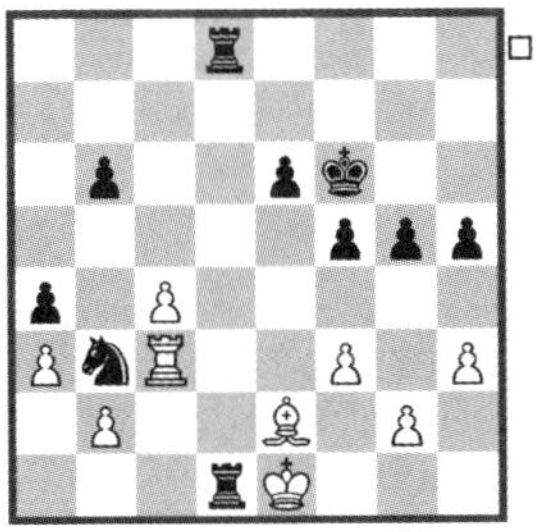

Position after: 31... ♖xd1+

32. ♗xd1 ♘c5 This is also hopeless for White.

31. ♖d1 ♖xd1+

31... ♖d4 Black supports the centralization before further advancing the majority – this is perhaps even more brutal.

32. ♗xd1 ♘d3+ 33. ♔f1 ♘xb2 34. ♗e2 ♘a4

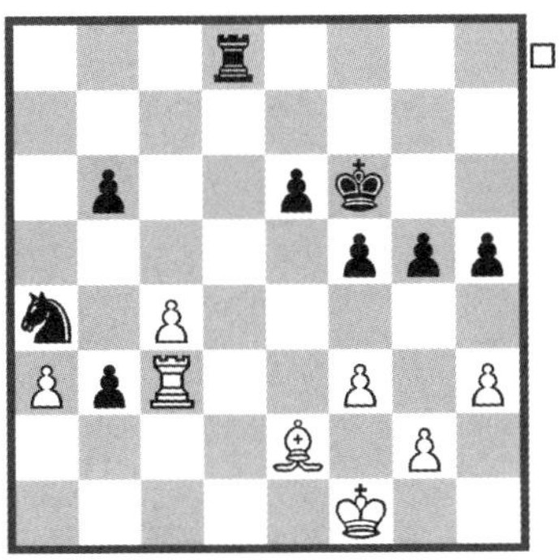

Position after: 34... ♘a4

35. ♖xb3

It may appear that White has managed to get some fresh air. However Black superbly converts his big advantage.

35... ♖d6 36. g4?!

White's idea is to somehow counter Black's kingside initiative. This is understandable, but it is definitely the wrong plan – this is a bad move which creates some new dark-squared weaknesses.

36. ♖b4 This looks better with the idea somehow to activate the a-pawn.

36... ♘c5 37. ♖b5 hxg4 38. hxg4

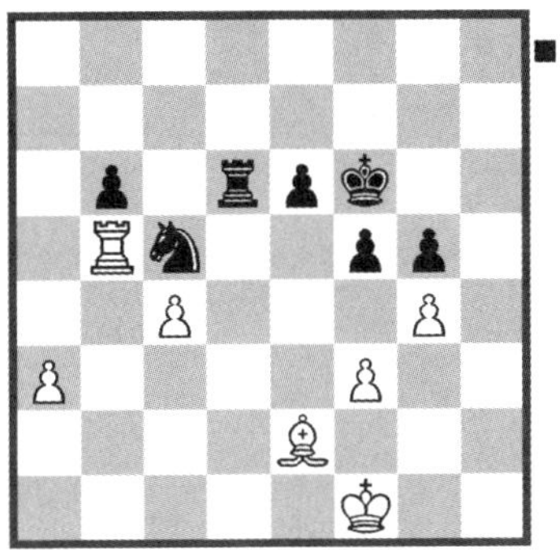

Position after: 38. hxg4

38... f4

Black has blocked the position; White's bishop is now desperately bad.

38... fxg4! 39. fxg4 ♔e5 Simpler and better. White is just lost.

39. ♔e1 ♔e5 40. a4 ♔d4 41. a5 bxa5 42. ♖xa5 ♖a6

A demonstration of power.

43. ♖b5

Position after: 43. ♖b5

43. ♖xa6 ♘xa6 This is just hopeless.

43... e5 44. ♔f2 e4 45. ♖b1 ♖a2

0-1

Game 119

♙ Tseshkovsky, Vitaly (2595)
♟ Romanishin, Oleg M (2580)
Tashkent 1980

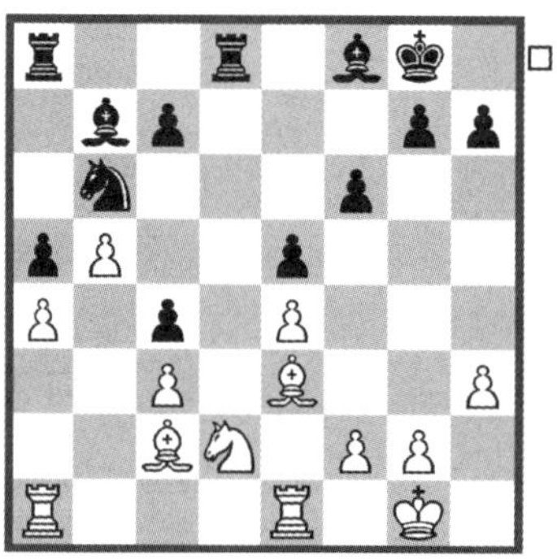

This can hardly be called an endgame. However such a beautiful example must not be omitted. It may appear that Black is okay because he has the d-file, and if White fights for the d-file then the pressure to the c4-pawn would be reduced. Alas, Black is actually completely lost. White has a perfect opportunity to switch the game to a simplified endgame where his majority will become the key factor.

21. ♘xc4! ♘xc4 22. ♗b3 ♗xe4 23. ♗xc4+

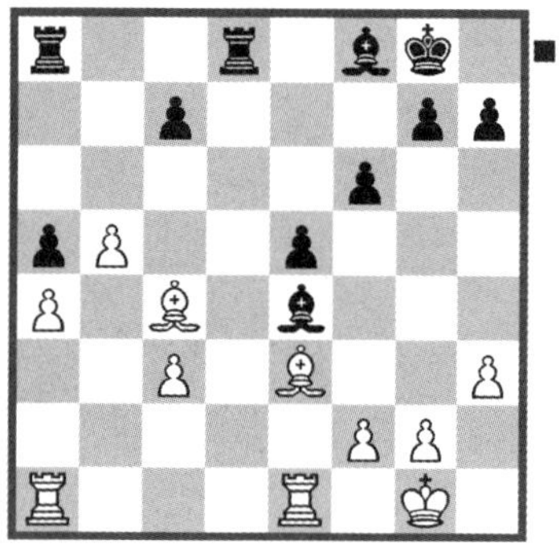

Position after: 23. ♗xc4+

23... ♗d5

This helps Black to centralize the king but he stays with the bad bishop.

If 23... ♔h8 then 24. ♔f1. White will patiently organize an opposition on the d-file and launch his majority.

24. ♗xd5+ ♖xd5 25. ♖ed1 ♖ad8 26. ♖xd5 ♖xd5

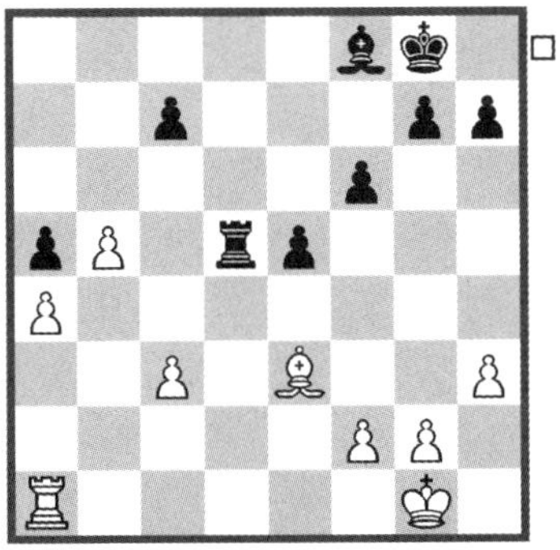

Position after: 26... ♖xd5

The game is simplified and White is winning. There is nothing that Black can do to stop White's queenside pawns. In addition the a5-pawn is horribly weak.

27. ♔f1 ♔f7 28. ♔e2 ♔e6 29. c4 ♖d8 30. c5!

Direct play. White has precisely calculated that the d5-square would give Black nothing.

30... ♗e7 31. ♖c1 ♔d5

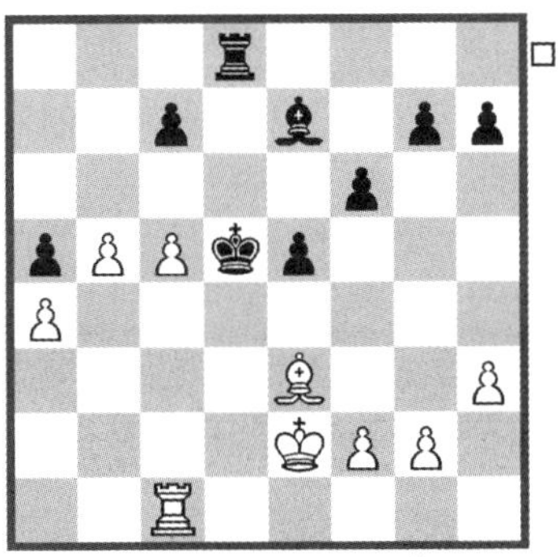

Position after: 31... ♔d5

32. c6

32. ♖d1+ ♔c4 33. ♖xd8 ♗xd8 34. b6 cxb6 35. cxb6 ♔b4 36. ♔d3!

Position after: 36. ♔d3!

36... ♔xa4 37. ♔c4 A forced way to win the game.

32... ♗d6 33. ♖d1+ ♔e6

33... ♔c4 This loses to 34. b6 ♔b4 35. b7.

34. ♗c5 f5 35. g4!

In this pawn endgame Black's only chance may have been to set up a barrier. After this move that chance is gone.

35... g6 36. gxf5+ gxf5 37. ♗xd6 ♖xd6

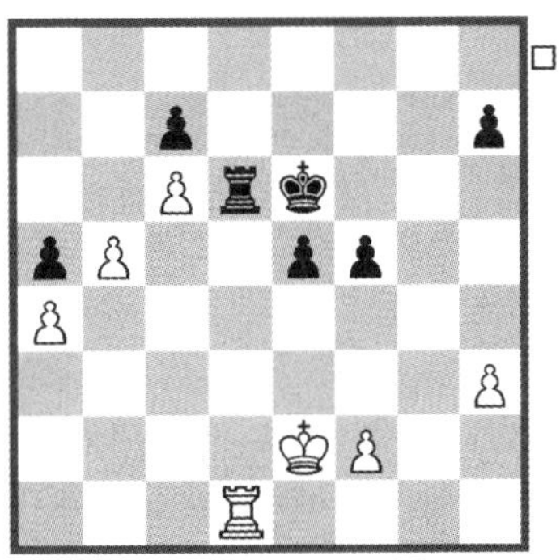

Position after: 37... ♖xd6

38. ♖g1

38. ♖xd6+ A clear win. 38... ♔xd6 39. ♔f3 The idea is ♔g3-h4-g5 winning easily.

38... ♖d4 39. ♖g7 ♖xa4 40. ♖xc7 ♖b4 41. ♖b7

1-0

Pawn Weaknesses

The concept of pawn weaknesses is relatively clear. Some isolated pawns shouldn't necessarily be considered as weaknesses. For example, pawns on a2/a7 are often hard to catch, so that's okay if they are isolated. The vulnerability also comes in the assessment of an isolated pawn.

How to handle such weaknesses? Should we advance such pawns if possible or not? Should we defend them or to seek counterplay somewhere? Should we trade pieces or not? All these and many other questions will be answered in this chapter.

Game 120

♙ Scholl, Eddie C
♟ Polugaevsky, Lev
Amsterdam 1970

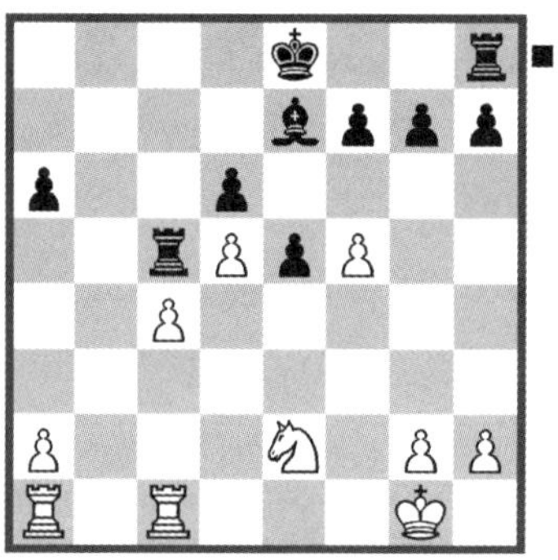

In our first example Black is winning. Although it may appear that the knight is better, this is an illusion. The knight is not on e4 and won't manage to get there. The most important factor is that White's structure is in ruins. Even the black bishop will soon become very strong.

22... ♔d7 23. ♖ab1 ♖hc8 24. ♖b7+ ♔e8!

24... ♖5c7 This is not precise due to the simple 25. ♖cb1.

25. ♖a7

What else?

25... ♖xc4 26. ♖xc4 ♖xc4 27. ♖xa6

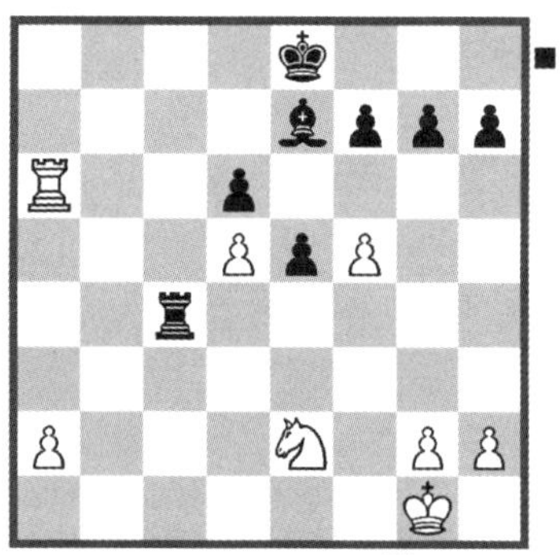

Position after: 27. ♖xa6

27... ♖c5 28. ♖a8+ ♗d8 29. ♘g3 ♖xd5

The rest is a matter of technique and style.

30. ♘h5 ♔d7 31. ♘xg7

With great effort White has kept the material balance. However the two connected passed pawns will decide the game.

31... e4 32. ♔f1

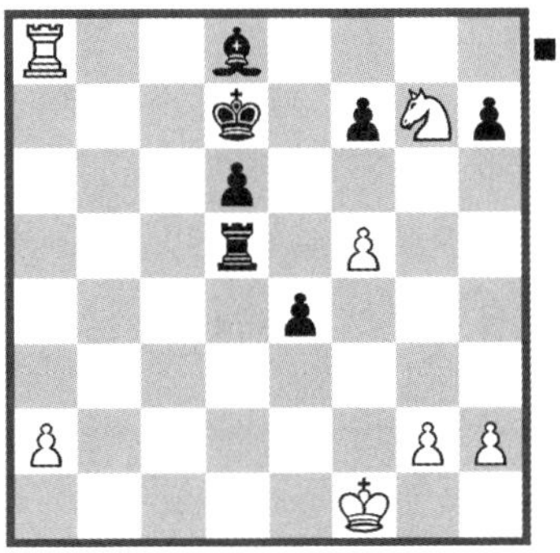

Position after: 32. ♔f1

32... ♖a5

Black decides to simplify his task. From a methodical point of view his decision is reasonable.

32... ♖d2 This also wins easily.

33. ♖xa5 ♗xa5 34. ♘h5 ♗c3

Preventing the check on f6.

34... d5 35. ♘f6+ ♔d6 36. ♘xh7 ♔e5 This also wins easily.

35. h4 d5 36. g4 ♔d6 37. ♘f4 ♔e5 38. ♘e2 ♗a5 39. a4 d4

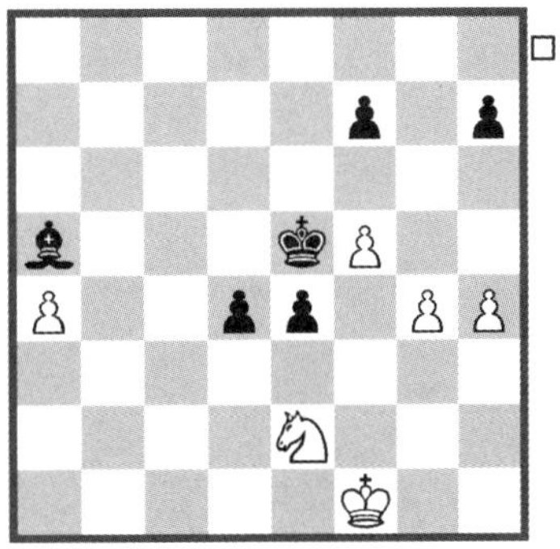

Position after: 39... d4

40. ♘c1 d3 41. ♘b3

And here White resigned.

0-1

Game 121

♙ Boleslavsky, Isaak
♟ Fine, Reuben
Radio 1945

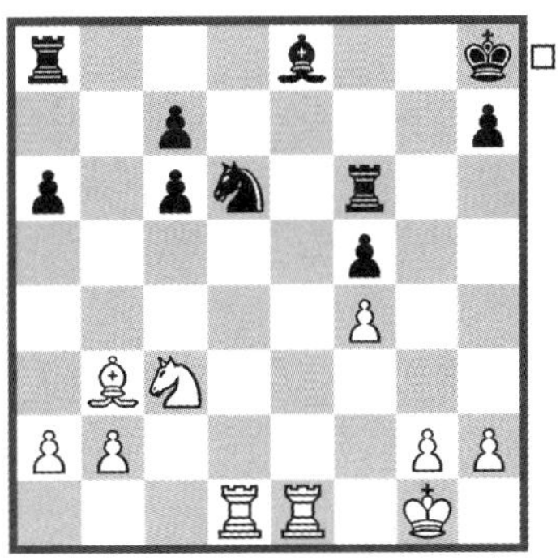

The evaluation is clear in our next position – White is winning. With such passive pieces and especially his ruined structure Black has no chances to survive. White's first move is natural – he penetrates.

24. ♖e7 ♖c8 25. ♖de1

The rook belongs to the e-file.

25... ♗g6 26. ♖1e6 ♖xe6

26... ♖ff8 27. ♗c2 Here for instance, the maneuver ♖e5-c5 would gain material.

27. ♗xe6 ♖e8 28. ♖xe8+ ♗xe8

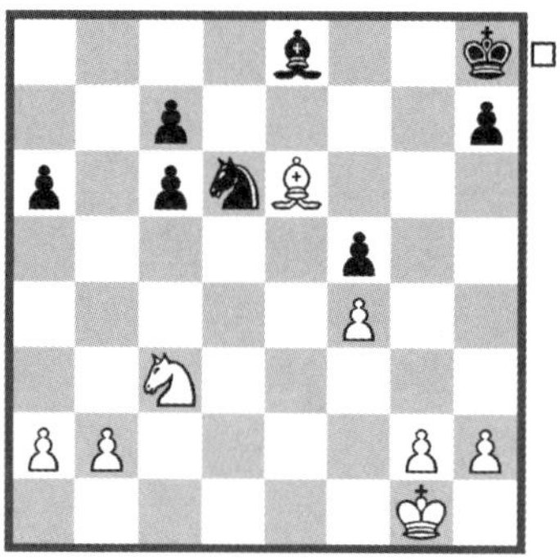

Position after: 28... ♗xe8

Reducing material has brought nothing for Black. Every type of endgame here is simply won for White. White has many different plans to convert: attacking the a-pawn, or the f-pawn, or using his majority on the kingside, or infiltrating with the king to the queenside.

29. ♘a4

The knight goes to the excellent blockading spot on c5.

29... ♔g7 30. ♘c5 a5 31. ♔f2 ♗f7

White can allow even this.

32. ♗xf7 ♔xf7 33. b3

There is no need for rush. White fixes the weak a5-pawn.

33... h5

Intending to exchange as many pawns as possible.

34. g3 ♔e7 35. ♔e3 ♘b5 36. ♘b7 c5

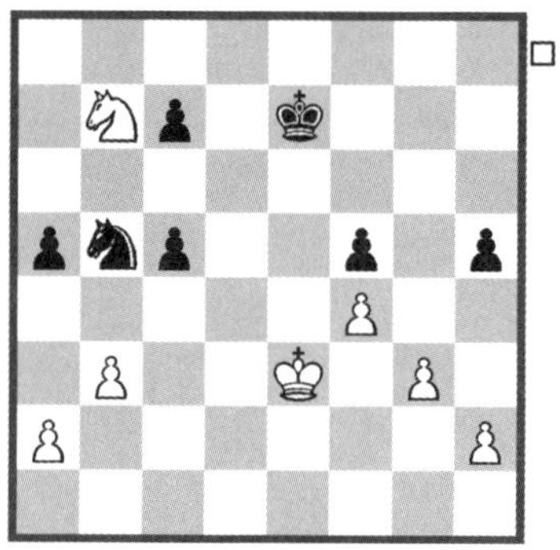

Position after: 36... c5

37. ♘xa5

Of course, this one!

37... ♔d6 38. ♘c4+ ♔d5 39. ♔d3 ♘d6

(see diagram next page)

Position after: 39... ♘d6

Desperation.

40. ♘xd6 cxd6 41. a3

Black resigned.

1-0

Game 122

♙ Smyslov, Vassily V
♟ Tal, Mihail
🌍 Moscow 1969

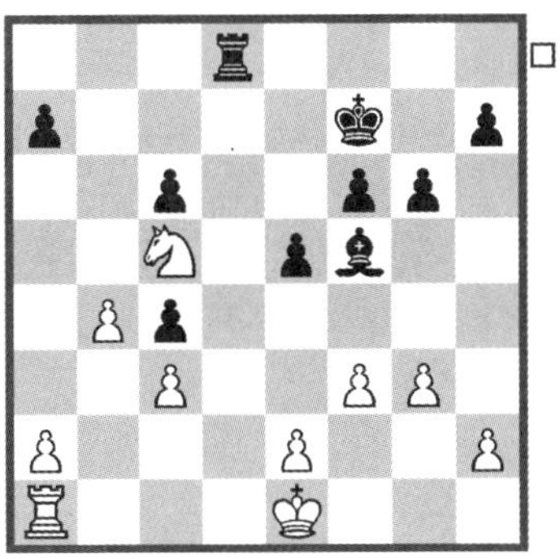

White is just winning here. The first thing that comes to mind is Black's damaged queenside, which is the key factor. Furthermore the knight must be the preferred piece rather than the bishop here. Each side has seven (!) pawns and in such situations, the knight easily prevails.

24. ♘b7

The knight goes to a5 to attack both the weak pawns on the c-file.

24... ♖d7

What else?

25. ♘a5 c5 26. bxc5 ♖d5 27. ♘b7

The knight dances and now changes direction. The game is over.

27... ♖d7 28. ♘d6+ ♔e7 29. g4

Position after: 29. g4

This move or e4 – it is a matter of style.

29... ♗e6 30. ♖b1 ♖c7 31. ♖b7

31. ♖b5 Another option, with a future possible activation of the king.

31... ♖xb7 32. ♘xb7 ♔d7 33. ♘d6 h6 34. ♔f2 ♔c6 35. ♔e3

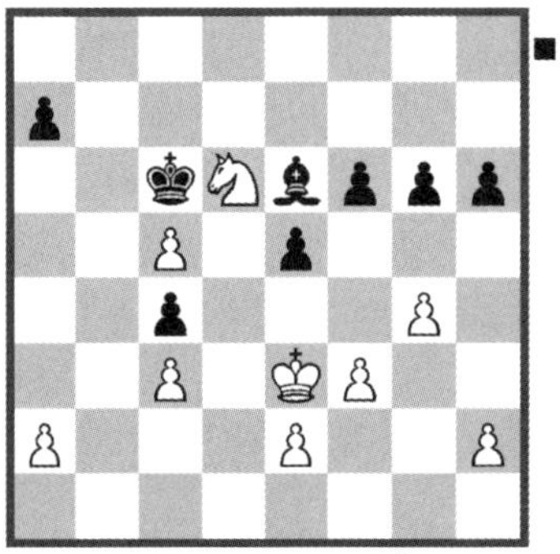

Position after: 35. ♔e3

The pawn is indirectly protected.

35... a5

A) 35... ♔xc5 36. ♘e4+ ♔b5 37. ♘xf6 ♔a4 38. ♔e4 ♔a3 39. ♔xe5+–

B) 35... f5 36. gxf5

Position after: 36. gxf5

36... gxf5 [36... ♗xf5 37. ♘xf5 gxf5 38. f4] 37. f4!+–

36. ♘e8 f5 37. ♘g7 ♗d7 38. gxf5 gxf5

(see diagram next column)

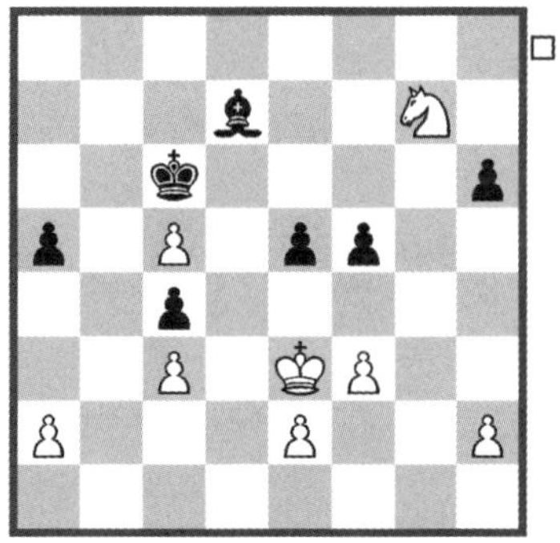

Position after: 38... gxf5

39. f4!

Again this move liberates the d4-spot and ends the game.

39... ♔d5 40. c6 ♗c8 41. c7 ♔d6 42. h4

1-0

Game 123

♙ Chigorin, Mikhail Ivanovich
♟ Pillsbury, Harry Nelson
London 1899

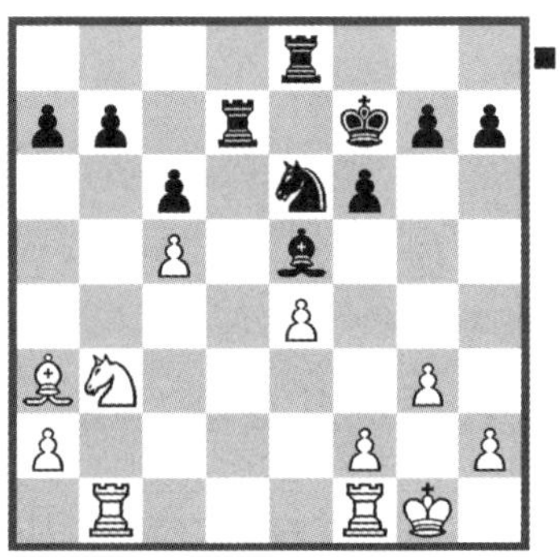

After indolent play White has achieved an unenviable situation. His minor pieces are strongly blocked in by the weakness on c5 and forced to protect it. First, Black eliminates White's chance to use his own majority on the kingside.

23... g5!

A very common approach in similar situations. White's f2-pawn stays separated from the e4-pawn. As a result White's majority becomes useless and furthermore, his separated pawns become weak!

23... b5 This is good as well, but from a method perspective I would rather suggest the played move.

24. ♖fd1

Trying to get relief on the file.

24... ♖ed8 25. ♖xd7+ ♖xd7

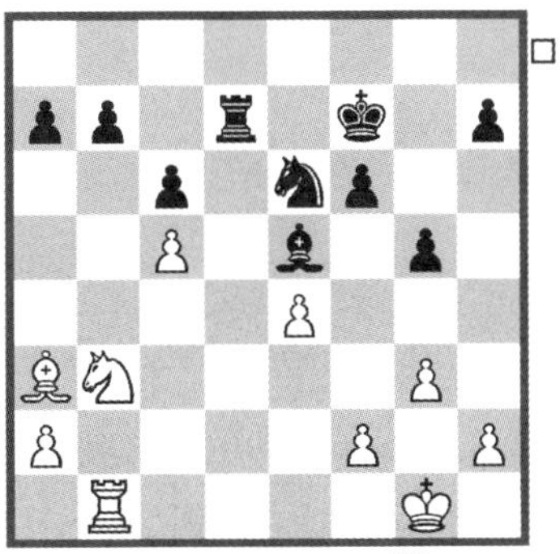

Position after: 25... ♖xd7

26. h3?

A primitive move preventing ...g4, but only temporarily.

26. ♘a5 ♘d8 27. ♔f1 This was a better way to show resistance but after 27... g4 White is still in big trouble.

26... ♗c7

Black has prevented ♘a5 and White is hopeless.

27. ♔f1 b5 28. ♗b4 h5!

Preparing ...g4 with fixing or ...h4 forcing exchanges on g3 with damage to White's structure.

29. ♔g2 ♖d3

First improving the pieces.

30. ♖c1

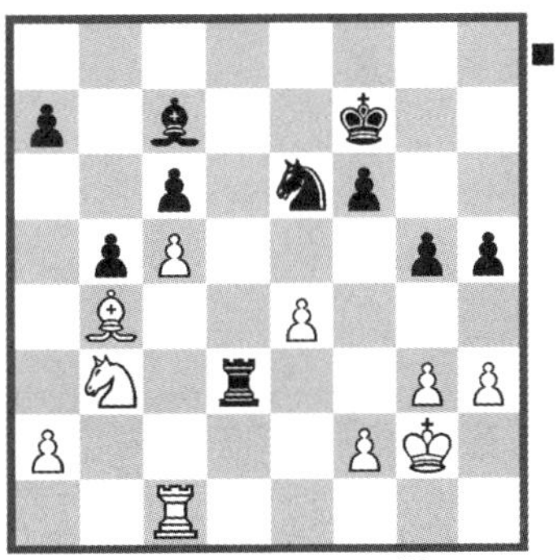

Position after: 30. ♖c1

30... ♘d4!

Once again an excellent and practical decision. With such a bad bishop White cannot offer any resistance. Black opts for exchanges to liberate his queenside majority and gain access to the c5-weakness.

31. ♖c3

31. ♘xd4 This loses a pawn after 31... ♖xd4.

31... ♖xc3 32. ♗xc3 ♘xb3 33. axb3

The situation has stabilized. White has gained some relief but the endgame is simply lost for him – Black is able to play on both wings against two weaknesses! For White, one weakness is that he must deal with the a-passer; the other is the fixed pawn on f2 (or g3).

33... a5! 34. ♔f3

Position after: 34. ♔f3

34... ♔e6?

A mistake. Instead, 34... a4 35. bxa4 bxa4 36. ♔e3 a3 37. ♔d3 a2 38. ♔c2 ♔e6 With Black's next move ...♗e5 he wins by force.

35. ♔e3 g4 36. hxg4 hxg4 37. ♔d3?

37. f4! gxf3 38. ♔xf3 a4 39. bxa4 bxa4 40. ♗b2 ♗e5

Position after: 40... ♗e5

41. ♗a3 ♗d4 42. ♔f4 This holds the position.

37... a4 38. bxa4 bxa4 39. ♗b4 ♗e5 40. ♗a3 ♗a1 41. ♗c1 f5!

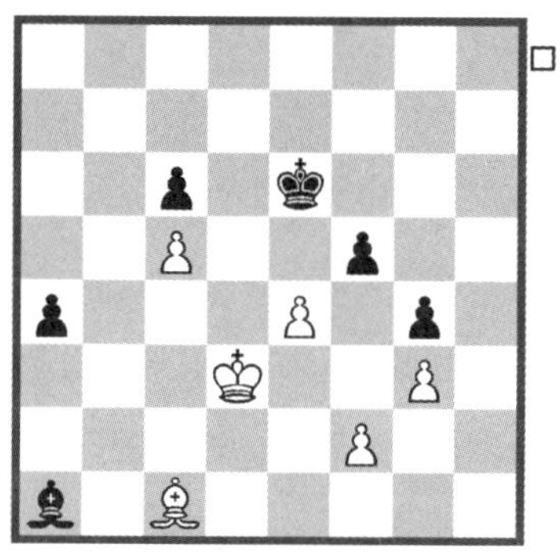

Position after: 41... f5!

This move opens the door to the king.

42. ♗a3 ♔e5 43. exf5 ♔xf5 44. ♔e3 ♔e5 45. f4+ ♔d5 46. f5 ♗e5 47. ♔f2 ♔e4

0-1

Game 124

♙ Sax, Gyula (2600)
♟ Andersson, Ulf (2625)
Reggio Emilia 1988

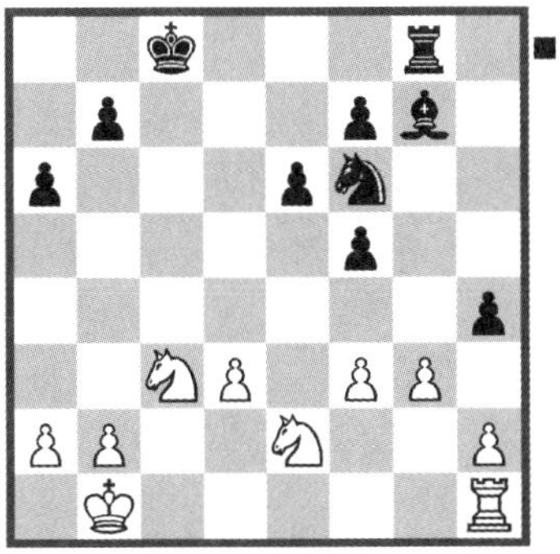

Black is dominant here due to White's pawn weaknesses. His d-pawn is isolated and there will soon be another weakness on the kingside.

24... ♖h8! 25. ♖g1 hxg3 26. hxg3 ♖h2 27. g4

What else?

A) 27. ♔c2 For instance, this move can be met with 27... ♘d7!.

B) 27. ♔c1 ♘d5!–+

27... fxg4 28. fxg4 ♔d7

(see diagram next column)

The first stage after the situation has stabilized is to activate the king

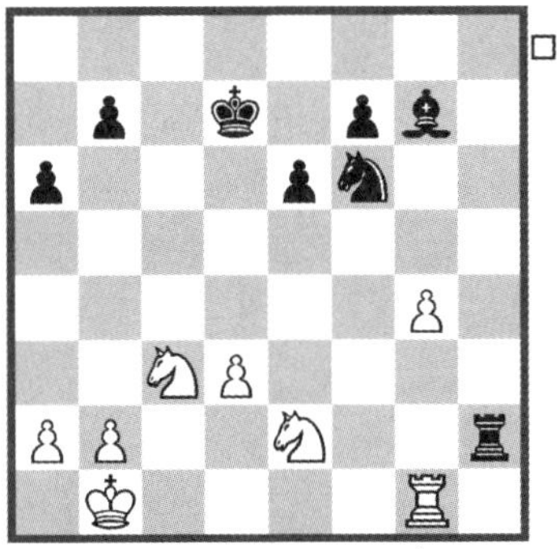

Position after: 28... ♔d7

29. ♔c1 ♘d5

Black also gets a moment to activate the knight.

30. ♔d1

30. ♘xd5 This fails to 30... ♖xe2–+.

30... ♘e3+ 31. ♔d2 ♘g2

It may appear that the knight only blocks the rook here, but in fact it threatens many dangerous jumps.

32. g5?!

This is understandable; White wants to install his knight on e4. The pawn on g5 would be protected by the knight and prevent ...f5. However this plan simply fails. The pawn is still on a dark square and is an object of attack.

32. d4!? This should have been worth a try.

32... ♘h4?!

32... ♘f4! Threatening to take on c3. 33. ♔e3 ♘h3

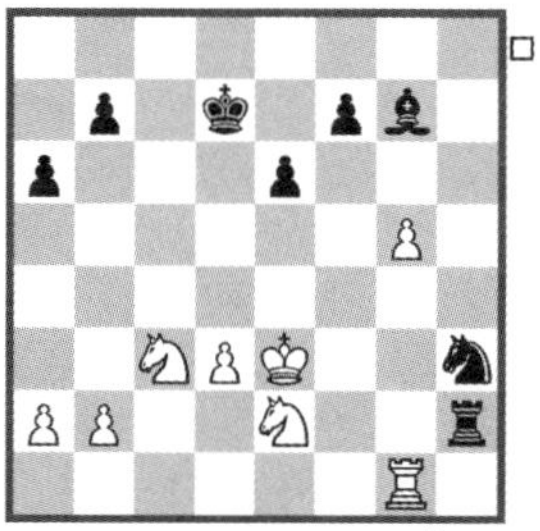
Position after: 33... ♘h3

34. ♖g3 ♘xg5 A tactical way to convert.

33. ♖f1 ♘f5 34. ♘e4

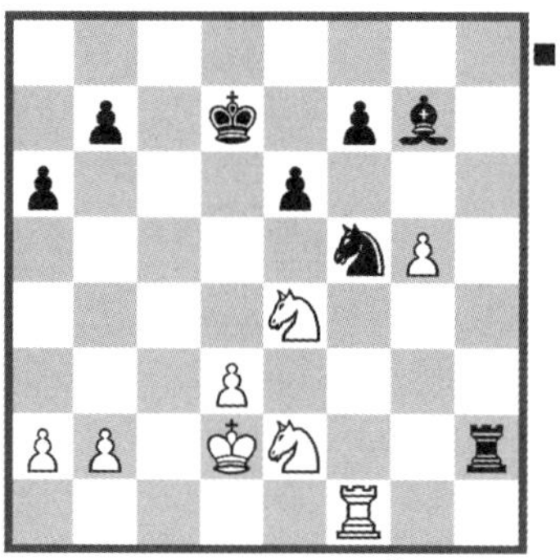
Position after: 34. ♘e4

It may look like White is okay here. However Black has many opportunities to enhance his initiative.

34... ♗d4

Keeping an eye on the e3-square.

35. b3 ♔e7

There is no need to rush. Black avoids some checks and preventively defends f7.

36. ♖f3 ♗b6 37. ♘4g3

White tries to get rid of the strong knight by exchanging pieces.

37... ♘d4 38. ♖f4 ♖g2

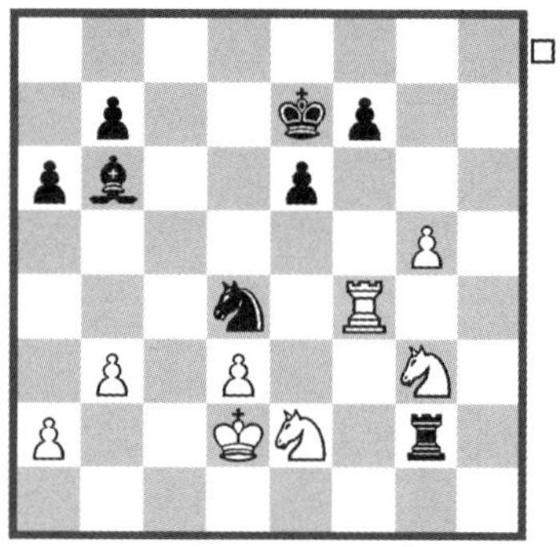
Position after: 38... ♖g2

All of White's pieces are hanging.

39. ♖e4 ♘xe2 40. ♘xe2 ♖xg5 41. ♔d1 ♗c5 42. ♖c4 ♗d6 43. ♘c3 f5!

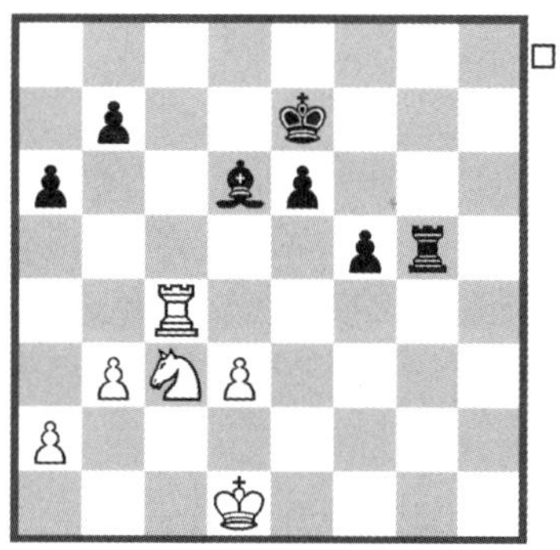
Position after: 43... f5!

Advancing and setting on a light square!

44. a4

Not having any good moves, White settles for a bad one. This move weakens the b3-pawn which is immediately exploited by Black.

44... ♖g1+ 45. ♔e2

The king goes closer to the passer but Black has the following.

45... ♖g2+ 46. ♔f3 ♖b2 47. ♔e3 ♖xb3 48. ♘e2 ♖b4!

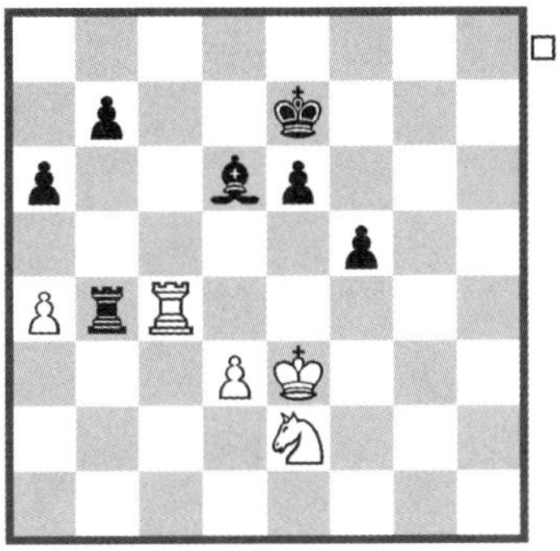

Position after: 48... ♖b4!

49. ♖xb4 ♗xb4 50. d4 ♗d6 51. ♘c1

0-1

Game 125

♙ Ivanchuk, Vassily (2720)
♟ Anand, Viswanathan (2690)
Linares 1992

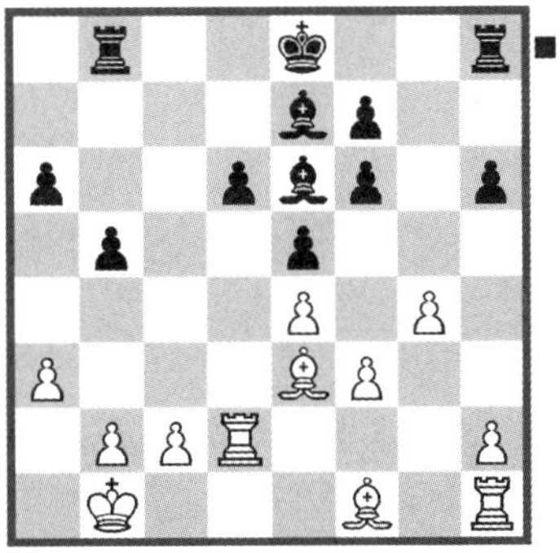

Black has more a compact structure. White's blockade on d5 is not strong. On the kingside White is not stable. Black has the possibility to seize the initiative with two breakthroughs.

18... h5!

This is the first breakthrough (another one, of course, is ...d5). Black gets rid of the separated pawn and opens the file for kingside activities. White must switch to defense.

19. ♖g1?

19. gxh5! ♖xh5 20. h4 This looks ugly but was necessary. 20... f5

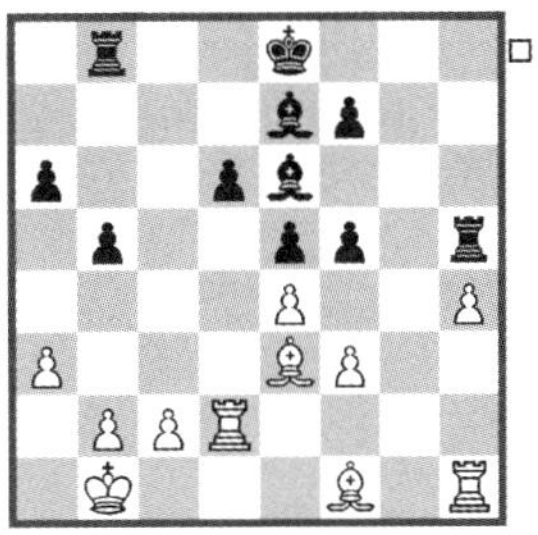

Position after: 20... f5

21. exf5 ♗xf5 This is better for Black but looks holdable for White.

19... hxg4 20. fxg4

Now White has one extra pawn island.

20... ♗c4!!

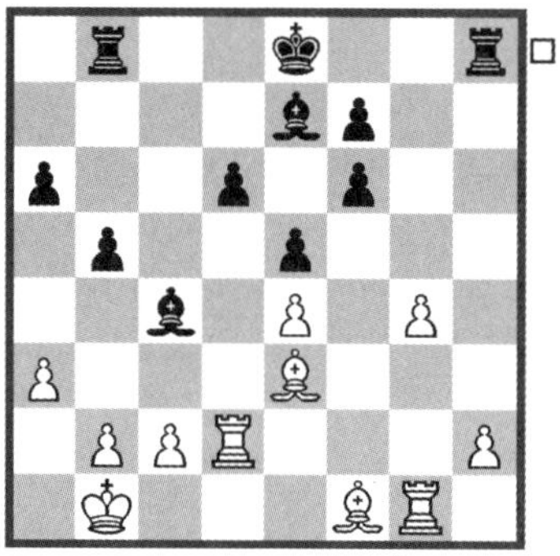

Position after: 20... ♗c4!!

This is the move that unlocks the doors on the kingside. Paradoxically, Black gives away his better bishop, but in return the white e4-pawn becomes weak and the rook gains access to the h3-square.

21. b3

21. ♗xc4 bxc4 This would have been even worse for White. Black gets the b-file while the c-pawn remains safe. White would be simply lost.

21... ♗xf1 22. ♖xf1 ♖h3 23. ♖e2 ♔d7!

Chess seems very simple ... when you look at the masterclasses from the giants. Black activates his king, preparing the liberating ...d5. Furthermore, the 8th rank is open for another rook. Now White is almost paralyzed. It is no wonder that he tries to complicate things with his next move.

24. g5

24. ♗d2 ♖bh8 25. ♖ff2 ♔e6 Preparing ...d5 or the maneuver ♗d8-b6 is hopeless for White.

24... ♔e6

Logical!

25. gxf6 ♗xf6

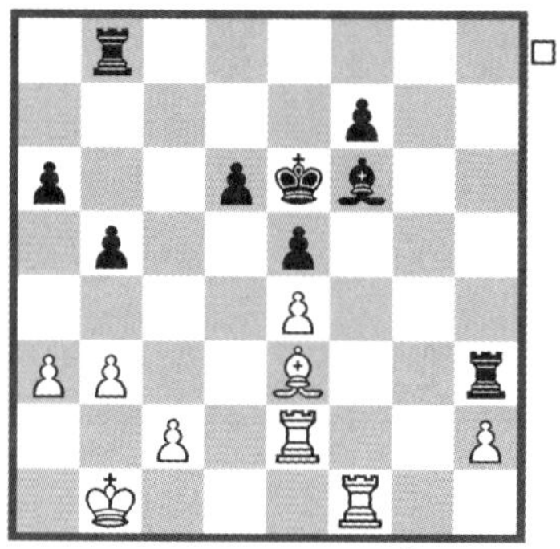

Position after: 25... ♗xf6

It is clear that Black has gained an advantage. He simply aims to create two connected passers which will end the game.

26. ♗d2 ♗e7 27. ♗e1 f6

The final preparing move.

28. ♗g3

28. ♖d2 ♖e3–+

28... d5! 29. exd5+ ♔xd5 30. ♖f5

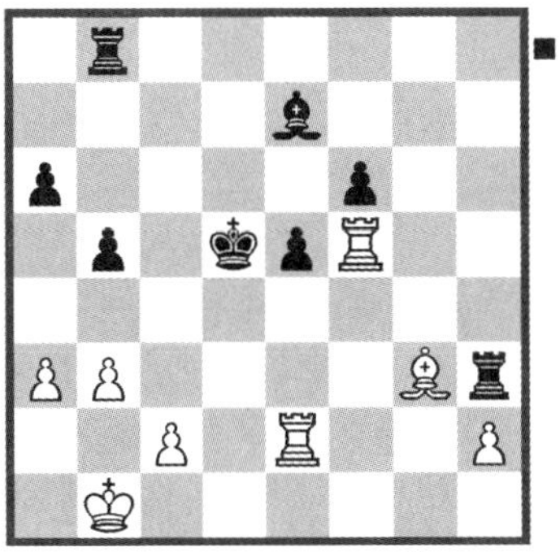

Position after: 30. ♖f5

A tricky move.

30... ♔c6!

Black is careful.

30... ♔e6? 31. ♗xe5!

31. ♖ef2 ♖h6 32. ♔b2 ♔d7

Now the king may go to a comfortable spot on e6.

33. ♖e2 ♗d6 34. ♖f3 ♖c8 35. ♗e1 ♔e6 36. ♖d3 ♖h7

(see diagram next column)

Probably as he was in time trouble Black went for patient maneuvering.

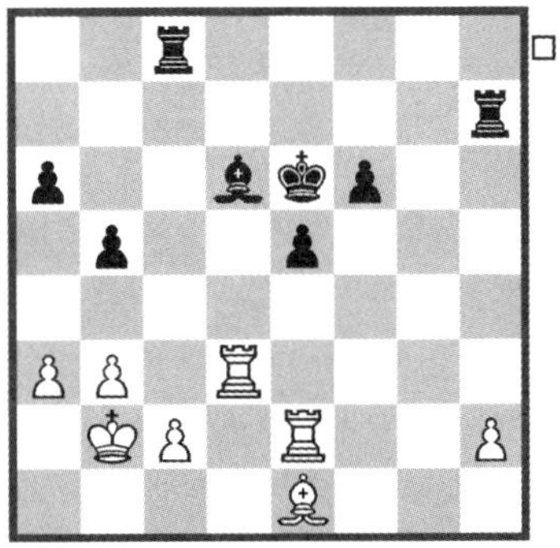

Position after: 36... ♖h7

37. ♖g3 ♗c5 38. ♔a2 ♖d7 39. ♖c3 ♖cc7 40. h4 ♖d1

After the time control has passed he goes for action.

41. ♗f2 ♗d6 42. ♖g3

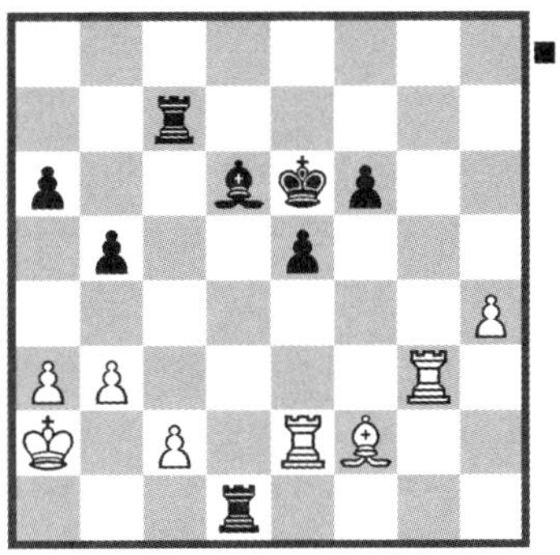

Position after: 42. ♖g3

42... e4!

A beautiful finish!

43. ♖xe4+ ♗e5 44. ♖xe5+ fxe5 45. ♔b2 ♖d2

0-1

Game 126

♙ Mecking, Henrique
♟ Petrosian, Tigran V
San Antonio 1972

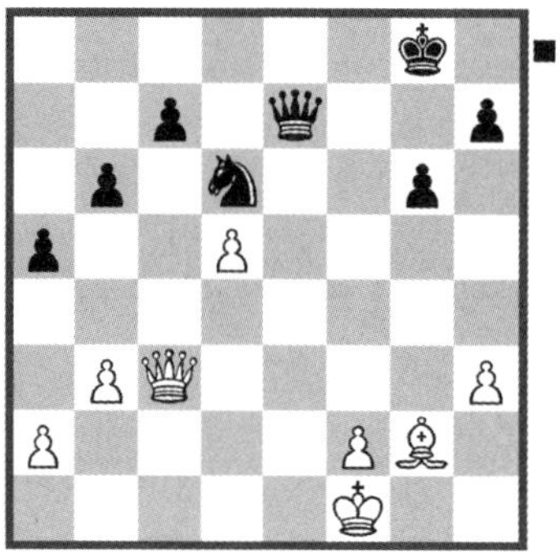

Here we see clearly Black's domination due to Capablanca's principle. However the more important fact is that White has a ruined structure. Although the engine may say that White can hold in practical chess, this is almost impossible. With his next move Black sets an exchange problem.

38... ♕g7!? 39. ♕c1!?

There are reasons both for keeping the queens and for trading them. I suggest you try to find as many of these reasons as possible.

39... ♕e5!?

Black gets a moment to centralize the queen. Again the psychological pressure is on White – whether to take on c7 or not.

40. ♗f3?!

40. ♕xc7 A direct and better approach. White must at some moment force play – waiting forever would lead to capitulation at some point, because Black can undertake long-term maneuvers whether with or without queens on the board. 40... ♕a1+ 41. ♔e2 ♕xa2+ 42. ♔e1!

Position after: 42. ♔e1!

42... ♕a1+ 43. ♔e2 ♕e5+ 44. ♔f1 This looks safe for White.

40... ♘f5

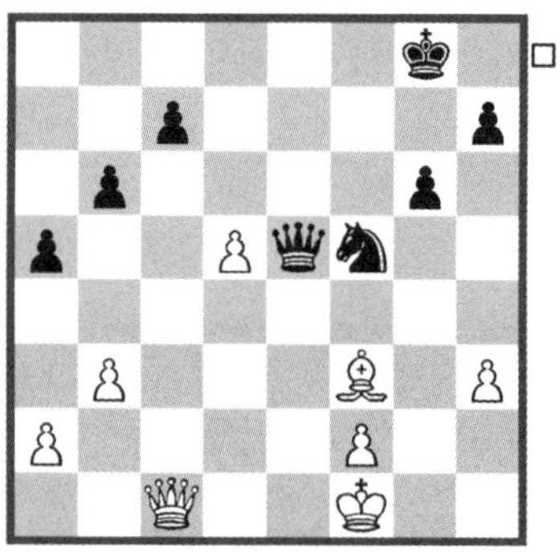

Position after: 40... ♘f5

41. ♕g5?!

41. ♗g4! ♘d4 42. f4

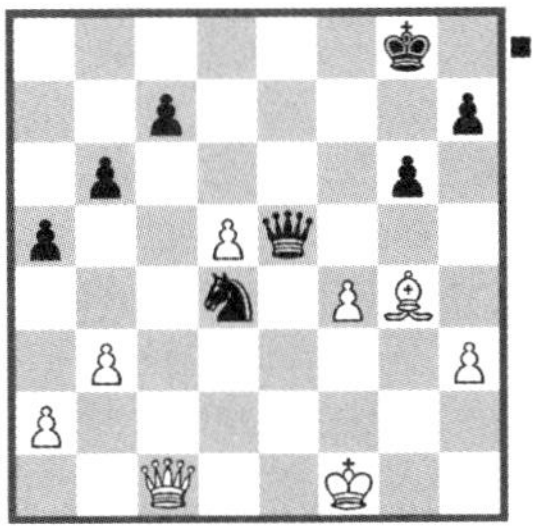

Position after: 42. f4

[42. ♗e6+? ♔g7! The bishop is misplaced with the kingside in danger.] 42... ♕d6 [42... ♕xd5 43. ♕xc7 This must be holdable.] 43. ♕e3 ♕xd5 44. ♕e8+ ♔g7 45. ♕e7+ This looks drawish.

41... ♔g7 42. ♔g2 ♕f6

Again Petrosian is consistent and confident.

43. ♕f4 ♕d6 44. ♕e4 ♔f6 45. ♕c4 ♕e5

Position after: 45... ♕e5

Black has achieved much obviously. There is powerful centralization.

46. b4?!

It is not surprising that White opts for drastic measures, twice missing the chance to capitalize at the right moment.

46. ♗e2 This looks like a better option, but is actually not good enough because Black keeps huge pressure and must be winning after the following. 46... ♘d4 47. ♗d3 ♕f4

46... axb4

46... ♕g3+! 47. fxg3 ♘e3+ 48. ♔f2

Position after: 48. ♔f2

48... ♘xc4 49. bxa5 ♘xa5 Black must be winning this endgame. Perhaps Petrosian did not want to trade queens and improve White's structure?!

47. ♕xb4 h5

Now he must show that his harmonized army can prevail. There is nothing apparent on the horizon.

48. ♗e4 ♘d6 49. ♗f3 ♔f7 50. ♕b3

(see diagram next page)

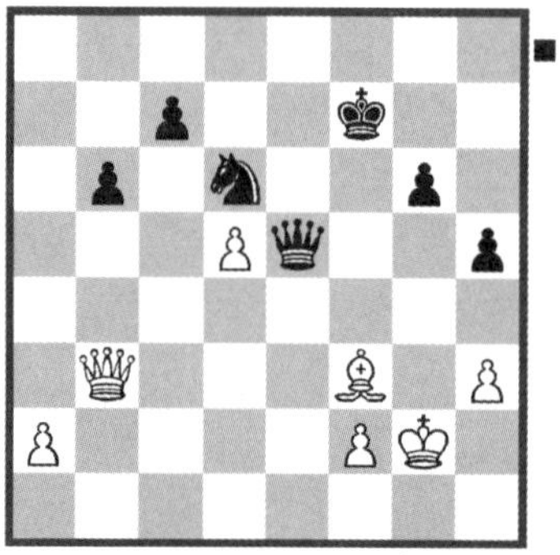

Position after: 50. ♕b3

50... ♔g7 51. ♕d3 ♔f6 52. ♗d1 ♘f5 53. ♗c2 ♔g5!?

Psychologically unpleasant for White.

53... ♕d4 However, this would have been better. Now 54. ♕b3 ♔e5 is equally unpleasant.

54. ♕d2+ ♕f4 55. ♕c3 ♘h4+ 56. ♔f1 ♘f3

Position after: 56... ♘f3

Black desperately fights to make some progress.

57. ♕d3?!

57. a4! Better – White has the possible idea of a5 at some timely moment.

57... ♕c1+!

Forcing the retreat of the bishop.

58. ♗d1 ♘e5 59. ♕d4?

59. ♕g3+! ♔f5 60. ♕b3 ♕c5 Black again achieves much since White does not have any harmony.

59... ♕c4+

White has finally blundered and Black takes advantage of it. Now the queens will be traded with the maximum number of White's weaknesses.

60. ♕xc4 ♘xc4 61. ♗c2

Position after: 61. ♗c2

What else?

61... ♘e5 62. ♔e2 ♔f4

White cannot stop the advance of the g-pawn which will create a passed

h-pawn.

63. h4 g5 64. hxg5 ♔xg5 65. ♔e3 ♘g4+

Position after: 65... ♘g4+

66. ♔f3 h4 67. ♗d1 ♘f6 68. ♗b3 ♔f5

The rest is a matter of technique – not difficult for Petrosian.

69. ♔g2 ♔g4 70. ♗d1+ ♔f4 71. ♗b3 ♘e4

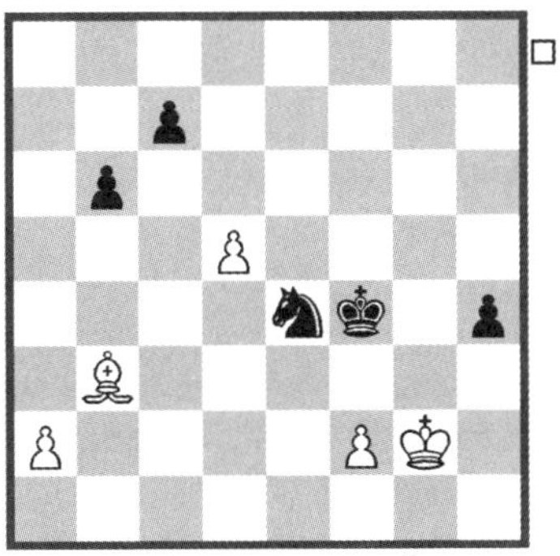

Position after: 71... ♘e4

72. ♗c2 ♘c3 73. ♗b3 ♘e4 74. ♗c2 ♘f6

There is no need to rush.

75. ♗b3 ♔g4 76. ♔h2 ♘e4 77. ♔g2

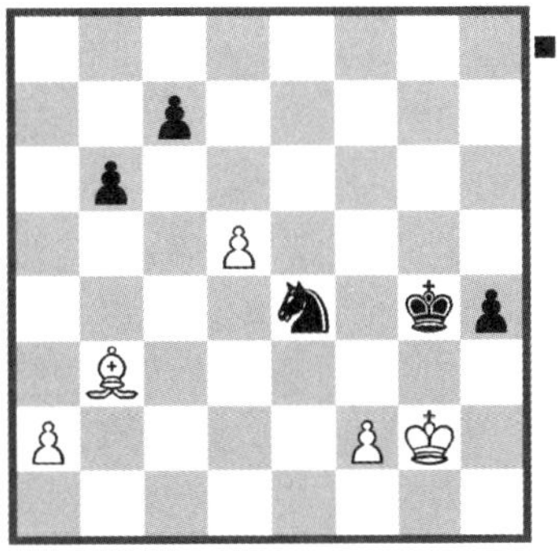

Position after: 77. ♔g2

77... h3+

This plan simplifies the win.

78. ♔g1 ♔f3 79. ♗d1+ ♔f4 80. ♗c2 ♘f6 81. ♗b3 ♘g4 82. ♗a4 h2+ 83. ♔g2 ♘xf2 84. ♔xh2 ♘d3 85. ♔g2 ♔e3 86. ♔g3 ♘c1

0-1

Game 127

♙ Gligoric, Svetozar
♟ Keres, Paul
Zuerich 1953

We can barely say that this is an endgame, but let's present this beautiful conversion. Black is dominant – White has many pawn islands, and especially weak is the a4-pawn. On the kingside however, there is a majority for White, but it cannot be used because of the weakening of the king's position.

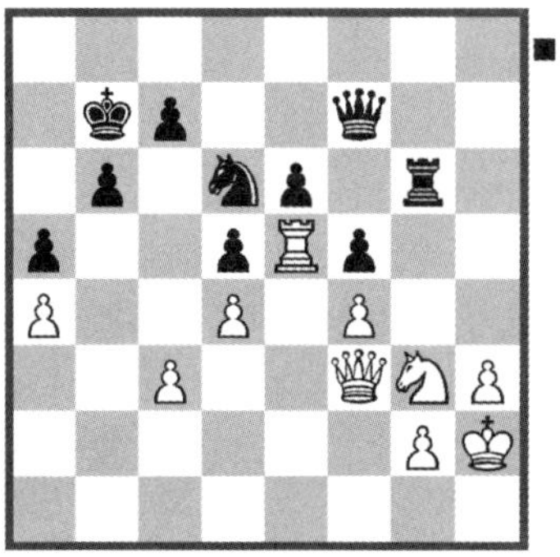

36... ♖h6!

Eliminating White's counterplay in relation to the move ♕h5 and preparing the next move with an invasion.

37. ♖e2 ♕d7 38. ♖a2 ♕c6 39. ♖a1 ♕c4 40. ♔g1 ♕b3 41. ♘e2 ♕c2

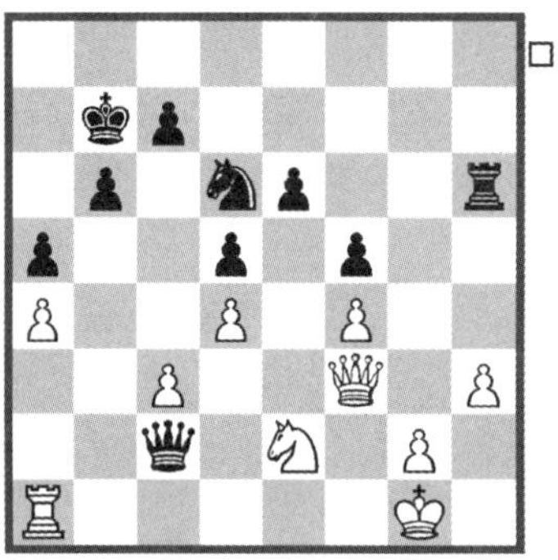

Position after: 41... ♕c2

A magical dance by the black queen. White can hardly prevent it.

42. g4

White goes for drastic measures. However, the black queen still affects the kingside.

42. ♕f2 A holding waiting policy with this move does not help. After, for instance 42... ♖g6 43. ♕f3 ♘e4 sooner or later there will be a collapse.

42... fxg4 43. hxg4 ♖h4 44. ♖c1 ♕h7!

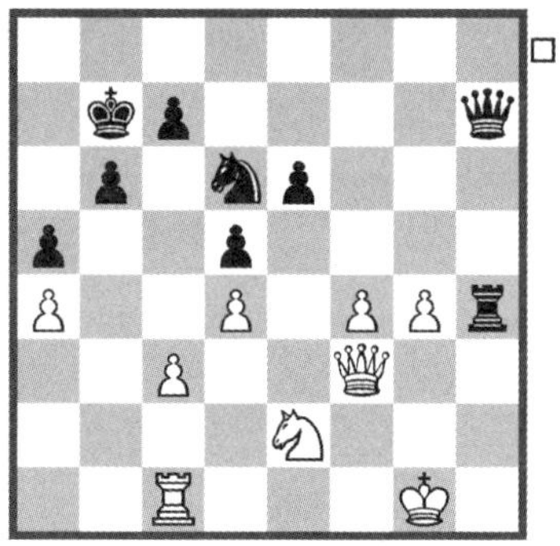

Position after: 44... ♕h7!

45. c4

Desperation.

45... ♖h3 46. ♕g2 ♕d3 47. cxd5 ♘e4 48. dxe6 ♕e3+ 49. ♔f1 ♖f3+

0-1

Game 128

♙ Estrin
♟ Lilienthal
🌍 Moscow 1951

Before I switch to endgames with typical isolated pawn structures I want to present a game that I love. Unfortunately it cannot be found in Megabase, so I want to show it.

1. e4 e5 2. ♘f3 ♘c6 3. ♗c4 ♗e7 4. d4 d6?! 5. dxe5!

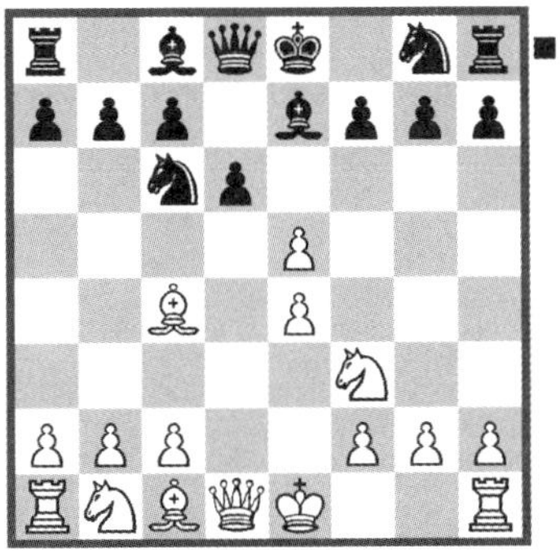

Position after: 5. dxe5!

Simple and strong.

5... dxe5 6. ♕xd8+ ♗xd8 7. ♘c3

We can hardly say that this is an endgame, but nevertheless let's carry on. Black is suddenly in trouble. He must protect the e5-pawn; ...f6 would weaken the light-squared complex. Unfortunately for him, on the c6-square is a knight instead of a pawn – so the d5-spot is accessible for the white pieces. Once we add to the list the disorder within the black army and the deficit in development, the diagnosis is clear.

7... ♗g4?!

7... ♘f6 This is preferable to get control over the d5-square.

8. ♗b5!

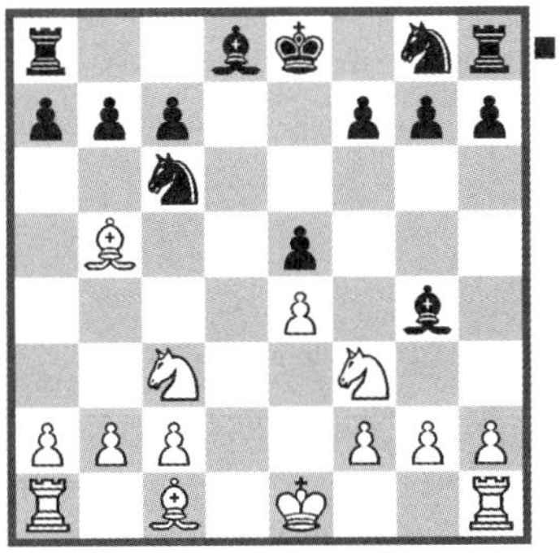

Position after: 8. ♗b5!

A classy reaction!

8. ♗e3! However, this would also have been very strong. Black will get nothing from doubling the white pawns.

8... f6

8... ♗xf3 This would be met for sure with the following. 9. ♗xc6+! bxc6 10. gxf3 White dominates – the doubled pawns in a group are not as weak as separated ones. Control of the c4- and c5-spots would finally result in material loss for Black.

9. ♗xc6+! bxc6 10. ♘d2!

Of course. White is ready to occupy the many weak spots on the kingside. At the same time the black bishop pair is useless and cannot compensate for the serious structural defect.

10... ♗e7 11. ♘a4 ♘h6 12. ♘b3 ♘f7 13. ♗e3 ♘d8 14. f3 ♗h5?

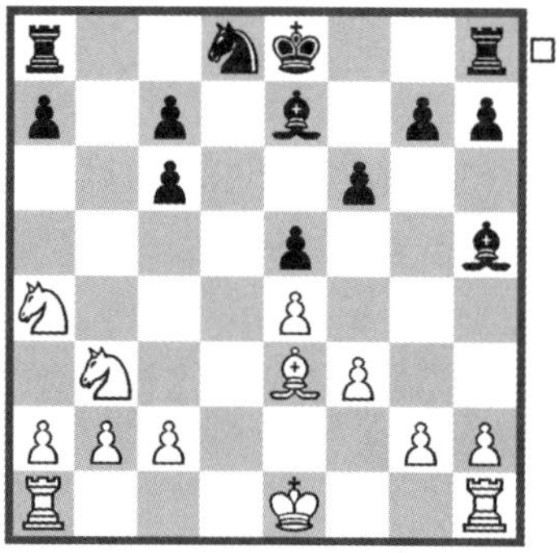

Position after: 14... ♗h5?

Of course, nonsensical. The bishop should be immediately transferred to the queenside. Here you should assure yourself that Black does not have some other defensive set-up that would help.

15. 0-0-0 ♗f7 16. ♖d3

Not only with the idea to double up, but also to use the d-file as a trampoline to get the c-file!

16... ♘b7 17. ♖c3

That game reminds me of the amazing game Nimzowitsch – Pritzel. You MUST check out this masterpiece. A similar maneuver occurred in that game, but Black has no weaknesses at the moment (that makes it even more impressive!)

17... ♗xb3 18. axb3

Whether a pawn or rook is employed – it is a matter of style.

18... ♔d7 19. ♖d1+ ♗d6

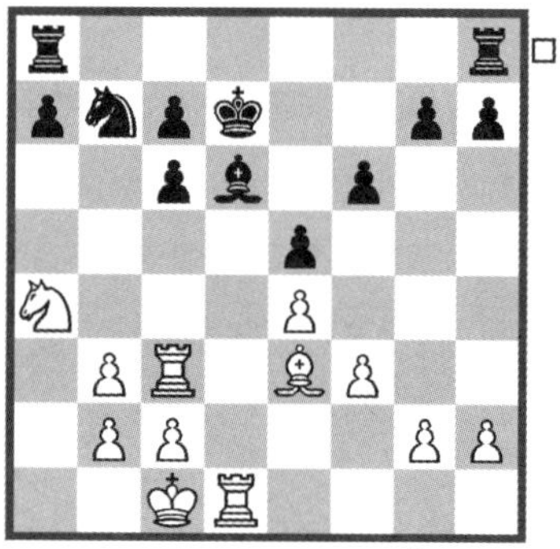

Position after: 19... ♗d6

Black is about to consolidate, bringing the rooks into the game. White acts quickly but logically.

20. ♘c5+

Trading does not help Black. Even the pawn endgame is winning for White (if the king reaches the c5-spot, of course).

20... ♘xc5 21. ♗xc5 ♖hd8 22. ♖c4! a5?!

An act of desperation. As usual, such moves only help the opponent.

To be fair, a neutral move such as 22... h5 would not have changed anything. White would play 23. ♗f2 and sooner or later the a-pawn would fall, after (if necessary) White sets both rooks on the a-file.

23. ♖a4 ♔e6 24. ♗f2 g6

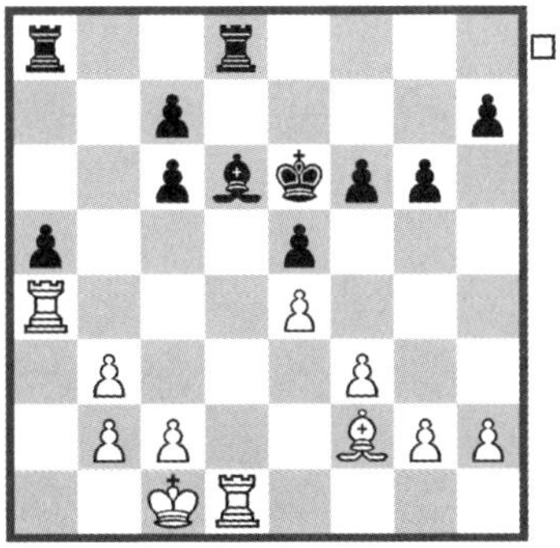

Position after: 24... g6

25. c3!

A methodical way to convert. White improves the king and attacks the weakness at the same time.

25... ♖ab8 26. ♔c2 ♖b5 27. c4 ♖bb8 28. c5!

Again, concrete play.

28... ♗f8 29. ♖xd8 ♖xd8 30. ♖xa5 ♗h6 31. ♗e1 ♗e3

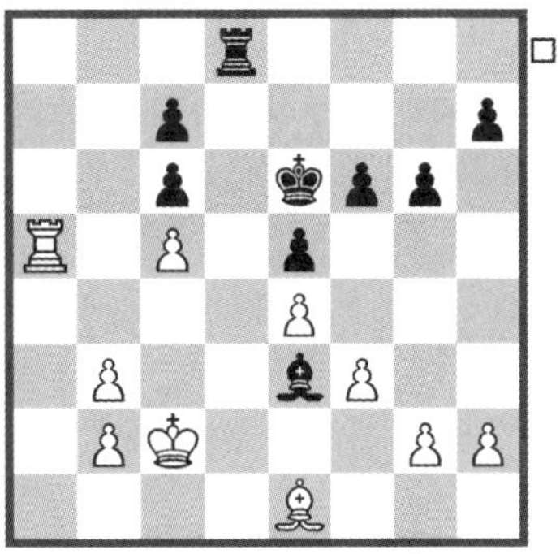

Position after: 31... ♗e3

Black has activated his pieces, but there is simply no compensation. White directly plays on the queenside launching his majority and converts without special problems.

32. b4 f5

A final attempt to get some counterplay.

33. ♖a6 ♔d7

33... fxe4 34. fxe4 ♔d7 35. ♖a3 (with ♖f3) – This changes nothing.

34. ♖a3 ♗d4 35. ♖d3

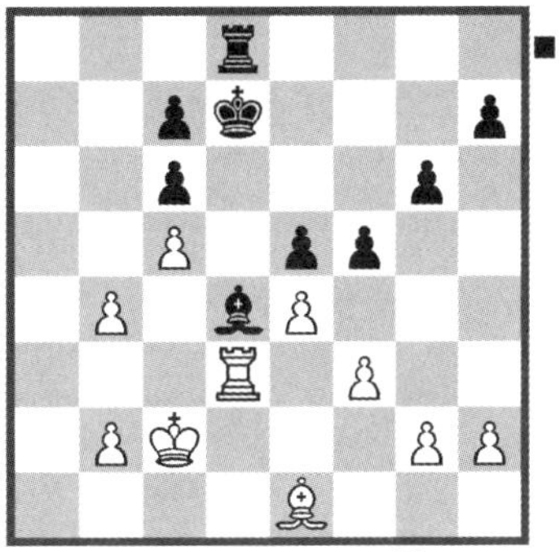

Position after: 35. ♖d3

35... fxe4

35... ♖f8 This is met with 36. exf5 followed by ♗c3.

36. fxe4 ♔e6 37. ♗f2

A concrete decision.

37... ♖f8 38. ♗xd4 exd4 39. ♖xd4 ♔e5 40. ♖d7 ♖f2+ 41. ♔c3

Black resigned.

1-0

Game 129

♙ Karpov, Anatoly
♟ Hort, Vlastimil
Budapest 1973

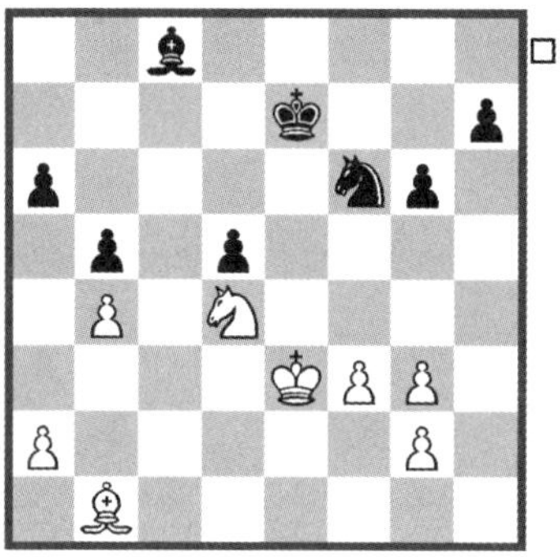

Let's switch now to positions with a typical isolated pawn as a weakness. As you already know, such a pawn becomes weak in the endgame when the traditional initiative (for the side having it) is gone. Despite White's majority on the kingside it may look useless; White is much better. In addition to the weak isolated pawn Black has the a6- and b5- pawns fixed on the light squares, with a severely weakened dark-squared complex. White's first moves are played with the instructive idea of launching the majority to restrict the black pieces.

33. g4! ♘d7

Black plans to eliminate White's dangerous knight. No other reasonable plan is evident.

34. f4 ♘f8 35. g5!

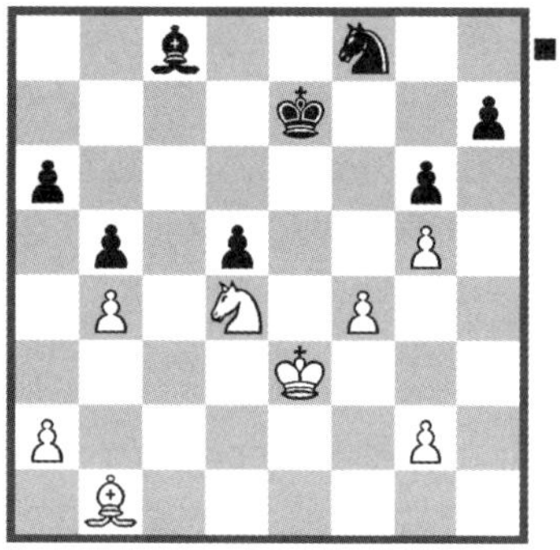

Position after: 35. g5!

35... ♔d6 36. ♔f3

Preparing g4 and practically provoking Black's next move.

36... ♘e6

Objectively Black has nothing better. Karpov has perfectly evaluated the position arising after trading the knights.

37. ♘xe6! ♗xe6 38. ♔e3 ♗g4

(see diagram next page)

White's pawns look to have been stopped, but White has another idea. Black is in zugzwang and soon his defense will collapse.

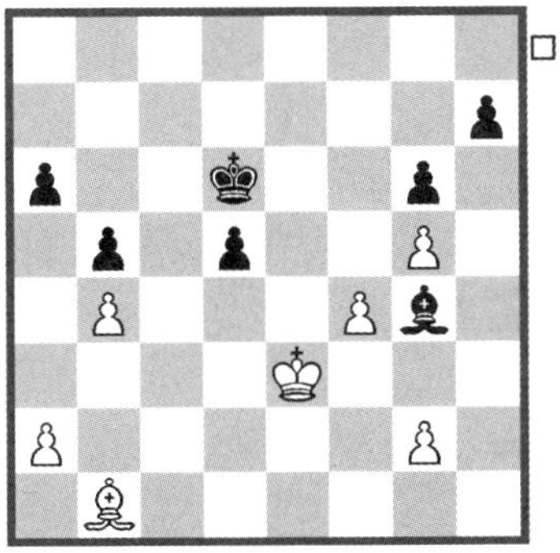

Position after: 38... ♗g4

39. ♗d3 ♗e6 40. ♔d4 ♗g4 41. ♗c2 ♗e6 42. ♗b3 ♗f7

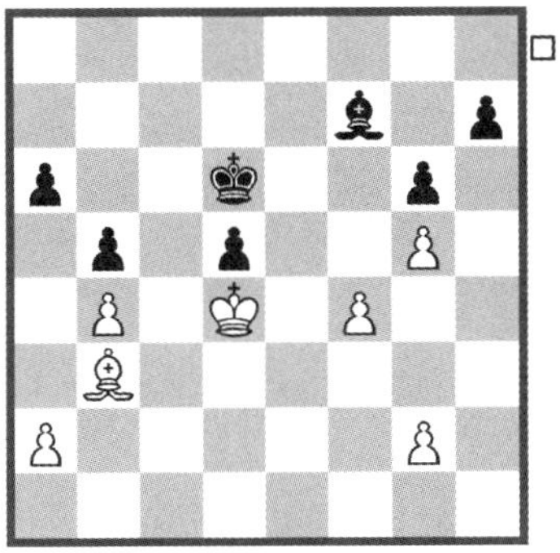

Position after: 42... ♗f7

The previous moves have been logical and now White transfers the bishop to a better diagonal.

43. ♗d1 ♗e6 44. ♗f3 ♗f7 45. ♗g4

Black resigned. He cannot avoid material loss. I suggest that you confirm for yourself that Black is lost; try to improve Black's play, then try to find a win for White.

1-0

Game 130

♙ Chloupek, Stanislav (2300)
♟ Stohl, Igor (2560)
Prague 1992

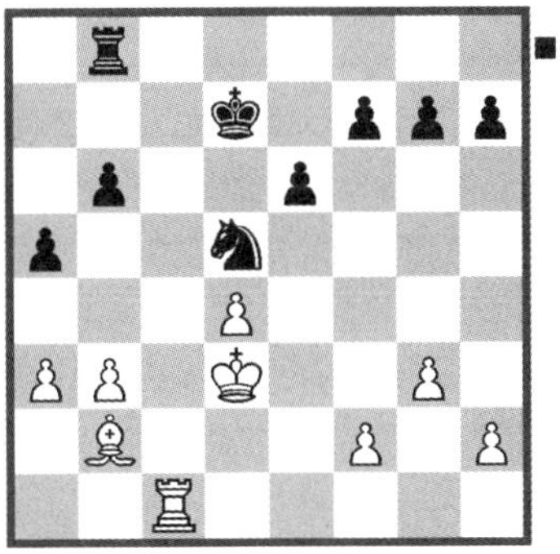

Black's domination is evident. The knight dominates on the square in front of the isolated pawn and there are chances to play on both wings. Black first takes measures to expand on the kingside.

34... g5 35. f3

35. g4 This would fix the black pawn on a dark square but the f4-square would become accessible for the knight.

35... h5 36. ♖c2 g4

Of course. Black fixes the white pawns on the bishop's color.

37. ♖f2 f5 38. ♗c1 b5

The rook is no longer on the c-file so Black now tries to gain an advantage on the queenside as well.

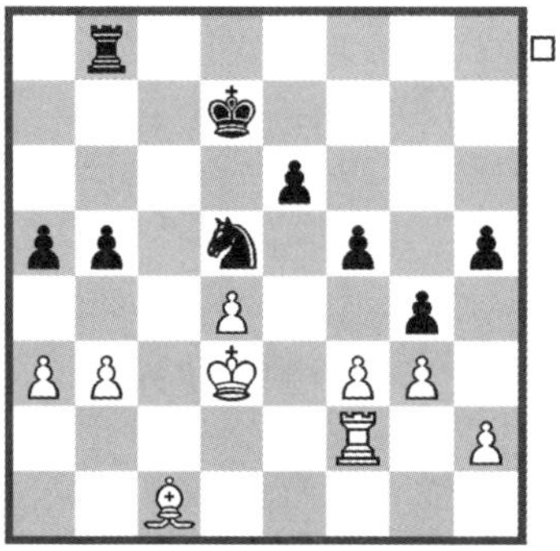

Position after: 38... b5

39. fxg4

Sooner or later this would be necessary.

39... hxg4 40. ♗f4 ♖c8 41. ♗d2

41. ♖c2 This loses after the following. 41... ♘xf4+ 42. gxf4 ♖h8!

41... a4!

Another fixing!

42. bxa4 bxa4

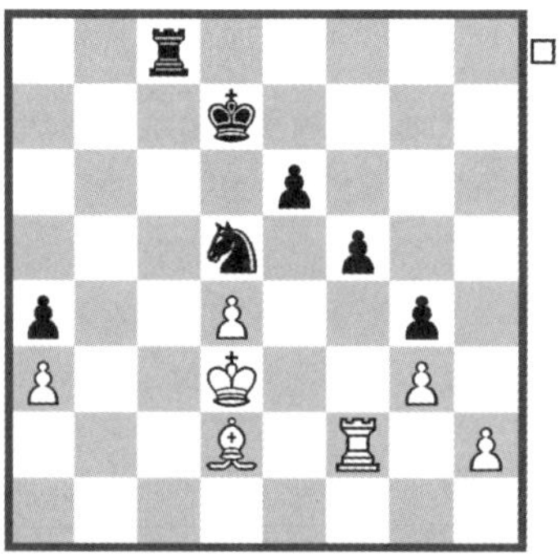

Position after: 42... bxa4

Black threatens ...♖b8 with ...♖b3.

43. ♗b4 ♖c1 44. ♖b2 ♘f6?!

Instead 44... ♖f1 with ...♖f3 would have been much better.

45. ♗c5 ♘e4 46. ♖b7+ ♔c6 47. ♖b6+ ♔c7 48. ♖xe6?

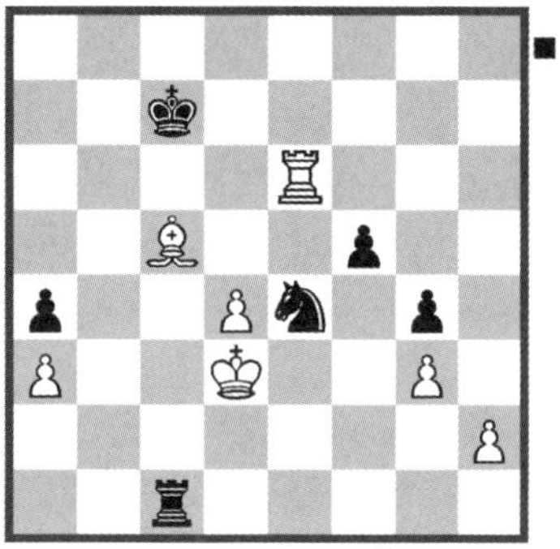

Position after: 48. ♖xe6?

White falls into a trap.

48... ♖xc5! 49. dxc5 ♘xc5+ 50. ♔d4 ♘xe6+ 51. ♔e5 ♔d7 52. ♔xf5 ♘d4+ 53. ♔xg4 ♘b5 54. ♔f4 ♘xa3

Position after: 54... ♘xa3

55. ♔e4 ♘c4 56. ♔d3 a3

0-1

Game 131

♙ Parma
♟ Puc
Ljubljana 1969

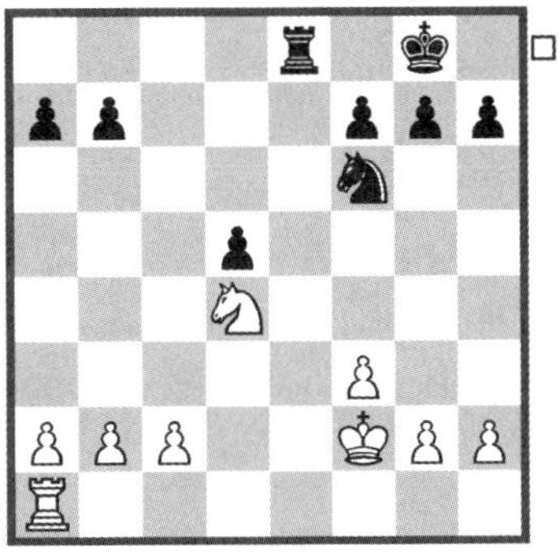

White dominates on the blockading d4-square and has more active pieces. It is important to know that further exchanges of pieces would be in Black's favor. Thus, White should try to keep both the knight and the rook on the board to achieve a lasting advantage.

23. ♖d1

The rook is ready for a frontal attack. There is also an idea to use the d-file as a trampoline to transfer the rook to the queenside.

23... a6 24. ♖d3 ♖c8

A very good defensive idea. Black practically forces White to close the 3rd rank.

25. c3

25. ♖b3 This achieves nothing in view of 25... ♖c7.

25... ♔f8 26. g4!

White targets the black knight wishing to destabilize the isolated pawn.

26... ♘d7

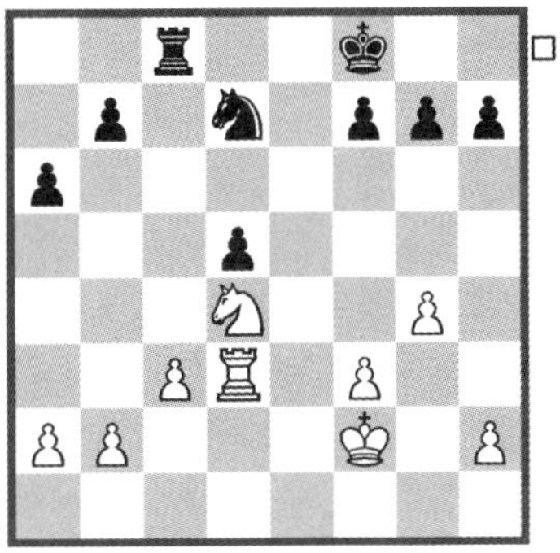

Position after: 26... ♘d7

27. ♘f5

The knight is good here to provoke a weakening advance. Furthermore there is an idea to switch to attacking the pawn instead of just blocking it.

27... ♘b6 28. b3

The pawn on c3 is safe, so it is good to restrict the b6-knight.

28... g6 29. ♘e3 ♖c5 30. ♔e2 h6

Black prevents any potential fixing after g5 where White would perhaps get the f6-square for the knight.

31. ♔d2

Position after: 31. ♔d2

31... ♔g7?

An incomprehensible move.

32. ♖d4

32. a4 Playing this immediately would also have been very good.

32... a5 33. a4 ♔f6 34. b4 axb4 35. cxb4 ♖c6

Position after: 35... ♖c6

36. a5!

White chooses the best way to gain material.

36... ♘c8

36... ♔e5 37. ♔d3 This changes nothing.

37. ♖xd5

37. ♘xd5+ ♔e5 38. ♔d3 This is probably more logical.

37... ♔e6 38. f4?!

White directly opts to advance his pawns, forgetting the king.

38... ♘d6 39. ♖c5+ ♔d7 40. ♖d5 ♔e6 41. f5+?!

Position after: 41. f5+?!

41... gxf5 42. gxf5+

Reducing the pawn material and isolating his own pawns – this is not a good recipe.

42... ♔e7 43. b5 ♖c8 44. a6?

If White's previous moves were dubious, this is a clear mistake.

Instead 44. ♔d3 with patient improving was needed.

44... bxa6?!

44... ♖a8!? 45. axb7 ♖b8 This would have been a much better option for Black. The passed pawn is less dangerous on the b-file.

45. bxa6 ♔d7 46. ♖a5 ♔c6 47. ♔d3

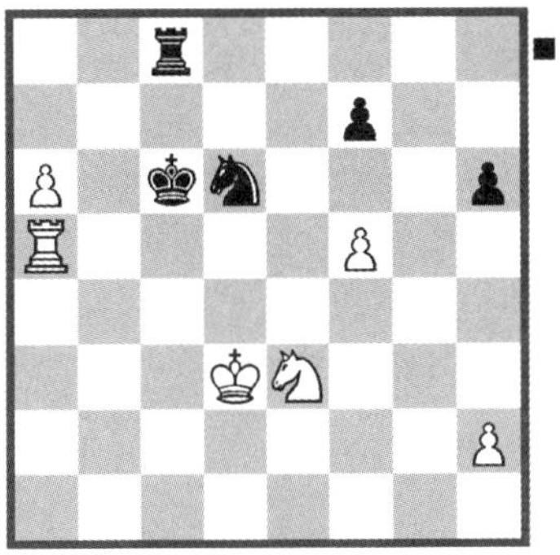

Position after: 47. ♔d3

Finally!

47... ♔b6 48. ♖a4 ♘b5

A very important moment. With such imprecise play White is close to losing the advantage, but now he has a chance to convert. Finally, in this situation, he finds a brilliant and the only possibility to convert.

49. a7! ♖d8+

A) 49... ♖a8 50. ♘c4++–

B) 49... ♘xa7 50. ♘c4+ ♔b5 51. ♖xa7 ♖xc4 52. ♖a5+!

Position after: 52. ♖a5+!

52... ♔xa5 53. ♔xc4 ♔b6 54. ♔d5 ♔c7 55. ♔e5 ♔d7 56. ♔f6 ♔e8 57. ♔g7 ♔e7 58. f6+ ♔e6 59. h3! h5 60. h4+–

50. ♘d5+!!

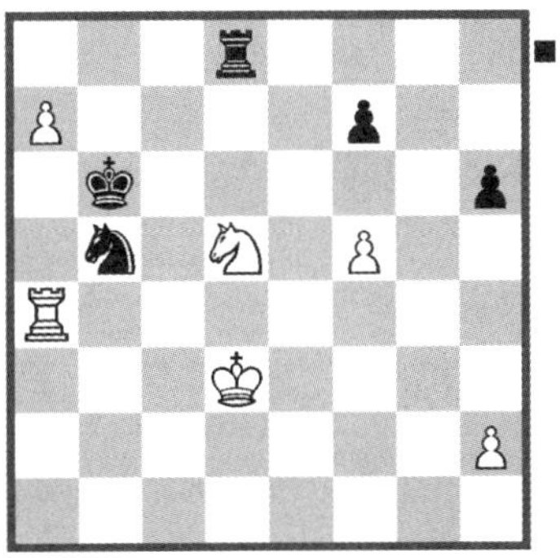

Position after: 50. ♘d5+!!

This is the well-hidden point.

50... ♔b7 51. a8=♕+! ♖xa8 52. ♖b4 ♖a5 53. ♘c3

By eliminating all the pieces, White wins

in the pawn endgame.

53... ♔c6 54. ♖xb5 ♖xb5 55. ♘xb5 ♔xb5 56. ♔d4 ♔c6 57. ♔e5 ♔d7 58. ♔f6

Position after: 58. ♔f6

58... ♔e8 59. ♔g7 ♔e7 60. f6+ ♔e6 61. h3

1-0

Game 132

♙ Szabo, Laszlo
♟ Penrose, Jonathan
Bath 1973

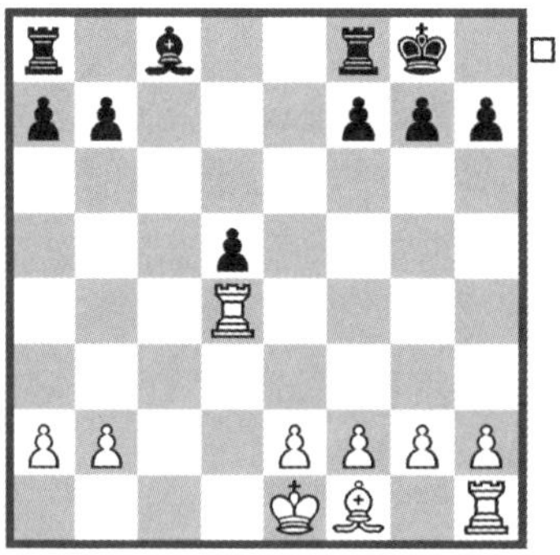

White's advantage is evident. He has the better bishop, better king, better rooks, and better structure.

16. e3

Of course.

16. ♖xd5? ♗e6 17. ♖a5? ♖fc8 Black has a strong initiative.

16... ♗e6 17. ♔d2 ♖fd8 18. ♗d3

Everything is going smoothly for White.

18... ♖ac8 19. f4!?

A risky move. Of course the "backward" e3-pawn is not a problem. I think it is too early to lose flexibility with such an advance.

19... f6 20. ♖c1 ♖xc1 21. ♔xc1

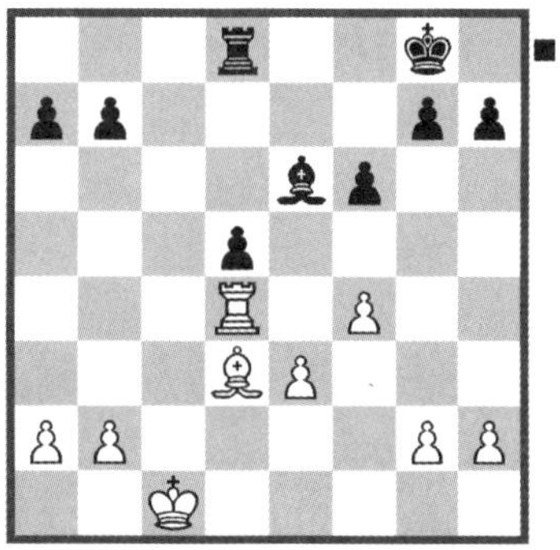

Position after: 21. ♔xc1

21... h6?!

Rendering the pawn safe but also creating holes.

21... ♔f7?! This is met by the following powerful response. 22. f5 ♗c8 23. ♗c4

22. ♔d2 ♔f8 23. ♖a4

White tries to create new weaknesses in Black's camp, provoking him to set his pawns on the light squares.

23... a6 24. ♖b4 ♖d7 25. ♔c3 ♔e7 26. ♔d4 ♔d8

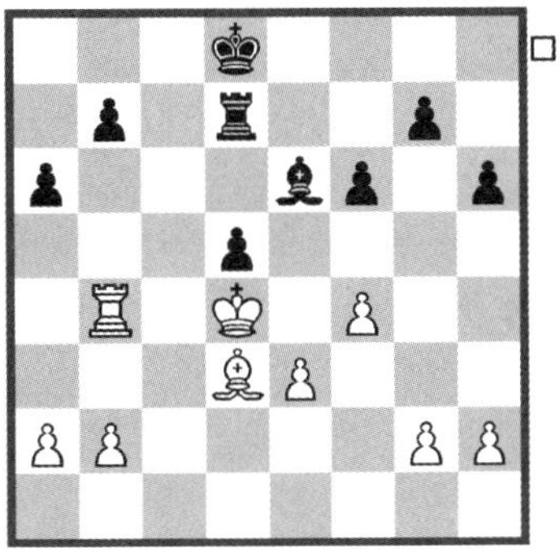

Position after: 26... ♔d8

White has achieved much. His king is on the desired square while both the rook and bishop have freedom to maneuver. The next stage would be to create weaknesses wherever possible.

27. ♗e2 ♔c7 28. ♗f3 b6 29. ♖b3 ♖d8 30. ♖c3+ ♔b7?!

A strange decision.

30... ♔d6 This is normal when after 31. b4 White would try to advance the pawns on both flanks to set a zugzwang or to create weaknesses.

31. g4

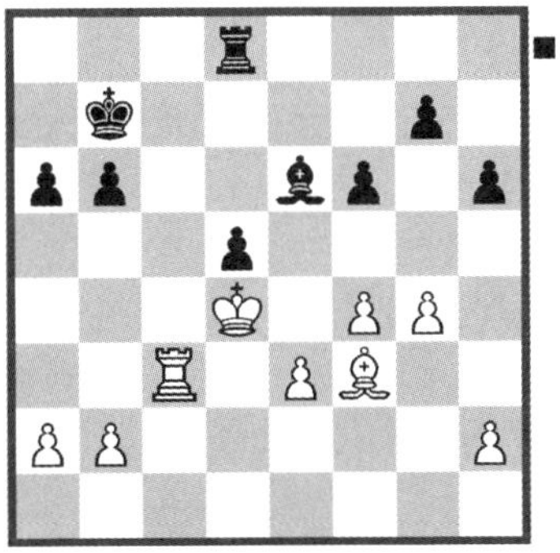

Position after: 31. g4

31... ♖d6

31... g5 This looks natural but it is bad. 32. f5! ♗f7 33. b4 White may combine threats of h4 with threats on the c-file to invade. It would be hopeless for Black to parry the various threats.

32. a3

32. f5! This would have been clearly good. White would even have the g4-g5 breakthrough with an arsenal of threats.

32... a5 33. h4 ♗f7 34. f5! ♖d8 35. ♖c2 ♖d7

(see diagram next page)

White sets the scene for the crushing g5. It cannot be parried well by Black because his king is stuck on the b7-square, far from the battlefront.

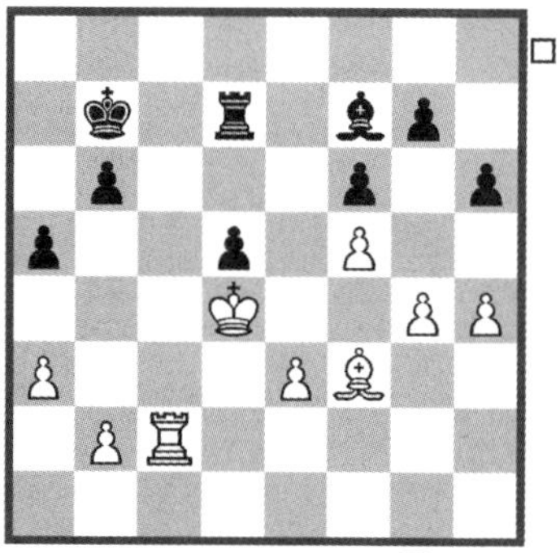

Position after: 35... ♖d7

36. g5

36. ♖g2 This is better. There was no need to rush.

36... fxg5 37. hxg5 hxg5 38. ♖g2

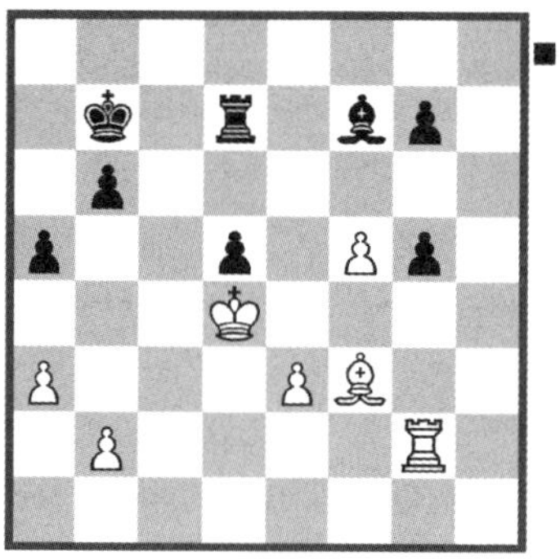

Position after: 38. ♖g2

38... ♖d6

38... g6 This would have been more resistant, although there is no doubt about the result after the following. 39. fxg6 ♗xg6 40. ♗xd5+

39. ♖xg5 g6 40. fxg6 ♖xg6

1-0

Game 133

♙ Kortschnoj, Viktor Lvovich (2650)
♟ Karpov, Anatoly (2690)
Merano 1981

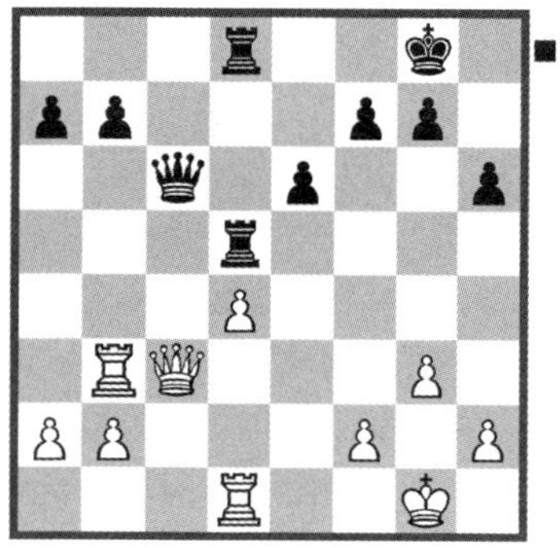

Here is a very well-known game from a famous clash between these two titans. Black is dominant, with his major pieces on the board; a frontal attack on the isolated pawn should decide the result. A deadly pin will sooner or later be applied with ...e5.

29... ♕d7!

The only way to keep the advantage. Black must keep the queens.

29... ♕xc3 30. bxc3! This gives White an important tempo and stability to the pawn. 30... b6 31. ♖b4 e5 32. ♖c4 White should hold without any specific problem.

30. f4?!

This move was widely criticized, but its intention to stop ...e5 is clear. Perhaps the commentators wanted to play without the pawn but with a safer king?! Objectively, White is lost anyway. And in any case, what else should have been played instead?

30. ♕f3 This may look better, but in the end after 30... b6 it should have no effect on the result.

30... b6 31. ♖b4 b5!

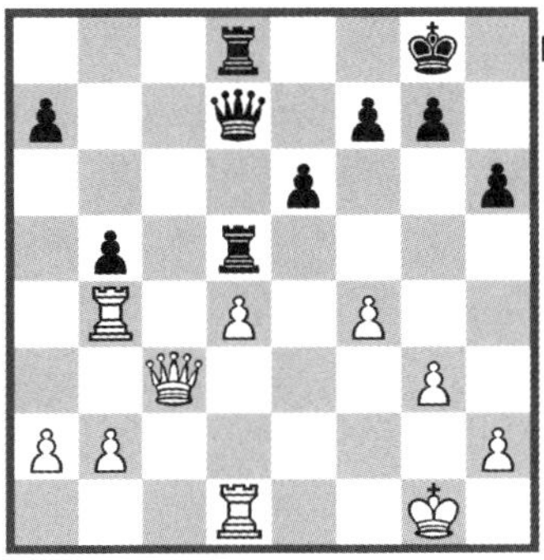

Position after: 31... b5!

This move excludes the white rook from play.

32. a4

White's intention to trade the pawn material and to complicate is reasonable.

32... bxa4 33. ♕a3 a5 34. ♖xa4 ♕b5 35. ♖d2

The previous moves have been natural. It is now time for Karpov to demonstrate his masterclass.

35... e5!

With most of the white army stuck on the queenside Black opens up the position on the kingside, attacking the white king.

36. fxe5 ♖xe5

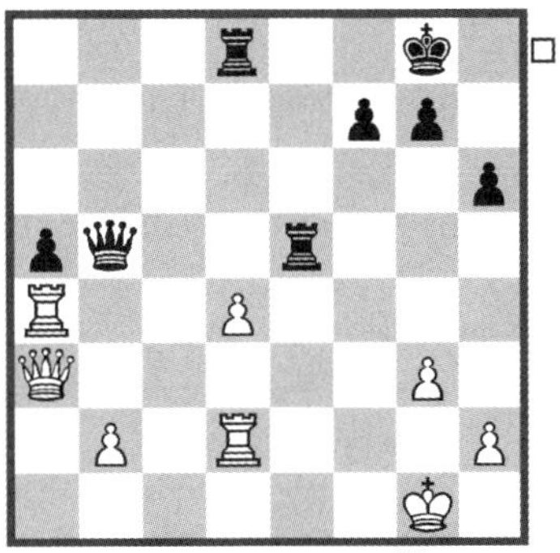

Position after: 36... ♖xe5

Threatening ...♖e1.

37. ♕a1

37. ♖f2 ♖f5 38. ♖xf5 ♕xf5 39. ♖xa5 ♕b1+

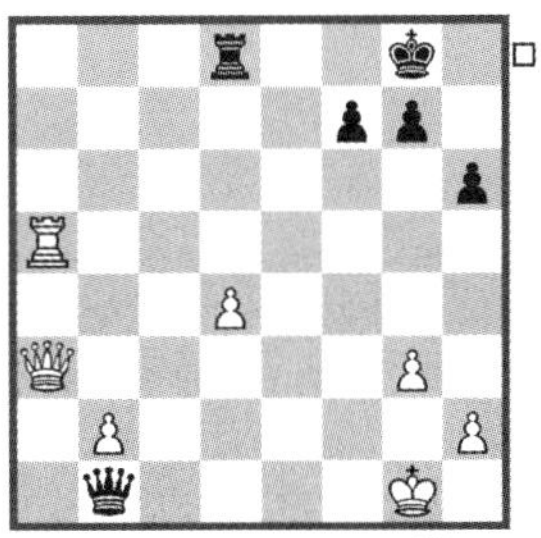

Position after: 39... ♕b1+

40. ♔g2 ♖xd4 This is simply won for Black.

37... ♕e8 38. dxe5 ♖xd2 39. ♖xa5 ♕c6

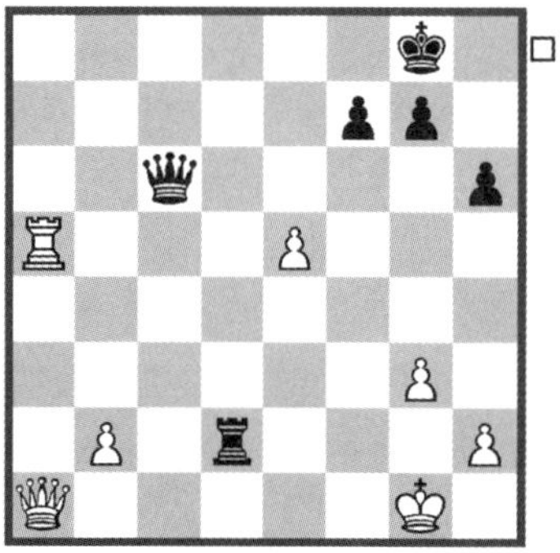

Position after: 39... ♕c6

It is game over.

40. ♖a8+ ♔h7 41. ♕b1+ g6 42. ♕f1 ♕c5+ 43. ♔h1 ♕d5+

0-1

Game 134

♙ Kuzubov, Yuriy (2623)
♟ Efimenko, Zahar (2689)
Kiev 2012

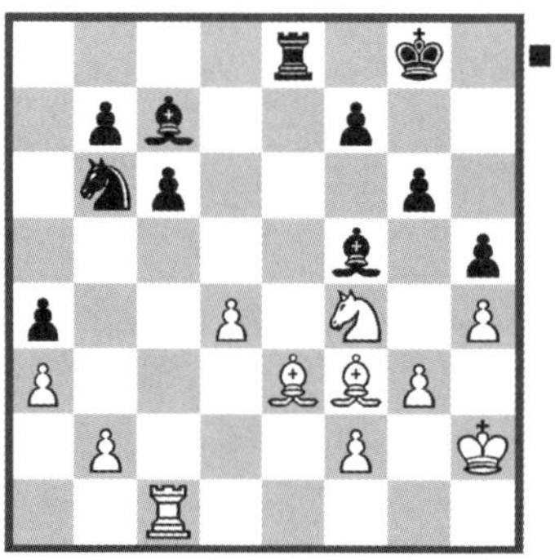

We know that exchanges are generally in favor of the side playing against the isolated pawns. However this is not always the case – some pieces must still be kept on the board! Our next two examples are instructive.

Here Black is better. Clearly, the white dark-squared bishop is his worst piece. So, let's trade the light-squared bishops and reach a dream endgame.

26... ♗e4! 27. ♔g2?

This is primitive and simply helps Black.

27. ♗d1 This should have been preferred. However 27... ♔g7 keeps a huge plus.

27... ♗xf4! 28. ♗xf4 ♗xf3+! 29. ♔xf3 ♘d5

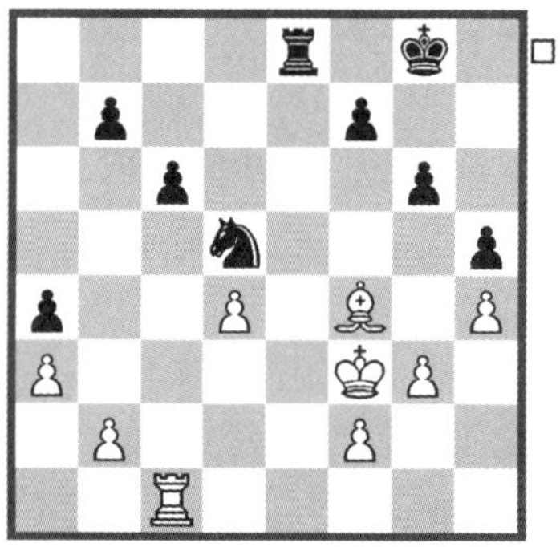

Position after: 29... ♘d5

Everything is clear. Black dominates with his knight and on the light squares. The presence of rooks does not help White.

30. ♗d2 f6!

Taking control over some of the dark squares and activating the king.

31. ♖c4 ♖a8 32. ♔e4 ♔f7 33. ♔d3 ♔e6 34. f3 ♖a6 35. ♗c1 ♔f5 36. ♔e2

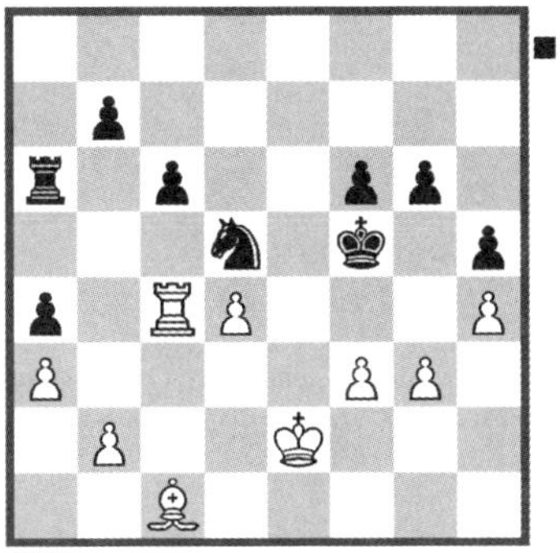

Position after: 36. ♔e2

36... g5!

Remember – an advanced pawn on the edge is always a target for attack.

37. ♔f2

37. hxg5 fxg5 Black wins by creating an outside passer after ...h4 or after weakening the light squares with ... g4.

37... g4

A matter of style.

38. fxg4+ ♔xg4 39. ♖c2 ♖b6!

The rook invades via b3 – poetry.

40. ♖e2 ♖b3 41. ♖e4+

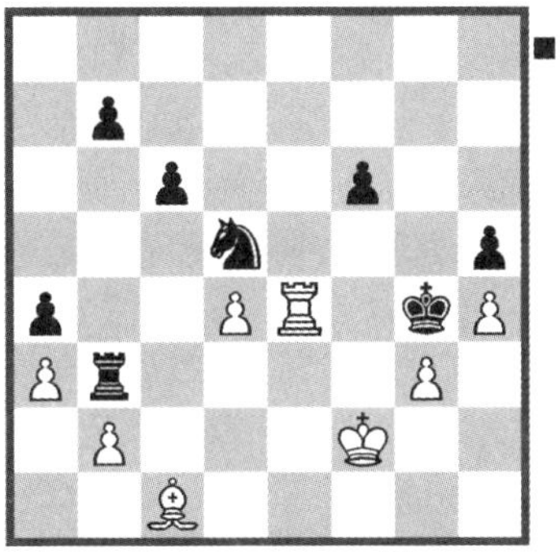

Position after: 41. ♖e4+

41... ♔h3

The quickest win.

42. g4

An act of desperation.

42... hxg4 43. h5 f5 44. ♖e1 ♔h2 45. h6 ♖f3+ 46. ♔e2 ♖h3 47. ♔f1 f4 48. ♖e2+ ♔g3 49. ♖g2+ ♔f3

0-1

Game 135

♙ Regedzinski, Teodor
♟ Rubinstein, Akiba
Lodz 1917

Black dominates on the blockading d5-square and has a winning position. White's pieces are in disorder and Black has a nice tactic to invade using many of the weakened squares.

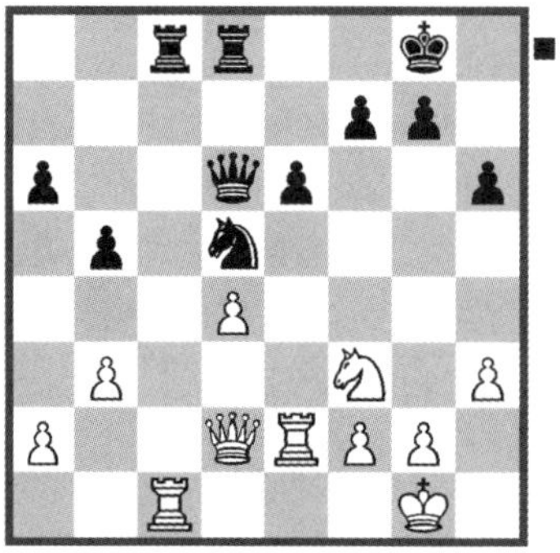

26... ♕f4!

Forcing an exchange and eventually penetrating.

27. ♖c2 ♕xd2 28. ♖exd2 ♖xc2 29. ♖xc2 ♘b4

Due to the attack on a2 White must leave the file.

30. ♖b2 ♖c8 31. ♔f1 ♖c1+ 32. ♔e2 ♖a1

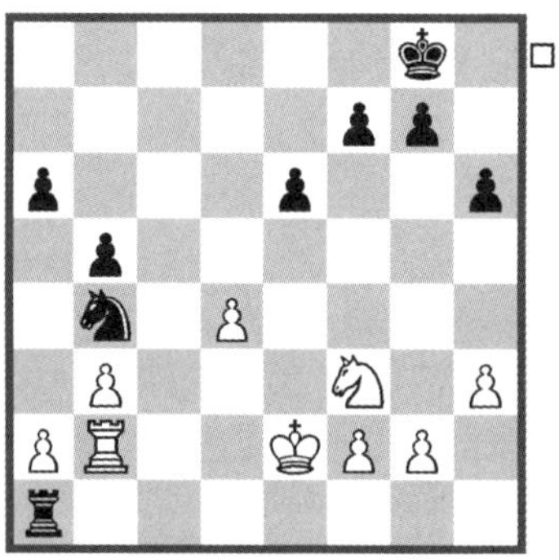

Position after: 32... ♖a1

33. ♔d2 ♖xa2

With Black's material gain, White is about to resign.

34. ♖xa2 ♘xa2 35. ♘e5 ♘b4 36. ♘d7 f6 37. g3 ♔f7

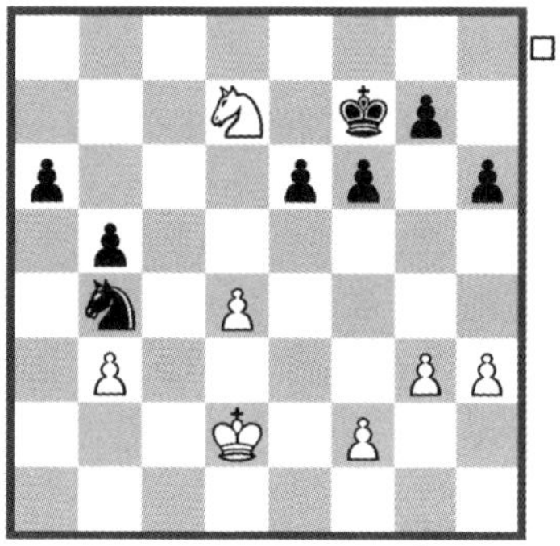

Position after: 37... ♔f7

38. ♘b6

38. ♘c5 This does not change anything after the following: 38... ♔e7 39. ♔c3 ♘d5+ with 40... ♘c7.

38... ♔e7 39. ♔c3 a5

0-1

Game 136

♙	Ivanchuk, Vassily	(2750)
♟	Aronian, Levon	(2744)
🌍	Morelia/Linares 2007	

This endgame is very interesting. White cannot exchange rooks in some favorable way. Taking on c5, of course, would be ridiculous in view of ...bxc5. Moreover, the rooks are needed to set up serious threats against the d5-pawn, because it is unclear whether White would be able to create a second weakness in a minor piece endgame. What is there to do? Ivanchuk's creativity helps him solve the problem in a fascinating way.

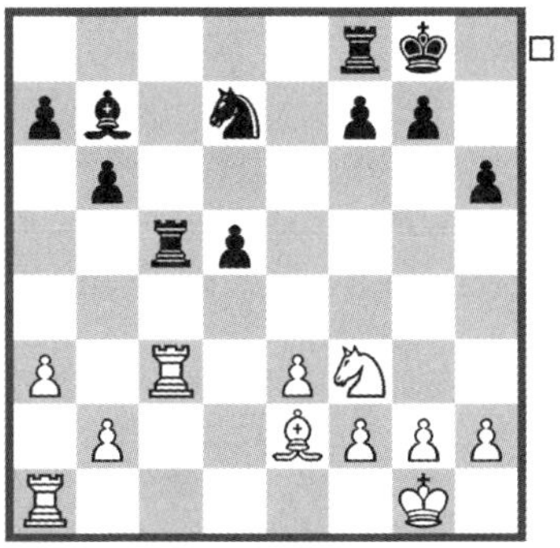

17. ♖cc1!?

White is ready to go for a frontal attack on the d5 weakness. White is not distracted by the temporary loss of the c-file and allowing Black to invade the 2nd rank. White has correctly evaluated that Black cannot gain any advantage from the c-file.

17... ♖fc8?!

17... ♖xc1+ 18. ♖xc1 ♖c8 This would have been safer for Black.

18. ♖d1! ♖c2 19. ♗b5! ♘f8

A logical retreat. The knight aims for the e6-spot.

20. ♖ab1

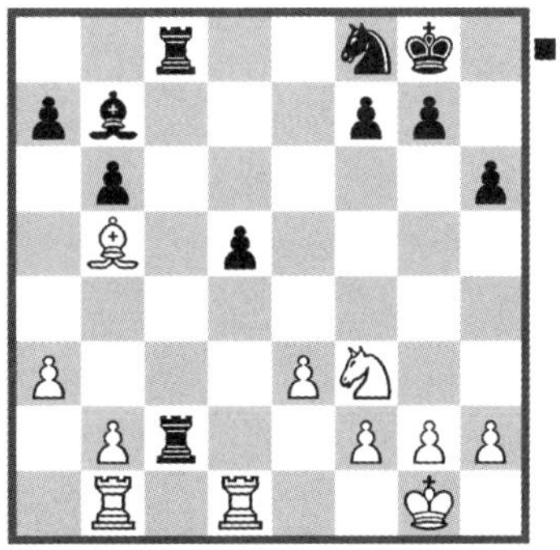

Position after: 20. ♖ab1

20... ♖2c7

20... ♘e6 21. ♗a4 ♖2c7 This switches to the game.

21. ♗a4 ♘e6 22. ♗b3 ♔f8 23. h3?!

The "don't rush" principle, but there are some better waiting moves .

A) 23. ♔f1?! Not this because of the following. 23... ♗a6+ 24. ♔e1 ♗c4 Black has excellent play.

B) 23. h4!? Perhaps this should have deserved more serious attention.

23... ♖c5 24. ♔h2 ♔e7 25. ♖d2

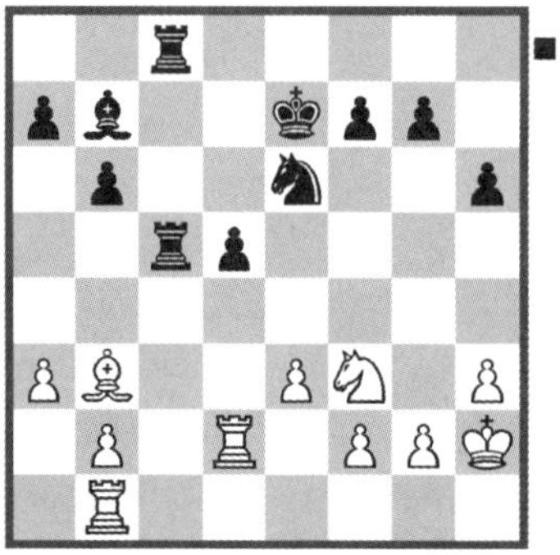

Position after: 25. ♖d2

25... ♖b5?!

There is no real benefit for Black with this move.

25... ♘g5!? An interesting move. 26. ♘xg5 hxg5 27. ♖bd1 ♔e6

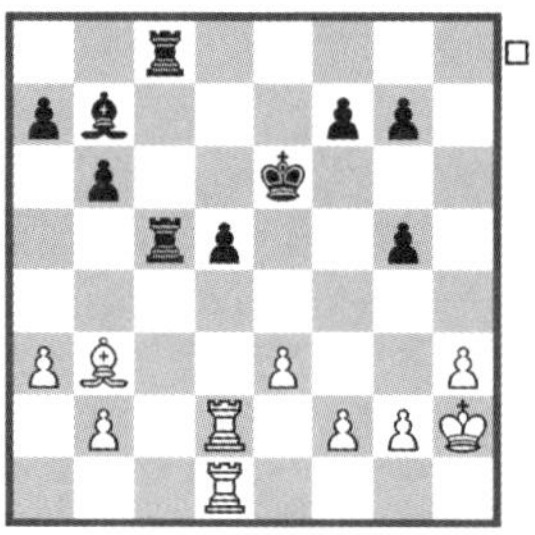

Position after: 27... ♔e6

This does not look so bad for Black. 28. e4 ♖c1 Black has some active chances.

26. ♗a2 ♖bc5 27. ♘e1!?

Controlling the c2-square, but also reorganizing the pieces, in order to block and attack the d5-pawn.

A) 27. ♖bd1

B) 27. ♔g3 A solid and natural patient move.

27... a5

27... ♖c1! Black doesn't have anything apparent from the c-file and should have traded rooks instead. With his centralized king he would have been fine in a minor piece endgame, with even the advance ...d4 on the agenda.

28. ♖bd1 ♖d8 29. ♔g3 ♖b5 30. f3

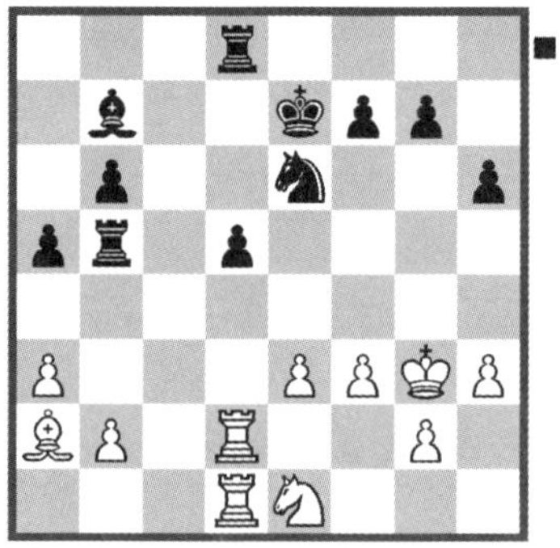

Position after: 30. f3

30... ♖c8?

A careless move. Black probably simply missed White's powerful possibility.

30... ♖c5 Instead this should have been played where White has nothing apparent.

31. ♘d3!

Surprisingly, the rook is trapped. Black is unable to avoid material loss.

31... d4

A) 31... a4 32. ♘b4 ♘c7

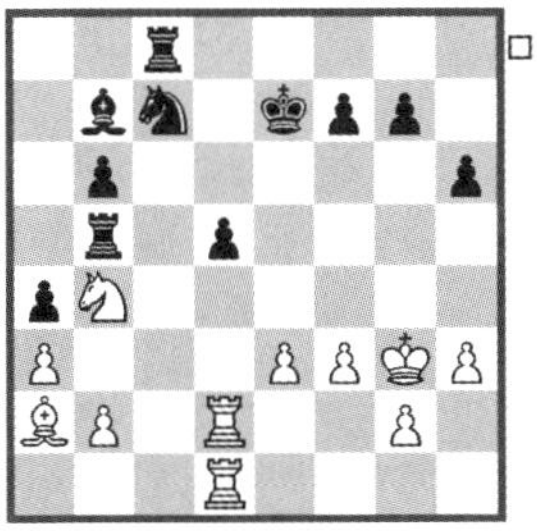

Position after: 32... ♘c7

33. e4! White wins.

B) 31... ♘c5 32. ♘f4 ♘a4 33. ♗xd5 ♗xd5

Position after: 33... ♗xd5

34. ♘xd5+ This is almost winning for White.

32. ♗xe6

32. e4 This is clearly another good move, perhaps an even better one.

32... ♔xe6 33. ♘f4+ ♔e7

(see diagram next column)

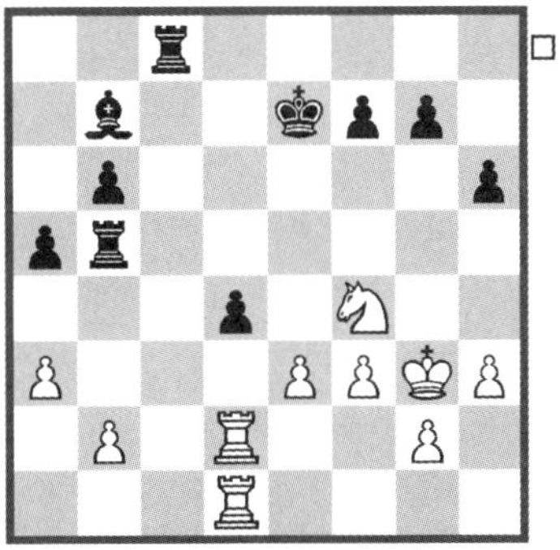

Position after: 33... ♔e7

34. ♖xd4 ♖c7 35. ♖1d2

After the storm has passed the situation has stabilized. White enjoys both a material and positional advantage. Black's bishop can do nothing although the position is "opened".

35... ♖bc5 36. e4

Of course, White restricts the bishop and launches his majority.

36... ♖c4 37. ♖d6! ♖4c6 38. e5!

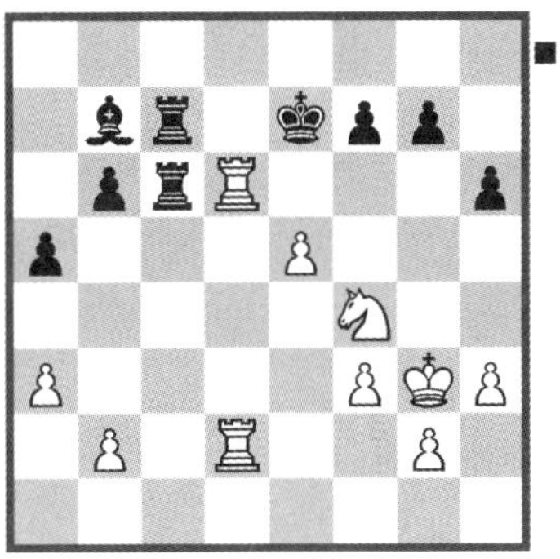

Position after: 38. e5!

38... ♖c2?

Perhaps demoralized, Black plays without a plan.

39. ♖xc2 ♖xc2 40. ♖xb6 ♗c6 41. b4 g5 42. ♘h5 axb4 43. axb4 ♗d5 44. ♘g7!

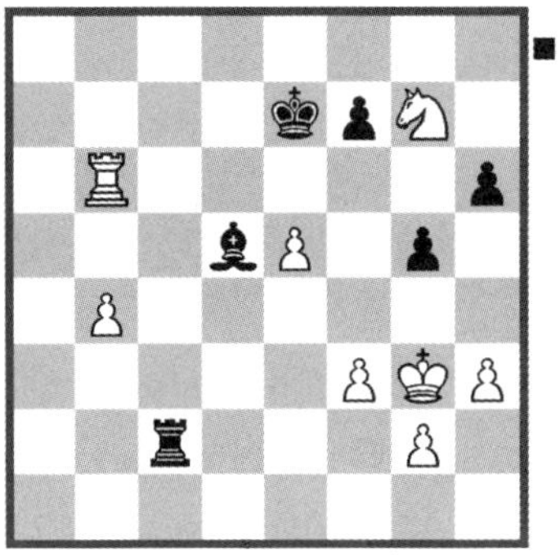

Position after: 44. ♘g7!

44... ♖e2 45. ♘f5+ ♔e8 46. ♘xh6 ♗e6 47. ♖b5 ♖b2 48. ♖b8+ ♔d7 49. ♖g8

1-0

Game 137

♙ Vaganian, Rafael A
♟ Bronstein, David Ionovich
Yerevan 1975

Here we see a more complicated endgame with the same evaluation – White is clearly better and holds a lasting advantage. Not only is there an isolated pawn, but the dominant knight over the bishops makes the evaluation clear.

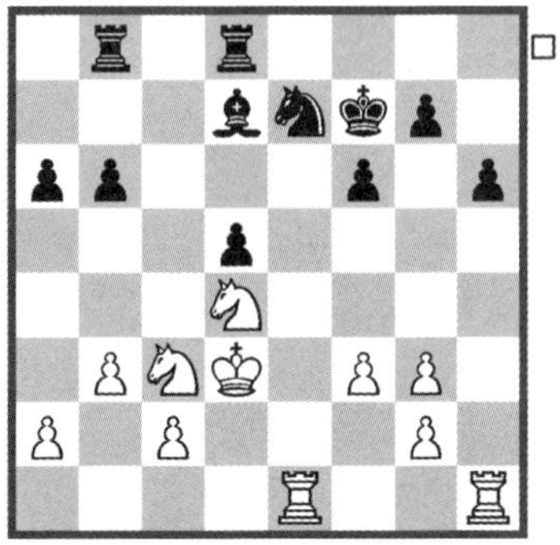

25. ♖h5!?

This move simply looks dangerous optically. White tries to cause some disorder in Black's camp. However, even with time-wasting, White cannot spoil anything.

25... ♗e8

25... ♘c6!? An attempt to exchange “a passive piece for an active one”, but this cannot be satisfactory for Black – he would simply again stay with “a bad piece against a good one".

26. ♔d2

A solid waiting prophylactic move.

26... ♖bc8 27. ♖e6

White tries to confuse Black, but Bronstein calmly eliminates any threats.

27... ♘c6 28. ♘ce2 ♗d7

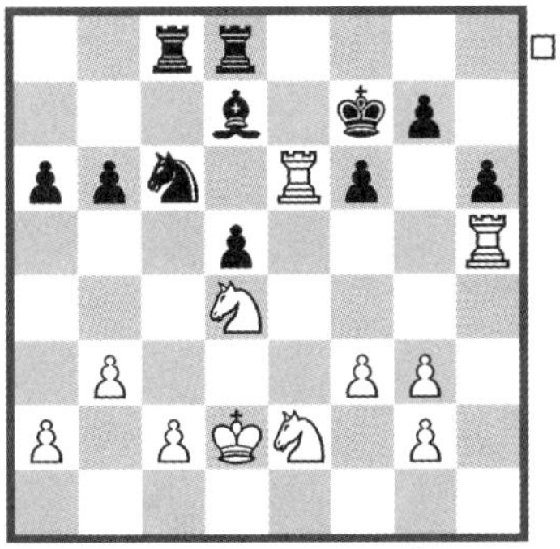

Position after: 28... ♗d7

29. ♖e3

29. ♘xc6 ♗xe6 30. ♘xd8+ ♖xd8 31. ♘d4 This is simpler. This was also the reason why White preferred to play with more pieces.

29... ♘e5 30. ♖h1 ♖c7 31. ♘f4 ♗c8

White has achieved some benefits. He has regrouped in a good way and is putting some pressure on the wide complex of central squares, including pressure on the d5 weakness. It is time to look for new resources, targets and possibilities.

32. g4!

Restricting the black minor pieces.

32... ♖e7 33. ♖he1 g6?!

Black is afraid of ghosts – White's ♘f5 would not be that dangerous for Black. There was no particular reason for this weakening move.

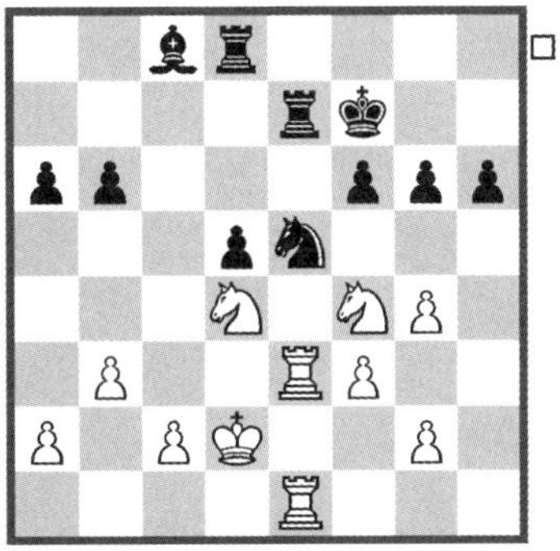

Position after: 33... g6?!

33... ♖ee8 Instead this would have been a good waiting move.

34. a4!

White now advances on the queenside and organizes an attack with the a-pawn. The idea is to crush Black's structure and create new weaknesses.

34... ♗b7

34... a5!? This weakens the b5-square.

35. a5!

35. ♘fe6?! ♖xe6 36. ♘xe6 ♔xe6 37. f4 d4

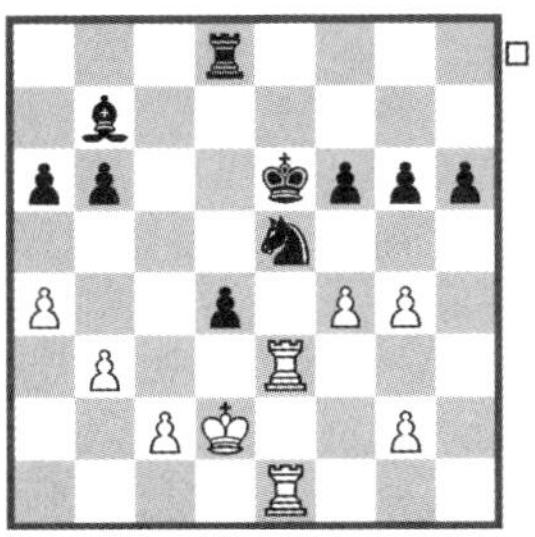

Position after: 37... d4

38. ♖3e2 [38. ♖h3 ♗xg2 39. ♖xh6 ♖g8] 38... d3 39. ♖e3 dxc2+ 40. ♔xc2 ♗xg2 This is unclear. Why go for complications if everything is going smoothly?

35... bxa5?!

Now White's task is much simpler.

35... b5!? This allows the following. 36. ♘fe6 [36. ♘d3 This is also good, of course, controlling the b4- and c5-squares.] 36... ♖xe6 37. ♘xe6 ♔xe6 38. f4 d4 39. ♖h3 ♗xg2 40. ♖xh6 ♖g8 41. fxe5 fxe5 42. c3 The difference with the variation with 35. ♘fe6?! is the vulnerability of the a6-pawn.

36. ♖a1 ♖c8 37. ♖xa5 ♖ec7

Comparing this to the previous diagram White has achieved much. Black's position is hopeless – he cannot hold all the weak points.

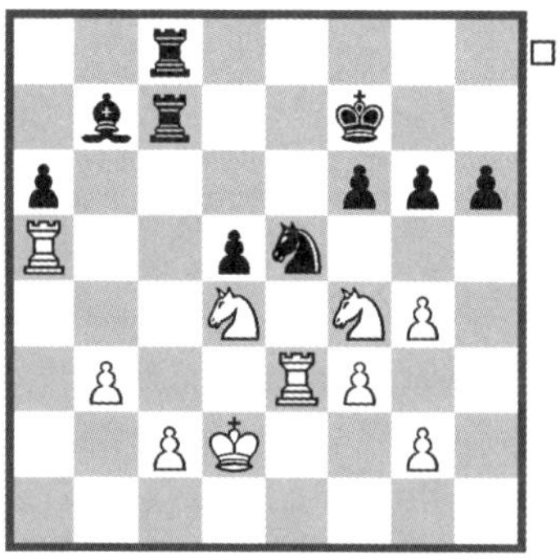

Position after: 37... ♖ec7

38. ♘fe6! ♖e7 39. ♘c5 ♖ce8 40. ♖c3

Black's rooks do nothing on the e-file.

40... ♗c8 41. ♘xa6

Finally there is a material advantage.

41... h5

Trying to find active play.

42. ♘c7

White parries simply.

42... ♖g8 43. ♖a8 hxg4 44. f4 ♘f3+ 45. gxf3 g3

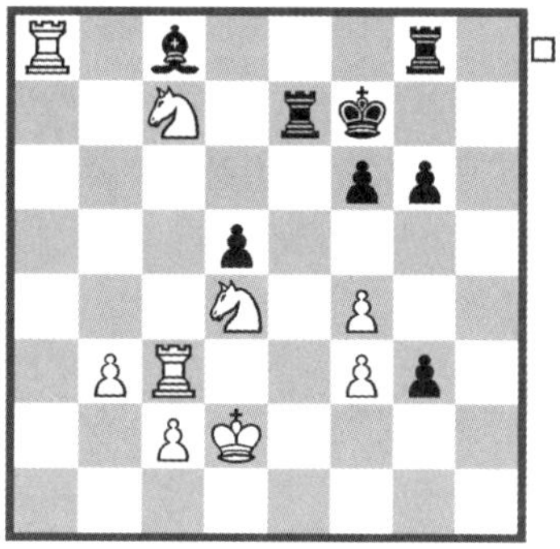

Position after: 45... g3

A desperate try.

46. ♖a1 ♖h8 47. ♖g1 ♖h2+ 48. ♔d3

The bishop cannot deliver check.

48... ♖f2 49. ♖xg3 ♖f1 50. ♔d2 ♖ee1 51. ♖e3

1-0

10

Two Weaknesses & Playing on Both Sides

From the great Aron Nimzowitsch we know that it would be good for us if the opponent has more than one weakness. This should eventually make our conversion easier, albeit not automatically.

We can capitalize from two weaknesses in the opponent's camp only if we have **"better communication lines"**. The prerequisite for this is to have more space and/or better activity. Then we would be able to "stretch" our opponent's defense and at some point in time they would simply be unable to deal completely with our simultaneous attack on both their weaknesses.

This chapter will enlighten and present clearly these ideas in action!

Game 138

♙ Zlatanovic, Boroljub (2373)
♟ Tadic, Stefan (2267)
Bajina Basta 2019

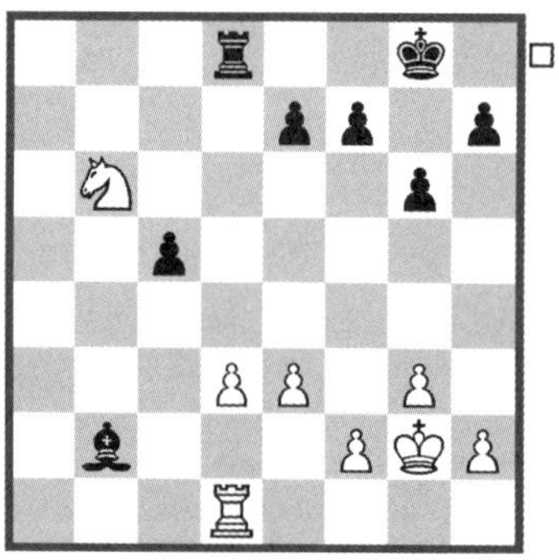

White appears better in the position on this diagram. Black's c5-pawn is weak and White may soon collect it. First, the king comes to the e2-square to protect the d3-square.

24. ♔f3 ♗c3 25. ♔e2 e6 26. ♖c1 ♗b4 27. g4!

I really think that this move is the best practical option – the c-pawn can be collected later. It is important to prevent Black's ...h5. There is also the positional threat of advancing g5 and then continue to play with minor pieces on the board. That would be a very dangerous set-up for Black – the holes on f6 and h6 can be used to infiltrate with the knight and the f7-pawn may become a serious weakness after installing the knight on the e5-square. Don't forget, the bishop is in a very passive position. At that moment I was sure that I could keep the c5-pawn alive and continue to play with the dominant knight over the bad bishop.

27. ♘a4 Of course this leads to collecting the c5 weakness after 27... ♖c8 28. ♖c4 followed by d4. However, I was not sure if the endgame would be winning – the distant passed pawn on the d-file would not be distant enough from the kingside pawns. Furthermore, I felt that I would fail to convert. If White transfers the endgame to a position with R+4:R+3 (pawns on e, f, g and h versus f, g and h) Black would be able to play ...h5, creating a set-up known to be the most promising in this type of endgame.

27... ♖d6 28. ♘c4 ♖a6 29. g5 ♖a2+ 30. ♔f3 ♔g7

Position after: 30... ♔g7

31. ♘e5!

The knight is extremely dangerous here. White already plans to attack the f7-pawn with the rook, obtaining the 7th rank somehow or going for ♖g1-g4-f4.

But not 31. ♘d6 ♖d2!.

31... ♖a3 32. ♔e4 f5+

Black's reaction is natural – the growing activity of White's pieces has forced him to play actively.

33. gxf6+ ♔xf6

The fixing is gone, but now Black has a broken pawn structure.

34. ♖c4

White has the idea after ♘g4 to transfer the rook to f4 with infiltration.

34... ♖b3

Position after: 34... ♖b3

35. h4!?

To prevent ...♔g5; the idea is to kick the black king back after checking on g4 and transferring the rook to the 7th rank. Another idea behind this move will become clear soon.

35... ♗a3 36. ♖c2

Preventing an exchange of rooks.

36... ♖b7 37. ♖a2 ♗b4 38. ♖a8

White's rook infiltrates.

38... ♗c3

However the bishop comes back into play.

39. ♘c4 ♖c7 40. ♘d6?!

Position after: 40. ♘d6?!

A tricky move made in zeitnot. Of course, such moves should not be played normally.

40... ♖d7 41. ♘c4 ♔e7

Black intends to play ...♗f6. Was it a mistake for White to launch his h-pawn? No!

42. ♖c8 ♗f6 43. h5! gxh5 44. ♖xc5

The situation has stabilized. White's advantages are tremendous; there is a clear plan of creating two connected passed pawns in the center. Nevertheless, accuracy is still needed.

44... h4 45. ♖h5 ♔f8

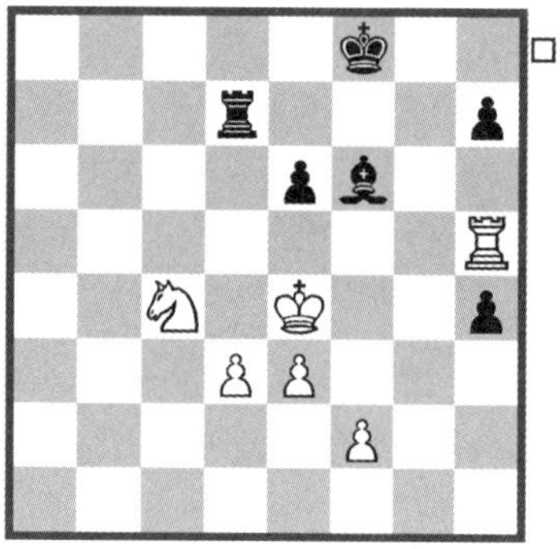

Position after: 45... ♔f8

Suddenly, Black has a tactical shot: ...♖d5.

46. ♖b5

White again simply keeps the rook. It goes on to attack the h-pawn from the front.

46... ♖d5 47. ♖b1 ♔f7 48. ♖g1

Preventing ...♔g6 and eventually ...♔h5. It appears the king should be safe on the h5-square. Safe and active!

48... ♖h5 49. f4 ♔e7 50. d4

Preparing the e5-outpost for the knight, if necessary. In any case, the bishop is restricted now.

50... ♖b5 51. ♘d2 ♖h5

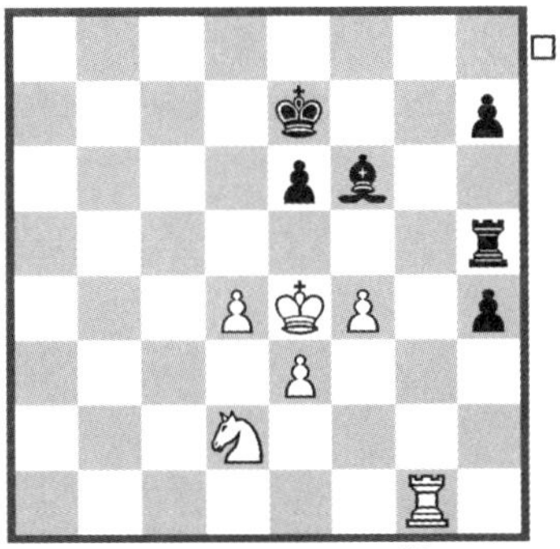

Position after: 51... ♖h5

52. ♖h1

52. ♘f3 ♔f7 It is not clear how White can improve with the knight on the f3-square.

52... ♔f7 53. ♔f3

With the idea of ♔g4, then ♘f3.

53... ♖a5! 54. ♖g1

If there is no immediate action White again prevents ...♔g6 – the "don't rush" principle in action.

54... ♖a3 55. ♔e4 ♖a5 56. ♘f3 ♖h5 57. ♘h2

(see diagram next column)

White can place the knight, of course, on the e5-square immediately, but he decides not to hurry.

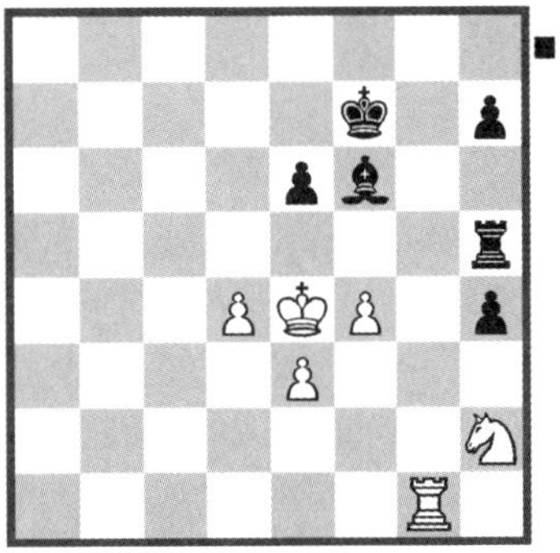

Position after: 57. ♘h2

57... ♗g7 58. ♘g4 ♔e7 59. ♔f3 ♗h8 60. ♖b1

The rook becomes active.

60... ♗g7 61. ♖h1

... But it goes back to the kingside.

61... ♗h8 62. ♖h3 ♔d6 63. ♖h2 ♗g7

Position after: 63... ♗g7

64. ♘e5

After a long preparation the knight finally comes to the e5-square.

64... ♔d5

64... ♗xe5 65. dxe5+

Position after: 65. dxe5+

65... ♔d5 [65... ♔e7 66. ♔g4 White wins.] 66. ♖d2+!

65. ♖d2!

Threatening e4!

65... ♗xe5 66. dxe5+ ♔c4 67. ♔g4 ♖h6

Position after: 67... ♖h6

68. ♔h3

68. ♔g5 This also wins. However, White followed another path in time trouble.

68... ♖g6 69. ♔xh4 ♔c3 70. ♖d6 ♔c4 71. f5

1-0

Game 139

♙	Smyslov, Vassily V	(2565)
♟	Karlsson, Lars	(2500)
🌍	Las Palmas 1982	

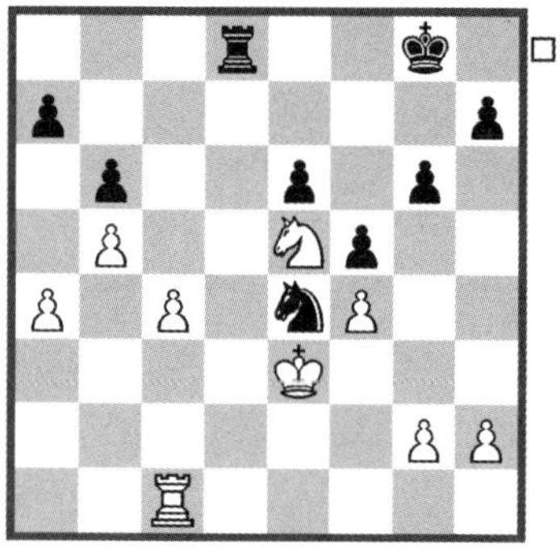

One may say that the mutual presence of backward pawns here makes the position balanced and equal. However this is an illusion – Black is completely lost. White's knight is a much more important piece. The key point is that White can play against two weaknesses – one is clearly the a7-pawn; the other will be created on the kingside as we shall soon see.

37. a5! ♘c5

37... bxa5 38. ♖a1 This is trivially lost for Black.

38. a6!

An instructive moment. If White takes on b6 then the only queenside target would be the b6-pawn. Now there are two targets, both the a7- and b6- pawns (due to the possible knight sacrifice)! White does not need the a-file at all.

38... ♔g7 39. ♖c2

Preparing a possible exchange of rooks.

39... ♘e4

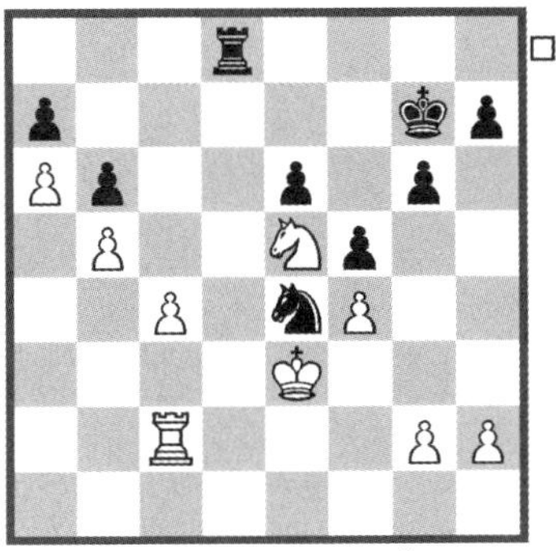

Position after: 39... ♘e4

40. g4!

Whatever White's plan is, it should be deferred. If you can improve the position before action, do so! White uses the fact that the black knight needs some pawn support to advance the pawn to g5. That would lead to fixing with a new weakness in Black's camp, at the same time restricting the black king.

40... ♔f6 41. g5+ ♔g7 42. ♘c6 ♖d7 43. ♖g2!

I like such prophylactic moves. White plans to advance the h-pawn and this move prevents ...h5.

43... ♔f8

43... h5 This helps White to an advantage because of the following. 44. gxh6+ ♔xh6 45. ♖xg6+

44. h4 ♔e8

Black can only wait.

45. ♖h2 ♔f8 46. h5

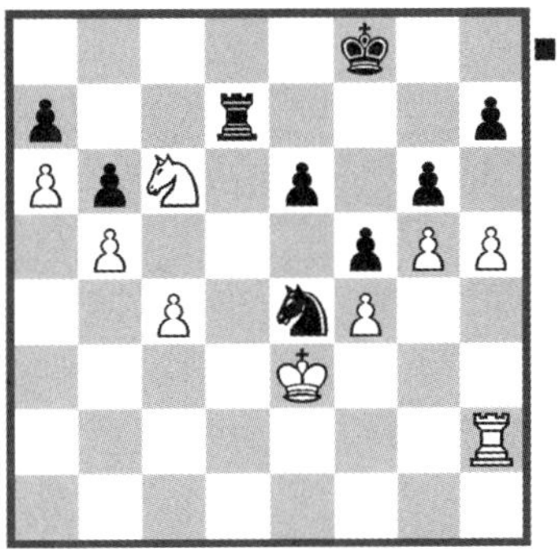

Position after: 46. h5

46... gxh5

46... ♔g7 47. hxg6 hxg6 48. ♖h6 White takes the g6-pawn.

47. ♖xh5 ♔g8 48. ♖h1 ♔g7 49. ♘e5 ♖d8 50. ♖h6

(see diagram next page)

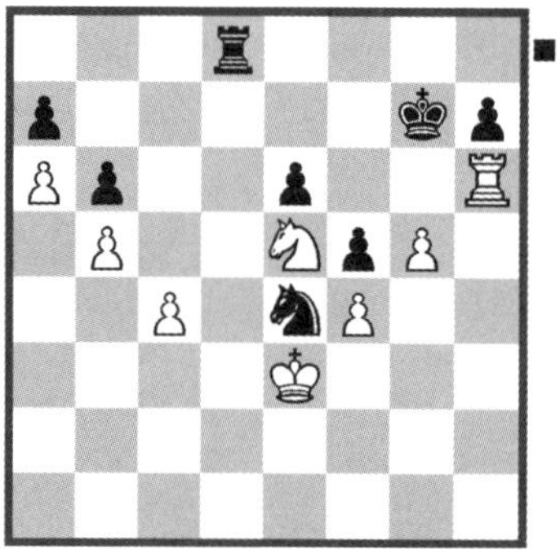

Position after: 50. ♖h6

50... ♖d6

50... ♖e8 This loses after 51. ♘c6.

51. ♔e2

"Don't rush!" – White does not play 51. ♘c6 instead because of 51... ♘d2.

51... ♘c3+ 52. ♔e1 ♖d1+

Desperation.

53. ♔f2 ♖d4 54. ♔f3 ♖d6 55. ♖f6

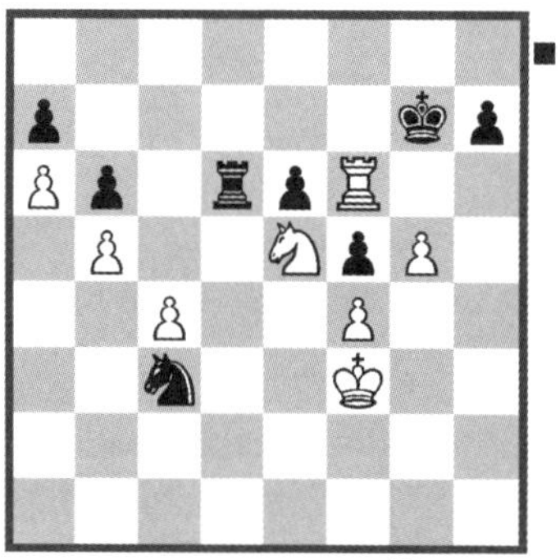

Position after: 55. ♖f6

Even this!

55... ♔g8 56. ♖f7 ♖d3+ 57. ♘xd3

Black resigned because the a7-pawn is lost.

1-0

Game 140

♙ Kotov, Alexander
♟ Pachman, Ludek
Venice 1950

White is dominant, but it is difficult to convert. Black has only one weakness, the one on c6. The knight is controlled by the bishop. Clearly, the white pieces need help from the king and pawns.

43. g4!

Take note of White's pawn set-up on the kingside – other advances are not so flexible and this is by far the best one! White wants to fix the potential weakness on h7!

43... ♔e6?!

It will become clear that this waiting strategy is a bad decision.

43... ♔g5!? This should have been played instead. 44. h3 f5!?

Position after: 44... f5!?

This secures the h7-pawn. 45. gxf5 ♔xf5 However this looks a bit strange because White has the chance to organize f3-e4.

44. ♔g2 ♖b7 45. ♖e8+ ♖e7 46. ♖h8 f6 47. h4

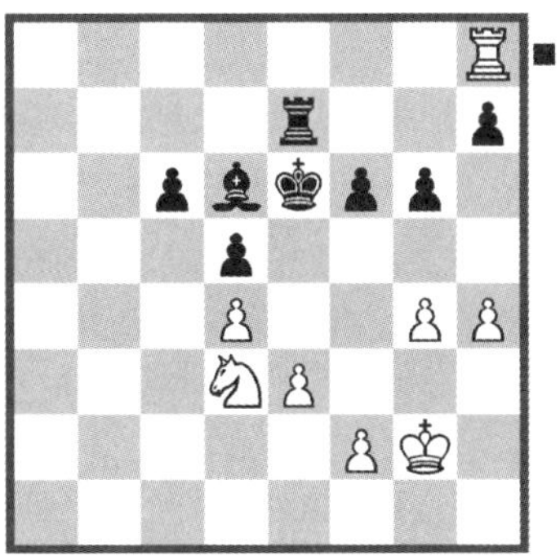

Position after: 47. h4

47... ♖b7 48. ♔f3 ♖f7 49. ♖e8+ ♖e7 50. ♖d8 ♖a7

After some waiting moves White activates the knight.

51. ♘c5+!? ♔e7 52. ♖c8 ♗xc5

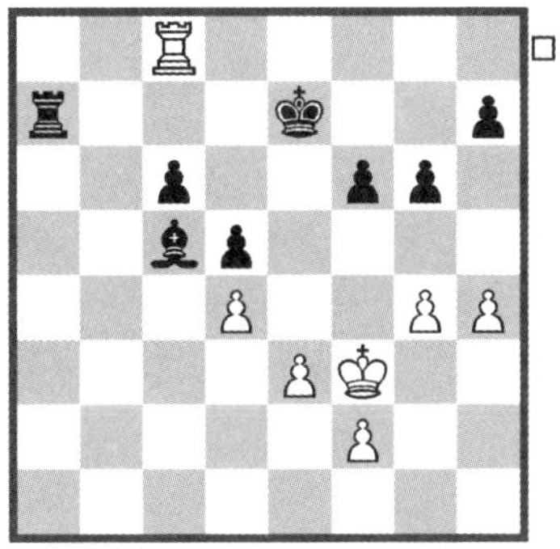

Position after: 52... ♗xc5

53. dxc5 ♔d7 54. ♖h8 ♔e6 55. ♖d8

White's much more active rook gives him some winning chances.

55... ♔e7?

A) 55... ♖d7? This loses to 56. ♖c8.

B) 55... ♖a4! Instead this would have been a good move. 56. ♖d6+ ♔e5

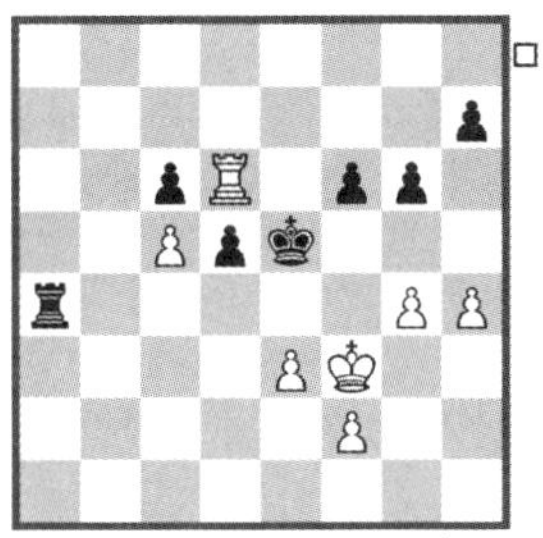

Position after: 56... ♔e5

57. ♖d7 [57. ♖xc6 d4! This leads to a relatively easy draw.] 57... f5! 58. g5

[58. gxf5 ♖xh4=] 58... d4! [But not 58... ♖xh4?? 59. ♖e7#.] 59. exd4+

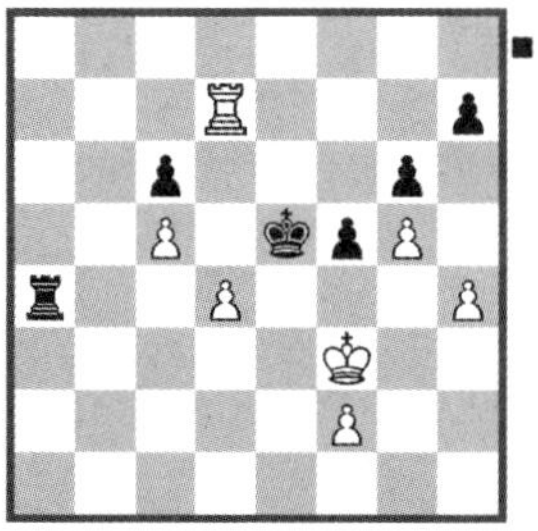

Position after: 59. exd4+

59... ♖xd4 60. ♖xh7 ♖f4+ Black has a holdable position.

56. ♖d6 ♖a6

Black is passive and White with his next move opens a path for the king.

57. g5!

Position after: 57. g5!

57... fxg5 58. hxg5 ♔f7 59. ♔g3 ♔e7 60. f3 ♖a3 61. ♔f4 ♖a4+ 62. ♔e5 ♖a3 63. ♖xc6 ♖xe3+ 64. ♔xd5

Position after: 64. ♔xd5

Black's position is about to collapse.

64... ♖d3+

64... ♖xf3 65. ♖c7+ ♔d8 66. ♖xh7 This is easily winning for White.

65. ♔e4 ♖c3 66. f4 ♖c1 67. ♖c7+ ♔d8 68. ♖xh7 ♖xc5 69. ♖f7

1-0

Game 141

♙ Shirov, Alexei (2500)
♟ Kinsman, Andrew PH (2340)
Paris 1990

The evaluation is clear – White is dominant due of course to the situation on the kingside. However Black's defense here is stable. In order to make progress White must create a weakness on the opposite side.

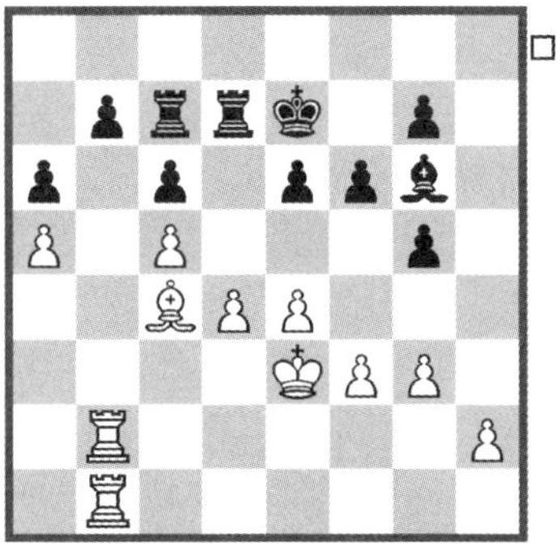

30. h4!

White is not afraid of isolating the h-pawn. He will gain the g-file for future actions.

30. f4! This move, with the same idea, would have been good as well.

30... gxh4 31. gxh4 ♗f7 32. e5 f5

32... fxe5 This does not help Black. After 33. dxe5 he has nothing from the d-file. Now even trading rooks would be good for White – he is practically a pawn up.

33. ♖g2 g6 34. ♖bg1 ♖c8

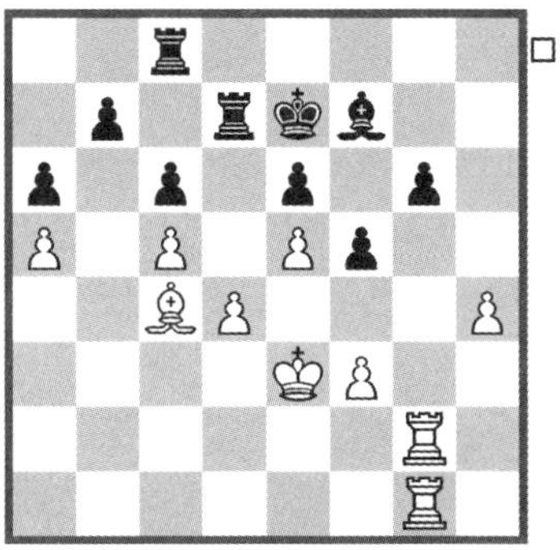

Position after: 34... ♖c8

35. ♖xg6!

Direct play and the quickest win.

35... f4+

A nice trick.

35... ♗xg6 36. ♖xg6 This leads to the loss of the kingside pawns and a quick defeat.

36. ♔d3!

36. ♔e4?? ♖cd8!

36... ♖cd8

Now this does not work.

37. ♖f6 ♖xd4+ 38. ♔c3 ♖d1 39. ♖g7

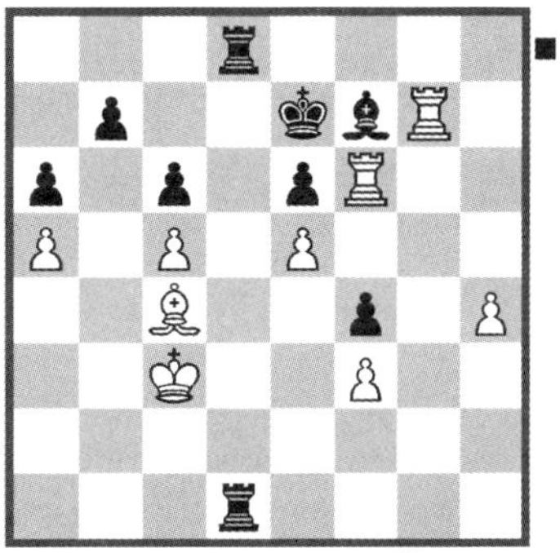

Position after: 39. ♖g7

The bishop is lost.

39... ♖c1+ 40. ♔b3 ♖b1+ 41. ♔c2

1-0

Game 142

♙ Lilienthal, Andor
♟ Bondarevsky, Igor Tsakharovich
🌍 Moscow 1940

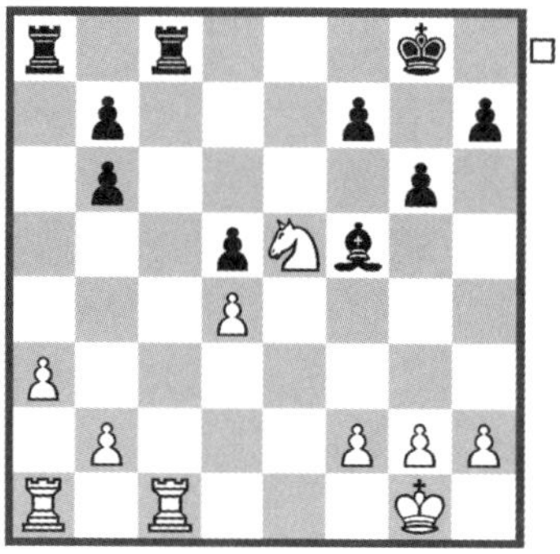

Here is a tense game from the last round of the Soviet Championship. Bondarevsky was a point ahead and Lilienthal needed win in the last round to finish in first place. Instead of sharp play he preferred a positional approach. Here White has a small but stable advantage due to his better knight. Black has weaknesses only on the queenside and it appears that White cannot attack them at all. However the small advantage becomes a substantial one, because here only White can play for a win! Black can only sit and wait.

White starts with kingside play, perhaps somewhat unexpectedly, but nevertheless it is very logical. The point is to gain space, restrict the bishop and eventually create some weaknesses there!

23. g4! ♗e6 24. h3?!

24. f3! Opening a path for the king is more precise. 24... h5? Now this fails easily to the following. 25. gxh5 gxh5 26. ♘d3 White dominates after ♘f4.

24... f6?!

Too classical, but not imaginative, although still okay.

24... h5!? This also deserves attention, aiming to reduce the pawn material.

25. ♘d3 g5

25... h5? Now this does not work in view of the following. 26. ♖e1 ♔f7 27. ♘f4

26. f3

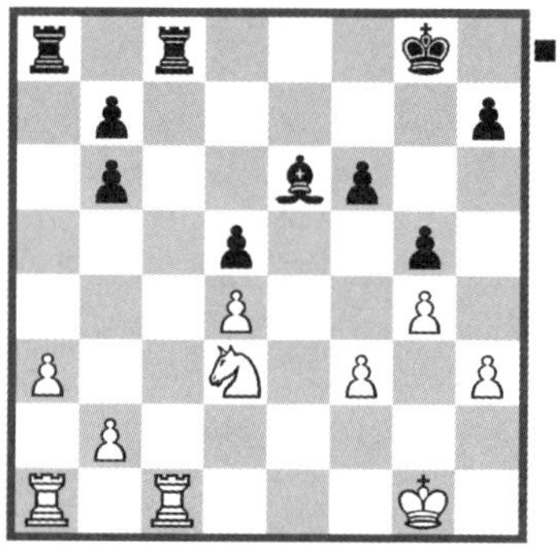

Position after: 26. f3

Black sets up a barrier on the kingside, but the bishop is restricted and White has many options to improve.

26... ♔f7 27. ♔f2 ♔e7 28. ♔e3 ♔d6 29. ♖xc8!

White eliminates a couple of rooks to

reduce Black's counterplay on the king-side.

29... ♖xc8 30. h4 h6

Necessary.

31. hxg5

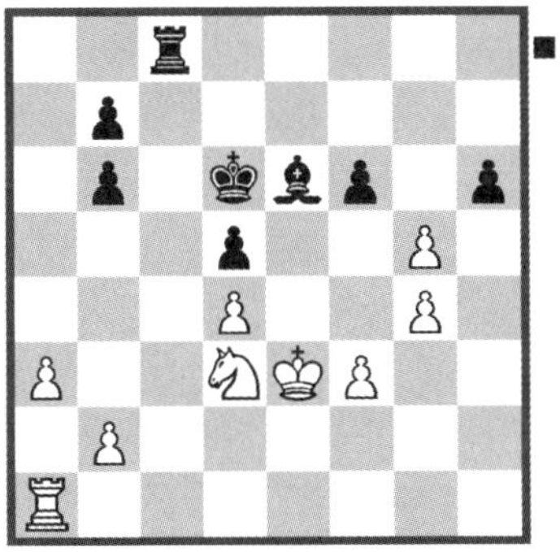

Position after: 31. hxg5

31... hxg5

31... fxg5 32. ♖h1 ♖h8 33. ♘e5 This is simply lost for Black.

32. ♖h1 ♖e8 33. ♔d2 ♗d7 34. ♖h6 ♖f8

White has achieved much, but Black's defense is still strong. White must r elocate his knight. In such situations it is useful to imagine that if you had a spare knight which you could put anywhere, where would this knight belong? Definitely in this case, on the e3-square, in order to attack the d5-pawn and to threaten a jump to f5!

35. ♘e1 ♔e7 36. ♘c2 ♖f7 37. ♘e3 ♗e6

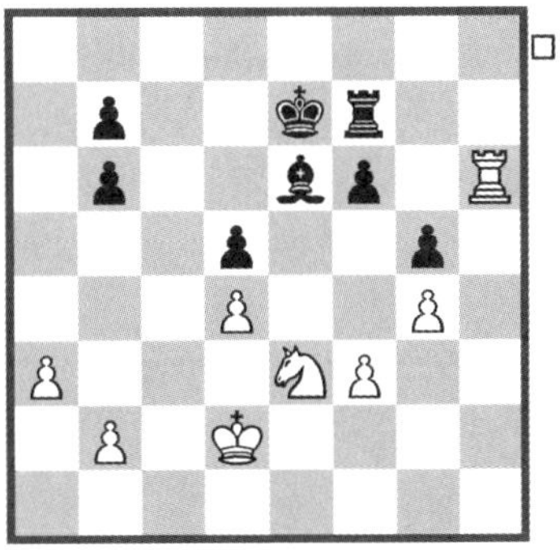

Position after: 37... ♗e6

Mission accomplished. It is time for the king now. Let's try on the queenside.

38. ♔c3 ♔d6 39. ♔b4 ♗d7

Black's defense is stretched – the bishop must control both the b5- and f5-squares. Thus White plays as follows.

40. ♘f5+

40. ♘f1 This leads to the same result.

40... ♔c7

40... ♗xf5 41. gxf5 ♔c6 42. a4 ♖f8 43. b3 ♖f7 44. ♖h8 Black is lost.

41. a4

Improvement after improvement!

41... ♗e6 42. ♘g3!

Position after: 42. ♘g3!

42... ♗d7 43. ♘h5 f5

And for a moment it looked as if Black might find some counterplay. However White makes a decisive impact.

44. ♘f6!

Putting additional pressure and closing the f-file. The game is over.

44... fxg4 45. ♘xd5+ ♔b8 46. fxg4 ♗xg4 47. ♘xb6

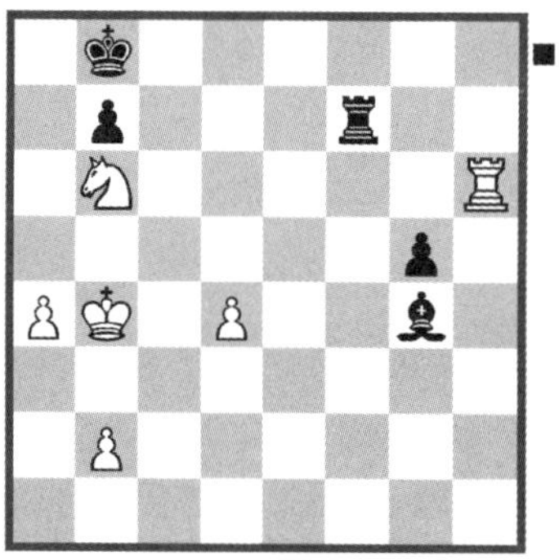

Position after: 47. ♘xb6

No, Black cannot hold this despite reducing the pawn material.

47... ♖f2 48. b3 ♗d1

A final desperate attempt.

49. d5 ♔c7

49... ♖f3 50. d6 ♖xb3+ 51. ♔a5 A picturesque position.

50. a5 ♖d2 51. ♖h7+ ♔b8 52. d6 ♖d4+ 53. ♔c5 ♖h4 54. d7 ♔c7 55. d8=♕+

Black resigned. A fantastic performance which helped Lilienthal to become the Soviet Champion ahead of Botvinnik, Smyslov, Keres and Kotov.

1-0

Game 143

♙	Hodgson, Julian M	(2550)
♟	Situru, Nathanael	(2385)
🌍	Jakarta 1996	

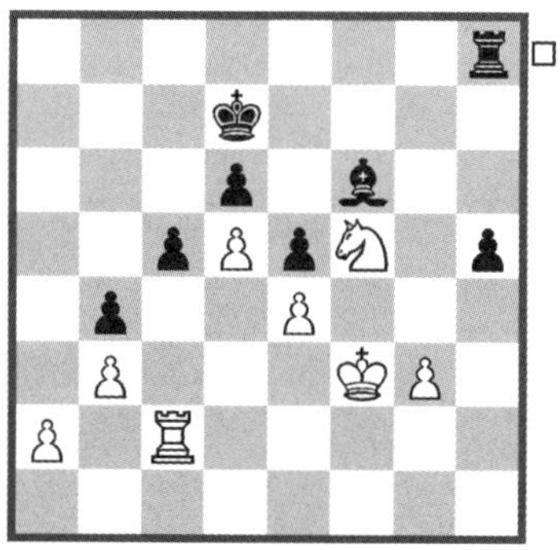

The knight is obviously superb in this position, while the bishop is clearly very bad. With his next move White sets up a very unpleasant pin on the h-file.

45. ♖h2 ♔c7

45... ♖a8 This is impossible. 46. ♖xh5 After this simple move, the d6-pawn falls. 46... ♖xa2 47. ♖h7+ White has an easy win.

46. ♔e2!?

A typical plan, but it's not accurately executed here. White cannot successfully play g4. So, exploiting Black's paralysis on the kingside White decides to attack on the queenside. The idea is to open the position there with a3.

46. ♔e3! This is preferable. 46... c4 47. bxc4 ♔b6 48. ♘xd6 ♔c5

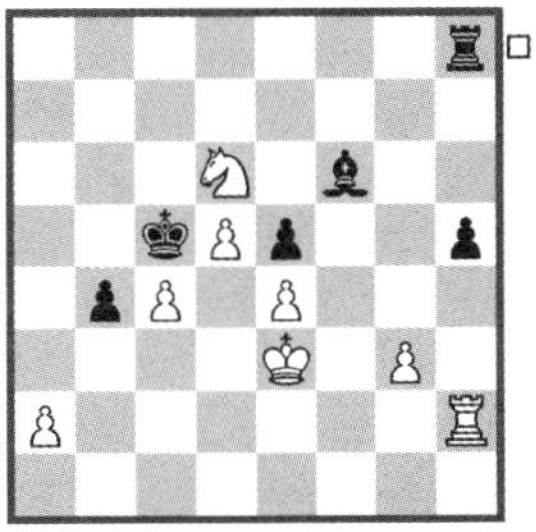

Position after: 48... ♔c5

49. ♘f5 ♔xc4 This fails to 50. ♖c2+ with an easy win.

46... ♔d7?

Black misses the chance.

46... c4! Instead this would have given Black some surprising relief. 47. bxc4 ♖a8 48. ♖xh5 ♖xa2+ 49. ♔d3 ♔b6! Black has enough compensation. Even in trivial positions you must be vigilant of any possible counterplay from your opponent!

47. ♔d3 ♔c7

Black must wait. There is nothing active that he can do.

48. ♔c2 ♔d7 49. ♔b2 ♗d8 50. a3

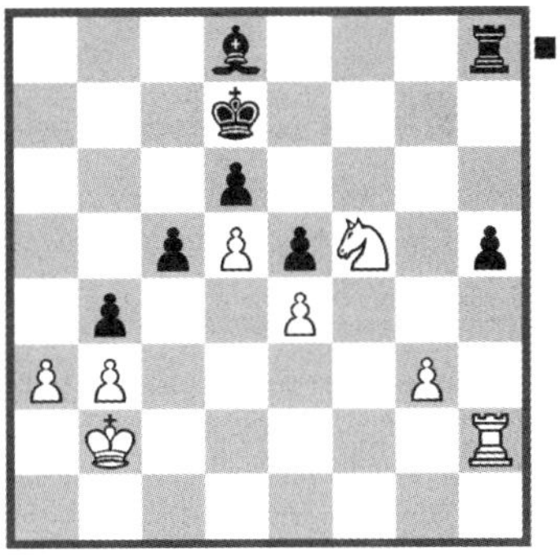

Position after: 50. a3

50... bxa3+ 51. ♔xa3 ♗a5

After implementing his plan of opening the a-file, the king comes to a better position.

52. ♔b2 ♗d8 53. ♖h1

White wants to transfer the rook to the a-file.

53. ♔c3 Simpler, with the same idea.

53... ♗f6 54. ♔c3

White puts the king onto its best square before he infiltrates.

54... ♗d8 55. ♔c4 ♗f6

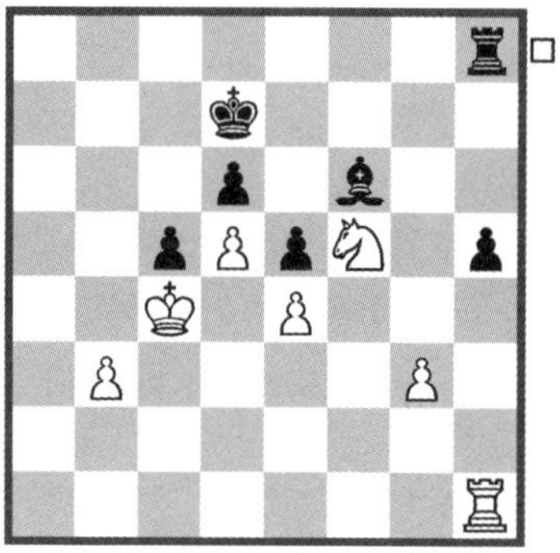

Position after: 55... ♗f6

56. ♖a1!

It is time for action!

56... ♗d8 57. ♖a7+ ♗c7 58. ♘g7!

This move ends the game!

58... ♔c8

58... ♖c8 59. ♘e6 This would have led to a nice zugzwang position.

59. ♘e6 ♗b8

59... ♗d8 60. ♖a8+ ♔d7 61. ♖xd8+ ♖xd8 62. ♘xd8 ♔xd8 63. ♔b5 63... ♔c7 64. ♔a6 This wins easily.

60. ♖g7 h4 61. gxh4 ♖xh4 62. ♔b5

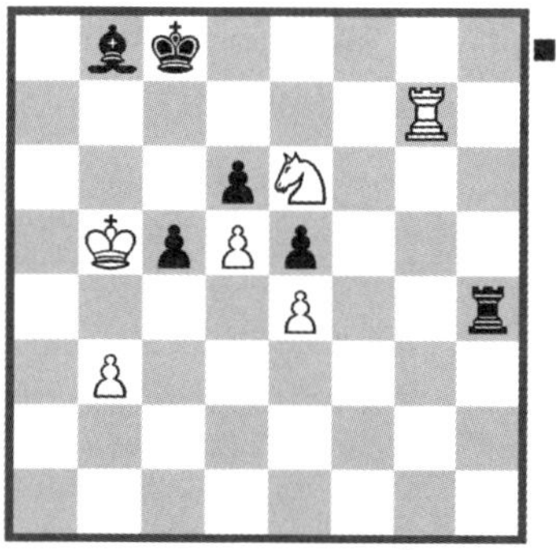

Position after: 62. ♔b5

Now you can see the importance of activating the king before infiltrating via the a-file!

62... ♖h8 63. ♔c6

Picturesque! Black resigned.

1-0

Game 144

♙	Ehlvest, Jaan	(2625)
♟	Hulse, Brian	(2355)
	New York 1993	

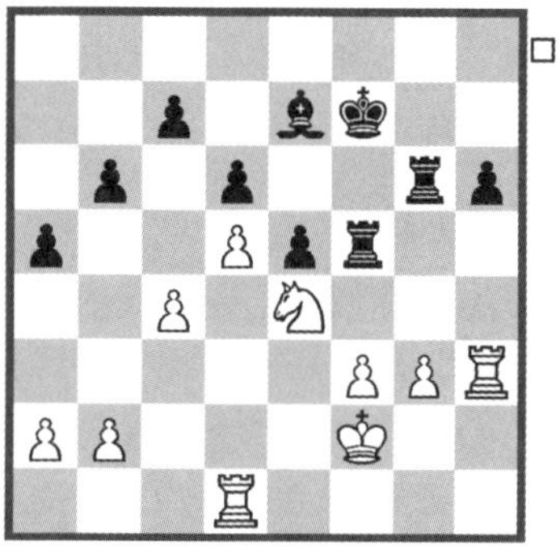

White clearly dominates due to his better knight. Furthermore, the white rooks are more dangerous especially after the next played move – they collaborate better with the knight. Black's pieces are stuck on the kingside, taking care of the weak pawn. This gives White a strong reason to open up another front.

38. a3!

The right moment. Black cannot set the rook on a8!

38... ♔e8 39. b4 axb4

A sad necessity.

40. axb4 ♔d7 41. ♖a1

White gets the a-file.

41... ♗f8 42. ♖ah1

However he finds nothing there and comes back to the kingside. There is no need to rush. The opening of the queenside will be exploited later.

42. ♖a8 Logical, but it's not the best here.

42... ♗g7

(see diagram next column)

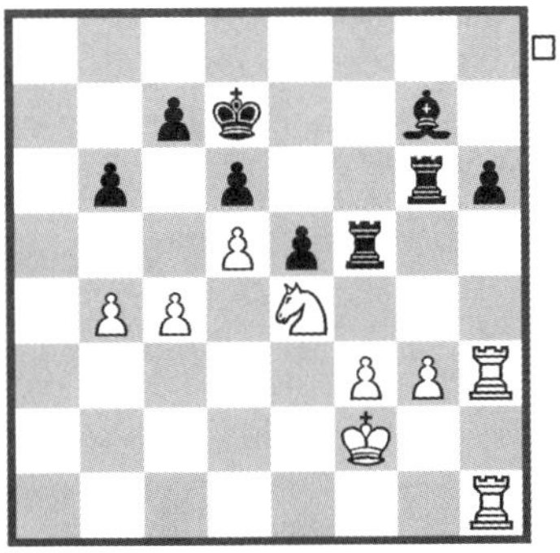

Position after: 42... ♗g7

43. ♖h5!?

White exchanges one pair of rooks in order to activate the king.

43... ♖xh5

43... ♖f7 White can still go for the plan implemented in the game.

44. ♖xh5 ♗f8 45. ♖f5 ♔e7 46. g4

Fixing!

46... ♗g7

Position after: 46... ♗g7

47. ♔e3

White activates the king.

47... ♗f6 48. ♖h5 ♔f7 49. ♖h1 ♔e7 50. ♔d3 ♗g7 51. ♘g3 ♗f8 52. ♔e4 ♖f6 53. ♘f5+ ♔e8

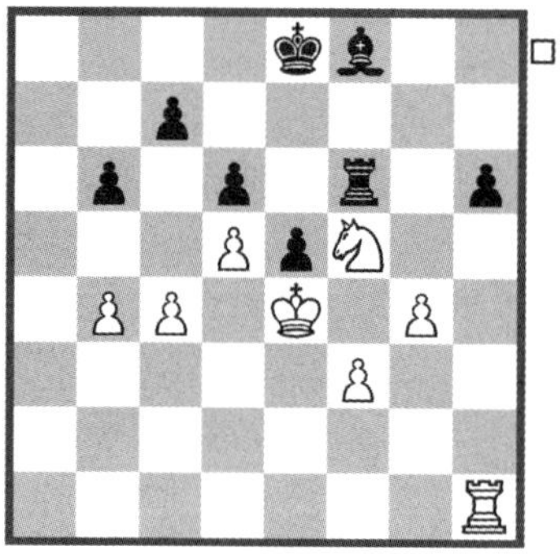

Position after: 53... ♔e8

54. ♖a1

Finally, White capitalizes from the opened file. The game is over.

54... ♔d7 55. ♖a8 ♖f7 56. b5!

A funny zugzwang!

56... ♖f6 57. ♔e3

The king goes to h5 and g6.

57... ♖f7 58. ♔f2 h5

A desperate attempt.

59. ♔e3 hxg4 60. fxg4 ♗e7

Position after: 60... ♗e7

61. ♖g8!

White prepares to advance.

61... ♗d8 62. ♔e4 ♖h7 63. ♖g7+

63. g5 This would have led to another win, of course.

63... ♖xg7 64. ♘xg7

1-0

Game 145

♙ Larsen, Bent
♟ Fischer, Robert James
Monte Carlo 1967

Black is better here due to his cavalry occupying the important central spots. Generally, Black should try to play on the queenside – the cavalry is simply more effective there. However first, he should play the following good move.

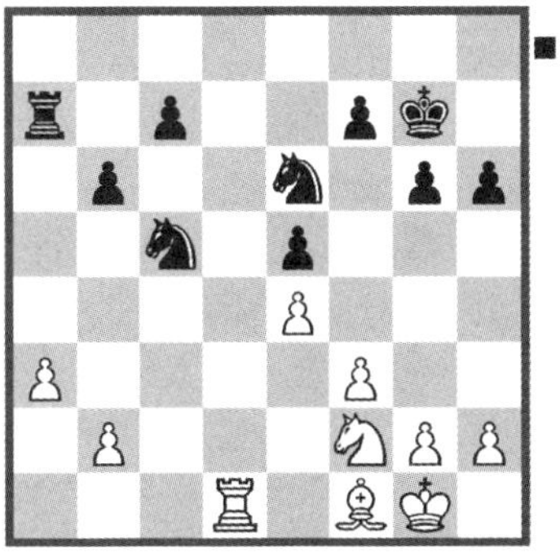

28... h5!

Black must first prevent ♘g4, which would cause the weakening ...f6; Black can transfer the knight to e3 and then c4 or d5.

29. ♖d5

A) 29. ♗c4 This looks solid but 29... ♘d4 dominates.

B) 29. ♘d3!? An interesting idea to obtain some relief from the black cavalry. However Black keeps a clear advantage after the following. 29... ♘xd3 30. ♗xd3 ♘d4

29... ♔f6

A classy response. Black does not create weaknesses.

30. h4

Not having any obvious moves White fixes the black pawns on the bishop's color.

30... ♔e7? 31. ♗c4

31. ♖xe5?? This loses after 31... c6 and the rook is trapped.

31... c6 32. ♖d2 ♘d4

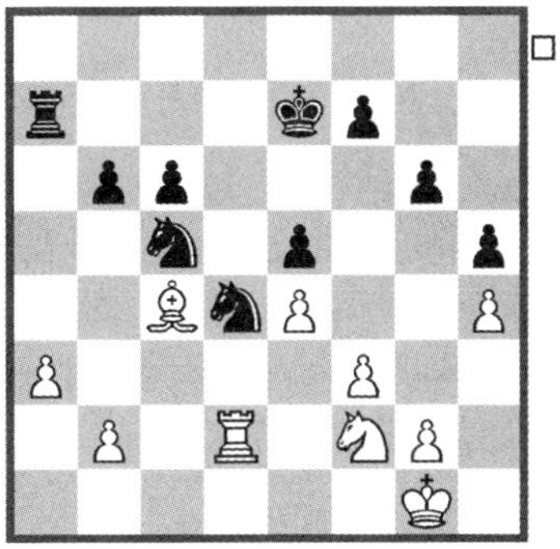

Position after: 32... ♘d4

Black has improved his position a lot and is ready to play on both wings because of his domination in the center.

33. ♔f1 f5?!

Too direct an approach. Black has more chances on the queenside. Thus, he should start by playing there first.

33... b5 34. ♗a2 b4!? 35. axb4 ♘xe4 An interesting possibility.

34. b4?

A logical mistake. White simply creates new weaknesses.

34. exf5!? A logical and brave move. White opens the position for the bishop

and reduces the pawn material. Furthermore there would be chances to create an outside passer. 34... ♘xf5 35. ♔g1 ♘xh4 36. ♖e2 ♔f6 37. ♖d2 A nice perpetual appears.

37... ♖d7

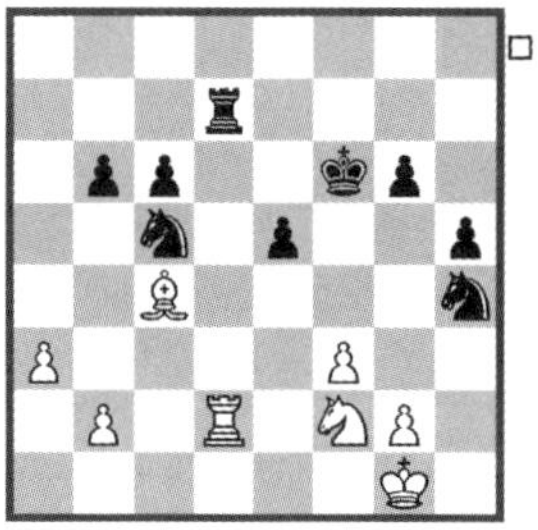

Position after: 37... ♖d7

38. ♖xd7! ♘xd7 39. a4 The threat is b4 and a5. 39... c5 40. ♘e4+ ♔e7 41. ♗d3 White transfers the knight to c4 and has full compensation for the pawn.

34... b5! 35. ♗g8

35. bxc5? bxc4 White is completely lost.

35... fxe4

Again concrete play.

36. fxe4

36. bxc5? This simply loses after the following. 36... e3 37. ♖d3 exf2 38. ♔xf2 ♖a8! 39. ♗a2 b4

36... ♘d7 37. ♖d3

(see diagram next column)

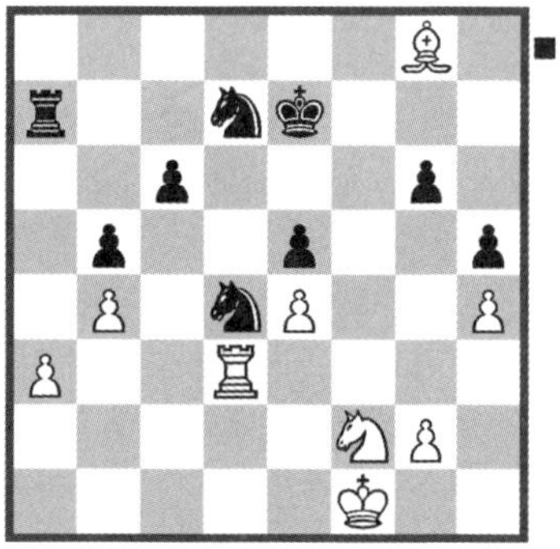

Position after: 37. ♖d3

37... ♖a6!

Played to defend the g6-pawn. It is also a practical waiting move. The point will become evident soon.

38. ♖c3 c5!

Again concrete play. This is the point of the previous move. The rook is moved from d3 and the strength of the strike is enhanced.

39. g4 c4

Black has created a passed pawn with a winning position.

40. gxh5 gxh5 41. ♗d5 ♘f6

White's bishop is centralized but in danger.

42. ♖g3 ♘xd5

The simplest.

43. exd5 ♖f6

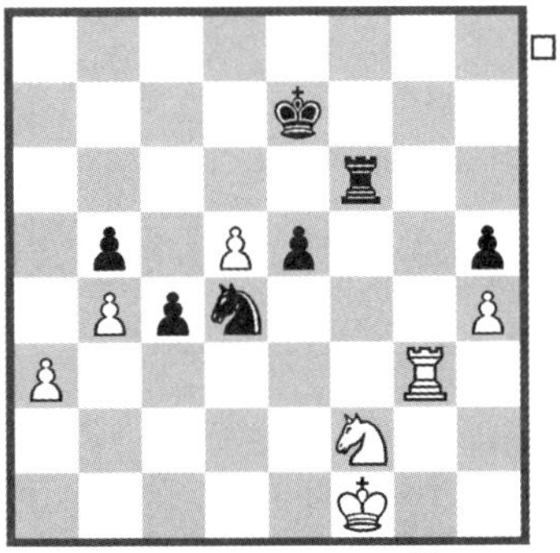

Position after: 43... ♖f6

Black has a brutal centralization against such weak pawns and passive pieces. The game is over.

44. ♔g2 ♘f5 45. ♖h3 ♖g6+ 46. ♔f3 ♘d4+ 47. ♔e3 ♖g2! 48. ♖h1 ♔d6 49. ♘e4+ ♔xd5 50. ♘c3+ ♔e6 51. ♖c1 ♖h2 52. a4 ♖h3+ 53. ♔f2 ♘b3 54. ♔g2 ♘xc1 55. ♔xh3 bxa4 56. ♘xa4 ♘e2 57. b5 c3 58. b6 c2 59. ♘c5+ ♔d5 60. ♘b3 ♔c6 61. ♔g2 ♔xb6

0-1

Game 146

♙	Mueller, Alexander	(2235)
♟	Delchev, Aleksander	(2548)
🌍	Bayern 2014	

Black's domination is clear. His king is closer to the center, his knight is well placed, and his bishop is better. A very important fact is that White's structure is damaged – the a4-pawn is exposed and about to fall. Exploiting this with his next move, Black takes control over the file.

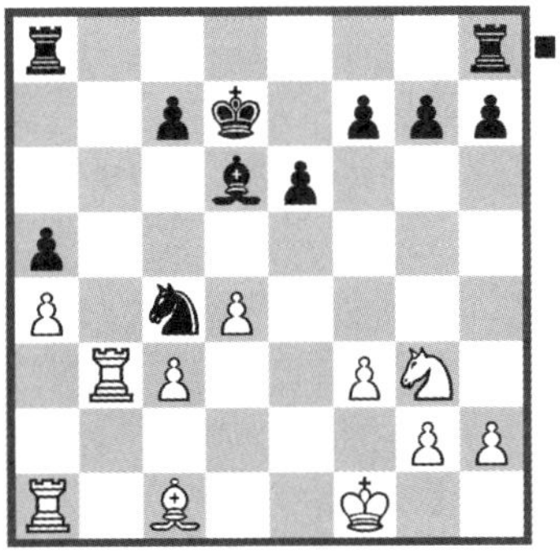

25... ♖hb8! 26. ♖xb8

26. ♖ab1 This simply loses to the following. 26... ♖xb3 27. ♖xb3 ♘b6 The a-pawn falls.

26... ♖xb8

Control over the file is added to the long list of advantages. White is strategically lost.

27. ♔e2 ♗xg3!

White's knight is the only piece that can fight for the weakened light-squared complex.

28. hxg3 ♔c6 29. ♔d3 ♔d5 30. ♖a2

Black has almost everything that he can wish for in this position. He wants to capitalize on the other side – attacking only on the queenside would not give him anything.

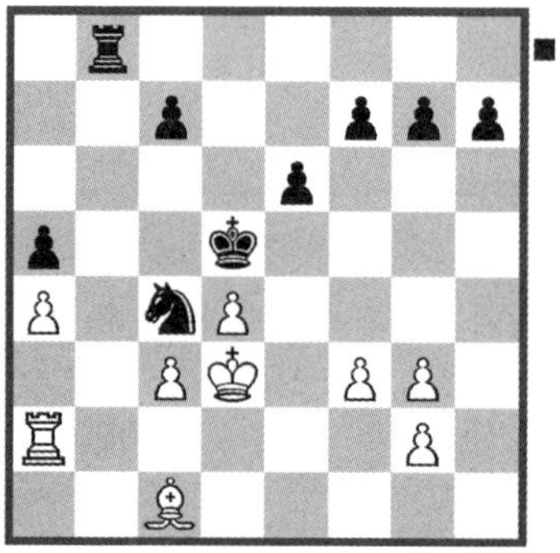

Position after: 30. ♖a2

30... h5!

It is always good to prevent any advance of doubled pawns! With this approach you would paralyze the entire group!

30... ♖b1 31. ♔c2 The rook must go back.

31. ♗f4 ♖b7 32. ♗c1 f6

There is no need to rush anywhere.

33. ♔c2 c6 34. ♗a3 g5 35. ♗c1

Position after: 35. ♗c1

With all his pieces on their best spots it is time to strike.

35... g4! 36. ♗f4

36. fxg4 hxg4 This would simply give Black the h-file and e-passer.

36... c5

36... e5 This is also an option, but the played move is more logical. White's passer is immobilized, whereas Black's one on the e-file will end the game.

37. dxc5 ♔xc5 38. ♗h6 ♔d5 39. ♔d3

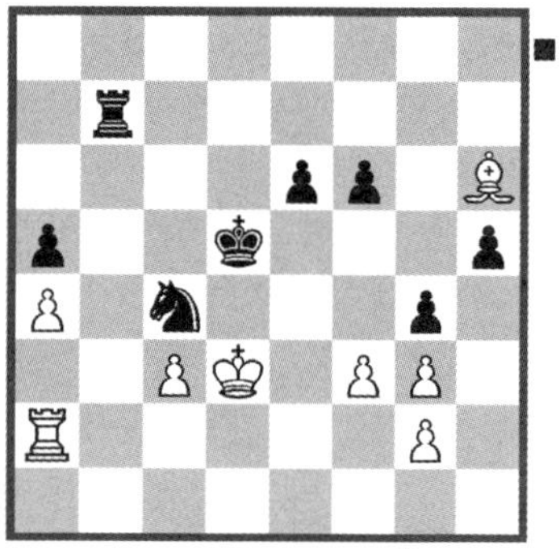

Position after: 39. ♔d3

Now Black can win easily

39... ♖b2 40. ♖xb2 ♘xb2+

0-1

Game 147

♙ Rosselli del Turco, Stefano
♟ Rubinstein, Akiba
🌍 Baden-Baden 1925

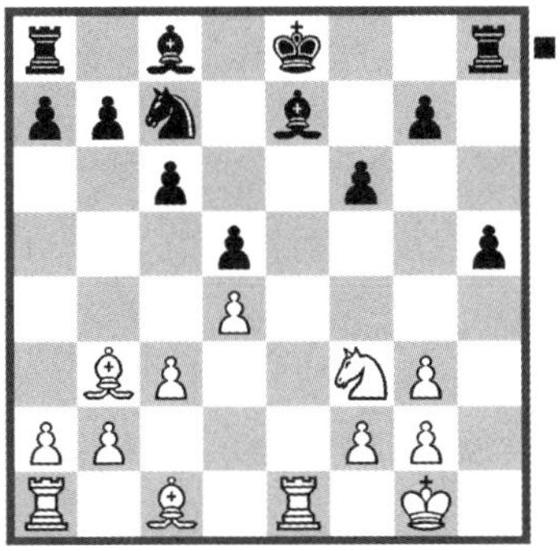

Let's conclude this chapter with an example by probably the best ever endgame instructor, the “Great Akiba”. White lacks harmony here and Black goes for initiative by gaining space on the kingside, at the same time eliminating any hidden threats.

15... g5!?

Concrete play. Black prevents ♗f4 and perhaps ♘h4.

15... ♗f5? 16. ♘h4! The idea is 17. ♗f4 and White wins.

16. ♗d2?

A big mistake.

16. ♗c2 This was normal instead.

16... ♗f5!

White’s ♗c2 is forbidden now.

17. ♖e3 ♔d7 18. ♖c1?!

White strangely misses the opportunity to double the rook. This gives Rubinstein the signal for action!

18... ♗d6 19. ♗c2 ♗xc2 20. ♖xc2

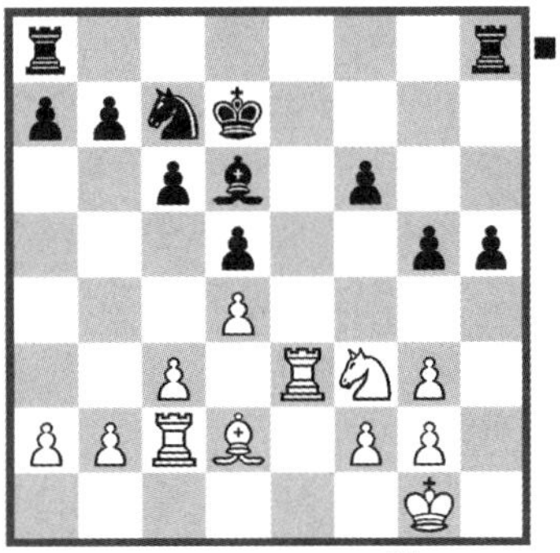

Position after: 20. ♖xc2

Black is dominant. White has lost a lot of time to trade bishops. As a result, Black has all his pieces better placed and has the initiative with good prospects on both wings.

20... ♖ae8!

Of course – White's rooks are not connected!

21. ♗c1 ♖xe3 22. ♗xe3 ♘e8

Black relocates the knight – the "principle of the worst piece" in action.

23. ♖e2 ♘g7 24. ♗d2 ♘f5 25. ♖e1

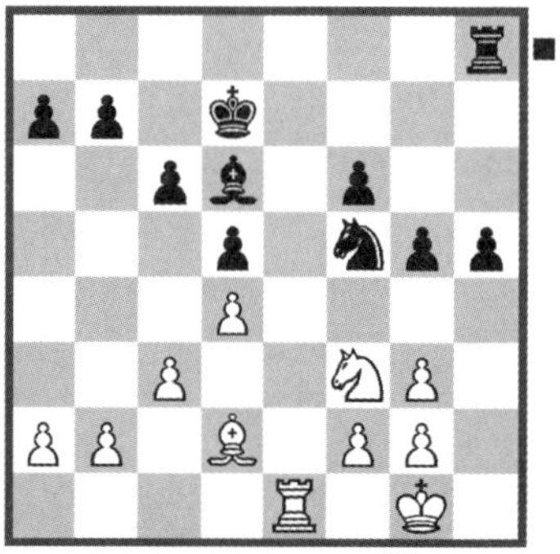

Position after: 25. ♖e1

A key moment in the game. With all his pieces perfectly placed it is time for pawn action! But where?

25... c5!

An absolutely amazing and shocking move! Yes indeed, it is usually bad to have isolated pawns in the endgame. However here, there is something more important. After exchanging pawns White cannot comfortably protect the pawn on g3! Another example where tactics come to the aid when strategic goals have been achieved. Moreover, take note – Black's action is expected on the kingside but instead, he strikes on the queenside, capitalizing on his central domination.

A) 25... g4 26. ♘h2 This is not dangerous for White.

B) 25... h4 26. gxh4 g4 27. ♘h2 g3

Position after: 27... g3

28. ♘f1 This also achieves nothing.

26. dxc5

White cannot allow c4, after which ♗d2 would be more restricted; Black would have more space and excellent prospects on the queenside.

26... ♗xc5 27. ♔f1□ h4! 28. gxh4 g4 29. ♘d4

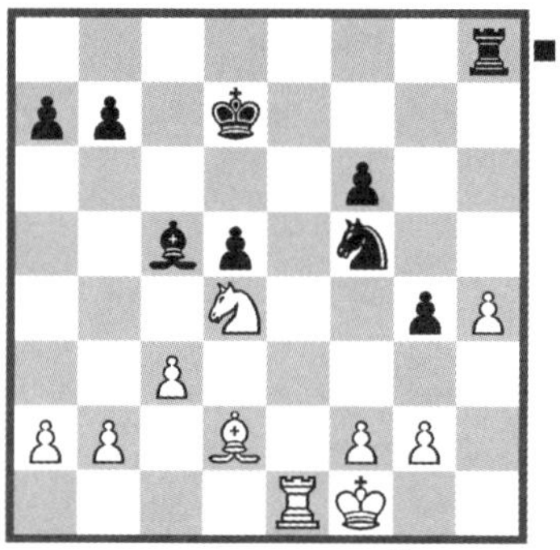

Position after: 29. ♘d4

29. ♘g1 ♖xh4 This is bad for White. Black threatens 30... ♖h1 followed by 31... g3 or 31... ♘g3.

29... ♗xd4!

The best way to retain material. In the endgame the knight would dominate over the bishop.

30. cxd4 ♖xh4 31. ♗c3 ♖h1+ 32. ♔e2 ♖h2 33. ♖g1 ♘h4 34. g3

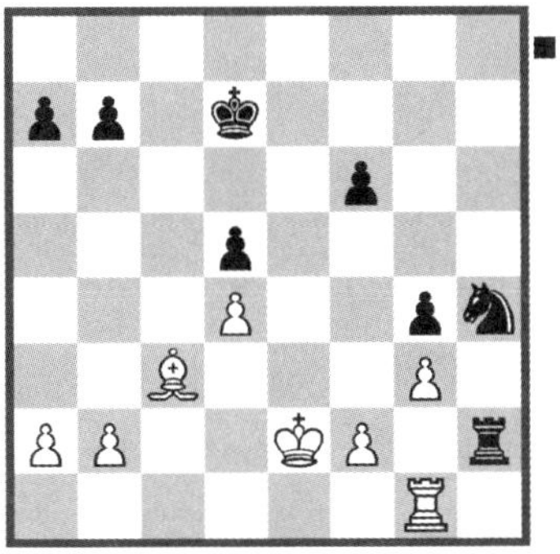

Position after: 34. g3

34. ♔f1 ♔e6 This leads to a funny zugzwang position. 35. g3 ♘f3 36. ♖g2 ♖h1+ 37. ♔e2 ♔f5 This is even more funny – the black knight paralyzes the white rook.

34... ♘f5!

The knight on f3 will simply be better placed. From f5 it attacks both the d4- and g3-pawns. Once again White cannot move his king and rook!

35. b3 ♔e6 36. ♗b2 a6 37. ♗c3

White can only wait, while Black can patiently improve his position.

37... ♘d6 38. ♔e3 ♘e4 39. ♗e1 ♔f5 40. ♖f1 ♖h8

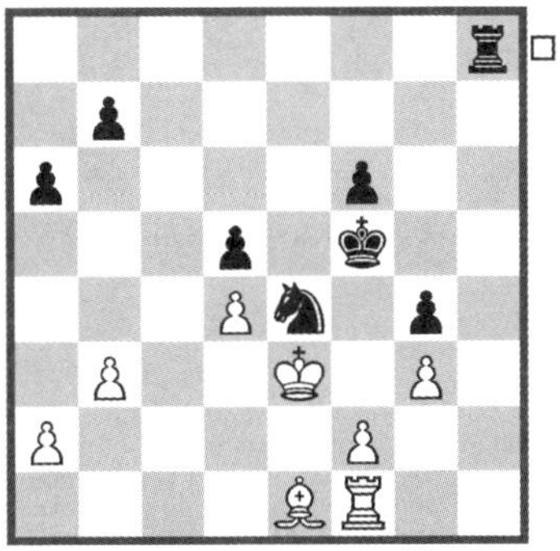

Position after: 40... ♖h8

The idea is to penetrate through the c-file or the e-file... if allowed.

41. ♔d3 b5 42. a3 ♖h7

In the next stage of the game Rubinstein demonstrates one of the most important endgame principles: "Do not rush!". Well, if your opponent is out of any real counterplay and forced to deal with many threats, it is very useful to patiently improve your position, switch to play on a different front and perhaps wait for your opponent's mistakes. Generally, patient play involves only moving pieces – pawn actions will come in if patient play does not result in a win.

43. ♗a5 ♖h8 44. ♗b4 ♖c8 45. ♗a5 ♘g5 46. ♗d2 ♘e4 47. ♗a5 ♔g6 48. ♗b4 f5!

(see diagram next page)

Patient play has not brought progress here and Black looks for a good moment for ...f4!.

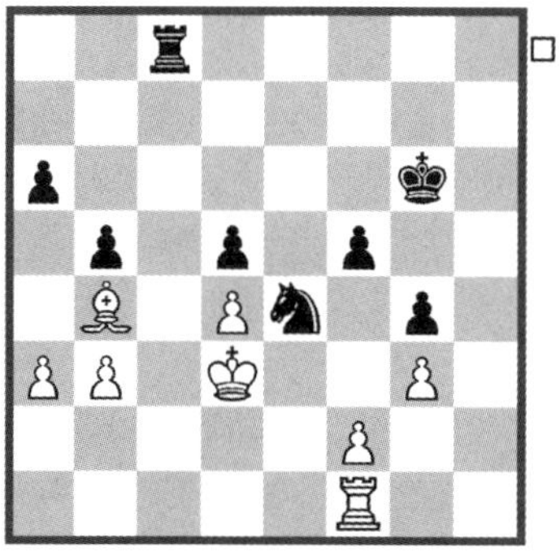

Position after: 48... f5!

49. ♗a5 ♖h8 50. ♔e3 ♖e8 51. ♔d3 ♖c8 52. ♗b4 ♖c7 53. ♗a5 ♖h7 54. ♔e3 ♖e7 55. ♔d3

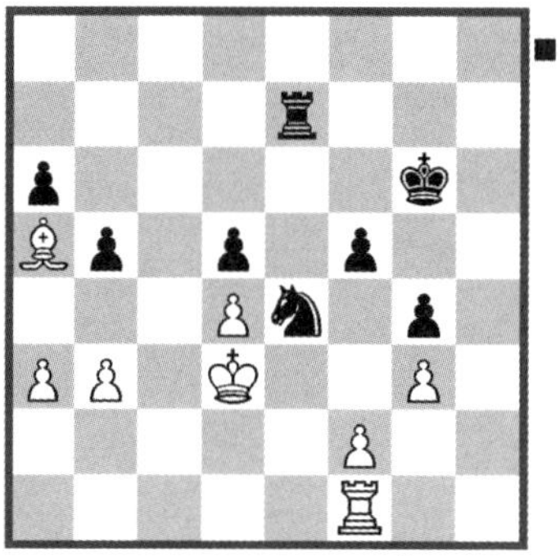

Position after: 55. ♔d3

55... f4!

White has not made a mistake and Black decides to go for direct play.

56. gxf4 ♖h7 57. ♗d2 ♘xd2!

Once again, direct play! Of course, the knight looks much better than the bishop, but after exchanging Black easily converts his great positional advantage into a full point.

58. ♔xd2 ♖h3 59. f3

What else?

59... gxf3 60. ♖f2 ♔f5 61. ♔e3 ♔g4 62. b4 ♖h1

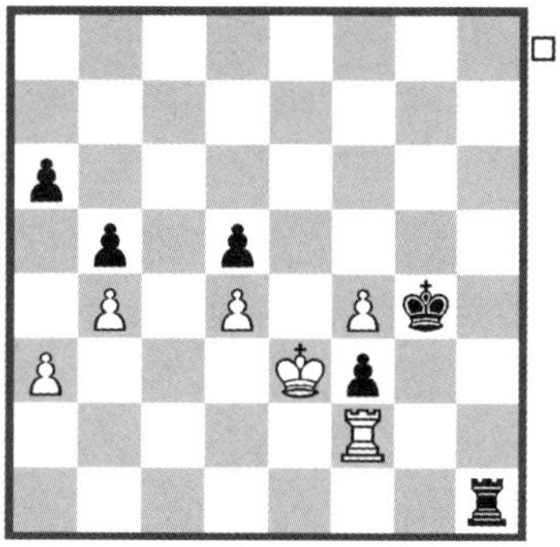

Position after: 62... ♖h1

63. f5

63. ♖xf3 ♖a1 This leads to a pawn endgame that is easily won for Black.

63... ♖e1+ 64. ♔d3 ♖e4

0-1

11

Opposite-Colored Bishops

It is recognized that drawing tendencies increase when the game transposes to an endgame with opposite-colored bishops. However, this is not automatically the case!

Here you will become familiar with a simple principle – he who has the better bishop **practically has an extra piece!** This is very drastic, of course – it is an exaggerated sentence, but it's in order to help you remember this important concept!

We will look at a few masterpieces where the masters of the endgame have managed to smoothly convert "drawish" endgames into wins!

Game 148

♙ Aronian, Levon (2754)
♟ Ivanchuk, Vassily (2746)
Nalchik 2009

I have decided to create this chapter because of the widespread endgame "theory" that opposite-colored bishops are automatically or usually drawish. This is not at all the case! Let's start the chapter with an uncommon material balance: a queen + bishop on each side. Later we will switch to the most common endgames: opposite-colored bishops with rooks. Of course, we will not present endgames with other minor pieces because it makes it harder to compare the bishops' strength.

Our first example is typical. Despite the fact that Black has the "better majority" he is clearly worse. The majority is useless – from c4 the white bishop will stop both the black pawns and attack the only vulnerable pawn in Black's position, the f7-pawn. To be honest, Black should not lose this.

26. ♔g2

There is no need to rush; the king goes to a safe position.

26... h5

Generally a good approach. Black sets his pawns on the light squares and makes additional space for the king. If White wants to advance, he will have to trade some pawns. The problem may be the possible vulnerability of the g6-pawn, but it appears safe.

27. ♕e4 ♗c3 28. ♕b7

White attacks both the pawns that he can target.

28... ♗f6

28... ♗a5!? This is also possible. The bishop will defend the b6-pawn; the queen will defend the f7-pawn. White would be forced to strike with his pawns, but then the white king would be exposed and there would be a chance for a perpetual. Evidently, Black did not want to play passively – an understandable decision.

29. ♗c4 ♕e7

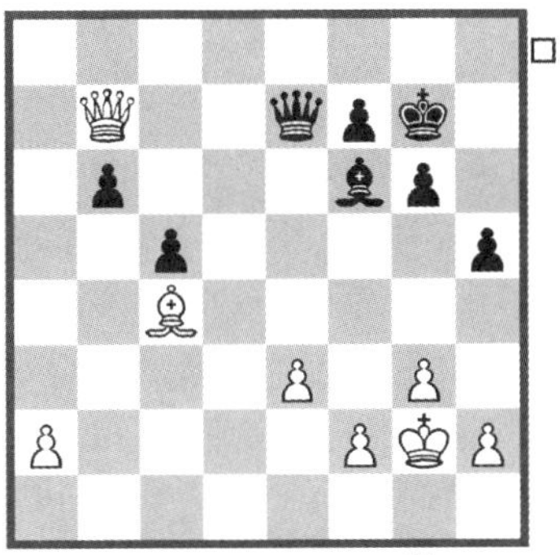

Position after: 29... ♕e7

This is the defense that Black prepared.

30. ♕d5

30. ♕xb6?? ♕e4+–+

30... h4!?

The idea is to trade several pawns.

30... ♔g8 Simply waiting is not so good. White can strike with 31. e4 and then f4 with e5.

31. e4 hxg3 32. hxg3 ♗d4 33. f4

Position after: 33. f4

33... f6??

The Ukrainian genius blunders for obscure reasons. He was not ready to wait, but here changing the structure is simply fatal.

33... ♕f6! 34. e5 ♕f5! This would give Black sufficient desired activity.

34. ♔f3

34. ♕g8+ Direct play. 34... ♔h6 35. ♕h8+ ♕h7 36. ♕f8+

Position after: 36. ♕f8+

36... ♔h5 [36... ♕g7 37. ♕c8 ♕e7 38. ♗e6 This would lead to paralysis. White is ready to advance his pawns and win with a mating attack.] 37. ♗e2#

34... ♔h6

34... ♕f8 Black prevents check but loses the b-pawn after 35. ♕b7+.

35. ♕g8 g5

Position after: 35... g5

This was Black's idea. His king is temporarily safe and he wants to eliminate the white king's pawn shield. However, this simply fails. Aronian finds the only winning move.

36. e5!

36. ♗f7? This gives nothing in view of 36... g4+! with an immediate draw.

36... fxe5

36... gxf4 This loses to 37. ♗f7.

37. ♗d3!

37. ♗f7? Playing this now is wrong because of the simple 37... ♕f6.

37... e4+ 38. ♗xe4 ♕g7 39. ♕e6+ ♕f6 40. ♕d7

Mate soon is unavoidable. Black resigned.

1-0

Game 149

♙ Rubinstein, Akiba
♟ Gruenfeld, Ernst
Karlovy Vary 1929

White's advantage is undisputed – he has a better structure, a better bishop and the possibility to create an h-passer. A very important fact is that a queenless endgame is not automatically drawish. White first improves on the kingside.

26. h4!

Restricting the black bishop and threatening g4+h5.

26... ♕d7 27. ♔g2 ♕d6 28. ♗b3

Freeing the diagonal for the queen.

28... ♕d7 29. ♕c4 ♕d2+ 30. ♔f3

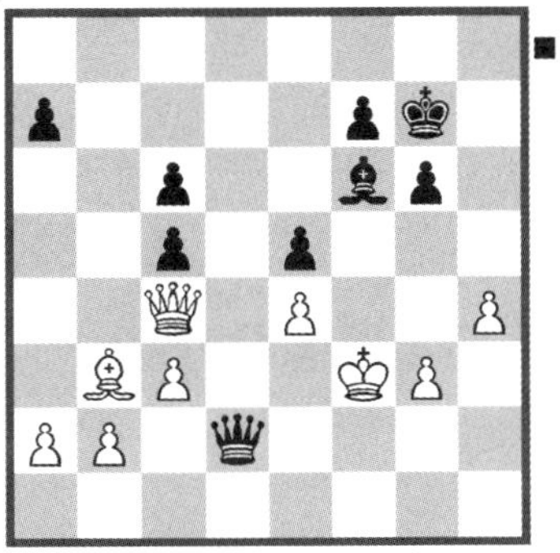

Position after: 30. ♔f3

30. ♔h3 This gives nothing in view of 30... ♕d7+.

30... ♔h6?

30... ♕d7 This was necessary. 31. ♕xc5? [31. ♔e2 This is probably a better try. Here one of the plans for White would be to evacuate the king to the queenside and then attack on both flanks.] 31... ♕d3+ Leading to a draw.

31. ♕xc5 ♕xb2 32. ♕e3+! ♔g7 33. ♕xa7 ♕xc3+

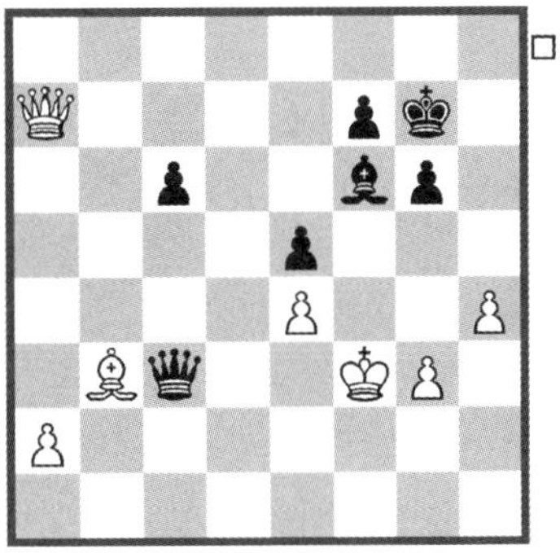

Position after: 33... ♕xc3+

The situation has crystallized. Black has not obtained any relief by getting rid of the doubled pawns. Moreover, he is lost. Black loses the f7-pawn and White can simply win after that by trading queens. White has the possibility to create another passer on the h-file.

34. ♔g4?

34. ♔g2! Correct. Now the king would be able to find a shield and from f6 the queen might be able to block some checks. 34... ♕d3 35. ♕xf7+ ♔h6 36. ♕xf6 ♕xe4+ 37. ♔h2+– The difference is evident. [37. ♕f3+–]

34... ♕d3 35. ♕xf7+ ♔h6

36. ♕c4

White tries his best.

36. ♕xf6 This leads to a perpetual as follows. 36... ♕xe4+ 37. ♔h3 ♕h1+

36... ♕d2?

Position after: 36... ♕d2?

36... ♕d7+! 37. ♔f3 ♕h3! Renewing the threats was necessary.

37. ♕f1 ♔g7 38. ♕d1 ♕g2 39. ♕f3 ♕d2 40. ♔h3

Now the white king is safe and White can continue with active play.

40... ♕d8 41. ♕c3 ♕d6

Position after: 41... ♕d6

42. g4?!

This weakens the king and looks risky. Still, it is not bad.

42. a4 This should have been preferred. Before striking on the kingside White should improve the situation on the queenside. White's king is placed on the kingside – that is why it was better to strike first on the opposite side.

42... ♗d8 43. g5! ♗b6 44. ♕f3 ♕f8

Finding nothing better, Black trades queens. He hopes that he can disturb the kingside pawn. Alas, White is simply winning.

45. ♕xf8+ ♔xf8 46. ♔g4 ♗e3 47. ♗a4!

A fine move. After the pawn comes to c5 the black bishop would be blocked.

47... c5 48. ♗b3 ♗d2 49. ♗c4 ♔g7 50. a4 ♔f8

Position after: 50... ♔f8

51. ♔f3

Rubinstein chooses a longer way. He thought that it would be safer.

51. h5 This would have been good enough to win, of course. 51... gxh5+ 52. ♔xh5 ♔g7 53. g6 ♗e1 [53... ♔f6 54. a5! ♗xa5 55. ♔h6+–] 54. ♔g5 ♗d2+ 55. ♔f5 ♗c3 56. ♗f7 White's king goes to the queenside, winning.

51... ♔e7 52. ♔e2 ♗a5 53. ♔d1 ♗b4 54. ♗e2 ♔d6 55. h5??

Practically anything else would have won!

55. ♔c2 For instance, this would have been one way. 55... c4 56. ♗xc4 ♗e1 57. h5

55... gxh5 56. ♗xh5 ♔e7 57. ♔c2 c4!

Position after: 57... c4!

58. ♗e2 c3?

58... ♔f7 59. ♗xc4+ ♔g6 60. ♔b3 ♗e1

Position after: 60... ♗e1

A huge difference – the white king is blocked. 61. ♗d5 ♔xg5 62. ♔c4 ♔f6 63. ♔b5 ♔e7 64. a5 ♔d8 Black's king goes back in time to save the game.

59. ♔b3 ♔f7 60. ♗d3 ♗a5 61. ♔c4 ♔g6 62. ♔b5 ♗d8 63. a5 ♗xg5 64. a6 ♗e3

Position after: 64... ♗e3

65. ♔c6 ♔g5 66. ♔b7 ♔f4 67. ♗b1 ♗d4 68. a7 ♗xa7 69. ♔xa7 ♔e3 70. ♔b6

Black resigned.

1-0

Game 150

♙ Kacakovski, Dimitar (2083)
♟ Zlatanovic, Boroljub (2378)
Struga 2018

Let's now switch to endgames with rooks on the board. The next example is from my praxis in a team match, where I wanted to bring my team a win by winning the game as Black. As an interesting anecdote: at that moment all the players had left the playing hall because of an electrical power cut. My opponent then said to me: "I think I can hold this endgame!" Before that I had felt that I could perhaps win, but after this I was sure that I would! Of course, the position is drawish, but White has one serious, and perhaps not obvious, problem – his disharmony! He cannot connect his pawns and bishop and the bishop cannot reach the d6-square. The bishop behind the pawns would cause disorder and I can organize an attack on the light squares. Black would simply try to combine an attack on the pawns, king and the unstable bishop. Everything will soon become crystal clear.

44... ♔c6 45. ♗d2 ♖h3+ 46. ♔c2?!

46. ♗e3 This is obviously better here.

46... ♗e4+ 47. ♔b2 ♔d5

Black has achieved some progress but not significantly.

48. ♗f4 ♔c4 49. ♗d2

Position after: 49. ♗d2

49... ♔d4

49... b5 This could have been played immediately instead. There is no serious difference.

50. ♗f4 ♗d5

With the idea of maybe ...♔e4.

51. ♔c1 ♔c3

Attacking the pawn and threatening mate. Nevertheless, White is okay, but at this moment it is clear that he does not have a plan for defense.

52. ♗d2+ ♔b3

Black's king is deep in the opponent's territory – psychologically it is very unpleasant.

53. ♖e2

Defending mate and threatening ♖e3.

53... ♖h4

Black avoids the exchange of rooks and threatens ...♖c4 at some point.

54. ♖e3+ ♔a2!

Position after: 54... ♔a2!

Strange, but the best try. Black wants to kick the white king to the kingside with checks. With the white king far from the b-pawn there may be an exchange sacrifice possibility to create a b-passer.

55. ♔c2 ♖c4+ 56. ♗c3

56. ♖c3? This is impossible because of 56... ♖xb4.

56... ♗e4+ 57. ♔d2 ♗f5

Now the white pieces are somewhat cramped.

58. ♖g3 ♖h4

Position after: 58... ♖h4

A check on h2 could be unpleasant.

59. ♖e3 b5

Sooner or later this would be needed. Black avoids ♗d4 with tempo, so that the rook may gain some freedom.

60. ♔c1 ♖c4 61. ♔d2 ♔b3

An unpleasant situation. White must wait with the rook.

Position after: 61... ♔b3

62. ♖g3 ♖h4 63. ♖e3 ♖h2+ 64. ♔e1

The king is driven away.

64. ♔d1 ♗g4+ The king will be driven toward the kingside.

64... ♔c4

With the threat of ...♗d3.

65. ♔d1

The king goes back to the queenside.

65... ♗c2+ 66. ♔c1 ♗d3 67. ♗d2 ♔d4

Position after: 67... ♔d4

68. ♖e1

68. ♔d1 This is possible here.

68... ♗e4

Black has achieved much. It appears that the e5-pawn will fall soon. White, close to time trouble, decides to defend it.

69. ♗f4?

A fatal mistake. Now White loses more than the important b4-pawn.

69. ♖g1 ♔xe5 70. ♖g5+ ♗f5 71. ♗e3 This should be holdable for White. The bishop comes to c5 and White would try to organize a blockade on the e3-square.

69... ♖c2+ 70. ♔d1 ♖c4 71. ♔d2

71. ♗d2 This loses to 71... ♗f3+.

71... ♖xb4 72. ♖d1

Position after: 72. ♖d1

Although it may look holdable, in actual fact it is dead lost for White. With a precise maneuver Black kicks the white king far away from the passer.

72... ♖b2+ 73. ♔e1+

73. ♔c1+ This loses quickly after 73... ♔c3.

73... ♗d3 74. ♖d2 ♖b3!

Position after: 74... ♖b3!

75. ♔f2 ♔e4 76. ♗g3 b4 77. ♖d1 ♖b2+ 78. ♔g1 b3 79. ♗e1 ♖c2

0-1

Game 151

♙ Keres, Paul
♟ Pirc, Vasja
🌍 Munich 1936

White's advantage is evident. However it is also clear that Black is safe. White's only chance to win is to attack the f7-pawn.

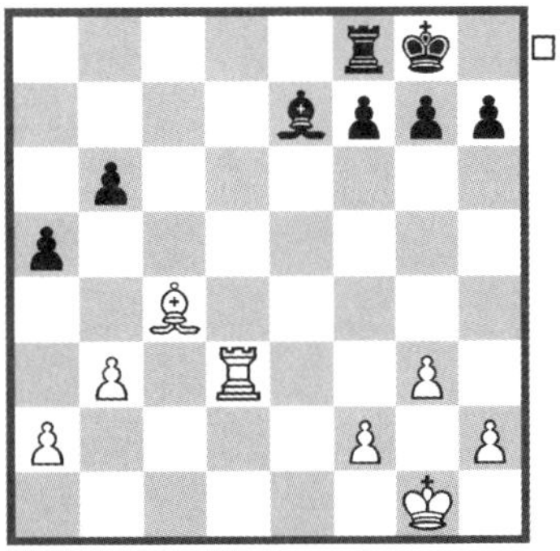

27. ♖d7 ♗c5 28. ♔g2 g6 29. g4!?

Preventing ...h5.

29... h6?!

If Black wanted to advance the g-pawn, it would have been better to do so immediately. 29... g5

30. h4 g5

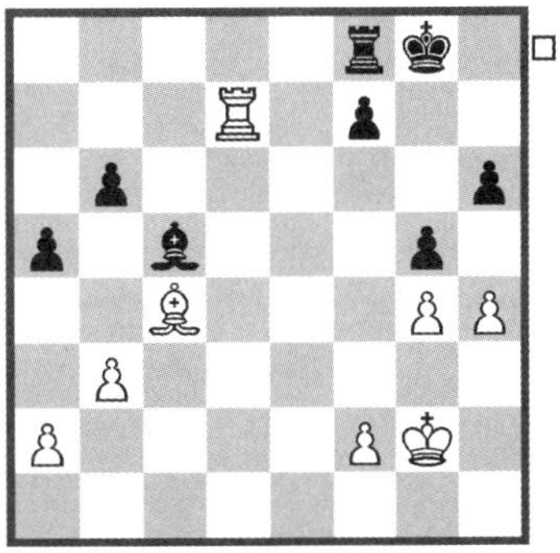

Position after: 30... g5

31. hxg5!

This keeps some chances.

31... hxg5 32. ♔g3

White must try f4.

32. ♔f3 ♔g7 33. ♔e4 ♔f6 This is equal.

32... ♔g7 33. f4 ♗e3?!

Black complicates for no reason.

33... gxf4+ 34. ♔xf4 ♔f6 35. g5+

Position after: 35. g5+

35... ♔g6 36. ♗d3+ ♔g7 37. ♔f5 ♖e8! The rook comes to e7 with a draw.

34. fxg5 ♗xg5 35. ♔f3

Position after: 35. ♔f3

Now the bishop cannot easily get to c5.

35... ♗d8?! ♔f4 ♔g6 37. ♗d3+ ♔g7

37... ♔f6?! 38. g5+ ♔e6?? 39. ♗f5#

38. ♔f5 ♔h6?!

Black plays with fire.

38... ♖e8 This is better. Black needs the additional spot for the king to defend f7. If the king is on g7 or g8 there would be the resource of g5-g6. 39. ♗c4 ♗e7 40. ♖b7 ♔f8

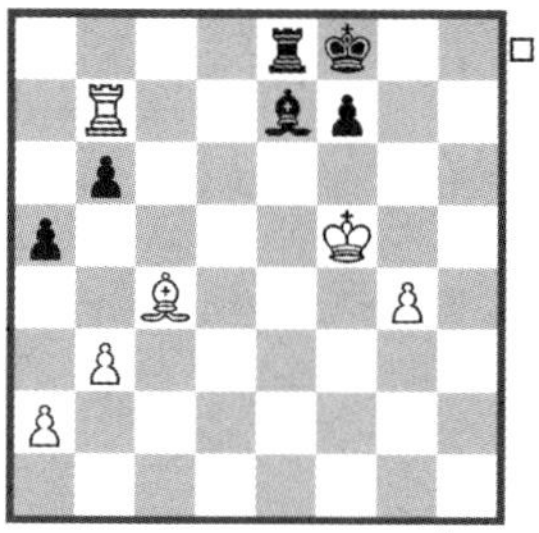

Position after: 40... ♔f8

41. ♖xb6 ♗b4 This is holdable for Black.

39. ♗c4

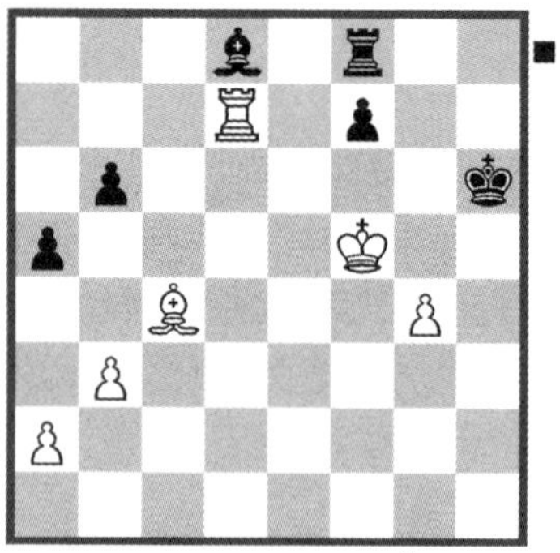

Position after: 39. ♗c4

39... ♔g7??

A final mistake.

A) 39... f6? Amazingly this loses after White employs a zugzwang. 40. a4 ♖e8 41. ♗e6

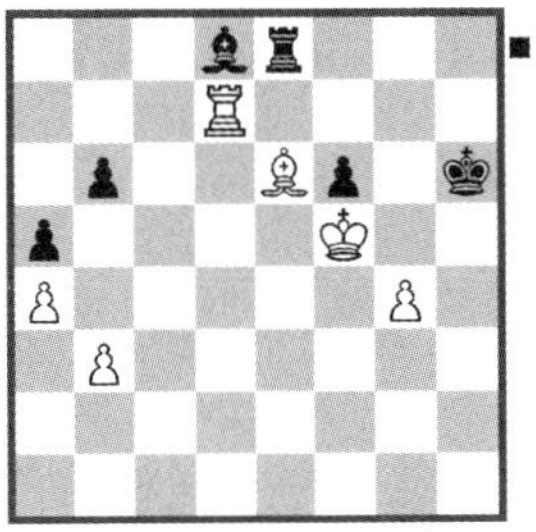

Position after: 41. ♗e6

41... ♖f8 42. ♗f7 ♖h8 43. ♗g6

B) 39... ♖g8! 40. ♗xf7 ♖f8 This should be holdable.

40. g5 ♔g8 41. g6

1-0

Game 152

♙ Ribli, Zoltan (2585)
♟ Browne, Walter Shawn (2550)
Tilburg 1978

A draw due to symmetry? No, White is better, much better! Why? Well, the white bishop is much better. From d5 it can attack f7, while at the same time the black bishop does absolutely nothing.

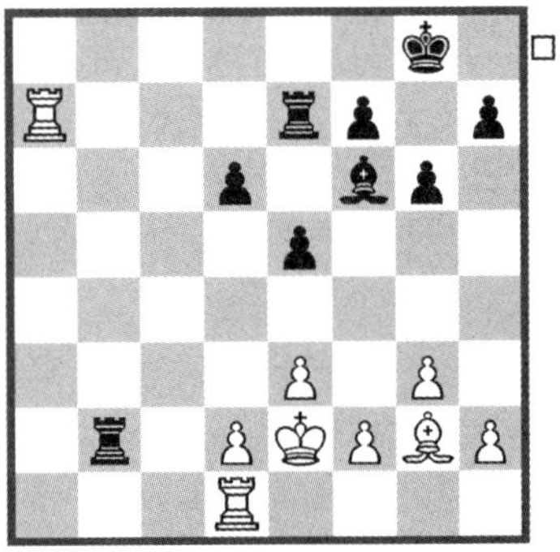

25. ♖a6

White naturally keeps the rooks on the board.

25... ♖d7 26. ♖c1

White wants to invade with the rooks on the 7th or 8th rank.

26... ♗e7?

Not obvious, but nevertheless a terrible mistake.

26... ♔g7! 27. ♗d5 [27. ♖c8 d5!] 27... ♖b8 There are no obvious ways to improve for White.

27. ♖c8+!

(see diagram next page)

With a forced array of moves White occupies the 7th rank to win.

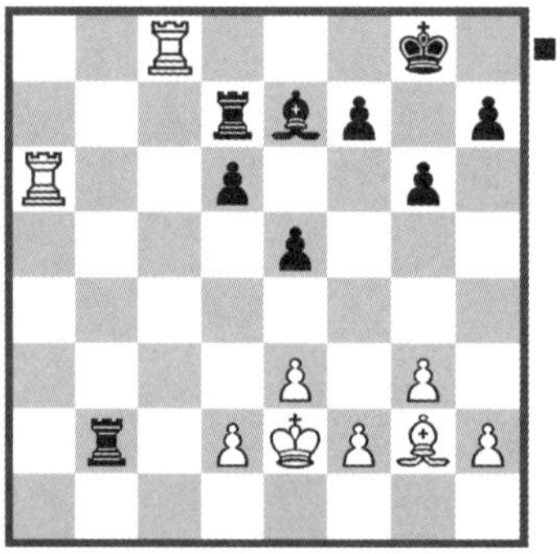

Position after: 27. ♖c8+!

27... ♔g7 28. ♗c6! ♖d8 29. ♖c7 ♗f6 30. ♗d5

Black loses a pawn.

30... ♖f8 31. ♖xd6?!

31. ♖aa7 Capturing the f7-pawn with a bishop would be more brutal.

31... ♗d8

Black gets the chance to prolong resistance.

32. ♖a7 ♖b6 33. ♖dd7 ♖f6

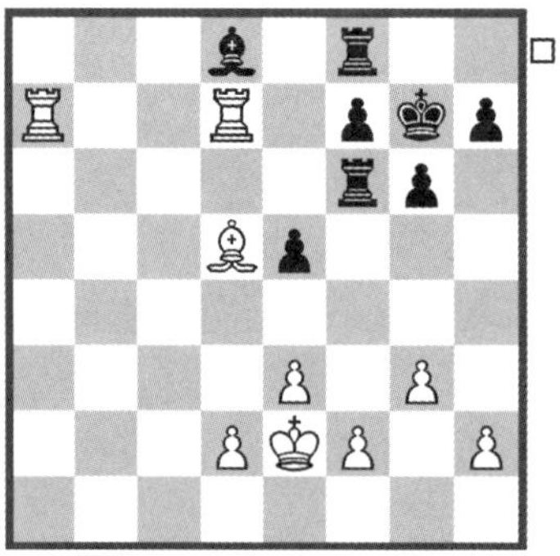

Position after: 33... ♖f6

Black has managed to defend f7 somehow. However with such paralysis there is no chance to hold. White can create a passer or advance on the kingside to remove the rook from f6.

34. g4

White chooses the second option.

34... h6 35. h4 g5 36. h5

Restricting is correct here. The h6-pawn is an additional weakness. At the same time the black king does not obtain any space.

36... ♗b6 37. ♖ab7 ♗c5 38. f3 ♗d6

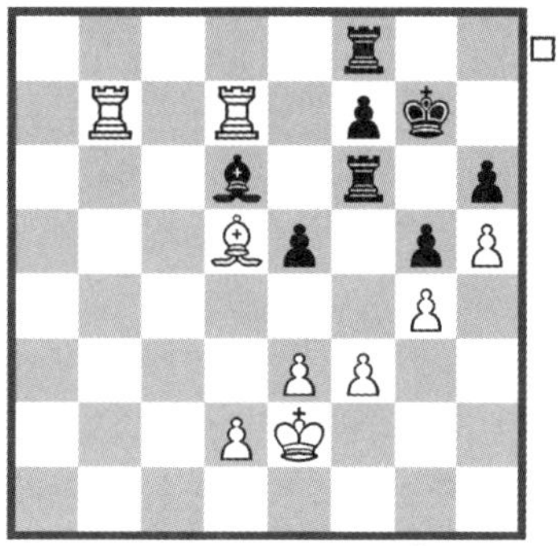

Position after: 38... ♗d6

White's pieces are on their best spots. There is no obvious pawn play. So, let's activate the king!

39. ♔d3 ♗c5 40. ♔e4 ♗d6 41. ♗c4 ♗a3

Sooner or later due to zugzwang Black loses another pawn.

41... ♔g8 42. ♖b6 ♗e7 43. ♖xf6 ♗xf6 44. ♔f5

Position after: 44. ♔f5

44... ♗g7 [44... ♔g7 45. ♗d5+–] 45. ♖xf7 ♖xf7+ 46. ♔g6+–

42. ♔xe5 ♖xf3

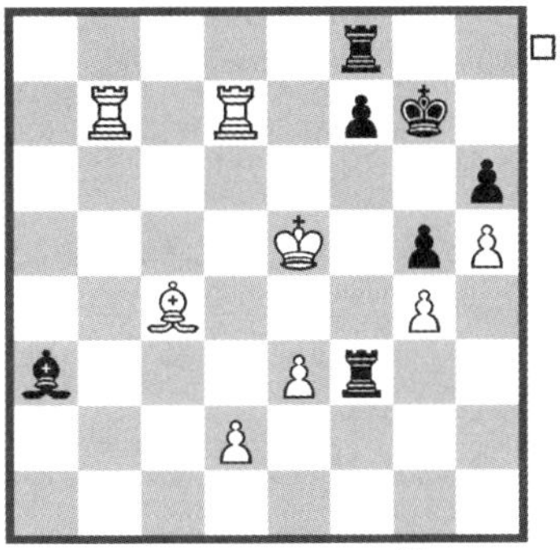

Position after: 42... ♖xf3

Black has managed to trade some pawns, but there is no relief. White does not need the f3-pawn. Furthermore, after the e5-pawn is gone White simply marches with the d-passer.

43. ♔e4 ♖f2 44. d4 ♗c1 45. ♔d3 ♖f3 46. ♖e7 ♗a3

(see diagram next column)

Position after: 46... ♗a3

47. ♖e6

The rook goes to g6. The technical issues to convert are simple.

47... ♗c1 48. ♔e2 ♖g3 49. ♖g6+ ♔h8 50. ♖xh6+ ♔g7 51. ♖g6+ ♔h8 52. ♗xf7

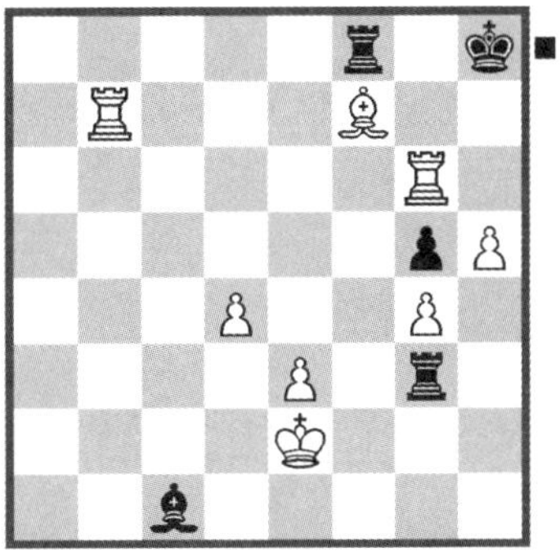

Position after: 52. ♗xf7

52... ♖xe3+ 53. ♔d1 ♗a3 54. ♗e6 ♗e7 55. ♔d2 ♖g3 56. ♗f5 ♖e8 57. ♖e6 ♖g2+ 58. ♔e3

Black resigned.

1-0

Game 153

♙ Alexander, Conel Hugh O'Donel
♟ Smyslov, Vassily V
London 1954

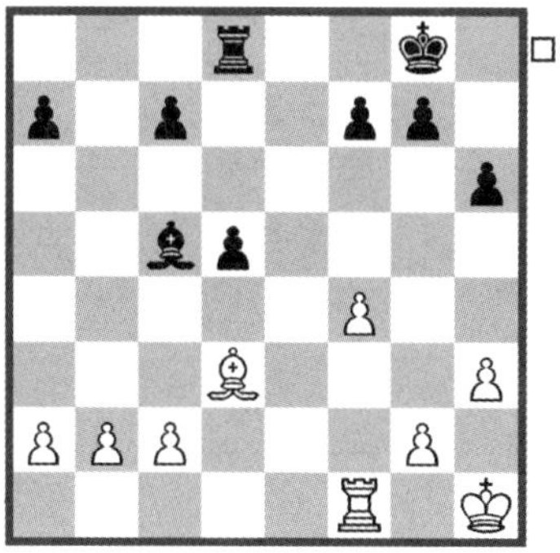

Our next endgame is balanced. Black has an extra pawn island, but the white bishop is restricted and White has some weak squares in his camp. White should simply occupy the file with a probable draw.

21. g3?!

21. ♖e1 Perhaps he did not play this in view of 21... ♗f2. However here White has the calm 22. ♖e7. Now White is safe after the following. 22... ♗g3 23. ♖xc7 ♖e8 24. ♔g1 ♖e1+ 25. ♗f1

21... ♖b8!

Before taking control over the e-file Black provokes a weakening.

22. b3 ♖e8

23. ♗b5?!

White finds a maneuver to remove the black rook from the file. However this results in new weaknesses in White's position.

23. ♔g2 This calm move should have been White's choice instead.

23... ♖e6

In order to push ...c6 on the next move.

24. ♖d1 c6 25. f5?! ♖d6 26. ♗d3

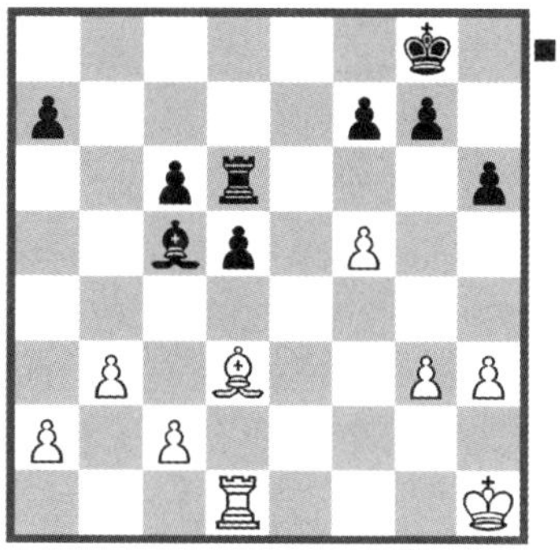

Position after: 26. ♗d3

Black's rook is no longer on the e-file. However White's position has become worse. Why? The f5-pawn restricts the bishop making it simply a big pawn. Black's counterpart has a wider radius now. Black's first task is to activate the king.

26... ♔f8!

The king gets to e7 before the white rook gets the e-file.

26... ♖d7 Occupying the file gives Black nothing because of the following. 27. ♖d2 ♖e7 28. ♖e2 There is equality after the exchange.

27. ♔g2

27. ♖e1? ♗f2

27... ♗b4

Black's bishop will control many important spots.

28. ♖f1

Having previously been reluctant to gain the file, White now spends much time retaining control of it.

28... ♔e7 29. ♖f2 ♖d8!?

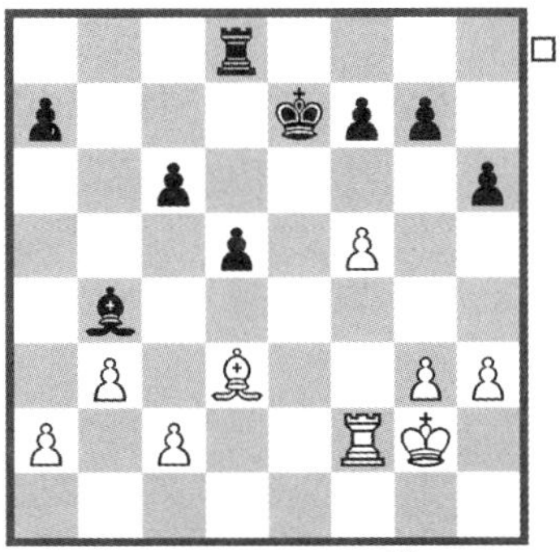

Position after: 29... ♖d8!?

29... ♗c3 This will prevent activation for White. However Black has problems with harmony after 30. ♖e2+ ♔d8.

30. ♔f3?

30. f6+! This would lead to safety for White. 30... gxf6 31. ♖e2+ ♔d6 32. ♗f5 White risks nothing. For instance, if necessary he can place his pawns on a4 and h5. Remember this approach: very often in opposite-colored bishop endgames a pawn means nothing; it is much more important to activate the bishop and control important squares.

30... ♔d6?

30... ♗c3! The correct move order.

31. ♖e2?

31. f6! g6 32. ♖e2 ♖d7 33. ♖e7! This results in a draw.

31... ♗c3 32. ♔f4

White's activity is illusory. There is nothing that can be gained on the kingside, nor from the e-file. Black uses the moment to activate his rook.

32... ♖b8! 33. h4 a5!

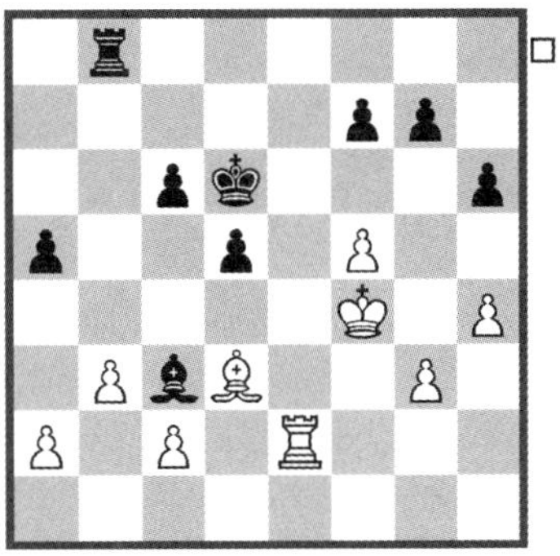

Position after: 33... a5!

The pawn marches to a3 – a very typical approach!

34. ♔g4 c5

34... a4 This is also possible, of course. White must not take when Black improves substantially.

35. ♔h5?!

White wanders. He will soon become the victim of an illusion. There is nothing that he can get from the advance.

35. ♖e3! Correct; threatening the black bishop.

35... a4 36. g4 ♗e5

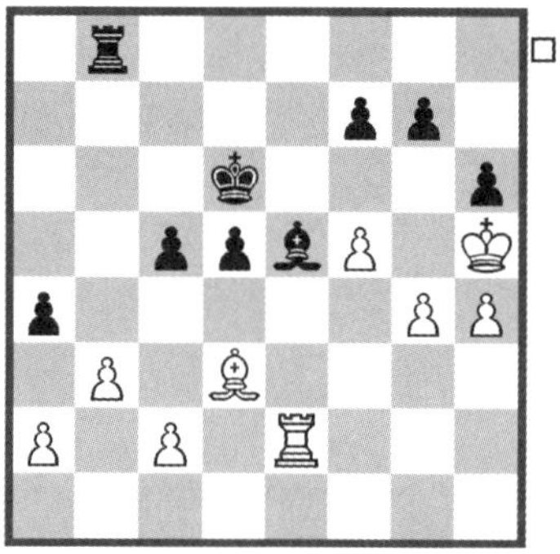

Position after: 36... ♗e5

Black closes the e-file and prepares to infiltrate with the rook. The target will be the a2-pawn.

37. g5?

37. ♖e1! ♖b4 38. ♖d1 Targeting the d5-pawn; this should give White some counter-chances.

37... hxg5 38. hxg5 ♖b4

Now even ...♗g3 is a threat. White's king is in danger.

39. ♖e3 ♖f4

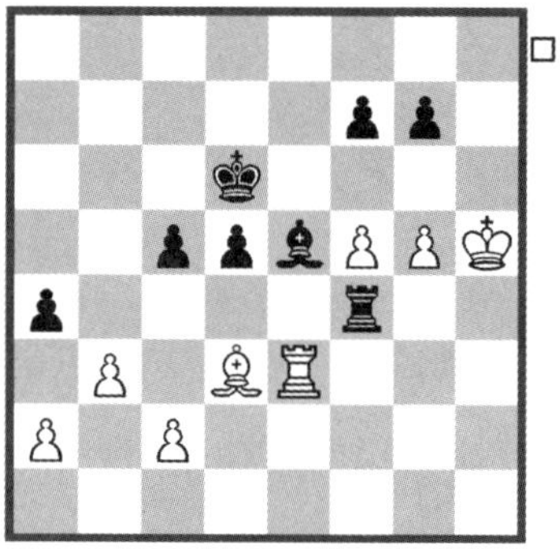

Position after: 39... ♖f4

40. c4?

A final mistake. Take a look at White's moves since the initial diagram. There has been a lot of wasted time, with many random moves. Even in the simplest position, you should aim for accuracy.

40. ♖e1 This would have been better. 40... c4 41. bxc4 dxc4 42. ♗e2 ♔c5 However this gives Black an enormous initiative and serious winning chances.

40... ♗d4

40... d4 41. ♖e2 a3 This would win too, threatening ...♖f3 and ...♗f4.

41. ♖g3 a3 42. cxd5

Here White resigned. The obvious 42... ♖f2 wins easily.

0-1

Game 154

♙ Reti, Richard
♟ Romanovsky, Peter Arsenievich
Moscow 1925

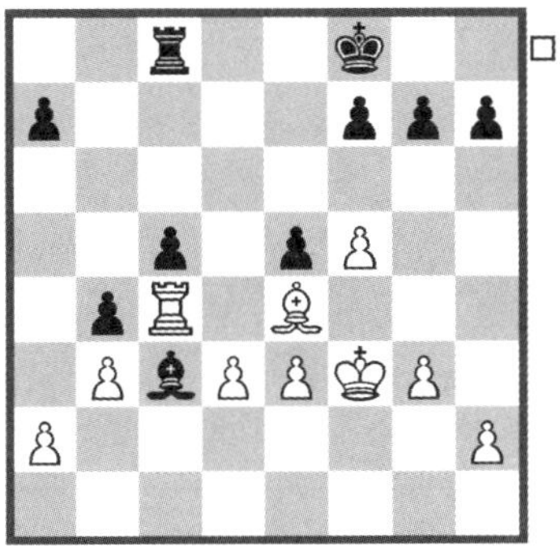

White is much better here. Black's bishop has no effect on the game, while its white counterpart works in many directions. White's next move is very methodical.

31. a4!

A very important move. White removes the pawn from a2 (who knows, maybe it will be attacked?!) and at the same time prevents Black's advance ...a5-a4. 31. f6! However this would have been a more direct move. Now, for instance the following is strategically lost for Black. 31... g6 32. g4 h6 33. h4

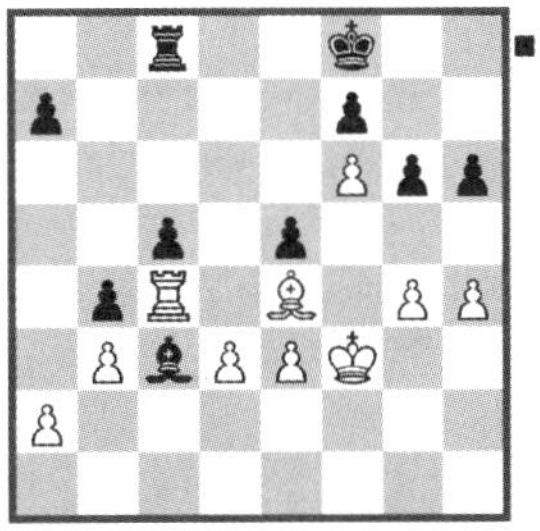

Position after: 33. h4

33... ♔e8 34. g5 h5 35. ♗d5

31... ♔e7 32. ♗d5 ♖c7 33. ♖h4 h6 34. ♔e4 ♔f6

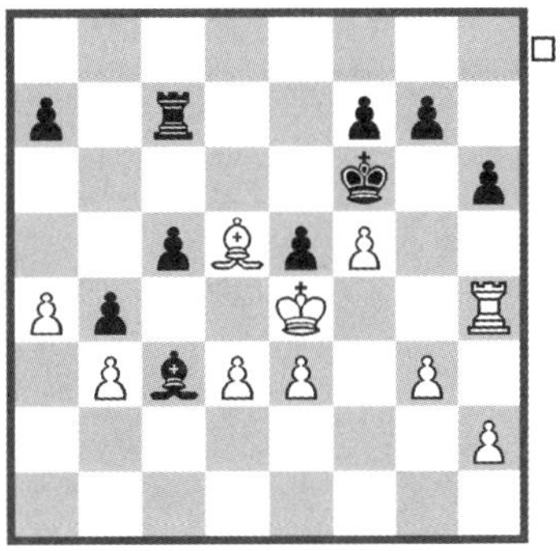

Position after: 34... ♔f6

The previous moves have been more or less normal. White must find a way to invade with his rook.

35. ♖h5! ♖d7 36. g4 g6

If Black waits, then White has h4 and g5 with a win.

36... ♖c7 37. h4 ♖c8 38. g5+ hxg5 39. hxg5+

Position after: 39. hxg5+

39... ♔e7 40. ♖h7 ♖g8 41. g6+–

37. ♖xh6 ♔g5 38. ♖h7

White threatens two or even three pawn checks!

38... ♔xg4

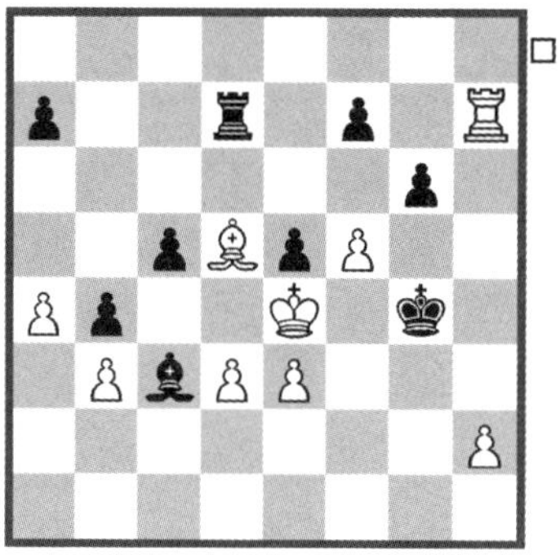

Position after: 38... ♔xg4

How to prevent mate in one?

39. ♗e6!!

Winning in style.

39. fxg6?? f5#

39... fxe6 40. fxg6 ♖d8 41. ♖xa7 ♔g5 42. g7 ♔h6 43. a5

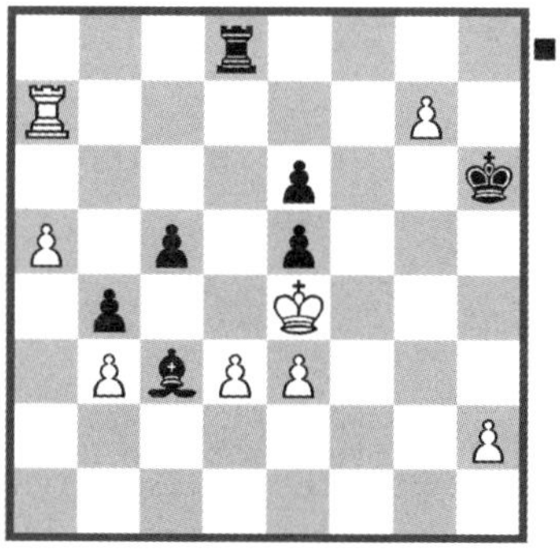

Position after: 43. a5

Picturesque! Despite his extra bishop Black cannot do anything!

43... ♔h7 44. a6 ♖d6 45. h4!

Now this pawn comes to help.

45... ♗e1 46. h5 ♗h4 47. h6

1-0

Game 155

♙ Von Gottschall, Hermann
♟ Nimzowitsch, Aron
Hanover 1926

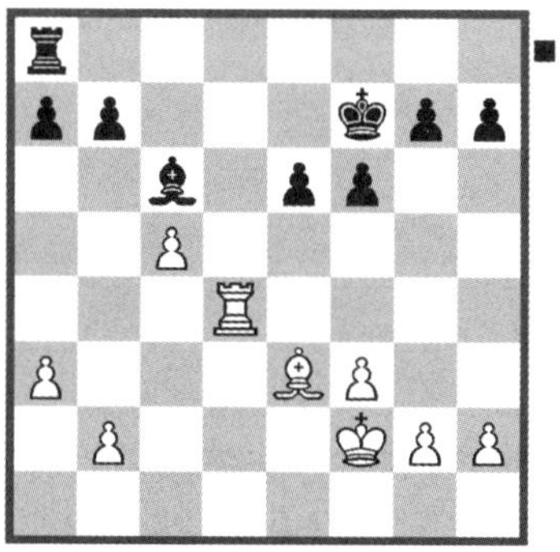

White has the file and a "better" majority; nevertheless Black is better. Yes, White cannot use his majority, especially after Black's next strong move. An even more important reason the black bishop is better is because it is effective on both flanks – it defends and attacks at the same time.

25... a5!

Neutralizing White's majority and keeping the pawns protected after the next move.

26. g3 a4!

27. f4?!

Such moves which create holes and open a path for the opponent's king and bishop must not be played. Nevertheless, White is not in big trouble here; he should hold a waiting policy. His position is worse, but eventually in the endgame the bishop (from b4) can connect the pawns and stop the potential e-passer. Therefore White should not have gone for such a drastic measure.

27. ♗d2 Better. White transfers the bishop to a better spot on c3.

27... h5!

Fixing with a possible strike.

28. h3 ♖h8

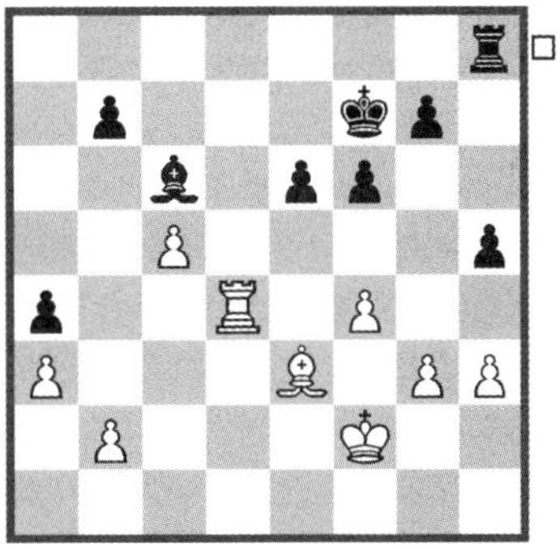

Position after: 28... ♖h8

"A mysterious rook move". It is clear that Black wants to prevent g4. His king is going to f5!

29. ♖d1 ♔g6 30. ♖d4 ♔f5 31. ♗d2

31... ♖f8!

Another "mysterious move" – amazing once again. Black wants to play ...e5, but it will not work.

31... e5? 32. fxe5 fxe5 33. g4+!

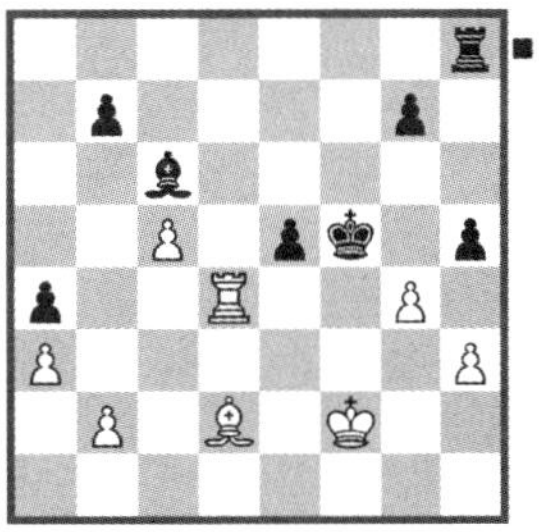

Position after: 33. g4+!

33... hxg4 34. hxg4+ ♔e6 35. ♖d6+ ♔f7 36. ♗c3 White is out of difficulties.

32. ♗e1 e5 33. fxe5 fxe5

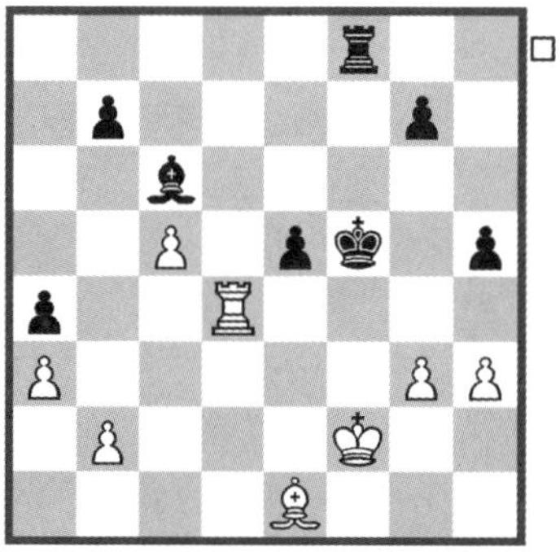

Position after: 33... fxe5

34. ♖h4

34. g4+?? ♔e6+ The rook falls. Now the point of the rook move is clear.

34... g5!

Black plays with great spirit.

35. ♖b4

35. ♖xh5?? ♔g6+

35... ♔e6+ 36. ♔e2 e4!?

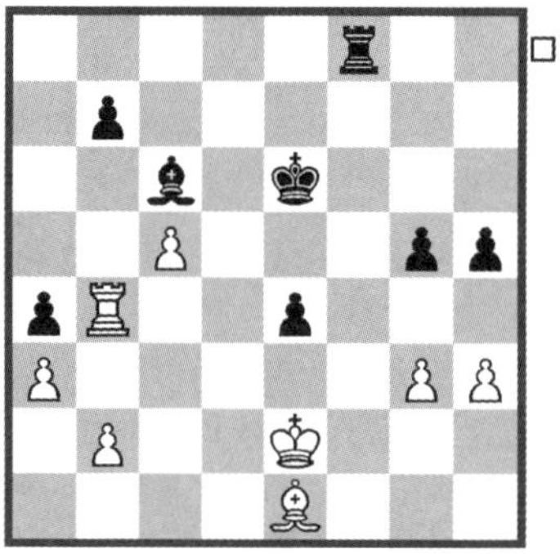

Position after: 36... e4!?

Sooner or later this looks necessary. However it would have been more logical to try without this move. But where and how?

37. ♗f2?

White must take the chance that his opponent has given him. It was necessary to play 37. ♖d4 with ♖d6.

37... ♖f3 38. ♖b6

What a move?!

38... ♔e5

Triangulation!

39. ♖b4 ♔d5

Black intentionally loses a move for the triangle.

40. h4

White prevents Black's possible ...h4 strike.

40. ♖b6 This can now be met as follows. 40... h4 41. gxh4 gxh4 42. ♗xh4

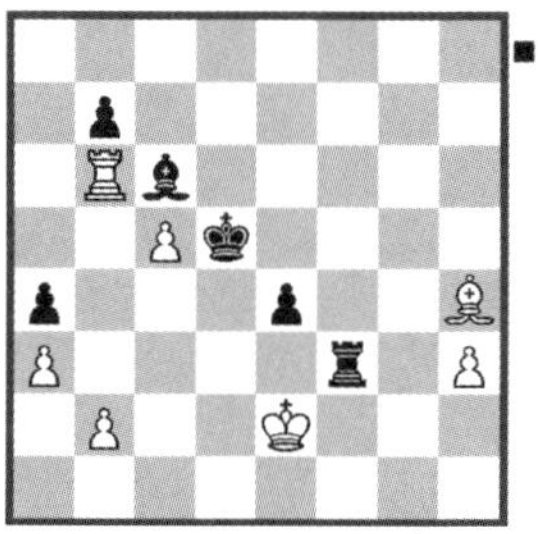

Position after: 42. ♗xh4

42... ♔xc5 This is played while also gaining a tempo on the rook.

40... gxh4 41. gxh4 ♖h3 42. ♖d4+

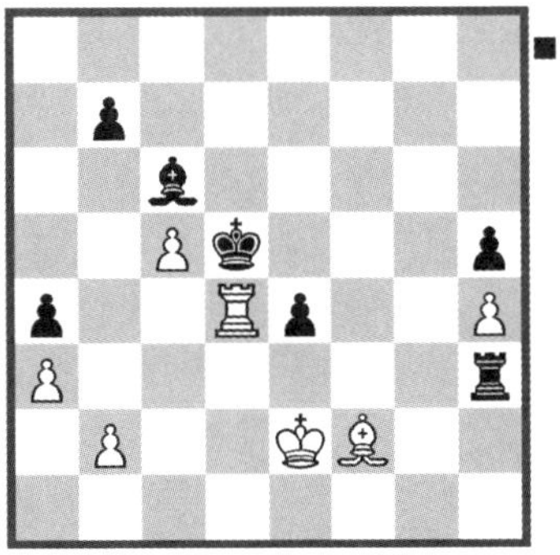

Position after: 42. ♖d4+

42... ♔e5 43. ♖d8 ♗d5

Black wants to use his bishop to secure the king.

44. ♖e8+ ♗e6 45. ♖d8 ♔f4

Step-by-step Black improves.

46. ♖f8+ ♗f5 47. ♖f7 ♖h2

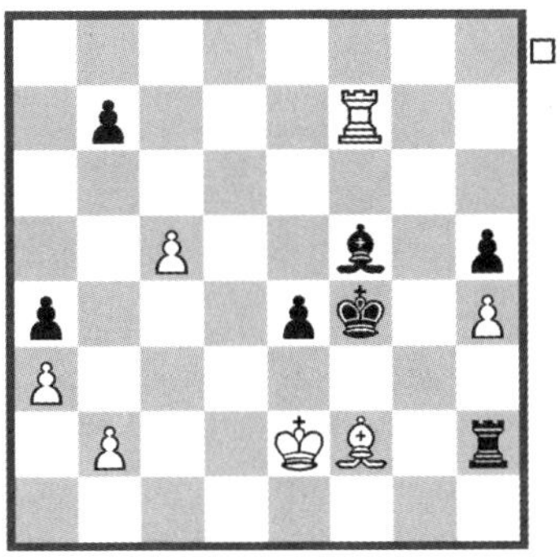

Position after: 47... ♖h2

48. ♖e7?

48. ♔f1 This was necessary here. Black would be forced to find some other way to convert.

48... ♗g4+ 49. ♔e1 ♔f3 50. ♖f7+ ♔g2

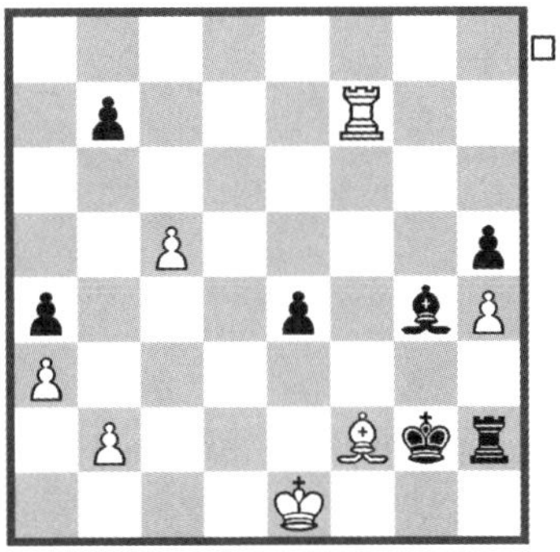

Position after: 50... ♔g2

51. ♔d2

51. ♗d4 This looks better but Black has the following response. 51... ♔h3

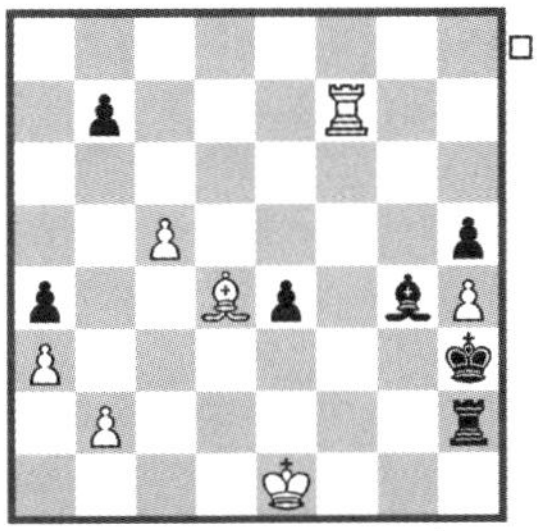

Position after: 51... ♔h3

52. ♖f2 [52. ♗f2 e3! wins.] 52... ♖h1+ 53. ♔d2 [53. ♖f1 ♖xf1+ 54. ♔xf1 ♔xh4–+] 53... ♗f3!

51... ♔f1 52. ♔e3 ♗f3

It is game over.

53. ♗g3 ♖xb2 54. ♗d6 ♖b3+ 55. ♔d4 ♔f2 56. ♖g7 e3

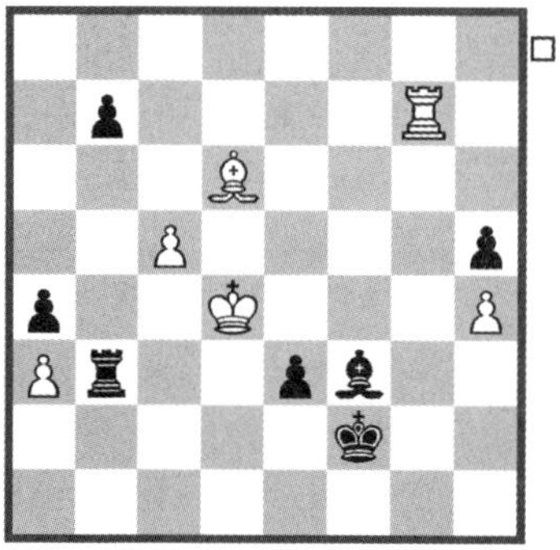

Position after: 56... e3

57. ♗g3+ ♔f1 58. ♖f7 e2 59. ♖e7 ♗c6

White resigned.

0-1

Game 156

♙ Zlatanovic, Boroljub (2330)
♟ Oberoi, Shelev (2146)
Chess.com 2021

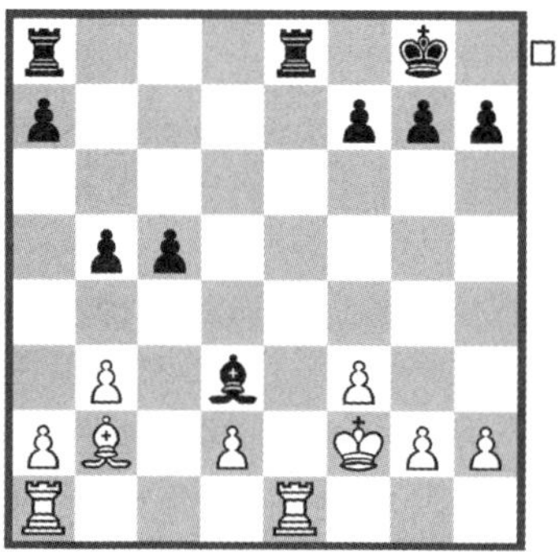

Here is a fragment from a recent hybrid game of mine. It may appear that Black is better because of his more compact structure and installed bishop. However in actual fact, White is preferable – not better, but preferable. White's bishop will soon be better – useful both in defense and attack. The point will soon become clear.

21. ♖ac1

White provokes ...c4.

21... c4 22. b4!

Now the point becomes clear. White will set his bishop on c3 where it will connect the pawns. Black's bishop is somewhat attacking but does not have any effect on the defense of the queenside. White has a4 on the agenda.

22... ♖ed8 23. ♗c3 ♖e8 24. ♗d4

There is no need to rush.

24... a6 25. ♖a1

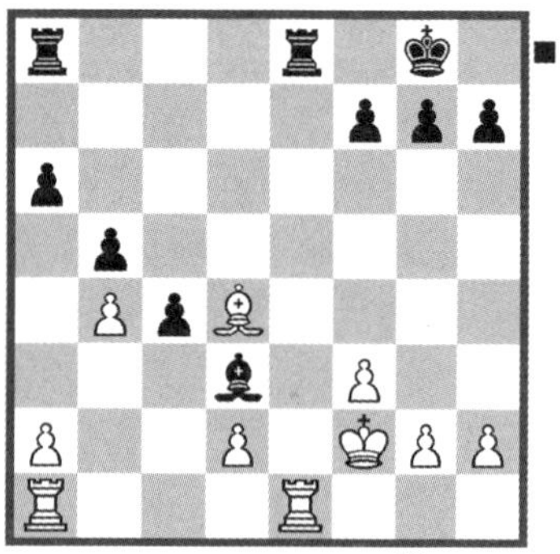

Position after: 25. ♖a1

25... f6

A natural move.

25... ♗c2 Playable here, to cut off White's plans. The game would be balanced.

26. ♗c3 ♔f7

This move should be criticized. Activation of the king should be undertaken later.

26... ♗c2! Again this move is a good choice.

27. a4!

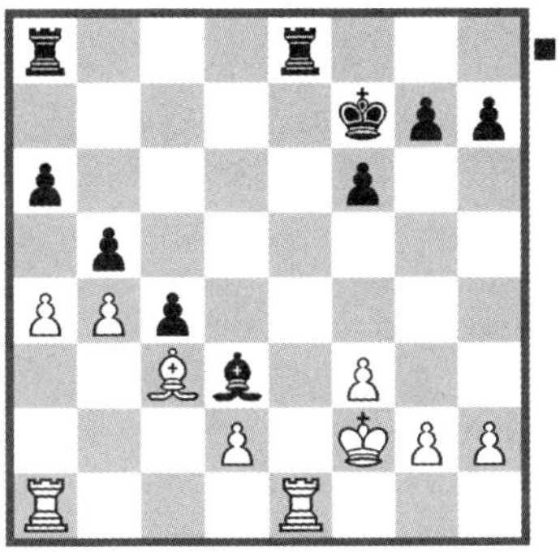

Position after: 27. a4!

Now Black's position becomes unpleasant.

27... bxa4?!

Whether to take or to wait is a matter of style. For me, waiting is more logical.

27... ♖xe1 28. ♔xe1 ♖e8+ 29. ♔f2 h5

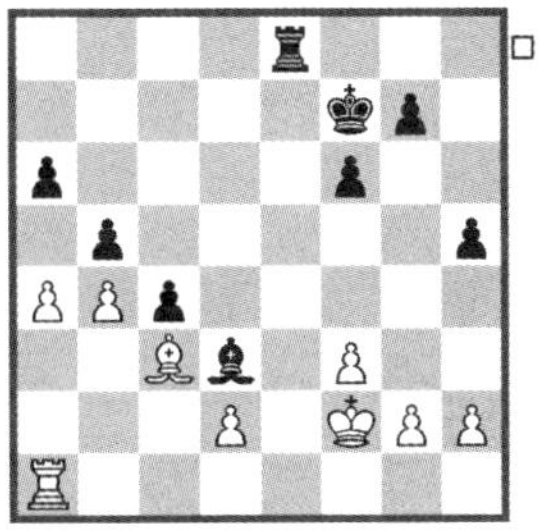

Position after: 29... h5

30. axb5 axb5 This is relatively safe for Black.

28. ♖xe8 ♖xe8 29. ♖xa4 ♖e6 30. h4!

It is time to expand and create some vulnerable spots in Black's structure.

30... g5!?

30... h5 This is also good.

31. ♖a5

Position after: 31. ♖a5

31... ♔g6

31... gxh4?! This was possible, but nevertheless after 32. ♖h5 Black's position looks ugly.

32. hxg5 fxg5

There is no longer the f6-pawn as a target, but White's bishop is working more effectively now.

33. g4 h6 34. ♖c5 ♖e2+ 35. ♔g3 ♖e6 36. ♗e5

I wanted to restrict the black rook before pushing f4.

36... ♖b6!

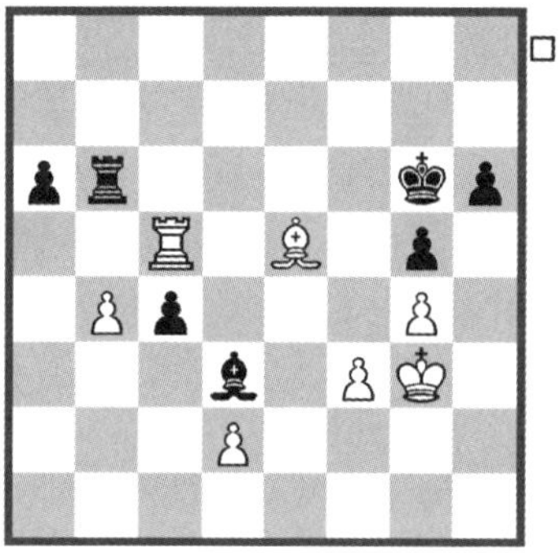

Position after: 36... ♖b6!

A good response.

37. ♗c3

There is no need to rush.

37... ♖e6 38. f4

Sooner or later this has to be played in order to make progress.

38. ♖c7 h5 This gives White nothing. I decided to keep the rook on the 5th rank for awhile.

38... gxf4+ 39. ♔xf4 ♖e4+ 40. ♔f3 ♖e6 41. ♖c7 ♔g5 42. ♔g3

Position after: 42. ♔g3

Not allowing ...♔h4 or ...♗e2 with the loss of a pawn. White threatens some annoying checks.

42. ♖c5+ ♔g6 This leads only to repetition.

42... h5??

What a blunder.

42... ♖d6 This is ok for Black, for instance, with waiting.

43. ♖c5+ ♔g6 44. ♖xh5?!

44. gxh5+ This is better. However I wanted to avoid having an "edge pawn". The idea was perhaps to use it as a shield.

44... ♖e1 45. ♖a5

(see diagram next page)

Position after: 45. ♖a5

45... ♖g1+?

45... ♖e6 This is better.

46. ♔f3 ♖f1+ 47. ♔g2 ♖e1

48. ♔f3?

White returns the mistake. I was afraid of ghosts.

48. ♖xa6+ ♔g5 49. ♔g3 ♖g1+ 50. ♔f3 ♖f1+

Position after: 50... ♖f1+

51. ♔e3 ♔xg4 52. ♔d4 This is winning. Black's bishop and king are very bad.

48... ♖f1+?

Black insists on checks.

49. ♔g3 ♖g1+ 50. ♔f4 ♖f1+ 51. ♔e5?

Position after: 51. ♔e5?

The festival of mistakes continues. White's king goes active but this allows Black to defend. However, you should know that this game was started at 2 am due to the time difference!

51... ♔g5?

Black errs at last.

51... ♖f6! This would have kept some defensive chances.

52. ♖xa6 ♔xg4 53. ♖a7 ♖e1+ 54. ♔d4 ♔f5 55. ♔d5

There is no need to rush.

(see diagram next page)

Position after: 55. ♔d5

55... ♖e8 56. ♖f7+ ♔g6 57. ♖f6+ ♔g5 58. ♖e6 ♖d8+ 59. ♔c6 ♔f5 60. ♖e5+ ♔f4 61. ♔c7 ♖a8

Position after: 61... ♖a8

62. b5

With all the pieces safe (I was concerned only not to blunder at 5 am) it is time to advance.

62... ♖a7+ 63. ♔b6 ♖a3 64. ♖e7 ♖a8 65. ♔b7 ♖a3 66. b6 ♗e4+ 67. ♖xe4+

The quickest win.

67... ♔xe4 68. ♔c7 ♖xc3

Position after: 68... ♖xc3

Desperation.

69. dxc3 ♔d3 70. b7 ♔xc3 71. b8=♕ ♔c2 72. ♕b4 c3 73. ♔d6 ♔d3 74. ♔d5 c2 75. ♕e1 c1=♕ 76. ♕xc1

1-0

Game 157

♙ Gufeld, Eduard (2525)
♟ Ermenkov, Evgenij (2520)
🌍 Jurmala 1978

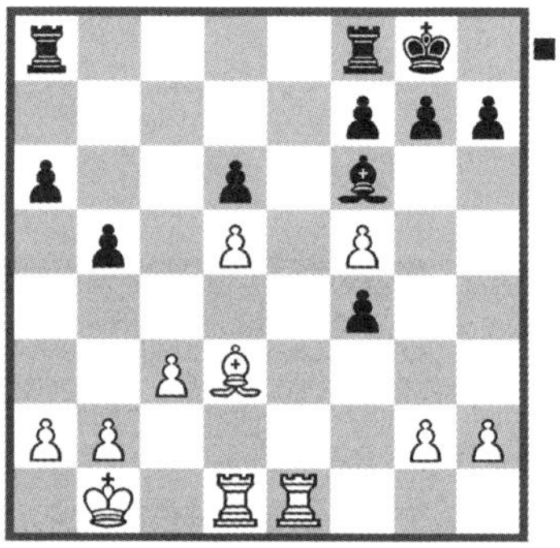

In the next example Black is optically preferable in a balanced position. It is easier for Black to play. White must find a way to activate his bad bishop and launch a queenside majority – not an easy task because the white king is there.

21... ♗e5

Obviously Black makes space for the king, blocking the file and liberating the majority at the same time.

22. ♖e4 ♖fc8 23. a4 ♖c5

A very good move, both defensive and attacking.

24. ♗e2

24. axb5 axb5 25. ♖b4

Position after: 25. ♖b4

This looks simpler. 25... ♖xd5 [25... ♖a5?! 26. c4! This gives White a plus after the following. 26... ♖a4! 27. ♖xb5 g5 28. fxg6 hxg6] 26. ♖xb5 The position is balanced.

24... g5

Black immediately advances on the kingside.

24... bxa4 25. ♖xa4 a5 This is also an interesting solution that is solid for Black.

25. fxg6

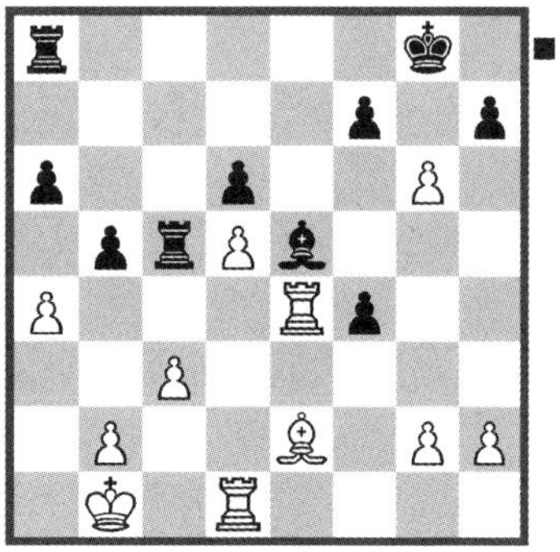

Position after: 25. fxg6

This is the lesser evil, rather than leaving the pawn vulnerable on f5.

25... hxg6!

This creates a dangerous grouping in the center and gives Black the h-file if needed.

26. ♔c2 ♔g7 27. ♖b4 bxa4!?

27... ♖e8!? This does not achieve anything because of the calm 28. ♗f1!. [28. axb5? ♗xc3!∓]

28. ♖xa4 a5

Black's queenside set-up is now safe.

29. ♖da1 f5

(see diagram next page)

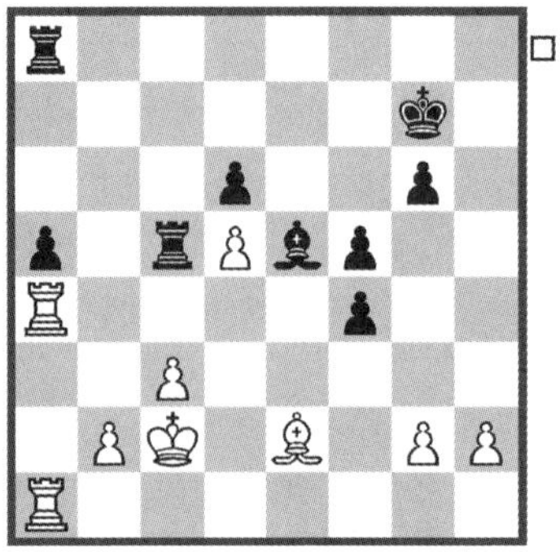

Position after: 29... f5

30. ♖1a2?!

An unclear move. White lacks a reasonable plan. Now it is clear that Black has an easier game.

30. ♖4a3 This should have been played instead. The idea is to advance b4. 30... ♔f6 31. b4 ♖c7 32. bxa5 ♖ac8 The game is balanced.

30... g5 31. h3 ♔f6 32. c4?!

Weakening a lot of dark squares.

32. ♖4a3 Again this would have been good. 32... ♖g8!? 33. ♖xa5 ♖xa5 34. ♖xa5 g4 35. hxg4 fxg4 This should be drawish.

32... ♖e8 33. b3?!

A move made without an idea.

33. ♖xa5 ♖xa5 34. ♖xa5 ♗xb2 35. ♗h5 The endgame is equal.

33... ♗d4

Position after: 33... ♗d4

34. ♔d3?

A direct and fatal mistake.

34. ♗f3 This was necessary instead. 34... ♖e3 35. ♖xa5 ♖xa5 36. ♖xa5 ♖c3+ 37. ♔d2 ♖xb3 This looks optically better for Black, but it is still equal.

34... ♗f2!

White probably missed this response. The bishop comes to e1 and Black invades via the e-file. The game is over.

35. ♖xa5 ♗e1

35... ♖xa5 36. ♖xa5 ♗e1 This wins as well.

36. ♖xc5 ♖e3+ 37. ♔c2 ♖xe2+ 38. ♔b1 ♖xa2 39. ♖c6 ♖xg2 40. ♖xd6+

(see diagram next page)

Position after: 40. ♖xd6+

40... ♔f7 41. c5 f3 42. ♖d7+ ♔e8 43. c6 f2 44. d6 f1=♕ 45. ♖e7+ ♔f8

0-1

Game 158

♙ Andersson, Ulf (2560)
♟ Stean, Michael F
Sao Paulo 1979

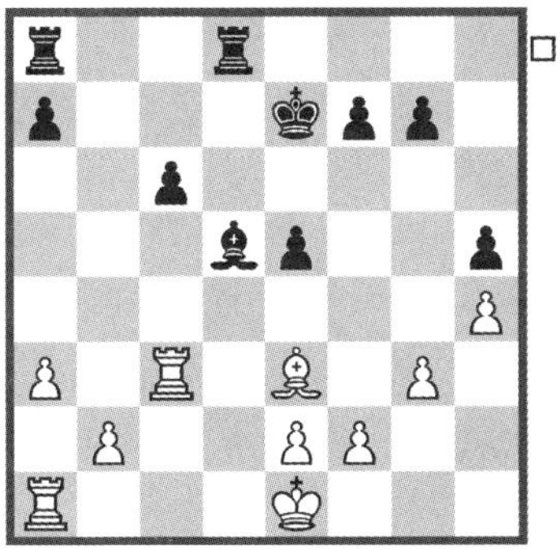

White is better here because of his more compact structure. Black's bishop is not good enough to compensate for this fully. However there is still no easy way for White to make progress. First, it is important to fix the opponent's pawns and prevent the annoying march ...a5-a4.

19. b4! ♖db8 20. ♗d2!

A very fine move to prevent ...a5.

20. ♖c5 This is bad because of 20... ♖b5.

20... ♔e6

Black threatens ...a5.

20... a5? 21. bxa5 ♖xa5 22. ♖e3 White wins a pawn.

21. ♖c5

There is no need to rush.

21... ♖b5 22. ♖cc1 f6 23. a4!

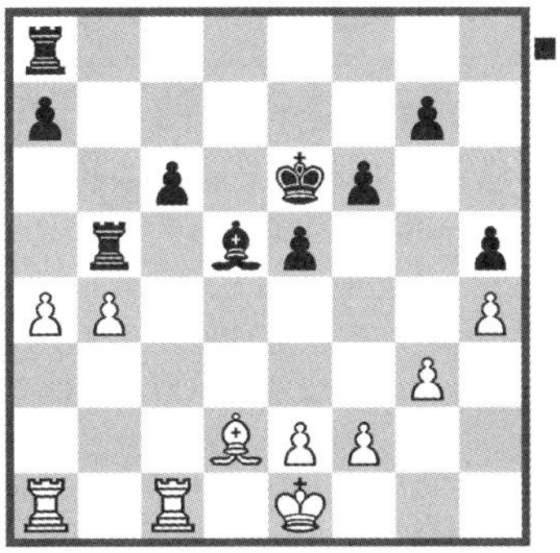

Position after: 23. a4!

23... ♖b7 24. ♖c5 ♖g8

Generally it is good for Black to play ...g5.

24... a6 A strictly defensive move and a solid one. However it is hard to opt for such a "weakening" move.

25. f3!

Restricting the black bishop, activating the king and preventing ...g5.

25... f5?

Black voluntarily weakens the dark squares in the center with no significant benefit.

A) 25... g5?? 26. hxg5 fxg5 27. e4

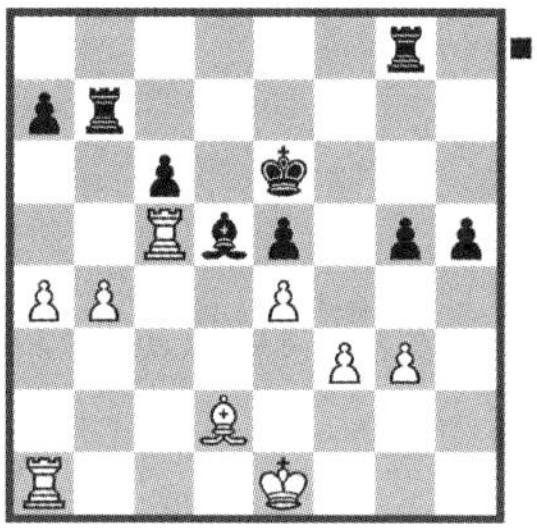

Position after: 27. e4

27... ♗b3 28. ♖a3+–

B) 25... e4! If Black wanted to play actively, this would have been the perfect option. The pawn stays on f6 to block the white bishop and create a shield for the black king. 26. fxe4 ♗xe4 27. ♖xh5 ♗d5 Having the white rook misplaced is obviously good for Black. However Black was not prepared to go for drastic measures.

26. ♔f2 ♖d8 27. ♗c3 e4

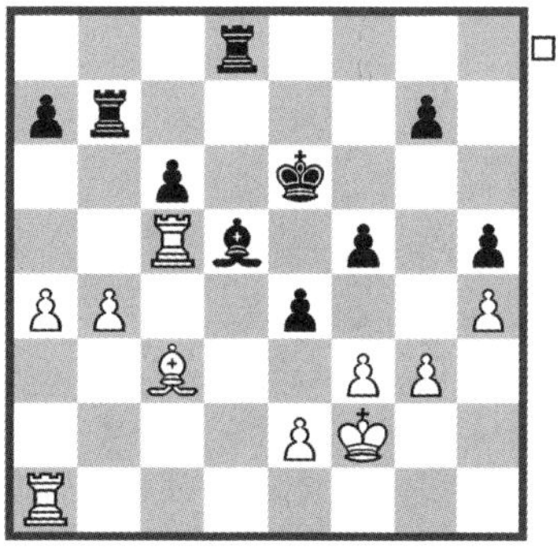

Position after: 27... e4

Black is consistent.

28. ♖d1 ♖dd7 29. ♔e3 g6 30. f4?!

White was focused on using the dark squares to invade the queenside. Nevertheless this move should not have been played now – one important reason being that it could have been played at any later time.

30. ♔f4 Clearly better. The idea is ♔g5 at some timely moment.

30... ♖d6 31. ♖b1

White prepares to regroup. The target is the a7-pawn!

31... ♖dd7?

Now Black's defense simply collapses. Black's pawn stays on a7 and will be taken.

31... a6! This was necessary here. 32. ♖a5 This can be parried as follows. 32... ♖a7 33. ♗d4

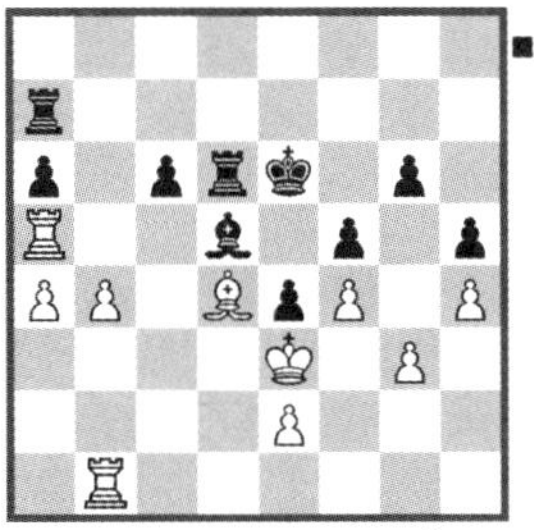

Position after: 33. ♗d4

33... ♖a8 Black's defense is still solid. 34. ♖a1 ♖dd8! Black can sufficiently defend the a8-rook.

32. ♗d4 ♔f7

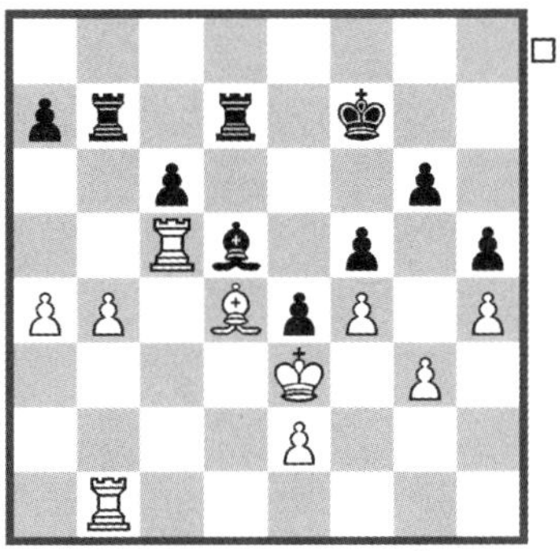

Position after: 32... ♔f7

33. ♖b2?

33. ♖a5! Preventing ...a6 once and for all.

33... ♔e6?

33... a6! 34. ♖a5 ♗c4 This complicates White's task.

34. ♔d2

The king reaches c3 and White would be able to regroup. The two rooks belong on a5 and a6 with a win. Black is unable to prevent this.

34... ♔f7

34... a6 35. ♖a5 ♗c4 Now this just fails to 36. ♔c3.

35. ♔c3 ♔e6 36. ♖a5 ♔f7 37. ♖a6 ♖e7 38. ♗c5

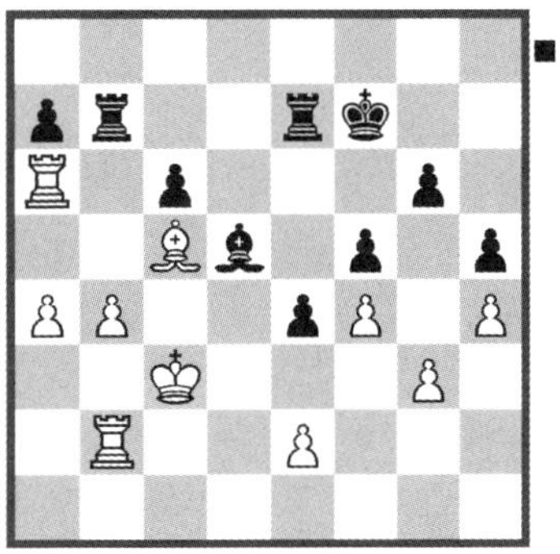

Position after: 38. ♗c5

38... ♖ed7 39. ♖d2 ♖bc7 40. ♗e3 ♖b7 41. ♗c5 ♖bc7 42. ♖c2

There is no need to rush.

42... ♖b7 43. ♔b2 ♖dc7 44. ♔a3

Finally. The king defends the a3-pawn, the bishop is free and will liberate c5 for the rook.

44... ♖d7 45. e3 ♖dc7 46. ♗d4 ♖d7 47. ♖c5 ♖bc7 48. ♔b2

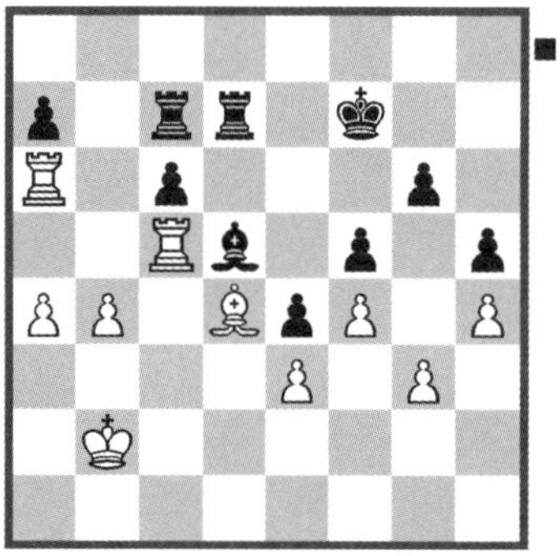

Position after: 48. ♔b2

There is no need to rush. Even the king should be improved before any operation. There is no reason to allow a move like ...♗c4, so the king goes to c3 to prevent it.

48... ♖b7 49. ♔c3 ♖b6 50. ♖ca5 ♖xa6 51. ♖xa6 ♗a2 52. ♖xc6

This is even stronger. The two threats ...♖a6 and ♖f6 cannot be parried. So Black resigned.

1-0

12 Exchange Problems

This chapter refers to a very specific problem in chess which is not related to any of the others presented here.

Nevertheless, there is a clear connection to the issue of majority, for instance – the side with the better majority should generally go for the exchange. However, should you trade a better piece for a worse one? There are many factors that you should take into account when deciding: consider carefully the pieces that are **remaining on the board** after the exchange, consider the current pieces' activities and space, and be aware of theoretically drawish endgames that may arise where the extra material cannot help you convert, etc.

Many of these factors will determine your decision and we will try to facilitate your decision-making by presenting some very important examples here.

Game 159

♙ Aronin, Lev Solomonovich
♟ Smyslov, Vassily V
🌍 Moscow 1951

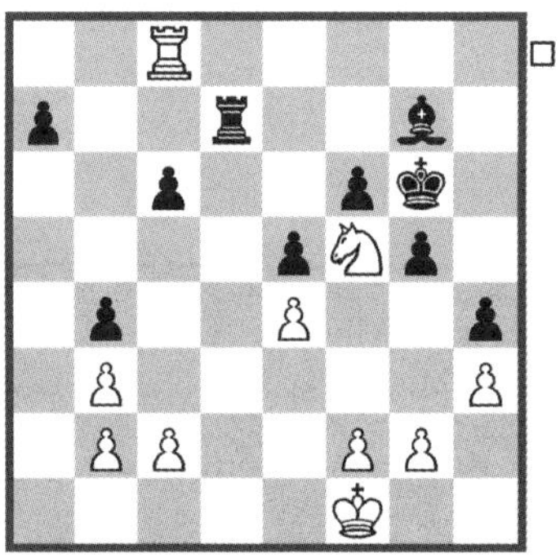

This is a completely winning situation for White. The knight dominates the rook and is ready to capitalize on the weaknesses, and the king is solid in the center. Instead of winning normally White decides to choose a forcing line.

42. ♖g8?!

A) 42. ♔e2 This clearly wins.

B) 42. ♖xc6 This wins as well.

42... ♔h7 43. ♖xg7+??

A terrible mistake. White simply missed Black's fascinating defensive idea.

43. ♖c8 This only wastes time with a trivial win.

43... ♖xg7 44. ♘xg7 ♔xg7 45. g4

Position after: 45. g4

This was White's idea. It appears that the kingside would be frozen with an easy win for White on the queenside, or that perhaps White's outside passer would be created on the h-file. Alas for White, the great Smyslov had something completely shocking in mind.

45... hxg3! 46. fxg3 g4!! 47. h4

47. hxg4 ♔g6 48. ♔g2 ♔g5 49. ♔f3 c5 This leads to a draw.

47... c5 48. ♔e2 ♔h7 49. ♔d3

Position after: 49. ♔d3

49... ♔h6

But not 49... ♔g6?? because the pawn on f5 would be taken with check and White would eventually win after the following. 50. ♔c4 f5 51. exf5+ ♔xf5 52. ♔xc5 a5 53. ♔d5

50. c3

50. ♔c4?? This would be fatal and Black would win due to a zugzwang as follows. 50... f5 51. exf5 e4

Position after: 51... e4

52. c3 a5 53. cxb4 axb4!

50... a5 51. cxb4 axb4

½-½

Game 160

♙ Padevsky, Nikola Bochev
♟ Barcza, Gedeon
Kecskemet 1966

White is evidently better here. The bishop is simply useless. However, the way to convert is not clear. White still cannot use his knight effectively.

28. ♕d3!

The correct approach. Without queens on the board White can more easily use his queenside majority and even the king may become active. On the other flank Black cannot achieve anything because of White's fixing with the h5-pawn!

28... ♕c5

28... ♕xd3+? This would of course have been a serious strategic mistake.

29. ♘e4 ♕b6 30. b4!

White gains space. This is looking dangerous for Black, although it's not really the case

30... ♔a7 31. ♔b3 ♕c7 32. f3

(see diagram next column)

There is no need to rush.

Position after: 32. f3

32... ♔b8 33. c5! ♔c8 34. ♘d2!

The knight goes to c4 from where it may threaten to jump to b6.

34... ♕d7?

Capitulation. Black must keep his queens on the board.

35. ♕xd7+ ♔xd7 36. ♔c4 ♔c6 37. a4 b5+

Position after: 37... b5+

This looks bad, but any other moves would not have helped Black. You should see if you can find a winning plan for White in other lines here.

38. cxb6 ♔xb6 39. ♘e4 a5

Once again the previous comment applies – another exercise for you.

40. b5 ♗f4 41. ♔d4 ♔c7

Position after: 41... ♔c7

42. ♔d3

White decides not to rush. The next moves were played to wait.

42... ♔b6 43. ♔c4 ♔c7 44. ♔d4 ♗c1 45. ♔d3 ♗a3 46. ♘d2 ♗b4 47. ♘c4 ♗e1 48. ♘e5

Position after: 48. ♘e5

48... f6 49. ♘c4 ♔d7 50. ♔e3 ♗b4 51. ♔d4 ♗e1 52. ♔e4 ♔c7 53. ♔f4 ♔d7 54. ♔g4 ♔c7 55. ♔f4 ♔d7 56. ♔e3 ♗b4 57. ♔e4 ♗e1

Position after: 57... ♗e1

58. g4

White goes for some flank activity.

58... ♗b4 59. ♔f4 ♗e1 60. ♔e3 ♗c3 61. ♔d3 ♗e1 62. ♔e4 ♗c3 63. f4! ♗e1

Position after: 63... ♗e1

64. f5!

This is the move that unlocks the door. Black's passed pawn is not a significant factor at all.

64... e5 65. ♔d5 ♗b4 66. b6 ♗e1 67. ♘d6 ♗f2 68. b7 ♔c7 69. ♔e6 ♗a7 70. ♘e4 ♔xb7 71. ♔f7 ♔c6 72. ♔xg7

Position after: 72. ♔xg7

72... ♔d5 73. ♘xf6+ ♔d4 74. ♔xh6 e4 75. ♘xe4 ♔xe4 76. ♔g6

1-0

Game 161

♙ Ivkov, Borislav
♟ Taimanov, Mark E
Belgrade 1956

The position may look double-edged but in actual fact it is not. White's majority is distant and in several types of endgame this may result in the creation of an outside passed pawn. Moreover, the black king is far from the battle-field. White's next move is simply perfect and direct.

28. b3!

An excellent and very practical decision. White offers Black a choice of three (!) different types of endgame: a rook, knight or pawn endgame. All of them are clearly in White's favor. Black's decides on a knight endgame.

28. ♘b3 a4 29. ♘d2 ♘b6 Black has some chances to survive.

28... ♘d6

A) A pawn endgame results after the following. 28... exd4 29. ♖xc4 ♖xc4 30. bxc4

Position after: 30. bxc4

This is lost for Black. The game may continue as follows. 30... ♔g6 31. ♔b2!

♔f5 32. ♔a3 ♔e6 33. ♔a4 ♔d6 34. ♔b5 White has a clear win.

B) The rook endgame is also hopeless for Black after the following. 28... exd4 29. ♖xc4

Position after: 29. ♖xc4

29... ♖d8 [29... ♖e8 30. ♖xd4 ♖e2 31. ♖d2 This is also winning for White.] 30. ♖c5

29. ♖xc8 ♘xc8 30. ♘c6 a4

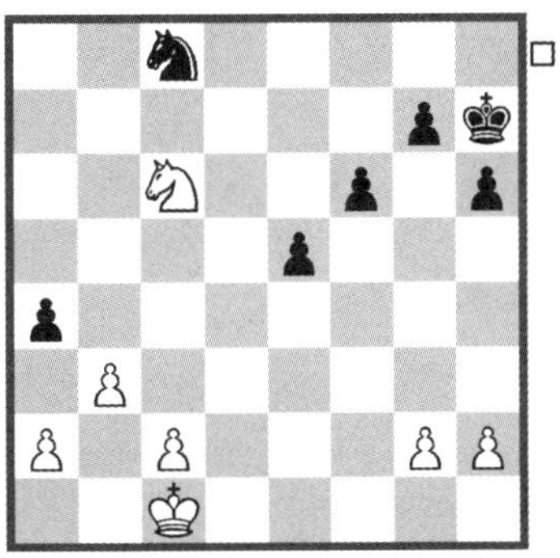

Position after: 30... a4

Practically, the best.

31. bxa4!

White is not afraid of disconnecting the pawns. Black has problems stopping this pawn.

31... ♔g6 32. a5 ♔f7 33. a6 ♔e6 34. a7 ♘b6

The previous moves were obvious.

35. ♘b4 ♔d6 36. c4 ♔c5 37. ♘d5 ♘a8

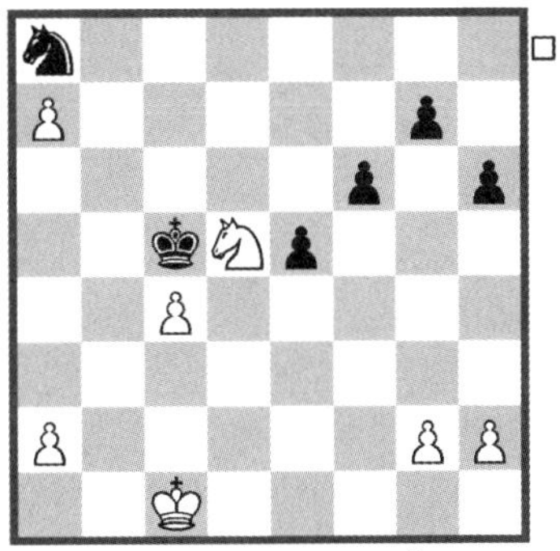

Position after: 37... ♘a8

38. ♘e3

38. ♔d2 Perhaps more precise. However this move is easily missed. Black is unable to play the following. 38... ♔b6. 38... ♔xc4 39. ♘e3+ ♔c5 40. ♘f5 ♔b6

Position after: 40... ♔b6

41. ♘xg7 ♔xa7 42. ♘f5 h5 43. h4 This

would give White two outside passed pawns on both flanks.

38... ♔b6 39. ♘f5 ♔xa7 40. ♘xg7 ♘b6 41. g4!

This move fixes the target on h6. The previous and next moves are clear.

41... ♘xc4 42. ♘f5 e4 43. ♘xh6 ♘e5

Position after: 43... ♘e5

44. h4

The quickest win.

44... ♔b6 45. h5 ♔c5 46. ♔d2 ♔d5

46... ♔d4 47. ♘f5+

47. ♘f5! ♘f3+

47... ♘xg4 48. ♘e3+!

48. ♔e2 ♘g5 49. h6

1-0

Game 162

♙ Dzindzichashvili, Roman
♟ Dementiev, Oleg I
Kaliningrad 1972

Due to the strong h6-pawn White is absolutely winning here. Moreover, Black also has problems on the queenside. It is clear that the power of the passer would increase with any exchange. Therefore White plays as follows.

51. ♗xd7! ♔xd7 52. ♗f4! ♗xf4 53. ♔xf4 ♔e7

Position after: 53... ♔e7

54. ♘f6!

An easy win!

54... ♘xf6 55. gxf6+ ♔xf6 56. b4! cxb4 57. ♔e3 b3 58. ♔d2

Black resigned.

1-0

Game 163

♙ Hansen, Lars Bo (2572)
♟ Holst, Allan (2358)
Copenhagen 2004

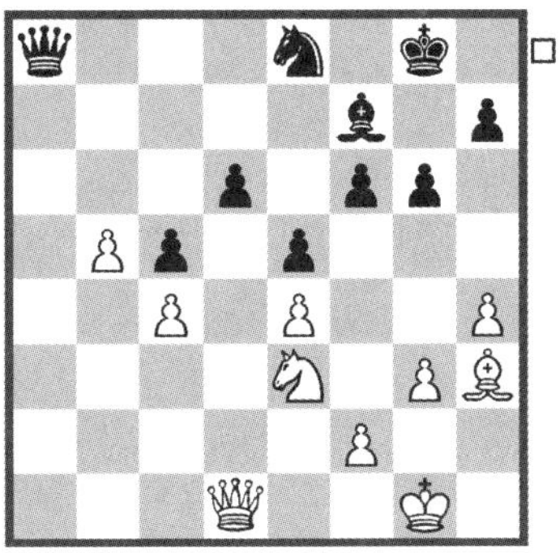

White is practically a pawn up and winning. Black is passive, with a useless backward pawn and is simply unable to properly deal with White's passer. Clearly, the conversion would be straightforward if the knight came to d5. Thus, the black bishop must be eliminated first.

32. ♗d7! ♕b8

32... ♕xe4 33. ♗xe8 ♗xe8 34. ♕xd6 This wins quickly.

33. ♗c6

33. ♗xe8 ♗xe8 34. ♘d5 This wins as well, but White wanted to eliminate the black bishop instead – it is a matter of style.

33... ♕d8 34. ♗d5 ♘c7 35. ♗xf7+ ♔xf7

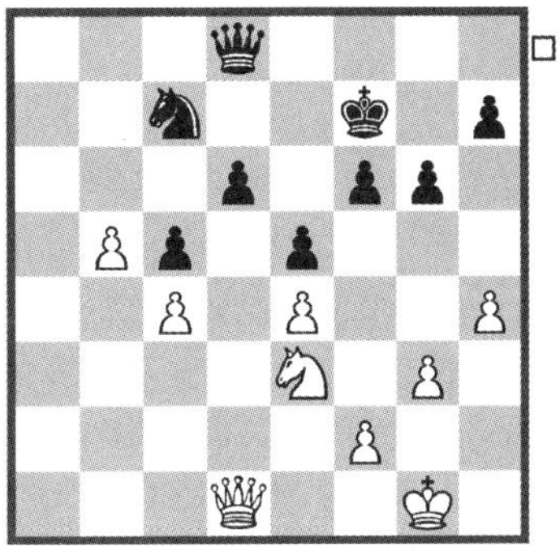

Position after: 35... ♔xf7

36. ♕a4

36. ♘d5 This wins too, but why trade the knights?

36... ♕b8 37. ♕a5 ♘e6 38. b6 ♘d8 39. ♕a7+ ♕b7 40. ♘d5

After eliminating Black's control of the d5-square White jumps.

40... ♔e6

(see diagram next page)

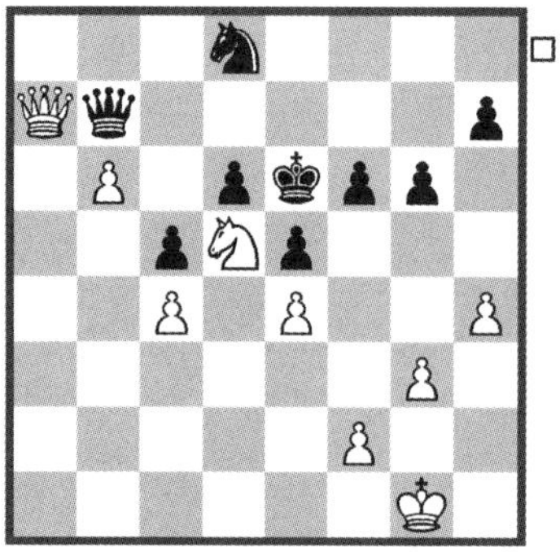

Position after: 40... ♔e6

41. g4

White improves his position on the king-side as well as surrounding the black king.

41... f5 42. exf5+!

White forces play and creates threats on the kingside.

42. f3 This could also have been played.

42... gxf5 43. g5 f4 44. ♕a3! ♔d7 45. ♕h3+ ♔c6 46. ♕f3

Position after: 46. ♕f3

46... ♔d7 47. ♘f6+ ♔e7 48. ♕h5

The quickest win.

48. ♕xb7+ ♘xb7 49. ♘xh7 Another simple and even more methodical win.

48... ♔e6 49. ♘d5 ♔d7 50. ♕xh7+ ♔c8 51. g6

Black resigned.

1-0

Game 164

♙ Faibisovich, Vadim Z
♟ Westerinen, Heikki MJ
🌍 Vilnius 1969

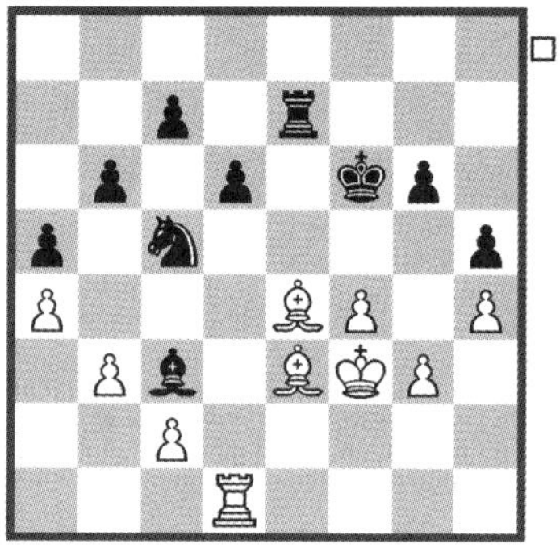

White is much better in our next endgame. But how to proceed? There are no obvious ways to invade, while the sole weakness, the g6-pawn, is easily defended.

43. ♗xc5!

Very brave, but a concrete and logical decision. White destroys Black's majority, tying up the black troops to the defense of the g6-pawn and invades with his king after this – White has so many advantages!

43... bxc5 44. ♖d5

The point of the plan.

44... ♖g7 45. ♖g5 ♗d2

Black can only sit and wait. This move prevents f5 at some point.

46. ♔e2 ♗c3

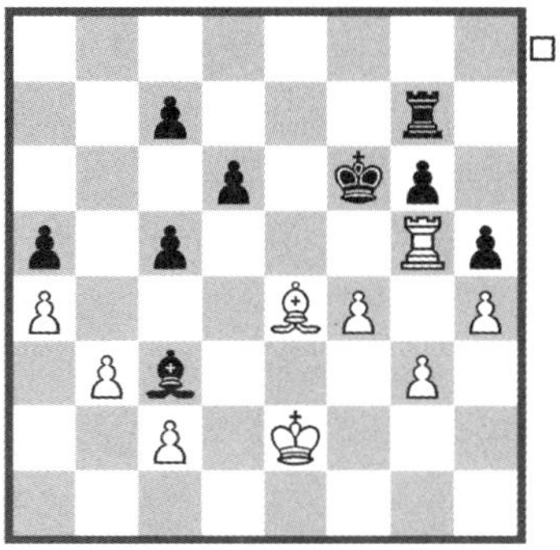

Position after: 46... ♗c3

47. ♔d3

But not: 47. f5? gxf5 48. ♖xf5+ ♔e6

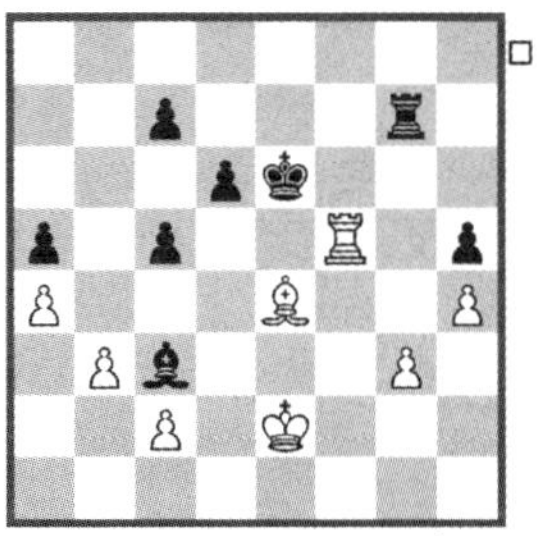

Position after: 48... ♔e6

49. ♔f3 ♗e5 with a draw. There is no need for pawn action – you should first fully activate all the troops.

47... ♗e1 48. ♔c4 ♔f7 49. ♔b5 ♗c3

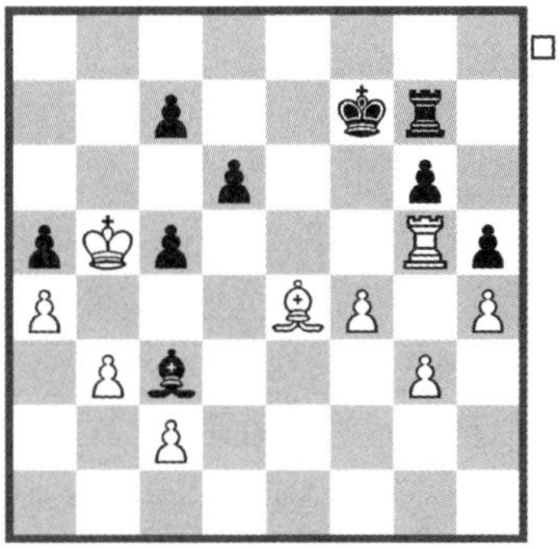

Position after: 49... ♗c3

50. ♖d5!

Now White switches to the a5 weakness. White prepares c3 to take the pawn and a win.

50... ♗e1 51. ♖d3 ♔f6 52. c3 ♖e7 53. ♗b7 ♖e2 54. ♔xa5 ♖c2 55. ♔b5

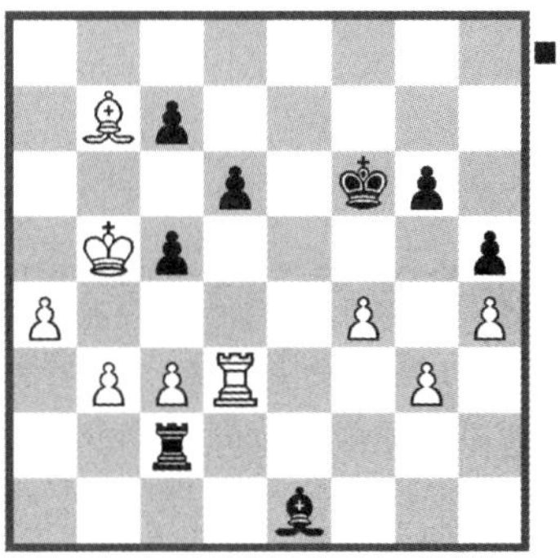

Position after: 55. ♔b5

55... ♗xc3

55... ♖xc3 56. ♖xc3 ♗xc3 57. ♗e4 This wins trivially.

56. a5 ♗e1 57. a6 c4 58. bxc4 ♗f2 59. ♖a3 c6+ 60. ♔xc6 ♖xc4+ 61. ♔xd6 ♗a7

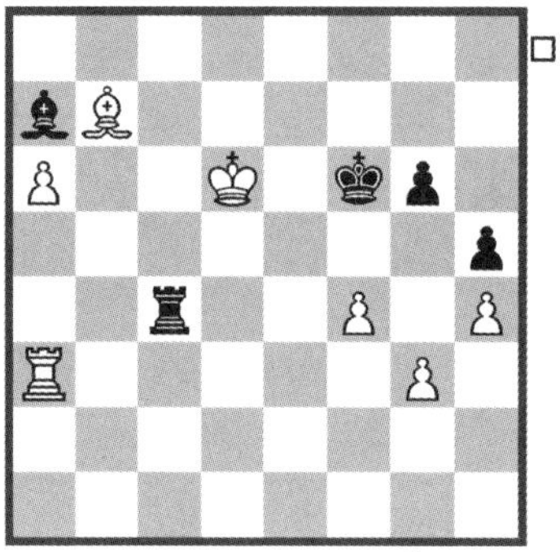

Position after: 61... ♗a7

The situation has stabilized. White has two extra pawns. The win is not complicated but there are some technical issues to solve.

62. ♗c6 ♖b4 63. ♔d7 ♖b1 64. ♖a5! ♖b3 65. ♖g5 ♖e3 66. ♔c7 ♖e7+ 67. ♗d7 ♗f2

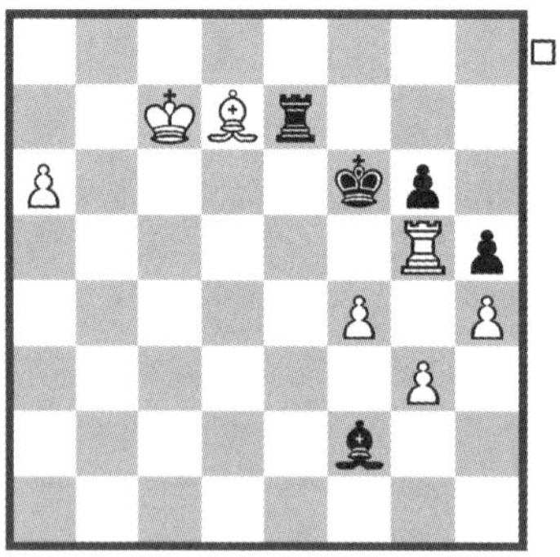

Position after: 67... ♗f2

68. f5!

Tactics serve strategy.

68... ♖e3 69. ♖xg6+ ♔f7 70. ♗e6+ ♔e7 71. ♖g7+

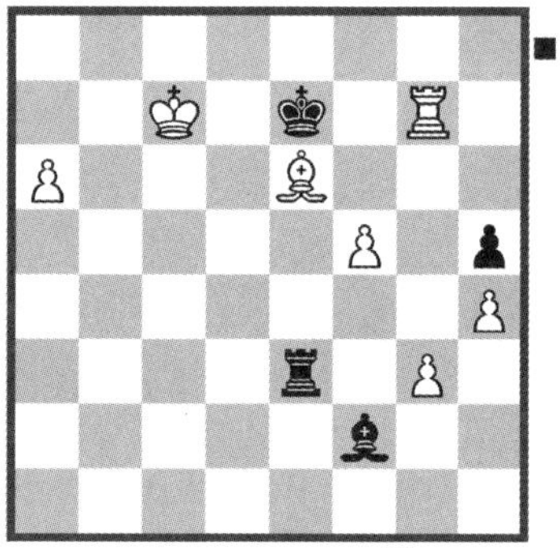

Position after: 71. ♖g7+

71... ♔f8 72. ♖f7+ ♔e8 73. a7

Black resigned.

1-0

Game 165

♙ Spassky, Boris Vasilievich (2640)
♟ Karpov, Anatoly (2705)
Montreal 1979

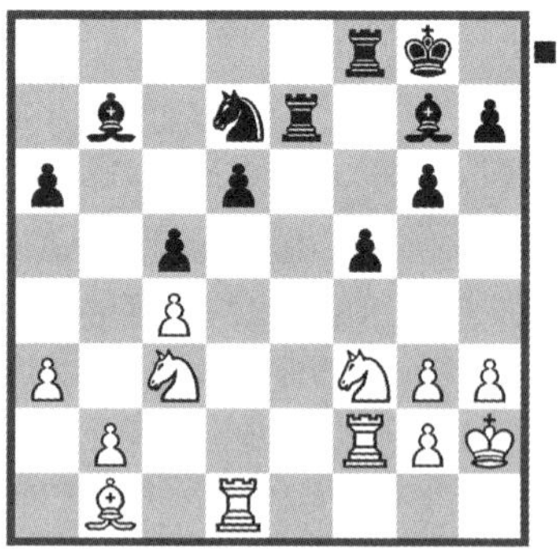

Spassky has played apathetically and achieved this unenviable situation. Black dominates due to his better structure and powerful bishop pair. Moreover, there is control of the important e-file. White attacks on d6, so Black on his move must make a concrete decision... and indeed Karpov found a convincing way to convert.

23... ♗xc3! 24. bxc3 ♖f6!

Black has voluntarily given away his most influential piece to damage White's structure, even on the queenside. The rook aims to protect the pawn from the f6-square, so having played 23... ♗xc3!, this is logical now. The bishop isn't blocked on g7, and the ♘d5-resource is prevented. The rest of the game will prove superbly that Karpov's decision was an excellent one.

25. ♖fd2

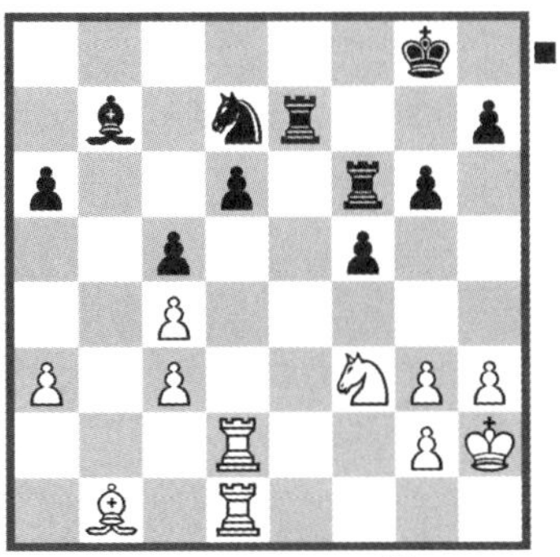

Position after: 25. ♖fd2

25... ♖e3

25... ♘e5 This is also possible. 26. ♘xe5 [26. ♖xd6? ♖xd6 27. ♖xd6 ♘xf3+

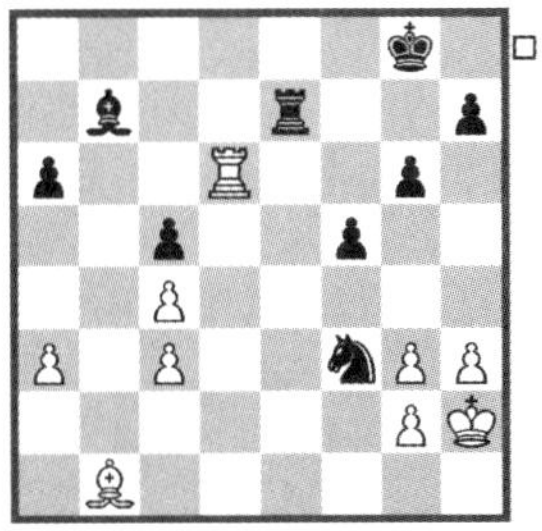

Position after: 27... ♘xf3+

28. gxf3 ♖e2+ This wins the poor bishop on b1.] 26... dxe5 This should lead to a win.

26. ♘g1?

Very passive.

26. ♖xd6 ♖xd6 27. ♖xd6 ♗xf3 28. gxf3 ♘e5 This gives Black a huge advantage.

26... ♔f7

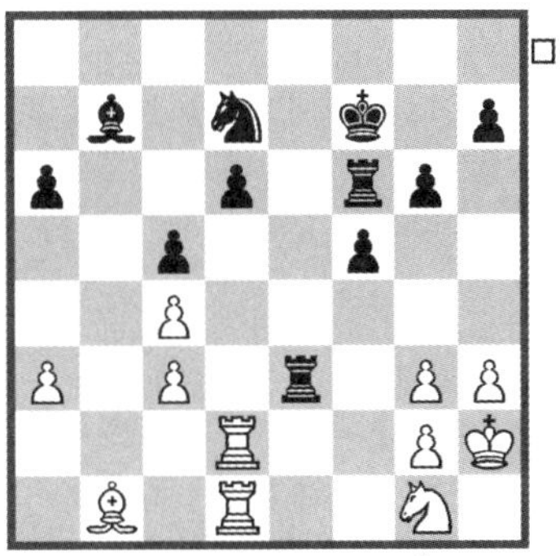

Position after: 26... ♔f7

26... ♘e5 This would have been very good, of course, perhaps even better than the played move. 27. ♖xd6 ♖xd6 28. ♖xd6 ♖xc3 White is in a terrible situation.

27. ♖xd6 ♖xd6 28. ♖xd6 ♔e7 29. ♖d3 ♖e1

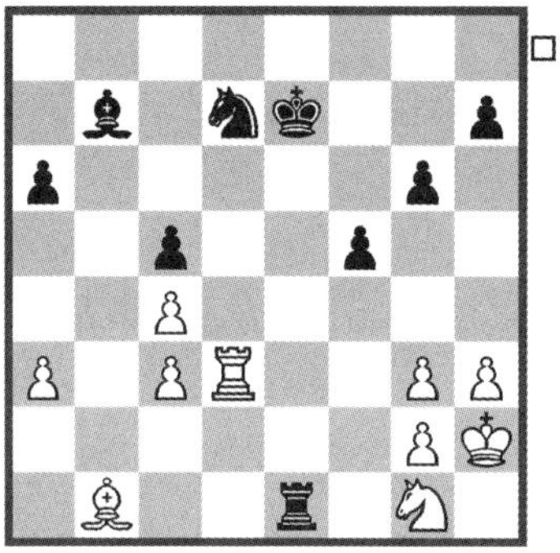

Position after: 29... ♖e1

30. ♗a2

30. ♗c2 ♘e5 31. ♖d2 ♘xc4 A line that superbly demonstrates that the white pieces are cramped in an open position.

30... ♖c1

30... ♖a1 31. ♖d2 ♘e5 This also wins.

31. ♘f3

Trying to make any active move.

31... ♗xf3!

Again a concrete decision and a logical solution to the exchange problem. Black could now play with a much better knight vs. White's poor bishop.

32. ♖xf3 ♘e5 33. ♖e3 ♔f6

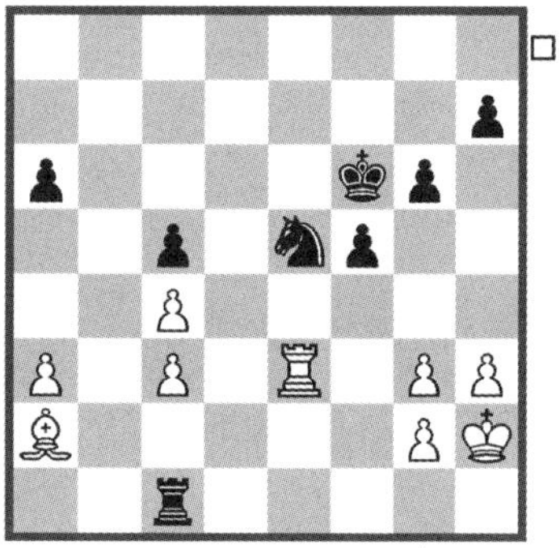

Position after: 33... ♔f6

The game is practically over. White has no moves.

34. ♗b3 a5 35. ♗a4 ♘xc4 36. ♖e8 ♖xc3

Position after: 36... ♖xc3

The rest is a matter of technique.

37. ♖c8 ♘e3

Everything wins.

38. ♗b5 c4 39. ♔g1 ♖c2 40. ♗c6 c3 41. ♗f3 g5 42. g4 f4

White resigned. The final position is a demonstration of brutal domination.

0-1

Game 166

♙ Azmaiparashvili, Zurab (2585)
♟ Montolio Benedicto, Cesar
San Sebastian 1991

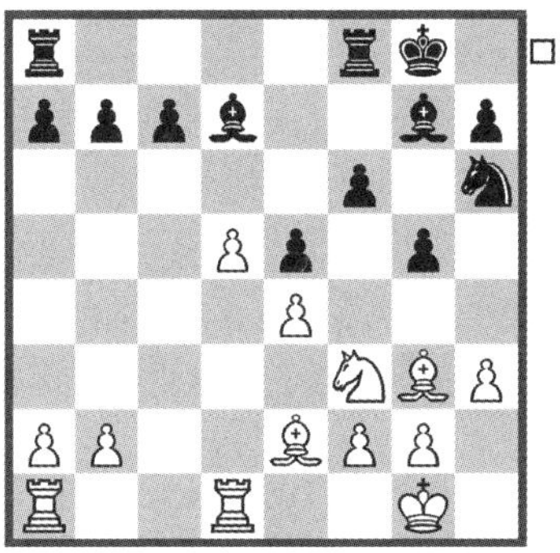

White is clearly much better. Black's army lacks harmony and his pawn structure is very damaged. The key squares are f5 and g4 and if White gets control over them then Black would be left without any play. Thus White plays as follows.

17. ♘d2! ♘f7

Black installs his knight on d6. Alas, this does not help at all.

17... f5 This achieves nothing. 18. f3!

Position after: 18. f3!

18... g4 19. hxg4 fxg4 20. ♘b3 Black is without play.

18. ♖ac1 ♖fc8 19. ♗g4!

Black's g7-bishop is a bad one, so let's force him to play with it. Your decision to exchange should be based on the pieces that will remain on the board, not on the pieces leaving the board!

19... ♗xg4 20. hxg4 ♘d6 21. f3

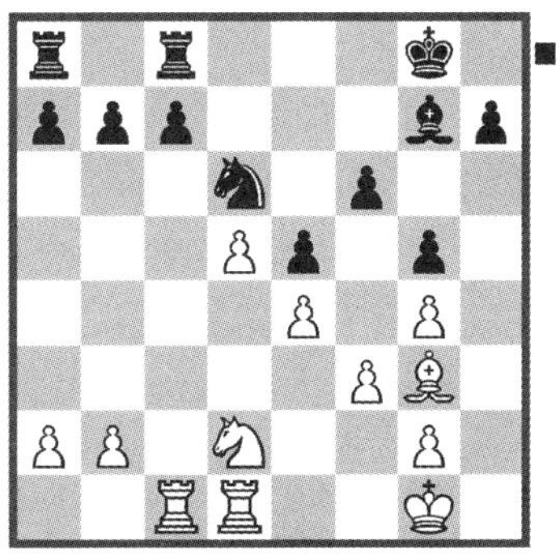

Position after: 21. f3

21... ♗f8 22. ♗f2 ♔f7 23. ♘b3 b6

New weaknesses have been provoked. It is now time to double up.

24. ♖c2

24. ♖c6 This is also ok. Yurab didn't want to intrude with the rook.

24... ♔e7 25. ♖dc1 ♔d7 26. ♘d2

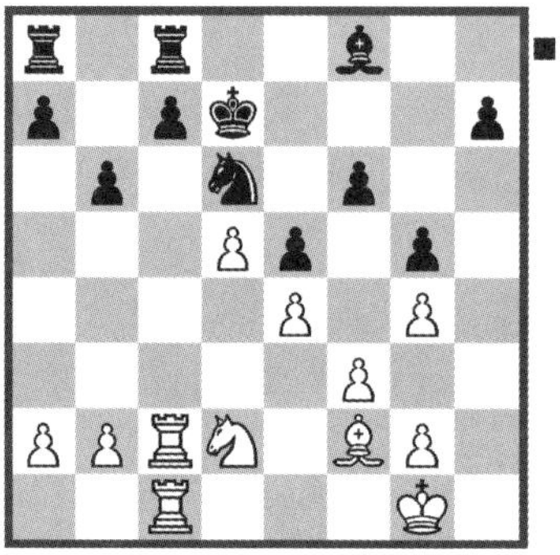

Position after: 26. ♘d2

The knight makes another journey. The targets are the f5- and h5-squares.

26... ♗e7 27. ♘f1 ♗f8

Black is paralyzed and can only wait.

28. ♘g3 ♗e7 29. ♖c6 ♖ab8 30. ♘h5 ♘e8 31. ♗e3 ♗d6 32. ♔f2 a5 33. ♖h1

Black cannot avoid material loss on the kingside, so he resigned.

1-0

Game 167

♙	Razuvaev, Yuri S	(2520)
♟	Azmaiparashvili, Zurab	(2460)
🌍	Minsk 1985	

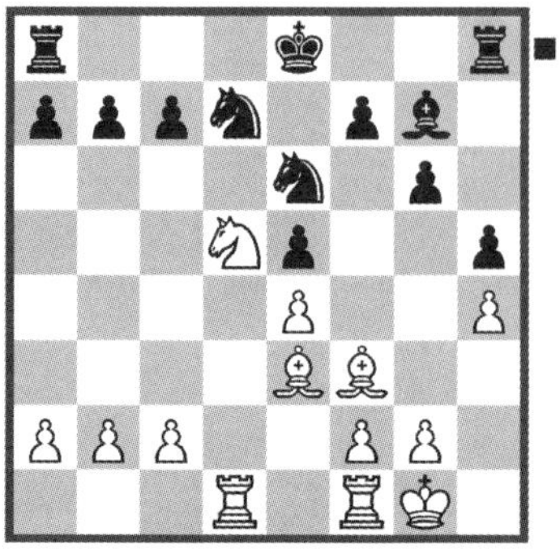

It may appear that the position is normal and balanced, or perhaps better for White due to his "bishop pair advantage". However Black has a powerful possibility to gain an initiative by occupying the soon-to-be weakened dark squares.

14... c6! 15. ♘c3

Alternatively 15. ♘b4 with ♘d3 deserved serious attention.

15... ♗f6! 16. g3 g5!

It is not often that you can see such an "anti-positional" but brilliant concept. The f5-square cannot be exploited. At the same time Black can exploit the dark squares as will become clear soon.

17. hxg5 ♗xg5 18. ♗xg5 ♘xg5

(see diagram next page)

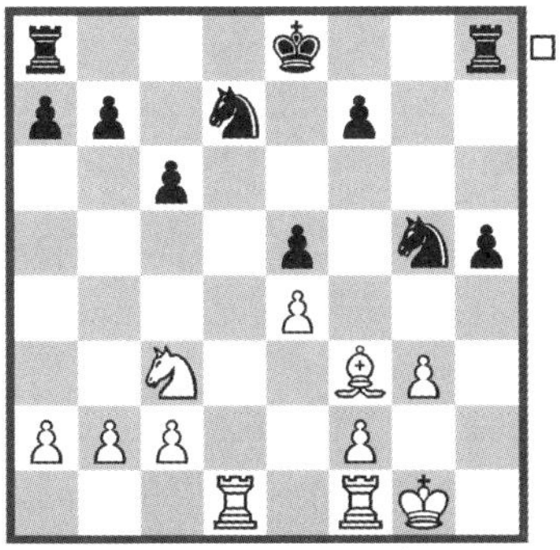

Position after: 18... ♘xg5

19. ♖d3

19. ♔g2 Transferring the rook to the h-file would have been natural. 19... h4 However, this keeps a plus for Black.

19... ♘c5 20. ♖e3 ♖d8

20... h4 This would have been more logical. It is not clear if the queenside rook belongs on the d-file. Perhaps after ...♔e7 this rook should go to the g-file.

21. ♖d1

If 21. ♗g2 then 21... h4.

21... ♖d4 22. ♗g2 h4

(see diagram next column)

An unpleasant choice for White. Advancing would be terrible. However after fxg3 the white pawn structure would be ruined and after gxh4 Black gets the f4-square and the g-file.

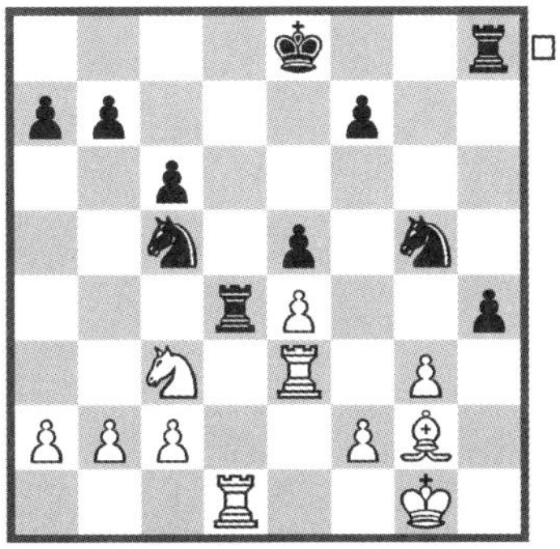

Position after: 22... h4

23. f4

White goes for active play.

23... ♘ge6 24. fxe5

24. f5 This should not be seriously considered. 24... ♘g5 White is hopeless.

24... h3

Of course, there is nothing wrong with the immediate 24... ♘d7.

25. ♗f1 ♘d7 26. ♖ed3 ♘xe5 27. ♖xd4 ♘xd4

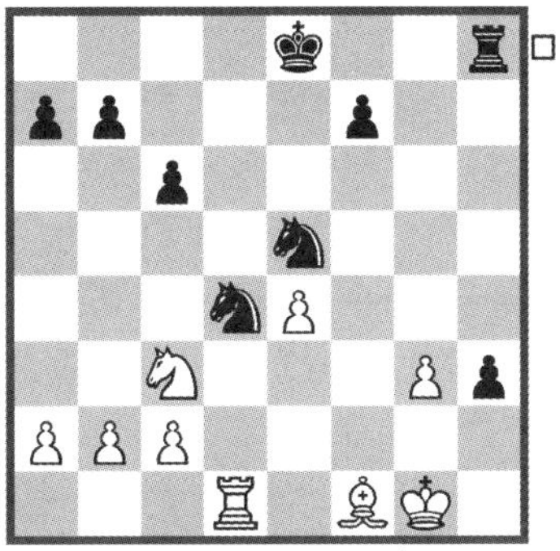

Position after: 27... ♘xd4

28. ♗e2

A) 28. ♗d3 ♖g8–+

B) 28. ♗xh3 This was White's last chance to hold. However, after 28... ♘xc2 White's vulnerable structure makes the evaluation clear – Black is fully dominant.

28... ♘xc2 29. ♔f2 ♘d4

Black's knights dance with style and power.

30. ♖h1 ♔e7

Now it is possible to play slowly.

31. ♘d1 ♔f6 32. ♘e3 ♘xe2

The simplest.

33. ♔xe2 ♔g5

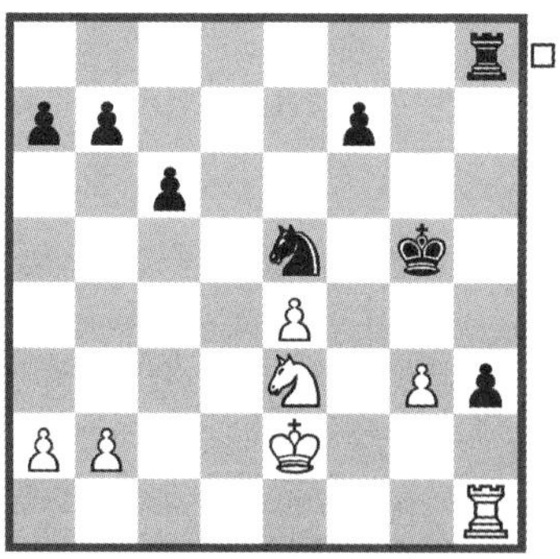

Position after: 33... ♔g5

White is almost in zugzwang.

34. ♖f1 h2 35. ♖h1 ♘g4 36. ♘f1 f5 37. ♘d2 ♖h3 38. exf5 ♔xf5 39. ♔f3 ♖h8 40. ♘c4 ♔g5

0-1

Game 168

♙ Seirawan, Yasser (2555)
♟ Sosonko, Gennadi (2595)
Bad Kissingen 1981

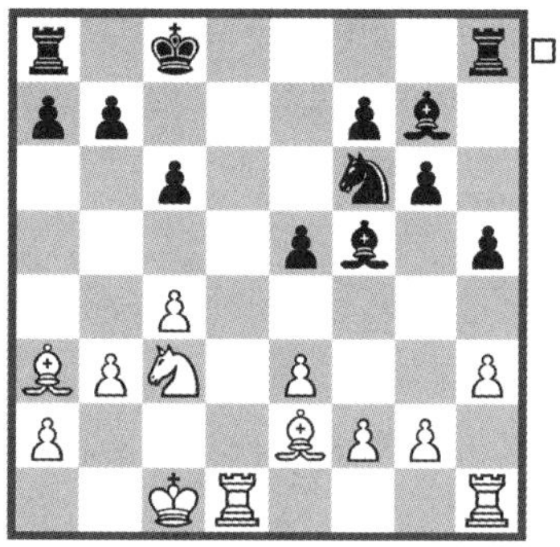

White is better here. Black lacks harmony and has some weak points. But how to exploit? Black wants to reduce material with ...♖d8 or ...♗f8 in order to neutralize White's initiative. Seirawan found one of the longest and deepest forced lines that I've ever seen, after which White obtains a stable and huge positional advantage.

14. g4! hxg4

14... ♗e6 This fails to 15. gxh5!.

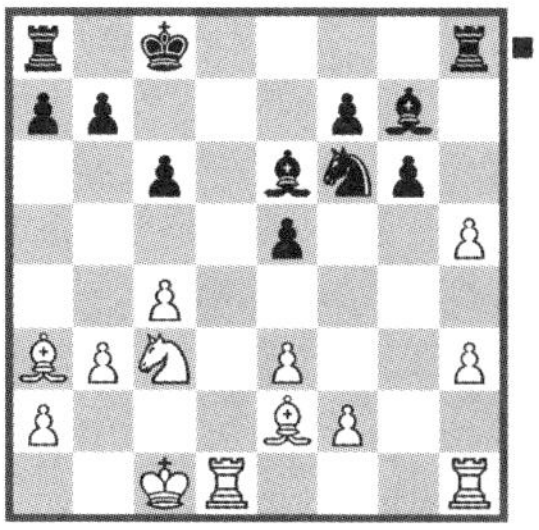

Position after: 15. gxh5!

15... gxh5 [15... ♘xh5 This is simply lost after 16. ♘e4 with the threat of ♘g5.] 16. ♖dg1 ♗f8 17. ♗xf8 ♖xf8 18. ♖g5 White wins.

15. hxg4 ♗xg4

A) 15... ♖xh1 16. ♖xh1 This is an even worse option for Black.

B) 15... ♘xg4 16. ♖xh8+ ♗xh8 17. ♖h1

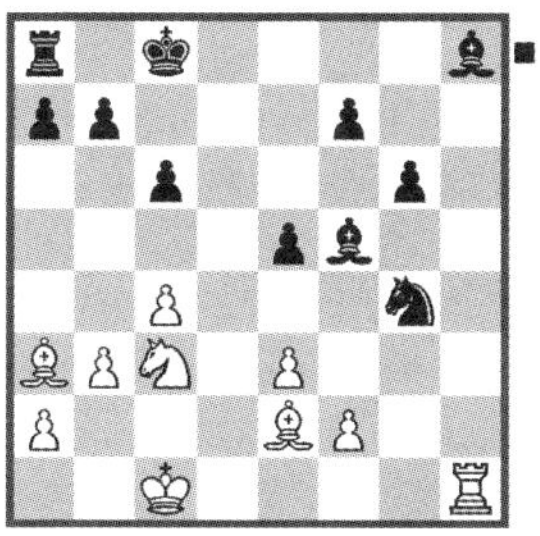

Position after: 17. ♖h1

17... ♔d7 18. ♖h7! The f7-pawn falls with a huge impact on Black's position.

16. ♖xh8+ ♗xh8

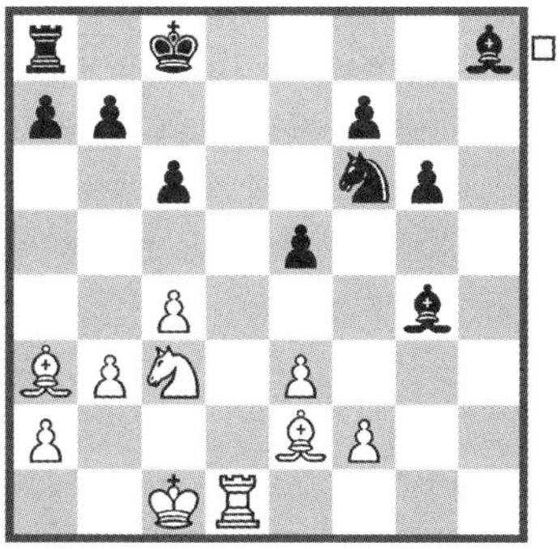

Position after: 16... ♗xh8

17. ♗e7!!

An amazing intermediate move and the point of White's plan.

17... ♗d7

The only move.

17... ♗xe2 18. ♖d8+ ♔c7 19. ♖xa8+–

18. ♖h1!?

18. a4! An engine move to fix Black's queenside pieces – let's assume it is stronger, but how can one find this? Anyway, I think Seirawan simply followed his plan.

18... ♗g7 19. ♗xf6 ♗xf6 20. ♘e4 ♗d8 21. ♖h7

(see diagram next page)

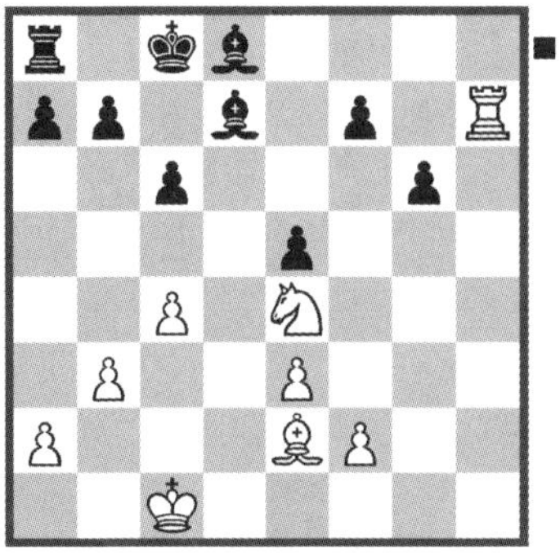

Position after: 21. ♖h7

21... ♗e8?

21... ♗f5! The move that neutralizes White's initiative. 22. ♘d6+ ♔d7

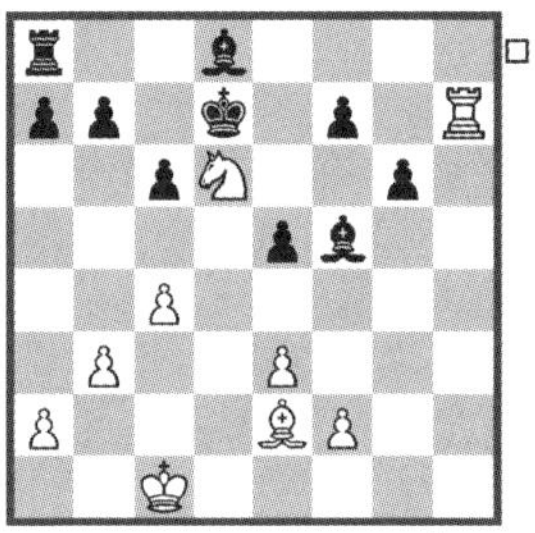

Position after: 22... ♔d7

23. ♘xf7 [23. ♘xf5 gxf5 24. ♖xf7+ ♗e7 25. ♖xf5 ♖f8 This leads to a draw.] 23... ♗e7! 24. ♘xe5+ ♔e6 25. ♘f3 ♔f6 Black has the threat of ...♗a3 and ♖d8, and according to the engine Black has a holdable position. However, during the game it is very difficult to go for this.

22. ♗g4+ ♔c7 23. ♗e6 ♗e7 24. ♗xf7 ♗xf7 25. ♖xf7 ♔d7 26. ♖g7 ♔e6

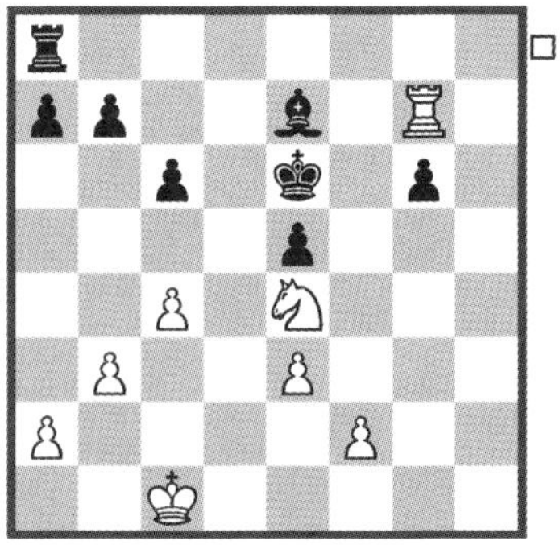

Position after: 26... ♔e6

As a result of the 13 (!) move long operation White has gained a strategically winning position. His first task is to consolidate and activate the king.

27. ♔d1 ♖f8 28. ♔e2 ♖f7 29. ♖g8 ♔f5 30. ♘g3+ ♔f6 31. ♖b8

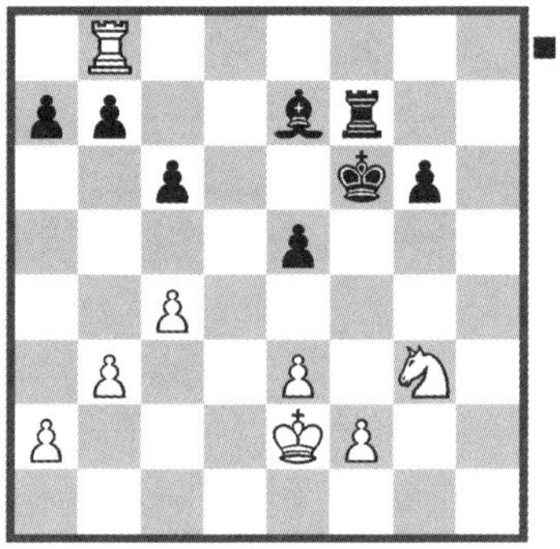

Position after: 31. ♖b8

White finds an active spot for his rook.

31... ♗f8 32. ♘e4+ ♔f5 33. f3

Securing control over the e4- and g4-squares.

33... g5 34. ♘f2 ♗d6 35. ♖g8 ♖h7

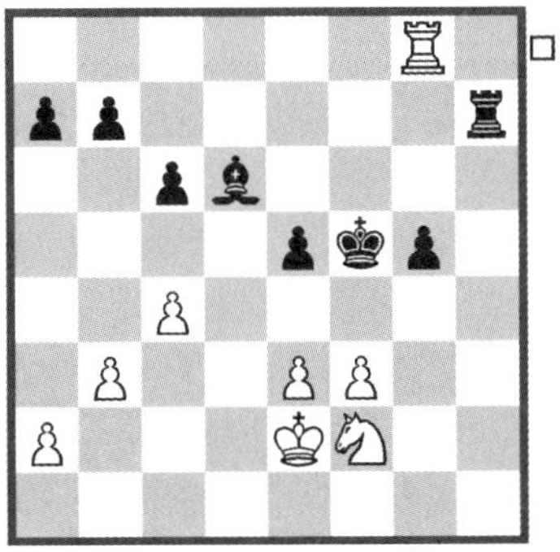

Position after: 35... ♖h7

36. a4?!

A logical move, removing the pawn from the 2nd rank, but it is not a direct continuation.

36. e4+! ♔e6 37. ♖g6+ ♔d7 38. ♘g4 Instead this would have been winning for White.

36... a6 37. ♘e4

Now this is strong – the a6-pawn is an additional target.

37. e4+ However, this is also good, as it was on the previous move.

37... ♗e7 38. ♖b8 b5

The idea is to reduce the pawn material. However White has a surprise – he takes the material under his own terms.

39. cxb5! cxb5 40. ♘g3+!

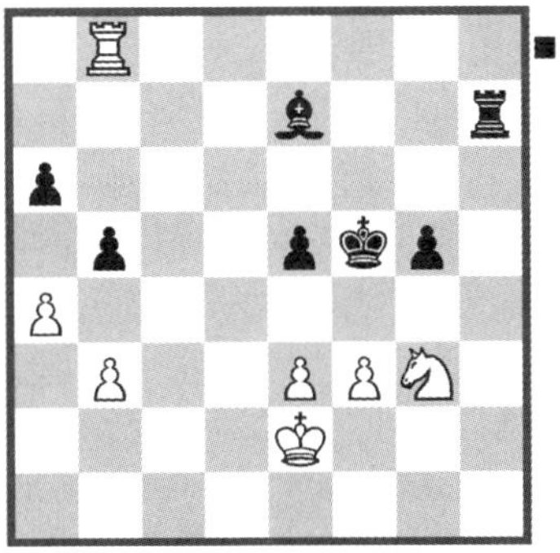

Position after: 40. ♘g3+!

40... ♔e6 41. ♖b6+ ♔d5 42. ♖xa6 b4

42... bxa4 43. ♖xa4!+–

43. ♘f5! e4

43... ♗f8 44. e4+ ♔c5 45. ♖e6 This wins easily.

44. ♘xe7+

The simplest.

44... ♖xe7 45. ♖a5+ ♔d6 46. ♖xg5

Position after: 46. ♖xg5

With two extra pawns the win is trivial. Black, alas, continued playing.

46... ♖c7 47. ♖g6+ ♔e5 48. f4+ ♔d5 49. ♖g5+ ♔d6 50. ♖b5 ♖c2+

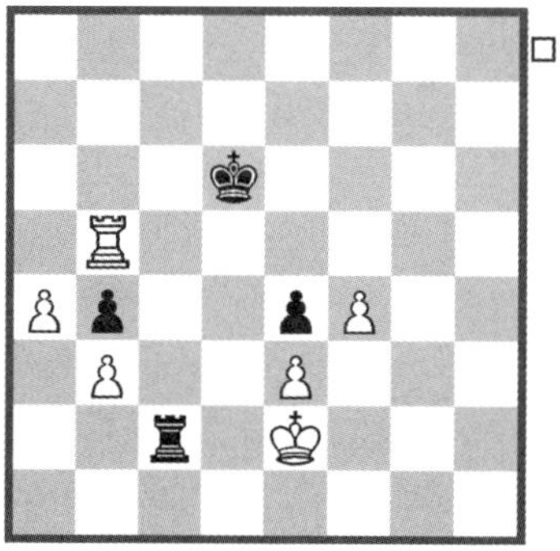

Position after: 50... ♖c2+

51. ♔d1 ♖c3 52. ♖xb4 ♖xe3 53. a5 ♔c5 54. ♖b8

54. ♖a4 This is another winning method, of course.

54... ♖h3 55. a6 ♖h1+ 56. ♔e2 ♖a1 57. ♔e3 ♖e1+ 58. ♔f2 ♖a1 59. b4+

Position after: 59. b4+

59... ♔d4 60. b5 e3+ 61. ♔f3 ♖f1+ 62. ♔g2 ♖a1 63. ♖e8

1-0

Do Not Rush!

Unlike the previous chapter, this chapter applies generally to all the others. The "do not rush" principle can be widely implemented, but one prerequisite is paramount – the opponent must not have any active play (or counterplay).

In such situations, it is methodical to implement the above-mentioned principle for many reasons: it reduces the chances of blundering, we can hide our plans, we can confuse our opponent (which may often cause some drastic reaction and accelerate our conversion of the advantage), or our opponent may be caught "asleep" and may not be ready to react against our plans, etc.

It is very important to understand the concept of “**choosing piece play"**. When the opponent has no active plan, you may have a situation where there are two possible plans (which is almost always the case!) – one based on piece play and the other on pawn play; in such situations, always choose the plan based on piece play. If this does not work, then you would still be able to switch to the other plan. On the other hand, if you choose pawn play and this plan fails, the structure and thus the situation would have been drastically changed and you would probably be unable to revert to the plan of piece play. It is better to have two chances to convert than one!

And, yes, a more patient conversion may cause the game to last longer than expected, but this should not matter at all – you would not be spending much energy "waiting for the opponent's mistake".

Game 169

♙ Mohrlok, Dieter A
♟ Gerusel, Mathias
Bad Pyrmont 1963

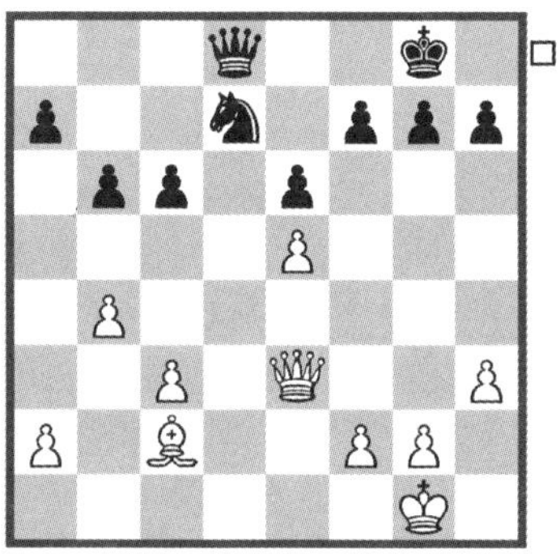

The material balance here should favor Black due to Capablanca's principle and the presence of seven (!) pawns on each side. However, after the next maneuver, White is dominant.

25. ♕d3!

Gaining an important tempo.

25... g6 26. ♕d6! ♕c8 27. ♗e4

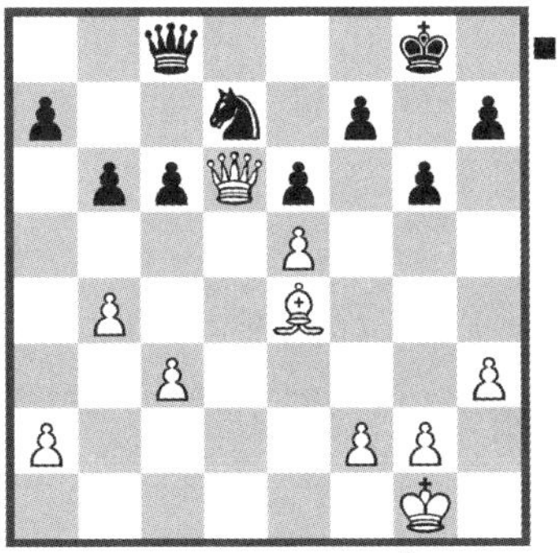

Position after: 27. ♗e4

27... ♘b8?

Too passive.

27... c5 This would have been better but Black's chances of survival are not great after the following. 28. b5! c4! 29. ♗c6! ♘c5 30. ♕e7

Position after: 30. ♕e7

30... ♕f8 Black must play this, when White can nevertheless combine play on both wings. 31. ♕xa7 ♕d8 32. a4 ♘b3

28. c4?

This leaves the b4-pawn unprotected and gives Black a surprising chance to escape.

28. a4! Black is in a hopeless situation.

28... a6?

28... ♕f8!

Position after: 28... ♕f8!

This was necessary and Black survives, for example as follows. 29. c5 [29. ♕c7 ♘a6! 30. ♕xa7 ♕xb4! 31. ♕xa6 ♕e1+ 32. ♔h2 ♕xe4 33. ♕xb6 ♕xc4 A draw results.] 29... bxc5 30. bxc5 ♘a6

29. g3

There is no need to rush anywhere.

29... ♔g7

29... ♕f8 This fails to 30. ♕c7!.

30. ♔g2 ♔g8 31. h4

White patiently improves his position on the kingside while the opponent's army is stuck on the opposite side.

31... b5

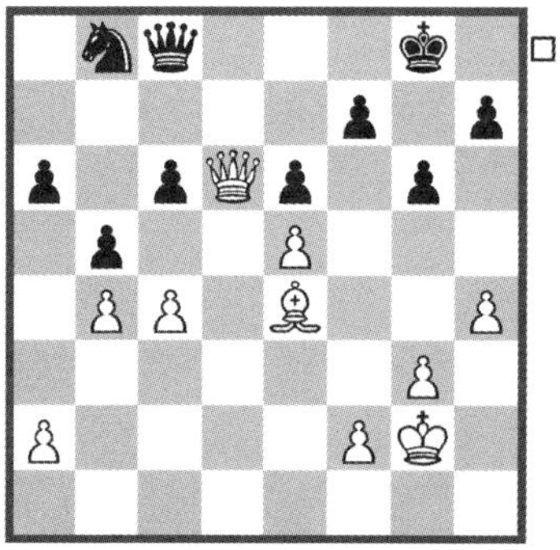

Position after: 31... b5

Black tries anything, but there is no liberation of course.

32. cxb5?

Strategically a very bad decision. Although this does not spoil anything, it is not to be recommended.

32. c5! This was the move instead, locking out the black pieces and keeping c6 as a target. The move does not require calculation. 32... a5 This should not concern White because the simple 33. bxa5 would lead win.

32... axb5

Black opts to make space on a6 for the knight.

32... cxb5 This is better, but ultimately it would not have helped Black. Black would open up the queen in this case and the knight would have the d7-spot in any case.

33. a3 ♕f8 34. ♕c7

There is no need to trade an active piece for a passive one.

34... ♕e8 35. ♗f3

Preparing h5.

35. h5 This could have been played without preparation, of course.

35... h5

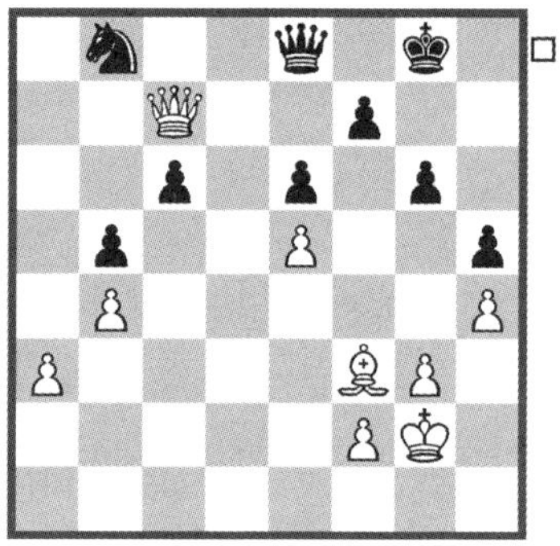

Position after: 35... h5

Black gains additional space and is ready to trade many pawns, should White expand on the kingside. However, this pawn, as usual, would become a hook upon which White could target his attack later.

36. ♗e4 ♔g7 37. ♔f3

White improves even his king. "Do not rush!"

37... ♔h8 38. ♔e3 ♔g7 39. ♔f4

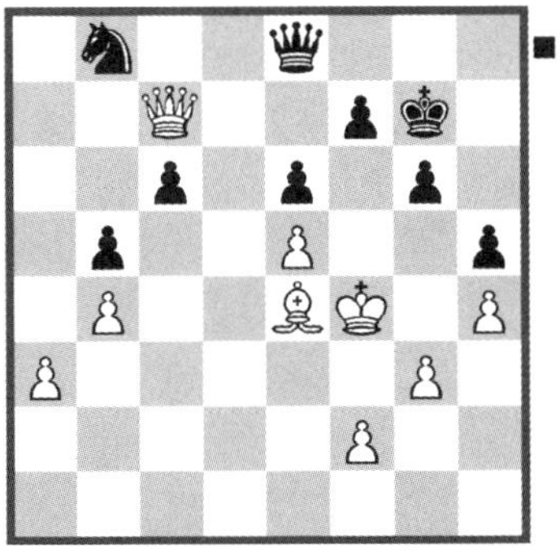

Position after: 39. ♔f4

39... ♔h6

39... ♔h7 40. ♔g5 ♔g8 This is also a possible defense. White's king cannot go any further.

40. ♕d6 ♔g7 41. ♔e3 ♔g8 42. f3

Finally White goes for the breakthrough, resulting in a passer on the h-file.

42... ♔g7 43. ♔f4 ♔h7 44. g4 hxg4 45. fxg4 ♔h6 46. ♗f3 ♔g7 47. h5

Position after: 47. h5

47... gxh5 48. gxh5 ♔h6 49. ♔g3 ♔g7 50. ♔g4 f5+

Black has reason to be afraid of White's growing initiative and opts for drastic measures. A waiting policy would not have helped him.

51. exf6+! ♔xf6 52. ♕f4+ ♔e7 53. ♕g5+ ♔d6 54. ♕c5+ ♔c7

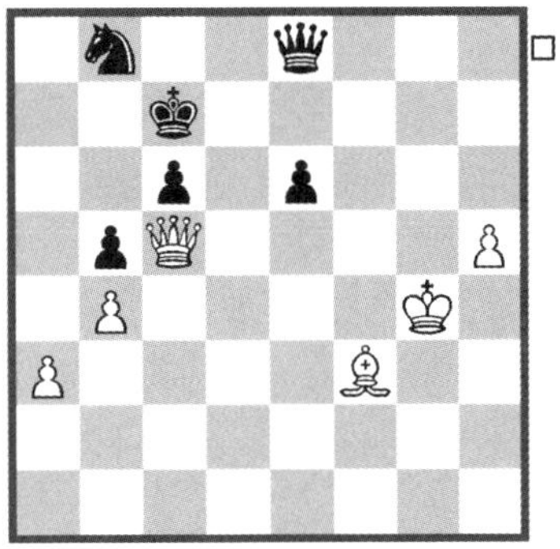

Position after: 54... ♔c7

55. h6

Fully centralizing his pieces, White advances.

55... e5 56. ♕a7+ ♔d6 57. ♕g7 ♕e6+ 58. ♔g3 ♕f5 59. h7 ♕f4+ 60. ♔g2

Position after: 60. ♔g2

60... ♕d2+ 61. ♔h3 ♕e3 62. ♕f6+

1-0

Game 170

♙	Delchev, Aleksander	(2571)
♟	Rotstein, Arkadij	(2471)
	Bayerisch Eisenstein 2019	

White is strategically winning here. Black has many weak points and there are numerous key squares that White can use. There may be technical problems for White as the weaknesses on b6 and d6 are relatively close. Thus White would probably be forced to a create weakness on the kingside.

29. ♖b5 ♖b8 30. ♕d3 ♖e8 31. ♖e1

White tries to confuse his opponent. There is no need to rush.

31... ♖ef8 32. ♖d5 ♖e8 33. ♖e4 ♖e7 34. ♕e3 ♖e8 35. ♖b5

Again!

35... ♖b8

Position after: 35... ♖b8

White is convinced now that he must organize pawn play on the kingside. However this would definitely result in both kings becoming vulnerable. Therefore let's first relocate the white king to a safe zone on the queenside before striking.

36. ♔f1! ♖b7 37. ♔e2 ♖f7 38. ♔d2 ♕d8 39. ♖d5 ♕c7 40. h4 ♖f6

Position after: 40... ♖f6

Black can only watch White's activities.

41. ♖b5 ♕c6 42. ♔c2 ♕c7 43. ♔b2 ♕c6 44. ♔a3 ♕c7 45. ♖d5 ♕c6 46. ♕d3 ♖bf7 47. ♔a2

Position after: 47. ♔a2

47... h5!?

Black is objectively lost so it is reasonable that he aims at some timely moment to do something active – he tries to face White's attack as strongly as possible. I suggest that you search for White's attack if Black is just waiting instead.

48. ♖e2 ♖e6 49. ♕e3 ♖ef6 50. ♕d2 ♕c7 51. ♖e4

White's pieces dance. There is no need to rush.

51... ♕c6 52. ♕e3 ♔h7 53. ♖b5 ♖b7 54. ♔a3 ♔g7

Position after: 54... ♔g7

55. g3

After long preparations, White strikes.

55... ♕c8 56. f4 exf4

Necessary.

57. gxf4

White now even has the e-file and the advance f5 is on the agenda.

57... ♕g4?

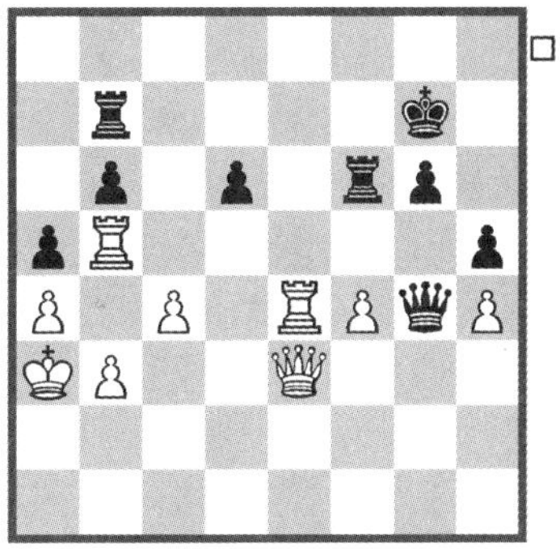

Position after: 57... ♕g4?

An active move, but it accelerates Black's defeat. We see this often.

58. f5 ♕d1

Threatening mate!

59. ♕c3!

Preventing mate and setting up a deadly pin.

59... ♖bf7 60. ♖e1 ♕g4 61. fxg6 ♖f8 62. ♖e7+

Black resigned. I decided to present this game without any variations.

1-0

Game 171

♙	Almasi, Zoltan	(2630)
♟	Zueger, Beat	(2470)
🌍	Horgen 1995	

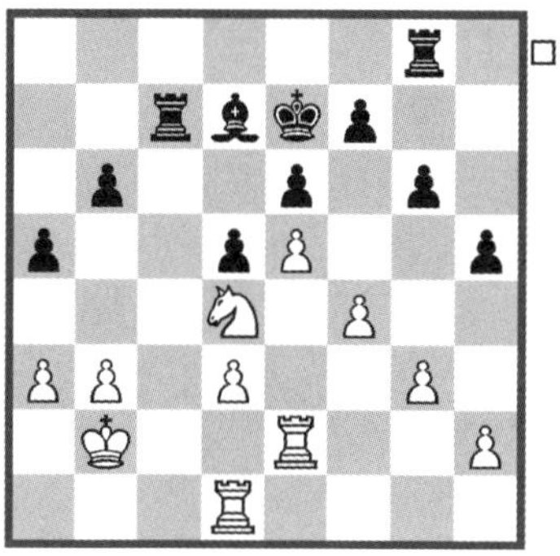

Our next examples relate to positions where one side dominates with a knight over a bishop. These are typical situations in which to implement the "don't rush" principle (conversely, the side with the dominant bishop generally goes for action in an open position).

Our next example is typical. The immoveable knight cements the position giving White chances on both wings. However it is not easy to convert. The obvious offer of a rook trade does not achieve anything because Black would wait with his rook on c5. White first eliminates any counterplay.

31. ♖f1!

Preventing ...g5.

31... ♖gc8

31... g5 32. ♖ef2!

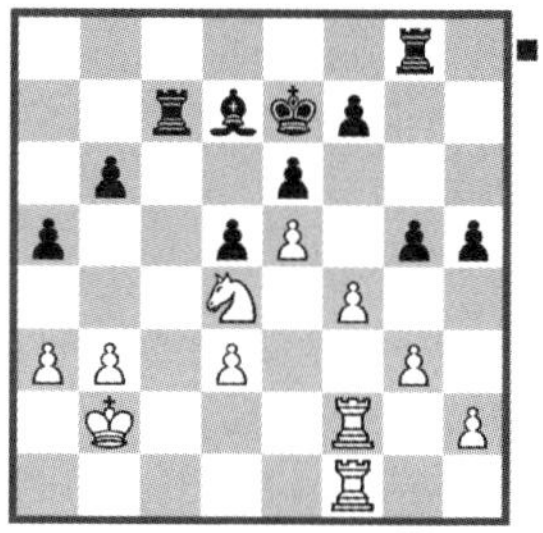

Position after: 32. ♖ef2!

32... g4 [32... gxf4 33. ♖xf4 ♗e8 34. ♘e2 White has a huge advantage.] 33. f5! Black's position looks hopeless.

32. ♖d2 ♗e8

After the threat of counterplay has been eliminated White must make a plan. First he offers the opponent a capture, which would be a mistake. It is important to keep in mind that any advance on the kingside would probably not achieve anything. Black is ready to trade a lot of pawns and even his minor pieces in case of the advance f5.

33. ♖c2

(see diagram next page)

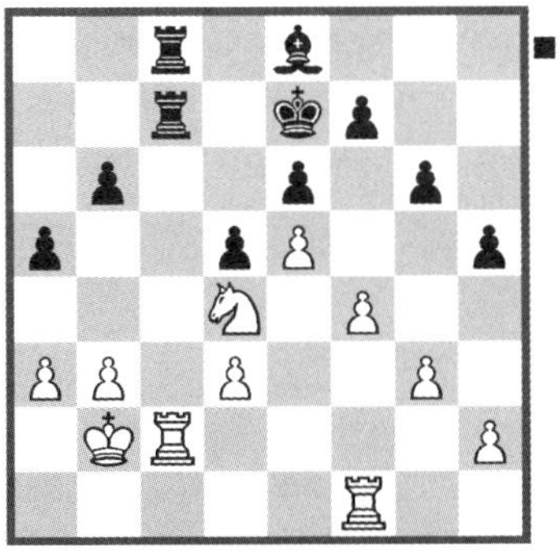

Position after: 33. ♖c2

33... ♖c5!

33... ♖xc2+? This would be a terrible mistake that helps White. With both pair of rooks on the board White must be more accurate.

34. ♖fc1 ♗d7 35. ♖f1 ♗e8 36. ♖ff2 ♗d7 37. ♔c1

White tries to confuse his opponent.

37... ♖8c7 38. ♔d2 ♖c8 39. ♖f1 ♖a8 40. ♖fc1 ♖ac8

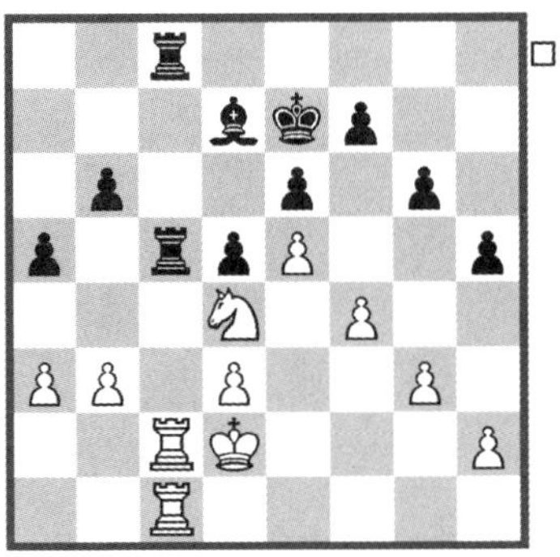

Position after: 40... ♖ac8

Black does not make a mistake. White tries another way to confuse.

41. ♘f3 ♔d8 42. ♘g5 ♖xc2+?

42... ♔e7! Why not this? White can force Black to take with d4 or b4 but both moves would cement the position, perhaps making any conversion impossible.

43. ♖xc2 ♖xc2+

Now this is necessary.

44. ♔xc2 ♔e7 45. ♔c3 ♗b5 46. ♘f3 ♔d7 47. ♘e1 ♔c6 48. ♘c2 ♔c7

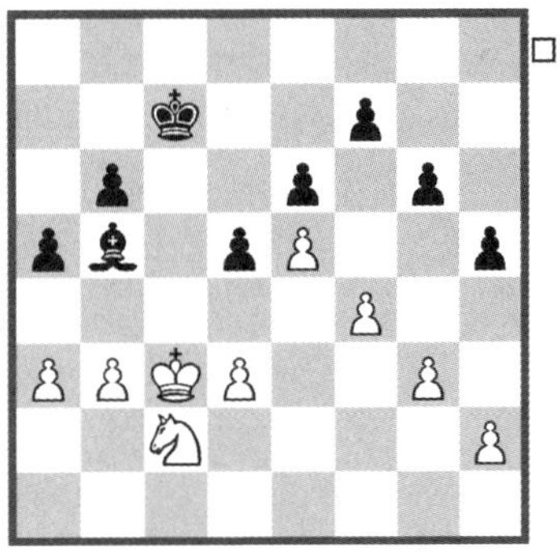

Position after: 48... ♔c7

49. b4?!

Not finding any obvious way to make progress, White advances.

49... ♗a4?!

Logically this must be risky.

49... axb4+ This looks better. Black's pawn on b6 would be safer and create a barrier together with the bishop.

50. ♘d4

White does not take. Both sides are consistent.

50... ♔d7 51. ♘f3 ♔c7 52. ♘g5 ♗e8 53. ♘h7?! ♗a4 54. ♘f6

Position after: 54. ♘f6

The knight does nothing here... except to set a trap.

54... ♗b5?

A fatal mistake.

54... axb4+! 55. ♔xb4 ♗d1! This was necessary instead. Black must defend either the d5- or h5-pawn in order to prevent a powerful strike.

55. bxa5 bxa5 56. f5!

This creates more weaknesses in Black's camp. He must wait.

56... ♔b6

Taking with any pawn would give White practically an extra passed pawn due to the doubled pawns on the f-file.

57. fxg6 fxg6 58. ♘h7 ♗e8 59. ♘f8 ♗f7

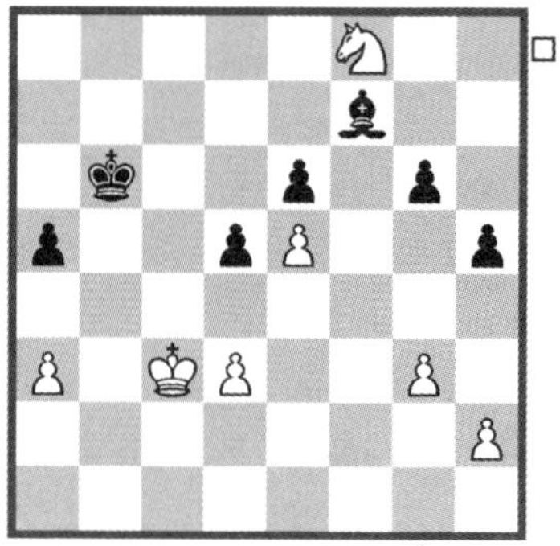

Position after: 59... ♗f7

60. h4!

A good fix.

60... ♔b5 61. d4!

61. ♔b3? ♔c5 62. ♔c3 d4+

61... ♔a4 62. ♔b2 ♔b5 63. ♔b3

Position after: 63. ♔b3

63... ♔b6

63... a4+ 64. ♔c3 ♔a5 Waiting does not help. White would transfer his knight to the queenside, say, to c3 and move his king to the kingside.

64. ♘d7+ ♔b5 65. ♘c5 ♔b6 66. ♔c3 ♔c6 67. ♘d3 ♔b5 68. ♘b2 ♔c6

Position after: 68... ♔c6

69. ♔d2 ♔d7

Black cannot set the bishop on f5. Even if this is possible, there would be a zugzwang.

70. ♔e3 ♔e7 71. ♔f4 ♗e8 72. ♔g5 ♔f7 73. ♘d3

(see diagram next column)

Now the knight comes to the battlefield.

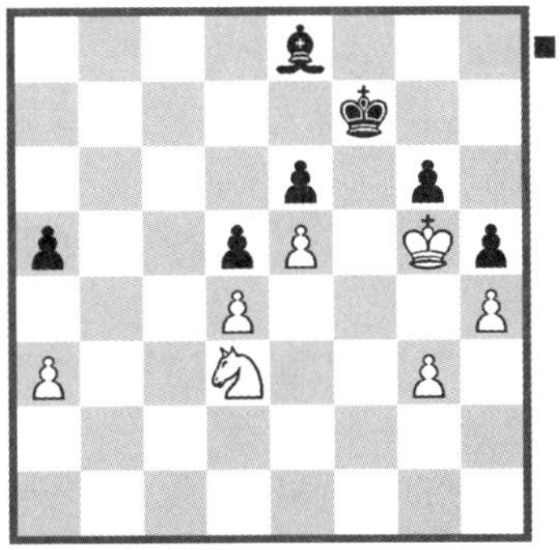

Position after: 73. ♘d3

73... ♗a4 74. ♘c5 ♗c2 75. ♘b7 a4 76. ♔h6

There is no need to rush even now.

76... ♔f8 77. ♘c5 ♔f7 78. ♔g5 ♗b3 79. ♔f4!

Position after: 79. ♔f4!

79... ♗d1 80. ♔e3

1-0

Game 172

♙ Sefc, Jan
♟ Petrosian, Tigran V
Vienna 1957

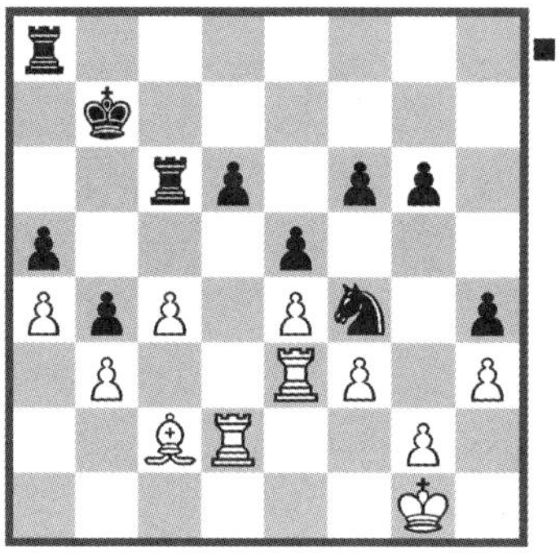

46... ♘e6

Black's domination is undisputed. Before trying something concrete, Iron Tigran prefers to dance with his knight – the usual method of implementing the "don't rush" principle.

47. ♖ed3 ♘d4?!

Black was sure that any sacrifice here would fail. In any case, there is no reason to offer such possibilities to the opponent. Objectively, White is lost and complicating in this way can only be in his favor.

48. ♔f1?!

48. ♖xd4 exd4 49. ♖xd4 ♔c7 50. f4 ♖e8 This looks very good for Black, but at the same time offers some relief for White.

48... ♖f8?!

Black insists.

49. ♔f2?! ♔c7?! 50. ♔f1?!

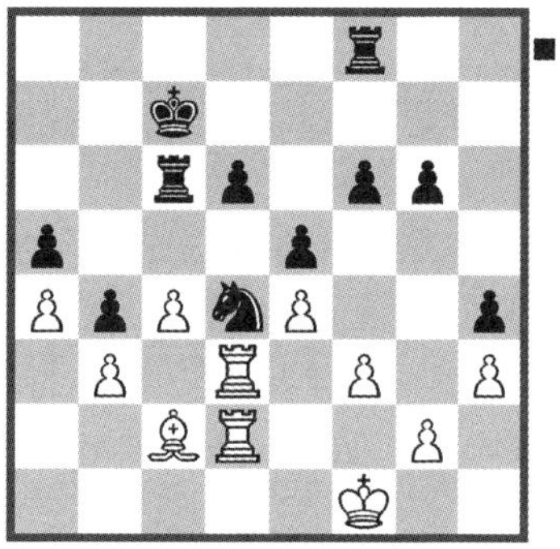

Position after: 50. ♔f1?!

50... ♔d7?! 51. ♔f2?! ♔e7?! 52. ♔f1?! ♖a6?! 53. ♔f2?! ♘e6!

Finally, the series of dubious moves is over and Black relocates the knight.

54. ♖e3 ♘c5 55. ♖d5 ♖aa8 56. ♔f1 ♘e6

Position after: 56... ♘e6

Achieving nothing, the knight goes to the right spot on f4. Black's chances are on the kingside.

57. ♖d2 ♘f4 58. ♖e1 ♖a7 59. ♖ed1 ♖d7 60. ♖e1 ♖h8

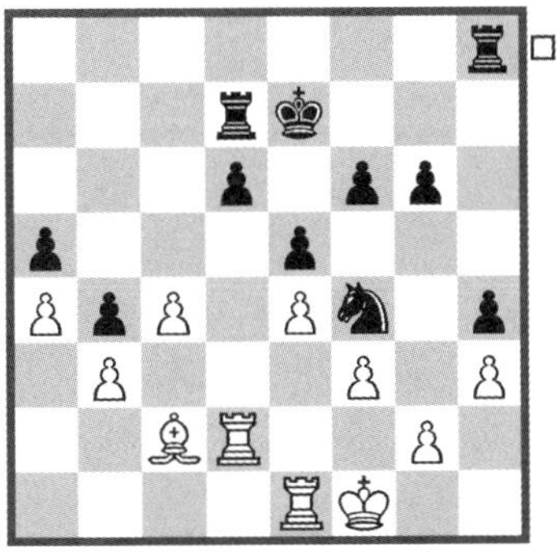

Position after: 60... ♖h8

61. ♖ed1 ♘e6 62. ♖e1 ♘d4?!

Again! Black risks giving White the chance to sacrifice the exchange, but he wants to set his king on c5.

63. ♖ed1?! ♔d8?! 64. ♖e1?! ♔c7?! 65. ♖ed1?! ♔c6?!

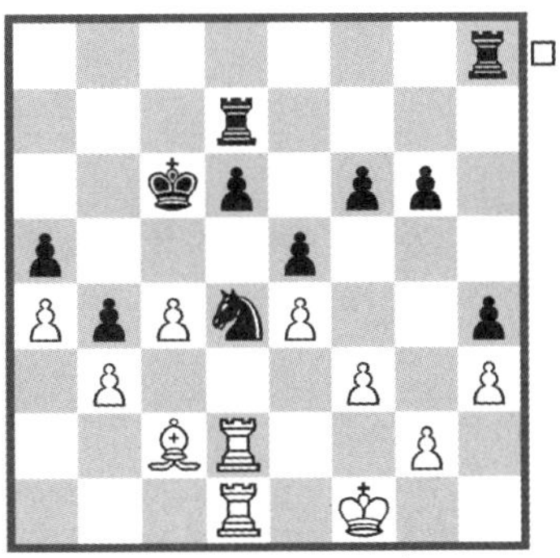

Position after: 65... ♔c6?!

66. ♖e1? ♔c5

There is no possible sacrifice anymore.

67. ♖e3 f5! 68. ♔f2 ♖h5?!

Position after: 68... ♖h5?!

So direct!

68... ♖g7 Another prophylactic move with the same idea.

69. ♔f1?!

This primitive holding waiting policy here achieves nothing. Black has many ways to improve.

69. exf5! gxf5 70. f4! A worthy try. 70... ♖e7! [70... e4 This looks natural but the position is unclear after the following line. 71. ♖e1 ♖e7! Preventing ♖ed1. 72. ♗d1! ♖h8 73. ♔e3 ♖g7 74. ♖xd4 ♖g3+ 75. ♗f3 There are mutual chances but Black should not prevail here.] 71. ♖xd4! ♔xd4 72. ♖d3+

(see diagram next page)

Position after: 72. ♖d3+

72... ♔c5 [72... ♔e4 73. ♖f3+ A repetition will ensue.] 73. ♖d5+ ♔c6 74. ♖xa5 This forces Black to find an only move, giving him serious winning chances. 74... ♖h8! Nevertheless Black must still work to win after the following. 75. ♗xf5 exf4 76. ♔f3 ♖e3+ 77. ♔xf4 ♖xb3 78. ♗e4+

69... ♖g5 70. ♔f2 ♖g3 71. ♔f1 ♖f7

Again there is no rush from Black's side.

72. ♔f2 ♖f8 73. ♔f1

Position after: 73. ♔f1

73... ♖h8

Finally Black goes for the correct plan.

74. ♔f2 ♖h5 75. ♔f1 ♖hg5 76. ♖f2 ♔c6

Before relocating the knight, the king goes to a safe place.

77. ♖d2 ♔c7 78. ♖f2 ♘e6 79. ♖ee2 ♘f4 80. ♖d2 ♔c6

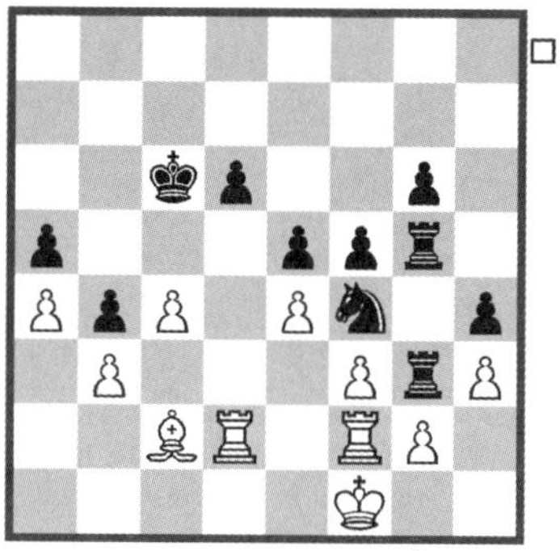

Position after: 80... ♔c6

White is in some kind of zugzwang.

81. exf5

What else?

81. ♗d1 fxe4 82. fxe4 ♖c3 83. ♗c2 ♖gg3 This leads to an invasion and a zugzwang.

81... gxf5 82. ♗d1 ♖g7 83. ♗c2 ♖3g5 84. ♗d3 ♔d7!

The king goes to e6 to liberate the rook.

85. ♗c2 ♔e6 86. ♗d3 ♖g3 87. ♗c2 ♖g8 88. ♗d3

Position after: 88. ♗d3

88. ♗d1 This loses after the following, for instance. 88... d5 89. cxd5+ ♘xd5

88... e4! 89. fxe4 ♘xd3 90. ♖xf5 ♘c5 91. ♖fd5 ♖xb3 92. ♖xd6+ ♔e7 93. ♖6d4 ♖c3 94. e5 b3 95. ♖xh4 ♖c1+ 96. ♔f2 b2

0-1

Game 173

♙ Flohr, Salo
♟ Bondarevsky, Igor Tsakharovich
Leningrad & Moscow 1939

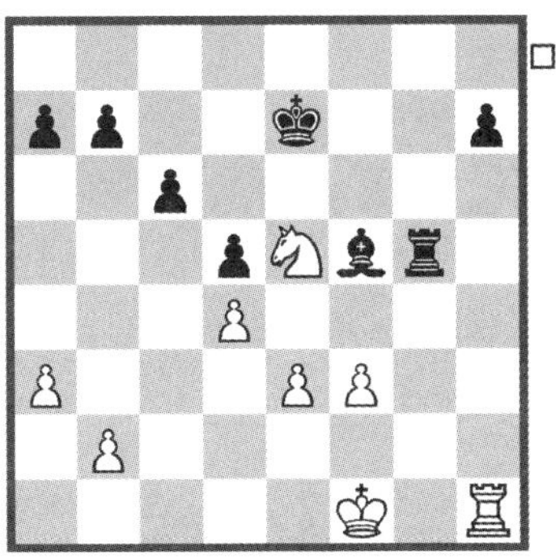

White is clearly better due to his very strong knight. His main task is to launch the central pawns and create a passer with different threats. Having only one rook on the board doesn't help much (while normally it's easier to win), because the bishop defends decently.

40. ♔f2 ♔f6 41. ♖h4 ♖g7 42. b4

After a few kingside moves there is an advance on the queenside – do not rush. White wants to advance his pawns on the queenside with the idea of fixing or organizing a minority attack.

42... ♔g5 43. ♖h1 ♔f6 44. ♖h2 ♖g5 45. a4 ♖g7

Position after: 45... ♖g7

46. a5

White opts for fixing. There is the potential threat of a6.

46... ♖c7 47. ♖h6+ ♗g6 48. ♖h1 ♗f5 49. ♖c1

White forces Black's next move.

49. ♔g3 A direct approach with ♔f4 and e4.

49... a6

49... ♖g7 This fails to 50. a6!.

50. ♖h1

After fixing Black's majority on the queenside White switches to the kingside.

50... ♖g7 51. ♖h2

Position after: 51. ♖h2

There is no reason to hurry anywhere. White wants to confuse his opponent.

51... ♖c7 52. ♖h6+ ♗g6 53. ♖h4 ♗f5 54. e4

Finally White advances.

54... dxe4 55. fxe4

(see diagram next column)

Position after: 55. fxe4

55... ♗g6

A logical retreat.

A) 55... ♗e6? 56. ♖h6+

B) 55... ♗c8 This can be met with the simple 56. ♔e3, improving the entire army.

56. ♖f4+ ♔e6 57. ♔e3

The strong central grouping gives White a clear edge and comfortable play without any risk. He can easily and patiently seize the initiative and improve smoothly without any particular resistance from Black. Black is practically forced to wait.

57... ♖g7 58. ♘d3!

The knight goes to the ideal spot on c5. At the same time the e-pawn is freed to march.

58... ♔d6 59. ♘c5 ♖e7 60. ♖f8 ♔c7 61. e5

Position after: 61. e5

Note White's formation – all his pieces and pawns are on the dark squares. The bishop cannot attack anything! White has set all his pieces perfectly and everything is ready for the king to infiltrate.

61... ♖e8

Black feels the danger but is paralyzed. White has no problem with exchanging – the king and knight are very active and the game is already won.

62. ♖xe8 ♗xe8 63. ♔f4 b6

A final try.

64. ♘a4! bxa5 65. bxa5 ♗f7 66. ♘c5

A blockading triumph and a brilliant strategy!

(see diagram next column)

Position after: 66. ♘c5

66... ♗c4 67. ♔g5 ♗e2 68. ♔h6 ♔d8 69. ♔xh7 ♔e7 70. ♔g6 ♗f1 71. ♔f5 ♗h3+ 72. ♔e4

Position after: 72. ♔e4

72... ♗g2+ 73. ♔e3 ♗f1 74. ♔d2 ♔f7 75. ♔c3 ♔g6 76. ♔b4 ♔f5 77. ♘b7

1-0

Game 174

♙ Donner, Jan Hein
♟ Karpov, Anatoly (2690)
Amsterdam 1981

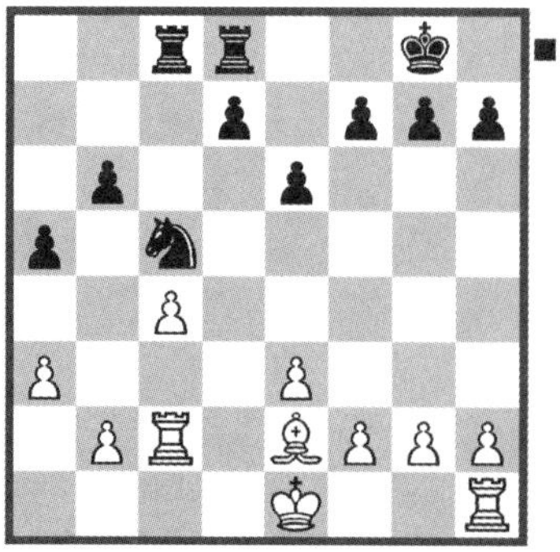

Black is better because of his dominant knight. He has chances to play on both wings, but first he must secure his knight's position.

21... a4!

Black sets the pawn on a light square but this is not a big problem for White.

22. f3 ♘b3

Not a necessary move at all.

22... ♔f8 Playing this immediately was better. The king comes to e7 and Black can start expanding.

23. ♗d3?!

Defending the rook in case of ...d5.

23. ♖c3 This was definitely a better way to secure the rook.

23... ♖c5 24. ♔e2 ♖dc8 25. ♖c3 ♘a5

(see diagram next column)

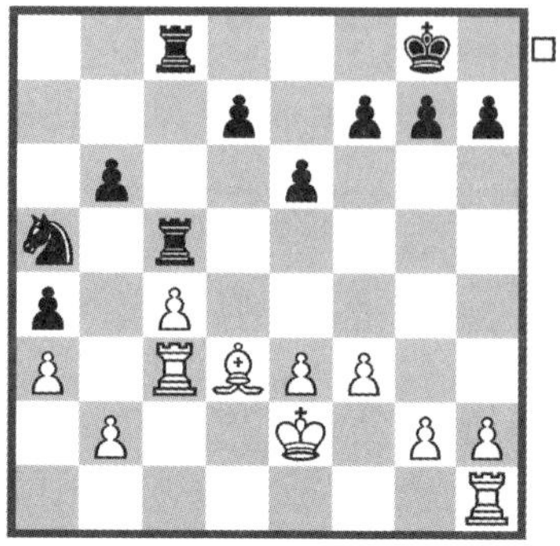

Position after: 25... ♘a5

Now we see that Karpov's plan was first to use the piece for active play. He attacks fully on c4. After White responds he will opt for another plan.

26. ♖hc1 ♔f8 27. ♔f2 ♔e7 28. ♔e2 h6

There is no need to rush.

29. ♔e1 ♖h5

I like such moves. Having more pawns on the light squares can only benefit Black. Time does not matter.

30. h3 ♖hc5 31. ♔f2 ♘b3!

Position after: 31... ♘b3!

The knight changes its spot. Black slowly switches to the kingside. At the same time Black prevents White's regrouping because the c1-square is taken.

32. ♖1c2 d6 33. ♔e1

33. h4 An attempt such as this to fight against Black's expansion will achieve nothing. 33... g5 This is possible here and after 34. hxg5 hxg5 the h-file belongs to Black.

33... g5 34. g3

A matter of style. It is generally better to wait with pawns that are not on the bishop's color.

34... ♖5c7 35. ♗f1 f5 36. ♔f2 ♖f8 37. ♗g2

Position after: 37. ♗g2

37. f4 ♔f6 This would give Black a chance to open the g-file after doubling.

37... f4

Black strikes, fixing the f3-pawn on a light square. White is strategically lost.

38. ♗f1

Any capture would be in Black's favor – the black rooks would more easily occupy the open files.

38... ♖c5 39. ♗d3 fxe3+ 40. ♔xe3 ♖e5+ 41. ♗e4 ♘c5

Closing the c-file and applying pressure on the e4-square.

41... d5? This fails to the following. 42. cxd5 exd5 43. ♖c7+ ♔f6 44. ♖2c6+

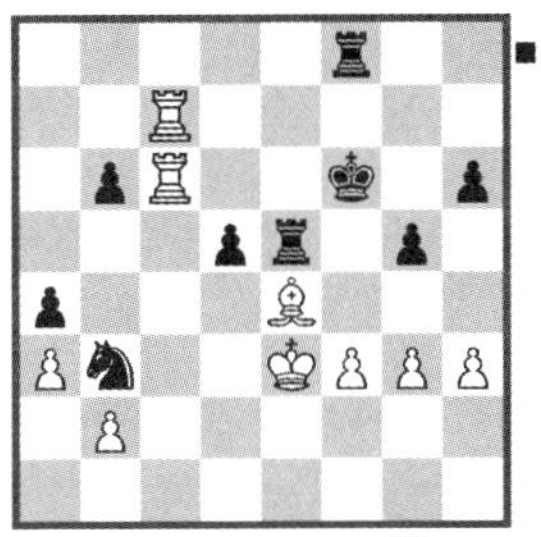

Position after: 44. ♖2c6+

44... ♖e6 45. ♖xe6+ ♔xe6 46. ♗c2

42. ♔d4

White eliminates the threat of ...d5.

42... ♘b3+

There is no need to rush.

43. ♔d3 ♔d7

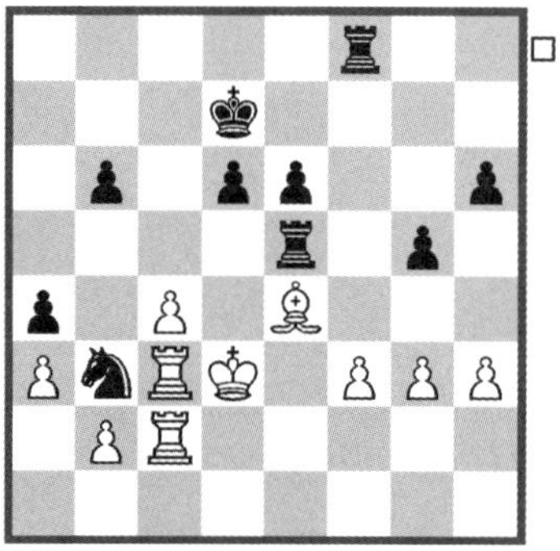

Position after: 43... ♔d7

Black changes his plan now.

44. ♔e3 ♘c5 45. ♔d4 ♖c8 46. ♖f2 ♘b3+ 47. ♔d3 ♖f8 48. ♖fc2 h5!

Finally. A powerful move that crushes White's fortress. Black threatens both ...g4 (undermining the bishop) and ...h4 (occupying the f4-spot).

49. ♔e3 ♘c5

Setting the pieces on their best spots before any decisive pawn action!

50. ♔d4

Position after: 50. ♔d4

50... g4

A matter of style. 50... h4 This would equally have led to a win.

51. ♖e3 gxf3 52. ♗xf3 ♘b3+ 53. ♔d3 ♖xe3+

The bishop falls on the next move. White resigned.

0-1

Game 175

♙ Soysal, Serkan (2381)
♟ Marjanovic, Dejan (2387)
Banja Vrujci 2017

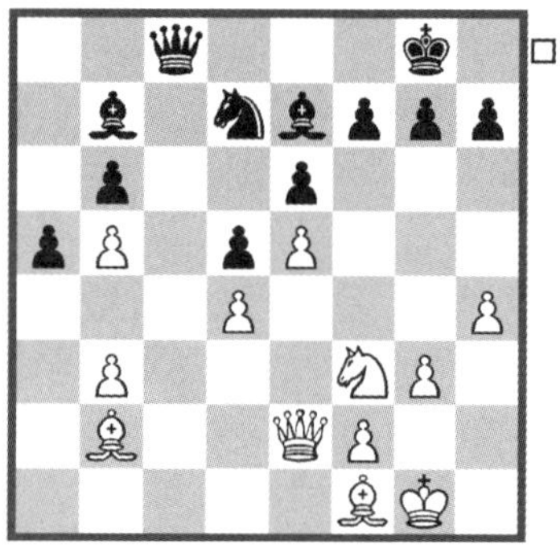

White is better here and has chances to organize some kingside play (either with pieces or with a pawn attack). At the same time White must deal with Black's chances on the queenside, which are not serious, however. The point is that White can afford to calmly organize his kingside play – the b5-pawn restricts almost the entire black army.

24. ♕d1!

A very fine starting move. The bishop goes to d3, the queen controls both diagonals toward a4 and h5, and also on the agenda is a possible battery on the b1-h7 diagonal.

24... ♘f8 25. ♗d3 ♗b4 26. h5! ♕c7

26... ♗c3 This achieves nothing because of 27. ♗a3.

27. ♔g2?!

White hesitates for no serious reason.

27. h6! This is simple and strong, either now or on the next move.

27... ♗c8?!

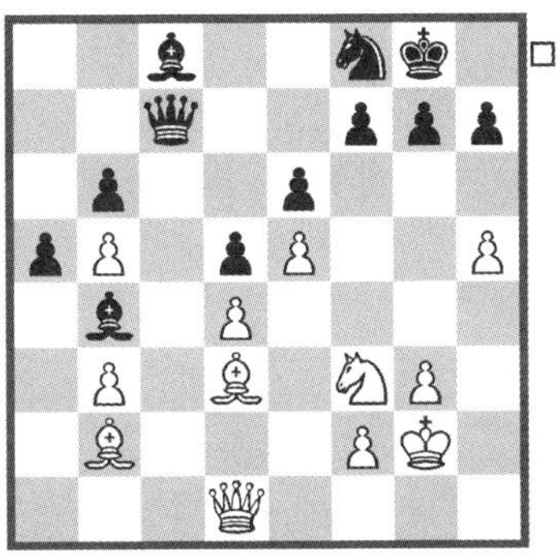

Position after: 27... ♗c8?!

27... h6!

28. ♘g5?

It seems that White was desperately wishing to provoke ...h6. The point is that this move would not have been bad for Black anyway.

28. h6! Instead this would have led to a strategically winning position.

28... ♗e7 29. ♕d2 ♗d7?!

29... h6!

30. ♘f3

The knight goes back. White admits that his 28th move has achieved nothing. However, White's advantage is stable, his opponent has no active play, and thus White can test out various plans.

30... ♕c8?!

30... h6!

31. ♕e2?! ♕a8?!

Position after: 31... ♕a8?!

32. ♗c1?!

White could have stopped Black's move, but he decided to allow it, thinking that after exchanging queens he would get the advantage of some vacated squares on the queenside. However it would have been better not to give Black a choice.

32... a4 33. bxa4 ♕xa4 34. ♗e3?!

Both the b5- and d4-pawns are stable. White wants to show that the black queen is practically out of play – the battlefront is on the kingside.

34... ♕b3?! 35. ♘h2 ♗e8 36. ♘g4 ♘d7

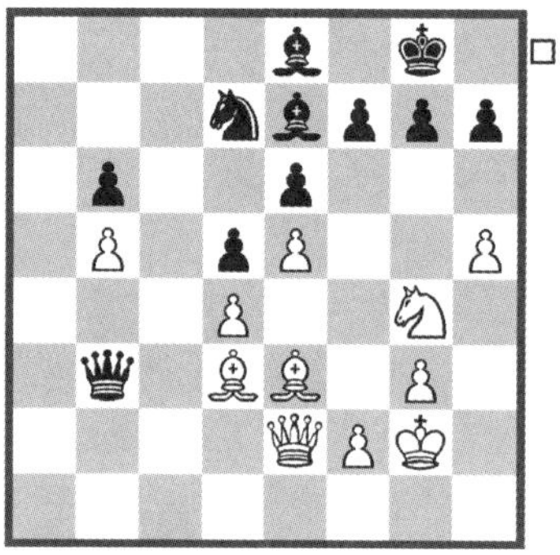

Position after: 36... ♘d7

Black must allow White's next move.

36... h6? This loses now after the following. 37. ♗xh6 gxh6 38. ♘f6+ ♗xf6 39. exf6

37. h6!

Finally creating some weaknesses in Black's position.

37... g6 38. ♘h2!

Black controls the f6-square, so the knight returns to f3.

38... ♕b4 39. ♘f3 ♕c3

Black's queen wanders.

40. ♕d1 ♘f8 41. ♕b1

Intending to play ♗d2 or to use the a-file for the queen's infiltration after removing the bishop from d3.

41... ♕b4?!

Position after: 41... ♕b4?!

42. ♕xb4

A concrete decision. White is not afraid of reducing material. Without queens on the board, the white pawns would be safer and the white pieces can be fully activated. Black should not offer to exchange queens, but White is able to force Black to do so.

42... ♗xb4 43. ♗g5 ♘d7 44. g4 ♗a3 45. ♗d8

One of Black's minor pieces must stay on d7, paralyzing the other.

45... ♗c1

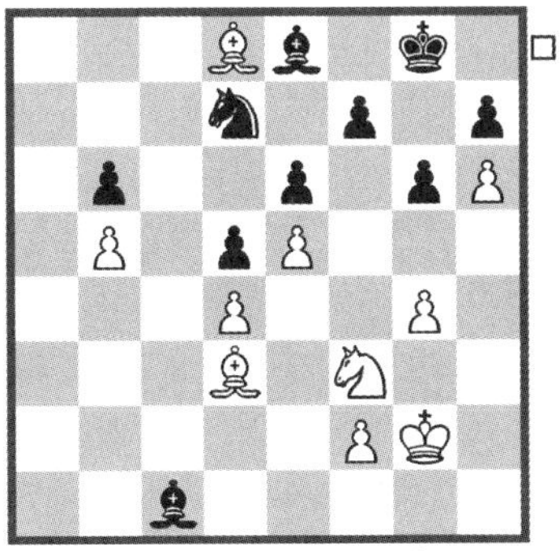

Position after: 45... ♗c1

46. g5!

Very inventively played. No, the game is not drawn due to the "blocked position". The knight goes to f6. After eliminating it, the white monarch can use the route via the e5-square!

46. ♗g5 ♗a3 47. ♔g3 White can prepare the advance f4-f5, but this would lead to a reduction of material and probably activate the black pieces. Furthermore, it is not clear if White can make progress even if Black decides to wait.

46... ♔f8 47. ♔f1 ♗b2 48. ♔e2 ♗c3 49. ♔d1

(see diagram next column)

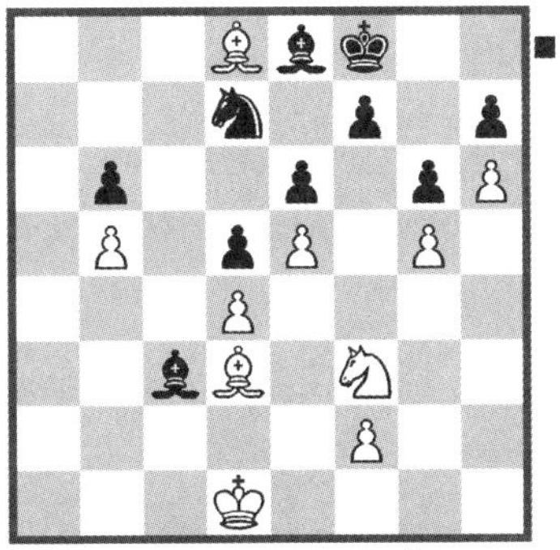

Position after: 49. ♔d1

49... ♗a5 50. ♔c2 ♗b4 51. ♔b3

After eliminating the threats to the d4-pawn, the white knight can go to f6.

51... ♗a5 52. ♗e2 ♘b8 53. ♗c7

Don't rush! White wants to put his pieces on their best squares before executing his plan.

53... ♘d7 54. ♗d6+ ♔g8 55. ♔c2 ♘f8

Position after: 55... ♘f8

55... ♔h8 This is another possibility. Test yourself and find a way to win here.

56. ♗xf8!

Once again a concrete decision. White has calculated till the end. The next moves are forced.

56... ♔xf8 57. ♘h2 ♗b4 58. ♘g4 ♗e7 59. ♘f6 ♗xf6 60. exf6 ♗d7 61. ♔d2 ♔e8 62. ♔e3 ♗c8 63. ♔f4 ♔d7 64. ♔e5 ♗b7

Position after: 64... ♗b7

It appears that White cannot break Black's defense, but the next maneuver proves otherwise.

65. ♗d3 ♗c8 66. f4 ♗b7 67. ♗xg6!

This blow could not be prevented.

67... fxg6 68. f7 ♔e7 69. f8=♕+ ♔xf8 70. ♔d6!

Black resigned.

1-0

Schematic Thinking

This concept is well-known to true masters. You have probably heard how the great Capablanca often preferred to apply it in endgames, simply by finding the best spots for his pieces. He is a very good mentor for this. Schematic thinking should be implemented when "there is nothing to calculate".

Moreover, very often after a storm has passed, it is very useful to "stop" and "take stock" – to take a look at the position through fresh lens which will "slow down" your thinking process. At such moments, re-establishing harmony is often very important and can be achieved by **schematic thinking.**

Generally, this principle should be implemented in "boring" positions, but everything will be clear after we have analyzed our examples in detail and provided you with some important ideas and patterns.

Game 176

♙ Euwe, Max
♟ Averbakh, Yuri L
Zuerich 1953

Let's start this chapter with a clear example. Black is absolutely winning here because of his strong b3-passer and the white bishop is excluded from the game. It may appear that White has compensation for this in the form of his active rook, but that is an illusion. Black plays a simple move here.

29... ♖e7

Now White has an unpleasant dilemma.

30. ♖xe7

30. ♖a8 This loses after the following. 30... ♖e1+ 31. ♔f2 ♖b1

30... ♘gxe7 31. ♔f2 ♔g8 32. g4 ♘d6 33. ♔e3

White sets up a barrier on the kingside which is irrelevant – the game will be decided on the queenside. But how to make progress? The answer is simple:

Black must eliminate the blockade on b2. Of course, this will entail a sacrifice. There is almost nothing to calculate. Black is winning and must play on the queenside!

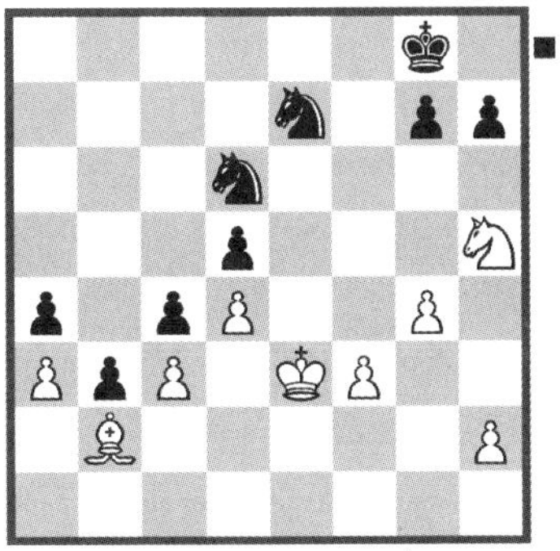
Position after: 33. ♔e3

33... ♘b5 34. f4 ♘c8 35. f5 ♘cd6 36. ♘f4 ♘xa3 37. ♗xa3 ♘b5 38. ♗c1

Position after: 38. ♗c1

38... ♘xc3!

38... a3?? 39. ♔d2 There is no win.

39. ♘e2 ♘b1

0-1

Game 177

♙ Ljubojevic, Ljubomir (2605)
♟ Karpov, Anatoly (2690)
Linares 1981

Black is clearly better (at least optically), but it is questionable if he can win. His knight collaborates better with his queen and the presence of seven pawns on each side helps Black. Nevertheless, White does not have any significant weaknesses and threatens to invade with his queen. In this position, there is almost nothing to calculate, and the scene is set for Karpov's amazing performance based on logic.

27... b6

A necessity. Black ensures that the c5-pawn is stable and prepares the queen for action.

28. ♕d3?!

With this move White simply forces Black to make the move that he wanted.

28. g4 This looks more logical. Now Black has the following options.

A) 28... ♕c6?! This is risky due to the complications arising after the following. 29. ♕d6+ ♕xd6 30. exd6

Position after: 30. exd6

30... ♘g8 [But not 30... ♘c6? where White surprisingly wins as follows. 31. b4!!

Position after: 31. b4!!

31... cxb4 32. g5 ♔c8 33. gxh6 gxh6 34. f5 exf5 35. ♗xh6 ♘e5 36. ♔c2 ♔d7 37. ♗f4 ♘g4 38. ♔b3 I suggest that you check the other lines.] 31. g5 ♔c8 32. b4 cxb4 33. c5 bxc5 34. ♗xc5 ♔d7 The idea is ...g6 and Black can still hold.

B) 28... ♕b7= A good move. 29. ♕d6+ ♔c8 Black is fine due to the threats along the longest diagonal.

28... g6! 29. hxg6

29. g4? gxh5 30. gxh5 ♘f5∓ Black has the safer king and pawns. Black's knight would be permanent on f5 and in fact the h5-pawn would be in danger, not the h6-pawn. This undisputed advantage would be definitely enough for Karpov to convert.

29... fxg6

Position after: 29... fxg6

30. a3

White feels Black's upcoming initiative on the kingside and is ready to go for active play on the queenside in return.

30. ♕e4 This is possible but after 30... h5 Black keeps a huge plus.

30... a5

Preventing 31. b4.

31. b3 h5

It is clear that Black has outplayed his opponent. The knight will be placed on f5 putting strong pressure on the g3-pawn and will be ready to jump closer to the white king.

32. ♕e4 ♘f5 33. ♗f2 ♕d7

Position after: 33... ♕d7

34. a4?

A waste of time.

34. ♔c2 This is better instead.

34... ♔c7!

An excellent move which underlines the problem of White's last move. White's queen cannot infiltrate because the black queen would come to d3 with destructive effect.

35. ♔c2

Now it is too late for this move. Black plays his next amazing multi-purpose move.

35. ♕a8? ♕d3 36. ♕a7+ ♔c8 37. ♕a8+ ♔d7 38. ♕b7+

Position after: 38. ♕b7+

38... ♔e8 39. ♕b8+ ♔f7 40. ♕b7+ ♘e7–+

35... ♕d8!!

Immediately reaching a much better position. The queen from d8 controls both the a8-square and the d-file. Furthermore the move 36... g5 is prepared. White is in big trouble.

35... ♕c6?! 36. ♕xc6+ ♔xc6 37. ♔d3=

36. ♔c1

A) If 36. ♕d3 then 36... ♕a8!.

B) 36. ♕f3 This allows an invasion after 36... ♕d4!! 37. ♕e2 ♕a1.

36... g5!

(see diagram next page)

Position after: 36... g5!

37. fxg5

37. ♔c2 g4! Creating a strong passer is immediately on Black's agenda.

37... ♕xg5+ 38. ♔c2 ♘e7 39. ♕h7 ♔d7

39... ♕g6+ Exchanging queens immediately is good, but Black wanted to spare a tempo.

40. ♕e4 ♕f5 41. ♕d3+ ♔c6 42. ♕xf5

Position after: 42. ♕xf5

42. ♗e1 This loses after 42... ♕xe5.

42... exf5!

Of course. Black's king will attack the e5-pawn very easily now. The game is decided. Karpov demonstrates his classy endgame technique in the next stage of the game.

42... ♘xf5 43. ♔d3 ♔d7 44. ♔e4 This looks safe for White.

43. ♗e3 ♘g6 44. e6 ♔d6 45. ♗g5

White's last chance is to attack the b6-pawn.

45... ♔xe6 46. ♔d2 f4!

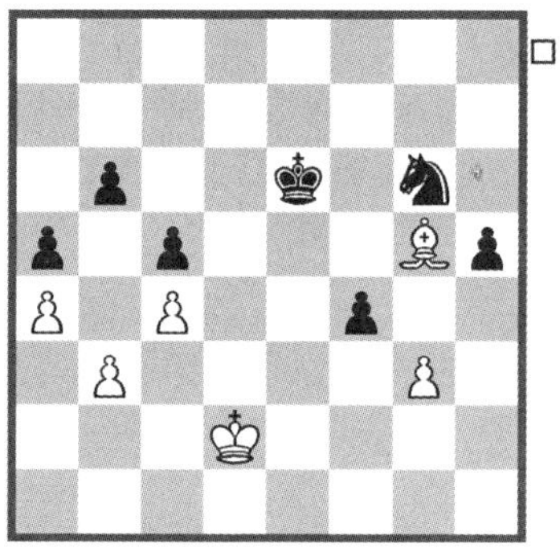

Position after: 46... f4!

47. gxf4 h4

47... ♔f5 Perhaps a more precise move order.

48. ♔e3 h3 49. ♔f3 ♔f5 50. ♔g3 ♘xf4! 51. ♗d8 ♘e2+ 52. ♔xh3 ♘d4 53. ♗xb6 ♘xb3

Black's king is close to the queenside pawns, while the white king could not be more distant.

Position after: 53... ♘xb3

54. ♗d8 ♔e4 55. ♔g4 ♔d3 56. ♔f4 ♔xc4 57. ♔e4 ♔c3

Karpov declines from collecting the pawn on a4 with his king. He chooses a safer plan. The pawn on a4 will fall later.

58. ♗f6+ ♔c2

Position after: 58... ♔c2

59. ♗e5

59. ♔d5 ♔d3 Black wins.

59... c4 60. ♔e3 c3 61. ♗f6 ♘c5 62. ♔e2

62. ♔d4 ♘xa4 63. ♔c4 ♘b6+ 64. ♔b5 a4

Position after: 64... a4

65. ♔b4 ♘d5+–+ Black has a nice fork at the end – a variation shown by Karpov.

62... ♔b3

0-1

Game 178

♙ Botvinnik, Mikhail
♟ Konstantinopolsky, Alexander
Sverdlovsk 1943

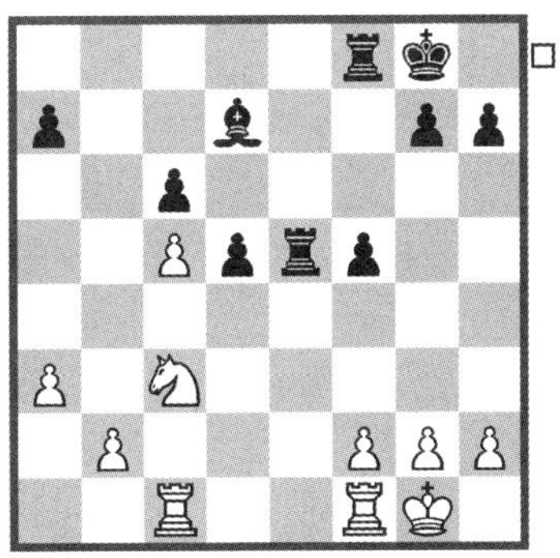

Here White is better. His knight is a much better piece and Black's bishop is restricted by the black pawns. White's task is clear – he must keep the position blocked, and not allow his opponent to activate the bishop, find targets and occupy the d4-spot. Whether to trade rooks or not in the meantime is not crucial, but it would be preferable for White to trade at least one pair of rooks.

20. f4!

White fixes the pawn on f5, and gets control over the e5-square.

20... ♖e7

20... ♖e6!? More precise. The difference is that the rook is now protected and Black can get the b-file with another rook. 21. ♔f2 [21. ♖fe1 This allows ...d4!.] 21... ♖b8 22. b4 a5 23. ♖b1

Position after: 23. ♖b1

23... axb4 24. axb4 d4 This is clearly a better option for Black. It is questionable if White can win at all.

21. ♖fe1 ♖fe8 22. ♖xe7 ♖xe7

The previous moves have been normal. The endgame is now dominant for White. His knight dominates and White's accessibility to the d4- and e5-squares makes the evaluation clear.

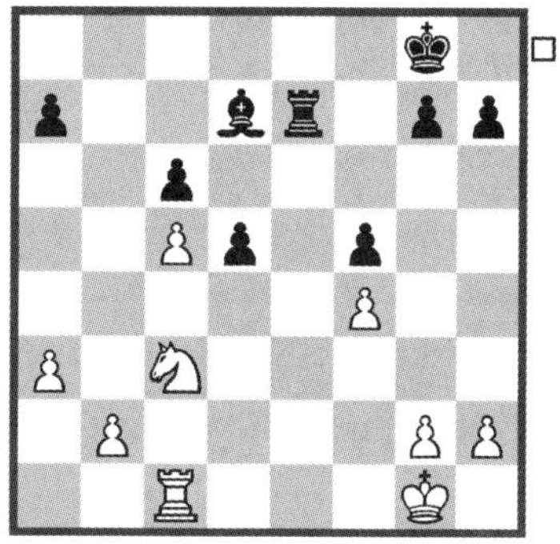

Position after: 22... ♖xe7

23. ♔f2

First, the king gets centralized.

23... ♔f7

24. ♖d1

White chooses the longer route to offer an exchange of rooks which will be in White's favor.

24. ♖e1? ♖xe1 25. ♔xe1 d4 26. ♘e2 ♔e6

Position after: 26... ♔e6

27. ♘xd4+ ♔d5 Black is not worse.

24... ♖e8 25. ♖d2 h6 26. ♖e2 ♖b8

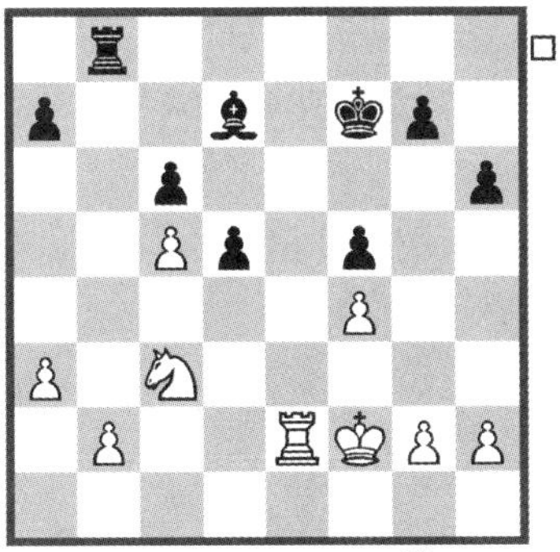

Position after: 26... ♖b8

Black must keep the rooks. Now White's king comes to the center.

27. ♔e3 ♖b3 28. ♔d4 ♔f6 29. ♘a2!

An excellent multi-purpose move. The knight attacks the rook and makes b4 possible. Furthermore the knight can be placed to d3 and e5 afterwards.

29... ♖b8 30. b4 g5 31. g3 gxf4 32. gxf4 a6 33. ♘c3

Position after: 33. ♘c3

White decides to keep the knight on c3 in order to prepare b5, at the same time putting pressure onto the d5-pawn.

33... ♖g8 34. a4 ♖g4 35. ♖f2 ♗e6 36. b5

With this thematic blow, the game is practically over.

36... axb5 37. axb5 cxb5 38. ♘xb5

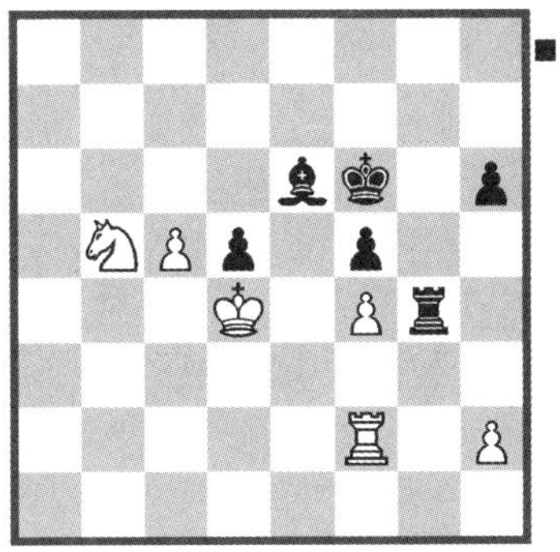

Position after: 38. ♘xb5

Of course, there is no reason to take the d5-pawn. The knight is better, so this pawn will fall later.

38... ♖g1 39. ♘c3

The knight closes the c-file (preventing the black rook from stopping the c-passer from the c1-square) as well as prevents a check from d1.

39... ♔f7 40. ♖b2 ♖f1 41. ♘e2 ♖e1 42. ♔e5

Again harmony. Once again the knight secures the king from checks and protects the c1-square, from where the black rook can stop the c-passer.

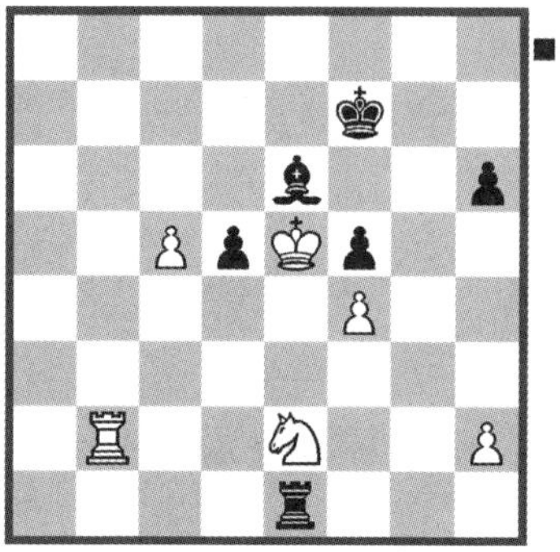

Position after: 42. ♔e5

42... d4 43. ♔xd4 ♔g6 44. ♘c3 ♔h5 45. ♖e2 ♖xe2 46. ♘xe2 ♔g4 47. ♔e5 ♗c8 48. ♘d4 h5 49. ♘xf5 ♗d7 50. ♘g7 ♗a4 51. f5 ♔g5 52. ♘e6+

1-0

Game 179

♙ Bondarevsky, Igor Tsakharovich
♟ Smyslov, Vassily V
Moscow 1946

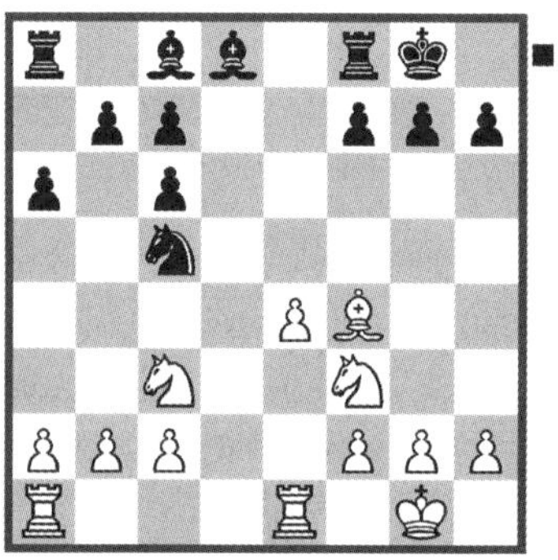

An interesting position. Here the players' skills are the key factor. Both sides have their pluses and minuses. Black wants to activate his bishop pair. Playing on the "wrong flank" (due to the pawn minority) does not distract Black at all.

12... f5!

An excellent decision. Smyslov plays directly, setting a positional trap. A less advanced player would have automatically advanced the e-pawn.

13. e5?

A terrible positional mistake. The pawn on e5 would be blocked. With precise play by Black, the blockading knight on e6 would be permanent. The pawn on e5 would actually restrict three white pieces: his bishop, knight and rook. White loses harmony after such a poor move and will soon become victim of an illusion.

13. ♗g5 ♗xg5 14. ♘xg5 h6 15. ♘f3 fxe4 16. ♘xe4 ♘xe4 17. ♖xe4 ♗f5

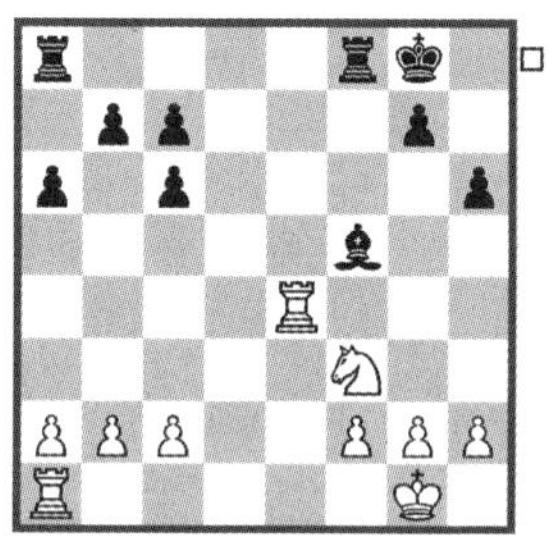

Position after: 17... ♗f5

18. ♖e2 [18. ♖e7 ♗xc2 19. ♖xc7 ♖f7] 18... ♗g4 19. ♖e3 This leads to a draw.

13... ♘e6 14. ♗d2 g5!

Black gains space on the kingside – a good strategy for the side having the bishop pair. This move restricts the white minor pieces and keeps the blockader on its perfect position on e6. White could play ♘e2 with the idea of exchanging the blockader after ♘f4 or ♘ed4. Thus, Black's last move is both aggressive and prophylactic.

15. ♘e2 c5!

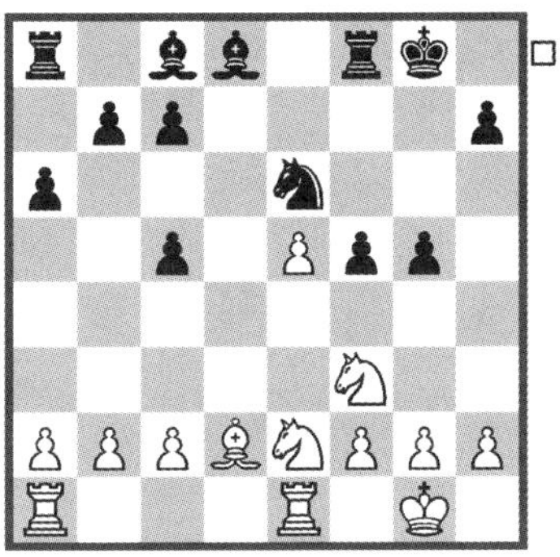

Position after: 15... c5!

The knight is safe now on e6.

16. ♗c3 b5

Gaining space on both flanks is a good strategy with the bishop pair advantage.

17. b3 ♗b7

You do not need to be an expert to see that Black is much better. His powerful pawn avalanche on both flanks will destroy everything in its way.

18. ♘g3

White intends to put this knight behind his opponent's pawn lines, perhaps hoping for an endgame with opposite-colored bishops. However this knight would be out of play on f6.

18... g4 19. ♘d2 ♗e7

Improving his position step-by-step. It is time to activate the rooks.

20. ♘h5 ♔f7 21. ♘f1 ♔g6!

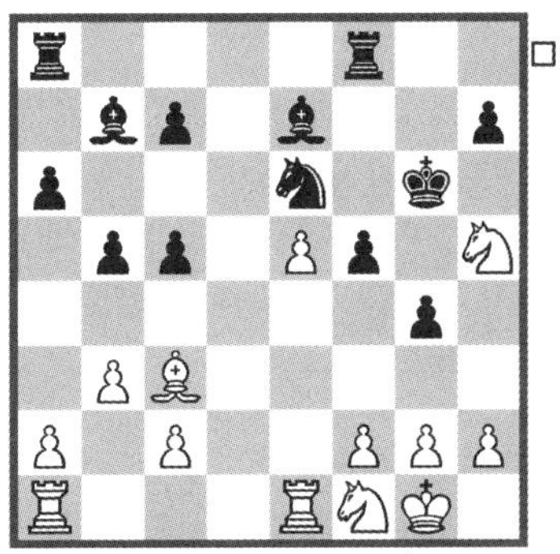

Position after: 21... ♔g6!

22. ♘f6 ♖ad8 23. ♖ad1

White's knight on f6 is out of play. If he wishes, Black could opt for an opposite-colored bishop endgame with an extra pawn (after the move exf6 this pawn will fall). Thus, Black decides to simplify the position by exchanging the rooks – his minor pieces will dominate perfectly, collaborating with his pawns on both flanks.

23... ♖xd1 24. ♖xd1 ♖d8 25. ♖xd8 ♗xd8 26. ♘e3?

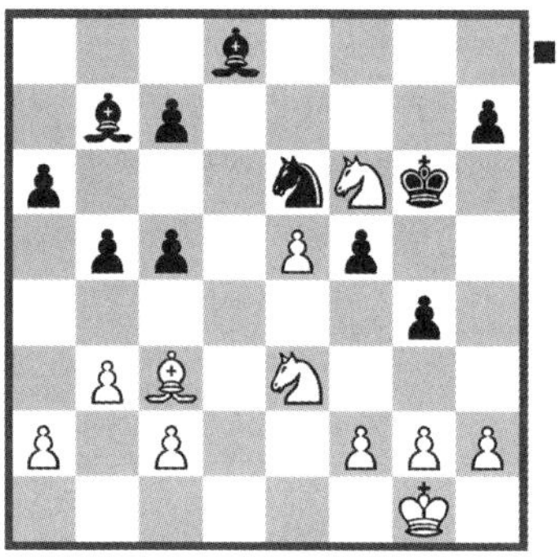

Position after: 26. ♘e3?

26... f4!

Taking the pawn on g4 is forbidden. Black's king gets even the f5-square now.

27. ♘d1 ♗xf6!

This is by far the simplest way to convert Black's huge positional advantage. The point is that Black would collect the white queenside pawns, while still keeping the white minor pieces paralyzed.

28. exf6 ♗e4! 29. ♗b2

(see diagram next column)

Position after: 29. ♗b2

29... b4!

Preventing activation of the knight on d1. White cannot escape; his queenside pawns cannot be saved.

30. f3 ♗xc2 31. ♘f2 gxf3 32. gxf3 ♗b1 33. ♘e4 ♗xa2

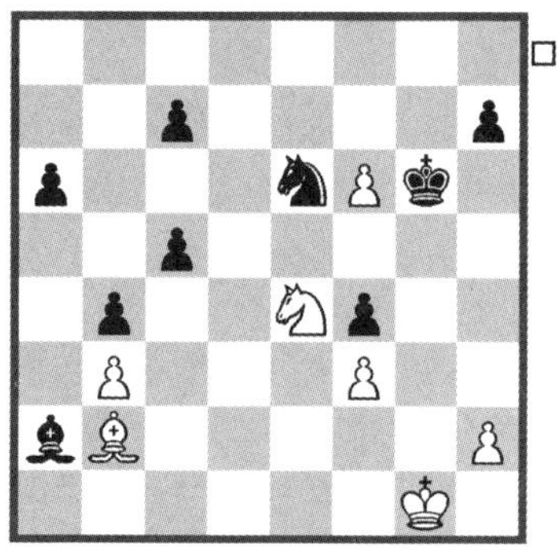

Position after: 33... ♗xa2

Even activated, the white knight is without active possibilities.

34. ♘d2 a5 35. ♔f2 ♘d4

35... c4 36. ♘xc4 ♗xb3 37. ♘xa5

Position after: 37. ♘xa5

37... ♗d5 This would have been a funny line! The roles are switched – now the black bishop paralyzes the white knight, fully this time!

36. ♗xd4 cxd4 37. ♔e2 ♔xf6 38. ♔d3 ♔e5

Position after: 38... ♔e5

39. ♔c2 a4 40. bxa4 c5 41. a5 c4 42. a6 d3+

White resigned.

0-1

Game 180

♙	Naiditsch, Arkadij	(2706)
♟	Blagojevic, Dragisa	(2516)
🌍	Valjevo 2011	

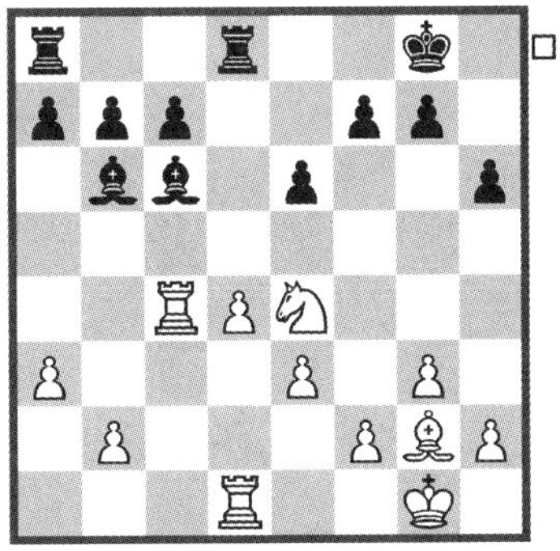

Here White has a significant advantage. The main achievement is the gain of space. Furthermore, the black pieces are without prospects, especially the bishop on b6. Black would rather capture the e4-knight and get a comfortable opposite-colored bishop endgame. Of course, White keeps his knight on the board, which would be more active than the bishop on b6.

20. ♘c3! ♗xg2 21. ♔xg2 c6

Once again with seven pawns on the board the knight is dominant over the bishop! Remember the postulate. In the endgame that arises Black wants to play

...c5 or ...e5, opening the position. White's first task is to prevent both strikes. Secondly, White wants to capitalize on his much better prospects for pawn play – Black is almost without chances to play actively. White's next move is typical and very instructive.

22. g4!

Absolutely instructive. White precisely advances the g-pawn; any other advance would have allowed Black to block the position.

22... ♔f8

22... g5 This is now bad because the pawns are set on the dark squares. White can strike with 23. h4 with a clear advantage.

23. h4 ♔e7

Black cannot avoid the fixing. 23... h5 24. g5! This is clearly better for White.

24. h5!

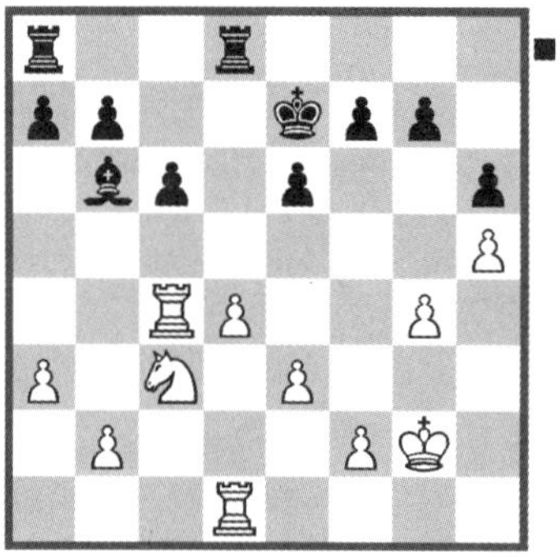

Position after: 24. h5!

24... ♖ac8 25. ♖c1

Preventing 25... c5.

25... ♗c7 26. f4

White has achieved much. Note that Black is out of any satisfactory pawn moves.

26... ♗d6 27. ♔f3 ♔d7

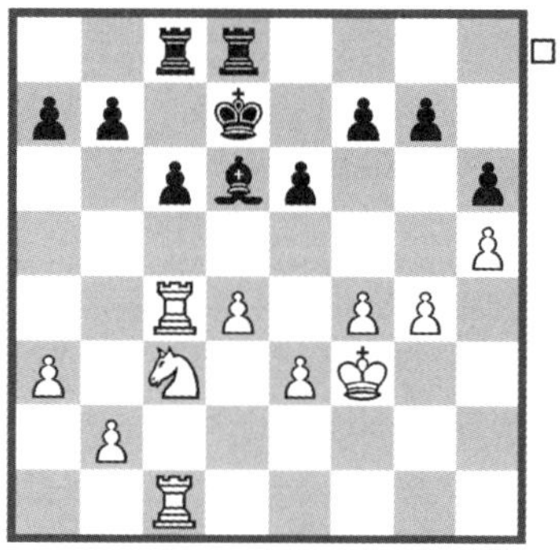

Position after: 27... ♔d7

How should White continue? His space advantage is evident, his pieces are very active, and the king is centralized. Naiditsch's next plan is very logical. It is based on preventing the position opening up. His rooks are busy on the queenside. White, of course, wants to play on the kingside. So, let's transfer the rooks there!

28. ♘e4!

The knight should be placed on d3 – from there it will prevent both ...c5 and ...a5.

28... ♗e7 29. ♘f2 ♗d6 30. ♘d3 ♖g8

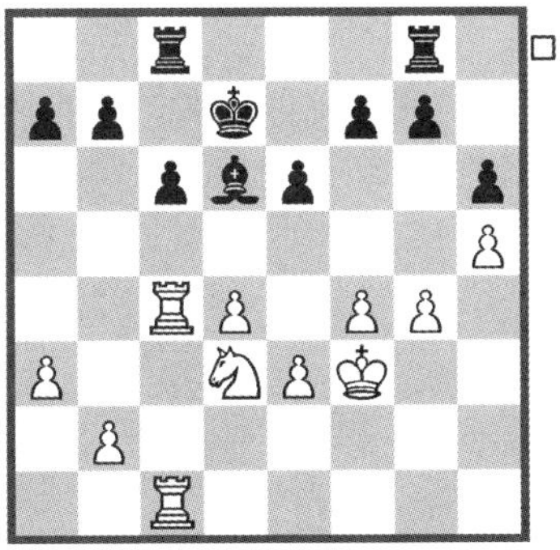

Position after: 30... ♖g8

31. ♖h1

Placing the knight on d3, White wants to employ his rooks. The previous move prevents ...g6 in some positions. White should not hurry with any action.

31... ♖a8

Black feels uncomfortable and makes the decision to activate his rooks via the a-file. Alas, there will not be time; White is quicker with his kingside play.

32. ♖c2

The rooks will double up soon.

32... a5 33. f5

White decides that it is time for action. It is a matter of style. He did not want to spend time or make any preparatory moves for the rook because it was still not clear which file would be opened.

33... ♖ge8

Black's option is solid. He wants to establish a defense on the e-file.

34. e4

Consistently gaining space.

34... e5?!

Position after: 34... e5?!

This is risky. Opening the d-file with the white rooks ready to be doubled cannot be good.

35. dxe5 ♗xe5 36. ♖d1 ♔c7 37. ♘xe5 ♖xe5 38. ♖cd2

Position after: 38. ♖cd2

White is infiltrated.

38... ♖ae8

Black hopes to obtain active play by doubling rooks.

38... ♖e7 This is met by the following. 39. f6! gxf6 40. ♖d6 ♖ae8 41. ♖xf6 ♖xe4 42. ♖xf7+ White plays for a win.

39. ♖d7+ ♔c8 40. ♖xf7 ♖xe4 41. ♖d3

After this simple move the white king is safe and Black is unable to save material.

41... ♖e2

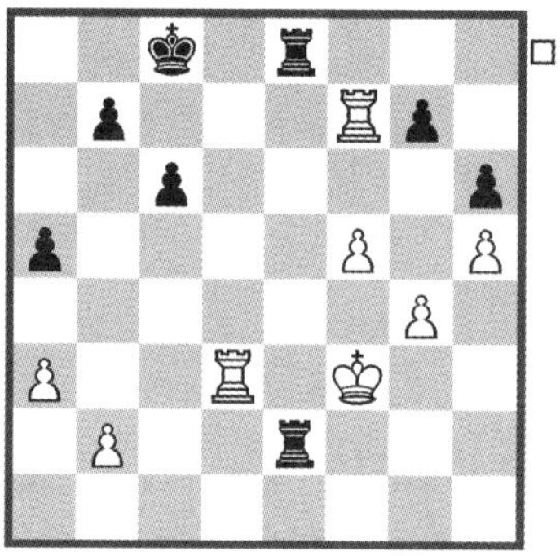

Position after: 41... ♖e2

42. b3?

White has missed a simple win and gives Black a chance to prolong the resistance.

42. ♖xg7! ♖xb2 43. ♖h7 Instead this is easily winning.

42... ♖h2?

A strange mistake. Black has played the last stage indolently.

42... ♖2e7 Instead this was necessary but nevertheless White can play for a win as follows. 43. ♖xe7 ♖xe7 44. g5

43. ♔f4 ♖f2+ 44. ♖f3

Black resigned.

1-0

Game 181

♙ Janowski, Dawid Markelowicz
♟ Capablanca, Jose Raul
🌍 New York 1916

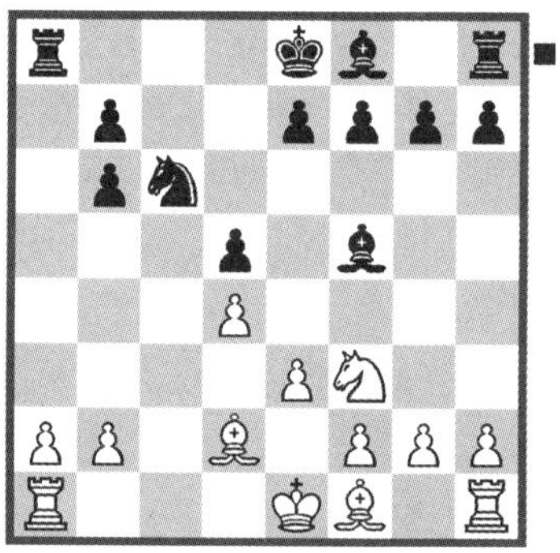

A very interesting and almost symmetrical position. The doubled pawns on the b-file make a difference. But is this a handicap for Black? White has a potential good spot on b5 (perhaps even b4), but Black has the a-file for his activities. Which will prevail? Black's next move is proof of Capablanca's genius, devoted to harmony and logic.

10... ♗d7!

Why does Black waste time for this retreat? First, the bishop controls the important b5-square. Secondly, this move helps Black to exploit the a- and c-files. The plan is to play ...b5 and transfer the knight to c4 with strong pressure.

11. ♗e2

11. ♗d3 Playing this and placing the king on e2 is clearly better. The king belongs in the center.

11... e6 12. 0-0 ♗d6 13. ♖fc1 ♔e7 14. ♗c3 ♖hc8

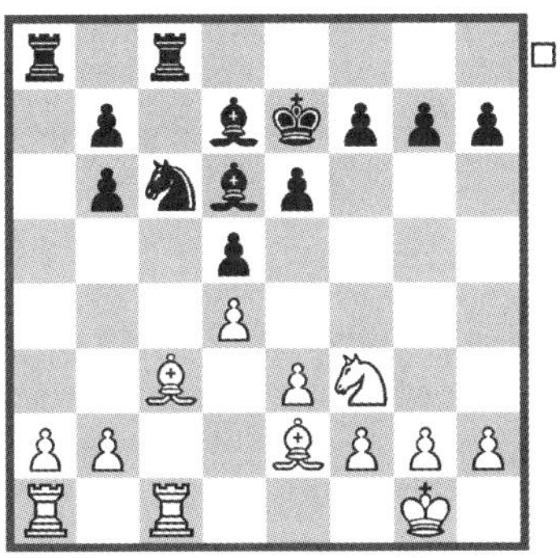

Position after: 14... ♖hc8

15. a3?!

A questionable decision, but White does not have anything concrete that is better.

Instead 15. ♘e1 and placing the knight on d3 looks logical.

15... ♘a5 16. ♘d2 f5!?

Black gains space on the kingside before any action on the queenside.

17. g3 b5 18. f3 ♘c4

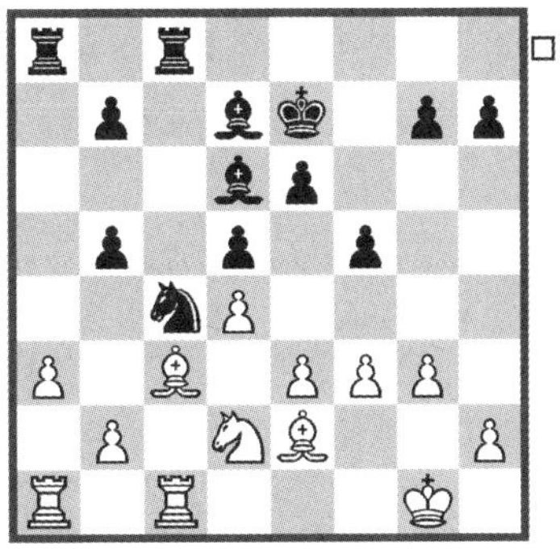

Position after: 18... ♘c4

Comparing this position with the initial diagram it becomes clear that Black has achieved much. Nevertheless White's position is without any weaknesses and his radical decision on the next move is not to be recommended.

19. ♗xc4?!

Not a question mark because the position looks blocked. However, this is an illusion.

A) 19. ♘xc4? This is bad because of the following. 19... bxc4 20. ♔f2

(see analysis diagram next page)

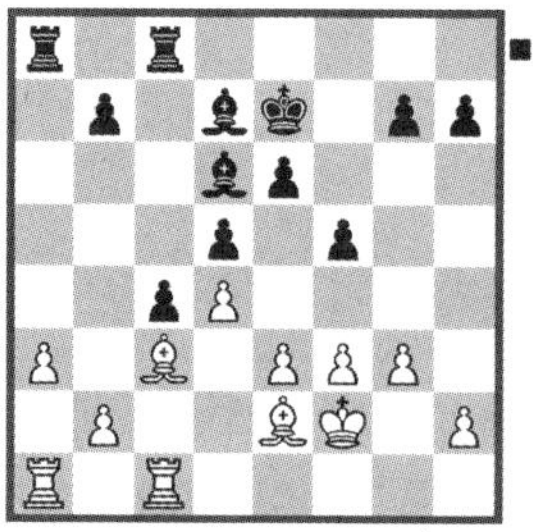

Position after: 20. ♔f2

20... ♗a4 Black's position looks dominant because of the possible ...b5-b4 advance.

B) 19. ♔f2 But why not this calm move?

19... bxc4 20. e4

Having the knight against the bishop, White definitely wants to block the position. However, the point nevertheless is that the bishop pair can prevail – with various important diagonals accessible.

20... ♔f7 21. e5 ♗e7

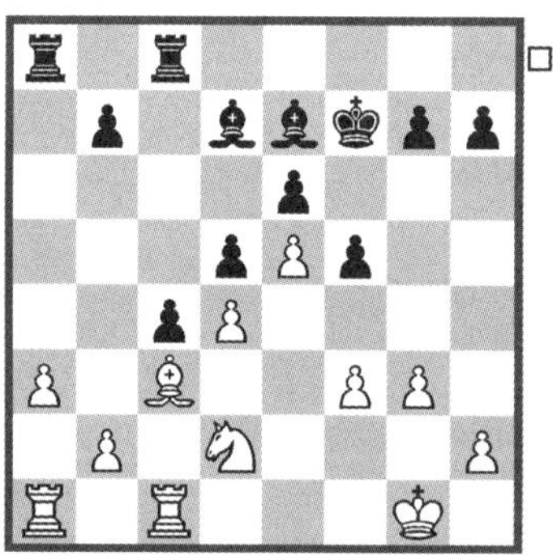

Position after: 21... ♗e7

22. f4?!

This is not logical. White should wait for Black's advance and then block. The point is that Black can play on both wings. Both the ...b4 and ...g5 advances are on the agenda.

22... b5 23. ♔f2 ♖a4

Black prepares ...b4.

24. ♔e3 ♖ca8 25. ♖ab1 h6

And now even ...g5.

26. ♘f3 g5 27. ♘e1 ♖g8 28. ♔f3

Position after: 28. ♔f3

White is forced to wait. There is nothing active that can be done.

28... gxf4?!

I need to criticize Capa for this move. It would have been logical to improve his pieces fully before opening the g-file.

28... ♗e8! The idea is to transfer the bishop to h5 before capturing. This would have been much more dangerous for White.

29. gxf4 ♖aa8 30. ♘g2?

30. ♘c2! Necessary. White would establish a firm blockade on the b4-square and be able with ♖g1 to counter on the g-file. His position would be safe.

30... ♖g4 31. ♖g1 ♖ag8

Now there is a deadly pin on the g-file.

32. ♗e1

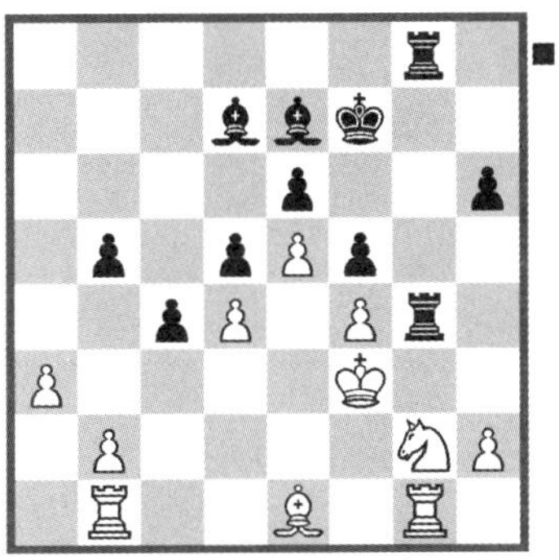

Position after: 32. ♗e1

32... b4?

Capablanca finds a different way to activate the light-squared bishop – via the a4-square.

32... ♗e8! Much stronger, transferring the bishop to h5 again.

33. axb4

33. ♗xb4 ♗a4 Black invades with devastating effect after 34. ♗xe7 ♗c2!.

33... ♗a4 34. ♖a1?

34. ♖c1 This is better, but 34... ♖4g7 keeps a plus. Black would have been forced to reorganize the troops and perhaps even switch the bishop to h5 or the rook to the queenside.

34... ♗c2 35. ♗g3?

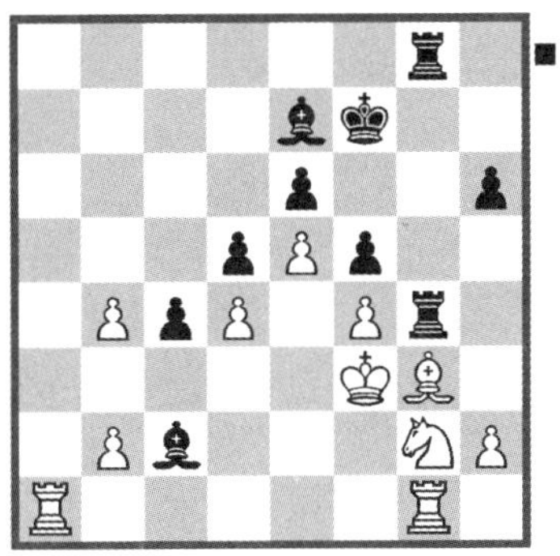

Position after: 35. ♗g3?

White closes the g-file ... but this is just temporary.

35. ♖a7! ♗e4+ 36. ♔e3 This is a much better version and there is no progress for Black evident.

35... ♗e4+ 36. ♔f2 h5! 37. ♖a7 ♗xg2 38. ♖xg2 h4

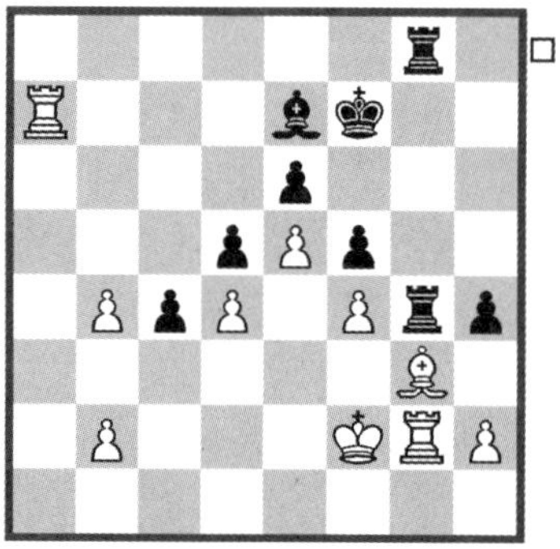

Position after: 38... h4

It is game over.

39. ♗xh4 ♖xg2+ 40. ♔f3 ♖xh2 41. ♗xe7 ♖h3+ 42. ♔f2 ♖b3 43. ♗g5+ ♔g6 44. ♖e7 ♖xb2+ 45. ♔f3 ♖a8 46. ♖xe6+ ♔h7

White resigned.

0-1

Restriction & Prophylaxis

The concept of prophylaxis is more or less clear. The point is to prevent the opponent's attack by strengthening your defensive lines, to eliminate weaknesses and potential weaknesses, to over-protect the king, and to patiently organize your attack by eliminating any potential counterplay, etc.

The concept of restriction is a more complex one. It is always surprising to me that there are players, even at the top level, who almost never implement this concept. Of course, they know about it, but their mindset simply forces them to choose direct play instead. Of course, a player's character and personality matter.

What I want to say simply is that you will sometimes get positions where you cannot find a direct way to play. What to do then? Well, in such situations, do not allow your opponent to play actively – restrict their active possibilities. And this does not only refer to keeping their pieces blocked, restricted or simply passive.

Moreover, even if you have an "obvious action" sometimes it is better simply to defer playing it, and instead restrict your opponent's possibilities. Many masters of the past, such as Rubinstein, Nimzowitsch, Karpov, and Andersson teach us that this concept can be a dangerous one. Of course, it can be based even on the opponent's personality and playing style – if they are an attacker and someone who likes direct play then it would probably be wise to restrict their actions. I must say that this concept is one of my favorites and here I present some of my "masterpieces".

Game 182

♙ Alekhine, Alexander
♟ Euwe, Max
London 1922

In this chapter we consider how to prevent the opponent's plans when you are not able to go for any action yet, or to wait for a better moment to start any action.

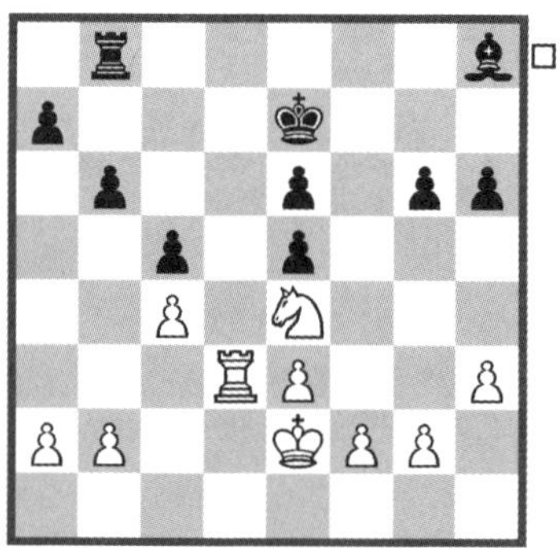

Let's start this chapter with a simple example. Black is paralyzed. White has managed to install his knight on the e4-square and to fix the black queenside pawns with c4. It is time to find a breakthrough. Although it appears that White should try to do so on the kingside, Alekhine finds it on the queenside. White is much better in this position. Surprisingly, the presence of so many pawns helps Black practically – White cannot easily penetrate.

23. a4!

White wants to create a weakness on the queenside and open the file for the rook to invade.

23... ♖c8

23... a5 This collapses immediately after 24. ♖b3.

24. ♖b3 ♔d7 25. a5 ♔c6

Position after: 25... ♔c6

What else?

26. axb6 axb6 27. ♖a3 ♗g7 28. ♖a7

After forced play that is characteristic of Alekhine, his rook penetrates.

28... ♖c7 29. ♖a8 ♖e7 30. ♖c8+ ♔d7 31. ♖g8

White's rook is in the opponent's camp and enjoys working hard.

31... ♔c6

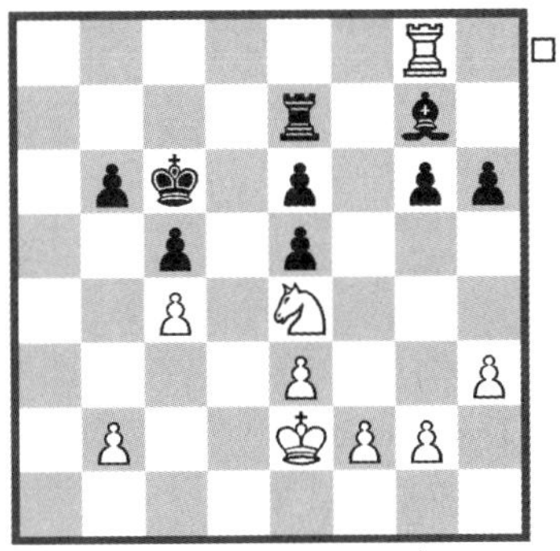

Position after: 31... ♔c6

32. h4

Now White decides to create some weaknesses on the kingside. Moreover after g4-g5 the bishop will be restricted, the point of which will become clear soon.

32... ♔c7 33. g4 ♔c6 34. ♔d3 ♖d7+ 35. ♔c3 ♖f7 36. b3

There is no reason to hurry.

36... ♔c7 37. ♔d3 ♖d7+ 38. ♔e2

Alekhine patiently plays, confusing the opponent.

38... ♖f7

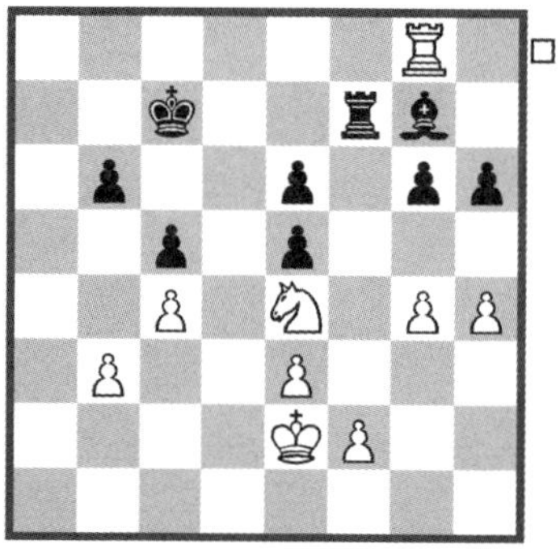

Position after: 38... ♖f7

39. ♘c3

The knight comes to b5, vacating the e4-square for the king. This is a decisive regrouping.

39... ♖e7 40. g5!

The knight has left the e4-square – now this pawn will keep the bishop paralyzed.

40... hxg5 41. hxg5 ♔c6 42. ♔d3 ♖d7+ 43. ♔e4

Position after: 43. ♔e4

Note Black's passive army. It is not often that you see such brutal domination.

43... ♖c7 44. ♘b5 ♖e7

44... ♖f7 45. ♖c8+ This would be a fine end to the game.

45. f3 ♔d7

45... ♔b7 46. ♘d6+ This wins in style after ♘e8.

46. ♖b8 ♔c6 47. ♖c8+

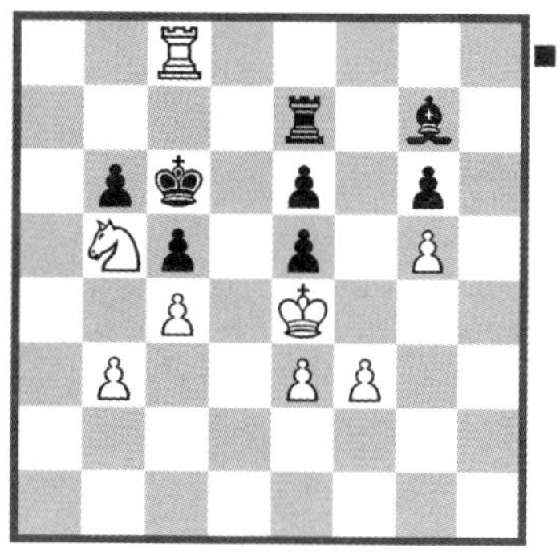

Position after: 47. ♖c8+

47... ♔d7

47... ♔b7 48. ♘d6+ ♔a7 49. ♖g8 This wins after the unavoidable ♘e8.

48. ♖c7+ ♔d8 49. ♖c6 ♖b7 50. ♖xe6

Black finally resigned.

1-0

Game 183

♙ Geller, Efim P (2590)
♟ Mikhalchishin, Adrian (2460)
Tbilisi 1978

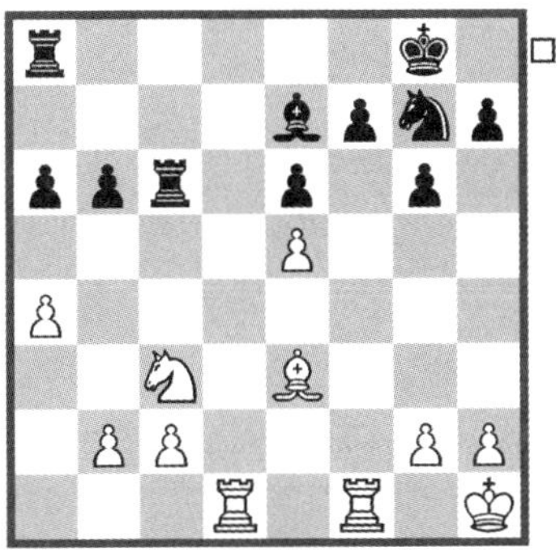

This example is more complicated, but nevertheless White's domination is evident. Moreover, the plan found by Geller suggests itself.

21. ♖d7! ♖e8 22. g4!

The move that secures the win. White excludes the black knight from the game. After this White will get time to organize any plan.

22... h5 23. h3

Of course.

23... hxg4 24. hxg4 b5

(see diagram next column)

A desperate try.

Position after: 24... b5

25. axb5 axb5 26. ♘e4

This move could have been prepared, but there is no need. White has calculated precisely.

26... ♖xc2 27. ♘f6+

The simplest. White takes a piece. Black cannot survive with the horribly weak dark squares and the angry white pieces.

27... ♗xf6 28. exf6 ♖xb2 29. fxg7 f5 30. ♖f3

Position after: 30. ♖f3

Intending ♖h3-h8.

30... fxg4 31. ♖f4 ♖c8 32. ♗c5

Black resigned. No sublines are needed at all.

1-0

Game 184

♙ Andersson, Ulf (2620)
♟ Lanka, Zigurds (2540)
Tilburg 1994

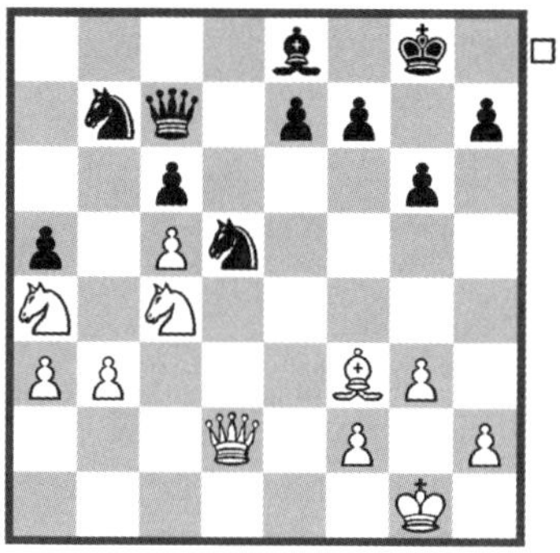

White is clearly dominant. Black's minor pieces are horribly placed. Furthermore, White has the better majority and can soon expand.

28. ♕d4

White first centralizes his queen, preventing some active moves such as ...e5.

28. ♗xd5? cxd5 29. ♕xd5 Of course this should not be even seriously considered in view of, for instance the following. 29... ♗xa4 30. bxa4 e6 White has released the pressure.

28... e6 29. ♘e5 h5?!

Preventing ♘g4 in this way is not advisable. White can later play against this pawn with h4, f3 and g4.

29... ♕e7 30. ♘g4 h5 This Is a better version for Black.

30. b4 axb4 31. axb4 ♕d8 32. ♘b6

White's last unit comes into play.

32... ♔h7

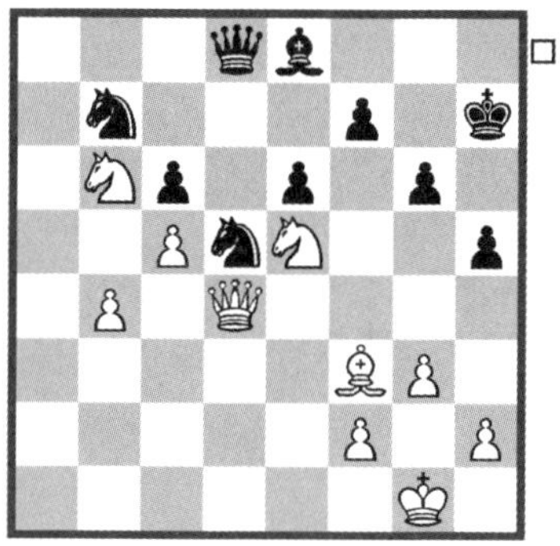

Position after: 32... ♔h7

33. ♘xd5!?

A strange decision. No doubt Andersson had worked out the winning plan before trading. Nevertheless this looks to only improve Black's structure.

33. ♗xd5 This is another, perhaps more logical, plan. After setting the knight on d4 White can push b5.

33... exd5 34. ♗e2

White relocates the knight to d4.

34... ♕f6 35. ♘f3

35. f4! Playing this first without rushing would have been even better. White should delay exchanging queens because he has more improving moves.

35... ♔g7 36. ♗a6 ♘d8 37. ♗c8

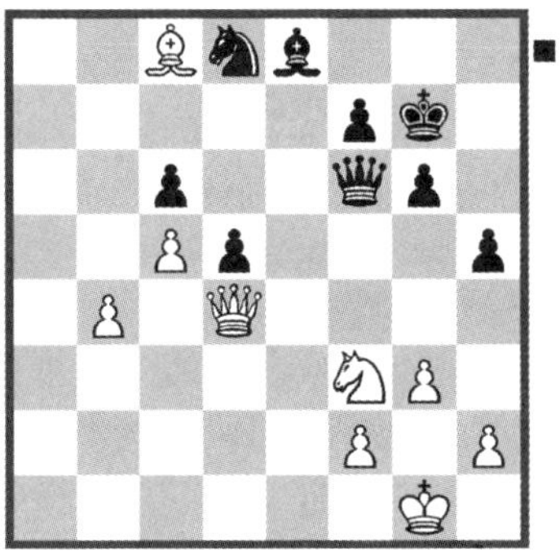

Position after: 37. ♗c8

This maneuver paralyzes the black minor pieces. White could have achieved the same with the pawn on f4, which would have been a much better version.

37... ♕xd4 38. ♘xd4 ♔f6 39. f4

Black is at a crossroads. Which piece should be activated? He opts for the bishop.

39... ♔e7?!

39... ♘e6! This must be preferable. 40. ♗xe6 fxe6 41. ♔f2 e5 42. fxe5+ ♔xe5 43. ♔e3 g5 This should be holdable for Black relatively easily.

40. ♔f2 ♗d7 41. ♗a6 ♔f6

41... ♘e6 This simply does not work. 42. ♔e3 ♘xd4 43. ♔xd4 After this the endgame is winning for White. He even has the h4 fixing motif. See if you can work out the winning plan.

42. ♔e3 ♔e7 43. ♗d3 ♗e8 44. ♔d2 ♗d7 45. ♔c3 ♗e8 46. ♗e2 ♗d7 47. ♗f3

The previous moves have been improving ones. On the other hand, Black cannot improve; White has achieved much. Black tries to change the character of the situation.

47... ♘e6

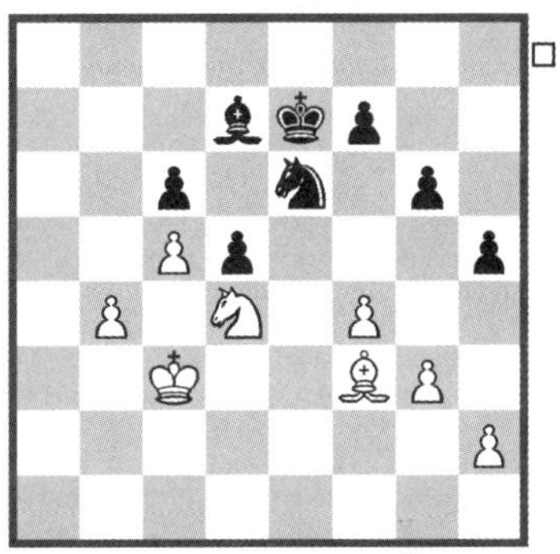

Position after: 47... ♘e6

48. ♗g2!?

This doesn't spoil anything, but capturing would have simplified the win.

48. ♘xe6 fxe6 49. ♔d4 ♔f6 50. ♗e2 ♗e8 51. ♗d3 ♗d7 52. h3 ♗e8

53. ♗c2 ♗d7 54. g4

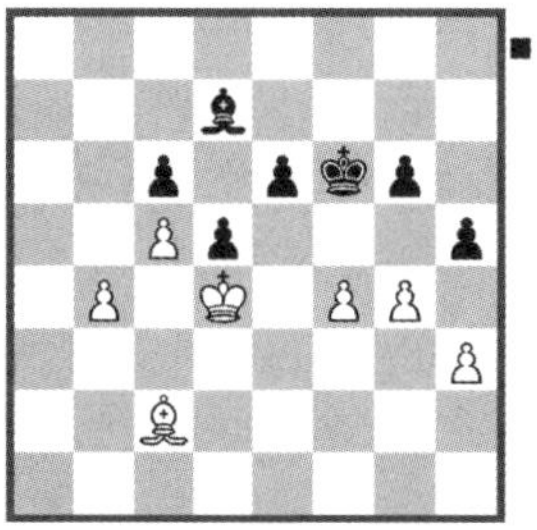

Position after: 54. g4

54... hxg4 55. hxg4 g5 56. fxg5+ ♔xg5 57. ♔e5 ♔xg4 58. ♔d6 ♗e8 59. ♔e7 ♗h5 60. ♗d1+

Position after: 60. ♗d1+

60... ♔g5 61. ♗xh5 ♔xh5 62. b5 This is one of the many beautiful lines.

48... ♘c7 49. ♗f1 ♔f6 50. ♗d3

Position after: 50. ♗d3

White prepares b5 and allows the next move.

White did not want to play 50. h4 because at some point Black would threaten ...♔f5-g4.

50... g5 51. fxg5+ ♔xg5 52. ♔d2

Before any action the king goes to e3.

52... ♘e6 53. ♘f3+ ♔f6 54. ♔e3 ♘g7 55. ♘d4 ♘e6 56. ♗e2

Position after: 56. ♗e2

White reminds Black of the h5 weakness. With weaknesses on both wings Black cannot resist.

56... ♘g7 57. ♗d1

Intending ♗a4.

57... ♔e5 58. h4

A methodical move.

58. ♗a4 A direct and easy win. 58... ♘f5+ 59. ♘xf5 ♔xf5 60. ♗d1

♔g5 61. h4+ 61... ♔g6 62. ♔f4 Now White just wins after g4. Black cannot stop both the c- and h-pawns in the pawn endgame.

58... f6 59. ♗c2 ♗e8

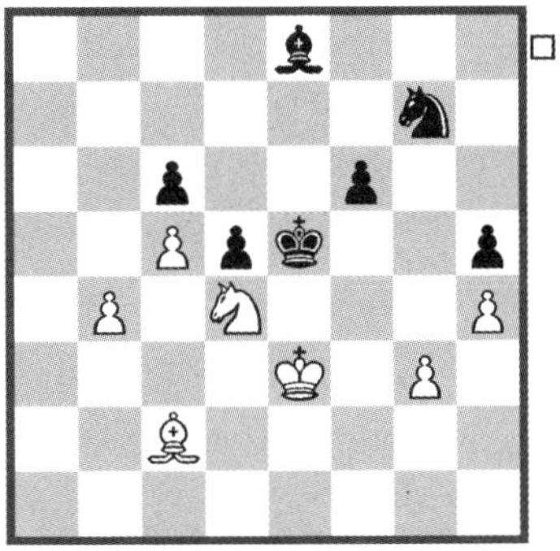

Position after: 59... ♗e8

Preventing ♗g6 and waiting.

60. ♗d3

60. ♗a4? Playing this now is a serious mistake. 60... ♘f5+ 61. ♘xf5 ♔xf5 62. ♗d1 ♔e5 Black plays ...d4 and holds.

60... ♗d7 61. ♘f3+ ♔e6 62. ♔f4

Black's king is driven back and White improves even his king. Black's bishop is equally bad, while he has problems with his knight which was "fianchettoed" on the queenside and now on the kingside.

62... ♔e7 63. ♘d4 ♔f7 64. ♗a6 ♘e6+

Necessary.

65. ♘xe6 ♔xe6

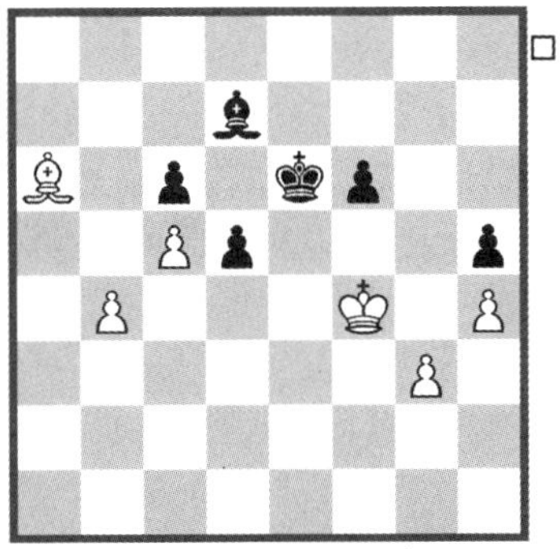

Position after: 65... ♔xe6

Black has saved his queenside pawns, but White switches side, simultaneously playing on both wings and creating passers to bring the win.

66. ♗e2 ♗e8 67. g4 hxg4 68. ♗xg4+ ♔e7 69. h5 ♔f7 70. h6

Position after: 70. h6

70... ♔g8 71. ♗f5

Fully paralyzing.

71... ♔h8 72. ♔e3 ♔g8 73. ♔d4 ♔h8 74. ♔c3

There is no need to rush.

74... ♔g8 75. ♔b3 ♔h8 76. ♔c3 ♔g8 77. ♔d4 ♔h8

Position after: 77... ♔h8

78. b5! cxb5 79. ♔xd5 ♗f7+ 80. ♔d6 ♗h5 81. c6 ♗f3 82. c7 ♗b7 83. ♔c5

1-0

Game 185

♙ Henneberger, Walter
♟ Nimzowitsch, Aron
Winterthur 1931

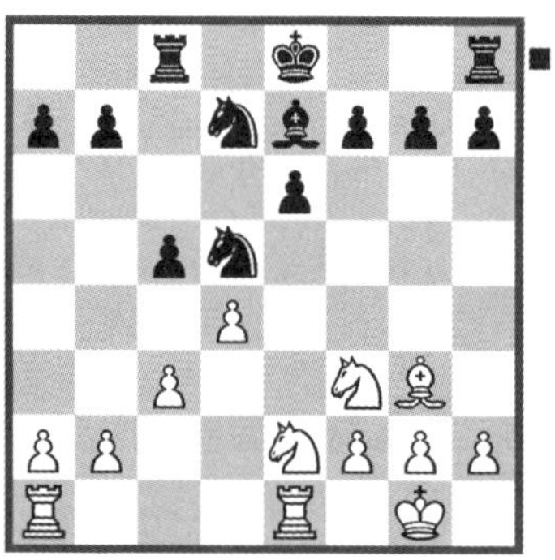

Black is already preferable in this position. White has played the opening apathetically and his cavalry is restricted by the c3- and d4-pawns. With his move, Black applies restriction.

15... c4!

A logical and powerful concept. First, Black gains space on the queenside. Secondly, this move secures the knight's excellent position on d5. Thirdly, it fixes the white pawns on the dark squares on c3 and d4 respectively, at the same time taking away any prospects for the white minor pieces.

16. ♘e5!?

A clever idea. White wants to exchange the d7-knight and later use the e2-knight to exchange the knight on d5.

16. ♘f4 This achieves nothing for White because of the following. 16... ♘xf4 17. ♗xf4 ♘b6 Black still controls the important d5-outpost!

16... ♘xe5 17. ♗xe5 f6! 18. ♗g3

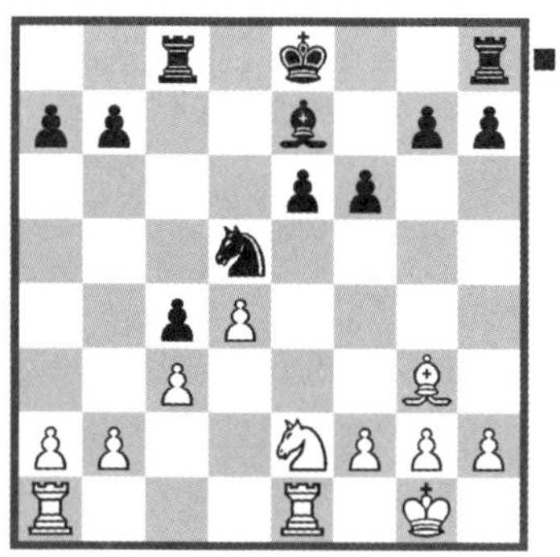

Position after: 18. ♗g3

18... g5!

It is very important to keep the knight on d5 alive. Black prevents the move 19. ♘f4. From this moment onwards the advantage is undoubtedly on Black's side. White would soon feel the lack of space and would not have any promising plans, both on the queenside and on the kingside.

19. f4?!

White still dreams of exchanging knights, which is natural. However, knowing his next moves, this move is inadvisable.

19... h6!

Of course.

19... g4 This looks natural, but Black is not better after the following. 20. f5! exf5 21. ♘f4 ♘xf4 22. ♗xf4

20. ♖ad1 ♔f7 21. ♖d2 b5!

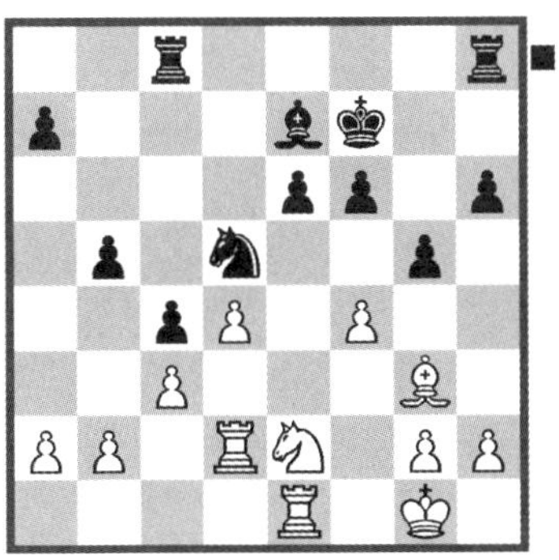

Position after: 21... b5!

White's pieces are cramped. White can only follow Black's activities. Black can organize active play on both flanks. On the kingside he wants to play ...g4 with ...f5, so he must still wait. It is time to organize queenside play – Black stands better there, because the white minor pieces cannot take part in the struggle.

22. ♖f1 ♖he8 23. ♖f3?

It is very difficult to comprehend the idea behind this move. Black uses the perfect moment to play the following.

23... g4! 24. ♖f1 f5!

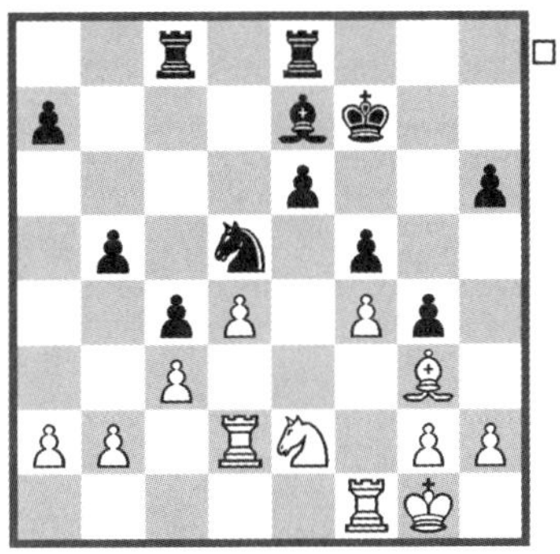

Position after: 24... f5!

Black has played ...g4 with tempo and following it with ...f5. From this moment onwards White is desperately lost. His minor pieces would rather be in different places ... but alas they are fully paralyzed.

25. ♗f2 ♖g8!?

Probably preventing the move h4 and preparing a possible kingside attack.

26. g3 h5 27. ♔g2 ♗d6

The best place for the bishop!

28. ♖c1 h4! 29. ♖dd1 ♖h8 30. ♖d2

What else is there to do?

30... ♔e7!

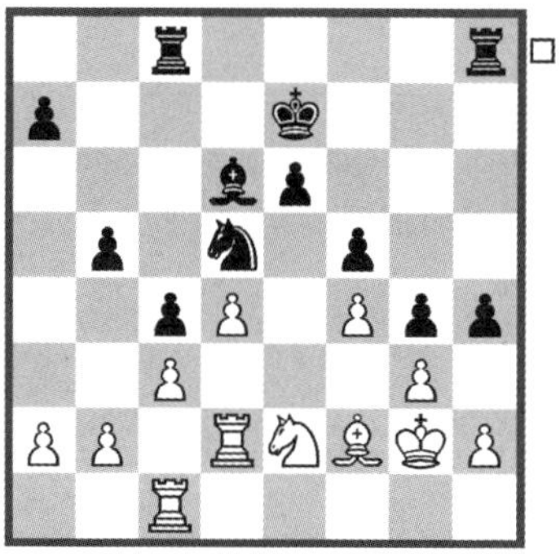

Position after: 30... ♔e7!

Black wants to set all his pieces on their best squares before any pawn action. The king goes closer to the d5-square (or even to a4) in order to be ready for instant action. If your opponent is in a hopeless situation and is so passive that they are reduced to following your activities, then you must dominate in the center and on both flanks. If you have better "communication lines" due to an advantage in space or mobility, then the most important point is "don't rush!" By playing patiently you would probably confuse your opponent, perhaps even wait for their mistake and reduce the chances for your own mistakes.

31. ♖dc2 ♔d7 32. ♖e1 ♖h7 33. ♖a1 hxg3!?

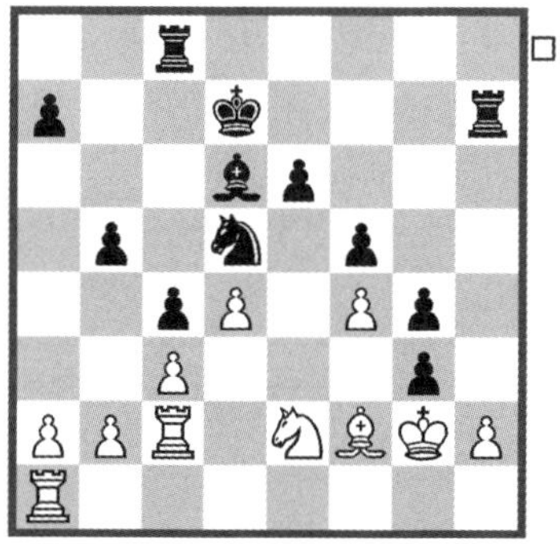

Position after: 33... hxg3!?

An interesting move order. It appears that Black wants to exchange rooks on the h-file and win the game on the opposite side.

34. hxg3 a5 35. ♖cc1 ♖ch8 36. ♖h1 ♖xh1 37. ♖xh1 ♖xh1 38. ♔xh1 b4!

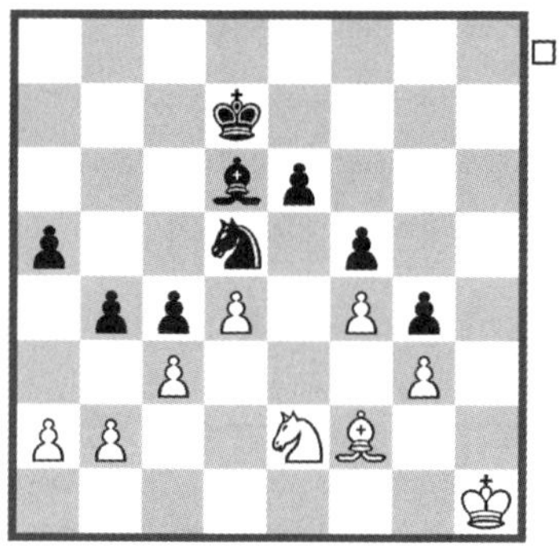

Position after: 38... b4!

Note the difference in activity between the black and white troops. Black is winning.

39. ♔g2 a4

Preparing both ...a3 and ...b3!. Instead, 39... b3 40. axb3 [40. ♘c1 a4; 40. a4

♗a3] 40... cxb3 41. c4 ♘b4 42. c5 ♘d3 This also wins.

40. cxb4 ♗xb4 41. ♔f1 ♔c6 42. ♗e1

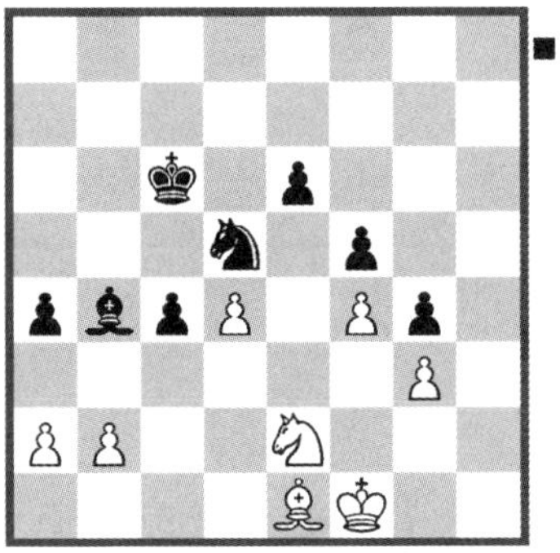

Position after: 42. ♗e1

42... ♔b5?

Nimzowitsch has played the perfect game, but this move is a mistake.

A) 42... ♘e3+ 43. ♔f2 ♘d1+ 44. ♔f1 ♗xe1 45. ♔xe1 ♘xb2 46. ♘c3 ♘d3+

Position after: 46... ♘d3+

47. ♔d2 ♘f2 48. ♔e3 ♘e4 49. ♘xe4 fxe4 50. ♔xe4 a3! This would have been the obvious continuation.

B) 42... a3 43. bxa3 ♗xa3 The idea is ...♗b2 and winning.

43. ♘c3+!

Now Black must make much more effort in order to win the game again.

43... ♗xc3! 44. bxc3 ♔c6

It is only possible to penetrate via the e4-square.

45. ♔e2 ♘f6 46. ♔e3 ♘e4 47. ♔e2 ♔d5 48. ♔e3

Position after: 48. ♔e3

It is clear that Black must install his king on e4 instead of the knight. However, how should he do so? Clearly the knight must be used to deflect the black troops, perhaps with some zugzwang motifs.

48... ♔d6!!

White's king creates a triangle in advance! Black's king cannot do the same – the squares d2 and f2 are taken up by the black knight!

48... ♘d6 This achieves nothing. 49.

♗d2 ♘b5 50. ♗e1 ♘a3 51. ♗d2 ♘b1

Position after: 51... ♘b1

52. ♗e1 Black has not achieved anything. It is clear that with White having the move in this position, there will be a zugzwang. Therefore, Black must lose a tempo. If the black king triangulates, then the white king would do the same! There will be no progress!

49. ♔e2 ♔c6 50. ♔e3 ♔d5 51. ♔e2

51. a3 ♘d6 52. ♗d2

Position after: 52. ♗d2

52... ♘b5–+

51... ♘d6 52. ♔e3 ♘b5 53. ♗d2 ♘a3

Mission accomplished!

54. ♗c1 ♘b1!

Position after: 54... ♘b1!

55. ♗b2 a3! 56. ♗a1

A picturesque situation. Both the minor pieces are paralyzed. However, what to do now? Black needs to lose a tempo to obtain the same position if White was having the move. White's king cannot triangulate because it must control the d2-square!

56... ♔d6 57. ♔e2 ♔c6 58. ♔d1 ♔d5 59. ♔c2

Position after: 59. ♔c2

59... ♔e4 60. ♔xb1 ♔f3 61. ♗b2! axb2!

61... ♔xg3? 62. ♗xa3

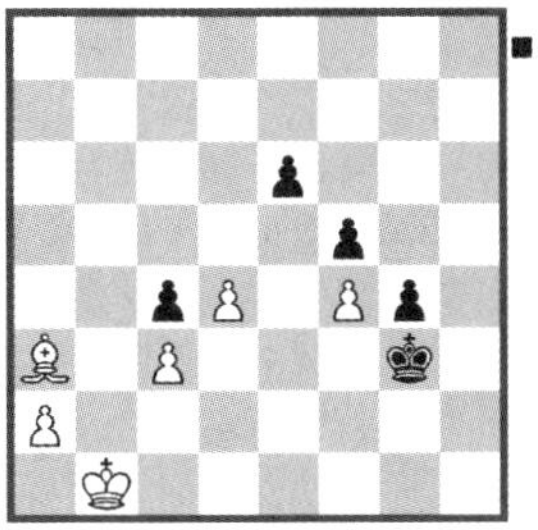

Position after: 62. ♗xa3

62... ♔f3 [62... ♔xf4 63. ♗d6+] 63. d5 exd5 64. ♗c5 Surprisingly, White will win!

62. a4 ♔xg3 63. a5 ♔h2!

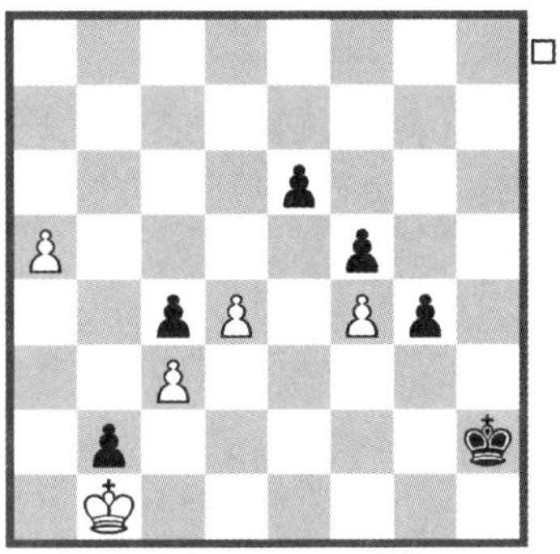

Position after: 63... ♔h2!

This move secures the win. The point will become apparent soon.

64. a6 g3 65. a7 g2 66. a8=♕ g1=♕+ 67. ♔xb2 ♕g2+!

After exchanging queens Black will promote first.

68. ♕xg2+ ♔xg2 69. ♔a3 ♔f3 70. ♔b4 ♔xf4 71. ♔xc4 ♔e3 72. d5 exd5+ 73. ♔xd5 f4 74. c4 f3 75. c5 f2 76. c6 f1=♕

White resigned.

0-1

Game 186

♙ Zlatanovic, Boroljub (2342)
♟ Ostojic, Nikola (2327)
Arandjelovac 2021

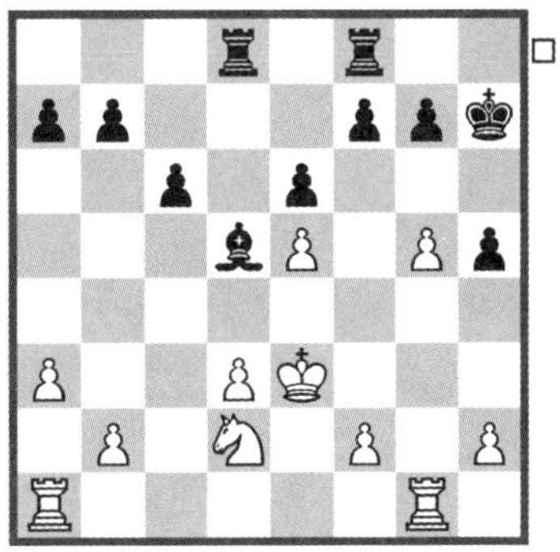

Methods of restriction and prophylaxis are widely implemented in my own games, as I am devoted to Nimzowitsch's and Petrosian's opus. For the end of this chapter I will present a few of my own games.

In this position it may appear strange that White is preferable. Why? The bishop looks very strong, doesn't it? The king may use the light squares to invade and there is a backward d3-pawn, right? Typically, yes. However, I decided to go for this endgame because of one reason that is not immediately apparent – the bishop cannot move, especially after the next move. Thus, the black rooks would be useless on the d-file.

22. ♖ac1 ♖d7

Not a bad move because the other rook can go even to a8 to prepare ...a5. Black must desperately find a way to activate the rooks. Otherwise White's upcoming initiative will become dangerous. White simply has a lot of useful moves.

22... f6? This would not have been a good way to open up the position. 23. gxf6 gxf6 24. exf6 ♖xf6 25. ♖g5

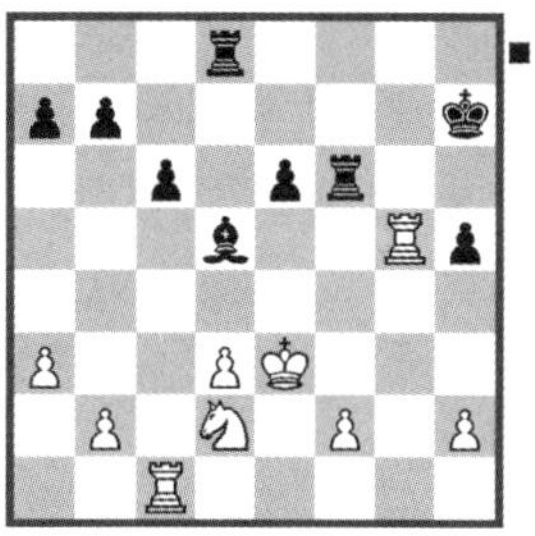

Position after: 25. ♖g5

25... ♔h6 26. f4 ♖df8 27. ♖f1 White is dominant.

23. ♖c3 ♔g6

This is risky, because the king simply cannot do anything.

23... b6 This would have been a good try. 24. b4 This would probably have been White's response. Here some crazy move such as 24... b5!? deserves attention because Black wants to advance ...a5 and not to allow b5.

24. h4 ♖fd8

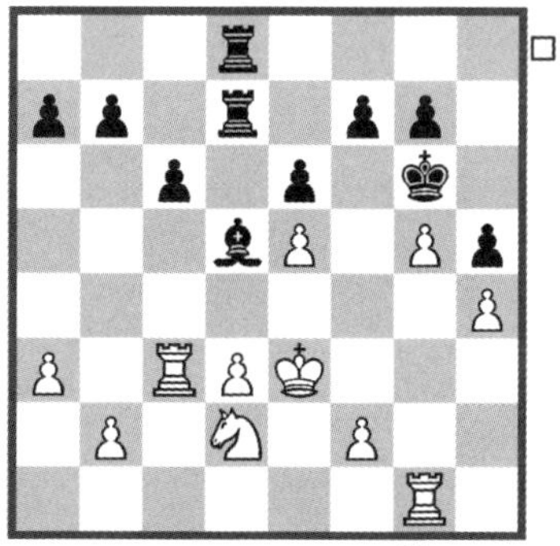

Position after: 24... ♖fd8

24... ♔f5?! 25. d4! The threat is g5 and the king must go back.

25. ♘f1!

The knight goes to g3 to paralyze the black king by controlling the f5-square and attacking the h5-pawn. There is a dangerous threat of ♘e2-f4, so Black must retreat.

25... ♔h7 26. ♘g3 g6

It has become clear that Black has lost a significant amount of time. White uses this fact to accumulate an advantage on the opposite side.

27. b4 ♔g7?!

A natural move which may be criticized.

27... b5!? Instead this should have been played with ...a5 next – this would have been an interesting plan again.

28. ♘e2 ♖a8

Finally Black wants to advance ...a5.

29. ♖b1

White prevents this.

29... ♔f8 30. ♘d4

Position after: 30. ♘d4

Comparing this diagram to the initial one it becomes clear that Black has been outplayed. White has achieved much; the black pieces are grouped behind the bishop which simply blocks them all.

30... ♔e7?

An irrelevant move which allows White to make the breakthrough.

Instead 30... a6 and 30... b5 would have been ugly, but were necessary defensive moves.

31. b5 cxb5 32. ♘xb5 ♗c6 33. ♘d6

(see diagram next column)

Position after: 33. ♘d6

Now White can organize the pressure on b7. After provoking ...b6 there would be an invasion through the c-file. In addition, there is a possibility to double on the f-file and attack the f7-pawn. Now it becomes clear why f4 was not played at all.

33... ♖xd6!?

Evidently this was Black's defensive intention. I really think that when the knight comes to d6, it's a necessity at some point. Nevertheless the position is not sufficiently blocked, and White can organize play on both flanks.

34. exd6+ ♔xd6

35. ♖b4!

A very good and important move. The rook will tie up a piece to defend the f7-pawn. Moreover, with forthcoming checks the black king may be driven back.

35... ♖e8 36. ♖f4 ♔e7 37. ♖d4

Now White wants at some point to transfer his king to e5 fully paralyzing Black.

37... e5

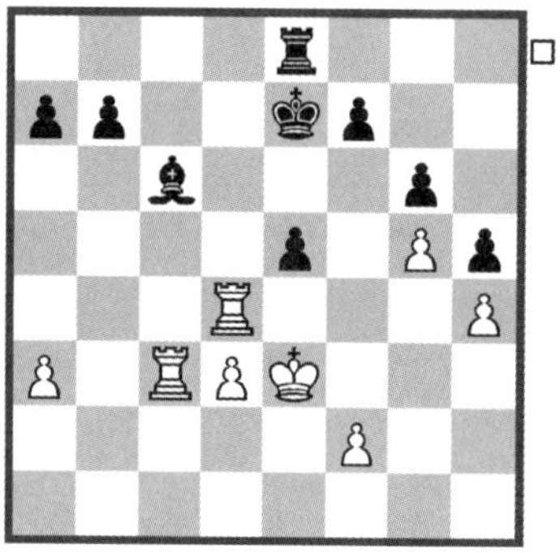

Position after: 37... e5

What else? Black has some fresh air, but White wants to provoke this move anyway. Now f4 will open up the position – with an exchange up, it's time to open the files to invade the opponent's camp!

38. ♖b4 ♔d6 39. ♔d2 ♖e6 40. f4 f5!? 41. gxf6 ♖xf6 42. fxe5+ ♔xe5 43. ♖c5+

Position after: 43. ♖c5+

43... ♔d6 44. ♖g5 ♔c7 45. ♔c3 b6 46. ♖d4!

Concrete play with the idea of invading. It may appear that the rook can be locked after Black's next move, but White has calculated precisely.

46... a5 47. ♖e5! b5 48. ♖e7+ ♔b6 49. ♖d8

The game is over. Black goes for a desperate attack.

49... ♖f4 50. ♖d6!

Position after: 50. ♖d6!

The point. Black's bishop falls in various lines after being pinned.

50... b4+ 51. axb4 axb4+ 52. ♔d2 ♔c5 53. ♖xg6 ♖f2+

(see diagram next page)

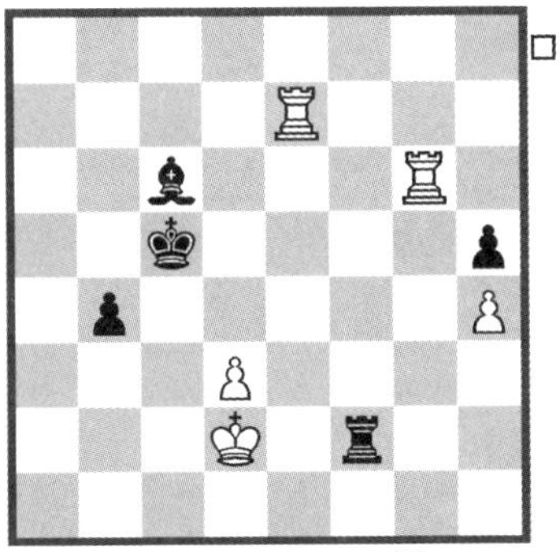

Position after: 53... ♖f2+

54. ♖e2

Simplification. Black must accept it.

54... ♖xe2+

A) 54... ♖f5 This loses after 55. ♖g5.

B) 54... ♖f4 55. ♖e5+ ♔d4 56. ♖xh5 ♖f2+ 57. ♔e1 It is time to resign.

55. ♔xe2 ♗e8 56. ♖g8 ♗f7 57. ♖b8 ♗d5 58. ♔e3 ♗e6 59. ♖e8

Position after: 59. ♖e8

There is no need to rush.

59... ♔d5 60. ♖b8 ♔c5 61. ♔e4 ♗d5+ 62. ♔e5 ♗c6 63. d4+ ♔c4 64. d5 ♗a4 65. d6

Black resigned.

1-0

Game 187

♙	Zlatanovic, Boroljub	(2334)
♟	Ilincic, Zlatko	(2326)
🌍	Pool 2022	

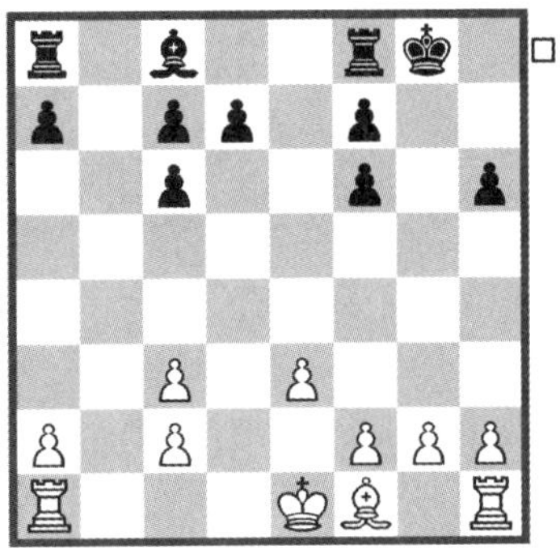

An important game against an idol from my youth, with the first place at stake. White is evidently better, with his better king, better development and more compact structure. It is important to occupy the b-file first, especially because this would keep the black bishop on c8 for awhile.

12. ♖b1! d6 13. ♔d2!

It is bad to activate the bishop first because there are many options for it. So, let's first move the king – it must go to d2.

13... ♖e8?

A serious mistake. Black wants to delay any activation of the bishop but this is bad. The idea is ...♖e5 with action on the 5th rank, but the subsequent strong response cuts off Black's plans.

13... ♗e6! This was necessary instead and gives White a small edge after the following. 14. ♗a6 [14. ♖b7 This can be parried as follows. 14... ♖ab8 15. ♖xc7

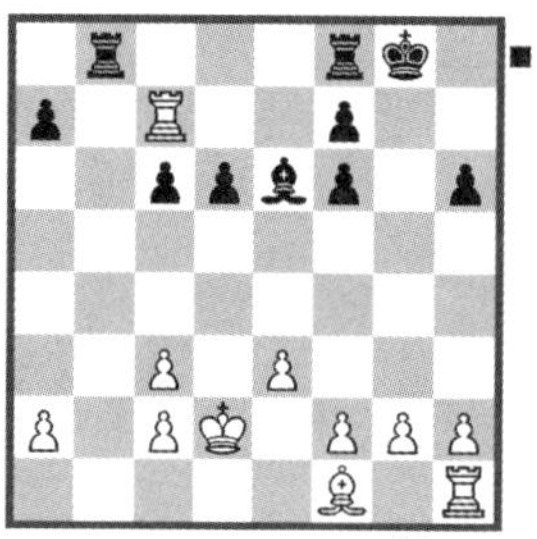

Position after: 15. ♖xc7

15... ♖b1 Black has compensation.] 14... ♖ab8 15. ♖b4 c5 16. ♖a4

14. ♗e2! a5

14... ♖e5 This is met with 15. ♗f3. ♖c5 [15... d5 This will simply close the 5th rank and White can go for 16. ♖b4 with an invasion on the queenside with a win; 15... ♗d7 This fails to the trivial 16. ♖b7.] 16. ♖b3! White has a huge advantage.

15. ♗f3 ♖a6

Black aims in this way to control all the squares on the b-file. Clearly, this rook would be out of play for a long time. Black is already strategically lost.

16. ♖b8 ♔f8

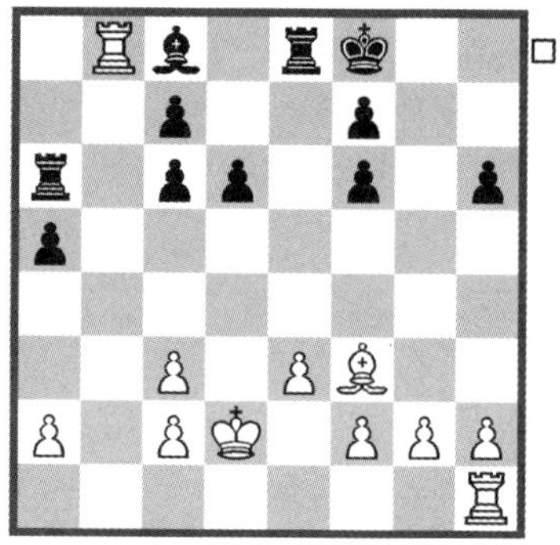

Position after: 16... ♔f8

17. ♖hb1 ♔e7

White can opt for many plans here. Most of these are connected with a strike on the kingside, using the fact that the black rook is stuck on the queenside. Before any active play White prophylactically sets some of his pawns on the dark squares.

18. a3! f5

There are no further good moves for Black. The played move prevents ♗g4.

18... ♗e6 For instance, this can now be met with the following. 19. ♖xe8+ ♔xe8 20. ♖b8+

Position after: 20. ♖b8+

20... ♔e7 21. ♖h8 White wins. The pawn is removed from the a2-square!

19. g3

Continuing with prophylaxis before any action.

19... ♖d8 20. h4 d5

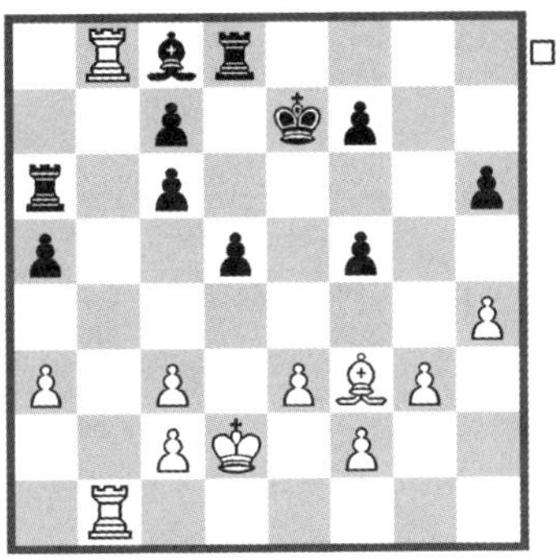

Position after: 20... d5

This is the move that White has been waiting for. It seems there is relief for Black, but in actual fact it accelerates his defeat. White now has a concrete way to crack Black's defense.

21. c4!

A very unpleasant move for Black. White gets rid of the doubled pawn, activating the king at the same time.

21... ♔d6

A) 21... d4 This simply loses after the following. 22. exd4 ♖xd4+ 23. ♔c3

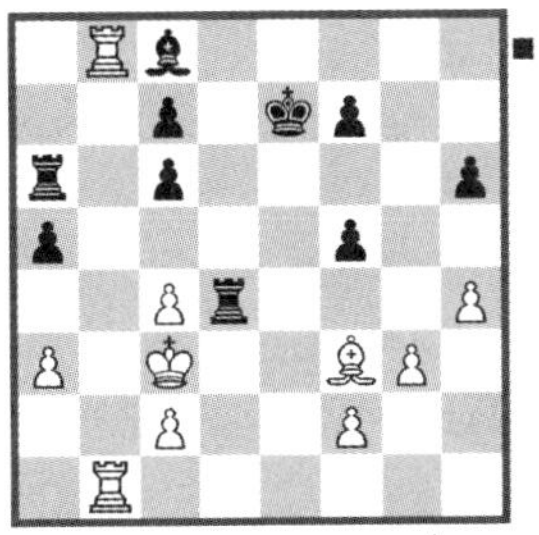

Position after: 23. ♔c3

23... ♖d8 24. c5 Black is paralyzed and White can combine numerous threats to win.

B) 21... dxc4+ 22. ♔c3 White is practically a pawn up on the kingside with all the previous advantages still present.

22. ♔c3 ♔e5 23. c5!

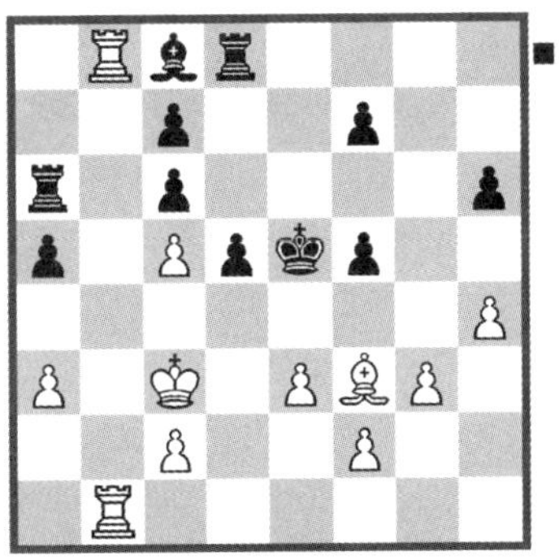

Position after: 23. c5!

There are many winning plans, but I had exactly this move in mind when I played c4. Black's rook is out of the game and he is lost.

23... ♖a7

It is time for White to find the winning plan. I wanted to transfer the rook to f4 and after attacking the f5-pawn with the bishop, then simply to pick it up.

23... a4 This allows, for instance the following line. 24. ♖1b7 ♗xb7 25. ♖xd8 ♖a5 26. ♖e8+ ♔f6 27. ♔d4

Position after: 27. ♔d4

27... ♖b5 [27... ♖a8 28. ♖xa8 ♗xa8 29. ♔c3 ♔e5 30. ♔b4 d4 31. ♔xa4 This easily wins.] 28. ♗e2 ♖b1 29. ♖b8 White has an easy win.

24. ♗g2 ♖g8 25. ♗h3 ♖e8 26. ♗f1

(see diagram next column)

There is no need to rush.

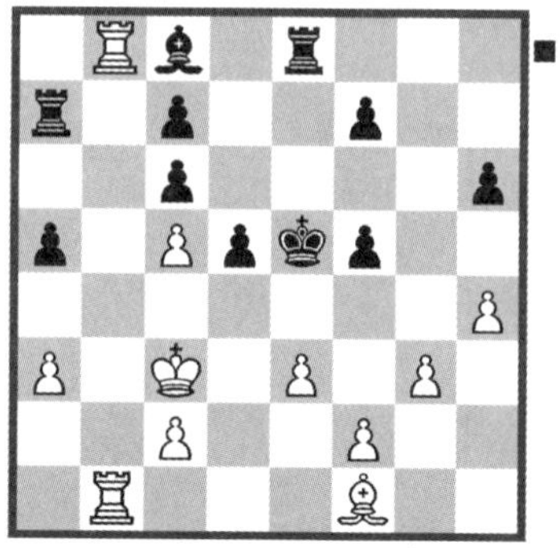

Position after: 26. ♗f1

26... ♖g8 27. ♖d1 ♖e8 28. ♖d4 ♗d7

This was Black's intention – to trade the rooks when the white rook is not on the b-file. However there is a surprise – White changes the rhythm of play while making immediate progress.

28... a4 This leads to a funny line. 29. ♖bb4 ♖a5 30. ♖xa4 ♖xc5+

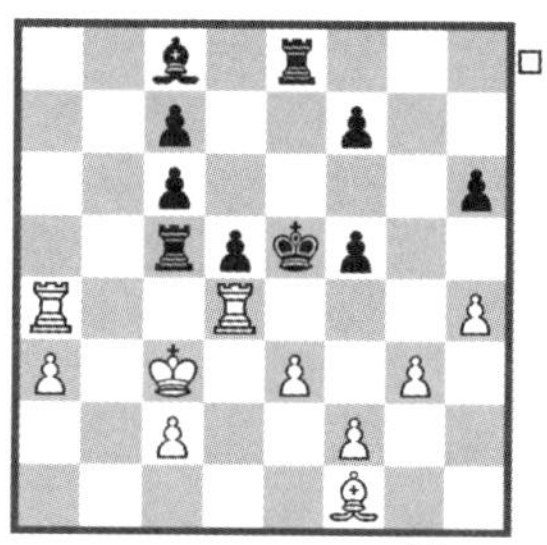

Position after: 30... ♖xc5+

31. ♔d2 The black rook is not trapped on c5!

29. ♖xe8+! ♗xe8 30. g4!

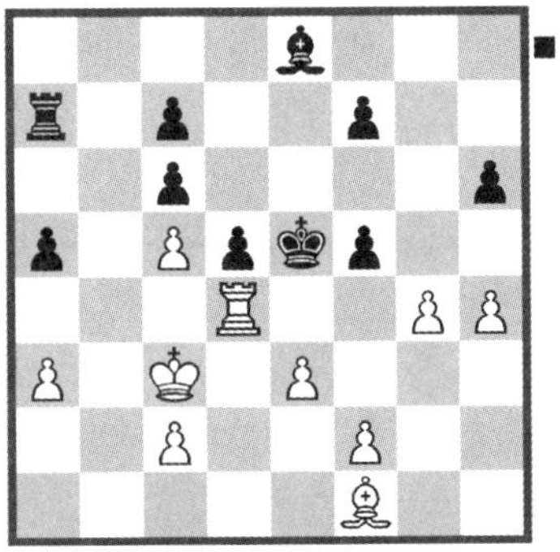

Position after: 30. g4!

30... fxg4

30... ♗d7 This is bad. 31. g5 hxg5 32. hxg5 The black king may even be mated in the center. For instance, there is a ♖h4-h6 motif with a final mate with f4.

31. ♖xg4 ♔f6

31... ♖b7 32. ♖g8 ♗d7 33. ♖h8 ♖b1 34. ♗d3 Black is lost. White will take the h-pawn and play f4. Black has nothing to attack.

32. ♖g8 ♗d7 33. ♖b8!

Picturesque – the point of White's plan. Black's rook is again out of play. White's rook works perfectly.

33... ♔g6 34. ♗e2 ♗f5 35. a4!

(see diagram next column)

Cementing the situation on the queenside. The pawn cannot be attacked.

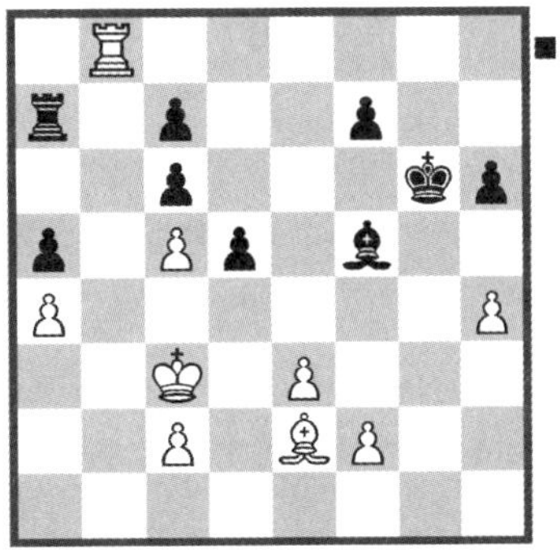

Position after: 35. a4!

35... ♔f6 36. ♔d2 ♔g7 37. ♗d1 ♔f6 38. ♔e2

The king goes to f4. There is no need to rush with pawn play.

38... ♗g4+ 39. f3 ♗h5 40. ♔d3

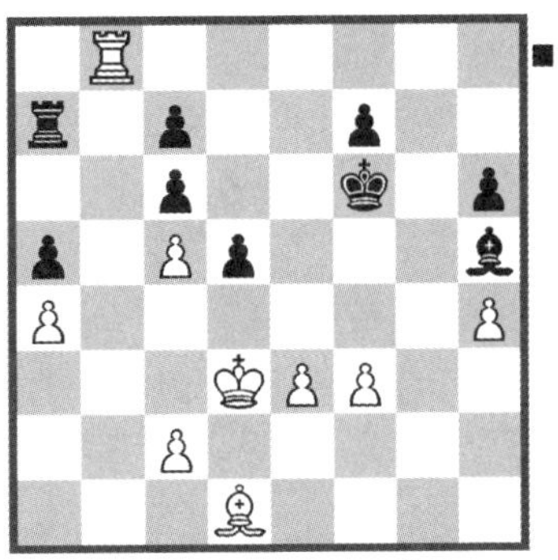

Position after: 40. ♔d3

Now the king comes to d4.

40... ♗g6+

40... ♔e5 This loses a piece after 41. f4+.

41. ♔d4 ♗f5 42. c4!

The most methodical plan. White practically has an extra kingside pawn after this exchange.

42... dxc4 43. e4 ♗h3 44. f4 ♗f1 45. ♗g4 c3 46. e5+ ♔g7 47. ♔xc3 ♗a6

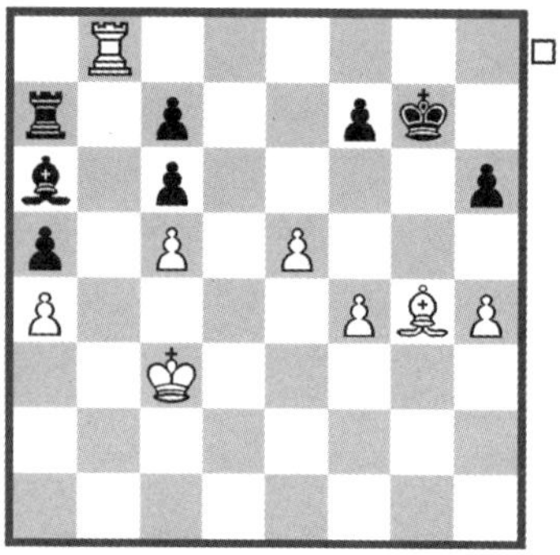

Position after: 47... ♗a6

The black rook will be liberated but it is too late.

48. f5 f6 49. e6 ♖b7 50. ♖a8

1-0

Game 188

♙ Zlatanovic, Boroljub (2377)
♟ Pobor, Milo (2175)
Paracin 2020

Here is a game that I played against a young and talented opponent, who was dynamically orientated. This is why I decided to play patiently, gradually improving, and not to allow him any chance for active play. Black's cavalry here looks more flexible. I started immediately to reactivate my own.

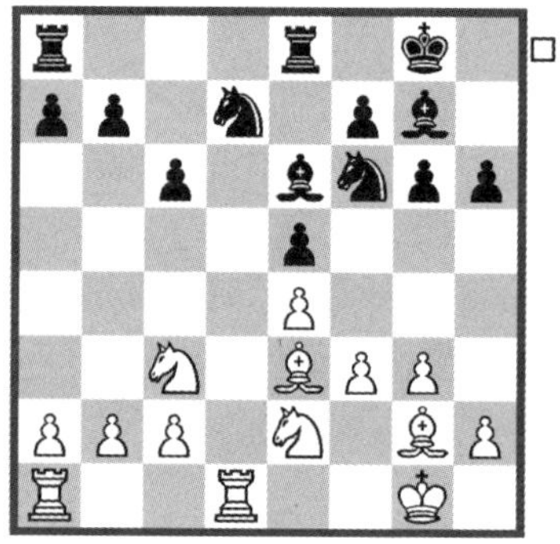

14. ♘c1

14. a4 This is typical and possible. I preferred to allow him ...b5.

14... ♘b6?

My opponent fails to find a plan. Tarrasch says: " The knight on b6 is always bad". After this move Black is unable to play either ...a5 or ...b5.

14... b5 Instead this is logical where after 15. ♘d3 there is an idea later after b3 and a4 to provoke ...b4 and occupy c4. [15. ♖d6 This achieves nothing after 15... ♖ec8.]

15. b3 ♘fd7 16. ♘d3 ♗f8 17. ♗f1

I regroup all my pieces toward the queenside. Both sides decided to go for active play in the center. Black can do nothing on the kingside. As for White's possibilities on the kingside, this will become apparent in awhile.

17... f6

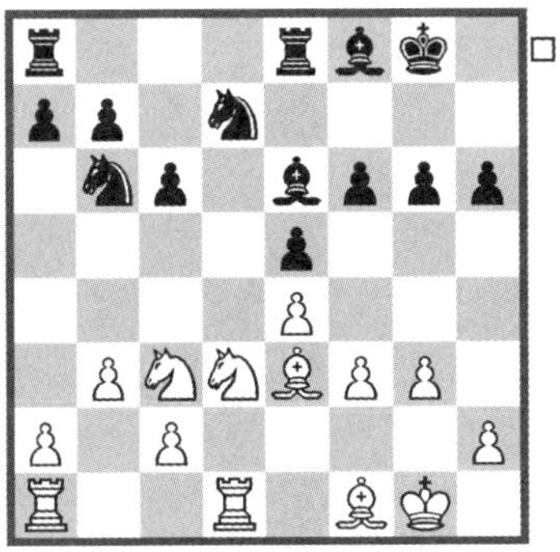

Position after: 17... f6

Bringing the king closer. On the other hand, with three connected pawns on the same rank there is an option to strike at the middle one and create holes!

18. h4! a5

A) 18... h5 This is risky because I would have the plan of ♗e2 and g4 at some timely moment. My pieces would gain easier access to the kingside.

B) 18... ♖ad8 Playing this with ...♘c8 looks to be a solid option.

19. a4 ♖ac8

Strange. Black apparently has the idea of c5-c4.

20. ♘b1!

The knight goes back. There are three reasons: first, to set the knights on b2 and d2 and to occupy c4; secondly, to play ♗d2 in case of the opponent's next move; and thirdly, after Black's potential ...c5, to play c4 and install the knight on d5.

20... ♘a8?!

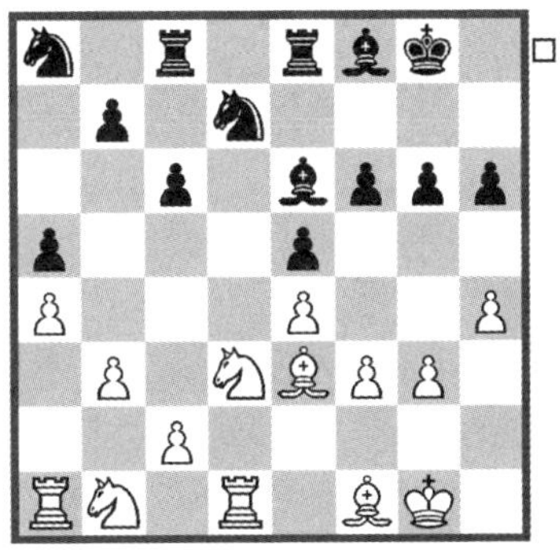

Position after: 20... ♘a8?!

20... c5 21. c4! ♘b8 22. ♘c3 ♘c6 This is bad because the c5-pawn will fall.

21. ♗d2!?

Played in Botvinnik's manner to provoke a weakness.

21. ♘d2 Playing this with ♘b2 and occupying the c4-square is clearly a good option. However I preferred the option with restriction.

21... b6

Now the knight at a8 can only go to c7.

22. ♗e3

The bishop comes back, liberating the d2-square for the knight. Moreover, the poor d7-knight is tied to protecting the b6-pawn. All my moves have been made with the same idea – to patiently improve while not giving my opponent the chance for any active play, at the same time restricting his active possibilities!

22... ♘c7 23. ♘d2 ♖b8 24. ♔f2

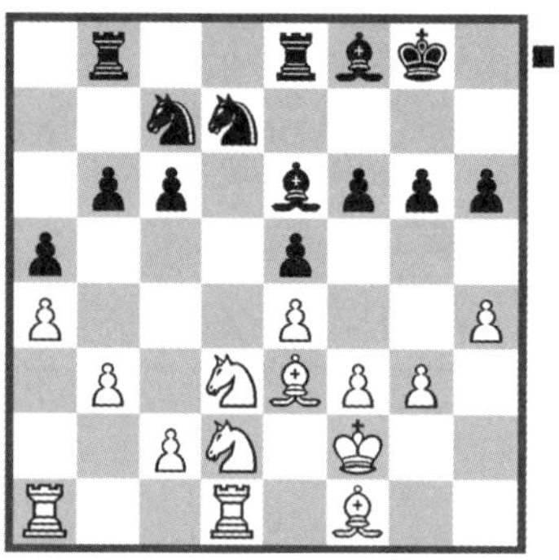

Position after: 24. ♔f2

The king should not be forgotten.

24... ♖ed8 25. ♗e2 ♗f7

Black tries to organize something. The point is that there is not much that he can organize. It is time for me to try to get the benefit of my prophylactic measures.

26. h5!?

Here my opponent was close to time trouble and I decided to go for active play. With a solid extra hour on my clock this is logical. However, there are also strong chess reasons for my decision. Black's pieces are stuck on the queenside.

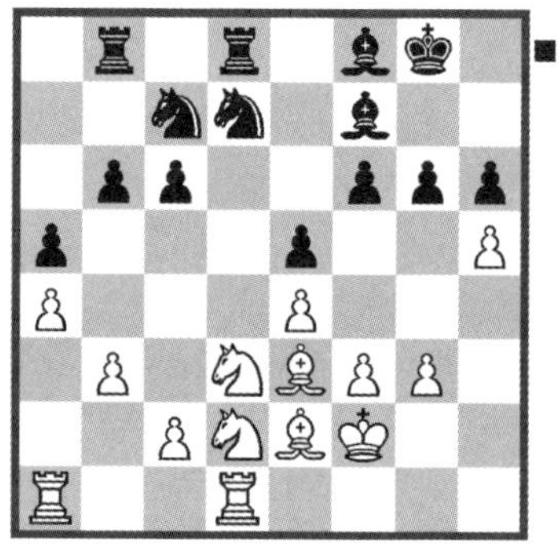

Position after: 26. h5!?

26... g5

26... gxh5 This is possible but risky. The following variation confirms this. 27. f4 ♘e6 28. ♖h1 ♘g7?!

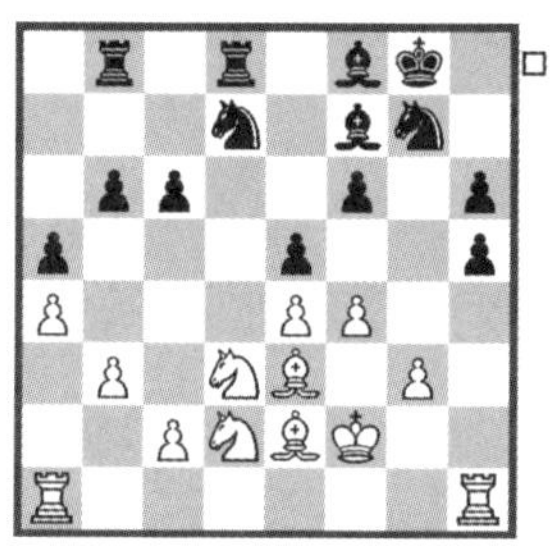

Position after: 28... ♘g7?!

29. f5 Black is in an awful situation.

27. f4 ♘e6?!

27... exf4 28. gxf4 ♘e6 This looks safer and better. 29. ♘c4 ♘dc5 The situation is unclear.

28. fxg5 fxg5?!

A) 28... hxg5?! 29. ♗g4 This is bad for Black.

B) 28... ♘xg5!? 29. ♗g4 ♘c5 A wild continuation and probably the best for Black.

29. ♘c4

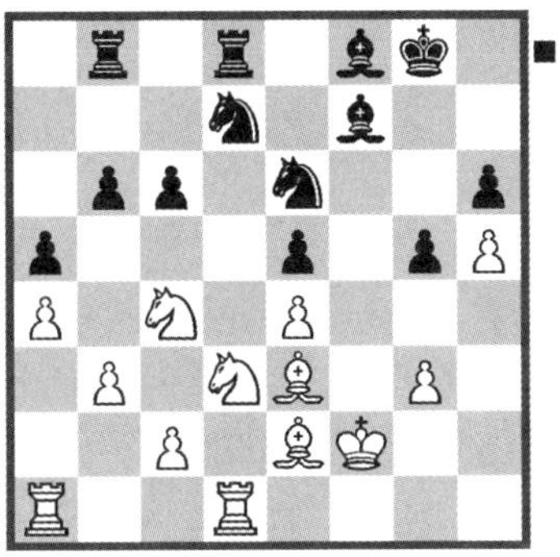

Position after: 29. ♘c4

29... ♘ec5?!

29... ♗g7 This is ugly, but a better defense. 30. ♘d6 White keeps a serious advantage.

30. ♘dxe5

30. ♘xc5 ♗xc5 31. ♗xc5 ♘xc5 32. ♔e3 ♗xc4 33. ♗xc4+ This is another way for a better endgame, but I did not want to go for an endgame with a light-squared bishop against a knight.

30... ♘xe5 31. ♘xe5 ♘xe4+ 32. ♔g2

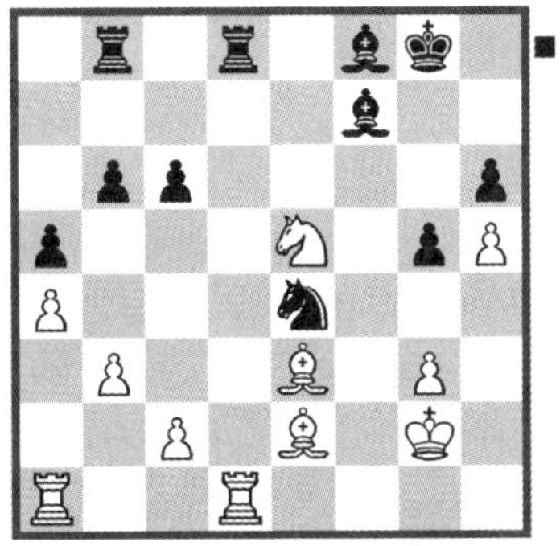

Position after: 32. ♔g2

32... ♗d5?

My opponent errs in time trouble.

32... ♖xd1 This was practically essential. 33. ♖xd1 ♘c3 34. ♖d2 ♘xe2 35. ♘xf7

Position after: 35. ♘xf7

35... ♔xf7 36. ♖xe2 Black would be in difficulties because many of his pawns are fixed on the bishop's color. Nevertheless, this would have been the lesser evil.

33. c4! ♗g7 34. cxd5 ♗xe5 35. dxc6!

Black probably missed this powerful shot.

35... ♘xg3 36. ♗c4+ ♔g7 37. ♖xd8 ♖xd8 38. ♗xb6

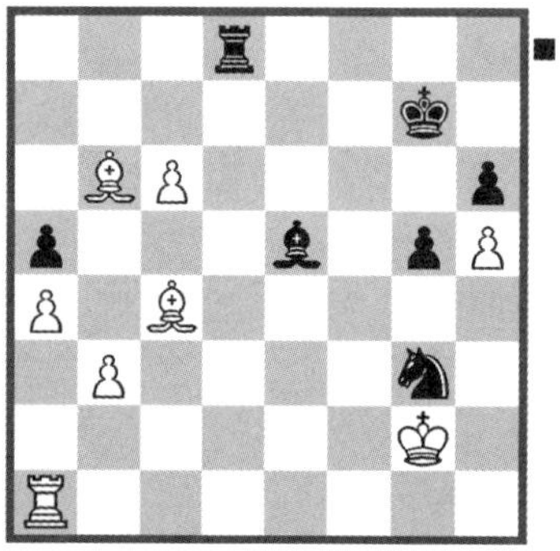

Position after: 38. ♗xb6

38... ♖c8 39. ♖e1 ♗d6 40. ♖e6 ♖xc6 41. ♖g6+ ♔f8

Position after: 41... ♔f8

The previous moves have been forced. After the storm has passed, White finishes the game with a fine move.

42. ♗d8!

Threatening mate in one.

42... ♔e8 43. ♗b5 ♔xd8 44. ♗xc6 ♔c7 45. ♗f3 ♘f5 46. ♖f6

1-0

Index of Games